RELIGIONS OF LATE ANTIQUITY IN PRACTICE

RELIGIONS OF

LATE ANTIQUITY

IN PRACTICE

Richard Valantasis, Editor

PRINCETON READINGS IN RELIGIONS

PRINCETON UNIVERSITY PRESS

PRINCETON AND OXFORD

Copyright © 2000 by Princeton University Press
Published by Princeton University Press, 41 William Street,
Princeton, New Jersey 08540
In the United Kingdom: Princeton University Press, 3 Market Place,
Woodstock, Oxfordshire OX20 1SY

Library of Congress Cataloging-in-Publication Data
Religions of late antiquity in practice / Richard Valantasis, editor.
p.   cm. — (Princeton readings in religions)
Includes bibliographical references and index.
ISBN 0-691-05750-8 (hardcover : alk. paper) — ISBN 0-691-05751-6 (pbk. : alk. paper)
1. Religions—History.   2. Europe—Religion.   3. Church history—Primitive and early
church, ca. 30–600.   I. Valantasis, Richard, 1946–   II. Series.
BL690.R46   2000
200'.9'015—dc21   99-049325

This book has been composed in Berkeley

The paper used in this publication meets the minimum requirements
of ANSI/NISO Z39.48-1992 (R1997) (*Permanence of Paper*)

www.pup.princeton.edu

Printed in the United States of America

1 3 5 7 9 10 8 6 4 2

1 3 5 7 9 10 8 6 4 2
(Pbk.)

DEDICATED TO

IRENE AND LOUIS,

FLORENCE AND HARRY,

OUR FIRST GUIDES IN

THE PRACTICE OF

RELIGION

PRINCETON READINGS

IN RELIGIONS

———

Princeton Readings in Religions is a new series of anthologies on the religions of the world, representing the significant advances that have been made in the study of religions in the last thirty years. The sourcebooks used by previous generations of students placed a heavy emphasis on philosophy and on the religious expressions of elite groups in what were deemed "classical civilizations," especially of Asia and the Middle East. Princeton Readings in Religions provides a different configuration of texts in an attempt better to represent the range of religious practices, placing particular emphasis on the ways in which texts are used in diverse contexts. The series therefore includes ritual manuals, hagiographical and autobiographical works, and folktales, as well as some ethnographic material. Many works are drawn from vernacular sources. The readings in the series are new in two senses. First, very few of the works contained in the volumes have ever been translated into a Western language before. Second, each volume provides new ways to read and understand the religions of the world, breaking down the sometimes misleading stereotypes inherited from the past in an effort to provide both more expansive and more focused perspectives on the richness and diversity of religious expressions. The series is designed for use by a wide range of readers, with key terms translated and technical notes omitted. Each volume also contains a lengthy general introduction by a distinguished scholar in which the histories of the traditions are outlined and the significance of each of the works is explored.

Religions of Late Antiquity in Practice is the seventh volume of Princeton Readings in Religions. The thirty-six contributors include leading scholars of the religious traditions of Late Antiquity, each of whom has provided one or more translations of key works, many of which are translated here for the first time. The works translated derive from ancient martyrologies and anonymous letters, from psalmbooks and sermons, and are drawn from all the major religious movements of Late Antiquity, including Manichaeanism, Neoplatonism, magic, monasticism, and the local religions of the Roman Empire, in addition to Judaism and Christianity. Each chapter begins with a substantial introduction in which the translator discusses the history and influence of the work, identifying points of particular difficulty or interest. Richard Valantasis provides a general introduction in which the major themes of the religions of Late Antiquity are introduced and analyzed.

Tantra in Practice and Judaism in Practice are currently in press, with volumes on the religions of North America and South America in progress.

Donald S. Lopez, Jr.
Series Editor

CONVENTIONS

[ ] in text indicates a restoration of a word or phrase not appearing in the original language text, or necessary for understanding in English

[. . .] in text indicates a lacuna in the original text

[Exod. XXXs] in text supplies biblical or textual reference to a quotation

[2A] brackets enclosing numbers indicate the page or section in the critical edition in the original language used as the basis for the translation

(?) in the text indicates the translator's best judgment, or the translation of an opaque word or phrase

LXX: signifies the Septuagint, the Greek translation of the Jewish Scriptures widely used by a variety of religious people in Late Antiquity

On the issue of standardization, consistency has been maintained within chapters but not throughout the volume, according to individual preferences and practices of the various contributing editors.

CONTENTS

Locating Religion in Society: Community

Regulating Religious Expression: Law

Creating Religious Ceremonial: Ritual

Singing Divine Praises: Hymnody

Sacrificing Self to God: Martyrology

Enlivening Thought: Philosophy and Theology

CONTRIBUTORS

Ellen Bradshaw Aitken teaches New Testament at Harvard Divinity School (Cambridge, Massachusetts).

Lawrence J. Altepeter just completed his Ph.D. in Historical Theology at Saint Louis University (St. Louis, Missouri).

Jason David BeDuhn teaches in the Department of Humanities, Arts, and Religion at Northern Arizona University (Flagstaff, Arizona).

Daniel Boyarin teaches in the Department of Near Eastern Studies at the University of California at Berkeley (Berkeley, California).

David Bundy teaches at Christian Theological Seminary (Indianapolis, Indiana).

Elizabeth Geraldine Burr teaches in the Department of Theology at the University of St. Thomas (St. Paul, Minnesota).

Virginia Burrus teaches at the Theological School at Drew University (Madison, New Jersey).

Elizabeth A. Castelli teaches in the Religion Department at Barnard College (New York, New York).

Robert Doran teaches in the Department of Religion at Amherst College (Amherst, Massachusetts).

David Frankfurter teaches in the Department of History at the University of New Hampshire (Durham, New Hampshire).

James E. Goehring teaches in the Department of Classics, Philosophy, and Religion at Mary Washington College (Fredericksburg, Virginia).

Nonna Verna Harrison teaches at St. Joseph of Arimathea College (Berkeley, California).

Arthur G. Holder is Dean of the Church Divinity School of the Pacific (Berkeley, California).

David G. Hunter teaches in the Department of Philosophy and Religious Studies at Iowa State University (Ames, Iowa).

Clayton N. Jefford teaches New Testament at Saint Meinrad School of Theology (St. Meinrad, Indiana).

Tracy Keefer is completing her Ph.D. in the Department of History at the University of South Carolina (Columbia, South Carolina).

Kathleen A. Kelley holds a Ph.D. in classics from the University of Wisconsin, Madison, and teaches at Saint Louis University School of Law (St. Louis, Missouri).

Derek Krueger teaches in the Department of Religious Studies at the University of North Carolina at Greensboro (Greensboro, North Carolina).

Blake Leyerle teaches in the Department of Theology at the University of Notre Dame (Notre Dame, Indiana).

Vasiliki Limberis teaches in the Department of Religion at Temple University (Philadelphia, Pennsylvania).

Matthew C. Mirow is a Golieb fellow in legal history at New York University School of Law and teaches at South Texas College of Law (Houston, Texas).

Teresa M. Shaw teaches in the Religion Department of Claremont Graduate University (Claremont, California).

Arthur B. Shippee teaches at Hartford Seminary (Hartford, Connecticut) and is completing his Ph.D. at Yale University (New Haven, Connecticut).

James C. Skedros teaches at Holy Cross Greek Orthodox School of Theology (Brookline, Masschusetts).

Carl P. E. Springer teaches in the Department of Classics at Illinois State University (Normal, Illinois).

Kenneth B. Steinhauser teaches in the Department of Theological Studies at Saint Louis University (St. Louis, Missouri).

Columba Stewart OSB teaches at Saint John's School of Theology and Seminary at Saint John's University (Collegeville, Minnesota).

Kimberly B. Stratton is a doctoral candidate in the Department of Religion at Columbia University (New York, New York).

Gail Corrington Streete teaches in the Department of Religious Studies at Rhodes College (Memphis, Tennessee).

Peter T. Struck teaches in the Classics Department of the University of Pennsylvania (Philadelphia, Pennsylvania).

Michael D. Swartz teaches at Ohio State University (Columbus, Ohio).

Maureen A. Tilley teaches in the Department of Religious Studies at the University of Dayton (Dayton, Ohio).

Richard Valantasis teaches in the Bible Department at Iliff School of Theology (Denver, Colorado).

David Vila teaches at John Brown University (Siloam Springs, Arkansas).

Frederick W. Weidmann teaches in the New Testament Department at Union Theological Seminary (New York, New York).

Megan H. Williams teaches in the Religion Department at Mount Holyoke College (South Hadley, Massachusetts).

RELIGIONS OF LATE ANTIQUITY IN PRACTICE

INTRODUCTION

Richard Valantasis

The religious landscape of postmodern Western European and American society has its origins in the religious movements of Late Antiquity. In Late Antiquity the major religions of the West (Judaism, first, then Christianity, and later Islam) developed the contours of religious society still operative today, and the primary categories and modalities of religion set in place then still function now. Rabbinic Judaism flourished during this period and moved throughout Europe, the Middle East, North Africa—it is a structure and theological argumentation that characterizes Judaism still. Christianity developed the theological categories that delimited orthodoxy until today, while putting into place an episcopal structure that continues to influence even those churches of the Protestant Reformation that have rejected that structure. Although not all Late Antique religions survived into the twentieth century as did Judaism and Christianity, the influence of other religious movements of Late Antiquity is still being felt. The Manichaean churches, so prevalent and pervasive in Late Antiquity (Lieu 1998; Gardner 1995), preserved early Christian literature—the apocryphal acts of the apostles—which provides an important window on the life and theology of alternative Christian communities. Augustine of Hippo, the Christian bishop so influential in Christian theology, was a Manichaean hearer for nearly a decade before converting to Christianity (Brown 1972). Hermetic philosophy and religion became part of the staple of Renaissance thinkers (McKnight 1991) and a fascination to the modern psychologist Carl Jung (Jung 1967).

We should not, however, be too convinced by the distinction between religion and politics or religion and society. Modern understandings of religion describe religion as a sphere of human activity separate and distinct from other activities, but such was not the case in classical Greece and Rome, nor was it a distinction in Late Antiquity. Social and political systems intertwined with what we would call religious practices in such a way that they appear to be seamless. Roman political identity became evident in religious practice and religious practice expressed and concretized social and political realities (Beard, North, and Price 1998, 214–16). The martyrologies best exemplify this seamless relationship between religion, politics, and society. The persecutions aimed not to remove a different religion; many different kinds of religious movements and cults coexisted in the Roman Empire (Frend 1967). Rather, the persecutions of Christians sought a means to establish their faithfulness and participation in the established Roman political and social establishment through the connection of Roman cult and Roman politics and society. The issue for the Romans remained the common identity of people under Roman authority, an identity that Christians rejected because of the exclusivity of their cult. Christian exclusivity signaled a rejection of Roman law and society and was met with drastically repressive measures. But at the center of the issue stands the seamless relationships of what appear to modern people to be separate spheres of activity, but that were not perceived as separate in Antiquity.

Throughout the Late Antique period (as in earlier Roman religious theorizing), there was a debate that marked the boundaries between acceptable and unacceptable religious practices. *Religio* articulated the acceptable religious practices of the dominant group, but dominance remained a fluid and shifting category throughout the period. *Superstitio* articulated the unacceptable religious practices of subordinate groups, whose practices varied from the acceptable and the dominant practices. The same practice, such as augury, could be defined as either *religio* or *superstitio* depending upon the perspective of the person characterizing the practice (Beard, North, and Price 1998, 214–18). This is much like the use of the word "cult" in modern discourse—a descriptive noun that can be made a derogatory epithet.

Late Antiquity

As a term, Late Antiquity bears two overlapping references. In the narrow definition, Late Antiquity follows upon the Later Roman Empire that began in 284 C.E., with the accession of Diocletian, and lasted until 395 C.E., with the death of the emperor Theodosius I (Cameron 1993, 1–12). In the study of Late Roman religions, this narrow sense has been expanded slightly to extend to the Arab invasions of the seventh century and the rise of Islam. This narrow understanding of Late Antiquity, even in the expanded sense, works well for social and political historians, but it is still not sufficient for historians of religion interested in religious practice. Students of religion recognize that religious practices change slowly and that over time the same practice develops new and different meanings. For those interested in the religious practices of Late Antiquity, the starting point must be earlier, that is, with the religious reforms and renewal begun by the emperor Augustus (63 B.C.E.–14 C.E.). In this broader sense, the focus of attention for religion in Late Antiquity remains the fourth century C.E. until the seventh century, but the religious practices themselves reach back further into the religious traditions of the Hellenistic and Roman periods. One example will show the need for this. The Christian martyrological literature of the third century develops themes of the first-century C.E. Maccabean literature. Although the literary tradition moves backward, the effect moved forward throughout the period following the martyrdoms themselves (before Late Antiquity by the narrow understanding) because these martyrdoms were read in public assemblies during Christian liturgies throughout the history of Christianity and especially in the period covered by this book. For the purposes of this collection of readings, Late Antiquity has been taken in the broader sense to give a wider purview to religious practices.

The Religions of Late Antiquity

Religious practice and religious affiliation formed an important part of Late Antique Life. Late Antiquity witnessed the growth and development of major religious movements while at the same time witnessing the transformation of ancient religious traditions under the influence of a plethora of multi-cultural social and political changes.

Christianity

The rise of Christianity stands out as the major religious development in Late Antiquity. Founded by Jesus (born 4 B.C.E.) and spread by followers both who associated with him in his Palestinian mission (the disciples) and who did not have any contact with him whatsover (Paul and the many later apostles and bishops), Christianity quickly moved from Roman Galilee and Palestine to the major cities of Asia Minor, Syria, Mesopotamia, Greece, Rome, North Africa, and southern Europe (Frend 1984). Christianity offered a system of salvation based upon a knowledge of God made evident in the life, sayings, and deeds of Jesus; a collection of sacred writings (the New Testament); a concern and provision for the poor and the disenfranchised; a thoroughly organized church structure that included both a hierarchy of leaders and provision for instruction of the majority of participants; a theological system that incorporated the most current forms of Neoplatonic thought and the most popular forms of textual interpretation; and a distinct means of self-definition that clearly delineated Christians from all other religious groups and their practices. Christian churches employed regional and empire-wide meetings (Church Councils) to regulate their internal life and to articulate the parameters of acceptable (orthodox) theology and practice. These councils created both unity among those who stood in what was deemed orthodox and schism from those deemed unorthodox. Schismatic churches and movements, however, continued to thrive alongside orthodox churches and movements so that condemnation by a council did not—even with imperial support— automatically disband the unorthodox communities or eliminate their religious practices.

Christianity appealed to people from widely differing classes and economic statuses, including the conversion during Late Antiquity of wealthy Romans matrons who financed religious foundations throughout the empire and especially in Jerusalem (Clark 1979). The significant quantity of written materials in many diverse genres attests to the vitality of Christianity's literacy from the very beginning and especially in the Late Antique period when leading intellectuals who were trained in classical culture took on important roles in church administration and theology (cf. Harris 1989). Christianity's relationship with imperial power and socially dominant groups shifts wildly over the course of these centuries, from persecuted minority in the martyrological literature to imperial protection under the Christian emperors. But it was not only the outside world that queried Christianity's relationship with the wider world: Christians themselves held various contradictory attitudes about the value or importance of the Roman world, its philosophical and cultural traditions, and its form of government (Cameron 1993, 1993a). The question of Christian accommodation to surrounding cultures has never been resolved.

The development of Christian religious hegemony constitutes one of the most dramatic changes in Western religious history and yet that translation from minor cult to imperial religion did not leave all forms of prior religious practice behind (Fowden 1993). Christianity certainly innovated, but that innovation resonated with established religious practices both Jewish and Roman.

Judaism

Judaism changed from an international traditional temple cult centered in Jerusalem's Temple to a household-focused religion oriented toward the transmission of the sayings of the Rabbinic sages (Neusner 1995). This change also signaled a shift from a religion recognized by the Roman authorities as venerable and ancient to one considered dangerous, rebellious, and worthy of persecution (Feldman 1993). The destruction of the Temple in Jerusalem in 70 c.e. by the Romans marked the beginning of the transformation of Judaism, which was made complete in Late Antiquity.

After the destruction of the Temple, the focus of religious practice shifted to creating a home environment in which the biblical Law (Torah) could be observed and obeyed. This transformation hinged on the role of the rabbis who interpreted the Torah and made it accessible for daily living. The rabbis produced the definitive sources for a post-temple Judaism: the Talmud (one in Jerusalem and one in Babylon) contains both the oral and written traditions of the Law formed around the Mishnah, a collection of their sayings, and school dialogues with their students organized under a number of different headings (agriculture, marriage, civil law, holidays, ritual regulations, and purity). The Talmud also contains various interpretative traditions (Midrashim) and mystical traditions (Kabbala) (Neusner 1995; Boyarin 1990).

Manichaeanism

Manichaeanism, a new religion in Late Antiquity, began in the eastern part of the Roman Empire but spread quickly from the Mediterranean basin, through Africa and the Middle East, and as far as Chinese Turkestan, where it survived until the tenth century C.E., and the Fukien province, where there is evidence that it lasted until the thirteenth century C.E. (Lieu 1998). Founded by Mani (216–276 C.E.) who came from Seleucia-Ctesiphon in Persia, the Manichaeans taught a clear distinction and cosmic conflict between light and darkness. A succession of revealers including Jesus, the Buddha, Paul of Tarsus, and Mani himself, taught the means of releasing light particles, which had been perniciously entrapped in matter, through various religious practices. The Manichaean communities consisted of various classes of participants: the elect, who were oriented toward living maximally to release the light, and the hearers, who assisted the elect in doing their salvific work. The Manichaeans promulgated various ascetical activities primarily oriented toward eating certain foods purported to be more full of the primal light and avoiding certain foods altogether. Manichaean literature (often preserved in luxurious and beautiful manuscripts) included a life of Mani (the Cologne Mani Codex), various hymns and songs, a catechism, and sermons by Mani. It is fortunate that both writings by Manichaeans (Gardner 1995) and the polemical literature against the them have survived (Brown 1972).

Roman Cults

Throughout Late Antiquity two primary kinds of Roman cult continued: those of the city of Rome itself, its colonies, and cities; and those cults in the wider eastern and western empire, which included other non-Roman cults. In the eastern Roman Empire, rooted as it was in Hellenistic religious traditions, traditional cults continued to be practiced. In the eastern empire, the major religious cults from the Hellenistic period onward included the cult of Asclepius, the healing god whose sanctuaries provided medical care from Spain through the Middle East; the ancient oracles consulted widely in a number of different forms; the mystery cult of Eleusis; the popular Egyptian cults of Sarapis and Isis; the cult of Mithras, which was prevalent in the Roman military; and, of course, the cult of the Great Mother (*Magna Mater*), which developed in the eastern Roman Empire but was also accepted in Rome itself. The Hellenistic Roman practice of making emperors divine and then granting them ritual cults and sacrifice eventually became the norm for both the eastern and western Roman Empire (Beard, North, and Price 1998).

In addition to these religious cults, the cults of Rome also survived throughout Late Antiquity. Although the Roman cults centered upon Roman practice and specific traditions that related primarily to the city of Rome, the cults of the city were exported to colonies and cities established under Roman rule and thereby they became part of the Roman colonial system. These cults included the cult of the goddess Roma, the cults of the genius of the emperor, and various cults of the god Jupiter. Roman emperors throughout Late Antiquity (including most of the Christian emperors) retained their Roman function as *pontifex maximus* (chief priest) of the Roman cults. It is reasonable to assume that over time these traditional cults both represented continuous religious practice and underwent changes in practice and understanding. The best example of this sort of transformation is the work of the emperor Julian (born 331 or 332 C.E.). Julian was raised as a Christian, but rejected his Christian faith when he became the emperor and then he began to revive the ancient Roman cult throughout the empire. His tolerance of all religions, as well as his official support of pagan cult, attempted to reinvigorate ancient religious practice. Julian, however, understood the effectiveness of Christian organization and the role of Christian doctrine in creating cohesive community, so he modeled his revived Roman cult on Christian principles of care for the poor and on Christian systems of hierarchic organizations with various orders of ministry. The religious practice that Julian fostered thus both resembled ancient practice while at the same time transforming it.

General Religious Practices

Some religious practices in Late Antiquity crossed recognized boundaries of religions. Asceticism stands out as the most significant. The term *asceticism* is a sport metaphor that means "training": in its base form it refers to an athlete training for an event. It signifies the gradual and purposeful transformation of a person's body aimed at improvement through various practices. By extension, throughout both the classical period and Late Antiquity asceticism refers to practices and training that improved the body and the mind. Often Late Antique asceticism involved renunciation of various foods, regulation of sexual intercourse, the development of certain virtues with a corresponding renunciation of vices, the manipulation of sleep patterns, the restriction of social engagement, and numerous other activities geared to self-improvement. Ascetics identified themselves as Christians, Manichaeans, Jews, philosophers (especially Neoplatonist), and theurgists. Although the practices may be the same in various religious environments, the significance of the practices varies according to the religious and social context of the ascetical practitioner (Wimbush and Valantasis 1995).

Ascent traditions also cross religious lines. The Late Antique understanding of a hierarchically organized cosmos that moves along a series of steps from dense matter up to ethereal spiritual elements and even to God enabled hierophants to lead initiants through various stages from the lower aspects of their embodied life to the higher. This ascent to the mental or spiritual realities, while disengaging from bodily existence, became a practice in Christianity, Judaism, Neoplatonic philosophy, theurgy, and Hermetism, among others. Ascent rituals enabled Late Antique people to relate to the heavenly and divine spheres in order to enhance their human life and social standing (Swartz 1996).

Magic had long been a part of religious practice in antiquity and it continued to be practiced in Late Antiquity as well. Sections of the Theodosian and Justinianic legal codes indicate that imperial decrees attempted to regulate or forbid the use of magic and yet the vast number of magical rituals that have been preserved from Late Antiquity attest to the continued practice of magic. Every powerful deity and force in any religion could be incorporated into magical rituals and this expansive understanding of the deities probably points the way to the various religious affiliations of the people using them. Even though Christianity attempted to eliminate magical rites, they persisted not only in the society but even within Christian practice itself, as some of the ritual texts assembled in this book bespeak. One function of magic clearly related to the healing of the body, but a Late Antique person could also seek out healing from Christian saints and holy persons, by incubation at an Asclepius temple, or from the many medically trained doctors who practiced in the cities of the Late Antique Roman Empire (Betz 1992; Meyer and Smith 1994).

Rhetoric formed an important part of Late Antique social, political, and religious practice. Public addresses were opportunities not only to display the rhetorical skill of a public figure or philosopher, but also a time to explore the issues facing a community and to celebrate the common life of a community. Christian sermons form an important part of the evidence for Late Antique attitudes and practices, but so do the public lectures of the famous orator Libanius and of the emperor Julian. The amalgamation of rhetorical skill with philosophical and theological questions created a rich supply of superb works of theology for Christians and Romans alike to the extent that the production of theology and philosophy became a kind of religious practice as, I am sure, was the exercise of listening to these religious declamations (Kennedy 1983).

Historical Overview

This historical overview simply presents the major emperors who had some impact on the study of the practice of religion in Late Antiquity (for more thorough information see Barnes 1981, 1982; Bury 1958; Cameron and Garnsey 1998). The emperor Augustus (63 B.C.E.–14 C.E.) built the infrastructure that underlay the spread of religion in Late Antiquity. Augustus created a single administrative structure stretching from Spain to Syria, including southern Europe (Gaul, and areas around the Danube and Rhine Rivers), Italy, Greece, Asia Minor, North Africa, Ethiopia, and Egypt. This administrative structure improved communication, travel, cultural and religious exchange, and created relative peace throughout the empire. These factors provided rich soil for the development of religious and intellectual life.

The period from the first century B.C.E. until the late third century C.E. witnessed many important historical occurences that had a continuing affect on the religions of Late Antiquity. These occurrences included such monumental events as the destruction of the Jewish Temple in Jerusalem in 70 C.E., the Jewish wars and the transformation of Jerusalem into a Roman city named Aelia Capitolina, the founding of Christianity and of rabbinic Judaism, the continued development of the imperial cult, and the introduction of foreign cults into Rome. Although the period between Augustus and Diocletian contains events of such great importance, this section deals primarily with the religious events in the period from the accession of Diocletian (284 C.E.) until the rise of Islam.

The reign of Diocletian witnessed the pressures between developing religions and the Roman cults. Diocletian inaugurated the most dramatic persecutions of the Christians because many of them refused to honor the traditional Roman religious rites. At times and in some places these persecutions were severe, often so severe that the reaction eventually was a decree of religious toleration, which was to last until the Christian emperors beginning with Constantine began to condemn alternative religious beliefs and practices both Christian and Roman.

These centuries were a period of intense fighting among Christians about the parameters of acceptable speculation about the divinity of Jesus Christ and the relationship of Jesus to the Creator Father. The emperor Constantine (285–337 C.E.) was the first emperor to profess Christianity, although it is not clear that Constantine rejected his former religious practices and beliefs as he became involved in Christianity (Barnes 1981). With the exception of Julian, all the other emperors of the period were Christians. Constantius II (324–361 C.E.), Constantine's son, aligned himself with a Christian theology that his father rejected. The emperor Julian (332–363) succeeded Constantius II, renounced his Christian faith and attempted to reinstate traditional Roman religion, especially of the philosophical variety, as the norm in the empire. His early death as well as his somewhat antiquarian and peculiar understanding of traditional Roman cult prevented his project from becoming successful.

Theodosius the Great (346–395) regulated religion to a significant degree, as his laws surely indicate. He was a pious Christian who opposed Christian heretical groups, magic and divination, Roman traditional religion, Manichaeanism, and other religious practices and beliefs inconsistent with his own faith. This sort of religious regulation was to continue as the norm in Western imperial policy.

The final emperor of significance to Late Antique religion is Justinian (482–565). Justinian continued the legal work that Theodosius began—work that included significant legislation of religious belief and practice especially against Judaism, traditional Roman religion, and heretical Christians. His reign constitutes the last of the Late Antique emperors and the first of the Byzantine Empire, which prided itself as the renewal of the ancient Roman Empire. Justinian built some of the finest Christian churches such as Saint Sophia in Constantinople (modern Istanbul in Turkey).

The Byzantine Empire begins to define itself religiously and politically in relationship to the emerging competitor to Christianity, Islam. The Prophet Muhammad (ca. 570–632 C.E.), who understood himself as the last of the great prophets of God that included Moses and Jesus, received revelations from God that he transcribed in a book entitled the Qur'an. The teachings of Islam revolve around four pillars: that there is one God, whose prophet is Muhammad; that Muslims (adherents of the religion Islam) should pray five times a day; that Muslims should give alms to the needy; and that Muslims should make at least one pilgrimage to Mecca during a lifetime, if it is possible. Initially, Islam spread throughout the Arabian peninsula and into Asia and the Pacific rim. During the sixth and seventh centuries, Arab tribes conquered much of the Middle East and North Africa and subjected both Christians and Jews to Muslim authority. These religious and political conquests mark the end of Late Antiquity.

The Geography of Late Antiquity

One reason for the modern fascination with Late Antiquity is the cultural pluralism found in Late Antiquity. Roman political organization linked widely divergent geographical areas and their indigenous cultures while at the same time imposing common cultural bonds that helped to create a common culture. The Roman Empire during the Late Antique period connected all of Western and Eastern Europe, the Near East, North Africa, most of the areas surrounding the Black Sea, Armenia, the Caucasus, and extended far into modern Iran and Iraq. The languages common to all those areas included Latin and Greek, but regional languages continued to be spoken and written; significant literature survives in such demotic languages as Punic, Coptic, Aramaic, Syriac, Armenian, and Georgian. Religion also played an important role in unifying disparate cultures. Manichaean literature survives in Coptic, Greek, Syriac, and Latin and the religion was known to have adherents throughout the Roman Empire and beyond. Similarly, Christian literature exists to some degree in every one of the demotic languages of the Roman empire. Although the degree of acculturation always needs careful delineation, the simultaneous uniformity and great diversity of cultures clearly marks the religions of Late Antiquity.

About This Book

My strategy in putting together this book was simple: to gather the texts that engaged creative scholars of Late Antiquity into an anthology for classroom use. These texts in the hands of today's scholars will certainly become resources for future study and research and they will become part of the ever-widening corpus of Late Antique texts available to students. I avoided including those texts that are handily and inexpensively available for classroom use. I have not for the most part duplicated the valuable work of the Penguin Library, the Loeb Library, the patristic sources of St. Vladimir's Press, the historical texts published by the Liverpool University Press, or the Cistercian Studies series. Nor have I attempted to supplement the many collections of texts on Roman and Greco-Roman religion. I wanted instead to bring fresh texts to bear and to gather a set of texts that would cohere and present a comprehensive picture without serious duplication of efforts. The texts gathered here, then, both encapsulate Late Antique religion and push the corpus of texts beyond the current parameters, while reflecting the superb scholarly work that has been emerging in Late Antique studies. I owe a profound debt of gratitude to the many contributors who have given so richly of their work.

The nine sections that organize and present these texts in this anthology stand only as a suggestion. Many of these texts would fit into a number of other categories and they certainly can exemplify still other ways of approaching the religious practices of Late Antiquity. However, it seems to me that the question of the individual and the invention of the individual emerges again and again as a central topic in Late Antiquity; biography is only one way of approaching that problematized personality. The biographies of Pachomius, Apollonius, and Plotinus provide evidence for the rich diversity in biographical writing. Another way uses the emerging and vast literature of asceticism, which not only invents the individual but attempts to refashion the person as well. Among the possible texts exemplifying ascetical practice, those of Evagrius Ponticus, pseudo-Athanasius, and Basil of Caesaria (for the eastern empire) and Columbanus (for the western) provide a solid overview. The inclusion of Manichaean ascetical material provides even more depth. The many new religious movements also demand attention because Late Antique religion is replete with new systems of organization and relationship. These new monuments vary widely but show the creative energy of Late Antique religious practice. The texts included here explore diverse ways of organizing (or reorganizing) religious social life in Judaism, Roman cults, Manichaeanism, and Christianity. The nature of religious communities and attitudes toward the city betray a Late Antique fascination with corporate life. That fascination includes new interpretations of social life in the city, as well as new means of understanding society (especially marriage and sexuality) within existing social relationships. Correlative to this interest in exploring social relationships is the attempt to regulate them through law. The laws presented here exemplify both macrocosm (imperial law) and microcosm (Christian ecclesiastical councils). And what study of religious practice could be complete without ritual and hymnody? The ritual practices presented in this section include Jewish and Manichaean liturgies as well as arguments about ritual practice among Spanish Christians and texts of magical healing. The hymns gather together the best of Latin and Greek Christian hymnography with Manichaean and Egyptian religious hymns. The next section reviews the religious persecutions of Christians and Jews, which produced an important body of literature that reveals the conflicting forces of Late Antique society. Last, the brilliant intellectual contributions of theologians, rhetors, philosophers, and other religious thinkers complete this exploration of the practice of religion in Late Antiquity. This section portrays the wide diversity of theological and rhetorical practice in sermons, iconography and its mirror in ekphrasis, oracles and oracular theology, theological treatises, and popular religious practices. The objective, again, was to present a comprehensive overview with fresh sources, reflecting the creative thinking of emerging leaders in the field. The result is an anthology of texts that I hope provides maximum flexibility and creativity for classroom use.

General Bibliography

Bagnall, Roger S. 1993. *Egypt in Late Antiquity.* Princeton: Princeton University Press.

Barnes, Timothy D. 1981. *Constantine and Eusebius.* Cambridge: Harvard University Press.

———. 1982. *The New Empire of Diocletian and Constantine.* Cambridge: Harvard University Press.

Beard, Mary, John North, and Simon Price. 1998. *Religions of Rome.* 2 vols. Cambridge: Cambridge University Press.

Benko, Stephen. 1984. *Pagan Rome and the Early Christians.* Bloomington: Indiana University Press.

Betz, Hans Dieter, ed. 1992. *The Greek Magical Papyri in Translation, Including the Demotic Spells.* 2nd ed. Chicago: Chicago University Press.

Boyarin, Daniel. 1990. *Intertextuality and the Reading of Midrash.* Indiana Studies in Biblical Literature. Bloomington: Indiana University Press.

Branham, R. Bracht, and Marie-Odile Goulet-Cazé, eds. 1996. *The Cynics: The Cynic Movement in Antiquity and Its Legacy.* Berkeley and Los Angeles: University of California Press.

Brown, Peter. 1972. *Religion and Society in the Age of St. Augustine.* London: Faber and Faber.

———. 1978. *The Making of Late Antiquity.* Cambridge: Harvard University Press.

———. 1981. *The Cult of the Saints: Its Rise and Function in Latin Christianity.* Chicago: University of Chicago Press.

———. 1982. *Society and the Holy in Late Antiquity.* Berkeley and Los Angeles: University of California Press.

———. 1988. *The Body and Society: Men, Women, and Sexual Renunciation in Early Christianity.* New York: Columbia University Press.

———. 1992. *Power and Persuasion in Late Antiquity: Towards a Christian Empire.* The Curti Lectures, 1988. Madison, Wis.: The University of Wisconsin Press.

Bury, J. B. 1958. *History of the Later Roman Empire from the Death of Theodosius I to the Death of Justinian.* 2 vols. New York: Dover.

Cameron, Averil. 1993. *The Later Roman Empire:* A.D. *284–430.* Cambridge: Harvard University Press.

———. 1993a. *The Mediterranean World in Late Antiquity* A.D. *395–600.* London: Routledge.

Cameron, Averil, and Peter Garnsey, eds. 1998. *The Cambridge Ancient History.* Vol. 13, *The Late Empire,* A.D. *337–425.* Cambridge: Cambridge University Press.

Clark, Elizabeth A. 1979. *Jerome, Chrysostom, and Friends.* Studies in Women and Religion, 1. New York: Edwin Mellen.

———. 1986. *Ascetic Piety and Women's Faith: Essays on Late Ancient Christianity.* Studies in Women and Religion, 20. Lewiston, N.Y.: Edwin Mellen.

Clark, Gillian. 1993. *Women in Late Antiquity: Pagan and Christian Lifestyles.* Oxford: Clarendon.

Cloke, Gillian. 1995. *'This Female Man of God': Women and Spiritual Power in the Patristic Age,* A.D. *350–450.* London: Routledge.

Cook, S. A., et al., eds. 1939. *The Cambridge Ancient History.* Vol. 12, *The Imperial Crisis and Recovery:* A.D. *193–324.* Cambridge: Cambridge University Press.

Cooper, Kate. 1996. *The Virgin and the Bride: Idealized Womanhood in Late Antiquity.* Cambridge: Harvard University Press.

Cox, Patricia. 1983. *Biography in Late Antiquity: A Quest for the Holy Man.* Berkeley and Los Angeles: University of California Press.

Dawson, David. 1992. *Allegorical Readers and Cultural Revision in Ancient Alexandria.* Berkeley and Los Angeles: University of California Press.

Feldman, Louis H. 1993. *Jew and Gentile in the Ancient World: Attitudes and Interactions from Alexander to Justinian.* Princeton: Princeton University Press.

Fowden, Garth. 1986. *The Egyptian Hermes: A Historical Approach to the Late Pagan Mind.* Princeton: Princeton University Press.

————. 1993. *Empire to Commonwealth: Consequences of Monotheism in Late Antiquity.* Princeton: Princeton University Press.

Fox, Robin Lane. 1987. *Pagans and Christians.* New York: Alfred A. Knopf.

Frankfurter, David. 1998. *Religion in Roman Egypt: Assimilation and Resistance.* Princeton: Princeton University Press.

Frend, W.H.C. 1967. *Martyrdom and Persecution in the Early Church.* Garden City, N.Y.: Doubleday.

————. 1984. *The Rise of Christianity.* Philadelphia: Fortress.

Gardner, Iain. 1995. *The Kephalaia of the Teacher: The Edited Coptic Manichaean Texts in Translation with Commentary.* Nag Hammadi and Manichaean Studies, 37. Leiden: E. J. Brill.

Harris, William V. 1989. *Ancient Literacy.* Cambridge: Harvard University Press.

Jones, A.H.M. 1986. *The Later Roman Empire 284–602: A Social, Economic, and Administrative Survey.* 2 vols. Norman: University of Oklahoma Press, 1964. Rpt. Baltimore: Johns Hopkins University Press.

Jung, C. G. 1967. *Symbols of Transformation (1911–12/1952).* Vol. 5 of *The Collected Works of C. G. Jung.* Bollingen Series. Princeton: Princeton University Press.

Kennedy, George A. 1983. *Greek Rhetoric under Christian Emperors.* Princeton: Princeton University Press.

Lieu, Samuel N. C. 1998. *Manichaeanism in Central Asia and China.* Nag Hammadi and Manichaean Studies, 45. Leiden: E. J. Brill.

MacCormack, Sabine G. 1981. *Art and Ceremony in Late Antiquity.* Berkeley and Los Angeles: University of California Press.

McKnight, Stephen A. 1991. *The Modern Age and the Discovery of Ancient Wisdom: A Reconsideration of Historical Consciousness, 1450–1650.* Columbia: University of Missouri Press.

Meyer, Marvin, and Richard Smith. 1994. *Ancient Christian Magic: Coptic Texts of Ritual Power.* San Francisco: HarperCollins.

Miller, Fergus. 1993. *The Roman Near East 31 B.C.–A.D. 337.* Cambridge: Harvard University Press.

Miller, Patricia Cox. 1994. *Dreams in Late Antiquity: Studies in the Imagination of a Culture.* Princeton: Princeton University Press.

Neusner, Jacob, ed. 1995. *Judaism in Late Antiquity.* Handbook of Oriental Studies: The Near and Middle East. 2 vols. Leiden: E. J. Brill.

Potter, David. 1994. *Prophets and Emperors: Human and Divine Authority from Augustus to Theodosius.* Cambridge: Harvard University Press.

Rouselle, Aline. 1988. *Porneia: On Desire and the Body in Antiquity,* trans. Felicia Pheasant. Oxford: Basil Blackwell.

Swartz, Michael D. 1996. *Scholastic Magic: Ritual and Revelation in Early Jewish Mysticism.* Princeton: Princeton University Press.

Veyne, Paul, ed. 1987. *A History of Private Life.* Vol. 1, *From Pagan Rome to Byzantium,* trans. Arthur Goldhammer. Cambridge: Harvard University Press.

Wimbush, Vincent L., and Richard Valantasis. 1995. *Asceticism.* Oxford: Oxford University Press.

Inventing the Individual: Biography

— 1 —

The First Sahidic *Life of Pachomius*

James E. Goehring

Pachomius (ca. 292–346 C.E.), an Upper Egyptian from the nome of Sne (Latopolis), converted to Christianity in 312/313 and embarked on an ascetic life, first in the village of Šeneset and then as an anchorite (withdrawn monk) under the tutelage of the nearby ascetic Palamon. He eventually moved to the deserted village of Tabennesi and there developed a new form of the ascetic life in which individual ascetics joined together to form a community separated from the world by an encircling wall. Life within the community was governed by a common rule. This new form of the ascetic life is known as coenobitic monasticism.

Much can be reconstructed of Pachomius's life as a result of an extensive though complex literary tradition (Rousseau 1985, 37–55). It includes numerous forms of a *Life of Pachomius,* rules, instructions, and letters (English translations in Veilleux 1980–1982). The *Life of Pachomius* exists in various editions in Coptic (Lefort 1925, 1933), Greek (Halkin 1932), Arabic (Amélineau 1889) and Latin (van Cranenburgh 1969). While the relationship among these *Vita* traditions is complex (Lefort 1943, XIII–XCI; Veilleux 1968, 17–114, 1980–1982, I.1–21; Goehring 1986, 3–23), it is generally agreed that the most complete early forms of the *Life* that survive are a Sahidic Coptic edition preserved most fully in Bohairic Coptic and Arabic translations (*SBo;* Veilleux 1980–1982, I.23–295) and a Greek form known as the *Vita prima* (*G¹*; Veilleux 1980–1982, I.297–423).

The fragmentary version of the *Life* translated here derives from a different Sahidic version known as the First Sahidic *Life of Pachomius* (*S¹*). Unfortunately, only an account of the beginning of the movement survives from *S¹*, and it is fragmentary. The unique evidence that it supplies, however, identifies the text as the most primitive surviving *Vita* tradition (Lefort 1943, LXXII; Veilleux 1968, 40–41). It offers valuable insight not only into the formative stages of the movement, but also into the literary formation of a saint.

The more complete early versions of the *Life* noted above (*SBo* and *G¹*) offer a relatively unified version of Pachomius's conversion and early development as an ascetic (Veilleux 1980–1982, I.23–47, 297–324). Born in the nome of Sne (Latopolis) in Upper Egypt in 292, Pachomius converted to Christianity in 312 as a result of kindness shown to him by Christians while he was being held in prison as a conscript for the war between Licinius and Maximin Daia. When he was freed, he proceeded to the nearby village of Šeneset (Chenoboskeion), where he was baptized. The Coptic version (SBo) indicates that he remained in the village for three years serving the local people during a period of plague.

Pachomius eventually decided to become an anchorite and apprenticed himself under the older ascetic Palamon who lived in the inner desert near the village. He remained with Palamon for seven years, practicing a hard asceticism of fasting and vigils. Then, while on a trip to the acacia forests for wood, he happened upon the deserted village of Tabennesi, where he was instructed in a vision to remain and build a monastery so that others might come and lead the ascetic life with him. He reported the vision to his spiritual father Palamon, who proceeded with him to the village to build a cell for him in accordance with the vision. Shortly thereafter, Palamon died.

The two versions agree that Pachomius's elder brother John soon joined him in Tabennesi, where they lived as anchorites and practiced a harsh asceticism of renunciation and self-mortification. After a time, Pachomius was moved to expand their dwelling into a larger monastery in order to receive others into the ascetic life in accordance with the instructions he had received in his vision. His brother John disagreed with this move and harsh words ensued. Pachomius recognized the carnal nature of his anger towards his brother and mortified himself in prayer the entire night, asking for forgiveness. The Coptic version (SBo) includes an episode in which the brothers are reconciled. Pachomius miraculously sends away a menacing crocodile, which results in John's acknowledgment of his brother's superior faith. John died shortly thereafter.

After accounts of Pachomius's successful victory over various demonic temptations, both versions next report the arrival of the first three disciples, Psentaesi, Sourous, and Psoi. The fame of the movement soon spread and others joined. In the account of the initial growth process, the Coptic version (SBo) notes in a brief passage that Pachomius accepted fifty ascetics from a place called Thbakat, whom, when he discovered that they had carnal minds, he expelled from the monastery. The Vita prima (G¹) includes a more extensive account of this incident, though it places it much later in the Life, after accounts of the organization of the community, the monks' relationship to the local priests, the building of a church in the village by the monks, Athanasius's visit to the Thebaid, Pachomius's hatred of Origen, the founding of a women's monastery, and a lengthy account of Theodore's entry into the movement.

The accounts preserved in SBo and G¹ indicate some initial difficulty in Pachomius's move from the solitary life of an anchorite to the more organized monastic community he envisioned. The difficulties, however, are reduced by the way in which they are treated in these two versions of the Life. In the dispute with his brother John, the SBo version indicates that Pachomius's anger was initiated by John, who sought to stop the expansion by spoiling the wall they were building.

Again in G^1, John appears to oppose the expansion and initiates the exchange of words by asserting that his brother is being conceited. In the Greek account, John does not reappear, though later versions of the *Life* in Greek report his death shortly thereafter. The *SBo* tradition likewise reports his death soon after the event, but not before John's acknowledgment of his brother's superior faith.

Similarly, the account of carnal brothers who had to be expelled appears in both traditions as but a brief episode in a monastery that has already begun to expand. In the *SBo* tradition, it is reported in two sentences after the accounts of the arrival of the first and second wave of faithful disciples. In G^1, it is removed even further from the beginnings of the coenobitic experiment. One is left with the impression that the community was well along in its development when this problem arose.

The First Sahidic *Life of Pachomius* (S^1) translated here offers a remarkably different account of these events. After an introductory section explaining the value of telling Pachomius's story for the edification of the brothers (Fragment 1), the best preserved portion of the text (Fragment 3) begins with the story of Pachomius and his brother, who in S^1 remains nameless. According to this version, the brothers were living as anchorites in Tabennesi when Pachomius received his vision to expand their dwelling and create a communal monastery. While the account of Pachomius's stay with Palamon may well have been in the lost sections of S^1, the fact that the vision occurs after his brother had joined him rather than before is important. The text further implies that Pachomius hid the nature of the vision from his brother when first asked about it. The account also indicates that the brothers began the expansion of the monastery together. There is no indication that John opposed the decision. One only learns that "a small matter came between them" while they were building the wall. Pachomius's brother complained that he was being pompous, which led to Pachomius's anger, and which he immediately regretted. Repenting, he spent the whole night in anguished prayer. While this episode ended the account of the dispute in *SBo* and G^1, S^1 reports that a second exchange of words and a second night of anguished prayer by Pachomius followed. At this point, he mastered his anger, or at least controlled it in the manner of the saints. As in the other accounts, John died shortly thereafter.

While the basic story remains the same in all three versions, the account in S^1 allows for a better understanding of Pachomius's brother's complaint. As opposed to the *SBo* and G^1 versions, the brother has already joined Pachomius prior to the latter's visionary instruction to expand the community. Pachomius initially keeps the vision from his brother, who nonetheless appears to have agreed with the expansion decision in the end. When the dispute arises, we are not actually told the cause. While the focus of the story is naturally on Pachomius's successful conquering of his anger, the account leaves open the possibility of his shared responsibility for the initial dispute. Such is not the case in *SBo* and G^1.

The story that sets S^1 uniquely apart, however, is the account of the first disciples who joined Pachomius's expanded monastic enterprise (Fragments 3, 10–

14, 19). They came from the neighboring villages, and they followed a rule established by Pachomius. They were each responsible for themselves, though a share of everything for their bodily needs was placed in a common pool and overseen by Pachomius. Pachomius took care of them according to the rule that he had established. For their part, they took advantage of his humility and service and treated him with contempt. Pachomius endured their behavior with patience for four or five years.

The text unfortunately breaks off after the rather long beginning of a prayer in which Pachomius entreats God, undoubtedly to ask for advice and aid in dealing with the problem. The account resumes (Fragment 4) with Pachomius setting limits with the brothers, and informing them that if they do not wish to follow the rule, they can go elsewhere. They mocked him and continued their brash behavior towards him. Pachomius then chased them out of the monastery. They appealed to the local bishop, who sided with Pachomius. At this point, the text again breaks off.

A small fragment (Fragment 5) reports Pachomius's temptation by demons, recalling the equivalent passages in *SBo* and *G*[1], which occur in these versions immediately after the account of his dispute with his brother. Fragment 6 begins with the report of Pachomius's expulsion of his sister's son from the monastery and moves on to a longer account of his careful and nourishing management style.

The early nature of the *S*[1] tradition is indicated by its unrefined account of the beginnings of coenobitic monasticism. While it shares the account of Pachomius's initial dispute with his brother with the other versions, it neither locates the source of the disagreement in the brother's rejection of Pachomius's call to expand their monastery (*SBo* and *G*[1]), nor affirms the brother's eventual recognition of Pachomius's superior faith (*SBo*). The latter points, which underscore Pachomius's sanctity at John's expense, suggest the work of a later editor eager to remove any hint of Pachomius's culpability.

The detailed account of Pachomius's initial failure with his first ascetic recruits likewise rings true. It is difficult to imagine that later editors would add such an episode at the beginning of the movement's history. On the other hand, their movement of it to a later period in the community's history makes considerable sense, since it then neither detracts from Pachomius's initial success nor challenges the divine authority inherent in his vision to expand the monastery. While the episode is preserved in shortened form in the later versions of the *Life* (*SBo* and *G*[1]), its placement after the arrival of the first faithful brothers removes the hint that experimentation and failure were involved in Pachomius's initial attempts to establish a coenobitic community. The account in *S*[1] suggests that considerable difficulty occurred in this move from the more traditional anchoritic form of ascetic practice to the innovative communal life.

The account of the beginnings of Pachomian monasticism translated here thus offers insight into the practice and difficulty of ascetic innovation in Late Antiquity. Together with the later traditions, it also serves to illustrate the nature of hagiography and its process of increasing sanctification. In the refining of the text, which functioned as ascetic guidebook, the historical guide was increasingly transformed into the ideal saint. It is a process that serves the primary religious and communal function of the text. Within the text, the reader can also find, among other things, evidence on the nature of ascetic practice, the significance of scripture, the place of vision and prayer, and the role of family connections in early Christian asceticism.

The text translated here as the First Sahidic *Life of Pachomius* (S^1) has been reconstructed from various sources. Only sixteen full pages and two half pages remain of a sixth-century manuscript identified as S^1 (Veilleux 1968, 40; Lefort 1933, 1–9). A later Coptic compilation known as the Third Sahidic *Life of Pachomius* (S^3), however, was formed by simply combining sections of *SBo* with S^1. Additional portions of S^1 can thus be reclaimed from the text of S^3. I have followed the work of Armand Veilleux in this regard, and the selections and section numerations repeat those made by him (Veilleux 1968, 40–41; 1980–1982, I.8–9). The Coptic text is drawn from the editions of L.-Th. Lefort (Lefort 1933; 1941). In the translation that follows, I have noted for each of the seven fragments, both whether it derives from S^1, S^3 or a combination of the two, and the location of the translated Coptic text. If a fragment contains text from both S^1 and S^3, I have indicated the shifts by enclosing the information in angle brackets within the translation itself. In the case of the first fragment, a very small emendation was made from yet another edition of the Coptic *Life of Pachomius* known as S^8. As this was done to complete fragmentary lines, I have not indicated it in the translation itself (cf. Lefort 1933, 253).

Good translations of this material exist in French (Lefort 1943) and English (Veilleux 1980–1982, I.425–43). I have consulted these translations and not shied away from using their interpretations and language when it seemed most appropriate. I have sought to keep the translation as literal as possible without being wooden. I am confident that I have erred in both directions. I have included words in square brackets that represent restorations to the text made chiefly by Lefort (Lefort 1943). While it is necessarily difficult always to match the missing Coptic with the appropriate square-bracketed English translation, I want the reader to be aware of the extent of the restoration in various places in the text. Words in parentheses were added for purposes of clarification. Biblical citations refer to the Greek Septuagint and New Testament texts and are also enclosed in square brackets.

FRAGMENT 1

S^3 supplemented by S^8; Lefort 1933, 253A12–254B36

[1] It is good for us and God's will that we make known to everyone the grace and gift that has come to us from God; especially to the brothers and those begotten of our fathers and their seed, who did not have contact with them in

the body, so that they may understand and strive to become sacrifices to God through purity of body and mind and (thus) truly be, both in this age and in the age to come, sons of our fathers, whose face they have not seen in the flesh.

[2] So Isaiah cries out to others who do not know their fathers, so that they may know them, saying, "Look to Abraham your father and Sarah who bore you, for he was one and I called him, and I blessed him, and I loved him, and I multiplied him [Isa. 51:2]." Let us not claim in ignorance that the Lord said in the gospel, "Call no man your father on earth, for you have one father, who is in heaven [Matt. 23:9]". To be sure, our Lord said this in the gospel for "those who consider the things of the earth, but our citizenship is in the heavens [Phil. 3:19–20]." Furthermore, the apostle, writing to others, says, "If we have had our fathers according to the flesh whom we respect, shall we not much more submit to the father of the spirits and live [Heb. 12:9]?" When he said, "If we have had fathers according to the flesh," he indicated that they are not fathers to them in (their own) time; just as it is written in the gospel that "the one who comes to me and does not hate his father and his mother, etc., cannot be my disciple [Luke 14:26)," so that we may know with assurance that the man who begets a man in the work of God is his father after God, both in this age and the next. Paul says again in another place, "Indeed, you have ten thousand guides in Christ, but not many fathers. For I am the one who begot you in Christ Jesus through the gospel [1 Cor. 4:15]." And we know that he begot them not only through the gospel, but through his (own) good and marvelous deeds. So also, instructing others, he said, "Everything noble, everything just, everything pure, everything good, every blessing, every virtue, every honor, think about these things. What you have learned and received and heard and seen in me, do; and the God of peace will be with you [Phil. 4:8–9]."

[3] This is clearly also the case with our father Pachomius, for he deserves to be called father (because our father) who is in the heavens dwells in him, as he (the apostle) confesses with his own mouth, saying, "It is not I who live, but Christ lives in me [Gal. 2:20]." Therefore, through the divine goodness that is in him, he encourages everyone who wants to obey him, saying, "Imitate me as I imitate Christ [1 Cor. 11:1]." Surely then all who imitate the apostle through their actions are worthy to be called father, because the Holy Spirit dwells in them. For God, the Lord of . . .

FRAGMENT 2

S³; Lefort 1933, 102A1–300

[4] . . . hair-[tunic] that he wore bound around his loins so that the ashes ate away at him, and he was in pain. He hardly ever wore his linen tunic. But from the time he gathered together the (monastic) community, he no longer wore the hair-tunic except at night.

[5] Just as the brothers were assigned to different houses and in each house had someone who was [res]ponsible for them as father, so [h]e too [li]ved in a house. He [di]ffered from the brothers [in n]othing. He did not have [the author]ity to get a tunic [for h]imself f[rom] the head [of the mona]stery, except [when the m]aster of the house in which [he lived] got it for him in accor[dance with the rul]es of the brothers that he [had established] from God.

FRAGMENT 3

S[1] and S[3]; shifts cited below within text

[6] ⟨S[3]; Lefort 1933, 106B35–107B23⟩ One day he and his brother were gathering the harvest on an island near the deserted village of Tabennesi to which they had withdrawn. That night, after they had finished praying according to their custom, he sat off by himself, a short distance from his brother, sad and troubled over the will [of] God [that he wanted] to kno[w]. And [while it was] still dark, behold, [a m]an of light stood before him and said to him, "Why are you sad and troubled?" He answered and said, "It is the will of God that I seek." He said to him, "Do you real[ly] desire the wil[l of] God?" H[e said to him], "Yes." He replied, "The [will of] God is [to serve] the [human] race [in order to] reconcile it to him." [He ans]wered again, a[s if he were ind]ignant, "I se[ek the] will of God, and you say, 'Serve men.'" And that one [answered] him th[ree times], "The wi[ll of Go]d is to ser[ve] men in order to ca[ll] them to him." And after that he (Pachomius) no longer saw him. He remembered the covenant he had made with God on the day alms had been brought to him [in pr]ison with his fellow [prison]ers, when he promised [hi]m, saying, "God, if you help me and deliver me from this distress I am in, I will serve the human race for your name's sake." And he was satisfied that it was a work of the Spirit of the ⟨S[1]; Lefort 1933, 1, 1–7, 28⟩ Lord that had arisen in his heart, for it agreed with the words spoken to him by the man of light who had addressed him. When his brother, who was not far from him, heard him speaking, he said to him, "With whom are you speaking?" for he could not see the one speaking with him. And hiding the matter from him, he (Pachomius) answered, "With no one."

[7] After he had seen the vision in which he was instructed to work on the souls of men "to present them holy to God [Col. 1:22]"—for this was the will of God that he had sought—he and his brother began to expand the place where they lived in order to set up a small monastery; for he (God) had appointed him to take in everyone who came to him to stay and practice the anchoritic life with him. And while they were building the wall of the monastery, a small matter came between them. His brother responded angrily, "Stop being so pompous!" When he heard these words, he became agitated. And when he realized that he had become angry over these few words, he grieved

deeply and said, "I am not yet [faithful], and still I am far from God whose will I promised to do."

[8] When evening came, he went down into an underground place in the deserted village where he lived. He put a brick under his feet and stretched his hands towards God, weeping the entire night from evening until dawn, saying, "Lord, help me. Remove this carnal thought from me so that I will not become angry at all, even if someone should strike me in the face. Am I more honored than my Lord, your beloved son, who became human for the salvation of us sinners? 'For (when) he was reviled, he did not revile; and when he suffered, he did not get angry [1 Pet. 2:23].' How much more ought not I, the sinner, humble myself? Seven times more than he! For he is a God without sin, and he suffered for us. And I am clay, a molded product of his hands. Why can't I suffer without anger?" And in this way he cried out to God all night long in these words, so that the brick on which he stood dissolved beneath his feet from the sweat that streamed down onto it from his face. For it was very hot down in that place, because it was summer. And when dawn arrived, he stopped praying and went again immediately with his brother to work on their building project.

[9] A few days later his brother again let fly a word against him. And when he heard the remark, he became angry. When he realized that he had again become agitated, he did as he had done the first time, spending the whole night praying so that the brick on which he stood turned to mud beneath his feet. And from that day on, he was not again made angry by a carnal thought; for God had granted him the request he had asked for from him. As James says in his letter, "Everything good and every perfect gift comes down from heaven, descending from the father of lights [James 1:17]." The Lord also exhorts everyone who loves him, saying in the gospel, "Ask, and you will receive; seek, and you will find; knock, and it will be opened to you. For everyone who asks will receive, and the one who seeks will find, and to the one who knocks, it will be opened [Matt. 7:7–8]." John too, writing in his letter to all believers, said, "This is the confidence that we have in him, that if we ask in accordance with his will, he will hear us [1 John 5:14]." And after his request had been granted by God, he became obedient like David, who says, "Forsake wrath, renounce anger [Ps. 36:8]." For truly, from that day on he did not get angry again as men of the flesh do, but if he became angry on occasion, he was angry after the manner of the saints. He also earnestly asked the Lord to give him the means to fulfill the other commandments that are written in the holy scriptures. After these events, his brother passed away.

[10] As for him, a few men came to him from the neighboring villages and built dwelling places for themselves in the area he had enclosed as a monastery and practiced the anchoritic life with him. And they formed a small group of men.

[11] When he saw that the brothers were gathering around him, he established the following rule for them so that each one would be responsible for

himself and take care of his own affairs. They would place a share of everything related to the needs of the body in a common pool, either for food or for strangers who might visit them, for they all ate together. And they gave their shares to him to manage for them. They did this freely and of their own will so that he could see to all their needs, because they judged him trustworthy and because he was their father after God. He established this rule for them in this way, adjusting it to their weakness, as the apostle says, "To the weak I became weak, that I might gain the weak [1 Cor. 9:22]." And writing to the Corinthians, he also said, "I fed you with milk, not solid food; for you were not ready, and even now you are not ready [1 Cor. 3:2]." This then was how he proceeded, for he saw that they were not yet inclined to bind themselves together in a perfect community, like that of the believers written about in Acts, "They were of one heart and one soul, and everything they possessed was held in common; no one said about the things that were theirs, 'They are mine.' [Acts 4:32]."

[12] Our father Pachomius nourished them as well as he could, as it is written, "A righteous father nourishes well [Prov. 23:24]." That which he received from them according to this rule, he managed in accordance with all their rules. If they happened to bring him fish or some other food, he took it and prepared it for them. And when he had finished preparing it for them and feeding them, he would sit down, (and) if it were his second day fasting, he would place a little salt on his hand and eat his bread with it. And this is how he always dealt with them, being a servant to them in accordance with the covenant he had made before God, as the Paul says, "For though I am a free man in everything, I have made myself a servant to all, so that I might gain more [1 Cor. 9:19]."

[13] As for them, since they did not stretch their hearts towards God, when they saw his humility and complaisance, they treated him with contempt and great insolence. Habitually when he told them to set some need of theirs in order, they would talk back at him and curse him, saying, "We will not obey you!" He did not pay them back, but, on the contrary, bore with them with great patience, saying, "They will see 'my humility and my affliction [Ps. 24:18],' and they will turn to God and repent and fear him." And this too he did in accordance with the word of Paul: "A servant of the Lord should not quarrel, but should be humble before everyone, a teacher who endures those who are evil, gently instructing those who talk back, so that God might grant them repentance and knowledge of the truth, that they might recover from the devil's traps, since they have been ensnared by him to his will [2 Tim. 2:24–26]."

[14] Once at harvest time, they went out together to reap for wages. And when mealtime arrived, he (Pachomius) harnessed a donkey to (go and) get them something to eat. When he got back, he prepared it for them, and they ate. And when evening came, they stopped working. And after they stopped, some of them jokingly got on the donkey, while others chased after it, laughing

and saying, "Pachomius, our servant, pack up the gear on your back and return it to the monastery." With a troubled heart and sighing, he packed up the gear and brought it back to the monastery. He was not troubled on account of the suffering they caused him, but because of their continuing insolence and the baseness of their souls.

[15] After a long time had passed during which he endured this sort of distress from them and their pranks—not a year or two, but four or five years—he saw that they were not returning to God at all in spite of the patience and forbearance that he showed them. At that point, one day in the evening he went off by himself and stood and prayed all night long. He was troubled over them, because they did not fear God in the work he was patiently doing with them.

[16] And praying, he called on God, saying: "Lord, God almighty, blessed God, blessed Father who is in the blessed Son, and blessed Son who is in the blessed Father, in the blessed Holy Spirit. You who fill every place by the power of your divinity. You from whom nothing is hidden, for all creation came to be through the word of your mouth and was created by the breath of your lips [cf. Ps. 32:6]. "Holy, holy, holy, Lord Sabaoth; heaven and earth are full of his glory [Isa. 6:3]." You who "sit on the Cherubim" and the Seraphim in the heavens, "whose eyes behold the abyss [Dan. 3:55]." You whom no one can bless and exalt and glorify as you deserve and in the manner in which you exist, seeing that you are invisible and invincible and all blessing. Lord, blessed God, the power of whose divinity no one can describe, seeing that we are earth and ash, and you created us out of nothing and gave us existence. For you and your beloved Son, our Lord, and the Holy Spirit are one, as it is written, "you are eager to guard the unity of the Spirit [Eph. 4:3]" of God who is holy and exalted and living, patient, compassionate, good, abounding in mercy. Lord God, faithful, righteous, true and delightful judge. Lord God, the strong of the strong, the resolute one, the awesome one, "who makes his angels spirits and his ministers a flaming fire [Ps. 103:4]." Lord, blessed God, you who created things visible and invisible, whether archangels or principalities or authorities or powers or dominions or thrones or glories [cf. Col. 1:16; Eph. 1:21]. Lord, blessed God, you "who created the heaven and the earth and the things that are in them [Ps. 145:6] ⟨S³; Lefort 1933, 114A27–115B38⟩," the light and the darkness, the sun and the moon and the stars, the sea and the rivers and all that is in them. Lord, blessed God, you who gave the man you created glory and beauty. You took clay from the earth and formed it with your own hands into a man after your image and likeness. You made him male and female. You breathed into his face the breath of life, and the man became a living spirit. You granted him speech on earth, so that he might obey your voice, keep your commandments, [do] all your will, and bless you all [the days] of his life [cf. Gen. 1:2–2:7]. [Lo]rd, bles[sed] God, you who made ma[n] his o[w]n master to choose for [himself in] accordance with his will, consc[ie]nce, and discern-

ment between evil and good. Lord, blessed God, you who gave the man you
formed wisdom, understanding, knowledge, and cleverness. Lord, blessed God,
you who created all the human races from one (man) to live upon the face of
the earth. Lord, Blessed God, you who put the fear and dread of the man you
created into all creatures: birds of the sky, animals of the land, fish and reptiles.
You made him master over all your creatures on the earth. Lord, blessed God,
you who created fertility and barrenness as you informed us in the holy scriptures. Lord, blessed God, you who formed us in the womb and brought us
forth from it. Lord, blessed God, you who cause all our growth and who nourishes us from infancy to old age. Lord, blessed God, you who, through your
will, give us bread to eat, water to drink, and clothing to wear. Lord, blessed
God, you who give us many and varied goods, from the seeds of the earth and
the fruit trees, from the animals and the birds, from the sea, rivers, and dew
of the heaven. Lord, blessed God, you who help all who love you, who seek
you, who keep your commandments in all things, and who are filled with all
the fruits of righteousness of your Holy Spirit according to the condition of
their heart. Lord, blessed God, you who sent to us in the world your holy
Word, the truth, the life, the true light, the invisible one who is in your likeness
in all things, our Lord, your beloved holy son Jesus Christ, who died for us
and rose so that he might raise us from our sins and trespasses through which
we died, and grant us the eternal and imperishable life that he promised us.
Lord, [blessed] God . . .

FRAGMENT 4

S³; Lefort 1933, 116A1–117B38

[17] . . . easily. [And so] I [spo]ke [with you earlier] so that perhaps [you
might repe]nt and [retur]n to the [Lord w]ho created [you when] you [did
not] know him. [So now, wh]en you are [called] to the syna[xis (community
prayers), you w]ill all come, [and you will not] behave in this way every d[ay
on account of me]. If you frequ[ently . . .] until you [. . . y]ou [. . .]. [And]
likewise, when you are called to eat, you will come together, and you will not
behave as you have behaved every day. If you happen to be working together
on some [n]eed of ours, [you will] all go toge[ther], and you will not b[e
negl]ligent a[s you have] been until [now]. If [you] do not (wish to) obey [the]
rules that I [have given] you, [y]ou are free men, and "[to] the Lord [bel]ong
the earth and i[ts fullness] [Ps. 23:1]." If [you] go elsewhere, you can do as
you wish. For I will no longer put up with you if you do not behave in accordance with all the rules I have given to you.
[18] And when he had finished speaking with them, they looked at one
another, and sneering and laughing, they said, "What's the matter with Pachomius today, with the harsh speech? For we will never obey him when he

speaks harshly." So they walked away from him, since they had no concern for him, trusting in the power of their flesh; for they were strong men. Afterwards, when they were called to prayer, whereas until that day they used to come one by one, from that time on no one came. For they had agreed among themselves, "Let's act in this way and see what he [does]." When he saw by their boldness and arrogance that they did not possess the fear of God and had decided not to listen to the voice of the one who spoke with them, he was emboldened by the Holy Spirit that was in him. And trusting in the words of the voice that had spoken and come to him, he got up without staff or weapon for fighting, having, at that moment, a door key in his hand, and he ran after them one by one in the name of God and threw them out of the monastery. They went as though being chased by a crowd or by a fire. To be sure, this act which led to their departure from that place was not an act of man, but rather, it was the Lord who acted against them, as David says, "Let God arise, and let his enemies scatter [Ps. 67:2]." Not only were the enem[ies scattered, but] they gave [themselves up as sl]aves to be be[aten. The m]an who [joins himself to] the spirit of [God does] as the [apostle] says, "[He who jo]ins himself to [the Lord is a] single spirit (with him) [1 Cor. 6:17]." Indeed, this is [why] Dav[id says], "S[trike who]ever is [my enemy] without cause [Ps. 3:8]."

[19] Thos[e men fled in the blindness of t]heir hearts and proceeded to the b[isho]p in the diocese of [Hew] whose name was Sara[pion]. They accused him (Pachomius), saying, "Pachomius threw us out of the monastery." The bishop looked at them, saw their size and strength, [and] sai[d] to them, "You are strong men. This is why Pachomius [. . . as]cetic practices to [. . . you]. I[f he] threw you [out of] the monastery, it [was not he] (who did it) but [God]. Most as[suredly he did] this because of some evil [deeds] that you did. For righteous men . . .

FRAGMENT 5

S[1]; Lefort 1933, 8A1–9B12

[20] . . . testifies in the [scriptures ag]ainst each one of the temptations, putting the devil to shame.

[21] Again one da[y] it happened that a very large throng of demons assembled together and [bro]ught for[ward in] his presence [a great] . . . [six lines missing] . . . together, just as a group of men would try to drag a large stone. This they also did so that perhaps he might laugh . . . [eleven lines missing]

[22] When the devil saw that he could not trick him in any of these (ways), he entered into a [v]er[y beautiful] woman, who [sa]id . . . [thirteen lines missing]

[23] She go[t up, went] and knocked for him. He opened the door, and when he looked and saw her, he immediately looked downward. [twelve lines missing]

FRAGMENT 6

S^3; Lefort 1933, 118A1–119B37

[24] He also saw his own sister's son involved in some wicked affairs while he (the boy) was living the anchoritic life with him in the (monastic) community. And when he saw him, he remembered the word that is written in the gospel, "If your right hand offends you, cut it off and throw it away [Matt. 5:30];" and so he threw him out. He continued to operate in this way all the days of his life, as he had been instructed by God to throw out obstacles and impediments from the house of the Lord.

[25] He was in fact like a shepherd caring for his flock. He nourished the weak in the pastures of righteousness, he bound up the broken (hearted) with the bandages of the gospel, and he brought those that wandered astray back to the sheepfold. The well-nourished and first born, he offered as a sacrifice on the altar of the Lord so that he (the Lord) might smell the fragrance, just as Noah had taken some clean animals and birds and offered them on the altar, and God smelled the fragrance [Cf. Gen. 8:20–21]. So also Paul says, "We are a fragrance of Christ to God [2 Cor. 2:15]." He (Pachomius) made every effort to avoid the reproach that Ezekiel the prophet addressed to the shepherds [Cf. Ezek. 34]. Rather, he tended the sheep, which the Lord had gathered together to him, in accordance with the apostle's command, "Instruct the ignorant, encourage the humble, sustain the weak, be patient with everyone [1 Thess. 5:14]." Actually, he appealed to the Lord's sheep to nourish (themselves) with good food, so that they might become a fragrance for him (the Lord) as he (the apostle) says, "I appeal to you, my brothers, to present your bodies as a living sacrifice, holy and pleasing to God [Rom. 12:1]," not only to become a fragrance through the purity of your body, but also through (the purity of) your heart, as David says, "The sacrifice to God is a broken spirit [Ps. 50:19];" and he urged them to become through their mouths an offering of praise. For he applied himself on behalf of everyone whom the Lord had gathered under him, in every blessing and every good work. And he worked with each individual according to his ability, making every effort so that if someone did reject him, no one else would later be able to bring him back to the work of the Lord. He operated in this way, watching that no one left him without being saved only to be saved by someone else, lest he be reproached in the age to come with the words, "After you threw me out as worthless, behold, someone else gave me life." This is the reason he so diligently worked on the brothers' souls. Some of them he reproached, others he comforted, and still others he rebuked not only in words, but as Paul says, "Do you want me to come to you with a rod, or with love and a spirit of gentleness [1 Cor. 4:21]?" With others again he showed patience with their indifference, teaching them "so that God might grant them repentance, and they might come to know the truth and escape the snares of

the devil [2 Tim. 2:25–26]." And all kinds of people living in sin, he endeavored, in the fear of the Lord . . .

FRAGMENT 7

S³; Lefort 1941, 113A1–115A15

[26] . . . thinking insi[de] that you are taking c[are o]f me and that yo[u contin]ue grievi[ng because] I did not accept it fro[m y]ou. No, I tell you. Bu[t do yo]u hate me? [I] do not [k]now. Fo[r i]f I behave[d like this], I would be leaving [beh]ind a grave scandal that might cause you also to behave in t[his] way on another occasion, and I might be bou[nd] to judgment before G[o]d. [Indee]d, many ti[mes . . .] a mo[nk] . . . [sixteen lines missing]

[27] ["I mortify my body and make it a slave, lest after preaching to oth]ers, I am [myself] rejected [1 Cor. 9:27]." Wh[en] the [brothers hea]rd this, they were frightened and [stopped] speaking w[ith him]. The hair mantle that [he was wearing], they [received] from him, as he had said, on the [day] he passed away. [one and a half lines missing]

[28] It happened again [one day] that one of the old men, the h[ouse]master in his house, became sick. [He] was a holy man. Our father Pachomius grieved incessantly and prayed to the Lord continually. And an angel said to him, "How long will you [grieve a]nd pray for [this brother]? Will you not find [an]other, if he passes away?" [A]nd he looked and saw three men of light, exalted, glorious, gray-haired men. They had come for the one who was ill. The angel said to him, "These are Abraham, Isaac, and Jacob, the patriarchs." And [im]mediately they took the so[ul] of the sick brother [and brought it to heaven with] great [g]lory.

[29] [So] also the apo[stl]e often ag[ain spoke] with him and [the gl]orious [one] who had spoken with him at the gate. He said, "Do you . . . [three lines missing]. . . . He saw . . . again oth[ers] . . . among those who . . . saint[s] in a revelation.

Bibliography

Amélineau, Émile. 1889. *Monuments pour servir à l'histoire de l'Égypte chrétienne au IVᵉ siècle: Histoire de saint Pachôme et de ses communautés.* Annales du Musée Guimet 17. Paris: E. Leroux.

Chitty, Derwas J. 1966. *The Desert a City: An Introduction to the Study of Egyptian and Palestinian Monasticism under the Christian Empire.* Oxford: Basil Blackwell. Rpt., London and Oxford: Mowbrays, 1977.

Goehring, James E. 1986. *The Letter of Ammon and Pachomian Monasticism.* Patristische Texte und Studien 27. Berlin and New York: Walter de Gruyter.

————. 1986. "New Frontiers in Pachomian Studies." In *The Roots of Egyptian Christianity,* ed. Birger A. Pearson and James E. Goehring, 236–57. Philadelphia: Fortress.

————. 1992. "The Origins of Monasticism." In *Eusebius, Christianity, and Judaism,* ed. Harold W. Attridge and Gohei Hata, 235–55. Detroit: Wayne State University Press.

————. 1999. *Ascetics, Society, and the Desert: Studies in Early Egyptian Monasticism.* Harrisburg, Pa.: Trinity Press International.

Halkin, François. 1932. *Sancti Pachomii Vitae Graecae.* Subsidia hagiographica 19. Brussels: Société des Bollandistes.

Lefort, L. Th. 1925. *S. Pachomii vita bohairice scripta.* Corpus Scriptorum Christianorum Orientalium 89. Paris: E typographeo reipublicae. Rpt. Louvain: Corpus Scriptorum Christianorum Orientalium, 1965.

————. 1933. *S. Pachomii vitae sahidice scriptae.* Corpus Scriptorum Christianorum Orientalium 99–100. Paris: E typographeo reipublicae. Rpt. Louvain: Corpus Scriptorum Christianorum Orientalium, 1965.

————. 1941. "Glanures pachômiennes." *Le Muséon* 54: 111–38.

————. 1943. *Les Vies coptes de saint Pachôme et de ses premiers successeurs.* Bibliothèque du Muséon 16. Louvain: Bibliothèque de l'Université.

Rousseau, Philip. 1985. *Pachomius: The Making of a Community in Fourth-Century Egypt.* Reprint, 1999, with new preface. Berkeley and Los Angeles: University of California Press.

Ruppert, Fidelis. 1971. *Das pachomianische Mönchtum und die Anfänge klösterliche Gehorsams.* Münsterschwazacher Studien 20. Münsterschwarzach: Vier-Türme-Verlag.

van Cranenburgh, H. 1969. *La Vie latine de saint Pachome, traduite du grec par Denys le Petit.* Subsidia hagiographica 46. Brussels: Société des Bollandistes.

Veilleux, Armand. 1968. *La Liturgie dans le cénobitisme pachômien au quatrième siècle.* Studia Anselmiana 57. Rome: Herder.

————. 1980–1982. *Pachomian Koinonia.* 3 vols. Kalamazoo, Mich.: Cistercian Publications.

2

Philostratus of Athens

The Life of Apollonius of Tyana

Megan H. Williams

The *Life of Apollonius* portrays a man who is both philosopher and religious figure, combining an ascetic lifestyle, exotic connections, political influence, and semi-divine powers. Apollonius of Tyana lived in the first century C.E.; he came from a small town in the backwater region of Cappadocia in eastern Asia Minor. Philostratus, writing in the early third century C.E., introduced many new elements into his story, creating what is virtually a biographical novel (Bowie 1978, 1663–67). Therefore it is difficult to use the *Life of Apollonius* as a source for the life of the first-century holy man. However, the text provides a wealth of information on the religious, political, and cultural ideals of the educated, elite Greek-speaking world of the third century (Francis 1995, 89). Furthermore, Philostratus's portrayal of Apollonius was influential in succeeding centuries, not only attracting worshippers to his shrine at Tyana and believers who used amulets bearing his image, (Bowie 1978, 1686 and n. 135) but also in setting a pattern for the biographical treatment of the philosopher-sage.

Philostratus of Athens was a prime representative of the educated elite who dominated the cities of the eastern Roman Empire in the second century and beyond. His other major work, *Lives of the Sophists,* consists of biographies of prominent members of this group. These men were highly trained in oratory and literary composition in a culture where public displays of eloquence were popular spectacles, arousing great excitement among the population and conferring tremendous influence upon successful performers. Furthermore, literary education, which was the basis for this sophistic culture, served as a common currency throughout the diverse regions of the Roman Empire where Greek was the *lingua franca.* It allowed the educated to assert their privileges wherever they went simply on the strength of their intimate knowledge of a common literary canon and their ability to speak and comport themselves in the appropriate manner. Philostratus himself was a member of a circle of intellectuals who gathered around the Empress

Julia Domna, a Syrian, wife of the Emperor Severus and mother of Caracalla (Anderson 1994, 4–6). These men were typical of Greek intellectuals whose literary culture allowed them to wield disproportionate influence with the emperors of the second and early third centuries (Anderson 1994, 2–3). Philostratus depicts Apollonius of Tyana according to his own ideal: he is on equal terms with philosophers from Greek cities, unintimidated by Roman emperors or Persian kings, a representative of correct religious practice, has pure Greek diction, and carries the Hellenic ideal wherever he goes.

Apollonius is represented throughout the biography as a philosopher, yet his teachings are not the focus of interest. Rather, it is his exemplary way of life and his semi-divine powers that make him a philosopher (Francis 1995, 106). This image of the pagan philosopher as holy man is a phenomenon of the third century. The historical Apollonius may have been a philosopher or a charismatic wonder-worker, but the combination of these two roles is a later development. Apollonius's lifestyle includes various ascetic practices: he gives up his inherited wealth; does not marry; abstains from sex, meat, and wine; wears distinctive linen clothing; and has long hair. However, this mode of living does not involve self-mortification or extreme measures such as fasts and vigils. Instead, it resembles the practices of those who consulted the gods at a pagan temple or through a divinatory rite: Apollonius lives his entire life in a state of ritual purity, prepared for contact with the gods. It is this way of life that allows him to claim access to divine wisdom, which is in turn the source of his reputation as a philosopher.

This emphasis on personal characteristics, lifestyle, and ethics over teachings is appropriate for the picture given of Apollonius as a follower of Pythagoras. Pythagorean philosophy was resurgent in the second and third centuries: though Pythagoras himself, a rather mysterious figure who lived in the sixth century B.C.E. in Greece and South Italy, had left no writings, Late Antique authors produced lives of Pythagoras as they imagined him and they even forged his sayings. His image was associated with an ascetic lifestyle, a cryptic and abbreviated manner of speech, and an interest in mathematics and astronomy as mystical wisdom. Pythagorean teachings form part of the Middle Platonic synthesis that governed philosophy from the second century onward: Stoic ethics, Platonic metaphysics, and Aristotelian logic and natural science were fused into a comprehensive, eclectic system, which became associated with the great names of classical Greek philosophy, Plato first among them. This philosophy had profound religious tendencies: among its central concerns were personal ethics and lifestyle issues such as diet, the quest for knowledge of the gods in this life, and the fate of the soul after death. Like the founder of this philosophical school, the Pythagorean initiate was expected to be an individual of mysterious, charismatic, even magical or semi-divine powers—not only a learned man but an avatar of divine wisdom.

Apollonius does not use his personal charisma to oppose, but rather to reform and to reinforce the religious and political status quo (Francis 1995, 108–18). Philostratus represents Apollonius as a favorite of good emperors and an opponent of bad ones, chiefly the hated Domitian, who persecuted many among the empire's elite in his paranoid fear of conspiracy (Flinterman 1995, 162–93). Apollonius's defiance of Domitian does not represent a criticism of the imperial system; the speech that he makes to Vespasian praising monarchy makes this clear (*Life of Apollonius* V.27–28; Bowie 1978, 1660–63). Furthermore, on the many occasions where Apollonius gives advice on religious practices, he informs the authorities of pagan temples on the correct ancient form of their worship, using his special knowledge to return the cult to its archaic form. His own avoidance of blood sacrifice and use of secret rituals for sun-worship are not recommended for others. Instead, they are part of what makes Apollonius uniquely authoritative in matters of traditional religious practice. In the same way, Apollonius criticizes Greek cities for falling away from their former glory, adopting debased foreign practices. For example, he attacks the Athenians for giving gladiatorial shows, a Roman custom, in the Theater of Dionysus beside the Acropolis, where the plays of Aeschylus, Sophocles, and Euripides first appeared. Finally, a major part of the *Life of Apollonius* provides an account of Apollonius's travels to Babylonia, Persia, India, Spain, and Egypt, and wherever he goes he finds Greek culture already there before him. The function of travel in the *Life*, therefore, is not to discover new, previously unknown sources of wisdom and spiritual power, but rather to confirm the absolute centrality of Greek literary and religious culture as the source of legitimacy everywhere—beyond the bounds of the Roman empire as well as within it.

But the *Life of Apollonius* is above all a very long, digressive, and heterogeneous text. It is impossible to give an impression of the diversity of its contents in a collection of brief excerpts or a schematic overview of the text's underlying assumptions. Though Philostratus has clearly imposed upon his sources his own view of what a philosopher and holy man ought to be, there are still signs of differing opinions as to what Apollonius was really like scattered throughout the text. Furthermore, the narrative often digresses to deal with tangential topics, such as the natural history and social habits of elephants, which receive a long discussion midway through Apollonius's visit to India. This grab-bag quality is yet another feature of the *Life* that is typical of Late Antiquity: to a modern reader's taste, the work seems disorganized, even confusing. In order to give something of the literary quality of the text, the excerpts below are longer and omit certain aspects of Apollonius's persona, rather than being a series of brief, isolated vignettes.

This digressive quality of Philostratus's account reveals another facet of the culture in which the biography of Apollonius was produced, one that can help to make coherent the image of an individual who is sophist, sage, and saint all at once. This is the importance of ancient rhetoric—the science of public speaking and literary composition—and the attitude towards learning that it imparted, in shaping Philostratus's writing style and his entire outlook. The art of rhetoric was essentially practical: despite the many abstruse theoretical treatises produced in Late Antiquity that claimed to render rhetorical principles scientific, rhetorical schooling remained centered on the tactics and techniques most likely to persuade. As the master discipline in ancient education and scholarship, rhetoric supported a piecemeal approach to learning. Facts, descriptions, fragments of narrative, and philosophical commonplaces—all were part of the successful persuader's armament. No great distinction was made among them, nor was there much call for an overarching systematization of learning. Instead, the clever, retentive mind of the rhetorically educated person would pick up an amazing array of disparate tidbits, from mythology and religion to geography, history, and statecraft. It is this whole ill-assorted inheritance that is evident in Philostratus's account of Apollonius's travels. The excerpts assembled here represent only a narrow selection of this material: they focus on Apollonius's early life, his asceticism, his travels and encounters with foreign sages and kings, and his dealings with Roman emperors.

APOLLONIUS'S YOUTH AND WAY OF LIFE

[I.1] Those who praise Pythagoras of Samos say that he was not an Ionian at all, but was once Euphorbus at Troy and was reborn after he died as Homer's poem tells. They say that he refused to wear garments made of mortal substance and maintained the purity of his diet by avoiding living things and the meat of sacrifices. For he refused to bathe the altars in blood but, as they report, he offered honey-cakes and frankincense to the gods and sang them hymns, for he knew that the gods enjoyed such things more than hecatombs and the sight of the sword resting upon the sacrificial basket. Pythagoras had friendly relations with the gods and learned from them how men could please or disgust them and he based his opinions about nature on his knowledge of the gods; for he said that while others merely form inferences about the divine and offer opinions to counter the opinions of others, he himself had received a visitation of Apollo, who acknowledged that he was the god in person. Furthermore he had associated with Athena and the Muses and with other gods, whose forms and names men did not yet know, though none of these confessed their identities. And whatever Pythagoras proclaimed, his followers took as law, and they respected him as one who had come from Zeus. They imposed silence upon themselves for the sake of the god, for they heard many divine and unspeakable things, which it was difficult to apprehend until they had learned that to be silent is also a form of speaking. . . . And they recount many other things about those who pursued philosophy after the manner of Pythagoras, but it is not appropriate for me to touch on them now, when I ought to hasten on to the story which I have set myself to complete.

[I.2] For Apollonius's philosophic discipline was akin to that which I have described, yet he was more divine than Pythagoras in wisdom and in his sallies against tyrants. He lived neither in ancient times nor just recently and yet men do not recognize him for the true wisdom, which he practiced through cultivation of both a philosophical mind and a purified and healthy body. Instead, each praises a different aspect of the man and then others, since he associated with the Magi of Babylonia and the Brahmans of India and the Gymnosophists of Egypt, call him a magician and slander him as practicing fraudulent wisdom. But these latter regard him in a distorted light, for Empedocles and Pythagoras himself and Democritus, though they conversed with magicians and they report many wondrous things, in no way were seduced by the magical art; Plato went to Egypt and intermingled much of what he took from the prophets and priests there into his own writings, as a painter who makes a picture employs diverse colors, yet he was not accused of magic, though he was envied by all men for his wisdom. For the fact that Apollonius perceived so many things in advance and had foreknowledge does not suffice for an accusation of this kind of wisdom, or else Socrates too would stand indicted for the things that he foreknew, informed by his daimon, and Anaxagoras for what he foretold. . . . Yet those who assign feats of wisdom to Anaxagoras would deprive Apollonius of what he foreknew according to wisdom; instead, they say that he did these things by magical arts. For all these reasons I have seen fit not to abandon the world in its ignorance, but to give precise information regarding the man, both the precise chronology of his words and actions and the general outlines of his wisdom, for which he attained the reputation of being a semi-divine, indeed a holy man. I have assembled my information from all the cities where he was loved, from all the temples where he restored rites that had fallen into disuse, from other writers' accounts of him, and from his own letters. For he sent these to kings, to sophists, to philosophers, to men of Elis, to Delphians, to Indians, and to Egyptians, concerning the gods, customs, and laws; in each area he set straight the errors of all. But now I move on to present these materials in detail.

[I.4] Now Apollonius's father was of the city of Tyana, a Greek city among the Cappadocian race; his father had the same name as he did, and his family was ancient and derived from the first settlers. The father was a wealthy man for the area, though the region is abundant. An apparition of the Egyptian demi-god Proteus appeared to Apollonius's mother while she was pregnant with him, the same Proteus who underwent so many transformations in Homer. She, not at all afraid, asked him whom it was that she bore, to which he replied, "Myself." Then when she asked, "But who are you?" he replied, "Proteus, the Egyptian god." Now anyone who has heard the poets hardly needs me to lay out who Proteus was and of what sort his wisdom: how he took on many forms, changing from one to another and was beyond capture and seemed to know and to foresee everything. But the reader must bear Proteus in mind, especially when the story as it goes along shows that the man it speaks of was greater than Proteus in foreknowledge and greater in his ability to escape from difficulty and danger just as he was close beset.

[I.5] It is said that Apollonius was born in a meadow, near which his temple has now been erected with great care. The manner in which he was born must not be overlooked; for at the hour of the birth a dream led his mother to walk out into the meadow and gather flowers; presently she came with her housemaids to take up the flowers: the maids scattered themselves over the field, but she fell asleep in the grass. There swans, which grazed in the meadow, formed a circle around her while she slept. The birds, as is their habit, cried out together in prayer and presently a breeze arose in the meadow; she was awakened by their song and gave birth, for any astonishment can suffice to bring about an early delivery. Then, too, the people round about say that at the moment Apollonius's mother gave birth to him, a lightning bolt seemed to fall upon the earth, then shoot back up into the ether and disappear above. By this, I think, the gods showed how distinguished he was to become and how he would rise above everything earthly and grow close to the gods, and they foreshadowed what sort of man he was to be.

[I.7] Now I will proceed to his youth: in grammar school, he showed himself to have a powerful memory and to be hard-working. He spoke pure Attic and his speech was not deformed by the influence of the nation among which he lived. All eyes were drawn to him, for at that time he was very attractive. When he was fourteen his father sent him to Tarsus to study with Euthydemus from Phoenicia. Euthydemus was a good rhetorician and taught him this art but, although Apollonius was pleased with his teacher, the customs of the city seemed to him amiss and not conducive to those who would be philosophers. For the inhabitants of Tarsus were preoccupied with pleasure above all else and loved to jeer at people and make fools of them, and paid more attention to their fine white linen than the Athenians ever did to wisdom. They used to recline along the banks of the river Kydnus like so many pompous waterfowl. . . . For these reasons Apollonius transferred his teacher, with his father's consent, to neighboring Aegae. There he found quiet appropriate to one who would study philosophy and a school more vigorous in tone and a temple of Asclepius, where Asclepius himself appeared visibly to people. At Aegae too there studied together Platonic philosophers, and Stoics after the school of Chrysippus, and Peripatetics; Apollonius also heard the instruction of the Epicureans, for he did not disregard any of these teachings. Pythagorean doctrines, however, he pursued with an aptitude that was beyond description. For his teacher himself was not terribly serious about Pythagorean teachings and did not pursue a rigorous life of philosophy; for the man was subject to the demands of his belly and his sexual desires and modeled himself on Epicurus. This teacher was Euxenus from Heracleia in Pontus. . . .

[I.8] So Euxenus, considering that Apollonius had conceived a great undertaking, asked him how he would begin it. Apollonius answered, "At the point where physicians begin, for when they purge the stomach, those who are not ill are prevented from becoming sick and those who are sick are cured." From then on, he refused animal foods as impure and dulling to the mind and ate instead sweetmeats and greens, saying that they were pure, inasmuch as the earth itself gave them. Furthermore, while he admitted that wine was a pure drink, since it came from a plant so readily tamed and cultivated by men, nonetheless he opposed it for filling the mind with conflict and entirely muddying the ether in the soul. Then after purifying his stomach with this diet, he took to walking shoeless by way of adornment and put on linen clothing, for he refused to wear anything made from a living creature, and he let his hair grow and lived in the temple. Those who came to the temple were amazed at him; and one day Asclepius told the priest that he rejoiced to cure illnesses while Apollonius watched. So the Cilicians and those from the surrounding regions came to see him, drawn by what they had heard. . . .

[I.13] When Apollonius heard that his father had died, he hastened to Tyana and there with his own hands he buried him beside the tomb of his mother, for she had died not long before. Then he divided the property, which was magnificent, with his brother, who was an unruly fellow and a drunkard. . . . But eventually Apollonius, like those men who gentle horses that are bad-tempered and difficult to lead, brought his brother around by persuasion and corrected his mistaken ways, though his faults were numerous. For his brother was a slave to dice and to wine, and was given to reveling with whores, and took great pains over his own hair, which he artfully dyed, strutting about and giving himself airs. Then when matters with his brother were well in hand, he turned to his other relatives and won over those who were in need by giving them his remaining inheritance, keeping only a little bit for himself. Indeed one might charge that Anaxagoras of Clazomenae was more philosophical towards herd-animals than men, since he abandoned his possessions to cattle and goats, and Crates of Thebes by throwing his money into the sea benefited neither men nor sheep. Furthermore, though Pythagoras was commended for the prescription that one ought to have intercourse with no woman except one's own wife, Apollonius said that Pythagoras had intended this for others and he himself would neither marry nor engage in any sexual congress. He exceeded in that regard even the restraint of Sophocles, for while that man said that when he arrived at old age he escaped from a harsh and raving master, Apollonius because of his virtue and self-control was not enslaved to this passion even in youth, but already as a young man ruled over a vigorous body and mastered its ravings. Nevertheless, some accuse him of sexual entanglements and say that having suffered an erotic disappointment he went abroad for a year among the Scythians. But this is completely false, for he neither visited the Scythians nor did he ever suffer such erotic passions, for even Euphrates did not accuse him of sexual misdemeanors, even though he composed false statements about him, which we shall expose in the account of Apollonius's relations with Euphrates; instead Euphrates quarreled with Apollonius because the latter rebuked him for accepting money and tried to lure him away from money-changing and trading in dime-store wisdom. But I must treat of these things in their own time.

[I.14] Once Euxenus asked Apollonius why he did not become a writer, since his nature was so noble and he possessed a style of such high quality. At this Apollonius, as if awakened from sleep, said, "Because I have not yet kept silence." And from that point on he began to keep silence, for he believed it to be necessary. Yet while he restrained his voice, his eyes and his mind noticed many things, and he committed all to memory; indeed, even when he was a hundred years old, he still surpassed Simonides in the capacity of his memory. He used to sing a certain hymn in honor of memory, which says that all things perish under the force of time, yet time itself is ageless and deathless because of memory. Moreover, during the time when he kept silence his company was not without grace: he would signal with his eyes and hand and a nod of the head his reactions to what was said, so that he did not appear gloomy or sullen, for he carried himself in a sociable and agreeable manner. He himself says that this period was the most arduous of his entire life, since he spent five years in this ascetic exercise; though he had many things to say, he said nothing, and though he heard many things that could have angered him, he paid no attention; he says that when he was aroused to speak up he led himself onwards by repeating the Homeric verse, "Bear up, my heart and tongue," and when others' logic struck him as faulty he set aside the urge to disprove them for the time being.

[I.16] [After his five years' silence, Apollonius stayed some time in Antioch]. ... When he had it in mind to converse, he avoided the places where he could find company and a disorderly crowd, saying that he did not require merely the society of other people for himself, but was looking for true men. He frequented the more solemn places and dwelt in those temples that were not closed up from disuse. At dawn he offered up to the sun a private form of worship of his own, which he only made known to those who had practiced the discipline of silence for four years. During the rest of the day, if the city was Hellenic and the holy places in it well-known, he would call together the priests and speak philosophy concerning the gods and set them straight on such matters, to the extent that they had departed from the form that had been ordained originally. But if the rites were barbarous and peculiar to the place, he would learn who had founded them and to what end they were established and these inquiries would show him how he might improve them; thus he would make suggestions, if he could devise a wiser form of worship than was presently in force. Then he would go off with his followers and bid them ask him whatever questions they wished. For he said that it was necessary for those who would philosophize to keep company with the gods at earliest dawn, and afterwards to make time for human intercourse. When he had spoken to his companions and satisfied their queries and had had enough of their company, he would get up to address the rest of the people, not before mid-day, but exactly at the time when the day stood still. And when he thought he had discoursed thus as much as was needful, he would be anointed and rubbed, and would cast himself into cold water, for he called the baths the old age of men; at any rate when the Antiochenes were shut out of the baths because of the terrible things that had been done there he said, "It seems to me that the Emperor has given you an extension of life in return for your crimes." Then too, when the Ephesians were planning to stone the archon for not heating the baths adequately he said, "You blame the archon, since you bathe wretchedly, but I blame you, for bathing at all."

APOLLONIUS'S TRAVELS

[I.18] After all this, the idea occurred to him to make a great journey and he began to think of the Indian race and the wise men among them, the Hyrcanians who are called Brahmans; he would say that it was appropriate for young men to travel and to set out for foreign lands. Along the way he could pick up an acquaintance with the Magi, who dwell in Babylon and Susa, and learn their wisdom while passing by. So he announced the plan to his followers, who were seven in number. But when they tried to convince him to adopt another plan and sought by any means to dissuade him from this impulse, he said to them, "I took counsel with the gods and told you their decisions; now I have tested you, to see if you are strong enough for what I plan to do. But since you have turned out to be mere pantywaists, I wish you the best of health and hope that you may continue your philosophical careers; for myself, I will be moving on, where wisdom and the gods lead me." With these words he set out from Antioch with a pair of servants, whom he had from his ancestral estate, the one a shorthand writer and the other a calligrapher.

[I.19] He arrived in the ancient city of Ninus, in which a statue is set up in a barbaric fashion; the altar is dedicated to Io the daughter of Inachus and she is represented with small horns sprouting from her temples. While he was staying there and deducing a great deal more about the statue than the priests and the prophets there knew, a man named Damis approached him, a native of Ninus's city. I mentioned him above, for Damis shared Apollonius's travels with him and participated in all his wisdom and preserved many particulars of the man. Damis was immediately drawn to Apollonius and said to him, since he was eager for the road, "Let us go, Apollonius, you following the god and I following you, for you may find that I am good for many things; though I can't claim to know everything, at least my knowledge is sufficient for Babylon; I know the number of its cities, since I visited there not long ago and I am familiar with the villages, in which there are many good things. Moreover, I know the various barbarian languages, though there are several of them: one for the Armenians, and one for the Medes and the Persians, and another for the Kadusii; I have learned all of them." The philosopher replied, "As for myself, my friend, I understand every language, without having learned any of them." At this the Ninevite was astounded. "Do not be amazed," said Apollonius, "if I know every language of humankind; for indeed I know also every silence of humankind." But at that the Assyrian did obeisance to him as if to a god, so impressed was he by what he had heard. He looked upon Apollonius just as if he were a divine being and remained with him, giving himself up to the acquisition of wisdom and memorizing whatever he learned. . . .

[I.20] . . . Now in order to give an accurate account and not pass over anything which Damis wrote, I thought also to speak of all the things they undertook while traveling through these barbarous regions, but the tale drives me on to greater and more wonderful things. Nevertheless, I must dwell a moment on a brace of worthy themes: the manliness which Apollonius displayed in wandering among such races of barbarians and brigands, who are in no way under the rule of the Romans, and the Arabian wisdom which allowed him to acquire an understanding of the speech of the animals. He learned this ability in the course of this very journey among the Arabian tribes, who best know and practice the skill. For it is common for the Arabians to listen to the birds prophesying, as we listen to oracles: they are able to understand the wordless speech of the birds, so they say, by eating the heart and the liver of dragons.

[I.26] Concerning the Magi, Apollonius has said enough himself, for he associated with them and learned certain things from them, and taught them others before he went away. But Damis knew nothing of the conversations that occurred between Apollonius and the Magi, for they forbade him to accompany Apollonius when he went to visit them. So he merely says that Apollonius visited the Magi at mid-day and in the middle of the night and when Damis asked him, "What of the Magi?" Apollonius answered, "They are wise, but not in all respects."

[I.27] But of Apollonius and the Magi later on. When he arrived at Babylon the satrap who presides over the great gates, perceiving that he had come seeking knowledge, held out a golden image of the king, to which one must do obeisance as if to a god in order to gain entrance to the city. Now those who come on embassies from the Roman government are never required to do this, but those who come as ambassadors from barbarian lands, or just to learn about the country, are sent away unreceived if they do not worship the image. Think, that to be a high court official among the barbarians involves such duties as these! So when Apollonius saw the image, he said, "Who is this?" When he heard that it was an image of the king, he said, "This man, to whom you do obeisance, would receive a great service if I were merely to praise him as good and noble." And saying this he went through the gates. But the satrap, amazed at him, followed after him, and taking Apollonius's hand asked through an interpreter his name and his house and his business and his purpose in coming to the city, and when he had written these things down on a writing tablet along with a description of his appearance he bid him wait there. . . .

[I.31] . . . Apollonius approached the Persian king and greeted him, and the king addressed him in the Greek language, and bid Apollonius sacrifice with him; for he was on the point of slaughtering a white Nisaean horse to the Sun, decked in rich trappings, as if for a ceremonial procession. Apollonius, however, replied, "Your Highness, go ahead and sacrifice as you normally do; but I will offer with you an offering according to my own custom." Then taking up some frankincense he said, "Oh Sun, send me wherever on earth seems fit to me and to you and may I make the acquaintance of good men, but may I neither learn of what is debased nor be lowered to such things myself." When he had said these things he cast the frankincense on the fire . . . and he left the place of sacrifice, in order to avoid participating in the shedding of blood.

A CONVERSATION ON DIVINATION
AT THE COURT OF THE INDIAN KING

[II.37] [Apollonius said,] ". . . And yet divination by means of dreams, which seems to be the most divine faculty of which humans are capable, comes more easily not to those who are befuddled by wine, but rather to those who receive such dreams undefiled and with all the mind's powers collected. For the interpreters of dreams, whom the poets call sellers of dreams, do not examine any dream without asking first what time it was when the dream appeared. If it was dawn and the dream came in the sleep of morning, they consider that the soul, being in a state of health, was able to prophesy, since it had time to drain off the wine; but if the dream came in the first onset of sleep, or in the middle of the night, when men's souls are immersed in wine and befuddled by it still, the interpreters in their wisdom reject the dream as a mere false show. And I can demonstrate conclusively that the gods also are of this opinion, and that they grant oracles to those whose souls are sober rather than drunken. For there was, Your Highness, a man among the Hellenes who was a prophet, by the name of Amphiaraus." The Indian king replied, "I know, for you speak perhaps of the son of Oiocles, who when he went up out of Thebes was swallowed up alive by the earth." Apollonius said, "This man, Your Highness, now provides oracles in Attica by granting dreams to those who seek them. His priests require anyone who seeks a dream to refrain from eating for one day, and from drinking wine for three, in order that the soul, being transparent to the light of prophecy, may draw in the oracles. But if wine was a good drug for bringing on sleep, then the wise Amphiaraus would bid the seekers to prepare themselves in the opposite manner, and they would be carried into his inner sanctum full of wine like earthen jugs. But I could mention also many other oracles, well respected by the Greeks, in which the priest prophesies from the tripod after imbibing water, not wine. Indeed you may consider me too as a bearer of the god, Your Highness, along with all those who drink only water: for we are taken prisoner by the nymphs of the springs and are bacchants in sobriety." The king said, "Then Apollonius, will you make me one of your sacred band?" Apollonius replied, "I would, but it would make you seem vulgar to those who are under your rule; for a man who wields kingly power will develop an ideal royal temperament if he practices a philosophy that is measured and somewhat indulgent; and this precept is demonstrated by your example. But what is severe and extreme, Your Highness, will appear vulgar and lowly in you as it would not in a private citizen; furthermore, the envious might consider it to be a sign of vanity."

APOLLONIUS AND THE INDIAN SAGES

[III.10] From there on, the road led for four days through pleasant and well-cultivated lands, until they were told that they were approaching the tower of the sages. Their guide then bid his camel to kneel and leapt off, terrified and covered in sweat. But Apollonius perceived exactly where he had come. He laughed at the Indian guide's fear, and said, "I suppose that this fellow, if he were to sail into a great harbor after crossing an immeasurable ocean, would be anguished at the sight of land and would fear to enter the haven." With these words he instructed his camel to sit down, for he was accustomed by then to this mode of travel. What had made the guide so afraid was the proximity of the sages, whom the Indians dread even more than their own kings: for even the king himself, to whom the land is subject, consults them about everything he says and does, just like those who send for advice to a god. And the sages instruct the king as to what is desirable for him to do, but forbid him and warn him away from what is to be avoided.

[III.11] They were about to halt in a neighboring village—it is not quite a stade distant from the hill of the sages—when they say that a young man arrived running, the blackest Indian they had seen, with a crescent shaped mark on his forehead above his brows that glimmered marvelously. . . .

[III.12] Running up to Apollonius the youth addressed him in the Greek language; this did not seem at all amazing since everyone in the village also spoke Greek, but when he said, "Greetings to the great man," the others were overtaken with wonder. Apollonius himself, however, was encouraged to believe that he had found what he came for, and looking at Damis, he said, "We have come among men who are truly wise, for they seem to have foreknowledge." At once he asked the Indian what he must do, for he already desired the company of the sages; the Indian youth replied, "The others must remain here, but you may come just as you are, for they have commanded it so themselves."

[III.13] The enigmatic and peremptory quality of his reference to these men already had a Pythagorean ring to it for Apollonius, and he followed eagerly. They say that the hill on which the wise men dwell is the height of the Acropolis of Athens; it rises up above the plain, and just like the Acropolis it is encircled by natural rock fortifications. . . . And around the hill they say that they saw a cloud, in which the Indian sages dwell, visible to those whom they wish to see them and concealed from all others. But if there are any other gates protecting the hill, they say that they did not see them. For the fog did not give way so that they could see whether the hill had any entrance or was shut quite fast.

[III.14] But Apollonius himself went up [to the hill]. . . . There he saw first a well, four fathoms deep, from the mouth of which there rose a bright blue light. When the midday sun stood above the well, this light emerged from the brightness of the well and spread upwards, in the form of a glowing rainbow. Apollonius later learned that the earth beneath the well was scarlet red and its water was considered mystical and sacred. For all the inhabitants of the surrounding regions of India believed that it had the power to enforce binding oaths. Next to this well there was a crater of fire, from which there went up a flame the color of lead; no smoke or fumes darted up from it, nor did it ever overflow this basin, but its bubbling was contained by the pit. There the Indians are purified of unintentional sins, so that the sages call the well "The Trial" and the fire "Forgiveness." They say that they saw two wine-jars of black stone which held the rains and the winds. The first jar, which contains the rains, is opened when drought takes hold of India and sends forth clouds and waters all the earth; but if the rains are excessive, it is closed and restrains them. The other wine-jar, which contains the winds, plays, I suppose, the same role as the bag of Aeolus; for the sages can open the jar and let loose one of the winds in season to blow upon the land and refresh it. Furthermore, they say that they saw images of the gods: not only Indian and Egyptian gods, which would have been no great wonder, but also images of the most ancient gods of the Hellenes, Athena Polias and Apollo of Delos and Dionysus of Limnae and Dionysus of Amyclae, and others of equal antiquity, all of them set up and worshipped by the Indians according to Hellenic customs. These sages say that they dwell in the center of India and they regard a certain mound as the very navel of their hill. On this mound they celebrate fire rituals, using fire which they say they draw out of the rays of the sun, and every day at midday they sing a hymn to the sun.

[III.15] . . . Damis says that the Indian sages were in the habit of making their beds upon the ground, after they had strewn the earth with a particular species of grass. He also says that he saw them walking about in the air as much as two cubits off the ground. They did this not merely for the sake of performing wonders, for they disdain those who seek human approbation, but rather they rise up with the Sun and walk about above the earth as a form of offering to the god. Moreover, they do not keep the fire, which they draw forth from the rays of the sun, burning upon an altar nor do they guard it in a fire-box, though it is a physical fire. Instead, as the rays that are emanated from the sun are reflected in water, so this solar fire hovers in mid-air and shimmers in the ether. . . .

[III.17] [After meeting Iarchas, the leader of the Indian sages, and his followers, Apollonius is invited to join them in their midday worship of the Sun.] They went to a spring of water, which Damis says that he saw later on and describes as like the spring of Dirce in Boeotia. There they first stripped themselves, then anointed their heads with a drug which resembled amber. This potion so warmed the Indians that their bodies steamed and the sweat ran off them in gushing streams, just as if they were washing themselves next to a fire.

Then they threw themselves into the spring; when they had washed themselves in it they proceeded to the temple, their heads garlanded with wreaths and their throats swelled with sacred song. There they assumed the form of a chorus and set Iarchas before them as their chorus-leader and together they raised their rods upright and struck the earth. The earth billowed like a wave and sent them up two cubits into the air. All the while they sang a song just like the paean of Sophocles, which they sing at Athens in honor of Asclepius. . . .

APOLLONIUS AND THE EMPEROR TITUS

[VI.29] When Titus had taken Jerusalem and filled the city with corpses, the neighboring peoples voted to grant him a crown. He declined this honor, however, saying that he had not done the deed himself, but had merely lent his forces to God, who had thus shown his anger. Apollonius praised this refusal, for it revealed Titus's understanding of both human and divine affairs and made him appear full of moderation, since he rejected a crown awarded for the shedding of blood. So Apollonius addressed a letter to Titus, which he sent to him via Damis, as follows:

"Apollonius to Titus, the Roman general, greetings. Since you have shown unwillingness to be acclaimed for acts of war and for the shedding of blood, I crown you with the garland of moderation, for you recognize the actions for which one properly deserves acclaim."

Feeling this compliment very warmly, Titus replied, "I am well aware that my father and I both owe you thanks; I will remember this, for while I have conquered Jerusalem, yet you have conquered me."

[VI.30] But when he had been proclaimed emperor in Rome and received the highest accolades for bravery, Titus entered equally into the Empire with his father [the Emperor Vespasian]. Nevertheless he kept Apollonius in mind, thinking that it would be worth much to him to see the philosopher even if they could be together only for a short time. So he asked Apollonius to come to Tarsus. When he arrived Titus embraced him and said, "My father wrote to me concerning all his conversations with you; here is the letter in which he writes that you were his benefactor and the cause of all our good fortune. Now, I am only thirty years old, yet I have deserved already what my father received only when he was sixty. I fear that perhaps I have been called to rule before I know how to obey and have assumed responsibilities that are too great for my capacity." Apollonius caressed his neck, for he was as well muscled as an athlete in training, and said, "And who will force so strong a bull to bow his neck under the yoke?" "He who from my youth raised me like a calf," Titus replied, speaking of his father and implying that he would only be ruled by the man who from boyhood had accustomed his son to obey him. "I am so pleased," said Apollonius, "first because you are prepared to follow your father's lead, for even those who are not his natural children are happy to be ruled by him, and then to see that you are anxious to safeguard his power, for this course will keep you safe as well. But when youth and age unite to rule, what lyre or flute could produce a harmony so sweet and well-blended? For when the respected elder joins with the youth, age will be strengthened and youth will not lack order."

[VI.31] "What counsel will you give me then, man of Tyana, concerning government and the exercise of monarchical power?" said Titus. Apollonius replied, "Only the advice you have already given yourself, for it is clear that you have submitted yourself to your father and are in agreement with him. But I will quote you a saying of Archytas on that head, for it is noble and worth learning by heart. Archytas was a native of Taranto, a philosopher of the school of Pythagoras; on the subject of the raising of children he wrote, 'Let the father be an example of virtue to the children, for the fathers will proceed all the more resolutely along the course of virtue, if they see that their children are coming to resemble them.' But I will introduce to you my own friend Demetrius, who will be your companion and instructor whenever you wish advice on the duties of the good ruler." Titus said, "What sort of wisdom, Apollonius, does this man possess?" Apollonius replied, "Freedom of speech and no fear of telling the truth to anyone, for these are the Cynic virtues." Titus seemed discomfited when he heard the name Cynic. But Apollonius, punning on the original meaning of Cynic, a "dog-like" philosopher, went on, "Even in Homer, Telemachus, when he was a young man, needed two dogs and Homer sent them with the young man to the marketplace of Ithaca as helpers, although they were unreasoning animals. But you will be accompanied by a dog who will bark on your behalf wisely, not irrationally—at others and at you yourself, if you go wrong." Titus said, "Then give me this dog to help me; I will even allow it to bite me, if it perceives that I am committing some injustice." Apollonius replied, "I will write him a letter, for he is a philosopher at Rome." Titus said, "Do write to him and I wish that someone would write on my behalf to you, too, so that you would share the road to Rome with us." Apollonius replied, "I will come whenever it is beneficial to us both."

[VI.34] Now the inhabitants of Tarsus had been angry with Apollonius for a long time, because they lacked the vigor to endure the vehemence of his rebukes, unrestrained and pleasure-loving as they were. But at this time they came to submit to the man in the following manner and to consider him their patron and the mainstay of the city. While the Emperor was sacrificing in public, the entire city united to ask of him a very great favor. He replied that he would repeat their request to his father and would himself represent their interests before him. But Apollonius was standing by and said, "If I were to prove to you some of these men here were opposed to you and your father and that they had sent emissaries to Jerusalem to foment rebellion, indeed that they were secret allies of your most open enemies, what counsel would you take?" "Why, what else," Titus replied, "but that they should die?" Then Apollonius said, "But is it not then shameful to impose penalties immediately, but to delay the granting of benefits and to carry out the one on your own account, but to hold back the other until you can consult your father?" The Emperor was persuaded and said, "I grant their requests, for my father will not be angry with me because I have been ruled by the truth and by you."

Bibliography

Anderson, Graham. 1986. *Philostratus: Biography and Belles Lettres in the Third Century* A.D. London: Croom Helm.

———. 1994. *Sage, Saint, and Sophist. Holy Men and their Associates in the Early Roman Empire*. London: Routledge.

Bowie, E. L. 1978. "Apollonius of Tyana: Tradition and Reality." *Aufstieg und Niedergang der römischen Welt* 2.16.2: 1,652–99.

Elsner, John. 1997. "Hagiographic Geography: Travel and Allegory in the *Life of Apollonius of Tyana*." *Journal of Hellenic Studies* 117: 22–37.

Flinterman, Jaap-Jan. 1995. *Power, Paideia and Pythagoreanism: Greek Identity, Conceptions of the Relations between Philosophers and Monarchs and Political Ideas in Philostratus' Life of Apollonius*. Amsterdam: J. C. Gieben.

Francis, James A. 1995. "Apollonius of Tyana: The Rehabilitated Ascetic." In Francis, *Subversive Virtue: Asceticism and Authority in the Second-Century Pagan World*. University Park: Pennsylvania State University Press.

Jones, C. P., trans. 1970. *Philostratus: Life of Apollonius*. Harmondsworth: Penguin.

Philostratus. 1870. *Vita Apollonii*. Ed. C. L. Kayser. Leipzig: Teubner.

———. 1939. *The Life of Apollonius of Tyana*. 2 vols. Trans. F. C. Conybeare. Loeb Classical Library. Cambridge: Harvard University Press.

3

Porphyry

On the Life of Plotinus and the Order of His Books

Richard Valantasis

Porphyry (232–305 C.E.), born in Tyre in Syria, became a leading scholar of the fourth century in Rome. His most famous accomplishment was the editing and publishing of the works of one of his famous teachers, the philosopher Plotinus (205–69 C.E.), who articulated the Neoplatonic philosophy popular in Late Antiquity. Porphyry's *On the Life of Plotinus and the Order of His Works* formed the biographical introduction to the edition of Plotinus's lecture notes organized by Porphyry into six *Enneads* (groups of nine treatises) and published in the beginning of the fourth century. Another edition of Plotinus's writings by another student, the physician Eustochius, existed, but Porphyry intended this biographical introduction to establish his publication as the definitive edition authorized by Plotinus himself. The biographical foreword serves as an introduction to the work, an argument for Porphyry's edition as primary, and a marketing device that justifies Porphyry's organization of Plotinus's notes; it is the only existent biography of the famous philosopher Plotinus.

The content of Porphyry's foreword is easily outlined. The introduction (sections 1–3) portrays Plotinus's attitude toward his body and describes his educational formation. The next division (sections 4–6) lists Plotinus's treatises chronologically. The third division (sections 7–9) describes Plotinus's relationships with his students and the fourth division (sections 10–12) characterizes his personality. The fifth division (sections 13–16) describes Plotinus's school. Sections 17–23 provide evaluations of his work by Amelius, Porphyry, Longinus, and an oracle. The final division (sections 24–26) outlines Plotinus's treatises as Porphyry has organized them into enneads. Plotinus played an important role in the philosophy and religious thought of Late Antiquity, but it is Porphyry's biography that provides an intriguing description of religious practice in Plotinus's social circle. Porphyry provides a description of the wide assortment of his personal religious practices, including the following. (1) Plotinus observed the birthdays of Plato and Socrates as religious holidays, even though he refused to allow anyone to observe his own birthday (section 2). (2) He held as a sacred covenant the agreement not to disclose the mystic teachings of his teacher Ammonius (section 3), even though Plotinus brought Ammonius's thinking to bear on his own philosophy and theology (section 14). (3) He permitted an Egyptian priest to summon Plotinus's personal daemon (a spiritual companion to humans) and to pronounce an oracle even though he himself refused to observe the lunar festivals (section 10). (4) Plotinus was clairvoyant and practiced these abilities in relationship to common daily problems (section 11). (5) Plotinus withdrew (*anachorein*) to country estates ascetically to practice his philosophy (sections 5 and 12).

Porphyry also provides an intriguing window into the social patterns of Plotinus's religious and philosophical life. Plotinus ran an orphanage for Roman noble children whose parents were dying (section 9); he resisted the magical rituals of jealous competitors (section 10); at the encouragement of Galienus the emperor, he tried to build a city named Platonopolis wherein the residents would live according to Plato's laws (section 12). These and many other elements in the treatise indicate the depth of religious commitment of Plotinus and his followers and their dedication to living out the social implications of their theology and philosophy. Porphyry's descriptions of Plotinus's students, his "hearers," shows the widespread interest in religious practice by doctors, poets, literary critics, senators, and rhetoricians, as well as many women students from among the Roman upper class.

This translation is only of Porphyry's introduction and is based on the critical edition of Plotinus's work by Paul Henry and Hans-Rudolf Schwyzer.

On the Life of Plotinus and the Order of His Books

[1] Plotinus, who is the philosopher of our times, seemed to feel shame that he was embodied. With such a disposition, he could bear to discuss neither his race, nor his parents, nor his fatherland. And he felt so unworthy to show himself to a painter or sculptor that he even said to Amelius, who wanted to insure that a portrait of him was produced, "Is it not sufficient to bear the image which nature has conferred upon us?," and even to expect him to agree to leave behind a longer-lasting image of an image as though it were something well worth seeing. So when he forbade the portrait and refused to sit for it because of this, Amelius, who had as his friend Carterius, who was the best painter of his day, sent him [Carterius] to produce the portrait and to present himself at the school meetings, for it was permitted for one who wished to frequent the [school] meetings, and he [Carterius] developed the habit of receiving by his increased attention the more striking mental images from his observation. Later, after drawing the likeness from the image that was stored

up in his memory, and after Amelius corrected the tracing toward the greatest likeness, Carterius's artistry produced a portrait of great likeness, without Plotinus's knowledge.

[2] Often suffering with a sickness of the bowel, he would not submit to an enema, saying that it is not becoming to an elder to undergo such a treatment, nor did he abide remedies from wild animals, saying that neither would he admit the nourishment from the bodies of tamed animals. He abstained from baths and he had his daily massage in his home. When his masseurs died during the intensification of the plague, and because he was unconcerned about such medical treatments, he soon developed the fiercest of sore throats. While I was in his presence nothing of this sort had yet begun to be manifest, but when I had sailed away, the condition became so savage, as Eustochius, who was the companion who also remained with him until his death, said to me when I returned, that even the sonority and euphony of his voice was stripped away when he became hoarse, and his sight became blurred and his hands and feet became ulcerated. So when his friends turned away from meeting him because he had the habit of greeting everyone from the mouth [a kiss?], he went to Campania to the estate of Zethus who was an old friend of his who had already died. And all of his necessities were provided for and attended to by Zethus's estate and from Castricus's estate at Minturnae, for Castricus had his property in Minturnae. And when he was about to die, as Eustochius explained it to me—since Euchtocius was living in Puteoli he came to him quite slowly—he said to him, "I am still waiting for you!" and he said, "Try to return the God in you to the divine in the Entirety." Then when a snake came forth from under the couch on which he was reclining and slipped into an opening there was in the wall, he threw out his spirit.

He had become, as Eustochius said, sixty-six years old at the completion of the second year of Claudius's reign. When he died, I, Porphyry, happened to be spending time in Lilybaeum, Amelius was in Apamaea of Syria, Castricus was in Rome, and only Eustochius was with him. If his sixty-six years are counted backward from the second year of Claudius's reign, the year of his birth falls in the thirteenth year of Severus's reign. He did not disclose either the month in which he was born or the day of his birth, since he did not deem it worthy for anyone either to sacrifice or to hold a banquet for his birthdays, although on the traditional birthdays of Plato and Socrates, he sacrificed and provided a banquet for his companions. At that time it was even necessary, for those of his companions who were able, to read a speech for those who gathered.

[3] These are the sorts of things that he often explained about himself in his conversations:

Until he was eight years old, even while he was studying with his schoolmaster, he would return to his nurse and uncovering her breasts, he was eager to nurse; but when at one point he heard "He's a disruptive child," he was ashamed and desisted.

When he was twenty-eight years old, he was led to turn to philosophy. After he was introduced to those philosophers who were then well-esteemed at Alexandria, he would return from their lectures downcast and full of grief, so that he even explained what he was experiencing to one of his friends who, perceiving the desire of his soul, sent him to Ammonius whom Plotinus had not yet experienced. And when he went to him and heard him, he said to his companion, "This is the one for whom I was searching." And from that day, he remained with Ammonius continually, and he acquired such an ability in philosophy that he was eager to try out both the Persian practice and that developed by the Indians.

When the emperor Gordian was about to march against the Persians, he entered the army; he had already reached his thirty-ninth year, for he had remained with Ammonius and studied with him for eleven whole years. And when Gordian was killed in Mesopotamia, barely escaping he arrived safely in Antioch. And in the reign of Philip the emperor, he, now being forty years old, went up to Rome.

Since Errenius, Origen, and Plotinus made a covenant by no means to disclose Ammonius's doctrines, which he had made quite clear to them in his lectures, Plotinus stood fast [in the covenant] while being engaged with some who approached him, still guarding Ammonius's doctrines as unheard [*anekpystos*]. While Errenius was the first to trespass the covenant, Origen followed and surpassed Errenius: he wrote nothing before the composition "Concerning the Daemons" and in Galienus's reign; [he wrote] "that the Emperor is the Sole Creator." Plotinus continued writing nothing for a long time, while crafting his lectures from his association with Ammonius. And in this way he completed ten whole years, being engaged with some, but writing nothing. His lecture was full of disorder and much silly talk, since, as Amelius relates it, he encouraged his companions to ask questions.

Amelius went to him after spending three years in Rome during the third year of Philip's imperium and remaining until the first year of Claudius's reign. He associated with him all of twenty-four years. When he came he had already developed skill from his association with Lysimachus. With laborius practice [*philosophia*] he surpassed all of those who were with him both through collecting and writing down almost all of the works of Numenius and through knowing the majority of them well. Having made notes from his attendance at his lectures, he put together about a hundred books of notes, which he offered to Hostilianus Hesychius of Apamea, who adopted him as a son.

[4] In the tenth year of Galienus's reign, I, Porphyry, having come from Greece with Antonius of Rhodes, understood that even though Amelius had been in Plotinus's company for eighteen years he [Plotinus] ventured to write nothing up to this point, except the notes whose quantity had not yet reached a hundred for him. But I, Porphyry, first associated with him when I myself was then thirty years old. From the first year of Galienus's reign, Plotinus was encouraged to write down the subject matter [*hypothesis*] which arose in the

discussions. During the tenth year of Galienus's reign when I, Porphyry, first made his acquaintance, Plotinus was found to have written twenty-one treatises, which also I found to have been published for a few people. Neither was the publication easy: it happened neither with a good conscience [*eusyneidetos*] nor openly nor in the easiest way, but with the thorough evaluation of those who would receive them. These written works were such that, since he did not inscribe them himself, another gave a title to each one. So these are the titles that prevailed. I have also placed the initial words of the treatises so that each of the indicated treatises is more easily recognized from the initial words. [Here follows the list of Plotinus's first twenty-one works in their chronological order.] So these are the twenty-one treatises that I, Porphyry, found were written when I first came to him. Plotinus was then in his fifty-ninth year.

[5] While I associated with him this year and another five succeeding years—for I, Porphyry, had been in Rome a little earlier than the decade [of Galienus's rule] when Plotinus was spending his summer in the country and when I was engaged in the conversations in another way—in those six years, many close examinations occurred in the conversations and both Amelius and I encouraged him to write, so he wrote: [here follows another listing of his books.] These are the twenty-four that he wrote in the six-year time frame of my, Porphyry's, presence with him, in which he took up subject matter from the occasional problems discussed, as we have made clear from the summing up of each of the books; with the twenty-one prior to my living [in Rome], all of the corpus becomes forty-five totally.

[6] While I was spending time in Sicily—I withdrew there [*anachorein*] around the fifteenth year of Galienus's reign—Plotinus, having written five books, sent them to me: Concerning Well-being [I.4]; Concerning Providence I [III.2]; Concerning Providence II [III.3]; Concerning the Cognition of Substances and What Is Beyond [V.3]; and Concerning Love [*eros*] [III.5]. So he sent these in the first year of Claudius's reign, and as the second year began, Plotinus, a little while before he would die, sent these: Of What Sort are Evils [I.8]; If the Stars Create [II.3]; What Is the Living Being [I.1]; and Concerning Well-Being [I.7]. With the forty-five prior [treatises] and the second writing, these become fifty-four.

The books have their power according to when he wrote them; those of his early life, then those at his peak, and finally those when subdued by his body. The first twenty-one are of a more shallow ability, not yet being able to reach a vigorous stature; those occurring in the middle [period of] publication manifest the apex of his power and are the twenty-four most accomplished, except for the shorter ones; the final nine were written in a subdued tone of his power and the last four more than the five prior to them.

[7] He had many hearers who were eager for, and were brought together by, philosophy: Amelius from Tuscany, whose name was Gentilianus. Plotinus, because of the [potential for substituting an "r" in his name] deemed him worthy to be called Amerius saying that it is more fitting for him to be named from *amereia* [indivisibility] than from *ameleia* [indifference].

There was also a medical practitioner, Paulinus of Scythopolis, whom Amelius called Mikkalos: he was full of misunderstanding. And he also had another medical person [as a hearer], the Alexandrian Eustochius, who, having met him toward the end of his years, stayed with him attending him until his death. Studying only the [teachings] of Plotinus, he acquired the skill of a genuine philosopher.

Zoticus, the poet and critic, was also with him. He rendered the corrected texts of Antimachus and translated the "Atlantis" into a quite successful poem. Losing his sight, he died a little before Plotinus's death. And Paulinus also died before Plotinus. He also has Zethus, an Arabian by race, as a disciple, who married the daughter of Theodosius, who was a friend of Ammonius. He was also a medical practitioner and showed a great deal of affection for Plotinus. Since he was politically involved and had political power, Plotinus tried to thwart [his political interests]. He treated him as a relative such that he even withdrew to his country house that was six miles from Minturnae, which Castricius—who is called Phirmis—acquired. Castricius was the one among us who most loved beauty and revered Plotinus and served Amelius in everything as a good household slave and devoted himself to me in everything as a true brother. So this one who chose the political manner of life revered Plotinus.

Even among those from the Senate there were not a few who preferred work in philosophy: Marcus Orontius and Sabinillus were his hearers. There was also Rogatianus from the Senate who advanced to such a renunciation [apostrophē] of this life that he gave away all of his belongings, and he sent away all of his household slaves, and even renounced his rank. When he was about to come forth as praetor when the attendants were present, he would neither come forth nor take heed of the liturgy, but neither did he choose to live in his own house, but rather, being accustomed to frequent some one of his friends, there he both ate and slept and was fed on alternate days. When he became gouty from the renunciation and heedlessness to his life—such that he was even borne about upon a seat—he recovered; even though he could not stretch out his hands, he used them much more easily than those who pursue the arts through their hands. Plotinus approved of him and he continued to praise him as being among the best, putting him forward as a wonderful example to those who philosophize.

Serapion the Alexandrian was also with him: he was at first a rhetorician and later attended philosophical discourses, but he was not able to avoid the defect of money and its lending. There was also me, Porphyry of Tyre, who was also one of his closest companions, whom he deemed worthy to restore his books to order.

[8] With respect to writing, he could not ever bear to change the written thing twice, but neither could he bear to read and to go through it thoroughly because his sight did not serve him for reading. And he wrote, neither forming his letters beautifully, nor clearly separating the syllables nor taking into consideration correct spelling, but he possessed the mind alone and, a thing at which we were all amazed, he continued to work his mind until the end. For

he would complete by himself the subject for reflection from the beginning to the end, later he would transmit into writing that which he examined. Writing this down, he would connect that which he had arranged in his mind [*psychē*] so that he seemed to transcribe the things that were written as from a book. When he both was speaking to someone and continuing the subject of his conversation, he retained his own subject of reflection, so as, at the same time discharging the requirement of the conversation and of the things proposed in his speculation, to preserve his thinking process unbroken. When the one with whom he was speaking left, neither did he repeat what was written because his sight was not strong enough, as we have said, for him to revise, but he would subjoin one after another, as though there were no interval of time intervening when the conversation occurred. So he was present to himself and to others at the same time. And he would never break his attention toward himself except in his sleep, which he would drive away both by his little food— for he would often not even touch bread—and his continuous turning of him- self toward his mind.

[9] He also had exceptionally devoted women hearers: both Gemina, in whose house he also lived, and her daughter Gemina, similarly named for her mother, and Amphiclea who became the wife of Ariston, Iamblichus's son— all were exceptionally devoted to philosophy.

Many men and women of great nobility, when they were about to die, bring- ing their own children, both male and female, gave them to him with all their belongings as to a kind of holy and divine guard. Therefore even his house was filled with young boys and girls. Among these were also Potamon, giving thought to whose education, he would listen many times while he recomposed even one poem. He maintained the accounts [of their estates], bearing up those who survived among them, and he was also concerned for their accuracy, saying that until they decided that they would not become philosophers, they needed to have their belongings and revenues untouched and preserved.

And nevertheless, while he was waking he never disturbed the intensity toward the mind, while yet providing for so many both concern and attention toward their life. And he was gentle and open to those who in any way whatever had acquaintance with him. Although he lived in Rome all of twenty-six years and was for many an arbiter in their disputes with one another, he never made any political enemy.

[10] Olympios of Alexandria, one of those who pretended to philosophize, who was for a little while a student of Ammonius, was contemptuous of him because of his own love for being the first. He was so disposed toward him that he attempted to have him star-struck by bewitching him. Since he perceived that his attack was turning against himself, he said to his acquaintances that the power of Plotinus's soul [*psychē*] is so great that it is able to drive away the attacks against him toward those who were attempting to hurt him. Plo- tinus, when he perceived Olympios's attempt, said to him that at that time his body was "as a purse closed by being drawn together" [Plato *Symposium,*

190e7–8] pressing his limbs together toward one another in him. And, often in danger of suffering something himself rather than of hurting Plotinus, Olympios ceased his attempts, for Plotinus had something more than others by birth.

A certain Egyptian priest who came up to Rome, having been introduced to him through a friend, and who wanted to give a demonstration of his own wisdom, encouraged Plotinus to come to view the presence before him of his summoned personal daemon. When he willingly obeyed, the summoning happened in the Isian temple, for the Egyptian said that only that place was found to be pure in Rome. And when the daemon was called to become a physical manifestation, a god, and not one of the daemonic type, came forth, so the Egyptian said, "You are blessed for you have a god as your daemon and not an associate [*synonta*] of the subordinate type." Since the observing friend, either because of jealousy or because of fear of something, strangled the bird that he was firmly grasping as a protection, it was granted neither to inquire further about anything nor to see the presence any longer. So, since Plotinus had the more divine daemon as an associate, he himself also continued to raise his divine eye toward him. He had from such a concern also written the book *Concerning our Assigned Daemons* in which he attempts to consider the question concerning the differences among daemonic associates.

When Amelius became fond of sacrifices and he would go around to the sanctuaries at the new month and festivals, and when at one time he requested Plotinus to accompany him, Plotinus said, "It is necessary for them to come to me, not for me to come to them." From what sort of thought process [*dianoia*] he could boast [*megalēgorein*] this way, neither were we able to understand, nor emboldened to inquire of him.

[11] He was possessed of such an abundant superiority in understanding character that when there was a theft of Chione's expensive choker—she lived with him [*synoikos*] together with her children honorably passing her widowhood—and when the household was gathered under his sight, he looked at all of them. "This one," he said, "is the thief," indicating a certain one. He was whipped and he completely denied it at first, but later confessed and, bringing forth the stolen item, he returned it.

He would also foretell concerning each of the children living with him how they would turn out, such that he even foretold concerning Polemon of what sort he would be, namely that he would be an erotic type and short-lived, just as it also turned out.

And once he perceived that I, Porphyry, was considering removing myself from life, and suddenly, he set upon me in the house in which I was living and he told me that that desire was not from a noetic condition, but from a sort of melancholic illness, so he urged me to go abroad. Trusting him, I went to Sicily having heard that a certain Probus, a man held in high repute, was living near Lilybaeum. And I myself both warded off such a desire and was hindered from being with Plotinus until his death.

[12] Galienus the emperor and his wife Salonina honored and revered Plo-

tinus especially. He made full use of their friendship because it was said that there was a certain city of philosophers in Campania, a city otherwise run down. He convinced them to reassemble it and to give the surrounding country to those who lived in the city, and for those who were about to live there, to use the laws of Plato, and to make the proper name of that city Platonopolis. He undertook to withdraw [*anachōrein*] there with some of his companions. And the plan would easily have happened for the philosopher, had not some of those companions of the king out of jealousy, or anger, or some other despicable cause, hindered him.

[13] In his conversations, he was competent in expressing his ideas and strongest at discovering and thinking through the issues brought forward, but he erred in certain words, for he would not say *anamimnēsketai* but *anamnēm-isketai,* and some other incorrect words, which he would retain even in his writing. When he was speaking, the proof of his mental capacity was the light whose illumination extended even as far as his face. He was lovely to look at, but at these times he was especially more beautiful to behold. He usually sweated slightly and his gentleness shone through and his kindness and his vigor with respect to questioning was evident. For instance, when for three days I, Porphyry, questioned how the soul conjoins the body, he prolonged his argumentation to the point that when someone whose name was Thaumasius came in to engage in general discussions and said that he wanted to hear him speak as he wrote in his books, but that he could not endure Porphyry's questioning and answering, he said, "But if when Porphyry questions we will not resolve his difficulties, we will not be able to say anything absolutely in the manner of the book."

[14] In his writing he was concise and thoughtful, both brief and abounding more in thoughts than words, expressing most things in the language of ecstatic and passionate utterance and speaking it more from sympathy to the concept than from tradition. Both unrecognized Stoic and Peripatetic doctrines are mingled in his writings. Even Aristotle's study *Metaphysics* is condensed in them. Neither did any of the studies escape him, neither geometric, nor arithmetic, nor mechanical, nor optical, nor musical studies. But he was not prepared to work at these subjects.

In the meetings he would have the commentaries either of Severus, or Kronius, or Numenius, or Gaius, or Atticus read to him, and for the Peripatetics, the commentaries of Aspasius, Alexander, Adrastus, and of those others he came upon. He would say nothing absolutely as it came out of one of these, but he had his own perspective and being utterly changed in his consideration [*theōria*] he brought also the mind of Ammonius to bear in the inquiries. He would quickly be filled up with these written materials, so, after giving the sense of the deep consideration in a few words, he would pass on. When Longinus's *On First Principles* and his *Lover of Antiquity* were read to him, he said, "Longinus is a literary person [*philologus*], but not at all a philosopher."

Once when Origen presented himself at the meeting, he blushed and wanted to leave, but when he was encouraged by Origen to speak, he said, "The desire shrinks back when the speaker knows that they know before he speaks that which he is about to say" and so after a little while, since he [Plotinus] had already discoursed, he dismissed them.

[15] When at Plato's feast I read a poem, "The Sacred Marriage," and someone said, "Porphyry is mad" because many things in it were expressed mystically with the esoteric language of divine inspiration, he said within hearing of them all, "You have demonstrated at once that you are a poet, and a philosopher, and a hierophant."

When the rhetor Diophanes read a defense of Alcibiades in Plato's *Symposium,* presenting the position that for the sake of studying virtue in the meetings he should submit to sexual intercourse with the one who desires erotic intercourse [*aphrodisias*] with the teacher, he [Plotinus] was agitated, often getting up to escape from the assembly, and restraining himself, after leaving the lecture hall, he appointed me, Porphyry to write the response. Since Diophanes did not want to give me his book, I wrote against him from my memory of his engaging in attempts to prove his point, and when I read it to the same gathered audience, I pleased Plotinus so much that he continuously announced in the meetings, "Cast off and become a light to men" [cf. Homer *Iliad* 8:282].

When Eubolius, the Platonic Successor, wrote from Athens, and sent compositions about some Platonic subjects he had them given to me, Porphyry, and he encouraged me to study them and to bring back my written responses to him. And he turned his attention toward the rules of the stars, not in any mathematical way, but more precisely toward those who cast astrological birth tables. After he discovered the unwarranted nature of their undertaking, he did not shrink from refuting many of the concepts contained in their compositions.

[16] During his time, there were not only many Christians, but also others—sectarians who rose above the old philosophy, those who followed Adelphius and Aculinus, those who possessed the majority of the compositions of Alexander the Libyan, Philocomus, Demostratus and Lydus, and those who produced the apocalypses of Zoroaster, Zostrianus, Nicotheos, Allogenes, Messos and many others of this sort—who both deceived and were deceived to the extent that they claimed that Plato did not approach the depth [*bathos*] of noetic reality. Hence he made many refutations of their doctrine in the [school] meetings, and he wrote the book that we have entitled *Against the Gnostics* while leaving it for us to critique the remaining doctrines. Amelius advanced to forty books writing against Zostrianus's book. And I, Porphyry, developed many refutations against Zoroaster, demonstrating fully that the book was spurious and new, and that it was fabricated by those who wanted to commend the sect through projecting the opinion that the doctrines that they themselves had chosen to rank first are those from the ancient Zoroaster himself.

The next chapters (17–22) present evaluations and reactions to Plotinus's thought. In Chapter 17, there is a defense of Plotinus's thought against the accusation that he plagiarized his work from Stoic and Platonic teachings. It includes a letter from Longinus supporting Plotinus's originality. Chapter 18 contains the description of Porphyry's initial rejection of and subsequent conversion to Plotinus's writings. Chapter 19 presents another letter from Longinus to Porphyry requesting authoritative texts of Plotinus's treatises and expressing Longinus's personal respect and admiration for Plotinus's thought. In Chapter 20, Porphyry inserts a long quotation from a work of Longinus that positively appraises the significance of Plotinus's work. Chapter 21 presents Porphyry's summary of Longinus's response to Amelius's and Porphyry's work and Chapter 22 presents an oracle of Apollo describing the divinization of Plotinus. The interpretation of the oracle by Porphyry continues:

[23] In these oracular statements, it is said that he was gentle and kind, and especially mild and soothing, which we also knew about him. And it is said that he kept his soul vigilant [agrypnos] and clean, and he always strove toward the divine which he loved with his whole soul, and that he did everything to be released to escape from the bitter waves of the blood-drinking life here. That God who has neither shape nor any form, who is enthroned above mentality and all intelligible things, appeared thus especially to this daemonic light who many times led himself up to the first and transcendent God by his thought and according to the roads Plato paved in his *Symposium*. And I, Porphyry, having reached sixty-eight years old, say that once I drew near and was united to him. The indwelling goal was manifest to Plotinus. For him the end and goal was to be united to and to draw near to the God who is above all things. When I was with him, four times in some degree he attained this goal in an ineffable actuality [and not merely in potentiality]. It was said that often when he was moved criss-crossedly, the gods made straight his road, sending down a solid radiant ray so that by the observation [epiblepsis] and by the visitation [episkepsis] from them he would write his writings. From both interior and exterior vigilance, "You saw clearly," it says, "your two eyes saw many things and beautiful, the things that no one among persons attentive to philosophy easily see." For indeed the contemplation of human beings might enable them to become better than human, such that it [the contemplation] might be more beautiful with respect to the divine knowledge, but yet not enabled to understand the depth [bathos] in the same way that the gods understand it. So the oracle explained these things that he produces and succeeded in some of them while he was still encased in a body. After his release from the body, he went to the daemonic assembly, for there lives affection, desire, mirth, and love [erōs] inflamed from God, and there the so-called judges of the souls are stationed, the children of God, Minos and Rhadamanthys and Aiakos. He was given to them not to be judged, but to be their associate, with the others as many as are the best. These are their associates: Plato, Pythagoras, and as many others who are set upon the dance of immortal love [erōs]. And there the blessed daemons have their birth, both participating in a life filled with good

things and mirth, and, since it endures completely, even being made blessed by the gods.

[24] In this way, then, have I narrated Plotinus's life. Since he entrusted to me to do the arranging and correcting of his books, I, even while he was still living, undertook it and I announced to the other friends that I would do this. First, I did not judge it right to leave the books in utter confusion [by being] chronologically ordered as published, but rather I imitated Apollodorus the Athenian who assembled the works of Epicharmus the comedian and published them in ten volumes, and Andronicus the Peripatetic who divided the works of Aristotle and Theophrastus by subject matter gathering similar subjects together. Thus also I, having fifty-four treatises, divided the works of Plotinus into six enneads—I was pleased by the perfection of the number six and by the ninth. And to each ennead I brought together similar subjects giving the first place to the easier questions.

Summary of Enneads as organized thematically: Ennead I gathers the ethical questions; Ennead II, physics and questions about the cosmos; Ennead III, the cosmos continued; Ennead IV, questions on the soul; Ennead V, the intellect, the things beyond the intellect, the intellect and the mind, and ideas; Ennead VI, treatises on being.

Bibliography

Brisson, Luke, Marie-Odile Goulet-Cazé, Richard Goulet, and Denis O'Brien. 1982. *Porphyre: Vie de Plotin*. Histoire des Doctrines de L'Antiquité Classique, 6. Paris: Librarie Philosophique J. Vrin.

Cox, Patricia. 1983. *Biography in Late Antiquity: A Quest for the Holy Man*. Berkeley and Los Angeles: University of California Press.

Hadot, Pierre. 1993. *Plotinus, or The Simplicity of Vision*. Trans. Michael Chase. Chicago: University of Chicago Press.

Henry, Paul, and Hans-Rudolf Schwyzer, eds. 1964. *Plotini Opera*. Oxford: Clarendon.

Miles, Margaret R. 1997. *Reading for Life: Beauty, Pluralism, and Responsibility*. New York: Continuum.

Smith, Andrew. 1974. *Porphyry's Place in the Neoplatonic Tradition*. The Hague: Martinus Nijhoff.

Valantasis, Richard. 1991. *Spiritual Guides of the Third Century: A Semiotic Study of the Guide-Disciple Relationship in Christianity, Neoplatonism, Hermetism, and Gnosticism*. Harvard Dissertations in Religion, 27. Minneapolis: Fortress.

Refashioning the Person: Asceticism

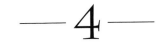

Evagrius Ponticus on Prayer and Anger

Columba Stewart OSB

Evagrius Ponticus was the most acute monastic psychologist of the fourth century C.E. He was also a remarkable teacher of prayer. For Evagrius, the workings of the passions had a direct bearing on both the possibility and the quality of prayer. This was especially the case with the passion of anger. Anger is part of the interpersonal terrain of monastic life, remaining an issue even after other passions such as gluttony or lust have been effectively managed. "Exhort the old to master their anger, and the young to master their belly," he writes in one of the texts translated below. Its effect on prayer was to obscure the mind, so preoccupying it that there was no psychic energy left to transcend resentment. Both perennial and deeply subversive, anger was a passion to be reckoned with over the long haul.

Evagrius was a monk of great learning and rich experience. Born around 345 in Pontus, the province of Asia Minor along the southern coast of the Black Sea, he was taught his theology by Gregory of Nazianzus (who ordained Evagrius deacon), and he accompanied Gregory to Constantinople in 380. Evagrius's ecclesiastical success seemed assured until guilt over a romantic attachment to a married woman of high station drove him from the imperial capital to refuge in Jerusalem. Staying on the Mount of Olives with Melania the Elder and her scholar-friend Rufinus of Aquileia, Evagrius was in a congenial intellectual environment shaped by the teachings of Origen, the great third-century Alexandrian exegete. Melania proved to be a wise director of souls and when she discovered the roots of Evagrius's troubles, she packed him off to the Egyptian monastic settlement of Nitria, which she had visited some years previously. Evagrius arrived in Nitria probably in 383; two years later he moved to Nitria's more austere outpost, the Cells (Kellia), where he remained until his death in 399. Among his teachers in the monastic life was Macarius the Great (the Egyptian), whom Evagrius described as "our holy and most ascetical (*praktikōtatos*) teacher" (*Prak.* 29).

Evagrius is best known as a systematizer of the spiritual theology of Origenist

Egyptian monasticism. His theological background was brought to bear on practical monastic wisdom, which he acquired in the desert, and the result is an ordered exposition of both the ascetical agenda and contemplative possibilities of the monastic life. A three-part overview of the monastic life in the works entitled *Praktikos, Gnostikos,* and *Kephalaia Gnostica* contains the basic elements that recur throughout his writings. Monastic life consists of ascetical attention to the eight besetting "thoughts" or passions (gluttony, lust, avarice, sadness, anger, listlessness, vainglory, and pride). This "practical" aspect of life facilitates the integration of emotions Evagrius describes with the Stoic term *apatheia,* "passionlessness." One who attains *apatheia* becomes capable of "knowledge," which for Evagrius means insight into the nature of things human and divine. Such a "Knower" (*gnōstikos*) can then become a teacher of others. The second and third parts of Evagrius's trilogy are directed to the Knower as teacher (the *Gnostikos*) and as explorer of hidden realities (the *Kephalaia Gnostica*). The sayings related to anger from the *Praktikos* and the *Gnostikos* are translated here.

Evagrius wrote two major treatises on prayer. In the 153 brief chapters of *On Prayer,* he describes both the impediments to and qualities of what he calls "pure prayer," i.e., prayer beyond words, images, and distorting emotion. The much longer *Antirrhetikos* is divided into eight sections, one for each of the eight principal thoughts. The title means rebuttal, and the work contains descriptions of various scenarios that may occur in monastic life and provides a biblical text that can be used as a prayer formula against the besetting passion. Book 5 of the *Antirrhetikos,* on situations related to anger, is translated here.

Evagrius's other surviving works include commentaries on the biblical texts most apt to monastic life (the Psalms, Proverbs, and Ecclesiastes), sentences on the monastic life intended for meditation (he prepared collections for both men and women), other descriptions of the eight principal thoughts, and biblical commentaries. Throughout, in sometimes wearying repetition, one finds the basic system sketched in the trilogy. Because Evagrius became suspect for his Origenist views around the time of his death (Guillaumont 1962), his works were often attributed to others and many have not survived in the original Greek. Modern study of Evagrius has been largely devoted to reclaiming Evagrian authorship and gathering together the scattered textual traditions.

Anger and Prayer

The most virulent allergen in the monastic life, according to Evagrius, is anger. The theme threads itself throughout his writings, dwarfing other issues that one might have expected to loom large in monastic awareness, such as food or sex. Evagrius emphasizes the vices of monastic maturity, which are anger and vainglory. Indeed, his works fairly crackle with the problem of anger. Part of the explanation for anger's prominence lies in Evagrius's anthropology: the traditional

Platonic/Stoic one in which a resistant or repelling tendency (*thumos*) functions along with desire (*epithumia*) as a life force. Evagrius's definition of anger is traceable to Aristotle and to Stoicism (*Prak.* 11). When used correctly, anger battles demons and invasive thoughts. When misdirected, anger attacks other human beings (*Prak.* 24). Because anger is so fundamental an aspect of the soul, when stirred up "it keeps the soul wild all day" (*Prak.* 11).

Anger is prompted by events of daily life. Memories linger in the memory, creating resentment toward others who are perceived to have offended in some way. (*Prak.* 11, 23, 26, 93; *Antir.* 5.36, 38, 42). Often anger arises from resentment about material goods or possessions (*Prak.* 99; *Gnost.* 8; *Antir.* 5.6, 15, 22, 30, 57). Evagrius notes the demonic double-whammy: having inflamed such anger, the demons then suggest it can be quenched by gaining possessions. Evagrius also comments on the way anger can arise as a reaction to persecution or criticism; one wonders how much of this relates to his own experience as an Origenist intellectual living among those who were often suspicious of learning (*Gnost.* 32; *Antir.* 5.34, 56).

Like lust, anger creates fantasies in the mind at the time of prayer and causes nightmares if not addressed (*Prak.* 11, 21, 91; *Antir.* 5.12). Most dangerously, it darkens the mind to a dangerous degree (*Prak.* 23–24), meaning that, according to Evagrius's highly visual theology, one becomes unable to see the light of God reflected in the mind or to have insight into things created or divine: everything is shrouded as if by fog or clouds or smoke. Evagrius opens his treatise *On Prayer* with these words: "I was feverish and enflamed with passions when, as usual, you revived me with the touch of your godly letter." Although he does not name the passions, a few lines later he remarks: "you desire chapters fixed in the mind through love and through lack of resentment" (*De orat.* Prol.). In one of his letters he admits his own recurring experience of being troubled by thoughts of vainglory and angry murmuring that deprive him of the light that illumines the mind at the time of prayer (*Ep.* 17). He writes, "Nobody who loves true prayer and at the same time is enraged or resentful can be other than insane: it is like wanting to have sharp eyesight while tormenting your own eyes" (*De orat.* 65).

Not only do problems with anger remain a part of the monastic emotional landscape, they often become more acute with age and even with spiritual progress. There are several reasons for this perennial quality. Anger is more susceptible to rationalization than passions like lust or avarice. There can be a pretense of justifiable outrage or resentment (cf. *De orat.* 24, 137). When other passions no longer occupy the center of ascetical attention, anger emerges into prominence. The emotional struggle shifts from the largely physical issues of sexual attraction and gluttony to the social one of anger. Evagrius notes in the *Praktikos* that when one attains to prayer without distraction, the warfare is around the irascible part of the soul (*Prak.* 63).

Anger therefore becomes a particular danger to those who teach others about the spiritual life, as he warns in the *Gnostikos*. The supreme virtue of the "Knower" is freedom from anger (*aorgēsia, Gnost.* 5). The point is not a throw-away remark. In that treatise of fifty brief chapters of advice for monastic teachers, Evagrius devotes nine of them to issues related to anger and approachability but only two to avarice (*Gnost.* 30, 38) and two to asceticism in general (*Gnost.* 37, 47). The only reference to gluttony applies to the young monks in the Knower's care (*Gnost.* 31), and a possible allusion to lust is quite vague (*Gnost.* 11). Evagrius notes the irony of claiming spiritual progress while being a deeply angry person (*Antir.* 5.46, 59, 62, 64). As he puts it in one of his many ocular similes, "One who has touched knowledge and is easily moved to anger is like someone who pierces the eyes with an iron pin" (*Gnost.* 5).

Therapeutic Strategies

Although anger arises from daily interaction with others and its violence is directed toward others, it is not cured simply by backing off from people. In fact, the temptation to flee other people is to be resisted (*Prak.* 22). Anger differs from lust, though both are triggered by interaction with others. With lust the issue is attraction, and the cure is greater distance from the desired object. For anger, which is fundamentally a reaction or repulsion, to withdraw would be a surrender to the driving force of the passion.

The same emphasis on the social context of anger is found in the cures for it. In the *Praktikos,* Evagrius notes that healing the intellect requires reading, vigil, and prayer; healing the desiring part of the soul involves hunger, toil, and withdrawal from others; healing the irascible part of the soul requires psalmody, patience, and mercy. This last is conceived very concretely as giving alms or providing hospitality to those in need (*Prak.* 15, 26, 91; *Gnost.* 7, 45). An emphasis on psalmody and practical kindness as the cures for anger recurs throughout Evagrius's writings. The emphasis on psalmody is significant: it is the standard prescription for soothing the passions, and especially that of anger (*De orat.* 83). Besides the content of psalmody there is its interplay of heart and body. It is impossible to engage all of the elements of singing while angry.

Note on the Translation

The translations of the *Praktikos* are entirely from the Greek, that of the *Gnostikos* almost entirely so. The Greek text of the *Antirrhetikos,* however, has not survived. Therefore, I have translated Evagrius's scenarios from the Syriac version and the biblical quotations from the Greek of the Septuagint and New Testament. I have noted where the text of the Syriac Bible ("Peshitta") differs significantly from the Greek. The headings to the various sections of the *Antirrhetikos* are given as they appear in the Syriac.

Because Evagrius's teaching on anger has very much to do with relations with one's monastic neighbors and because he wrote primarily for monastic men, I have retained the masculine terminology of "brothers" when it refers to monks. Biblical quotations and more generic statements are rendered inclusively.

Works Translated

Praktikos, chapters 11, 15, 20–26, 63, 91, 93, 99–100. Greek text: Guillaumont 1971.
Gnostikos, chapters 5, 7–8, 10, 31–32, 45, 47. Greek text of all except chapters 7 and 10: Guillaumont 1989. Syriac text of chapters 7 and 10: Frankenberg 1912, 512–20.
Antirrhetikos, Book 5: "Against the Demon of Anger." Syriac text: Frankenberg 1912, 512–20.

Praktikos

[11] The passion of anger is very fast. It is said to be a boiling of fury and a movement against one who has offended or is thought to have offended. It makes the soul rage all day long, but it is especially during prayers that it seizes the mind and depicts the face of the one who has grieved [it]. When it endures and is changed into resentment, it provokes disturbances by night, a wasting away of the body, pallor, and attacks by poisonous beasts. These four things, which occur in the wake of resentment, can also be found accompanying many thoughts.

[15] A wandering mind is stabilized by reading, vigil, and prayer; enflamed desire is quenched by hunger, labor, and withdrawal; stirred-up anger is calmed by psalmody, patience, and mercy. These things are to be done at the proper time and in the proper measure: for things that are immoderate and untimely do not last, and things that do not last do more harm than good.

[20] Anger and hate increase wrath, but mercifulness and gentleness diminish even what already exists.

[21] "Let the sun not go down on your anger" [Eph. 4:26], lest the demons arising by night frighten the soul and make the mind weaker for the next day's combat. For frightening visions are generated from the disturbance of the *thumos* [the irascible part of the soul], and nothing else makes the mind more prone to distraction than a disturbed *thumos*.

[22] Whenever the irascible part (*to thumikon . . . meros*) of our soul has latched onto an excuse and become upset, at that moment the demons suggest to us the benefits of flight lest we resolve the causes of our sadness and free ourselves from upset. But when the desiring part (*to epithumētikon*) is heated, then they try to make us sociable by calling us hard and wild, so that in our desire for bodies we actually encounter them. One must not obey the demons, but do the opposite.

[23] Do not give yourself over to the thought of anger by fighting in your imagination the one who has grieved you. Nor give yourself to the thought of

fornication by continually fantasizing about pleasure. For the first darkens the soul, and the second entices it to the burning of passion; both make your mind filthy. And when at the time of prayer you are fantasizing images and unable to offer pure prayer to God, you at once fall in with the demon of *accidie* (listlessness). This one most of all falls upon dispositions such as these, tearing the soul into pieces like a dog does to a fawn.

[24] The nature of anger is to battle demons and to fight for any sort of pleasure. Therefore the angels suggest to us spiritual pleasure and its blessedness, and exhort us to turn anger against the demons. They, for their part, push us toward worldly desires and urge anger, against its nature, to fight human beings so that the mind is darkened and, falling from knowledge, becomes a betrayer of the virtues.

[25] Pay heed to yourself lest you ever drive away one of the brothers because you were angry. For you will not evade in your life the demon of sadness, who will always be a stumbling block for you at the time of prayer.

[26] Gifts quench resentment: trust in Jacob, who overcame Esau with gifts when he was going out to meet him with four hundred men. But we who are poor fulfill the need at table.

[63] When the mind begins to make its prayers without distraction, then all of the battle occurs, day and night, around the irascible part (*to thumikon meros*) of the soul.

[91] It is necessary to interrogate the ways of those monks who have made a straight path before us and to set ourselves to follow them. For we can find much that they said or did well. Among those things is this: one monk said that a diet which is quite dry and regular, when joined to love, leads the monk quickly to the haven of impassibility (*apatheia*). The same monk delivered a brother troubled in the night with apparitions by assigning him care of the sick, along with fasting. When asked, he said that there is nothing like mercy for extinguishing passions of this kind.

[93] The vessel of election, the old man Macarius the Egyptian, asked me: "Why is it that when we are resentful toward humans we obliterate the power of memory in our soul, but when we resent demons we are blameless?" I was at a loss for words to reply, and asked him for the reason. He said, "In the first case, anger is used against nature; in the second, it is used in accordance with nature."

[99] Another of the monks said: "I strip away pleasures in order to cut off any pretexts for anger. For I know that anger is always fighting for pleasures, disturbing my mind, and driving away knowledge." One of the old men said, "Love does not know how to hold on to stores of food or money." The same said, "I do not know if I have ever been deceived by the demons twice in the same way."

[100] It is impossible to love all of the brothers equally. But one can deal with all of them with passion (*apathōs*), free from resentment and hate. We are to love the priests next to the Lord, for they purify us with the holy mys-

teries and pray for us; and we are to respect our old men like the angels, for they are the ones who anoint us for our contests and heal the bites of the wild beasts.

Gnostikos

[5] All of the virtues prepare the way of the Knower, but above all is lack of anger. For one who has touched knowledge but is readily moved to anger is like someone who pierces the eyes with an iron pin.

[7] The Knower will strive always to give alms and will be ready to do good. If lacking money, he will use the instrument of his soul [i.e., the body]. For, in every way, even without money, it is his nature to do good, which is what the five virgins who had unlit lamps were not doing.

[8] It is shameful for a Knower to be involved in a dispute, whether as victim or perpetrator. If he is the victim, it means he has not endured; and if he is the perpetrator, it means he has done wrong.

[10] Let the Knower, when teaching, pay heed whether he is free from anger, resentment, sadness, bodily sufferings, and care.

[31] Exhort the old to master their anger, and the young to master their belly. Psychic demons fight against the former, and most of the time bodily demons fight against the latter.

[32] Shut the mouth against those who slander in your hearing, and do not be surprised at being blamed by many: for this is a temptation from the demons. The Knower must be free from hatred and resentment even if not wanting to be.

[45] The pillar of truth Basil of Cappadocia said, "The knowledge that comes from human beings is strengthened by attentive study and exercise, but the knowledge that comes from God is strengthened by righteousness, lack of anger, and mercy. Even the impassioned can receive the first kind, but only those free from passion are capable of the second, they who at the time of prayer behold the light proper to the mind shining upon them."

[47] The angel of the church of Thmuis, Serapion, said, "The mind is perfectly purified when it has drunk spiritual knowledge; love heals the enflamed parts of the *thumos* [the irascible part of the soul]; and abstinence (*enkrateia*) stops the flow of evil desire.

Antirrhetikos. The Fifth Treatise: Against the Demon of Anger
From the Book of Genesis

[1] Against the soul that does not know that a gift readily quenches a brother's long-standing grudge.

Jacob said to Esau, "If I have found favor before you, receive the gifts from my hands. For the sake of this I looked upon your face, as someone might look upon the face of God, and you will be pleased with me. Take my gifts that I have brought to you, because God was merciful to me and is everything to me" [Gen. 33:10–11].

[2] Against the thoughts of anger that arise along the way of living rightly.
"Do not get angry on the way!" [Gen. 45:24].

[There is no heading for Exodus in the original manuscript.]

[3] Against the thought of false witness generated by anger.
"You shall not bear false witness against your neighbor" [Exod. 20:16].

[4] Against the thought that is from the Adversary that raises up and enkindles fury against the brothers.
"You shall not entertain an idle rumor" [Exod. 23:1].

[5] Against the thought that was raised up from anger and wants to revile the brothers.
"You shall keep away from every unrighteous word" [Exod. 23:7].

[There is no heading for Leviticus in the original manuscript.]

[6] Against the thought that depicts a brother in the mind who through hatred said something bad or heard something hateful. This is like what John the prophet, seer of Thebes [John of Lycopolis], explained can happen if hatred is about possessions or provisions. However, hatred on account of human glory is uprootable only with difficulty.
"You shall not hate your neighbor in your mind, but with a reproof rebuke your neighbor, and do not suffer sin because of your neighbor" [Lev. 19:17].

From Numbers

[7] Against the soul that considers perfect humility to be unnatural.
"And the man Moses was more humble than everyone on the earth" [Num. 12:3].

From Samuel

[8] Against the soul that does not realize that revilings arising from humans occur when God gives it over to testing.
"David said to Abishai and to all his servants, 'Look, my son who went out from my loins seeks my life (*psychē*), and now there is the Benjaminite. Let

him revile, because the Lord told him. It may be that the Lord will look upon my lowliness and will reward me with good things instead of his reproaches this day' " [2 Sam. 16:11–12].

From Psalms

[9] Against the soul that has strayed from humility but wants to relearn the ways of the Lord.

"He will lead the humble in judgment, he will teach the humble his ways" [Ps. 24:9].

[10] Against the soul that is receiving thoughts of anger and assembling evil accusations and false suspicions against the brothers.

"Cease from anger and set aside fury: do not be anxious, for it makes you do evil; for those who do evil will be utterly destroyed, and those who wait for the Lord, they will inherit the earth" [Ps. 36:8–9].

[11] Against the thought stirred up in backbiting of the brothers and shrouding the soul with a cloud of fury.

"Sitting you slander your neighbor; and against your sibling you place a stumbling block" [Ps. 49:20].

[12] Toward the Lord so that the mind knows that at night frightful visions occur from the tumult of fury, and so that it understands also that they are extinguished through mercy and patience.

"You made me know your commandment more than my enemies, because it is mine forever. I have understood more than all of my teachers, because your testimonies are my meditation" [Ps. 118:98–100].

[13] Against the demon that incites fury against the brothers and also convinces us to sing this chant, where the commandment of patience which we do not keep is written. He does this to mock us when we sing a commandment, which in practice we do not keep.

"How shall we sing the song of the Lord on alien soil?" [Ps. 136:4].

From the Proverbs of Solomon

[14] Against the thought that is gathering wicked ideas against a brother such as negligence or blasphemy or not doing something he should.

"Do not contrive bad things against your friend who dwells with you and trusts you" [Prov. 3:29].

[15] Against the thought that arises from hate and wants to dispute with a brother about transitory matters.

"Hate stirs up strife, but love covers all who do not love strife" [Prov. 10:12; cf. Peshitta: "hate stirs up judgment and hate hides all those who are unjust"].

[16] Against the thought that is pushing us to utter a curse against a brother.

"Righteous lips conceal enmity; but those who utter curses are without understanding" [Prov. 10:18].

[17] Against fury stirred up against a brother and making unseemly things [in] the mind at the time of prayer.

"A blessed soul is wholly simple but a wrathful person is not sincere" [Prov. 11:25].

[18] Against the thought that raises up our wrath about a flock not going straight on its path.

"The righteous have pity on the souls of their flocks, but the feelings of the impious are unmerciful" [Prov. 12:10].

[19] Against the thought suddenly raised up by anger and disturbing the mind on a foolish pretext.

"The senseless immediately [on the very day] announce their anger, but the scrupulous hide their own shame" [Prov. 12:16].

[20] Against the thought that ponders treachery against a brother.

"A treacherous person is made for prey, but one who is pure is a worthy possession" [Prov. 12:27].

[21] Against the soul in the course of a flowing wrath that by thoughts stirs up the mind to be enkindled with fury, even after the thought of this passion fades. Time passes, [but] the memory of a word or of a past matter obscures and submerges the mind.

"In the ways of righteousness is life, and the ways of remembrance of wrongs are toward death" [Prov. 12:28].

[22] Against the thought of anger that shakes and uproots the spirit of patience, and makes us consider deeds of evil doing. The power comes from the desire for possessions, in place of which humility ought to be stirred up.

"The long-suffering are great in understanding, but the short-tempered are exceedingly senseless" [Prov. 14:29].

[23] Against the thought of anger that prevents us from humbly returning an answer to those who reprove us appropriately.

"Anger destroys even the wise; but a deferential answer turns away fury, and an offensive word raises up anger" [Prov. 15:1].

[24] Against the thought that incites us to strife against the brothers and hinders us from withholding accusations.

"A wrathful person stores up arguments, but a long-suffering one soothes even the [argument] about to start" [Prov. 15:18].

[25] Against the soul that thinks a thought of anger is not loathsome to God, but [only] the sin that may come from it.

"An unrighteous thought is loathsome to the Lord, but the words of the pure are holy" [Prov. 15:26].

[26] Against the thought that incites us to like furious people and words of anger.

"Do not be associated with wrathful persons, do not dwell with angry friends, lest you learn their ways and find a stumbling-block for your soul" [Prov. 22:24–25; for 24b the Peshitta reads "do not go in with someone of angry speech"].

[27] Against the soul that has been wronged and thus wants to do wrong. This is the sign of an evil passion of the soul that likes worthless things.

"Do not say 'I will do to them as they did to me and I will repay them the wrongs they did to me'" [Prov. 24:29].

[28] Against the mind that has neither mercy nor pity on its enemy when it sees him in bitter poverty and does not want to soften its enmity by means of the table.

"If your enemies hunger, feed them; if they thirst, give them a drink. For by doing this you heap coals of fire upon their heads, and the Lord will reward you with good things" [Prov. 25:21–22].

From Qoheleth

[29] Against the thought of the soul that is quickly enflamed to wrath and suddenly embittered toward the brothers.

"Do not make haste in your spirit to become wrathful: because wrath lies in the breast of the foolish" [Eccles. 7:9].

[30] Against the soul that does not want to let go of pretexts for rage but desires food, garments, riches, and passing glory. Such as these are overshadowed by stirred-up anger, which does not depart from the heart but plunges the mind into the ruin of ruins.

"Put away wrath from your heart, and lead away evil from your flesh, because youth and lack of understanding are vanity" [Eccles. 11:10].

From the Song of Songs

[31] Against the demon that through many trials seeks to extinguish our love for the brothers.

"Many waters will not be able to extinguish love, and rivers will not wash it away" [Song of Sol. 8:7].

From Isaiah

[32] Against the thought that incites me to write words of harm, which strike the heart of the one who distresses us.

"Woe to those who write evil, for in writing they write evil" [Isa. 10:1; the Peshitta reads: "Woe to those who are decreeing decrees of deceit and writing iniquity"].

From the Lamentations of Jeremiah

[33] To the Lord because of thoughts of anger, that they no longer provoke us.

"You have judged, Lord, the judgments of my soul, you ransomed my life. You saw, Lord, my troubles, you judged my judgment; you saw the whole of their vengeance in all of their thoughts about me" [Lam. 3:58–60].

From the Gospel of Matthew

[34] Against thoughts of anger that our fathers and brothers harbor toward us when they persecute us on account of the Name of the Lord.

"Blessed are those who are persecuted because of righteousness, because theirs is the Kingdom of Heaven" [Matt. 5:10].

[35] Against the thought that from weariness of mind is violently moved against a brother.

"Any who are angry with their neighbor will be liable to judgment" [Matt. 5:22].

[36] Against the mind that is enraged over one who has struck it, and because of a second blow does not want to let go the thought, which it has because of the original blow.

"Whoever strikes you on the right cheek, turn to them your other also" [Matt. 5:39].

[37] Against the thoughts provoking us to hate and curse our enemies.

"Love your enemies, bless those who curse you, do well by those who hate you, and pray for those who threaten you with violence: thus you will be children of your Father in heaven" [Matt. 5:44, variant reading].

From the Gospel of Luke

[38] Against the thought of anger that is not receptive to the repentance of a brother but is still embittered against him.

"If your neighbor sins, rebuke the offender, and if your neighbor repents, forgive; and if seven times a day your neighbor sins against you and seven times turns back to you saying, 'I repent,' then forgive" [Luke 17:3–4].

From the Gospel of John

[39] Against the mind that entertains thoughts of anger against the brothers and perverts the commandment of love which is called "new."

"I give you a new commandment, that you love one another. Just as I have loved you, so you also are to love one another" [John 13:34].

From the Letter of the Romans

[40] Against the thoughts of anger that are embittered toward love.

"Who will separate us from the love of Christ? Will hardship or distress, or persecution, or famine, or nakedness, or peril, or sword?" [Rom. 8:35].

[41] Against the thoughts of jealousy that rejoice in the misfortune of our enemies.

"Rejoice with those who rejoice, weep with those who weep; be of one mind among yourselves" [Rom. 12:15].

[42] Against the thought that holds on to a grudge and endeavors to repay evil to the one who grieved it.

"To no one return evil for evil, but take heed of good things before all people" [Rom. 12:17].

From the First Letter of the Corinthians

[43] Against thoughts of anger that counsel us to take advantage and to cheat.

"Why not then be wronged? Why not then be cheated? You yourselves wrong and cheat, and [do this] to other disciples!" [1 Cor. 6:7].

[44] Against the thought of anger that is enraged about someone who curses us [when we are] in service.

"If you were a slave when called, do not be concerned with yourself. But if you can become free, then that obliges you. For the one who has been called a slave in the Lord is freed in the Lord" [1 Cor. 7:21–22].

[45] Against the soul that is not allowed into the frankness of love and is separated from it by the thought of anger.

"If I speak with the tongues of humans and of angels but I do not have love, I am a noisy gong or a clanging cymbal. And if I have prophecy and see every mystery and all knowledge and if I have total faith so as to move mountains but I do not have love, I am nothing. And if I give away all of my possessions and if I hand over my body to be burned, but I do not have love, I gain nothing. Love is patient, love is kind, love is not jealous; love is not boastful or arrogant or rude; it does not seek its own, it is not irritable, it does not think evil; it does not rejoice in wrongdoing but rejoices in truth. It bears all things, believes all things, hopes all things, endures all things. Love never fails" [1 Cor. 13:1–8].

From the Letter to the Galatians

[46] Against the soul that is suddenly angered but wants to find in itself the border of knowledge of the truth.

"The fruit of the Spirit is love, joy, peace, patience, kindness, generosity, faith, lowliness, and self-control" [Gal. 5:22–33].

[47] Against the thoughts that cast us into sadness because of the failings of the brothers.

"Bear one another's burdens and thus fulfill the law of Christ" [Gal. 6:2].

[48] Against the thoughts of the soul that thinks with anger about people who receive many good things from others and then complain about them.

"Let us not weary of doing good, for in its own time we will harvest if we do not give up" [Gal. 6:9].

From the Letter of the Ephesians

[49] Against the thoughts of anger that do not allow us to be reconciled with the brothers and depict before our eyes reasons that seem justifiable. These are really shame, fear, and pride, in case the one who sinned never falls again into those same original offences. This is a sign of the cunning of the demon who will not allow the mind to be free from a grudge.

"Do not let the sun go down on your anger and do not make room for the devil" [Eph. 4:26–27].

[50] Against thoughts of any kind that are generated from rage about matters of whatever sort.

"Put away from yourselves all bitterness, wrath, anger, wrangling, and slander, along with all evil" [Eph. 4:31].

The Letter That Was to the Philippians

[51] Against the thoughts of anger that dare to murmur about the service of the brothers.

"Do everything without murmuring and arguing" [Phil. 2:14].

From the Letter of the Colossians

[52] Against the thoughts that are from inflamed rage and are bringing forth blasphemy and treachery from their fervor.

"Now put off all such things—wrath, anger, evil, blasphemy, and unseemly language—from your mouth. Do not lie to one another" [Col. 3:8–9].

The First Letter of the Thessalonians

[53] Against the thoughts that want to repay evil for evil.

"See that no one repay someone evil for evil, but always pursue good toward both one another and all things" [1 Thess. 5:15].

From the First Letter of Timothy

[54] Against the soul that does not know the aim of the command of God and in the sway of thoughts of anger perverts it.

"The aim of the command is love from a pure heart, a good conscience, and a sincere faith" [1 Tim. 1:5].

From the Second Letter That Is Timothy's

[55] Against the mind that stirs up battle in the intellect by means of the thoughts.

"A slave of the Lord must not be quarrelsome, but must be gentle toward everyone" [2 Tim. 2:24].

[56] Against the thought of anger that befalls me because of persecution— I am persecuted by my fathers and by my own kind because of the name of the Lord.

"And all those wanting to live piously in Christ Jesus will be persecuted" [2 Tim. 3:12].

From the Letter of Philemon

[57] Against the thought that is stirring up anger in us about a brother who is receiving money or something else for his needs and not diligently accounting for it.

"If he has wronged you in any way or owes you, I will repay it" [Philem. 18].

From the Letter of James

[58] Against the soul that is quick to anger but seeks the righteousness of God.

"Let everyone be quick to listen, slow to speak, slow to anger: for human anger does not accomplish God's righteousness" [James. 1:19–20].

[59] Against the thought that fills the mind with anger though [the mind] wants to see itself in the wisdom of God.

"The wisdom from above is first pure, then peaceable, kindly, willing to obey, full of mercy and good fruits, impartial, and sincere. The fruit of righteousness is sown in peace by those making peace" [James. 3:17–18].

[60] Against the thought that is moved to slander of the brothers and disdains the Lawgiver as if he did not justly establish this law, which he commanded when he said, "do not slander your neighbor."

"Do not slander anyone, brothers and sisters. The one who slanders a brother or sister or judges them slanders the law and judges the law. If you judge the law, you are not a doer of the law but its judge. There is one lawgiver and judge who can save and destroy" [James. 4:11–12].

From the Letter of Peter

[61] Against the mind that wants to repay evil with evil or reproach with reproach, and does not want by means of blessings to forget thoughts of reproach or slander.

"Do not repay evil for evil, or reproach for reproach, but instead bless [them], because for this you were called that you might receive blessing" [1 Pet. 3:9].

From the Letter of John

[62] Against the mind that says the fear of God is in it but hates its brother.

"The one who claims to be in the light but hates brother or sister is in darkness until now" [1 John 2:9].

[63] Against thoughts that are begotten from hate and make the mind murderous toward a brother.

"Everyone who hates a brother or sister is a murderer, and you know that murderers do not have eternal life dwelling in them" [1 John 3:15].

[64] Against the mind that professes to love God [but] in the sway of hatred toward a brother has denied the first love.

"Any who say 'I love God' and hate brother or sister are liars: for any who do not love their brother or sister whom they have seen cannot love the God whom they have not seen" [1 John 4:20].

Blessed is Our Lord Jesus Christ our God, who has given us victory over the thoughts of the demon of anger so that we may defeat it!

Bibliography

Bamberger, John Eudes. 1972. *Evagrius Ponticus. The "Praktikos" and "Chapters on Prayer."* Cistercian Studies Series 4. Kalamazoo, Michigan: Cistercian Publications.

Evagrius. For works and editions see *Patrologia Graeca* 2430–82; several recent editions have appeared in the series Sources chrétiennes, Paris: Editions du Cerf.

———. On Prayer (*De oratione*). Greek text: *Patrologia Graeca* 79.1165A–1200C; revised edition in Tugwell 1981. English translation: Bamberger 1972, 52–80, and Tugwell 1987, 25–47.

Frankenberg, Wilhelm. 1912. *Euagrius Ponticus*. Abhandlungen der königlichen Gesellschaft der Wissenschaften zu Göttingen, Philologisch-historische Klasse. Rev. ed., vol. 13, 2. Berlin.

Guillaumont, Antoine. 1962. Les "Kephalaia Gnostica" d'Evagre le Pontique et l'histoire de l'origénisme chez les grecs et chez les syriens. Patristica Sorbonensia 5. Paris: Editions du Seuil.

Guillaumont, Antoine and Claire. 1971. Evagre le Pontique: "Traité pratique" ou "le moine." Sources chrétiennes 171. Paris: Editions du Cerf.

————. 1989. Evagre le Pontique: "Le Gnostique" ou "À celui qui est devenu digne de la science." Sources chrétiennes 356. Paris: Editions du Cerf.

Tugwell, Simon. 1981. Evagrius Ponticus: "De oratione." Oxford: Faculty of Theology.

————. 1987. Evagrius Ponticus: "Praktikos" and "On Prayer." Oxford: Faculty of Theology.

5

Pseudo-Athanasius

Discourse on Salvation to a Virgin

Teresa M. Shaw

The Greek treatise translated here is devoted to the praise of and practical instruction in Christian female virginity. The various manuscripts bear two different titles: *Discourse on Salvation to a Virgin* and *On Virginity or On Asceticism* (Von der Goltz 1905, 60–65). The treatise belongs to a sizable body of fourth- and fifth-century texts sharing its genre, themes, and topics. It was in the fourth century that the various institutional forms of Christian asceticism and monasticism began to appear most distinctly against the landscape of what was already a broader cultural and religious phenomenon, as many of the texts collected in this volume testify. From this period we have a wealth and variety of sources related to the disciplined religious life—which was by no means uniform—of individuals and communities. These include: hagiographical treatments of extraordinary persons, instructions and rules, theological or theoretical treatments of ascetic themes such as sexual chastity or fasting, arguments for or against a particular type of discipline (for example, spiritual marriage), collections of anecdotes about and sayings of holy persons, and sermons or letters offering advice or encouragement. In many cases, of course, a particular text might incorporate elements from several of these.

The treatise *On Virginity*, often referred to by the common Latin title *de virginitate*, is one of the more distinctive genres among this literature. In the texts produced by the dozen or more authors that are usually counted after the beginning of the fourth century (Camelot 1952; Aubineau 1966, 23–213), we find both a striking consistency of thematic elements and a dramatic assertion of individual concerns and controversies as well as expressions of particular ascetic practices. The most common elements of the *de virginitate* include praise of virginity as angelic or above nature; identification of the virgin as the bride of Christ; comparison of the virtue or freedom of virginity to the lower achievement and troubles associated with marriage; use of good and bad examples from scripture and history; warnings against going out in public; warnings against associating with men or with married women; warnings against certain wicked people, heretics, or false virgins or monks; advice on ascetic practices (fasting, chastity, prayer, etc.); advice on care of the body; instructions for proper appearance, clothing, and demeanor; and reflections on the meaning of female virtue, female nature, and female sin.

These features do not necessarily appear in all texts of the type, and they receive more or less emphasis and elaboration depending on the author. For example, one treatise might focus on the practical aspects of the virgin's daily life while giving less attention to the ideology of virginity, while another might concentrate heavily on the relationship of the virgin to Christ, her bridegroom, embellishing the discussion with sensual descriptions of the virgin's longing for Christ or Christ's jealousy over his virgin bride. Some authors seem especially concerned to blunt the influence of rival teachers and ascetic leaders, who are labeled heretics, deceivers, and frauds, while others offer few clues to their personal concerns and particular situations.

The *Discourse on Salvation to a Virgin* translated here contains all of the features listed above. But there are some surprising and curious elements that have fueled the scholarly debate over authorship. The work opens with a statement of Trinitarian faith and an account of creation (1), and continues with a call to imitate Christ by taking on a life of hardship and sacrifice in this world in order to inherit the kingdom. The author returns several times to the idea that suffering and endurance of trials in this world lead to eternal rest, comfort, and the "imperishable crown" of the kingdom, while relaxation and the pursuit of worldly comfort lead not only to evils in this life but also to eternal punishment in Hades (3, 15–19, 23–25). Practical details of the virgin's life are the subject of advice and exhortation: she should fast regularly and practice almsgiving (6–8, 12, 24); she should avoid eating with worldly women and "buffoons" (13) and should not go out except when absolutely necessary (22); her clothing should cover her from head to toe and be inexpensive and plain (11); and she is to avoid the baths and be silent in church (11, 23). While the virgin takes no thought of the flesh and mortifies her body, nevertheless the author insists that she ease her regimen if she becomes ill (6–8, 12). While she should not raise her face toward anyone she sees, nevertheless she should greet a holy person who comes into her home by prostrating herself before him and washing his feet (11, 22). The virgin should live under a rule and under the authority of an elder woman and is instructed to seek the counsel of her elders in everything she does (14, 23).

Much of the short text focuses on prayer and the liturgical life of the Christian virgin and the virgins who are with her as her "soul mates." Valuable information about the hours of prayer, the practice of psalmody, and prayer before meals colors the text (12–14, 16, 20). Keeping watch over her daily routine, diet, associations, and activities is not enough, for the virgin must be especially vigilant concerning idle, strange, or even evil thoughts (*logismoi*), which, according to the author, are really suggestions from the enemy meant to thwart and deceive. Thus the enemy will whisper praises leading to pride or suggest that the virgin need not work so hard to be saved, which leads to negligence (8, 23). The virgin is represented as the bride of Christ (2, 23), the true widow (10), the wise virgin with oil in her lamp ready to greet the bridegroom (23), the servant of Christ and dancer in his chorus (2, 7, 8, 16, 22, 25), and the manly and virtuous one who has cast off "womanish" ways (10).

The most prominent features of the *Discourse on Salvation,* then, are the detailed instructions on the hours of prayer and the recitation of psalms, the emphasis on suffering in the world and rewards in heaven, the danger of thoughts, and the value of regular fasting. Other topics that might be treated elaborately in another text receive only slight attention here, including the heavenly bridegroom motif, the contrast between marriage and virginity, and the danger of associating with men. (Indeed, the virgin greets the male holy visitor as if he were Christ and washes his feet). Finally, there is no real theological argument for the origin and value of virginity in the scheme of creation and salvation of the type that one finds, for example, in the treatises of Basil of Ancyra and Gregory of Nyssa. Neither is there any reference to heretics or theological opponents such as one finds in other ascetic works attributed to Athanasius, or in the writings on virginity by Jerome, Chrysostom, Gregory of Nyssa, and others. The closest our author comes is his very general warnings against "worldly," "vain," or "foolish" people and those who through either praise or criticism of her askesis might cause the virgin to turn away from her discipline and lose her crown.

Scholars continue to comb through the treatise's content, style, and manuscript evidence in order to prove or refute its claim of Athanasian authorship. Athanasius was the bishop of Alexandria from 328 to 373 C.E., a prominent leader and a key witness to a crucial period in Egyptian asceticism. While many ascetic texts bear his name as author, a significant number of these are regarded as unauthentic (Brakke 1994, 1995; Aubineau 1955). Scholars have long debated the authenticity of the *Discourse on Salvation,* with the majority expressing doubt. In modern scholarship, Pierre Batiffol, for example, argued against Athanasian authorship in 1893 and again in 1906, basing his conclusions on the writer's style, theological formulas, and ascetic inclinations. Others have since concurred with Batiffol's assessment (Burch 1906; Delehaye 1906; Lebon 1925; Puech 1930, 3:116–18; Bardy 1935; Aubineau 1955; Brakke 1994). Batiffol noted that the Trinitarian formula of chapter one, "three hypostases, one divinity," is not otherwise characteristic of Athanasius, but is rather more Cappadocian. He gives most weight, however, to the type of asceticism found in the treatise, with its emphasis on fasting, fulfilling all commandments, and choosing the road to salvation by rejecting the world. Specifically, he argues that the rigorous lifestyle advocated by the treatise suggests that it should be associated with the "enthusiastic" asceticism of the Eustathians, who were condemned at the Council of Gangra in the mid-fourth century for their elitist and rigorous asceticism. For example, he interprets the author's advice to "fast for the entire period" (for one's whole life), and his recommendation that all food is pure "as long as it is non-animal" (8, 12) to suggest that the treatise advocates an absolutely vegetarian diet and fasting every single day, including traditional non-fasting days such as Sunday. And the fact that the treatise gives so much attention to private or small group prayers, synaxes, and psalmody—and mentions the virgin's presence in church only once—indicates to Batiffol the same kind of arrogant scorn for the institutional church that those condemned at Gangra supposedly exhibited.

The fullest argument in support of the authenticity of the treatise was made by Eduard von der Goltz, who published an edition and lengthy commentary in 1905. Perhaps most importantly for our purposes, von der Goltz sought to locate the ascetic practice evidenced in the text firmly in the Egyptian context of the fourth century and to demonstrate that the behaviors singled out by Batiffol as suspicious were in fact common to most ascetic groups at the time (von der Goltz 1905, 119–20). Whatever arguments can be made about the author's style and authenticity, I agree with von der Goltz that the disciplines advocated in this treatise are far from extreme, particularly when compared to other texts of its type. The so-called "vegetarian rule" is not explicitly ordered for every single day of the year; even if it were, this does not set our author apart from many other advocates of fasting who regularly warned against eating meat. And the emphasis on private prayer and chanting of psalms proves only that the setting of the text is monastic—the author does mention the virgin's behavior in church, with no hint of criticism. Even the discussion of earthly marriage and heavenly marriage to Christ seems rather mild compared to the vehemently scornful descriptions of the problems of marriage in, for example, Jerome or John Chrysostom. In one puzzling passage, it should be noted, however, the author observes that just as woman's body is "defiled" by a man so a virgin is "defiled" by worldly habits. Unfortunately the author does not elaborate, and it is difficult to know how to interpret this defilement.

In sum, the *Discourse on Salvation* fits squarely within the genre of the *de virginitate,* and its contents are consistent with a fourth-century date. The text makes clear that the virgin lives under a rule and (ideally) under the authority of an elder female monastic. It is not clear whether the women live together in a family home or in a separately designated monastic dwelling. The virgin has occasion to meet catechumens, wealthy women, and poor women and to receive visits from a male "saint" or a "just man" who, apparently, offers some type of instruction or lesson. The author mentions other virginal "soul mates" with whom she shares meals and joins in prayer and chanting.

In the translation below I have followed von der Goltz's text with corrections by Lake and Casey (1926). I have chosen to leave the word *askesis* untranslated, but it may be read as "training," or "discipline," with the athletic sense of physical effort. For the generic personal pronoun I have opted to use "she," as the treatise is concerned with female virginity.

On Virginity, or On Asceticism

[1] First of all, believe in one God the Father, ruler of all, and maker of all things visible and invisible, and in his only-begotten Son, Jesus Christ, who is

from the substance of the Father and in respect to all things of equal power with the Father, and before the ages; and in the Holy Spirit who is in the Father and Son, sent from the Father and given through the Son. Father, Son, and Holy Spirit, three hypostases, one divinity, one power, one baptism. For our God himself, the Father of all, in six days made the heavens and the earth and the sea, and all that is in them. He adorned the heavens with the sun and moon and very beautiful stars, and founded the earth attractively above the waters, adorning it with plants and trees of every kind. And by his command go forth rivers flowing like honey and streams everlasting. He commanded the earth and it brought forth flesh, and he made all the beasts of the earth according to their species and the birds of the air according to their species. He commanded the waters and they brought forth fish, and he created the huge sea monsters. After everything else, he created the human and granted everything to him for the purpose of stewardship. And the Lord God said to his Son: "Let us make human according to our image and likeness." And the Lord God formed the human, taking dust from the earth and he put him in the paradise of delight. Then the Lord God put a trance on Adam and he slept and he took one of his ribs and filled in flesh in its place. And he fashioned the rib that he took into a woman and he led her to Adam and Adam said: "Now she is flesh of my flesh and bone of my bones; she shall be called woman because she was taken from her man. For this a man shall leave his father and his mother and will cling to his wife and the two will be one flesh" [Gen. 1:26; 2:7–8; 21–24).

[2] Listen, you servant of Christ and all who desire to be saved, and pay attention to my words; let your ears receive divinely inspired sayings. "This mystery is great" [Eph. 5:32] as the blessed Paul says, because when anyone one clings to his wife the two become one body. Thus in turn every man or woman who clings to the Lord is one spirit with him [1 Cor. 6:17]. If those joined to the world leave father and mother and are joined to mortal persons, how much more so should the abstinent virgin leave all earthly things and cling to the Lord alone. And the apostle himself testifies for me when he says: "The unmarried woman concerns herself with the things of the Lord, that she may be holy in body and in soul; but the one who marries concerns herself with the things of the world—how she will please her husband—and she has divided interests" [1 Cor. 7:34]. Consequently I say this, that every virgin or widow who practices abstinence, if she has her concern in this world, this concern is her husband. Even if she has possessions or property, this preoccupation contaminates her thoughts. For just as the body is defiled by a man, so also worldly habits defile the soul and the body of the one who keeps abstinence, and she is not holy in body and in spirit. But the one who concerns herself with the work of God, Christ is her bridegroom. For she who is betrothed to a perishable husband does the will of her husband; thus it is said that "the woman does not have authority over her own body, but her husband does" [1 Cor. 7:4], and further: "just as the church is subordinate to the Lord, so also wives are completely subordinate to their husbands" [Eph. 5:24]. Now

based on these worldly affairs, if we desire, we understand also that which is above. But the one who is joined to the heavenly bridegroom carries out the will of her bridegroom.

[3] For this is the will of Christ, that the one who is joined to him carries around nothing whatsoever of this age, gives thought to nothing of earthly matters but only takes up the cross of the one crucified for her sake, and has thought and concern night and day to sing unceasing hymns and doxologies; that she keeps the eye of understanding illuminated, knows his will and does it, and keeps her heart simple and mind pure; that she is merciful, so that just as he [Christ] is compassionate and merciful, so also we follow him; that she is gentle and quiet, long suffering, not returning evil for evil, enduring many injuries just as he [Christ] was injured by the Jews and endured; that she submit to beatings and trials, for he [Christ] also suffered these things. When he was beaten by the servants of the high priest, he did nothing, but said only: "If I spoke wrongly, testify to the wrong; but if I spoke well, why do you beat me" [John 18:23]? Was he not able, he who commanded the earth so that it swallowed Dathan and Abiron alive [Deut. 11:6], also to command the earth to swallow the one who extends his hand and strikes his own creator? But he endured patiently, leaving behind a model for us, so that we might follow in his footsteps. But you, human, do you not bear to be mistreated by a fellow human being? Imitate your master. For if that one who is God suffered to be beaten by a sinful person for your sake, are you vexed because your fellow human abuses you, and do you seek to take vengeance? O great folly and mighty thoughtlessness! For this reason indeed chastisement was prepared by us, and by ourselves we kindle the fire. Because indeed although we are rational we liken ourselves to irrational beasts. He came to this world in great humility, and although he was rich he became poor for our sake, so that we might be enriched by that poverty. And although he was God he became human for our sake, and was born from Mary the Theotokos [the Godbearer], so that he might set us free from the power of the devil.

[4] For which reason the one desiring to be saved makes herself a fool in this world in order to be called wise in the presence of God. For those people who know how to give and take and buy and sell and to engage in business and to withhold the goods of their neighbor and to take advantage and to lend money and to make one obol two, these people are called wise, but God calls such people foolish and witless and sinful. Listen to what God himself has said through the prophet Jeremiah: "The people, they are foolish children, [skilled] in doing evil, but of doing good they have no knowledge" [Jer. 4:22]. And the blessed Paul: "The wisdom of this world is foolishness with God, and the one wishing to be wise should become foolish in order to be made wise" [1 Cor. 3:18–19]. And again the same one says, "Brothers, do not be infants in intellect, but be childlike in regard to evil" [1 Cor. 14:20]. For God wants us to be foolish in regard to worldly things but wise in regard to heavenly things; for even our opponent the devil himself is wise in evil things, and we must work

wisely against him with a view to prevailing over his deceitful schemes. For the savior says in the Gospels, "Be as wise as the serpents and as pure as the doves" [Matt. 10:16]. But the one who is called wise by him, this is the one who contrives to do the will of God and keep his commandments.

[5] Humility is a great salvific remedy, for Satan did not fall down from heaven on account of lust or adultery or theft, but pride cast him down into the bottom of the abyss. For thus he said: "I will raise myself up, and I will place my throne face to face with God, and I will be like the most high" [Isa. 14:13–14], and on account of this saying he was cast down, and his inheritance became the everlasting fire. Therefore pride is of the devil, but humility is of Christ; for the Lord himself says, "Let the one among you who wants to be great become the servant of all" [Matt. 20:26]. For God is the God of the humble.

[6] We love fasting earnestly; fasting is a great protection, along with prayer and almsgiving, for it delivers a person from death. Just as on account of food and disobedience Adam was thrown out of paradise, so in turn through fasting and obedience the one who desires enters into paradise. Adorn your body with this virtue, O virgin, and you will please the heavenly bridegroom. Those who are attached to the world and who beautify their bodies with perfume, incense, and sweet smells, and in extravagant cloth and gold in order to please men are unable to please God. But Christ does not expect any of these things from you, but only a pure heart and an undefiled body mortified by fasting. But if some people should come and say to you, "do not fast often, lest you become weaker," you shall not believe them, nor even listen to them, for the enemy is provoking them. Remember what is written [Dan. 1:3–16], when the three youths who were with Daniel were led captive by Nebuchadnezzar, king of Babylon, and other young ones along with them, and he ordered them to eat from his table and drink from his wine. Daniel and the three youths did not want to be polluted from the king's table, but said to the eunuch in charge of them, "Bring us [food] from the seeds of the earth, and we will eat." And the eunuch said to them "I am afraid of the king who has ordered your food and drink himself, lest your faces seem gloomy to the king, especially compared to the young ones who eat from the king's table, and he will punish me." But they said to him, "Test your servants for about ten days, and give us [what we ask]." And he gave them vegetables to eat and water to drink, and their appearance seemed excellent in comparison to the youths who ate from the king's table.

[7] See what fasting does: it heals diseases, dries up the bodily fluids, casts out demons, chases away wicked thoughts, makes the mind clearer, the heart pure, and the body sanctified, and places the person before the throne of God. And lest you think that these things are said lightly, you have the testimony in the Gospels, spoken by the savior. His disciples asked him, "Lord, teach us, by what method are unclean spirits banished?" And the Lord said, "This type are not cast out except by fasting and prayers" [Mark 9:29; Matt. 17:18–20]. Whoever, then, is troubled by an unclean spirit, if she decides to make use of

this remedy—I speak of fasting of course—the constrained wicked spirit flees right away because it fears fasting. For demons delight fully in drunkenness and the relaxation of the body. Fasting is a mighty force and mighty are the virtuous actions accomplished through it. Otherwise, from where do people discharge great power, and from where are wonders accomplished through them, and from where does God give healing to the sick through them, if not surely from askesis and humility and a good way of life? For fasting is the life of the angels, and the one who makes use of it has angelic status. And do not suppose, beloved one, that fasting is just superficial; for the one who fasts from food alone does not succeed, but the one who abstains from all evil things, by this is fasting accounted. For if you fast and do not keep your mouth from saying an evil, hot-tempered, false or perjurious word, or if you rail against your neighbor—if these things come out of the mouth of one who is fasting, it will be of no benefit, but even all of her effort is lost. You, therefore, servant of Christ, and all who want to be saved, if you fast, purify yourself from all love of money; for whoever loves money is not able to love God. "For the love of money is the root of all evils" [1 Tim. 6:10].

[8] Earnestly flee vainglory and haughtiness. If a thought should whisper to you that because you have advanced in virtue you have become great and distinguished, do not believe it; for the enemy is the one who thwarts and the one who suggests vainglory. Do not endure the thought that praises you. And if the thought whispers to you saying, "You should not want to work so hard, you have the power to be saved," do not listen to it. For it is the enemy who suggests slackening and negligence, in order to throw you off from your virtuous way of life. Many are the devices coming from the enemy against the servants of God; he provokes people to come and give praise with words so that their hearts will be self-exalted. But you, do not accept human praise. And if someone says to you, "you are blessed," say to that one, "if I leave this body by dying nobly, then I will be blessed, but at present I do not believe that I am blessed." We humans shift like the wind. Often [the enemy] suggests to you that you have contempt for those who eat; do not give heed to him, for he is a stranger. Consider yourself to be the least of all, so that you might lead many into the kingdom of heaven, and you will be lifted up in the presence of God. But the enemy also suggests great askesis, in order to make your body weak and useless. So let your fast have due measure. Fast for the entire period, except in case of necessity. But at the ninth hour of the day, continuing in hymns and prayers, take your bread and vegetables prepared with oil. Everything is pure as long as it is non-animal.

[9] You, O virgin, let no one observe your askesis, not even one of your own relatives. But if you do something, do it in secret and your heavenly Father, who sees what is secret, will give you your due [Matt. 6:4]. If you reveal your life, vainglory is generated in you and you are penalized. But if you should discover a harmonious soul suffering for God like you, reveal yourself secretly to this one only—there is no vainglory there. For you speak in order that a

soul might be saved; you will receive a high reward if a soul is saved through you. Speak of profitable things to those who have the desire to hear. But if one should hear and not act, do not speak at all. For the Lord says, "Do not give holy things to dogs, nor cast your pearls before swine" [Matt. 7:6]. God calls those who lead dishonorable lives dogs and swine; but the words of God are precious pearls given only to the worthy.

[10] O blessed soul that hears these words written in this book and practices them! I declare to everyone who hears these words and practices them that her name will be written in the book of life and that she will be found in the third rank of the angels. If you should pray or sing psalms or read, sit by yourself; let no one hear except you alone and one or two virgins, if you have soul mates. For Christ says, "Wherever two or three are gathered in my name, I am there in the midst of them" [Matt. 18:20]. Put away the womanish mentality and take up courage and manliness. For in the kingdom of heaven there is no male and female [Gal. 3:28], but all well-pleasing women take on the rank of men. Disregard youthful appearances, so that you might take on the dignity of the noble widow. The blessed Paul says, "Honor the widows, the true widows; the one who is a true widow and is left all alone has placed her hope in God and abides in supplications and prayers night and day. But the one who lives indulgently has died while she lives. Let her be counted as a widow who is not less than sixty years old, having been the wife of one man, if she has raised children, practiced hospitality, washed the feet of saints, relieved the afflicted, if she pursues every good. But refuse younger widows, for when they behave wantonly toward Christ they want to marry, receiving condemnation because they violated their first pledge" [1 Tim. 5:3–12].

[11] But you, if you do not put on youthful airs, you are not called younger, but you are even called aged and have honor like an elder. Let the material of your clothing not be high-priced. Your outer garment should be black, not dipped in dye, but its own natural color or the color of onyx; and your veil should be without fringe, likewise its own color, and your sleeves wool, covering your arms up to the fingers. The hairs on your head [should be] cut all around and your little headband should be woolen, with the head bound tight and the hood and cape without fringe. If you should by chance meet someone, let your face be veiled, covered up, bent down, and do not lift your face toward a person, but only toward your God. When you stand for prayer keep your feet hidden by your shoes, for this is seemly for a sacred person. Do not strip naked, but night and day let your outer garment cover your flesh. Not even another female should see your naked body except in absolute necessity; but neither shall you see yourself with your body uncovered. For from whatever time you agree to practice abstinence for God, your body is sanctified and a temple of God. There is therefore no need for the temple of God to be uncovered in front of someone. If you are healthy you shall not go to the bath except in absolute necessity, and do not immerse your whole body into the water, because you are sanctified for the Lord God. And you shall not defile your

flesh with any worldly thing, but wash only your face, hands, and feet. When you wash your face, do not wash with both hands, nor rub the cheeks, nor add any herbs or salts or things like these, for worldly women do these things. But wash in pure water.

[12] You shall not anoint your body with costly ointments nor put expensive perfumes onto your outer garment. If your body should become weaker, take a little wine for your stomach [1 Tim. 5:23]. But if, God forbid, you should fall ill, take care of yourself; do not give an occasion for people to say "this illness befell her because of asceticism." But lest someone says this to you, be considerate of yourself, so that you might recover quickly and assume your rule again. Continue all the years of your life in fasting, prayer, and almsgiving. Blessed is the one who hears these things. Night and day let the word of God not be far from your mouth. Let the practice of the Holy Scriptures continually be your work. Have a Psalter and learn the psalms. Let the rising sun see the book in your hand, and after the third hour complete the synaxis, because the wood of the cross was joined together in this same hour; in the sixth hour complete your prayers with psalms and weeping and supplications, because in this very hour the Son of God was hung on the cross; in the ninth hour, again in hymns and doxologies confessing your transgressions with tears, beseech God because in this same hour the Lord hanging on the cross gave up his spirit. And after the synaxis of the ninth hour eat your bread, giving thanks to God at your table in this way: "Blessed be God who nourishes me from my youth, 'who gives nourishment to all flesh' [Ps. 136:25]. My heart is full with joy and glad thoughts, that 'having enough of everything at all times we might abound in every good work' [2 Cor. 9:8] in Jesus Christ our Lord, with whom to you be glory, honor, and power together with the Holy Spirit unto the ages of ages. Amen."

[13] And when you sit at the table and start to break bread, while crossing yourself three times, giving thanks in this way, say: "We give thanks to you our Father for your Holy resurrection, for through Jesus your Son you have made it known to us; and just as this bread, which is at first scattered, becomes one when it is gathered together on this table, in this way may your church be gathered together from the ends of the earth into your kingdom, for yours is the power and the glory unto ages of ages. Amen." If two or three virgins are present with you, let them give thanks for the bread lying before you and join you in prayer. But if a catechumen should happen to be at the table, let her not pray with the faithful, and do not sit to eat your bread with her. Nor further will you sit to eat your morsel with careless women and buffoons, except when necessary. For you are sanctified for the Lord God; your food and drink are also sanctified, for they are sanctified through prayer and holy words. Pious and God-fearing virgins shall eat with you. You shall not take a meal with vain women, nor shall you keep a pretentious woman as a friend. For the Holy Scripture says, "Whoever touches pitch will be stained, and whoever keeps company with a vain person will become like that one" [Sir. 13:1]. When a

wealthy woman sits down with you at the table, if you should see a poor woman, you shall invite her to eat and you shall not be ashamed in front of the wealthy woman. Do not love the glory of people more than the glory of God. For God is the God of the poor and the contemptible. Blessed is the soul that keeps these things.

[14] It is not good for a young [virgin] to live with another young [virgin]; at any rate they accomplish no good, for the one disobeys the other and the other one despises the other. But a young [virgin] under the authority of an elder woman is good. For the elder will not submit to the will of the young [virgin]. Woe to the virgin who is not under a rule. For she is like a ship that has no captain. With the steering handles broken off and having no guide, it is cast here and there by the waves, until it collides with the rocks and is straightaway demolished. Every virgin who does not have someone she respects is like this. Blessed is the virgin who is under a rule. For she is like a fertile vine in paradise, and when the gardener comes he prunes her branches and he irrigates and chops away the rotten weeds around her. So she who has someone taking care of her renders her valuable fruit in the proper season. Observe [these things] and offer doxologies at the table, and the food and drink will be sanctified for you. Then when you get up from the table, again giving thanks, say three times: "The merciful and compassionate Lord gives nourishment to those who fear him [Ps. 111:4–5]. Glory to the Father and Son and Holy Spirit." And after the doxology again complete your prayer by saying thus: "O God, ruler of all, and our Lord Jesus Christ, the name above all names, we give thanks to you and praise you, because you consider us worthy to partake of your goods, of fleshly nourishment. We beg you and ask you, Lord, that you might give us heavenly nourishment as well, and grant that we might tremble at and fear your awesome and honorable name, and not disobey your commandments. May you store your law and your ordinances in our hearts, and sanctify our spirits, our souls, and our bodies through your beloved Son, our Lord Jesus Christ, with whom to you be glory, honor, and power unto the ages of ages. Amen."

[15] There are many people who are mindless and nourish themselves like wild beasts, getting up in the morning and searching for someone to take advantage of, someone to oppress, in order to fill their shameful bellies. They do not know how to praise God at the table. Regarding them the divine Paul says: "These ones are the enemies of the cross of Christ, whose goal is destruction, whose god is the stomach; and their glory is in their shame, with minds set on earthly things; but our citizenship is in heaven" [Phil. 3:18–20]. These people are worse than even the beasts and the brute animals; for the brutes and the beasts know the God who created them and they praise him. But these humans, formed by his hands and bearing his image, do not know the one who created them. They acknowledge him with their mouths, but they deny him by their deeds. "Do you believe that there is a God? You do well; even the demons believe and shudder. Faith without works is dead" [James 2:17–19].

For what does a person profit from acknowledging that there is one God, if her worthless deeds deny him? How can someone claim to have a master, and not serve him? For by this [service] one obeys one's Lord. Even slaves know who purchased them and they honor them. We also owe honor to him, not only in word but also in deeds. Our Lord Jesus Christ testifies to this in the Gospel when he says: "Not everyone who calls me 'Lord, Lord' will enter into the kingdom of heaven" [Matt. 7:21]. And further: "You shall not take the name of the Lord your God in vain" [Exod. 20:7]. And again he enjoins us by saying: "Let everyone who invokes the name of the Lord abstain from injustice" [2 Tim. 2:19]. But do you want to be convinced that the beasts and brute animals know God and praise him? Listen to the Holy Spirit commanding them in the hymn: "Praise the lord, you beasts and all brutes" [Dan. 3:81, LXX]. If they did not praise him, the Spirit would not have commanded them. And it is not only these who praise God, but also every creature that is apparent and visible to the eye; all confess him together without ceasing.

[16] And you then, servant of God, whether you stand up or sit down, whether you perform some task, whether you eat, whether you go to your bed to sleep, whether you get up, let the hymn to God not be absent from your lips. Blessed are the ears that receive these words. If the twelfth hour arrives, you shall celebrate a greater and longer synaxis, with your virgin soul mates. But if you have no soul mates with you, complete it by yourself, with God who is with you and hears you. It is good to pour forth tears before God. Remember the twelfth hour, because in this hour our Lord descended to Hades. And seeing him, [Hades] shuddered and was astonished, saying: "Who is this, who descends in authority and great power? Who is this, who shatters the bronze gates of Hades and crushes the steel bars [Ps. 107:16]? Who is this, who descends from heaven and is crucified and yet is not subject to me, Death? Who is this, who loosens the chains of those under my power? Who is this, who by his own death destroys me, Death?"

[17] For this reason we ought ourselves to be attentive in that hour and to entreat the Lord with tears in the night; for the tear is a great virtue, a mighty action; great sins and crimes are erased by means of tears. Even the Holy Gospel testifies for me, for when the savior was handed over to the Jews, Peter denied him with an oath three times before the crowing of the cock. Turning, the Lord gazed at Peter, and Peter remembered the words of the Lord, how he said to him: " 'Before the cock crows, you will deny me three times;' and he went out, and wept bitterly" [Luke 22:61; Matt. 26:72–75]. You see the remedy of tears, you have observed what sort of crime it wipes away. For what is worse than this evil, that he denied his own master with an oath three times, and he wiped away such a great crime by means of tears. You see what great power tears have. Now, that was written for our admonition, so that we might acquire eternal life by imitating it. Most people do not have the gift of tears, but all who keep their minds above, who disregard earthly matters, who do not take precautions for the flesh, those who do not know if there is a world at all,

those who mortify their bodily members that are upon the earth—to these ones alone is given the grief of tears. For because they have a pure mind and sharp sight in their intellect, while still being upon the earth they see the punishments in Hades and the eternal torments in which sinners are punished, and they see the eternal fire and "the outer darkness, the weeping and gnashing of teeth" [Matt. 25:30]. But they also see the heavenly gifts, which God gives to the saints, and the glories, the crowns, the holy robes, the royal garments, the radiant chambers, the indescribable luxuries, and eternal life. And what do I say still? The most wondrous thing of all: the one who has a pure mind discerns even God himself with their interior eyes. How, then, would the one seeing these things not wish to weep and mourn? For she weeps and laments so that she might be delivered from such punishments, while at the same time she weeps and prays while beseeching, so that she might be deemed worthy of those heavenly goods.

[18] For this reason the saints despise this world, because they know what good things they are about to inherit. So therefore the one who has rest in the world should not hope to receive eternal rest, since the kingdom of heaven is not for those who find rest in this world. It is rather for those who pass through this life in great affliction and constraint. They do not receive it as a gift, but those who are accounted worthy receive it after much labor and intense sweat. Whatsoever they suffer here, it does not concern them; for when they enter that place they forget the pain and the distress that they endured in this vain world, because of the wondrous and indescribable rest given to them. What do you say, human? Look, there are two roads set before you, life and death. Go whichever way you wish. And look, [here are] fire and water. Stretch out your hand for whichever you want [Sir. 15:16–17]. It is up to you if you wish to gain life and it is up to you if you wish to gain death. Now death is the world, and life is justice. And the world is as far from justice as death is from life. If you walk in this world, you walk in death and you are, according to the Holy Scripture, far from God [James 4:4]. If you walk in justice, you walk in life, and death does not touch you. With the just there is no death, but [rather] translation. [The just one] is transferred from this world into eternal rest. And just as someone might leave a prison, so the saints exit this wretched life into the good things that have been prepared for them. "What the eye has not seen nor the ear heard, nor sprung up in the human heart, what God has prepared for those who love him" [1 Cor. 2:9]. Sinners not only labor wickedly here, but also in turn the fire awaits them there; and for such ones there is double reason to cry. For not only are they in constraint here, but even there they do not receive freedom. For this reason the Holy Scripture said, "When the sinner is turned around, they disappear" [Prov. 12:7]. There are constraints on all sides for this one, both grief there, and trials here. There is no human being who does not work hard in this wearisome life; both the poor and the rich, both the slave and the free, both the sinner and the just, all struggle in a similar manner. And one encounter will befall all, whether sinner or just here in this world.

[19] But there [in the next world] it is not the same, but [there are] different ranks. For one is the effort of the just in this world, and the other that of the sinner. Now the just person works hard, not in order to fill the stomach—for the just one does not take care of the flesh at all, or even think that she bears flesh—but she works night and day searching for God, not getting her fill of sleep, with bread and water not satiating her soul, wandering in the desert, mortifying the body with great suffering, until she receives the imperishable crown, which is reserved for her. But the sinner works and wears himself out not for the purpose of righteousness, but for his miserable flesh, for a shameful woman. He struggles this way and that, not satisfied with what he has, passing his time in evil and envy. But foolish people understand nothing of these things; for the matters and many concerns of the world blind them and they go astray, until the stern warrior is sent to them [Wis. 18:15], who does not marvel at any person nor accept any bribe [Deut. 10:17]. Their souls will be unmercifully carried away by the angels with force and they will receive their sentence from God. Because they are vain, they also struggle in vain in this world. They occupy themselves with the things of this world and for this reason they head for eternal ruin. For they did not give heed to God when they were on earth, nor was it a concern for them to consider the fear of God; for this reason God does not have concern for them either. For God is just and just is his judgment [Ps. 119:137]. When he comes to judge the world, then he will render to each according to their works. Blessed is the heart that receives these things.

[20] In the middle of the night you shall awaken and sing hymns to the Lord your God, because in this hour our Lord arose from the dead and sang hymns to his Father. For this reason we are commanded to sing hymns to God. When you rise up, recite this verse before everything else: "In the middle of the night I rose up to sing praise to you regarding the execution of your justice" [Ps. 119:62]. And you should pray, and begin to recite the entire fiftieth psalm, until you finish. And let these things be prescribed for you each day. Recite as many psalms as you are able to recite while standing, and with the psalm let a prayer and genuflection be completed, with tears confessing your sins to the Lord and asking that they be forgiven. Then after three psalms, recite the alleluia. But if there are also virgins with you, let them sing psalms as well, and one after the other carry out their prayers. Just before dawn say this psalm: "O God, my God, I rise early for you, my soul thirsts for you" [Ps. 63:1]. Then at daybreak: "Bless all the works of the Lord, sing praise to the Lord" [Dan. 3:57, LXX], "Glory to God in the highest" [Luke 2:14], and so on.

[21] But let us preserve love, the greatest of all. "You shall love the Lord your God with all your heart, and all your soul, and your neighbor as yourself. Upon these two commandments hang all the law and the prophets" [Matt. 22:37–40]. God is love, and he first loved humans; and he delivered himself for us, so that we might be delivered from all lawlessness. If, therefore, our Lord himself died for us, we also ought to lay down our souls for each other [1 John 3:16]. God is love, and the one who has love has God [1 John 4:16]. For he himself said: "By this all people will know that you are my disciples, if

you love one another" [John 13:35]. For however much a person struggles, if she does not have love for the neighbor, she struggles in vain. Thus you shall show love to your neighbor, not in word only but also in deed. You shall not keep someone's offense in your heart, otherwise your prayer does not ascend pure. "Do not let the sun go down on your anger" [Eph. 4:26]. Have gentleness, have patient endurance, forbearance, and a childlike [simplicity]. For the Lord says, "Unless you turn and become like children, you will not enter into the kingdom of heaven" [Matt. 18:3].

[22] You shall not be sad when some trial befalls you, nor will you be sad over loss, nor over an outrage, for "the sadness of this world produces death" [2 Cor. 7:10]. You shall be sad only over your sins, but over other little matters you shall not be sad. Do not raise your voice when you are angry at someone, for the servant of the Lord has no need to quarrel [2 Tim. 2:24]. Cursing shall not escape from your mouth, not insolence, nor abuse. For your mouth is sanctified by hymns and praises to God. It is not good for you to go out, except in great necessity. Love silence as much as you are able. Do not forget the servants of God, nor let them be left out of your heart. If a saint should come to your home, receive him in such a way as the Son of God. For our Lord Jesus Christ says, "The one who receives you, receives me" [Matt. 10:40]. If a just man should come into your house, you shall face him with fear and trembling, and you shall prostrate yourself on the ground at his feet. For you do not prostrate yourself to him, but to God who sent him. You shall take water and wash his feet and you shall listen to his words with all reverence. Do not feel confident in your self-control, lest you fall. But be fearful, for to the extent that you are fearful, you do not fall. It is best for the abstinent one to eat her bread in private. If you should sit at table with [other] virgins, eat with them everything that they have set out; for if you do not eat, you appear as if you are judging them. And if they are drinking wine, and you do not [normally], drink a little for their sakes. But if they are eminent elder women and they urge you to drink more, do not listen to them, but say to them: "You have spent your youth in great askesis, but I have not yet advanced even to the first degree." You have no need to be admonished concerning hospitality and almsgiving, for you will do these things on your own.

[23] Keep silent in church, and do not laugh at all, but pay attention only to the reading. If the thought should arise in your heart that you should do something, do not do it hastily, lest the enemy deceive you. Do everything with the counsel of your elders. When you sing psalms or when you pray, do not allow strange thoughts to enter into your heart. I entreat you, beloved one, pay attention to and heed these commandments written in this book; and observe what is written not only with your exterior eyes, but also with your interior eyes. And attend to each one of the commandments, and fulfill it. For if you keep these commandments, you will be found worthy of the royal bridal chamber. Do not utter in your heart, "How can I fulfill all of these?" Let your thoughts not lay hold of cowardice, but rather observe these commandments

with all eagerness. For God's commandments are not burdensome to those who fear God. At all times let oil not be lacking in your lamp, lest the bridegroom should ever come and find it extinguished. For you do not know when he comes, whether at first watch of the night or in the morning. So be ready, in order that when he comes you will meet him along with the wise ones, having oil in your lamp, that is, your good works [Matt. 25:1–13]. At all times remember your end; each day keep death before your eyes. Remember before whom you must stand.

[24] Askesis is burdensome and abstinence grievous, but nothing is sweeter than the heavenly bridegroom. Here we suffer a little, but there we will receive eternal life. For holy Paul says, "The sufferings of the present time are not comparable to the future glory to be revealed to us" [Rom. 8:18]. It is good to flee from the crowd and withdraw in solitude. Abstinence is a great virtue, purity a great glory, wondrous panegyrics of virginity. O virginity, incomprehensible riches! O virginity, imperishable crown! O virginity, temple of God and dwelling place of the Holy Spirit! O virginity, precious pearl hidden from many, and discovered by only a few! O abstinence, beloved by God and praised by the saints! O abstinence, hated by many, but commended by those worthy of you! O abstinence, fleeing from death and Hades and held in the grasp of immortality! O abstinence, joy of the prophets and glory of the apostles! O abstinence, life of the angels, and crown of holy persons! Blessed is she who possesses you, blessed is she who persists in you with endurance; because by laboring a little, she will greatly delight in you. Blessed is she who fasts for all of this time, because when she dwells in the Jerusalem above she will dance with the angels and have rest with the holy prophets and apostles.

[25] I have written these things to you, beloved sister, choral dancer of Christ, for the support and profit of your soul. Therefore do not deviate from these instructions either to the right or to the left. For if one hears these words and disregards them, there is a great judgment against her. But you, most precious sister who possesses this book, may God grant that you keep these words, that you live by them, that you abide in them, with an enlightened intelligence, a pure mind, and with the eyes of your understanding illuminated, so that you may receive the imperishable crown that God has prepared for those who love him. Through our Lord and savior Jesus Christ, to whom be the glory unto ages of ages. Amen.

Bibliography

Athanasius. [On Virginity]. "Athanasiana Syriaca I: 'Un Λόγος περὶ παρθενίας attribué à saint Athanase d'Alexandrie.'" Ed. and trans. J. Lebon. *Le Muséon* 40 (1927): 205–48. English translation in Brakke 1995, 303–9.

———. [Letter to Virgins]. In *S. Athanase. Lettres festales et pastorales en copte*. Ed. and trans. L.-Th. Lefort, 150: 73–99, 151: 55–80. Corpus Scriptorum Christianorum Orientalium 150–51. Louvain: L. Durbecq, 1955. English translation in Brakke 1995, 274–91.

———. [Letter to Virgins Who Went to Pray at Jerusalem and Returned]. "Athanasiana Syriaca II: Une lettre attribuée à Saint Athanase d'Alexandrie." Ed. and trans. J. Lebon. Le Muséon 41 (1928): 169–216. English translation in Brakke 1995, 292–302.

Aubineau, Michel. 1955. "Les Ecrits de saint Athanase sur la virginité." Revue d'Ascétique et de Mystique 31: 140–73.

———. 1966. Introduction to Grégoire de Nysse: Traité de la virginité. Sources chrétiennes 119. Paris: Editions du Cerf.

Bardy, G. 1935. "Athanase." Dictionnaire de spiritualité ascétique et mystique, doctrine et histoire I.2: 1047–52.

Basil of Ancyra. De vera virginitatis integritate. Patrologia Graeca 30, 669–809.

Batiffol, Pierre. 1893. "Le περὶ παρθενίας du pseudo-Athanase." Römische Quartalschrift 7: 275–86.

———. "Recension." 1906. Revue biblique 3: 295–99.

Bouvet, Chanoine J., trans. 1972. "Discours de salut à une vierge." Spiritualité orientale, no. 9. Begrolles-en-Mauge: Abbaye Notre Dame de Bellefontaine.

Brakke, David. 1994. "The Authenticity of the Ascetic Athanasiana." Orientalia 63: 17–56.

———. 1995. Athanasius and the Politics of Asceticism. Oxford Early Christian Studies. Oxford: Clarendon.

Brown, Peter. 1988. The Body and Society: Men, Women and Sexual Renunciation in Early Christianity. Lectures on the History of Religions 13. New York: Columbia University Press.

———. 1985. "The Notion of Virginity in the Early Church." In Christian Spirituality: Origins to the Twelfth Century, ed. Bernard McGinn, John Meyendorff, and Jean Leclercq, 427–43. World Spirituality 16. New York: Crossroad.

Burch, H. Hacher. 1906. "An Early Witness to Christian Monachism." American Journal of Theology 10: 738–43.

Camelot, P. Thomas. 1952. "Les Traités 'de virginitate' au IVᵉ siècle." In Mystique et continence: Travaux scientifiques du VIIᵉ Congrès international d'Avon, 273–92. Etudes Carmelitaines. Brugges: Desclée de Brouwer.

Cameron, Averil. 1989. "Virginity as Metaphor: Women and the Rhetoric of Early Christianity." In History as Text: The Writing of Ancient History, ed. Averil Cameron, 184–205. Chapel Hill: University of North Carolina Press.

Cooper, Kate. 1996. The Virgin and the Bride: Idealized Womanhood in Late Antiquity. Cambridge: Harvard University Press.

Delehaye, H. 1906. Review of Von der Goltz, ed., De virginitate. Analecta Bollandiana 25: 180–81.

Elm, Susanna. 1994. "Virgins of God": The Making of Asceticism in Late Antiquity. Oxford Classical Monographs. Oxford: Clarendon.

Gregory of Nyssa. 1966. De virginitate. Ed. Michel Aubineau, Grégoire de Nysse: Traité de la virginité. Sources chrétiennes 119. Paris: Editions du Cerf.

Jerome. 1910–1918. Epistula 22. In Eusebii Hieronymi Epistulae, ed. Isidorus Hilberg, 54: 143–211. Corpus Scriptorum Ecclesiasticorum Latinorum 54–56. Vienna: Tempsky.

John Chrysostom. 1966. De virginitate. Ed. Herbert Musurillo and Bernard Grillet. Jean Chrysostome: La virginité. Sources chrétiennes 125. Paris: Editions du Cerf.

Lake, Kirsopp, and Robert P. Casey. 1926. "The Text of the De Virginitate of Athanasius." Harvard Theological Review 19: 173–90.

Lebon, J. 1925. "Pour une édition critique des oeuvres d'Athanase." *Revue d'histoire ecclésiastique* 21: 524–30.

Migne, J. *Patrologia Graeca* 28.252A–282B.

Puech, Aimé. 1930. *Histoire de la littérature grecque chrétienne*. 3 vols. Paris: Les Belles Lettres.

Shaw, Teresa M. 1998. *The Burden of the Flesh: Fasting and Sexuality in Early Christianity*. Minneapolis: Fortress.

Van Eijk, Ton H. C. 1972. "Marriage and Virginity, Death and Immortality." In *Epektasis: Mélanges patristiques offerts au Cardinal Jean Daniélou*, ed. Jacques Fontaine and Charles Kannengiesser, 209–35. Paris: Beauchesne.

von der Goltz, Eduard F., ed. 1905. Pseudo-Athanasius. *De virginitate. Λόγος σωτηρίας πρὸς τὴν παρθένον (De virginitate): Eine echte Schrift des Athanasius*. Texte und Untersuchungen zur Geschichte der altchristlichen Literatur 29,2a. Leipzig: J. C. Hinrichs.

6

Basil of Caesarea

The "Prooemium" of the *Regulae fusius tractatae*

Lawrence J. Altepeter

Included within the Basilian corpus are a significant number of works that focus specifically upon asceticism and the ascetical life, the most important being the *Moralia* and the monastic rules. There are actually three collections of "Rules" in the corpus: the "Long Rules," *Regulae fusius tractatae* (*Rft*), the "Short Rules," *Regulae brevius tractatae* (*Rbt*), and a translation made by Rufinus, *Basili regula a Rufino latine versa*. The *Rft* and *Rbt* are not systematic works, but rather compositions that were developed over extended periods of time, undergoing repeated revisions in response to questions raised by monks, ascetics, and other sincere Christians (Fedwick 1979, 15). Rufinus (ca. 345–410 C.E.) was primarily a translator of Greek theological material into Latin. His translation of Basil (ca. 330–379) actually represents an early phase in the development of the rules, containing elements of both the *Rft* and *Rbt,* preserving a "primitive" version of Basil's rules (Rousseau 1994, 354–59). Somewhere in the developmental process the "Prooemium" was affixed to the beginning of the *Rft*.

Whether or not the "Prooemium" was actually composed by Basil is a matter of debate. What is evident is that if the text did not emanate from the pen of the Caesarean bishop himself, at the very least it bears the heavy imprint of the Basilian school of thought.

Traditionally identified as "Rules," the *Rft* has been classified by scholars as everything from a collection of "spiritual essays" (Frazee 1980, 27) and "Scriptural commentaries" (Murphy 1930, 25) to "monastic catechisms" (Zöckler 1897, 287). While it may not "constitute a monastic Rule in any strict sense" (Rousseau 1994, 354), the *Rft* is certainly a document similar to a Rule in intent if not in form. In the "Prooemium" we are told that what is to be presented is "something concerning salvation." What follows are fifty-five detailed responses to questions concerning the living of the pious life. More than mere responses, the answers are legislative and exacting in their expression. The answers in the *Rft* are presented more as maxims on the pious life than as mere replies, and it is in this way that the *Rft* approaches the genre of monastic rules.

Basil's influence upon the development of Christian monasticism and asceticism—both eastern and western—has been widely acknowledged. He is credited with the introduction of monasticism into Asia Minor (Jackson 1989, xviii), the creation of "true cenobitical monachism, receptive of both sexes and all classes" (Wagner 1962, ix), and was designated the lawgiver of Greek monasticism, as well as exerting a significant influence over the western monastic lawgivers John Cassian and Benedict of Nursia (Quasten 1960, 25–213). The *Regulae fusius tractatae* is important in that it provided a stencil by which later monastic Rules were developed. Consisting of essentially seven sections, the text deals with questions relating to (1) obedience to the scriptural commandments of love, (2) *apotagē* (renunciation), (3) *enkratia* (self-mastery), (4) community order, (5) work, (6) superiors, and (7) the use of medicine (Vogüé 1979, 52). While the main body of the text provides valuable insights into the practical components of Basilian monasticism, it is in the "Prooemium" that the undergirding theological premises are exposed.

The purpose for writing the *Regulae fusius tractatae* is, as stated simply by the author, "to learn something concerning salvation." Each of the fifty-five questions discussed in the text has as its ultimate goal the winning of salvation. The final picture resulting from that lengthy discussion is of an extremely rigid and disciplined life. It is in the "Prooemium" that the necessity for such an existence is fully explained.

The "Prooemium" wishes to make fully clear to its audience that the goal of salvation cannot merely be hoped for, but in fact, must be actively pursued. Any refusal or hesitation on the part of the aspirant shall result in the denial of all future rewards. This understanding of salvation as a reward to be earned is based upon the image of God as judge—one of the most prevailing theological images throughout both the text of the *Rft* and its "Prooemium."

Further, according to the "Prooemium," God is not only a judge, but also a judge to be feared. Those who are found in fault on "that fearsome and manifest day of the Lord" are not only excluded from the heavens, but are banished to the "Gehenna of fire and eternal darkness." Yet God is also a merciful father to be loved. The concept that God is both a God of wrath and a God of mercy is fundamental to the "Prooemium."

Underlying these two attributes is the fact that God is a just God. As a righteous judge, the sentence that God proclaims, be it a reward or a punishment, is directly related to an individual's earthly activities. God may be a God of mercy—"Blessed are the merciful, for they shall obtain mercy"—however, God is also a God of justice: "Do you see how judiciously he employs mercy? Neither being merciful without judgment, nor judging without mercy. For the Lord is merciful and just." The judgment of God can be of wrath or of mercy; the reward can be eternal life or everlasting punishment.

Therefore, as the "Prooemium" explains, it would be a grave mistake to picture

God only as a God of mercy. Such an incomplete image may lead one to live a less-than-pious life in the hopes of obtaining unwarranted forgiveness in the future. Such forgiveness would be unjust, and the God of the "Prooemium" is a God of righteous judgment. It is important, therefore, that God not only be loved but also feared.

The "Prooemium" emphasizes the judgment of God because salvation—entrance into heaven or banishment to hell—is ultimately determined as a result of God's righteous judgment, and that judgment is based upon an individual's obedience to God's will. It is really of no consequence whether one fears God as a slave, honors God as a beneficiary, or loves God as a parent; what is imperative is that one lives in obedience to the will of God, regardless of the motive. It is not one's disposition that God judges, but the degree to which one lives in conformity to God's will. Therefore, what the "Prooemium" insists upon is a "life according to the commandments."

Relying upon Scripture, Basil perceives God as a merciful, yet just deity, a God that requires obedience to the divine will and rewards or punishes accordingly. Salvation can, therefore, only be realized by those who comply with the will of God. Exactly what it is that God wills is contained within the Scriptures in the form of precepts and commandments. To live in obedience to the will of God is to live in accordance with the precepts of Scripture. Thus, in a very real sense, the Scriptures hold within them the key to salvation. Through a careful reading of the Bible, humanity can learn both what it must do and from what it must refrain, in order to win a seat in Paradise.

Numerous precepts are laid down in the Scriptures and all are to be taken seriously. Compliance with only some of the divine commandments is not sufficient; salvation can only be realized if all are heeded. According to the "Prooemium," the myriad of divine commandments contained within the Bible form an interconnected whole. When one commandment is broken, others are simultaneously transgressed. While all of the commandments may be interconnected, none are superfluous. The occasion for each and every one of the divine precepts is the realization of salvation. Each of them is directed towards this purpose and, therefore, each must necessarily be observed.

In the "Prooemium" no leeway is provided in the call to obedience. On more than one occasion the text warns its audience that all must carry out each and every detail that has been commanded, and that "it is not without danger to neglect any precept." Anything short of absolute devotion to God is insufficient for those who endeavor to live the life of piety. In order to remain continuously steadfast in one's observance of all of God's precepts, a constant focus is required. It is precisely in the hopes of creating an environment where such a focus may be realized that the *Regulae fusius tractatae* was written.

Surprisingly enough, despite the significant role that it played within early Christian asceticism and monasticism, a critical edition of the *Regulae fusius tractatae* has never been produced. The translation of the "Prooemium" that follows is based upon the edition found in PG 31, cols. 889–901, and is a more literal rendition of the Greek than that found in the two early English translations (Clarke 1925, 145–51 and Wagner 1962, 223–31).

The "Prooemium" of the *Regulae fusius tractatae*

Since by the grace of God we have gathered together in this place in the name of our Lord Jesus Christ—those having set upon the one and same goal of a life of piety and who are now quite clearly desirous to learn something concerning salvation—I for my part am compelled to proclaim the righteous acts of God, remembering night and day the words of the apostle: "for a period of three years, night and day, I did not stop admonishing each one of you with tears" [Acts 20:31]. The present is the most suitable time for us and this place offers quiet and complete rest away from outside disturbances. Let us, therefore, pray together so that we might give provisions to our fellow servants in due measure; for you, having received the word, like good soil, produce in return the perfect and multiple fruit of righteousness, as it is written.

Therefore, I beseech you through the love of our Lord Jesus Christ, who gave himself for our sins, let us undertake at length the care of our souls; let us grieve over the idleness of the previous life; let us contend on behalf of the things to come for the glory of God, and of his Christ, and of the honorable and Holy Spirit. Let us not remain in this laziness and laxity, always throwing away the present on account of laziness, and continuously putting off to tomorrow the beginning of work, then being found by the one who seizes our souls, unprepared of good works, we are cast from the joy of the nuptial chamber. Then we weep fruitless and unprofitable tears afterwards, lamenting a life spent in doing evil, when repenting is no longer possible. "Now is the acceptable time," says the apostle, "now is the day of salvation" [2 Cor. 6:2]. This is the age of repentance, that of reward; this of endurance, that of consolation. Now God is the helper of the ones turning away from the evil way; then he will be the fearful and undeceivable examiner of the actions, words, and thoughts of humans. Now we have the benefit of [his] patience; then we will know [his] righteous judgment, when we rise again some unto eternal punishment, some unto eternal life, and each shall receive according to their action. How long shall we defer obedience to Christ, who has called us to his heavenly kingdom? Shall we not become sober again? Shall we not call ourselves back from the accustomed manner of life to the rigid discipline of the Gospel? Shall we not take before [our] eyes that fearsome and manifest day of the Lord, on which those who come to the right hand of the Lord because of good acts shall be received into the kingdom of heaven; but those placed on the left because of an absence of good works, they shall be concealed in the Gehenna of fire and eternal darkness? "There is," it says, "weeping and gnashing of teeth" [Matt. 25:30].

We say that we truly desire the kingdom of heaven, yet we do not give heed to that by which it is attained; rather we admit no toil on behalf of the commandment of the Lord. Yet we, in the vanity of our minds, assume to attain equal honor with those opposing sin until death. Who sitting or lying asleep in the house during the season of sowing, has filled his bosom with sheaves at the coming of harvest? Who has gathered grapes from a vine that he neither planted nor worked for? The fruits are for those who labor; honors and crowns are for the victors. Who would ever crown one who did not strip before the adversary?

According to the apostle, it is not only necessary to prevail but to compete lawfully; that is, not to neglect even the small things commanded but to do each as ordered. For it is said, "Blessed is that servant, who the Lord having come shall find, not doing just anything, but doing thus" [Luke 12:43]; and again, "If you made offerings forthrightly, but did not divide it forthrightly, you have sinned" [Gen. 4:7 LXX]. But we, believing that we have fulfilled one of the commandments to some degree (for I would not say that they have fulfilled [it]; for they [the commandments] hold firm to one another according to the sound meaning of Scripture so that if one is broken then the rest are also [broken] out of necessity) do not expect [God's] wrath on account of the disregarded [commandments], but on account of the [one] good act, we indeed wait for honors. The one retaining one or two of the ten talents entrusted to him, but restores the rest, is not commended as prudent because he has restored the greater part, but is exposed to be unrighteous and greedy because he withheld the smaller part. But why do I say "he withheld"? When the one entrusted with one talent returned that same one whole and untouched as he had received it, he was condemned because he did not add to that [which was given to him]. The one who has honored his father for ten years, but later casts only one blow, is not honored as benefactor, but is condemned as a parricide. "Go," said the Lord, "make disciples of all nations, teaching them, not to keep some [commandments] and to be neglectful of some, but to keep all just as I have commanded you" [Matt. 28:19–20]. And the Apostle likewise writes, "Giving no occasion of offense in anything, that (our) service have no blame, but in everything commending ourselves as the servants of God" [2 Cor. 6:3–4]. For if all were not necessary to us for the goal of salvation, all of the commandments would not have been written, nor would all have been declared by necessity for observance. What advantage are other virtuous actions to me, if I am destined to be liable to hell, for calling [my] brother stupid? For what is the advantage of being free from many [powers] if one is enslaved under one power? For it is said, "Whoever sins is a slave of sin" [John 8:34]. And what gain is there of not suffering from many [diseases] if the body is corrupted by one disease?

So then, someone will say, is it not in vain that the multitudes of Christians, who do not observe all of the commandments, keep any of them? In this interest it is good to remember the blessed Peter, who, after so many virtuous acts and such great blessings, on account of only one [wrong act] is told, "If I do not wash you, you have no part with me" [John 13:8]. But I might say, that same [act] showed neither indifference nor neglect, but was a reflection of [Peter's] honor and reverence.

And yet someone might say, it is written, "Everyone who calls upon the name of the Lord, they shall be saved" [Joel 2:32]; so that the calling upon the name of the Lord is sufficient to save the one calling. But let this one hear the words of the Apostle, "How then shall they call upon [him], in whom they do not believe?" [Rom. 10:14]. And if you believe, hear the words of the Lord: "Not everyone who says to me, 'Lord, Lord' shall enter into the kingdom of heaven, but the one who does the will of my father who is in heaven" [Matt. 7:21]. And wherever one does the will of the Lord, but not as God wills, nor doing it in a disposition of love towards God, the zeal of his effort is in vain, according to the declaration of him, our Lord Jesus Christ, who proclaims, "he that acts to be seen by men; truly I say to you, he has received his reward" [Matt. 6:5]. Wherefore Paul the apostle was taught to say, "Even though I give away all my goods to feed [the poor], and if I give my body that I may be burned, but I do not have love, I profit nothing" [1 Cor. 13:3].

Actually, I perceive three different dispositions, because of unavoidable necessity, that lead to obedience. Either for fear of punishment we turn away from evil, and we possess a slavish disposition; or, seeking the gain of reward, we fulfill the ordinances for the sake of our own profit, and by this we resemble hired laborers; or for the good for its own sake and the love of the one who gave the law to us, rejoicing because we have been deemed worthy to serve the glorious and good God, we thus possess the disposition of sons.

Nor will the one who keeps straight the commandments out of fear, and always wary of the penalty of sloth, do some of the commandments given him and disregard some, but he will fear equally the punishment that comes upon every disobedience. And he is called blessed who in all things crouches in fear out of [divine] reverence, and he stands steadfast in the truth, being able to say, "I have always seen the Lord before me, because he is to the right hand of me, in order that I might not waver" [Ps. 15:8 LXX] thus never choosing to neglect that which is binding. Again "Blessed is the man who fears the Lord." [Ps. 111:1 LXX] Why? Because "He shall delight greatly in his commandments" [Ps. 111:1 LXX]. Indeed those who are fearful do not neglect any of the commandments or do them carelessly.

But neither will the hired man choose to transgress any orders. For how would he gain the pay of his work in the vineyards, not fulfilling everything that had been agreed upon? For if he is deficient in anything of necessity, he makes it [the vineyard] useless to the property owner. Thus, as long as there is damage, who would pay the wage to the wrongdoer?

The third service is according to love. Now what son, having the goal of the father's good pleasure, making him happy in greater things, will choose to grieve him on account of the smallest matters? He will be all the more so, remembering the words of the Apostle, "And do not grieve the Holy Spirit of God, whereby you are sealed" [Eph. 4:30].

Therefore, in what kind of classification should the ones who transgress most of the commandments be placed? They neither serve God as a father, nor believe [in him] as the one who promises great things, nor serve [him] as a master. "If I am then a father," he [the prophet] says, "where is my honor? And if I am a Lord, where is my fear?" [Mal. 1:6]. For the one that fears the Lord shall greatly delight in his commandments. But "through the transgression of the law," he [the apostle] says, "you dishonor God" [Rom. 2:23]. How then, preferring life according to pleasure to [life] according to the commandments, can we assume for ourselves a life of blessedness, citizenship with the saints, and merriment with the angels in the presence of Christ? Certainly such fantasies are childish thinking. How will I be with Job, not meeting ordinary affliction with graciousness? How [will I be] with David, not showing long-suffering to the enemy? How [will I be] with Daniel, not seeking God with continuous self-mastery and laborious petition? How [will I be] with each of the saints, not walking in their footsteps? Who is such an undiscriminating judge, as to deem the victor and one who never contended worthy of equal crowns? What general ever called to an equal portion of the spoils with the conquerors, those that did not appear at the battle?

God is good, but also just. And worthy repayment is of the just, as it is written, "Do good, Lord, to the good and the upright in the heart. But those who turn to crooked ways the Lord shall lead away with the doers of lawlessness" [Ps. 124:4–5 LXX]. [God] is merciful, but also a judge. He [the psalmist] says, "for the Lord loves mercy and judgment" [Ps. 32:5 LXX]. And therefore, he [the psalmist] says, "Mercy and judgment I shall sing to you, Lord" [Ps. 100:1 LXX]. We have learned upon whom there is mercy; for he says, "Blessed are the merciful, for they shall obtain mercy" [Matt. 5:7]. Do you see how judiciously he employs mercy? Neither being merciful without judgment, nor judging without mercy. For the Lord is merciful and just. Therefore, let us not know God by halves, nor let us receive his loving kindness as an occasion for laziness. On account of this, thunder; on account of this, lightning—that [his] goodness not be despised. The one who makes the sun rise, also condemns with blindness. The one who gives the rain showers, also rains fire. Those are of [God's] goodness, these are of [God's] severity; let us either love [God] on account of those, or fear [God] on account of these, so that it may not be said to us, "Do you despise the riches of his kindness and forbearance and long-suffering, not knowing that the kindness of God leads you to repentance? But on account of [your] hard and impenitent heart, you are storing up wrath for yourself on the day of wrath" [Rom. 2:4–5].

Since then it is not possible to be saved, unless you do acts according to the commandment of God, it is not without danger to neglect any precept (for it is a terrible arrogance to make oneself a critic of the Lawgiver and to approve some of the laws, but rejecting others), therefore, let us who bear patiently the struggle of piety, who honor the quiet and calm life as a fellow worker in the keeping of the Gospel decrees, both common folk and council members, take heed that no commandment escape us. For if it is necessary for the man of God to be perfect (as it is written and [our] words have already shown), before all else he must be purified by means of every commandment "unto the measure of the stature of the fullness of Christ" [Eph. 4:13], since according to divine law, that which is mutilated even though clean, is unacceptable in a sacrifice to God.

Anyone believing to be lacking at all, let him bring this forward to be considered in common. For through the laborious examination of many [people] the hidden is discovered, for God, clearly, according to the promise of our Lord Jesus Christ, grants us discovery of the inquiry through the teaching and provocation of the Holy Spirit. Just as "necessity is laid upon me, and woe is me if I should not preach the gospel" [1 Cor. 9:16], so also equal danger is placed on you if you leave off the inquiry in laziness, or if you act lazy and careless in keeping the tradition and in fulfilling it through acts. For that reason the Lord says, "The word which I spoke, that shall judge him on the last day" [John 12:48], and "The servant who did not know the will of his lord, who did things worthy of blows, shall be flogged a little, but the one who knew, yet did not prepare himself according to his will, shall be greatly flogged" [Luke 12:47–48]. Therefore, let us pray that I may dispense the word without reproach, and the teaching may bear fruit in you. And since we know that the words of the divinely inspired Scriptures will stand before us at the tribunal of Christ ("I shall reprove you," he says, "and I shall place your sins before your face" [Ps. 49:21 LXX]), let us soberly heed that which is spoken and zealously seek to put forward the divine teachings into deeds, for we do not know on what day or hour our Lord will come.

Bibliography

Amand de Mendieta, Emmanuel. 1949. *L'Ascèse monastique de saint Basile de Césarée: Essai historique*. Maredsous: Editions de Maredsous.

Basil of Caesarea. 1925. *The Ascetic Works of Saint Basil*. Trans. W. K. Clarke. London: Society for Promoting Christian Knowledge.

———. *Saint Basil: Ascetical Works*. 1962. Trans. M. Monica Wagner. The Fathers of the Church 9. Washington, D.C.: Catholic University of America Press.

———. *Basili regula a Rufino latine versa*. 1986. Ed. Klaus Zelzer. Corpus scriptorum ecclesiasticorum latinorum 86. Vienna: Hoelder-Pichter-Tempsky.

———. The "Prooemium" of the *Regulae fusius tractatae*. *Patrologia Graeca* 31: 889–901.

Clarke, W. K. 1913. *St. Basil the Great: A Study in Monasticism*. Cambridge: Cambridge University Press.

Fedwick, Paul Jonathan. 1979. *The Church and the Charisma of Leadership in Basil of Caesarea*. Studies and Texts 45. Toronto: Pontifical Institute of Mediaeval Studies.

———. 1978. *St. Basil the Great and the Christian Ascetic*. Rome: Basilian.

Fox, Margaret Mary. 1939. *The Life and Times of St. Basil the Great as Revealed in His Works*. Washington, D.C.: Catholic University of America Press.

Frazee, Charles A. 1980. "Antolian Asceticism in the Fourth Century: Eustathios of Sebastea and Basil of Caesarea." *Catholic Historical Review* 66: 16–33.

Gribomont, Jean. 1953. *Histoire du texte des Ascétiques de saint Basile.* Bibliothèque du Muséon 32. Louvain: Publications Universitaires.

————. 1984. *Sainte Basile: Evangile et église. Mélanges.* 2 vols. Spiritualité orientale et vie monastique 36–37. Bégrolles-en-Mauges: Abbaye de Bellefontaine.

Jackson, Blomfield. 1989. "Prolegomena." *The Nicene and Post-Nicene Fathers.* Vol. 8. 2d series. Ed. Philip Schaff and Henry Wace. Grand Rapids: Eerdmans.

Morison, Ernest Frederick. 1912. *St. Basil and His Rule: A Study in Early Monasticism.* London: Frowde.

Murphy, Margaret Gertrude. 1930. *Saint Basil and Monasticism.* Catholic University of America Patristic Studies, 25. Washington, D.C.: Catholic University of America Press.

Quasten, Johannes. 1960. *Patrology.* Vol. 3. Westminister: Christian Classics.

Rippinger, Joel. 1977. "The Concept of Obedience in the Monastic Writings of Basil and Cassian." *Studia Monastica* 19: 7–18.

Rousseau, Philip. 1994. *Basil of Caesarea.* Berkeley and Los Angeles: University of California Press.

Vogüé, Adalbert de. 1979. "The Greater Rules of Saint Basil—A Survey." In *Word and Spirit, a Monastic Review, 1: In Honor of Saint Basil the Great 379.* Still River, Mass.: St. Bede's Publications, 49–85.

Wagner, M. Monica. 1962. "Introduction." *Saint Basil: Ascetical Works.* Trans. M. Monica Wagner. The Fathers of the Church 9. Washington, D.C.: Catholic University of America Press.

Zöckler, O. 1897. *Askese und Mönchtum: Zweite, Gänzlich Neu Bearbeitete und Stark Vermehrte Auflage der "Kritischen Geschichte des Askese."* Frankfurt: Heyder und Zimmer.

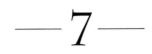

7

Sermons of Columbanus

Arthur G. Holder

Although the origins of Christianity in Ireland are obscure, there is surely some truth in the legends that accord an important role to the missionary preaching of Patrick, a Romanized Briton who came to Ireland in the early part of the fifth century. From that time forward, the Irish church had a strongly monastic flavor. Tales of the early Egyptian monks inspired many Irish women and men to seek the spiritual "desert" of the ascetic life. Following the example of Abraham who heard God's call to "Go from your country and your kindred and your father's house" (Gen. 12:1), many of these Irish ascetics went into voluntary exile, either within Ireland itself or in lands faraway. Wandering across land and sea in search of what they called their "place of resurrection," they spread the Christian gospel in a peculiarly Celtic form that placed equal emphasis on austerity and on learning.

The most prolific and influential representative of early Irish Christian asceticism was Columbanus, whose name in Latin means "dove." He was born in the province of Leinster around the middle of the sixth century. According to his biographer Jonas, the youthful Columbanus attracted the lascivious attention of some local girls and was advised by an anchoress that he should flee the neighborhood in order to preserve his chastity. Despite his mother's protestations, Columbanus became a monk, first at Cleenish on Lough Erne and later at the renowned monastery of Bangor, near present-day Belfast. In 591, inspired by the Irish ascetic ideal of wandering pilgrimage, he set out with twelve companions for France. There he established Luxeuil and two other monasteries, all of which attracted numerous converts. Soon, however, Columbanus incurred the wrath of the French bishops by preaching against the laxity of the Gallic church and by steadfastly advocating the Irish method for calculating the date of Easter. Finally expelled from Burgundy by King Theuderic in 610, Columbanus and his monks made their way across France and Germany into Switzerland, preaching to pagans and heretics and founding numerous monasteries along the way. In 612, he crossed the Alps into Italy and founded a monastery at Bobbio (near Milan), where he died on November 23, 615.

The earliest writings of Columbanus are a commentary on the psalms and some hymns composed during his years in Ireland; unfortunately, these have not survived. While in France, he produced two quite stringent monastic rules, as well as a penitential by which the Irish practice of private confession was first introduced into continental Europe. Five of the letters attributed to him can be accounted as genuine; three (including one to Pope Gregory the Great) deal with the paschal controversy, a fourth consoles the monks from whom Columbanus was about to be driven away into exile, and the fifth is a long and strident admonition warning Pope Boniface IV against the dangers of the "Three Chapters" schism. The most recent scholarship (Lapidge 1997) indicates that the metrical poetry previously attributed to Columbanus is spurious, but at least two non-metrical poems do appear to be genuine. Finally, there is a remarkable collection of thirteen sermons, which Clare Stancliffe calls "the only coherent exposition of Irish ascetic spirituality to have come down to us from the formative period of early Irish monasticism" (Lapidge 1997, 199).

These sermons were probably preached during Columbanus's last years, to a monastic audience in either Bobbio or Milan. Taken as a series, they constitute a *protrepticus*—an exhortation to moral virtue. As Jean Leclercq has noted, Columbanus's two great themes are the decrepitude of this world and the compelling duty of loving God and neighbor (Leclercq 1968, 35–37). The world's decrepitude is illustrated with many analogies, foremost among them the comparison of life (*vita*) in this world to a mere roadway (*via*) that ought not to be confused with that eternal homeland (*patria*), which is humanity's true destination. With mystic fervor, Columbanus spoke of love for God as a kind of longing adoration, imploring Jesus "that knowing you, we may love only you, love you alone, desire you alone, meditate on you alone by day and night, think always of you" (Sermon 12.3). Love for neighbor takes many forms, but above all it implies generosity in almsgiving and utter disdain for every earthly possession: "Do not be stingy with things that are fleeting, lest you lose things that are eternal; the whole world does not belong to you, who were born naked and are buried naked" (Sermon 3.4).

The approach to asceticism in these hortatory sermons is complex and somewhat paradoxical. Columbanus clearly means to deny the world any ultimate value, but in doing so he nonetheless affirms the critical importance of life in this world as preparation for the life that is to come. And even if his teaching calls for self-denial and the renunciation of much that appears fundamental to human nature, it is supported by quite rational arguments presented in a highly polished rhetorical style indicative of considerable erudition. Finally, there is in these sermons a careful balancing of nature and grace in a way that may be characterized as semi-Pelagian. Columbanus never fails to stress the need for discipline, effort, and perseverance, but even so, he eagerly affirms that humanity is dependent upon God in order to live virtuously: "Strive to be what one was created to be, and call upon God's grace to aid one's own effort; for by oneself alone it is impossible for anyone to obtain what was lost in Adam" (Sermon 3.2).

Columbanus's ascetic teaching contains much that can be traced back to classical sources, especially neo-Platonic doctrines concerning the world's transience and the imperative to discipline the body in order to prepare the soul for eternity. But in his sermons Columbanus never quotes a classical author. His authorities are the church fathers, and above all the verses of the Bible, which he understood as "testimonies of the divine oracle" (Sermon 12.1). In the gospels he found the Savior's admonitions to be charitable, to keep vigil, and to pray to the Father in heaven. In the apostolic epistles he found counsels of perseverance and examples of faithful discipleship. In the Psalms, and in the Song of Solomon, he found poignant prayers of longing and holy desire: "We will run after you" (Song of Sol. 1:4); "My soul has clung after you" (Ps. 63:8); "Draw me after you" (Song of Sol. 1:4). These verses, Columbanus says, are the songs that Christians sing while they travel "as wayfarers, as pilgrims, as guests of the world" (Sermon 8.2), moving along the roadway of this present life to their true homeland, which lies above.

The text translated is from *Sancti Columbani Opera,* edited by G.S.M. Walker.

Sermon 3: How the Monk Ought to Please God

[1] What is best in the world? To please its Maker. What is his will? To fulfill what he has commanded—that is, to live rightly and dutifully seek the eternal; for duty and uprightness is the will of the One who is dutiful and upright. How does one attain to this? By striving. Therefore we must strive with dutifulness and uprightness. What helps us to maintain this? An understanding that, sifting through everything else and finding nothing solid to cling to among the things of the world, has reason to turn toward the one thing that is eternal. For the world will pass away, and daily it is passing away and whirling toward its end (for what does it possess that it does not assign to an ending?) and in a certain manner it is propped up on pillars of vanity. But when an end of vanity comes, then it will fall and will not stand. But no one says of the world that it does not end. Thus by death and destruction all things pass away and do not endure. What then should the wise person love? A lifeless form, partly mute and partly resounding, which one sees and does not understand? For if one could understand, perhaps one would not love; but in this also it offends, in that it does not show itself. For who understands, either of oneself or of another who has been made a flower of the earth and earth from earth, how it is fitting that God should make his own child and an inhabitant of heaven out of what will shortly become earth and dust, and will never profit unless the soul intervenes?

[2] If God has allowed someone to understand what sort of life one ought to live in order to become eternal instead of mortal, wise instead of stupid, and heavenly instead of earthly, first let that person have a pure discernment employed in living well, and let that person see not what is, but what shall be. For what is not, shall be, and through the things that are seen one ought to ponder things unseen, and strive to be what one was created to be, and call upon God's grace to aid one's own effort; for by oneself alone it is impossible

for anyone to obtain what was lost in Adam. But what good is it to acquire discernment and not use it well? The person who uses it well is the one who lives so as never needing to repent [if possible] or failing to repent [when necessary]; for delayed penitence charges one with evil doing, while a good conscience commends one's life. What then does a pure discernment have the good sense to love? Surely that which makes it love all other things, which abides forever and never grows old. According to the principle of truth, no other external thing ought to be loved except that which is eternal and the eternal will, which is inspired and animated by the eternal, wonderful, ineffable, invisible, incomprehensible One who fills all things and surpasses all things, who is both present and elusive. A wise person ought to love nothing that is here, because nothing endures; for eternal things are there with the Eternal, and perishable things are here with the mortal. Thus it is perilous to live among things that are deceitful and deceptive, and not to see the true things that you ought to love, and moreover to see things that call to you as they are fleeing away, and as though in a dream entice you to sin with them, and (a loathsome thing) leer at you with their charms, and thus steal away the things that deserve to be loved, as though they do not exist.

[3] Obviously, then, anyone who lives among deceivers ought to be careful, for one will not escape unless one flees them and cautiously behaves oneself properly. How will we flee the world which we are not supposed to love, we who are in the world and are taught to die to it, but on the contrary enfold it within ourselves with a certain invidious lust, when we should have been (as it were) trampling it underfoot? To trample upon the world is to conquer oneself, to die to vices before one dies to nature, in the soul rather than in the body; for no one who spares oneself can hate the world; for only in oneself does one either love or hate the world. There is nothing left to love about the world, if one has died to bodily desires. Let us die by such a death, because bodily death grips everyone, but this one only a few. For there are few who live in such a way as to die daily; and while one has not always been, nor can one always be, in the world, but lives only for some very brief period of time, each person ought to live in such a way as to die daily, so that, doubtful of this death, one may think only of the eternal and heavenly things among which, if one merits, one shall be eternal and heavenly. For the things that were before the world are the very things that will also be after the world and forever, and they are even yet, but they are not apparent, for they are hidden from us to such a degree that it is not lawful for human beings to speak of them; "for they do not reach or enter into the heart or ears of a human being, nor can they be perceived by human sight." [1 Cor. 2:9] O how deplorable a condition! The things we were supposed to love are separated from us, both unascertained and unknown, in such a way that as long as we are human and situated in this prison of the body it is completely impossible for us to see, hear, or ponder the things that are truly good and eternal. What then shall we do? Let us love and seek even the things unknown, lest perhaps we ignore them and lose them

forever; for the person was born for no purpose, who continually ignores those things that are continual and remains eternally unaware of those things that are eternal. O you wretched human being! You ought to hate what you see, and you are ignorant of the thing you should love. Your life is a snare for you, and you are entangled whether you will to be or not; in yourself you possess that by which you are fettered, but in yourself you do not possess that which sets you free. Will you not beware of yourself, wretch, and have no confidence in yourself—you who are ensnared by yourself, but not set free by yourself? Although you have eyes, you are held fast like the blind, and willingly led to your death.

[4] O intolerable blindness! O incomparable anguish! O most miserable wretchedness! You favor your adversaries, willingly hand yourself over to those who persecute you without mercy, and gladly conspire with those who bind you and hand you over to death. Who ever proceeds to death cheerfully? Who is willingly led to be slaughtered or beheaded? Woe to you, human wretchedness! Would that you were slaughtered or beheaded, and not tormented forever. What is blinder than you, O wretched humanity! You see things so that you go astray, for you can see only as far as heaven, not beyond it; on this side of heaven, you have knowledge, beyond heaven you have no knowledge. Hard and impenetrable ignorance, who will tell you things that cannot be told? Miserable humanity, what will come to your aid? Hear what a wise person has said: "If a few things are not sufficient for a person, more will not do any good." [Sulpicius Severus, *Dialogus* 1.18] You have heard, I think, the Lord saying in the gospel: "Go, you accursed, into eternal fire" [Matt. 25:41]. And do you remember why they are sent into the fire? Be merciful, you wretched human being, and perhaps you will be able to drag yourself away from the son of perdition; do not be stingy with food, do not be stingy with perishable clothing, do not prefer your possessions to yourself. You should love yourself more than your possessions, your soul more than your property; for you alone are wretched, and not your property, so you ought to love yourself more than things that do not belong to you. For what is yours, except your soul? Do not be willing, then, to lose your only possession for the sake of nothing. Do not be stingy with things that are fleeting, lest you lose those that are eternal; the whole world does not belong to you, who were born naked and are buried naked. O incurable madness! What fleeting thing that does not belong to you do you love with so much affection that you would lose forever the eternal thing that is your own? Therefore ponder death, which puts an end to the pleasures of the world, and see where it hurls the winsome delight of the rich. Extravagance, jesting, lust, debauchery cease, and the earth receives the naked corpse, which is going to be destroyed by worms and putrefaction, while the most wretched soul is given over to eternal torments. What is more lamentable than this condition? What is more miserable than this wretchedness, which follows the vanities of this life to perpetual corruption and ruin? Surely one hour's endurance would be better than delayed penitence for eternal time?

Therefore fear death this side of heaven, and beyond heaven eternal fire; this one you see, that one you do not see, but nevertheless you believe in him who has seen it. For our Lord Jesus Christ is true, to whom be honor and glory unto ages of ages. Amen.

Sermon 4

[1] "Every discipline," according to the Apostle, "seems for the present to be a thing not of joy but of sorrow; but later it yields the pleasant fruit and peaceful gain of reward for those who have been trained by it" [Heb. 12:11]. For what indeed is learned here without sorrow and toil, in the time of our greatest dullness and weakness? But if temporal kinds of discipline take away the sweetness of present joy, what should we expect from this discipline of our school? This is actually the discipline of disciplines, and by means of present sorrow it procures the pleasantness of eternal time and the delight of eternal joy. For what kind of discipline is there that is free from the sorrow of chastisement? How much grief and sorrow is contained in the artisan's crafts? How much toil? How much work awaits those who practice a trade or even those who build? With how many lashings, with what afflictions are musicians' students taught? With how much weariness and how many sorrows are physicians' disciples troubled? And with what sorts of uneasiness are the lovers of wisdom constrained, and with what narrow straits of poverty the philosophers? Finally, with how many dangers are government offices sought after? In all these, although it may be after the toils of countless miseries, a most peaceful outcome is patiently expected, in consideration of which the aforesaid misfortunes, although not without sorrow, although with much bitterness, are endured. For even though discipline is accompanied by sorrow, nevertheless its outcome issues in joy, and toil is involved with ease, and in a strange way sadness is very patiently endured for the sake of joy, bitterness for the sake of sweetness, toil for the sake of ease, uneasiness for the sake of ease. For although they do not know if they will achieve the outcome of any discipline, nevertheless for an uncertain hope of future joy they bear present sorrow not scornfully, and not sluggishly do they pursue hard toil. For who among them is sure of ever being the master of that discipline in which toil is borne? Or of becoming a partaker of this joy for which sorrow is endured?

[2] And so, if so many and such kinds of things are tirelessly endured for the sake of things that are temporal and uncertain, what ought we to bear for the sake of things that are eternal and true and certain, whose outcome is eternal? For if those who pursue temporal disciplines are uncertain how much time there may be for them to benefit from the discipline once it has been acquired, yet they are absorbed in following it with no sluggishness at all, and are thus more persistent than we, although they are doubly in doubt, for (as I have said) they are uncertain if they will achieve the discipline's outcome, on

account of the uncertainty of life and the dullness of discernment, and once the discipline has been acquired they are no less in doubt again how long they may employ it. For they are as certain of giving up the discipline shortly as they are uncertain of carrying it through. Therefore (as we have said), they bear with temporary pursuits and unperfected skills, sorrows and sadnesses, narrow straits and toils, dangers and peregrinations, injuries and weariness, although they know very well how uncertain and fragile are the things for which such misfortunes are borne; if the discipline of our school involves tribulations, if it involves troubles, sorrows, and bitternesses, will it be wondered at, will it be deemed a thing to be avoided? Is it not impossible for any thorough schooling or any profession to be acquired without discipline? Or can discipline be attained without bitterness? Therefore, since these things are so, "let us prepare the soul" not for joy, not for ease, but (as the wise man says) "for trials" and tribulations, and for sadnesses and toils. [Ecclus. 2:1] Christ was tried, injured, reviled, and he suffered; and do you think of ease on earth? See and understand how difficult it is to conquer the world, when a saint is not delivered from it except through the death of Christ. "If it is so hard for the just to be saved, where shall the sinner and the ungodly person appear?" [1 Pet. 4:18] Listen to the Lord saying to the disciples, "In the world you will have affliction" [John 16:33], and again, "And you will weep and mourn, but the world will rejoice and you will be sad" [John 16:20].

[3] See the sorrow of our discipline; understand that one does not pass from joy to joy or from ease to ease, but from mourning to joy, and from tribulation to ease. Therefore we must patiently bear brief sorrow, that we might obtain eternal joy; and "the slightness of our tribulation must be endured with gladness, so that we may lay hold of the eternal life of boundless glory" [2 Cor. 4:17]. For if, as we have very often said, these things befall on account of things that are fleeting, but do not prevail, what shall weary or prevail over us who carry on the business of heavenly kingdoms? We should yield neither to joys nor sadnesses, neither to pleasure nor bitterness; for the world is full of both, and the Captain of our war has prevailed over both. And let us see how dangerously the unclean yields to those things to which the clean and unstained has not yielded; with Christ let us refuse the world's honors, and the devil's "kingdoms with all their glory" [Matt. 4:8]. Let us disdain to receive whatever is of the devil, and to that king of brief joy let us say, "May the things that are yours perish with you" [Acts 8:20]. Let us be "sad even unto death" [Matt. 26:38] with Christ, "so that our sadness may be turned into joy" [John 16:20]. Let the world laugh with the devil, let their joy be far from us; if we wish to rejoice now, let us rejoice partly in hope, but hereafter we shall truly have joy—sorrowing for our sins, joyful on account of the hope of eternal life; sorrowing on account of Christ's absence, exulting likewise, because we read "we shall see him as he is" [1 John 3:2]. For although we are filled with the sorrow of present miseries, although we are saddened by the multitude of our sins, nevertheless victory over both is abundant rejoicing and a singular joy;

and although for a while "we are on pilgrimage away from the Lord" [2 Cor. 5:6], so that for a brief time's warfare we might be crowned for eternity, we should not be too sad, knowing that we will soon go to be with him, and will dwell with him forever. For this he created us, that reigning with him forever we might praise him for ages of ages, and steadfastly continue to give him thanks. Therefore, since we know these things, in no toils, in no tribulations let us faint, by no sorrows let us be overcome, by no wars let us be wearied, by no anxieties of discipline let us be left destitute, and on the other hand let us be undone by no delights, by no blandishments let us be beguiled, and as with the Apostle's voice let us say, "May no one and no thing separate us from the love of Christ, no tribulation, no distress, no persecution, no hunger, no nakedness, no peril, no death whether by sword, by fire, by cross, or by murder, nothing sad, nothing sweet, nothing hard, nothing soft, may none of the world's vanities separate us from Christ, that we may abide in him here and for eternal ages of ages. Amen" [cf. Rom. 8:35–39].

Sermon 5

[1] O human life, frail and mortal, how many have you deceived, how many have you seduced, how many have you blinded! While you fly away, you are nothing; while you are seen, you are a shadow; while you arise, you are smoke. Daily you fly away and daily you return; you fly away in returning and you return in flying away—dissimilar in outcome, similar in origin; dissimilar in affluence, similar in transience; sweet to the foolish, bitter to the wise. Those who love you do not know you, and those who despise you are the ones who truly understand you. Therefore you are not true but false; you show yourself as though you were true, you draw yourself back as if you were false. What then are you, human life? You are a highway for mortals [Gregory the Great Homiliae in evangelia 1.1.3] and not their life, beginning from sin and proceeding unto death; for you would be true if the sin of the human being's first transgression had not cut you short, and then you became tottering and mortal, because you have assigned all your wayfarers to death. Thus you are the way to life, not life; for you are truly a way, but not a level one—long for some, short for others; wide for some, narrow for others; joyful for some, sad for others; for all alike, hastening and irreversible. You are a way, but you are not a way manifest to all; for many see you, but few understand you to be a way. For you are so subtle and so seductive, that few are able to know that you are a way. Therefore you are to be questioned and not believed or trusted; you are to be traversed, not inhabited, wretched human life. For on a highway one does not dwell, but walk, that those who walk upon the way may dwell in their homeland.

[2] Consequently, then, mortal life, you are dwelt in, loved, and possessed by the foolish and the lost, despised by the sensible, avoided by those who are

to be saved. And so you ought to be feared, human life, and much avoided, because you are so fleeting, so unstable, so perilous, so short, and so uncertain, that you will be dissolved like a shadow or a mirage or a cloud or something null and void. Therefore, O mortal life, while you are nothing except a way, a mirage, fleeting and empty, or a cloud, uncertain and frail, and a shadow, like a dream, we must make our way through you so warily, so cautiously, so briskly, as all people with understanding must hasten like those on the way to their true homeland, confident of what has been passed, wary of that which lies ahead. For it profits you nothing to climb what you have climbed, unless you surmount what lies ahead; for this life is to be considered as a way and an ascent. Let us not seek on the way what is to be in the homeland; for toil and weariness attend the journey, rest and ease are made ready in the homeland. And so we must beware, lest perhaps we come to be at ease along the way, and fail to reach our true homeland. For indeed there are not a few so much at ease on this journey that they seem to be not so much on the way as in the homeland, and they travel not so much willingly as reluctantly to a homeland that is surely already lost. For they have consumed their homeland on the way, and for the price of a brief life they have purchased eternal death. Unhappy folk, they take joy from a deceptive bargain; they have loved the perishable property that does not belong to them, and neglected their own eternal goods. Wherefore, however delightful they may be, however enticing, however beautiful they may be, let us shun the earthly things that do not belong to us, so that we lose not the eternal things that are our own; let us be found faithful in the things that do not belong to us, so that in those that are properly our own we may be made inheritors, by the gift of our Lord Jesus Christ, who lives and reigns for ages and ages. Amen.

Sermon 8

[1] See, now we must speak of the end of the way; for we have already said that human life is a way, and we have shown how doubtful and uncertain it is, and that it resembles a shadow because it is not what it is; likewise, we have already said how unpredictable and how obscure it is; but, with the Holy Spirit's help, our discourse must be prolonged with reference to the end of our life. For it is characteristic of wayfarers to hasten to their homeland, and likewise for them to have anxiety on the way, and ease in the homeland. Therefore let us, who are on the way, hasten to the homeland; for our whole life is like a journey of a single day. The first thing is for us to love nothing here; but let us love what is above, desire what is above, understand what is above, seek the homeland that is above; for our homeland is there, where our Father is. Thus we have no homeland on earth, because "our Father" is "in heaven" [Matt. 6:9]. Indeed, though by virtue of his power and in the greatness of his deity he is everywhere, so that he is deeper than the ocean, steadier than the earth, broader

than the world, purer than the air, higher than heaven, brighter than the sun; nevertheless he is manifestly in heaven, where he is "the bread of angels" [Ps. 78:25], who as members of his household inhabit the blessed palace of the highest heaven and enjoy the sight of God. But since our weaker nature was not able to bear the pure nature of the invisible God, for that reason the compassionate God, in whom are all things and beyond whom there is nothing [Hilary of Poitiers *De trinitate* 2.6], assigned to the heavenly virtues the knowledge of himself in the first region, which he enclosed within the first heaven that he tempered with the waters that were above; for if the nature of that first heaven had not been tempered by the aforesaid waters, it could by no means have been endured by lower natures when the virtue of the High God was enkindled; and thus while everywhere present to all, God remains invisible. For he is greater than everything that can be seen, and greater than all things, for he created all things out of nothing; and, thus, when seen he is invisible, because who he is and how great he is, is known to himself alone. Yet let us implore him, since God the Trinity, although invisible, although incalculable, is present so as to be known to each one according to the merit of our purity. Let us implore him here, I say, so that we may enter that place more intimately, or understand more clearly, and singing along the way let us say, "We will run after you in the odor of your perfumes" [Song of Sol. 1:4], and "My soul has clung after you" [Ps. 63:8], and "Draw me after you" [Song of Sol. 1:4]; that with these songs we may quickly pass through the world, and being guided from above may spurn things present, and thinking always of heavenly things may despise the things of earth; for unless we eagerly long for heavenly objects of desire, we will of necessity remain mired in earthly ones.

[2] And so, that we may not be occupied with human things, let us occupy ourselves with things divine, and like pilgrims let us always sigh for the homeland, always desire the homeland; for the end of the way is what wayfarers long for and desire, and thus, since we are wayfarers and pilgrims in the world, let us always be thinking of the end of the way (that is, of our life), for the end of our way is our homeland. But there all who travel in this world are allotted diverse fates according to their merits; and the good wayfarers are at peace in the homeland, but the bad ones will perish away from it; for many are those who lose the true homeland, because they love the way more. Let us not love the way more than the homeland, lest we should lose the eternal homeland; for we have such a homeland that we ought to love it. Therefore let that decree endure among us, that on the way we so live as wayfarers, as pilgrims, as guests of the world, mired in no carnal lusts, longing for no earthly objects of desire, but let us fill our souls with heavenly and spiritual forms, singing with energy and vigor, "When shall I come and appear before the face of my God?", for "my soul has thirsted for the mighty living God" [Ps. 42:3], and "My soul is like a waterless land before you" [Ps. 143:6], and saying with Paul, "I desire to be dissolved and be with Christ" [Phil. 1:23], let us know that although we are pilgrims away from the Lord while we are in the body [2 Cor. 5:6], we are

nevertheless present before the eyes of God. Wherefore, scornful of all idleness, and laying aside all lukewarmness, let us strive to please the One who is present everywhere, so that with a good conscience we may happily pass over from the way of this world to the blessed and eternal homeland of our eternal Father, from things present to things absent, from sad things to joyful things, from things that are fleeting to those that are eternal, from earthly things to those that are heavenly, from the province of death to the province of the living, where we shall see heavenly things face to face, and the Ruler of rulers ruling his realms with an upright rule, our Lord Jesus Christ, to whom be glory for ages of ages. Amen.

Sermon 12: On Compunction

[1] In the preceding discourses we have tried in some way to give an indication of the need for compunction, and by talking to ourselves, as it were, we have wished to stir up the idleness not only of our own but of every heart. But since poverty of faith and the will of the flesh, along with the lusts of the world, despise these lessons of chastisement and gives them a lukewarm hearing, they must be rehearsed very often; for if faith were not wavering, even one of the aforesaid testimonies of the divine oracle would more than suffice. Thus those who neglect what they have heard both believe and do not believe; otherwise, if today (as someone says) you should be told that a judge of this world wants to burn you alive tomorrow, what anxiety, I ask, what fear would be hanging over you? [Gregory the Great *Homiliae in evangelia* 2.26.11] And having heard these things, if you had the interval of one day free, how many things would you do, how would you bend over backwards, and where would you run, how abject and how mournful and how ragged would you be as you wandered about? Would you not pour out all your money on those by whose intervention you thought you might be able to escape? Would you not make all your goods the ransom for your soul [Prov. 13:8] and keep nothing back, although you were stingy and greedy, but spend it all, give it all away for the sake of your life? And if someone tried to stop or detain you, would you not say, "Let it all perish for my deliverance, and let nothing remain, if only I may live"? Why would you do this? Because you did not doubt that tomorrow you would burn according to the sentence of a most strict judge. But here you are doubting something because you do not know how soon it will come to pass; nevertheless, you cannot but know that it will come, although you pay no attention to it. Therefore you must awaken, keep watch, and pray, in accordance with the command of our Savior Jesus Christ, our God, who says, "Take heed for yourselves, lest perhaps your hearts be weighed down with wine-drinking and drunkenness and the cares of this life, and that day come upon you unexpectedly; for as a snare it will come upon all who dwell on the face of the whole earth. Therefore keep watch at all times, that you may be deemed worthy to

escape all these things that will take place, and to stand before the Son of Man"
[Luke 21:34–36].

[2] If we hear these things and believe, our watchfulness shows our faith,
and as the squalid and listless lethargy of deadly lukewarmness is dispelled, let
the pronouncement of the Lord and Savior quicken our senses, so that we may
always be prepared to lay aside all mortal cares, because we await the coming
of the last day, on which we will be caught up either to punishment or to glory;
and let the aforesaid word of the Lord, in which he taught us continually to
be watching and praying, focus the vision of our minds, so that we may not
be like those who believe and do not believe, and like those who hear and do
not hear; and let us tirelessly plead for the ineffable mercy of the kind and
good God through Jesus Christ his Son, from the bottom of our heart let us
beseech, let us pray that he may deign so to inspire us with his love that he
may join us to him forever, bind us inseparably together, raise us up from the
ground, and unite our senses to heaven even while we are situated in this body
of death [Rom. 7:24]; and may we await his coming without reproach, so that
when he appears we may run to welcome him with joy and great confidence
in his love. How blessed, how happy are "those servants whom the Lord will
find keeping watch when he comes!" [Luke 12:37] Blessed watch, in which
one watches for God the Creator of the universe, who fills all things and surpasses all things! Wretched though I am, but nonetheless his humble servant,
would that he would deign so to arouse me from the sleep of idleness, so to
enkindle with that fire of divine love, that the flame of his love, the longing of
his affection beyond measure, would blaze up beyond the stars, and the divine
fire would always burn within me! Would that I had the fuel with which to
sustain, feed, and keep that fire burning continually, and to nourish that flame
which cannot be quenched, and knows nothing but increase! Would that I
were of such deserving, that my lamp might always burn by night in the temple
of my Lord [Exod. 27:20–21], that it might give light to all who enter the
house of my God!

[3] Lord, give me, I pray you, in the name of Jesus Christ your Son, my God,
that love that cannot fail, so that my lamp can burn and cannot be quenched,
in order that it may burn for me and give light to others. May you, O Christ,
deign to light our lamps, our Savior most dear to us, that they may shine
continually in your temple, and perpetually receive light from you, the perpetual light, so that our darkness may be illumined, and the darkness of the
world may be driven away from us. So bestow your light on my lamp, I pray
you, my Jesus, that by its light there may appear to me the holy of holies that
contains you the eternal Priest of things eternal, entering there among the ranks
of that great temple of yours, that I may continually see, behold, and desire
only you, and by loving may contemplate you alone, and before you my lamp
may always shine and burn. Show yourself, I beg, to us who implore you, most
loving Savior, so that knowing you, we may love only you, love you alone,
desire you alone, meditate on you alone by day and night, think always of you;

and may you deign to inspire us with your love so far as it befits you to be loved and cherished as God; that your love may possess all our inward parts, and your ardor may occupy us completely, and your charity may fill all our senses, so that we may know how to love nothing else more than you who are eternal; that so much charity may be in us that it cannot be quenched by the many waters of this air and this earth and this sea, according to that saying, "And many waters cannot quench love" [Song of Sol. 8:7]; which can surely be partly fulfilled in us also, by your gift, our Lord Jesus Christ, to whom be glory for ages of ages. Amen.

Bibliography

Clarke, H. B., and Mary Brennan, eds. 1981. *Columbanus and Merovingian Monasticism.* Oxford: British Archaeological Reports.

Lapidge, Michael, ed. 1997. *Columbanus: Studies on the Latin Writings.* Woodbridge, England: Boydell.

Leclercq, Jean. 1968. "The Irish Invasion." In Jean Leclercq, François Vandenbroucke, and Louis Bouyer, *The Spirituality of the Middle Ages,* 31–45. New York: Seabury.

Munro, Dana Carleton, trans. 1895. *Jonas of Bobbio: Life of St. Columban.* Philadelphia: University of Pennsylvania Press.

Ó Fiaich, Tomás. 1974. *Columbanus in His Own Words.* Dublin: Veritas.

Walker, G. S. M., ed. 1957. *Sancti Columbani Opera.* Scriptores Latini Hiberniae, vol. 2. Dublin: Dublin Institute for Advanced Studies.

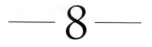

8

Manichaean Asceticism

Jason David BeDuhn

Coptic Manichaean Psalm-Book: A Psalm of the Vagabonds
Psalm-Book, Part II, 170.16–171.24

The Coptic Manichaean *Psalm-Book* is a very large collection of psalms, only half of which have been edited to date. Produced in Egypt in the fourth century C.E., some of it was translated into Coptic from Greek, with many Greek loan-words retained, while other portions seem to have been translated directly from Syriac. Within the pages of this collection, psalms are grouped according to an eclectic set of categories. This psalm belongs to a class known as the *psalmoi sarakōtōn*. The exact meaning of the latter word is uncertain, as it is otherwise unattested in Greek. The form *sarakōte* appears in Coptic texts (probably as a loanword) with the meaning of a wanderer, a vagabond, or someone generally uncouth. Most likely, then, the word is used as a humble designation for the homeless, wandering, long-robed Elect. For the majority of these psalms, no specific ritual situation can be associated with their content, and they may have been chants recited by the Elect as they walked along through town and country-side.

The Manichaean Elect were considered the embodiment of Christ's radical commandments, the ones who actually put into practice the ascetic moral demands of his call. This psalm is comprised of a pastiche of gospel metaphors, each of which the Elect who recited it claimed for themselves. Yet several details make this a distinctly Manichaean composition. There is, first of all, the critique of the concept of "church" towards the end of the psalm, hinting at the polemical context in which Manichaeans and Christians vied for the mantle of Christ. The true meaning of church, this psalm declares, is love, which it contrasts to "the eye of malice." Secondly, there is the characteristic Manichaean emphasis on "the commandment," the rules of Elect life, which alone preserved the believer from "the flood" of human drives and desires. Finally, there is the refrain that insists that no one should burden the Elect with toil. The Elect are totally given over to "the

Rest," an absolute cessation of harmful interaction with the world. They can do no physical labor, because that entails inflicting force on the surrounding world. There is a double meaning to "toil" here: on the one hand, work; on the other, trouble or bother of any kind. These are God's chosen; those who give them trouble do so at their own risk.

This composition is perhaps one of the best examples of a Manichaean responsorial hymn. The refrain drives the rhythm of the piece; in the original Coptic it has a very elegant, ten-syllable cadence (*empōrte lawe wah hise aran*). The individual verses were probably called by a lead singer, with the refrain given in chorus as the response. A final line is appended as a prayer for a person named Mary. The majority of the psalms in the Manichaean Coptic *Psalm-Book* contains brief codas on behalf of various individuals in the community, and Mary is by far the most prevalent of these figures. She is often referred to as "the blessed" Mary and the most likely scenario is that she is a martyr of the Egyptian Manichaean community, or perhaps a deceased leader.

No one can produce fresh English translations of these psalms, as I have done, without being influenced by the brilliant and often eloquent translation of C.R.C. Allberry, *A Manichaean Psalm-Book, II* (Stuttgart: Kohlhammer, 1938). My own renditions are frequently indebted to Allberry's turn of phrase.

A Psalm of the Vagabonds

We are men of the Rest. Let no one give us toil.

It is Jesus that we seek, the one whose model we have received. Let no one give us toil.

Our binding is upon our loins, our testimony is in our hand. Let no one give us toil.

We knocked at the door, the door opened to us; we went in with the bridegroom. Let no one give us toil.

We were counted in the number of the virgins in whose lamps oil was found. Let no one give us toil.

We were counted in the number of the right hand; we ceased to be in the number of the left hand. Let no one give us toil.

We were counted in the number of these sheep, we ceased to be in the number of the goats. Let no one give us toil.

We quit the broad way; we [found the] narrow way. Let no one give us toil.

[. . .] path we have found [. . .] we have found the [path that leads] to the height. Let no one give us toil.

We have found the treasury that is in the skies, in which there is no [. . .]. Let no one give us toil.

We have found a rest that has no toil, a joy in which there is no grief. Let no one give us toil.

We have found a treasure that is not taken away from [us, a gain] in which there is no loss. Let no one give us toil.

Behold, the commandment, behold, knowledge, too [. . .] them. Let no one give us toil.

Good the tree, good the fruit, good [the] sweet taste, also. Let no one give us toil.

One, two, three: this is the [perfect] church; [let] us come in to the church whose name is in the whole world. Let no one give us toil.

This whole world has gone astray because of this name, "church." Let no one give us toil.

They knew not the church, they fell into the fire; they did not understand. Let no one give us toil.

Desire: the flood; the eye of malice: the fire. Let no one give us toil.

The commandment is the ark; love is the church. [Let us] abide with these things for ever and ever.

May victory and rest meet the soul of Mary.

Coptic Kephalaion 79: Concerning the Fast of the Holy Ones Kephalaia 191.9–192.3

The Chapters of the Teacher (n.Kephalaion m.p.Sah, generally referred to as the *Kephalaia)* is a collection preserved in Coptic of Mani's oral lessons and answers delivered in response to the inquiries of his disciples. It is intended as a supplement to Mani's writings, but for the modern researcher it must stand in their stead, as all of Mani's works are lost. In this short chapter from that collection, Mani informs his audience of the positive outcomes of fasting, of which there are four: mastery of the body, filtering of the divine substance from food, secure containment of the released divine substance in the body without bringing harm to it, and restraint from harmful behavior in the world. This peculiar combination of effects only makes sense within the larger Manichaean understanding of the role of an ascetic elite in liberating the divine substance, which is mixed with evil in the world, by means of a ritual meal. The trapped divine substance is referred to in this passage as the Living Soul, and as the Cross (of Light). Bits of it are found in all living things; so when people eat, "this soul comes into them daily," and they further afflict it. Only the "holy ones," generally referred to as the Elect, discipline their bodies sufficiently to metabolize food harmlessly and safely extract the Living Soul for its ultimate liberation. Daily fasting before and after the ritual meal is one component of the total system of Elect disciplines, called here the Rest. Manichaean laypersons, mentioned here as "the Catechumens of the faith," were not expected to adhere to such a rigorous way of life. They fasted once a week on Sunday and supported the liberating work of the Elect through an institutionalized alms-service for them. Principal among the alms, of course, was the food that the layperson supplied for the Elect to purify.

My new translations from the *Kephalaia* are indebted to the pioneering work of H. J. Polotsky and A. Böhlig, *Kephalaia* (Stuttgart: Kohlhammer, 1940), whose standard page and line numbers are given in square brackets at the beginning of each paragraph, and especially to Iain Gardner, *The Kephalaia of the Teacher* (Leiden: Brill, 1995), a work I found to be a veritable thesaurus for particularly recalcitrant Coptic phrases.

Concerning the Fast of the Holy Ones

[191.11] Once again the Illuminator speaks to his disciples: The fast in which the holy ones fast is useful for [four] great works. The first work: the person who is holy subjects his body in the fast, subduing the entire rulership that exists in it. The second: this soul, which comes into him daily in the metabolism [*oikonomia*] of his food, becomes pristine, and is purified, separated, and cleansed from the mixture [*synkrasis*] with the darkness that is mixed in with it. The third: that person becomes a holy one in every deed—the mystery of [the children] of light, those [in] whom nothing perishes, nor [. . .] of the food, nor do they smite it, but are holy. [There is nothing] in them that defiles, [Or possibly *is defiled*] since they dwell in the Rest. The fourth: they make a [. . .] of the Cross; they restrain their hands from the hand [that harms and] destroys the Living Soul.

[191.27] [The] fast is useful to the holy ones for these four great works, if they persist, that is, remain in [it] daily, and they cause the body to fast in all its limbs [in a] holy fast. [The Catechumens of] the faith, those who do not have the power [to fast] daily, they fast rather [in] the day of the Lord [*kyriakē*]. They also have participation [in the works] and the fast of the holy ones through their faith and their alms-service.

Coptic Kephalaion 80:
The Chapter of the Commandments of Righteousness
Kephalaia 192.3–193.22

In this chapter, Mani, the "Illuminator," instructs his disciples in how to perfect their way of life within the faith. The Elect, also known as the Righteous, must first of all observe the Three Seals (192.6–15). Here, "*enkrateia* (restraint) and purity" constitute the Seal of the Breast, the "rest of the hands" or restraint of them from the "Cross of Light" corresponds to the Seal of the Hands, and abstention from meat and wine equate with the Seal of the Mouth. Although the language of seals is not employed, the content and structure of the passage clearly matches expositions of the Three Seals found in other Manichaean and anti-Manichaean literature. Secondly, the Elect may not withdraw from the world as a typical ascetic might, but must actively promote and disseminate the faith through teaching and preaching (192.16–25). The Manichaean layperson, or Catechumen, also undertakes two tasks. The first includes fasting, prayer, and supporting the Elect with alms (192.29–193.3). The second entails sponsoring a family member or some other dependent to become an Elect, or to "give them to Righteousness" (193.4–11). The parallel structure between the three Elect commandments and the three religious observances of the Catechumens is matched in the respective second duties of each, both of which involve the interdependence of the two grades of believer. The parallelism is broken when the text goes on incongruously to enumerate a "third occasion" for Catechumen merit (may we suspect a redactional seam here?), namely the construction or donation of buildings for religious use (193.11–14).

The Chapter of the Commandments of Righteousness

[192.6] [Once more] the Illuminator speaks to his disciples: Know [and] understand that the first righteousness that a person will do to become truly righteous is this: that he embraces restraint [enkrateia] and purity; and he acquires for himself the rest [of the] hands, so that he will restrain his hands from the Cross of Light; [and] the third is the purity of the mouth, so that he will purify his mouth from all flesh and blood, and does not taste anything at all of the name wine or liquor. This is the first righteousness which a person will do in his body [to be] called righteous among all men.

[192.16] The second righteousness that he should do, moreover, is this: that he adds to it [. . .] wisdom and faith so that [. . .] from his wisdom he gives wisdom to every person who will hear it from him; and also from his faith he gives faith [to] these who belong to the faith; from his [love also] he bestows love, [and] showers it upon them, so that he might join them to him. For, when that one produces a great treasure for himself [. . .] in righteousness, by this second godliness he causes other [treasures] to be sent to those resembling him in righteousness.

[192.25] Just as this righteous one, if he fulfills the second [righteousness], becomes a perfect Elect, so too, if the Catechumen shall be a Catechumen of the faith, he is perfected by two patterns of behavior.

[192.29] The first task of the catechumenate that he does is the fast, the prayer, and the alms-service. The fast in which he fasts is this: that he fasts on the day of [the Lord (kyriakē) from] the things of the world. [And] the prayer [is this: that] he prays to the sun and moon, the great [illuminators]. The alms-service, moreover, is this: that he places it [. . .] in the holy one, and he gives it to them in righteousness.

[193.4] [The] second task of the catechumenate [that he] does is this: the person will give a child of the church to Righteousness [i.e., the Elect class] — or [he gives] his kinsman, [or a member] of [his] household, or he redeems one when he finds him in affliction, or when he buys a slave—and he gives him to Righteousness, so that of all the good that he does, this one whom he gave as a gift [to] Righteousness, that Catechumen who [gave him] will have a share [*koinōnē*] in them. [i.e., the good deeds].

[193.11] Thirdly, the person will build a dwelling place or will establish a place so that it will be made for him a share of alms in the holy church.

[193.14] If the Catechumen fulfills these three great tasks, these three great alms [which one] gives as a gift to the [holy] church [. . .] these alms will make [. . .], and that Catechumen himself, who gave them to them, he [. . .], he receives a share in them. For the Catechumens who will give [. . .] there is a great love and a portion of all gifts and goods in the holy church. They will find many rewards.

Coptic Kephalaion 91:
Concerning the Catechumen Who Is Saved in a Single Body
Kephalaia 228.5–231.11

This chapter enunciates a model of the perfect Manichaean Catechumen and appeals for adherence to this model through a unique promise of reward, for this is "the Catechumen who is saved in a single body" and not subject to painful transmigration as would normally be expected for any non-Elect. In the account, the Elect who questions Mani explicitly declares his intention to preach this model to the Catechumens (228.16–19) so that they will emulate it. Having described an extreme ideal that would make a Catechumen for all intents and purposes an Elect (228.22–229.20), Mani goes on to characterize a second, slightly lower class of Catechumen who also may aspire to escape from rebirth (229.20–230.5). This second portrait seems to correspond to the actual norm promoted in the sermons, catechetical instruction, psalms, and other forms of discourse in the Manichaean tradition. The Catechumen is expected to practice *enkrateia,* specified here as vegetarianism, fasting, prayer, and giving alms from one's income to the Elect. In support of the latter, Mani reminds his audience that donors will, in effect, be endowing their wealth upon their own kin, since at least some of these will have become Elect, as encouraged in *Kephalaion 80.* Catechumens who live up to these ideals will not have to "come to a body (again)." Instead, their souls will be refined and purified in the same way as the soul-material extracted from the food eaten by the Elect in the ritual meal (230.11–20). Mani is aware, however, that many will not live up to these standards, and he holds out the promise of some mitigation of a person's future hardships in accordance with the amount of effort invested in reforming one's life and supporting the work of Mani's church (230.20–30). Mani twice alludes to the fact that he has covered this subject already in his book, the *Treasury of Life,* which unfortunately is no longer extant.

Concerning the Catechumen Who Is Saved in a Single Body.

[228.8] Once again that Elect speaks to this Apostle: I heard you, my lord, saying that there is a Catechumen who shall not come to a body other than this one alone; but at the time when he comes out of his body, his [soul is purified] in the firmaments, which are above, and he travels to the place of rest. Now I entreat you, my lord, that you instruct me about the deeds of that Catechumen who does not come to another body. What are, or what is, his type? Or what is his sign, so that I will know it and can inform my other brothers, that they might proclaim it to the Catechumens, so that they will be edified by that, and will ascend in peace to the good?

[228.20] Then the apostle says to him: I am the one who will instruct you about the deeds of those Catechumens of the faith who do not come to a body [again].

[228.22] The sign of that perfect Catechumen is this: You find [his] wife in the house with him being handled by him like a stranger. His house, moreover, is reckoned by him like an inn; and he says, "I dwell in a house for rent for [some] days and months." His family and kinsmen are reckoned by him [as] it is necessary [for] men who are strangers, accompanying him, walking with him in the road, as he [. . .] they will separate from him; and every [possession which he handles of] gold and silver and vessels of [value in the] house, they become like loaned items to him: [he] accepts them, and he is served by them, [and] afterwards he gives [them to] their owner. He does not place his trust in them, nor his treasure. He has removed his thought from the world; he has placed his [heart] in the holy church. At all times his thought is placed upon God. Now the one who surpasses all these things, in whom the guardianship and the care and the love of the holy ones exist, he guards the church like [his] house, even more than his house. He has placed his whole treasure in the Electi and the Electae. For this is that which [the] savior pronounced through the mouth of his Apostle: "From today those who have a wife, let them become like those who do not; those who buy as if they do not buy; those who rejoice as if they do not rejoice; those who weep as if they do not weep; those who [find] profit in this world as if they do not take advantage." These are the things that [. . .] proclaimed, the ones that [. . .] were uttered; and they were uttered concerning these perfect Catechumens who are released from this single body, and go to the height, resembling the Elect in their citizenship. This is the sign of those Catechumens who do not come to a body [again].

[229.20] There are others, too, embracing restraint [*enkrateia*], having [kept] every beast from their mouth, being eager for the fast and the daily prayer, assisting the church with that which reaches their hand, through alms. The potential for evil doing [translation suggested by Gardner 1995, 237] is dead in them. [They cause] the movement of their feet to the church more than to their house; their heart is upon it at all times. Their manner of sitting and their manner of arising is in the way of the Elect. They have stripped all of the things of the world from their heart. [Now] that man whose mind is placed in the holy church [. . .] every hour (?), and his gifts [. . .] and his donations and the presents that give profit [to] his life, he directs [lit. steers, sails] them to the holy church—into these, even, who come in to the church, [i.e., become Electi/Electae] be they his children or his wife or a kinsman of him. He rejoices over those more, and he loves [them], bestowing all of his treasure upon them.

[230.6] Look, this, therefore, is the sign and the type of these Catechumens who do not come to a body [again]. Like the good pearl, about which I have written for you in the *Treasury of Life,* the one that is priceless: this is also, indeed, the way these Catechumens are, these Catechumens who do not come to a body [again].

[230.11] But the time when they will come forth from their body, they journey on their way and traverse in the place above, and go in to the life. They are purified in the skies, and they are plucked as a ripe fruit is plucked from the tree. This is just the way of this alms-offering that traverses the Elect: it is transformed in many forms, is purified, and travels into the land of the living. This is the way, indeed, that the souls of the Catechumens resemble [the alms-offering], these who do not come to a body [again].

[230.20] Now concerning all of the remaining Catechumens, I have written down in the *Treasury of Life* the way that they are released, and are purified, each of them according to his deeds, according to his approach towards the church. This is the way that his ascent causes his healing and his purification to approach him.

[230.26] Because of this, indeed, it is fitting for the Catechumen that he pray always for repentance and forgiveness of sins from God and the holy church, because of his sins, the [first] and the last, so that his deeds will be collected, [the] first and the last, and be reckoned to his share.

[231.1] Then, when his disciples heard these words from [him], they blessed him, they glorified him with great blessings. They say to him: Blessed are you, our father, and glorious. Blessed is the hope that awaits us because of you. For a great thing is this that you have given to the souls: to the Elect you have revealed the deeds and the commandments of election by which they will live; and even the Catechumens you did not abandon, but have taught them every step, stage, and degree so that by them they will come up to the good—each according to his [power]—and reach the land of the living.

Bibliography

Allberry, C.R.C. 1938. *A Manichaean Psalm-Book II*. Stuttgart: Kohlhammer.

BeDuhn, Jason David. 1992. "A Regimen for Salvation: Medical Models in Manichaean Asceticism." *Semeia* 58: 109–34.

———. 1995. "The Battle for the Body in Manichaean Asceticism." In *Asceticism,* ed. Vincent Wimbush and Richard Valantasis, 513–19. London: Oxford University Press.

———. 1999. *The Manichaean Body in Discipline and Ritual*. Baltimore: Johns Hopkins University Press.

Gardner, Iain. 1995. *The Kephalaia of the Teacher*. Leiden: E. J. Brill.

Polotsky, H. J., and A. Böhlig. 1940. *Kephalaia*. Stuttgart: Kohlhammer.

Ries, Julien. 1985. "L'Enkrateia et les motivations dans les Kephalaia Coptes de Medinet Madi." In *La Tradizione dell'Enkrateia: Motivazioni Ontologiche e Protologiche,* ed. Ugo Bianchi, 369–83. Rome: Edizioni dell'Ateneo.

———. 1986. "La Doctrine de l'âme du monde et des trois sceaux dans la contraverse de Mani avec les Elchasaites." In *Codex Manichaicus Coloniensis,* ed. L. Cirillo and A. Roselli, 169–81. Consenza: Marra editore.

Founding Religious Movements:
Organizations

—— 9 ——

Talmudic Texts and Jewish Social Life

Daniel Boyarin

Judaism in Late Antiquity revolves about the Talmud, a collection of the oral and written traditions of the rabbis. The Talmud (and rabbinic Judaism in general) communicates its religious and social meanings through two modes of discourse, controversy about religious practice (halakha) and narratives about the lives of its heroes (aggada). The selections that follow provide several rich examples of the aggadic genre to illustrate the modes of expression characteristic of this Late Antique branch of Judaism.

Creeds and theological discussion are entirely absent from this form of Jewish religious life and discourse. The theological interests revolve about the practices central to Jewish living in the household, the schools, the family, the political sphere, and among the men and women in the wider community, Jewish as well as practitioners of other religions. The interaction of rabbinic saying with biblical text stands as the salient feature of these writings. The rabbis interact with rabbis from other generations, with famous rabbis and their families and students, with competing interpretations of the sayings, and they interact by piling up interpretation upon interpretation and text upon text. This intricate interaction creates space for new and exciting interpretations and conclusions.

One of the very important issues to consider in reading these texts is how these expressions of religious life are related to the religious life-world of Late Antiquity with its enormous watershed of transformation of a society from its traditional religion to Christianity and the ways that those Jews who did not become Christian participated—or not—in those transformations. These texts present the confrontation between Jews and other religious practitioners by sometimes rather surprising twists, as in the relationship of Antoninus and Rabbi and the arrest of a rabbi for being a sectarian (that is, a Christian). At each point the question of Jewish identity in the face of other religions emerges as central and that identity, in turn, reverberates with the social lives of other people within their religious community and beyond it.

The bibliography indicates places these texts have been explained at length in order to extract their religious and social meanings. Not meant as definitive interpretations, those readings, it is hoped, will stimulate further thought on the many and various ways to interpret these texts. The source for each text is indicated immediately following the title.

When Antoninus Met Rabbi

The Babylonian Talmud, *Avoda Zara* 10b, following ms.
Journal of Theological Studies Rabbinowitz 15

Every day [Antoninus Caesar] used to serve Rabbi. He used to feed him and give him drink. When Rabbi wished to get up on his bed, [Antoninus] would kneel down before the bed and say: "Get up on me to your bed." [Rabbi] said: "It is not appropriate to demean the kingship so." [Antoninus] said: "May I be a couch under you in the Next World!" [Rabbi] said: "Yes." [Antoninus] said: "Will I come into the Next World?" [Rabbi] said: "Yes." [Antoninus] said, "But is it not written: 'There will not be a remnant left of the house of Esau' [Obad. 1:18]?" "That applies only to one who behaves as Esau." [Antoninus] said, but is it not written: 'Edom is destroyed with its kings and all of its princes' [Exek. 32:29]?" "Its kings—but not all of its kings! All of its princes—but not all of its ministers!"

There is also a tannaitic tradition that says this: "Its kings—but not all of its kings! All of its princes—but not all of its ministers! Its kings, but not all of its kings, that is, except for Antoninus the son of Severus. All of its princes but not all of its ministers, that is, except for Ḳeṭi'a bar Shalom."

And what is the story of Ḳeṭi'a bar Shalom?

There was a certain Caesar who hated Jews. He said to his courtiers: "If someone has a wart on his leg, should he cut it off and live or leave it and suffer?" They said to him: "Let him cut it off and live!" Ḳeṭi'a bar Shalom said to him: "First of all, you won't be able to defeat all of them, for it is written, 'I have scattered them as the four winds of the heavens' [Zech. 2:10]—What is this 'as the four winds'? It ought to read 'to the four winds'! Rather it means that just as the world cannot exist without winds, so the world cannot exist without Israel. And secondly, they will call you a king who cuts."

[Caesar] said: "You have spoken well, but anyone who defeats the thing [in argument] gets thrown into a hollow furnace."

When they were taking him out [to be executed], a certain Matron said to him: "Woe to the ship that goes without the toll." He fell on the end of his foreskin and bit it off. He said, "I have paid the toll, and I will pass. . . ."

A voice was heard [from heaven]: Ḳeṭi'a bar Shalom is invited to the Next World!" Rabbi cried out and said: "There are those who acquire the next world in one instant, and those who acquire the next world only after many years!"

Antoninus served Rabbi, and when Antoninus died, Rabbi said: "The tie is rent!"

The Tale of Rabbi El'azar the Son of Rabbi Shim'on

Babylonian Talmud Baba Metsia 83b–85a

Rabbi El'azar the son of Rabbi Shim'on found a certain officer of the king who used to catch thieves. He asked him, "how do you prevail over them? Aren't they compared to animals, as it is written 'at night tramp all the animals of the forest' (Ps. 104:20)?" There are those who say that he said it to him from the following verse: "He will ambush from a hiding place like a lion in a thicket (Ps. 10:9)." Said he to him, "perhaps you are taking the innocent and leaving the guilty." He said to him, "how shall I do it?" He said to him, "Come I will teach you how to do it. Go in the first four hours of the morning to the wine bar. If you see someone drinking wine and falling asleep, ask of him what his profession is. If he is a rabbinical student, he has arisen early for study. If he is a day-laborer, he has arisen early to his labor. If he worked at night, [find out] perhaps it is metal smelting [a silent form of work], and if not, then he is a thief and seize him." The rumor reached the king's house, and he said, "Let him who read the proclamation be the one to execute it." They brought Rabbi El'azar the son of Rabbi Shim'on, and he began to catch thieves. He met Rabbi Yehoshua, the Bald, who said to him, "Vinegar son of Wine: how long will you persist in sending the people of our God to death?!" He said to him, "I am removing thorns from the vineyard." He said to him, "Let the Owner of the vineyard come and remove the thorns." One day a certain laundry man met him, and called him, "Vinegar son of Wine." He said, "Since he is so brazen, one can assume that he is wicked." He said, "Seize him." They seized him. After he had settled down, he went in to release him, but he could not. He applied to him the verse, 'One who guards his mouth and his tongue, guards himself from troubles' (Prov. 21:23). They hung him. He stood under the hanged man and cried. Someone said to him, "Be not troubled, he and his son both had intercourse with an engaged girl on Yom Kippur." In that minute, he placed his hands on his guts, and said, "Be joyful, 0 my guts, be joyful! If it is thus when you are doubtful, when you are certain even more so. I am confident that rot and worms cannot prevail over you." But even so, he was not calmed. They gave him a sleeping potion and took him into a marble room and ripped open his stomach and were taking out baskets of fat and placing it in the July sun and it did not stink. But no fat stinks. It does if it has red blood vessels in it, and this even though it had red blood vessels in it, did not stink. He applied to himself the verse, "even my flesh will remain preserved" [Ps. 16:8–9].

To Rabbi Ishma'el the son of Yose there also occurred a similar situation.

Eliahu [the Prophet Elijah] met him and said to him, "How long will you persist in sending the people of our God to death?" He said to him, "What can I do; it is the king's order?" He said to him, "Your father ran away to Asia Minor; you run away to Lydia."

When Rabbi Ishma‘el the son of Yose and Rabbi El‘azar the son of Rabbi Shim‘on used to meet each other, an ox could walk between them and not touch them. A certain matron said to them, "Your children are not yours." They said, "Theirs are bigger than ours." "If that is the case, even more so!" There are those who say that thus they said to her: "As the man, so is his virility." And there are those who say that thus did they say to her: "Love compresses the flesh." And why did they answer her at all? Does it not say, "Do not answer a fool according to his foolishness"? In order not to produce slander on their children that they are bastards.

Said Rabbi Yohanan, "Rabbi Ishma‘el the son of Yose's member was like a wineskin of nine kav; Rabbi El‘azar the son of Rabbi Shim‘on's member was like a wineskin of seven kav." Rav Papa said, "Rabbi Yohanan's member was like a wineskin of three kav." And there are those who say: like a wineskin of five kav. Rav Papa himself had a member that was like the baskets of Hipparenum.

Said Rabbi Yohanan, "I have survived from the beautiful of Jerusalem." One who wishes to see the beauty of Rabbi Yohanan should bring a brand new silver cup and fill it with the red seeds of the pomegranate and place around its rim a garland of red roses, and let him place it at the place where the sun meets the shade, and that vision is the beauty of Rabbi Yohanan. Is that true? But haven't we been taught by our master that, "The beauty of Rabbi Kahana is like the beauty of Rabbi Abbahu. The beauty of Rabbi Abbahu is like the beauty of our father Jacob. The beauty of our father Jacob is like the beauty of Adam," and that of Rabbi Yohanan is not mentioned. Rabbi Yohanan did not have splendor of face. Rabbi Yohanan used to go and sit at the gate of the ritual bath. He said, "When the daughters of Israel come out from the bath, they will look at me in order that they will have children as beautiful as I am." The Rabbis said to him, "Are you not afraid of the Evil Eye?" He replied, "I am of the seed of Joseph, our father, of whom it is said, 'A fruitful son is Joseph, a fruitful son by the spring (Gen. 49:22),' " and Rabbi Abbahu said [of this verse, "Do not read it, 'by the spring' but 'safe from the Eye'." Rabbi Yosef the son of Rabbi Hanina learned it from here, " 'And they will multiply like fish in the midst of the Land' (Gen. 48:16), just as the fish of the sea, the water covers them and the Eye does not prevail over them, so also the seed of Joseph, the Eye does not prevail over it."

One day, Rabbi Yohanan was bathing in the Jordan. Resh Lakish saw him and thought he was a woman. He crossed the Jordan after him by placing his lance in the Jordan and vaulting to the other side. When Rabbi Yohanan saw Rabbi Shim‘on the son of Lakish [Resh Lakish], he said to him, "Your strength for Torah!" He replied, "Your beauty for women!" He said to him, "If you repent, I will give you my sister who is more beautiful than I am." He agreed. He wanted to cross back to take his clothes but he couldn't. He taught him Mishna and Talmud and made him into a great man. Once they were disputing in the study house: "the sword and the lance and the dagger, from whence can they become impure?" Rabbi Yohanan said, "from the time they are forged in the fire." Resh Lakish said, "from the time they are polished in the water." Rabbi Yohanan said, "a brigand is an expert in brigandry." He said to him, "What have you profited me. There they called me Rabbi and here they call me Rabbi!" He became angry, and Resh Lakish became ill. His sister came to him and cried before him. She said, "Look at me!" He did not pay attention to her. "Look at the orphans!" He said to her " 'Leave your orphans, I will give life' [Jer. 49:11]. For the sake of my widowhood!" He said, " 'Place your widows' trust in me' [loc. cit.]." Resh Lakish died, and Rabbi Yohanan was greatly mournful over him. The Rabbis said, "What can we do to set his mind at ease? Let us bring Rabbi El'azar the son of Padat whose traditions are brilliant, and put him before him [Rabbi Yohanan]." They brought Rabbi El'azar the son of Padat and put him before him. Every point that he would make, he said, "There is a tradition that supports you." He said, "Do I need this one?! The son of Lakish used to raise twenty-four objections to every point that I made, and I used to supply twenty-four refutations, until the matter became completely clear, and all you can say is that there is a tradition that supports me? Don't I already know that I say good things?" He used to go and cry out at the gates, "Son of Lakish, where are you?" until he became mad. The Rabbis prayed for him and he died.

And even so, Rabbi El'azar the son of Shim'on did not trust himself, perhaps God forbid, such an incident would befall him again. He accepted painful disease upon himself. In the evening, they used to fold under him sixty felt mats, and in the morning they would find under him sixty vessels full of blood and pus. His wife made him sixty kinds of relishes and he ate them. His wife would not let him go to the study house, in order that the Rabbis would not reject him. In the evening, he said, "My brothers and companions [i.e., his pains], come!" In the morning, he said, "My brothers and companions, depart!" One day his wife heard him saying this. She said, "You bring them upon you. You have decimated the inheritance of my father's house." She rebelled and went to her family home. Sixty sailors came up from the sea and came to him carrying sixty purses and they made him sixty relishes, and he ate them. One day she said to her daughter, "Go see what your father is doing." He said to her, "Ours is greater than yours." He applied to himself the verse, "From afar she will bring her bread (Prov. 31:14].

One day he went to the study house. They brought before him sixty kinds of blood, and he declared all of them pure. The Rabbis murmured about him, saying is it possible that there is not even one doubtful case among those? He said, "If I am right, let all of the children be boys, and if not, let there be one girl among them." All of them were boys. They were all named after Rabbi

El'azar. Our Rabbi said, "How much procreation did that wicked woman prevent from Israel!"

When he was dying, he said to his wife, "I know that the Rabbis are furious with me and will not take proper care of me. Let me lie in the attic and do not be afraid of me." Rabbi Shmuel the son of Rabbi Nahman said, "Rabbi Yohanan's mother told me that the wife of Rabbi El'azar the son of Rabbi Shim'on told her that 'not less than eighteen and not more than twenty-two [years] that he was in the attic, every day I went up and looked at his hair, when a hair was pulled out, blood would flow. One day I saw a worm coming out of his ear. I became very upset, and I had a dream in which he said to me that it is nothing, for one day he had heard a rabbinical student being slandered and had not protested as he should have.'" When a pair would come for judgment, they would stand at the door. One would say his piece and then the other would say his piece. A voice would come out of the attic and say, "I find for the plaintiff and not for the defendant." One day his wife was arguing with her neighbor. She said to her, "May you be like your husband, who is not buried." Some say that his father appeared to the Rabbis in a dream and said, "I have one chick that is with you, and you do not want to bring it to me." The Rabbis went to take care of his burial, but the townspeople did not let them, because all of the time that Rabbi El'azar was lying in the attic, no wild animal came to their town. One day, it was the eve of Yom Kippur, and the people of the town were worried and they went to the grave of his father. They found a snake which was surrounding the opening of the tomb. They said, "Snake, snake, open your mouth and the son will come in unto his father." The snake opened for them. Our Rabbi sent to her to propose to her. She said, "A vessel which has been used for the holy, shall it be used for the profane?" There they say, "In the place where the master hangs his battle-ax, shall the shepherd hang his stick?" He sent to her, "Indeed in Torah he was greater than me, but was he greater than me in deeds?" She sent to him, "As for Torah, I know nothing; you have told me, but as for deeds, I know, for he took upon himself suffering."

As for Torah, what did he mean? When Rabban Shim'on the son of Gamliel and Rabbi Yehoshua the Bald used to sit on benches, Rabbi El'azar the son of Rabbi Shim'on and our Rabbi, used to sit in front of them on the ground and ask and answer. And the Rabbis said, "We are drinking their water, and they sit on the ground?" They built them benches and put them upon them. Rabban Shim'on ben Gamliel said, "I have one chick among you and you wish to cause him to be lost from me!" They moved Rabbi down again. Rabbi Yehoshua ben Korha said, "Shall he who has a father live, and he who has none shall die?" They took Rabbi El'azar down as well. He became upset. He said, "They think we are equals. When they put him up, they put me up; when they put him down, they put me down." Until that day, when Rabbi would say something, Rabbi El'azar the son of Rabbi Shim'on used to say, "There is a tradition that supports you." From that day onward, when Rabbi said, "This is my answer," Rabbi El'azar the son of Rabbi Shim'on said, "This is what you will answer; you have surrounded us with vain words, answers that are empty." Rabbi became upset. He came and told his father. He said, "Don't feel bad. He is a lion the son of a lion, and you are a lion the son of a fox. . . ."

Rabbi happened to come to the town of Rabbi El'azar the son of Rabbi Shim'on [after the latter's death]. He asked, "Does that righteous man have a son?" They answered, "He has a son, and any prostitute who is hired for two [coins], would pay eight for him." He brought him and ordained him "Rabbi" and gave him over to Rabbi Shim'on, the son of Issi, the son of Lakonia, the brother of his mother [to teach him Torah]. He taught him and spread a mantle over his head. Every day he would say, "I wish to return to my town." He said to him, "They call you 'sage,' and place a golden crown on your head, and call you 'Rabbi' and you say, 'I wish to return to my town?' " He said to him, "Here is my oath that I leave that be." When he became great, he went and studied in the Yeshiva of Rabbi Shemaia. He heard his voice and said, "This one's voice is similar to the voice of Rabbi El'azar the son of Shim'on." They said to him, "He is his son." He applied to him the verse, 'The fruit of the righteous is a tree of life; and he that wins souls is wise (Prov. 11:30).' " "The fruit of the righteous is a tree of life:" this is Rabbi Yose the son of Rabbi El'azar the son of Rabbi Shim'on, and "he that wins souls is wise:" this is Rabbi Shim'on, the son of Issi, the son of Lakonia.

When he died, they brought him to the burial cave of his father. A snake surrounded the cave of his father. They said, "snake, open the door and the son will enter to be with his father." It did not open for them. The people thought that it was because [the father] was greater than the son. A voice came from heaven saying that it was because [the father] suffered in a cave, and the son did not suffer in a cave.

Rabbi happened to come to the town of Rabbi Tarfon. He asked, "Does that righteous man have a son?" [for Rabbi Tarfon] had lost his children. They said to him, "He has no son, but he has the son of a daughter, and any prostitute who is hired for four, hires him for eight." He said to him, "If you return [to Torah], I will give you my daughter." He returned. There are those who say that he married her and divorced her, and those who say that he did not marry her at all, in order that people would not say that he returned for that. And Rabbi, why did he go to such lengths? For Rabbi Yehuda said that Rav said and there are those who say it in the name of Rabbi Hiyya the son of Abba in the name of Rabbi Yohanan and those who say it in the name of Rabbi Shmuel the son of Nahmani in the name of Rabbi Yonathan, "Anyone who teaches the son of his friend Torah, will be privileged to sit in the Yeshiva on High. . . ." Said Rabbi Pamak in the name of Rabbi Yohanan, "Anyone who is a disciple of the wise and his son is a disciple of the wise and his grandson is a disciple of the wise, the Torah will not cease from his progeny forever."

On Social Accommodation

Yerushalmi Shabbat 1: 3; 3c

They said to Rabbi Ḥiyya the Great: Rabbi Shim'on bar Yoḥai teaches, " 'You shall buy food from them [Edom = Rome] for money, and eat, and also buy water from them for money, and drink' [Deut. 2:6]: Just as water [is that] which has not been modified from its original state [literally, its creation], so also everything that has not been modified from its original state." He rejoined to them, "But their liverwort, dried apricots, pickled vegetables, and parched corn are permitted." All of the first three are not problematic because you can soak them in water and they return to their original state, but what about parched corn? Rabbi Yosi the son of Rabbi Bun in the name of Rav said, "Any food that can be eaten raw as it is, does not enter into the category of forbidden foods cooked by the Gentiles, and one may use it raw for rituals that normally require cooked foods." How, then, does Rabbi Ḥiyya the Great explain the verse: "You shall buy food from them for money, and eat"? If you feed him, you have bought and defeated him, for if he is harsh with you, buy/defeat him with food, and if [that does] not [work], then defeat him with money.

They say that is how Rabbi Yonatan behaved. When he saw a powerful personage come into his city, he used to send him expensive things. What did he think? If he comes to judge an orphan or a widow, we will find him propitious towards them.

On Surviving Religious Persecution

Tosefta Ḥullin, 2.24

It happened that Rabbi Eli'ezer was arrested for sectarianism [Christianity], and they took him up to the bēma to be judged.

The ruler said to him, "A sage such as you having truck with these matters!?"

He said to him, "I have trust in the judge."

The ruler thought that he was speaking of him, but he meant his Father in Heaven. He said to him, "Since you trust me, I also have said, 'Is it possible that these gray hairs would err in such matters?' Dimus! Behold, you are dismissed."

When he had left the bēma, he was troubled that he had been arrested for sectarianism. His disciples came in to comfort him, but he was inconsolable. Rabbi Akiva came in and said to him, "Rabbi, I will say before you a word; perhaps you will not be troubled."

He said to him, "Say!"

He said to him, "Perhaps one of the sectarians said something to you of sectarianism, and it caused you pleasure."

He said to him, "By heaven, you have reminded me. Once I was walking in the marketplace of Tsippori, and I found there Ya'akov the man of Kefar

Sikhnin [a place not known today], and he recounted a saying of sectarianism in the name of Yeshu' the son of Pantiri, and it caused me pleasure, and I was caught by the words of sectarianism, for I violated that which is written in the Torah, 'keep her ways far away from you, and don't come near the opening of her house, for she has brought many victims down! [Prov. 5:8].'"

On Reading Torah

Babylonian Talmud, Berakhot 61b; Oxford Opp. Add. Folio 23

Rabbi Akiva says, "With all your soul", even if he takes your soul.

Our Rabbis have taught: Once the wicked kingdom made a decree that people should not be occupied with Torah, and anyone who occupies himself with Torah will be stabbed with a sword. Papos the son of Yehudah came and found Rabbi Akiva sitting and teaching, gathering crowds in public, and a scroll of the Torah in his lap.

Papos said to him, "Akiva, Aren't you afraid of this nation?"

He said to him, "You are Papos ben Yehuda of whom they say: 'great sage'? You are nothing but a dunce. I will say for you a parable. To what is this matter similar—to a fox who was walking on the banks of the sea, and he saw the fish gathering together. He said to them, 'Why are you gathering?' They said to him, 'Because of the nets and the weirs that people bring to catch us.' He said to them, 'Come up onto the land, and we will dwell together, I and you, just as our ancestors dwelled together!' They said to him, 'You are the fox of whom they say that you are the wisest of animals? You are nothing but a dunce! If now that we stand in the place of our life it is so [that we are endangered], in the place of our death even more and more.' And you also, 'If now we sit and study Torah about which is written, "For it is your life and the length of your days to dwell on the land" [Deut. 30:20]—and it is so [that we are endangered], if we go and become idle from it, all the more so.'"

They have said not many days passed before they arrested Rabbi Akiva and chained him in the prison. And they arrested Papos the son of Yehuda and chained him with him.

He said, "Papos! What brought you to here?"

He said to him, "Blessed art thou, Rabbi Akiva, for you have been arrested for the words of Torah. Woe to Papos, who has been arrested for *superstitio* [false religion]."

Bibliography

Baer, Yitzhaq. 1961. "Israel, the Christian Church, and the Roman Empire from the Time of Septimius Severus to the Edict of Toleration of A.D. 313." In *Studies in History,* ed.

Alexander Fuks and Israel Halpern. Scripta Hierosolymitana 7, 79–147. Jerusalem: Magnes.

Baker, Cynthia. 1996. "Bodies, Boundaries, and Domestic Politics in a Late Ancient Marketplace." *Journal of Medieval and Early Modern Studies* 26, no. 3 (Fall): 391–418.

Blidstein, Gerald J. 1984. "Rabbis, Romans, and Martyrdom—Three Views." *Tradition* 21, no. 3 (Fall): 54–62.

Bowersock, Glen W. 1995. *Martyrdom and Rome.* The Wiles Lectures Given at the Queen's University of Belfast. Cambridge: Cambridge University Press.

Boyarin, Daniel. 1989. "Language Inscribed by History on the Bodies of Living Beings: Midrash and Martyrdom." *Representations,* no. 25 (Winter): 139–51.

———. 1990. *Intertextuality and the Reading of Midrash.* Bloomington: Indiana University Press.

———. 1992. " 'This We Know to Be the Carnal Israel': Circumcision and the Erotic Life of God and Israel." *Critical Inquiry* 18, no. 2 (Spring): 474–506.

———. 1993. *Carnal Israel: Reading Sex in Talmudic Culture.* The New Historicism: Studies in Cultural Poetics 25. Berkeley and Los Angeles: University of California Press.

———. 1994. "Jewish Masochism: Couvade, Castration, and Rabbis in Pain." *American Imago* 51, no. 1 (Spring): 3–36.

———. 1995. "Homotopia: The Feminized Jewish Man and the Lives of Women in Late Antiquity." *differences* 7, no. 2 (Summer): 41–71.

———. 1997. "Masada or Yavneh? Gender and the Arts of Jewish Resistance." In *Jews and Other Differences: The New Jewish Cultural Studies,* ed. Daniel Boyarin and Jonathan Boyarin, 306–29. Minneapolis: University of Minnesota Press.

———. 1997. *Unheroic Conduct: The Rise of Heterosexuality and the Invention of the Jewish Man.* Contraversions: Studies in Jewish Literature, Culture, and Society. Berkeley and Los Angeles: University of California Press.

———. 1998. "Gender." In *Critical Terms for the Study of Religion,* ed. Mark C. Taylor, 117–35. Chicago: University of Chicago Press.

Cohen, Aryeh. 1989. "Towards an Erotics of Martyrdom." *Journal of Jewish Thought and Philosophy* 7: 227–56.

Doran, Robert. 1980. "The Martyr: A Synoptic of the Mother and Her Seven Sons." In *Ideal Figures in Ancient Judaism: Profiles and Paradigms,* ed. John J. Collins and George W. E. Nickelsburg. Septuagint and Cognate Studies 12, 189–221. Chico, Calif.: Scholars Press.

Green, William Scott. 1979. "Palestinian Holy Men: Charismatic Leadership and Roman Tradition." In *Aufstieg und Niedergang der Römischen Welt II, Principat 19,2,* ed. Wolfgang Haase, 619–47. Berlin: Walter de Gruyther.

Hasan-Rokem, Galit. 1998. "Narratives in Dialogue: A Folk Literary Perspective on Interreligious Contacts in the Holy Land in Rabbinic Literature of Late Antiquity." In *Sharing the Sacred: Religious Contacts and Conflicts in the Holy Land First-Fifteenth C.E.,* ed. Guy Stroumsa and Arieh Kofsky, 109–29. Jerusalem: Yad Ben Zvi.

Neusner, Jacob. 1987. *Judaism and Christianity in the Age of Constantine: History, Messiah, Israel, and the Initial Confrontation.* Chicago Studies in the History of Judaism. Chicago: University of Chicago Press.

———. 1988. *Why No Gospels in Talmudic Judaism?* Brown Judaic Studies 135. Atlanta: Scholars Press.

Satlow, Michael L. 1996. " 'Try to Be a Man': The Rabbinic Construction of Masculinity." *Harvard Theological Review* 89: 19–40.

—10—

Julian "the Apostate"
Against the Galileans

Elizabeth Geraldine Burr

Against the Galileans was written by the fourth-century C.E. emperor Julian "the Apostate" in the winter of 362/3 during his very brief reign (11 December 361 to 26 June 363), in the city of Syrian Antioch, the staging point for his ill-fated Persian campaign. The historical background to this text revolves around the process of "Christianizing the Roman empire," which began at the imperial level with Constantine (311–337) and continued under his Arian son and successor, Constantius II (337–361). Despite the resulting high conversion rate, however, even by the 380s "a majority of the empire's total population" remained unconverted (MacMullen 1984, 119). Thus Julian's reign occurred at a critical moment in the course of the gradual transformation of classical culture, often represented as a contest between Christianity and paganism.

Julian himself has been an object of fascination, whether positive or negative, from his own time down to the present. Born in 331, he was six years of age when his father and eight other relatives were murdered on the orders of the Christian emperor Constantius as potential usurpers. This traumatic experience undoubtedly helped motivate Julian's later hatred of Christianity. Raised as a Christian with his half-brother Gallus, Julian also received a classical education. In 354 Gallus was executed by Constantius II, but Julian was spared. Julian studied rhetoric in Asia Minor with Libanius and then Neoplatonism under such teachers as Aedesius, Chrysanthius, and most importantly the theurgist Maximus of Ephesos. His actual conversion to paganism is dated to 351 (Bowersock 1978, 29), though he did not publicize it until 361 after the death of Constantius. Ranked as Caesar in 355, Julian was commissioned by the emperor to drive the German tribes out of Gaul and reclaim the area; his brilliant performance culminated in his troops' acclamation of him as Augustus (co-emperor), an action none too pleasing to his cousin the emperor. Confrontation with Constantius, occupied on the Persian front, was averted by the emperor's sudden death in

Cilicia en route to meet Julian and his troops. Progressing eastward, Julian had already sent letters to the senators at Rome as well as to several Greek cities announcing "his design to restore the Hellenic religion" (Wright 1923, III:xv). Julian's reign as emperor began in Constantinople.

Among his first imperial acts were the edict of restitution, referring to pagan temples, and proclamation of religious toleration, reiterating Constantine's Edict of Milan (313). Other measures included the cancellation of clerical privileges, discrimination against Christians in certain official contexts, and the transfer of wealth from the church to the state, in addition to other municipal, legal, and financial reforms. In June 362 Julian promulgated his so-called education edict, which authorized the emperor to oversee teaching appointments, followed closely by a rescript prohibiting Christians from teaching classical literature on the grounds that they disbelieved what they taught. By this measure he intended to exclude Christians from classical culture, viewed as inextricably connected with classical religion; they could not have one without the other (Wilken 1984, 175–76).

Julian's efforts to revitalize Hellenism are further documented in a number of letters to official addressees, both individual and collective. Part of his reformation of paganism entailed the adaptation of certain features of the church, notably organized charity. Scholars are divided on the question of what Julian's ultimate purpose was in regard to Christianity. A recent assessment describes Julian's policy as directed toward the destruction of Christianity "as a social and cultural force" rather than against Christians themselves (Smith 1995, 216). Although he may have tolerated occasional popular anti-Christian violence, Julian never organized a state-administered program of persecution (Braun and Richer 1978, 173).

The key writing from the works of Julian that affords access to the emotional and intellectual basis for his policy toward Christianity is *Against the Galileans,* composed in a city (Antioch) whose citizens (at least half of whom were Christian) treated him with marked disrespect during his stay of about eight months there. Originally occupying three books, this treatise is extant only in fragments; condemned in 448 or 529, little more than a third of it survived in the partially preserved refutation by Cyril of Alexandria written during the 430s under Theodosius II. Most of the surviving text derives from Book 1.

Concluding a series of three major pagan critiques of Christianity, Julian's treatise succeeded Celsus's *True Doctrine* from ca. 180 C.E. and Porphyry's *Against the Christians* and *Philosophy from Oracles* from the later third century. Julian's treatise is indebted to both predecessors, though perhaps more so to Celsus (Meredith 1980, 1148). The majority of Celsus's arguments are reused; even if lacking in originality, however, the work remains a "highly interesting and significant writing" (Geffcken 1914, 111–12). Based on the extant excerpts, an overview of their contents can be presented with respect to three themes: (1) The first concerns how God is known to us; here Julian seeks to discredit the biblical notion of revelation, with its particularist associations, in favor of the natural knowledge of God that is available to all. (2) Julian then compares the Greek and Jewish concepts of God in order to demonstrate the inferiority of the jealous, irrational, impotent Jewish God. The creation account in Plato's *Timaeus* proves the necessity of a plurality of lesser, "national" gods, each dedicated to the welfare of its people, whereas the Jews have erroneously identified their national god with the supreme universal God. (3) The beliefs and practices of the "Galileans," a pejorative term for Christians, are targeted in the final portion of the text we have. Problematic and inferior as the Jewish religion is, it has the merit of fidelity to ancestral tradition. The Christians, however, are inferior to the Jews because they have apostatized from their Jewish roots. This desertion Julian attributes to their cultural ignorance; Christians adhere to an atheistic pseudo-religion devoid of *paideia* (education or learning). Mosaic monotheism does not allow for the polytheistic position that Jesus is also God. Christian deviance from Jewish doctrine is signified by the Christian belief in a Trinitarian God compounded with the cult of the martyrs, which Jesus himself would have disavowed. Julian uses inconsistencies between New Testament texts to undermine further the Christian doctrine of Jesus' divinity. Christian apostasy is visibly evident in the refusal to follow Jewish dietary laws or to practice circumcision, divination, and sacrifice. The historical Jewish practice of sacrifice in Jerusalem linked Judaism most positively with Hellenism in Julian's eyes, and inspired his unsuccessful effort to rebuild the temple in Jerusalem. That project would have served simultaneously to revive Jewish sacrifice and to counter the claim of Christians to be the true inheritors of a Judaism otherwise invalidated by the loss of the temple.

Whatever the admixture of nontraditional elements in Julian's traditional polytheism, it seems clear that a primary factor behind the composition of *Against the Galileans* was Julian's deep fear of Christian universalism as a force poised to annihilate the Hellenic synthesis of cult and culture.

In chronological order, the major critical editions and translations of *Against the Galileans*, whether published separately or together with other works of Julian, are as follows:

Neumann, C. J. 1880. *Juliani imperatoris librorum contra Christianos quae supersunt.* Leipzig: Teubner.

Asmus, J. R. 1904. *Julians Galiläerschrift.* Freiburg: Universitäts Buchdruckerei von U. Hochreuther.

Wright, W. C. 1923. Reprints 1953–1993. *The Works of the Emperor Julian,* 3 vols. Cambridge and London: Harvard University Press.

Bidez, J., et al. 1924–1964. *Julien: Oeuvres complètes,* 2 vols. in 4. Paris: Les Belles Lettres.

Masaracchia, E. 1990. *Giuliano imperatore Contra Galilaeos.* Rome: Edizioni dell'Ateneo.

Against the Galileans

[39A] It seems right to me to explain to all humanity the grounds on which I was persuaded that the fabrication of the Galileans is a human fiction maliciously contrived. Containing no divine content, it has misled people by abus-

ing the myth-loving, childish, unthinking part of the soul into believing that
tall tales are true.

[41E] My purpose being to discuss all of what they call their most important
doctrines, first let me say that, if my interlocutors wish to oppose me as though
in a law court, they must neither inquire about irrelevant matters nor accuse
me in turn until they have defended their own position. For it is better and
clearer if they keep the business of correcting any of my views separate when
they wish to do that, and when they are defending themselves against my
correction they do not then also bring accusations against me.

[42E] It is worthwhile to review briefly the topic of how and from what
source a concept of God came to us in the first place, then to compare the
statements made about the divine among the Hellenes and the Hebrews, and
after this to question again those who are neither Hellenes nor Jews but adherents of the Galilean sect, as to why they chose the Jewish way rather than
ours, and moreover how it is that they have not remained faithful to Jewish
teaching but have fallen away from that and turned to their own way. Acknowledging nothing that is noble or excellent in Hellenic tradition or in He-
braic tradition, handed down by Moses, they have plucked from both of these
nations certain deadly features that were grafted onto them: the godlessness of
Jewish self-indulgence on the one hand, and on the other the trivial and negligent lifestyle resulting from our laxity and vulgarity. The resulting product
they wished to be known as the finest religiosity.

[52B] That human knowledge of God is not taught but rather arises by
nature can be proved first by the desire for the divine common to all human
beings, whether private or public, individual or collective. For without instruction we have all come to believe in some divine being about which it is difficult
to know anything definite; and for those who do know it is not possible to
proclaim their knowledge to all [. . .]. In addition to this concept shared by
all human beings, there is another one as well. For all of us are somehow so
attached to heaven and to the gods who appear there that, even if someone
came up with another god, he would certainly designate heaven as its dwelling
place. The point would not be to remove that god from the earth but, as it
were, to locate that king of the universe in the most esteemed place of all,
imagining him to be watching over things here from there.

[69B] Why should I call Hellenes and Hebrews here as witnesses? There is
no one who does not lift up their hands to heaven, whether invoking God or
gods; anyone with a general grasp of the divine inclines in that direction. This
is a natural experience. For noticing that nothing about the heavens increases
or diminishes, or alters or suffers from any disorder, but rather the heavenly
movement is musical and the heavenly disposition harmonious, the lunar
phases and the solar risings and settings ordained at predetermined times, they
naturally understood heaven to be God or God's throne. Inasmuch as such an
entity is not multiplied by any addition or diminished by any deprivation, it is
fixed beyond all change and variation, free from degeneration and generation,

immortal and indestructible, pure and unblemished. Eternal and perpetually in motion, as we observe, moved either by a higher and more divine soul present within it (just as our bodies are moved by the soul in us) or by motion inherited from God himself, it revolves around the great maker, wheeling in a boundless circle, its course unceasing and everlasting.

[44A] Yes, the Hellenes fabricated strange and unbelievable stories about the gods. They said that Kronos consumed his children and then threw them up again. They also told of illicit unions, of how Zeus slept with his mother and then, having had a child by her, married his own daughter, or rather did not marry her but, after crudely having intercourse with her, passed her on to another man. Then there is the story of the dismemberment of Dionysos and the rejoining of his limbs. The myths of the Hellenes tell stories like this. [75A] With them compare the Jewish teaching about the garden of Eden planted by God and the man Adam formed by God and then the woman created for the man. For God said, "It is not good that the man should be alone; let us make him a helper as his partner [Gen. 2:18]." In no respect did she help him, however; instead she seduced him and proved an accessory to his and her own fall from the luxury of the garden.

[75B] This myth is quite incredible. How could God not have known that the one created by him to be a support would become a liability rather than an asset to the one acquiring her? And what type of language shall we say the serpent used in conversation with Eve? Human language? In what respect do these stories differ from the myths fabricated by the Hellenes? Further, is it not the height of absurdity that God would withhold from the human beings whom he had made the ability to discriminate between good and bad? What could be more ridiculous than a person unable to distinguish good from evil? If that were the case, clearly he would neither shun what is evil nor cleave to what is good. In sum, God prevented human beings from tasting of wisdom, than which nothing could be more valuable to them. For it is apparent even to the unintelligent that the capacity to decide between good and evil is a function proper to wisdom; thus the serpent was a benefactor rather than a corrupter of the human race. In addition, it must be stated that this God is jealous. For when he saw that the humans had become sharers in wisdom, so that they might not (in his words) taste of the tree of life, he drove them out of the garden with these explicit words: "See, the man has become like one of us, knowing good and evil; and now he might reach out his hand and take from the tree of life, and eat, and live forever [Gen. 3:22]." [94A] Therefore, unless each of these stories is a myth with a secret interpretation, which I hold to be true, they are full of blasphemous statements about God. For not knowing that she who was created as a helper would be the cause of the fall, and prohibiting knowledge of good and evil, which alone seems to contain the human mind, and finally being jealous lest mortals having eaten from the tree of life should become immortal, all show excessive malice and envy. . . .

[99E] Moses says that the creator of the universe selected the nation of the

Hebrews, devoted his attention and care to it alone, and gives himself charge only over it. But concerning the other nations, how or by which gods they are administered, he has made no mention at all, unless it were agreed that he assigned the sun and the moon to them. I shall return to these matters in a little while, except to note here that Moses and the prophets after him and Jesus the Nazarene, but also Paul, who outdid every other wizard and trickster anywhere, maintain that he is the God of Israel only and of Judea and these are his elect. Listen to their own speeches and first to those of Moses: "And you shall say to Pharaoh, Israel is my firstborn son. I said to you, Let my people go that they may worship me. But you would not let them go [Exod. 4:22–23]." And a little further on: "And they say to him, The God of the Hebrews has called to us; therefore we will go a three days' journey into the wilderness so that we may sacrifice to the Lord our God [Exod. 5:3]." And a little later he speaks again similarly: "The Lord, the God of the Hebrews, has sent me to you saying, Let my people go, so that they may worship me in the wilderness [Exod. 7:16]." [106A] Not only Moses and Jesus, but even Paul has manifestly declared that from the beginning God cared only for the Jews, his elected inheritance; that Paul should have said this is astonishing, though. For like the sea polypus [octopus?] who changes its colors according to the rocks, Paul changes his opinions about God according to circumstances. On one occasion he stoutly maintains that the Jews are God's sole possession; whereas on another occasion, when urging the Hellenes to ally themselves with him, he says, "He is not the God of the Jews only, but also of the Gentiles, yes of the Gentiles too [Rom. 3:29]." It is therefore just to inquire of Paul why, if he was the God not only of the Jews but also of the Gentiles, he profusely sent the gift of prophecy to the Jews, as well as Moses and the anointing oil and the prophets and the law and the strange and portentous aspects of their myths. For you hear them crying out, "Mortals ate of the bread of angels [Ps. 78:25]." Finally he also sent Jesus to them; but to us he sent no prophet, no anointing oil, no teacher, no herald proclaiming the prospective benevolence, which would eventually, sometime, extend even to us from himself. Rather for myriads or, if you wish, thousands of years he disregarded those worshipping in such ignorance, from east to west and from north to south, what you call idols, all of humanity except for a tiny people who not two thousand years earlier had jointly colonized one section of Palestine. Indeed if he is the God of us all and the maker of all equally, why did he overlook us? Therefore it is fitting to suppose that the God of the Hebrews is not the maker of the whole world exercising authority over the cosmos but that, as I said before, in a humbled position he exercises a limited sovereignty promiscuously with the other gods. Shall we still defer to you because you or someone from your family line imagined the God of the universe, if only to the extent of a mere notion? Are all these matters not individual? Your God is zealous. Why, though, does his zeal lead him to punish the children for the sins of their fathers?

[115D] Now look at our doctrine again in contrast to yours. Our theologians say that the creator of everything is the common father and king, but the remaining functions have been distributed among national gods and guardian deities of cities, each of whom governs their own allotment according to their nature. For in the father all things are perfect and all are one, whereas one capacity or another prevails among the particular deities, so that, for example, Ares governs the belligerent nations, Athena those that conduct war wisely, and Hermes those that are sagacious instead of daring. Thus each of the nations governed by these gods conforms to the nature of its own god. If experience does not testify to our doctrines, then let them be considered delusory and unpersuasive, and let yours be commended. But if the opposite is emphatically the case and from time immemorial experience testifies to our assertions, and nothing seems to accord at all with yours, then why are you so stubbornly contentious? . . .

[152B] Marvelous is the law of Moses, that is, the renowned Decalogue. "You shall not steal, you shall not murder, you shall not bear false witness." Now let each of the commandments, which he says have been written down by God himself, be quoted here verbatim: "I am the Lord your God, who brought you out of the land of Egypt." The second comes after this: "You shall have no other gods before me. You shall not make for yourself an idol [Exod. 20:2–4]." And he declares the reason why: "For I the Lord your God am a jealous God, punishing children for the iniquity of their fathers down to the third generation [Exod. 20:5]." "You shall not take the name of the Lord your God in vain." "Remember the sabbath day." "Honor your father and your mother." "You shall not commit adultery." "You shall not murder." "You shall not steal." "You shall not bear false witness." "You shall not covet anything that belongs to your neighbor." [Exod. 20:7–8, 12, 14, 13, 15–17]

[152D] By the gods, is there any nation at all that does not think it necessary to keep these commandments except for "You shall not worship other gods" and "Remember the sabbath day"? Indeed penalties are laid down for the transgressors. In some cases they are harsher, in others about the same as those ordained by Moses, and there are places where they are milder.

[155C] However, after the commandment "You shall not bow down to other gods," he speaks a grave slander against God: "For I am a jealous God," he says [Exod. 20:5]; and again elsewhere, "Our God is a devouring fire [Deut. 4:24]." So then you regard a human being who is jealous and malicious as deserving reproach, but if God is called jealous you deify the epithet? And yet when the matter is so obvious, how can you reasonably tell lies about God? For if God is jealous, then all the gods are worshipped, and all the rest of the nations worship their gods, against God's will. Therefore, if God is so envious and opposed to the worship of any gods other than himself alone, how did he not stop it? Is it because he could not do so, or from the beginning did he not wish to prevent the other gods from being worshipped? The first alternative is sacrilegious, that is, to declare that he lacked the power, while the second alternative agrees with our practice. Give up this frivolity, and do not weigh yourselves down with such grave blasphemy. For if God wills that no one else be worshipped, why do you bow down to this illegitimate son of God whom he has never yet acknowledged or regarded as his own? And this I shall demonstrate easily. You, though, impute to him a spurious son, why I do not know. . . .

[194D] So then would the more perceptive of you not deservedly be despised, and the more senseless pitied who, following the lead of the "perceptive," have fallen into such an abyss of destruction as to cast off the eternal gods and cross over to the corpse of the Jews? . . . For the spirit that reaches human beings from the gods does so rarely and comes into being in a few, and it is not easy for every man to partake of it in every season. In this connection the prophetic spirit has failed among the Hebrews, nor is it preserved among the Egyptians any longer. And it seems that our own oracles are reduced to silence, submitting to the cycles of time. Surely our humane master and father Zeus, observing this, has given us the possibility of inquiring by means of the sacred arts, with which we may find enough help to answer our needs.

[200A] I almost forgot to mention the greatest gift of Helios and Zeus; yet reasonably I saved the best for last. Indeed it does not belong uniquely to us Romans but I think is common to the Hellenes, our relatives, as well. For truly Zeus generated Asklepios among the perceptible gods from himself, and made him known to the earth through the life of the fruitful Helios. Having advanced upon the earth from heaven, Asklepios appeared in the single form of a human being at Epidauros. Then multiplying himself in his emanations, he stretched out his saving right hand over the whole earth. He arrived at Pergamon, Ionia, and afterward Tarentum; later he came to Rome. He went off to Kos and from there to Aigai; soon he is everywhere on land and sea. Without visiting each of us individually, he nevertheless restores erring souls and bodies that have fallen ill.

[201E] But what comparable gift do the Hebrews boast that they have received from God, those to whom you have been persuaded to desert from us? If at least you still adhered to their doctrines, you would not have been entirely unfortunate, though in a worse state than before when you were with us; yet your sufferings would have been endurable and tolerable. For you would be worshipping one God instead of many, not a human being or rather many miserable humans. And despite your subjection to a rough and cruel law including much savagery and barbarity in contrast to our moderate and humane ordinances, as well as your inferiority to us in other respects, yet you would be holier and purer in your sacred rites. Now, however, what has happened is that, like leeches, you have drunk the most infected blood from there and neglected the cleaner part. [191D] Jesus, who seduced the worst among you, has been spoken of for just slightly over three hundred years; and during the time that he lived he performed no noteworthy deeds, unless it is thought that healing the crippled and blind and exorcising demoniacs in the villages of Bethsaida and Bethany can be considered great works. [205E] You do not even know whether he mentioned purity. Yet you rival the wrath and venom of the Jews in ruining temples and altars; and you cut the throats not only of those of us who remained faithful to our patrimony, but also of some of your own people who had wandered off like you but were called heretics for not lamenting over the corpse in the same manner that you do. These practices arise from yourselves, however, for in no way did either Jesus or Paul transmit such commandments to you. Why not? Because they never expected that you would ever reach such a pinnacle of power; they were satisfied if they deceived slaves and through them women and men such as Cornelius and Sergius [Acts 10, 13]. If you can demonstrate that either one of them is mentioned by any of the recognized writers of the time—for these events occurred under Tiberius or Claudius—then regard me as one who lies about everything.

[209D] I do not know why I was as if impelled to go off on this tangent. My point of departure was the question, Why did you desert to the Jews, disobliging our gods? Was it because the gods conferred kingship on Rome whereas the Jews were granted freedom only briefly and then perpetually enslaved while sojourners? Consider Abraham; was he not a stranger in a strange land? And Jacob; did he not first serve the Syrians as a slave, then the Palestinians, and as an old man the Egyptians? Does Moses not say that he brought his people forth from the house of slavery, out of Egypt, with an outstretched arm? And once they had settled in Palestine, did they not change their fortunes more rapidly than witnesses say the chameleon changes the color of its skin, at one moment submitting to the judges, at another serving foreign tribes? After that they instituted the rule of kings—let the subject of how this happened be left aside for now. For God did not willingly accede to their desire for a monarchy, as the Scripture says, but under their compulsion he warned them that they would be badly governed. However, they did at least dwell in their land and farmed it for a little over three hundred years. From that time onward, they were enslaved first by the Assyrians, then the Medes, later on the Persians, and finally ourselves. Even the Jesus proclaimed among you was one of Caesar's subjects. If you disbelieve my words, I will demonstrate their truth shortly; or let me declare it right now. At any rate you affirm that he was registered with his father and his mother when Quirinius was governor [of Syria; Luke 2:2].

[213B] Once he became a human being, what blessings did he establish for his own Galileans? For they say that they did not want to obey Jesus. But why? How did that hardhearted and stiffnecked people obey Moses; whereas Jesus, who enjoined the spirits and walked on water and drove out demons—about whom you relate that he created heaven and earth, though none of the disciples dared to say this about him, with the exception of John, who did not do so plainly or clearly, yet let it be conceded that he did say it—why could Jesus not win the devotion of his own friends and relatives for the sake of their salvation?

[218A] I shall return to this question when I begin to investigate separately the wonderworking and over-elaboration of the Gospels. But now give me an answer to the question whether it is better to enjoy uninterrupted freedom, to govern most of the earth and sea over a period of two thousand whole years, or to be slaves and to live under the yoke of a foreign power? No one is so shameless as to prefer the second alternative. Likewise, will anyone suppose that winning victory in war is worse than suffering defeat? Who is so bereft of sense? Then if what I am saying is true, show me one Hebrew general comparable to Alexander or to Caesar. He is evidently not among you. And, by the gods, I know all too well that I am insulting those men; yet I mentioned them because of their familiarity. For most of the people are ignorant of our lesser generals, though each one of them is more admirable than the whole lineup of Hebrew generals.

[221E] Moreover, with reference to the institution of the state and the character of the law courts, the administration of the cities and the beauty of the laws, advances in knowledge and training in the liberal arts, were those [aspects of civilization] among the Hebrews not wretched and barbaric? And yet the sorry Eusebius wishfully imagines hexameter verses among the Hebrews and prides himself on their diligent study of logic, having heard the word "logic" from the Hellenes. What sort of medical art ever came to light among the Hebrews like that of Hippocrates and some other schools that developed later among the Hellenes? Does their wisest Solomon resemble the Hellenes' Phocylides or Theognis or Isocrates? How would that be possible? If you compared the counsels of Isocrates with the proverbs of Solomon, you would certainly discover that the son of Theodorus is better than their wisest king. But Solomon also practiced theurgy, they say. What of it? Did this Solomon not worship our gods too, seduced by his wife as they tell the story? O magnitude of virtue! O abundance of wisdom! He did not prevail over pleasure, and the eloquence of a woman misled him. If this man was tricked by a woman, then do not call him wise; if you have confidence in his wisdom, do not suppose that he was seduced by a woman but that, persuaded by his own judgment and understanding and the instruction he had received from the god who was shown to him, he worshipped the other gods as well. For envy and zeal do not approach the finest humans and are that much more absent from angels and gods. After all, you attend to demi-powers, which are not erroneously called demons since ambition and vanity exist in them; but in the gods there is no such thing.

[229C] If it is enough for you to read your own Scriptures, why do you sample the learning of the Hellenes? And yet it would be better to exclude people from that learning rather than from eating meat sacrificed to idols. For the one who eats is not injured at all by such meat, even according to Paul, though the conscience of the brother who observes him might be scandalized [1 Cor. 8] according to you, O wisest and most arrogant of men. This learned literature has caused every noble person brought forth by nature among you to revolt from godlessness. Therefore, anyone endowed with the smallest particle of goodness has very rapidly revolted from your godlessness. So then it would be better to prohibit people from ingesting knowledge rather than sacrificial meat. It seems to me, however, that you yourselves know the difference between your writings and ours with respect to intelligence, and that from perusing yours no man would become noble or even merely equitable; whereas from ours every man would improve on himself even if he lacked any natural endowment at all. Someone who is well endowed, though, and has the good fortune to be educated by our literature, becomes an absolute gift of the gods to humanity. He may kindle the light of scientific knowledge, or establish a type of constitution, or defeat numerous enemies, or most notably traverse great distances on land and sea, thus being manifest as a hero.

[229E] A clear proof of this would be to select children from your whole community, training or preparing them in your Scriptures. If they end up as men more excellent than slaves, then consider my talk foolish and deranged. But then you are so unfortunate and senseless that you think your books are sacred despite the fact that they would never make anyone more prudent or more courageous or more excellent than their former self. Yet the writings through which one could gain courage, prudence, and justice, these you assign to Satan and the servants of Satan.

[235B] Asklepios heals our bodies; the Muses together with Asklepios and Apollo and the eloquent Hermes instruct our souls; Ares and Enyo join with us on the battlefield; Hephaistos allots and distributes the arts and crafts; and Athena, the motherless virgin, with the help of Zeus regulates all of this. Reflect then on whether we are not your superiors in each of these areas—I mean in the arts and wisdom and understanding—that is, in the practical arts, or the mimetic arts dedicated to the beautiful (as, for example, those of sculpture, painting, or home economics), or the healing art of Asklepios, whose oracles fill the earth, oracles that the god allows us to share in continually. Truly Asklepios healed me many times when I was sick by suggesting remedies; and Zeus is witness to these things. So then, if not having devoted ourselves to the spirit of apostasy, we are better off than you are in relation to soul and body and external matters, why do you dismiss our culture and embrace theirs?

[238A] Further, why do you neither adhere to the Hebrews' traditions nor welcome the law that God has given to them, forsaking their heritage more than our own and devoting yourselves to what the prophets proclaimed? For if anyone wishes to ascertain the truth about you, they will discover that your piety is composed of Jewish audacity and Gentile apathy and coarseness. Extracting from both parties not their best features but their worst ones, you have produced a border of evils. For the Hebrews have exact regulations concerning religious observances and sanctuaries, and numberless precepts requiring a priestly way of life and character. Their lawgiver commanded them not to serve all the gods but only one, whose "portion is Jacob and Israel, an allotment of his inheritance [Deut. 32:9];" but I think he added another saying: "You shall not revile the gods [Exod. 22:28]." It was the disgusting audacity of succeeding generations, wishing to do away with all popular piety, that determined that blasphemy is consistent with failure to worship the gods. This is the one thing that you adopted from them, since otherwise you and they share nothing similar. Thus from the innovative doctrine of the Hebrews, you snatched their blasphemy toward the gods whom we revere; while from our religion you have discarded both the pious devotion to all higher nature and the affection for our ancestral traditions, retaining only the custom of eating everything "just as . . . the green plants [Gen. 9:3]." If truth be told, you aspired to surpass our boorishness (in my view this happens to all nations, and reasonably so), intending to conform to the lives of our lower orders: hucksters, tax collectors, dancers, and keepers of mistresses. . . .

[327A] And you are so benighted that you have not even adhered to the traditions passed on to you by the apostles, which were corrupted and made less godly by their successors. At least neither Paul nor Matthew nor Luke nor Mark dared to say that Jesus was God. But when the upright John learned that the people of many Greek and Italian cities had to a large extent caught this disease and, I think, when he heard that the tombs of Peter and Paul were themselves being reverenced, albeit covertly, he first dared to refer to Jesus as God. Having said a little about John the Baptist, he returned to the Word whom he was proclaiming: "And the Word," he affirms, "became flesh and lived among us" [John 1:14]; out of shame he does not explain how. As long as he calls him God and Word, he does not use the name Jesus or Christ at all. But as if surreptitiously and stealthily spiriting away our ears, he says that John the Baptist put forth this testimony in the name of Jesus Christ, that this is the very one in whom we must have faith as God the Word. That John says this about Jesus Christ, I myself do not dispute. And yet to some of the impious, it seems that Jesus Christ is emphatically other than the Word proclaimed by John. However, that is not so. For the one whom John names God the Word, this one he confirms was recognized by John the Baptist as Jesus Christ. Consider then how discreetly, softly, and secretly he inserts into the drama the finishing touch of impiety; he is such a treacherous trickster that he rises up again to declare, "No one has ever seen God; the only-begotten Son, he who is in the bosom of the Father, that one has made him known [John 1:18]." Is this then God the Word made flesh, the only-begotten Son who is in the bosom of the Father? And if he is the same one, which I believe, then you too have surely seen God. For "he lived among you and you beheld his glory [John 1:14]." Then why do you say further that no one has ever seen God, since you have seen if not also God the Father at least God the Word. But if the only-begotten Son and God the Word are two different persons, which I have heard from some members of your sect, then not even John seems to have spoken so boldly.

[335B] Nevertheless, this harmful teaching began with John. And who could feel sufficient loathing for the many additional teachings that you have discovered one after the other? Everywhere you have amassed tombs and memorials, and yet nowhere in your writings are you told to honor tombs obsessively. But you have advanced in wickedness to such a degree that you think it unnecessary to hear the words of Jesus the Nazarene in this regard. Therefore, listen to what he says about tombs: "Woe to you, scribes and Pharisees, hypocrites! because you are like whitewashed tombs, which on the outside look beautiful but inside they are full of the bones of the dead and of all kinds of filth [Matt. 23:27]." So then if Jesus said that tombs are full of uncleanness, how is it that you call upon God when you visit them? . . .

Bibliography

Athanassiadi, P. 1992. *Julian: An Intellectual Biography.* London and New York: Routledge.

Bidez, J. 1930. *La Vie de l'empereur Julien.* Paris: Les Belles Lettres.

Bowersock, G. W. 1978. *Julian the Apostate.* Cambridge: Harvard University Press.

Braun, R., and J. Richer, eds. 1978. *L'Empereur Julien: De l'histoire à la légende.* Paris: Les Belles Lettres.

Browning, R. 1976. *The Emperor Julian.* Berkeley and Los Angeles: University of California Press.

Geffcken, J. 1907. *Zwei Griechische Apologeten.* Leipzig and Berlin: Teubner.

———. 1914. *Kaiser Julianus.* Leipzig: Dieterich.

Labriolle, P. de. 1948. [1934]. *La Réaction païenne: Etude sur la polémique antichrétienne du Ier au VIe siècle.* 2^d ed. Paris: L'Artisan du Livre.

MacMullen, R. 1984. *Christianizing the Roman Empire.* New Haven: Yale University Press.

Malley, W. J. 1978. *Hellenism and Christianity.* Rome: Università Gregoriana.

Meredith, A. 1980. "Porphyry and Julian against the Christians." *Aufstieg und Niedergang der Römischen Welt* 2.23.2, 1,119–49.

Rosen, K. 1997. "Kaiser Julian auf dem Weg von Christentum zum Heidentum." *Jahrbuch für Antike und Christentum* 40: 126–46.

Smith, R. 1995. *Julian's Gods: Religion and Philosophy in the Thought and Action of Julian the Apostate.* London and New York: Routledge.

Wilken, R. 1984. *The Christians as the Romans Saw Them.* New Haven: Yale University Press.

— 11 —

A Thriving Native Cult in the Fifth Century
and Its Demise under Coptic Monks

David Frankfurter

This lively and rather lurid account of violent conflict in Egypt between native religion and Christian monks in the fifth century also offers some of the most historically dependable information on the shape of native piety at this period (see Besa, *Life of Shenoute* 83–84 [in Bell 1983]; Wipszycka 1988, 142–57; Frankfurter 1998, 20–22). To be sure, the story is rife with hagiographical and other literary devices, such as the characterization of traditional believers as practitioners of child-sacrifice (2), an old accusation against unfamiliar religions that Christian authors had come to use against heterodox sects (see Winkler 1980; McGowan 1994), and the story's fiery denouement (9), which is meant to recall the biblical prophet Elijah's invocation of fire from heaven to incinerate the priests of Baal (1 Kings 18). But in many important details the story diverges from hagiographical boilerplate; and it is in these details that we can perceive, if not an historical native cult, at least memories of native religion as it continued in various rural pockets through the fifth century.

The author describes a temple structure without permanent staff—the chief priest must come from elsewhere to address the crisis posed by the monks, (7, 10)—but with an image of the god accessible to villagers—through which, perhaps, a priest might speak oracles (4). The inside of the temple is restricted to priests (4–5)—called *ouēēb* (pure) (10)—while the popular veneration of the local god is sustained and expressed through domestic ritual (1) and through festivals (7). The populace is not kept in passive thrall to deity and priesthood, as historians of a Protestant bent used to assume, but rather actively engaged in the maintenance and defense of the cult (5–6). Indeed, one individual, in the face of the monks' onslaught, apparently gains the mantic capacity to channel the voice of the god (9). All these aspects of the cult of Kothos conform to what we know of native religion from archaeological and other sources from Late Antiquity (See Frankfurter 1998, 131–36). The monks' attack on the temple and its devotees likewise mirrors testimonies to such practices in Libanius of Antioch and in imperial edicts. The monk Besa's specially worded invocation of "God, the Christ, who brought Peter out of prison" to release Macarius and three fellow monks from a temple building (8) actually conforms to a species of Coptic Christian "release" spells well-represented among the various ritual manuals of Coptic Christianity (cf. Meyer and Smith 1994, 265 [127, 1.24], 283 [131, ll.20–45]).

The name Kothos alone remains elusive. Shenoute of Atripe lambasted traditional folk of his region for venerating Kronos, an alternative name for Petbe, an Egyptian protector-god of some popularity in Late Antiquity. Petbe could well have been honored as "commander-in-chief" [*archistratēgos*] (10) (See Frankfurter 1998, 116–19). But Kothos may simply be a type for an Egyptian local god in upper Egypt.

Apa Pinution, the deacon of Macarius, the bishop of Tkōw, relates this story of his master's powers to Dioscorus of Alexandria while on board a ship bound for Chalcedon. This translation is D. W. Johnson's, reprinted with permission from Peeters Publishers, Belgium.

There Was a Village on the West Side . . .

[V.1] There was a village on the west side of the river in which they worship an idol called Kothos, which is mounted in the niches of their houses. And when they go inside their doors, they are accustomed to bow down their head and worship him. [Circumstances] being thus then, the priests [*presbyteros*] of the village came and told my father everything the pagans were doing, how they were seizing the children of the Christians and slaying them for their idol, Kothos.

[2] For instance, one day they waylaid them and he saw them performing the lawless acts by slaying the little children and pouring [out] their blood upon the altar of their god, Kothos. They seized some of them and handed them over to the tribunal. They interrogated them, and they revealed [the truth] without torture, saying, "We call out to the children of the Christians and deceive them and give them morsels of bread and little things to eat in order to shut them up in hidden places so that no one outside would hear their voices. And in this way, we slay them and pour their blood upon the altar and take out their intestines and stretch them [to make] strings for our harps and we sing to our god on them. We also burn the rest of their bodies and reduce them to ashes. And everywhere we know there is treasure, we take a small quantity of ashes and cast them upon it. And we sing on the harps with the little children's intestines for strings. The treasure comes to light at once, and we take what we want." And thus, the men who had been seized [. . .] gave a large sum of money to be delivered, since all the leaders of that district were money-lovers.

[3] When Father Macarius heard these things from the priests, he arose, he

and two others. And I was walking with him while the two priests were in front of us. And when we had come northward in the region for about five or six miles, I saw one of their temples by some vineyards beside the road. And my father went toward the temple. The priests said to him, "Our father, do not let these godless men kill us and [simply] write us off." But he said to them, "Will they be able to pay [compensation] to God for us? As the Lord lives, [even] if they kill me I shall not stop without going inside."

[4] But he had not yet reached the door of the temple when the demon who dwells in Kothos the idol cried out, "Make haste and cast Macarius of Tkōw out of this place, for a tremor has come over me when I saw him. And if he spends one more hour in this place, I shall go away from this very place, and you will never find me."

[5] And when they heard these things from the demon, they came out with rakes in their hands. And their wives too went up on the roof and threw stones down upon us. They said to him, "You are Macarius of Tkōw, the evildoer. What have you come to search for in this place? Our god has already told us about your hatred for him. Get away from us. What is your business with us?" The holy man said to them, "If I do not have business with you, what is your business with the children of the Christians whom you slay for your god?" And they said, "It is not the truth." And he said, "If it is not the truth, allow me to go inside your temple and examine it." And they said to him, "Come."

[6] But the priests were afraid. They did not come inside with us. And when we had gone inside, they made haste and threw themselves upon us. They numbered twenty, while we were [only] four. They said, "Your life-span stops today. Behold, your slaughtering place." At once they leapt upon my father first. They bound him like a guileless sheep. [Afterward], they made ready to offer us three up on the altar of their god.

[7] And their wives were making remarks of this sort, "Let us keep the festival today with these Christian evildoers." Some of them said, "It is fitting that, before we slay them, we notify the high priest first and summon him to the festival to our god Kothos." And the rest agreed with him in this matter. Now, the name of their high priest [archiereus] was Homer. And when the one who had been sent had gone, I said to my father with whom I was chained, "Will you continue to endure thus without praying that we escape? For behold the hour of our slaughter is at hand." But he said to me, "Do not be afraid, Pinution. God, the Christ, will help us."

[8] While we were still speaking, behold, Besa knocked at the door. But they did not open for him. And he cried out, "God, the Christ, who brought Peter out of prison when he was bound with two chains, the iron gate having been made to open for him by itself without a key, may you open the door of this temple without a key." And in an instant, the door of the temple opened. He came inside with fourteen other monks with him. And when the pagans saw them, they were troubled and became like these inanimate stones. Immediately our chains fell off.

[9] Father Besa said to my father, "Do one of these two things. Either pray and I will set the fire, or set the fire and I will pray." My father said, "No. Rather, let us pray together, and the fire will come down from heaven and consume this temple." And when the two stood at prayer with the brothers who were with them, a voice came down from heaven, saying, "Save yourselves from this temple." And when we were a little way from the door of the temple and had not yet turned our gaze back, a great wall of fire broke out in the temple. And an hour had not yet elapsed before the fire devoured the foundations of the temple. The walls of the temple fell and its stones came down. The fire consumed it right down to its foundations. My father looked back and cursed that land, saying, "Let there be no seeds for sowing in it [. . .] for ever. Rather, let it become parched, with wild animals and serpents breeding in it." And at this point, behold, a demon entered a man. He went to the village with the man crying out, "Do not let any pagan remain in the village, for behold, Macarius of Tkōw and Besa, the disciple of Father Shenute, have come."

[10] And when my father met Homer, their high priest, on the road, he knew that he was their leader for whom they had sent. My father said to him, "Why did you not come to the celebration of our slaughter, when we were about to be slain for your god Kothos?" He said, "You, an old man, are not worthy to be made a libation to our god." At once, my father made a sign to the brothers, "Seize him!" But that unclean priest [ouēēb] cried out, saying, "Great god Kothos, commander-in-chief of the air, the brother of Apollo, save me! I am your high priest." My father said to him, "I shall burn you alive and also your god Kothos."

[11] And when we went into the village, the multitude of the orthodox came out ahead [of us], singing psalms. Then he gave the command, and a fire was kindled. He threw Homer into it. He was burned along with the idols that had been found in his house. And [of] the rest of the pagans, some became Christians and received baptism. But others did not wish to receive [it]. Rather, they threw everything they owned into the depths of the cisterns and wells and fled with only their idols to the desert. And they counted the idols that had been destroyed that day and found them to number 306. As for those who fled, the Christians dwelt in their houses. Behold, the things that I saw and heard, I have related to you, my father, the archbishop.

Bibliography

Bell, David N. 1983. *Besa: The Life of Shenoute.* Cistercian Studies Series 73. Kalamazoo, Mich.: Cistercian Publications.

Frankfurter, David. 1998. *Religion in Roman Egypt: Assimilation and Resistance.* Princeton: Princeton University Press.

Johnson, D. W. 1980. *A Panegyric on Macarius, Bishop of Tkōw, Attributed to Dioscorus of*

Alexandria. 2 vols. Corpus Scriptorum Christianorum Orientalium 415–16, S. Coptici 41–42. Louvain: Corpus Scriptorum Christianorum Orientalium.

McGowan, Andrew. 1994. "Eating People: Accusations of Cannibalism against Christians in the Second Century." *Journal of Early Christian Studies* 2: 413–42.

Meyer, Marvin, and Richard Smith, eds. 1994. *Ancient Christian Magic: Coptic Texts of Ritual Power.* San Francisco: Harper.

Winkler, John J. 1980. "Lollianos and the Desperadoes." *Journal of Hellenic Studies* 100: 155–81.

Wipszycka, Ewa. 1988. "La Christianisation de l'Egypte aux IVe–VIe siècles. Aspects sociaux et ethniques." *Aegyptus* 68: 154–55.

─ 12 ─

The Cologne Mani Codex

Ellen Bradshaw Aitken

The Cologne Mani Codex (hereafter *CMC*) purports to be an autobiography of the prophet Mani and provides information about Mani's early life among a Jewish-Christian baptist sect in southern Babylonia. It also relates Mani's separation from that sect, the revelations he received from his heavenly twin, the Syzygos, and his missionary activities.

CMC is a miniature codex, a pocketbook, measuring 3.5 cm. × 4.5 cm.; it is thus one of the smallest books extant from antiquity (Henrichs and Koenen 1970, 100–101). One hundred and ninety-two pages, each with twenty-three lines and minute script, have been preserved, but with significant lacunae in pages 1–24 and pages 116–45; pages 146 to the end are too fragmentary to permit reconstruction. The codex itself is dated to the fourth or early fifth century C.E., but the text was probably compiled not long after Mani's death in 270. Its provenance is unknown, but it is quite plausible that *CMC* was produced at Lykopolis in upper Egypt, known as an important center of Manichaeism (Henrichs 1979, 340). The codex was opened first in modern times by Dr. Anton Fackelmann in 1969; it was read and then published by Albert Henrichs and Ludwig Koenen (see the account in Henrichs 1979).

CMC is a Greek text, translated from a now-lost Syriac original (Henrichs 1979, 352–53). New Testament quotations are not translated from the Syriac, but taken directly from a Greek text (Henrichs and Koenen 1975, 83). *CMC* appears to have known gospel traditions from Tatian's *Diatessaron* (Henrichs and Koenen 1978, 175), Marcion's canon of Paul's writings (Betz 1986, 222), and some of the apocryphal acts of the apostles (Henrichs 1981, 725). Some of the sayings attributed here to Mani are known from other Manichaean sources as well. It is possible to distinguish three literary stages in *CMC* prior to its translation into Greek: (1) the quotations from Mani's own writings; (2) excerpts from works by Mani's disciples, appearing here under the names of those disciples; and (3) the work of a final redactor, responsible for creating the framework and genre, compiling quotations and excerpts, and writing new material (Henrichs 1981, 726–27). Excerpts from followers of Mani, notably Timotheos and Baraies, are frequently marked by subtitles and ornaments in the manuscript (Henrichs 1979, 351–52).

The pages of CMC contain a running title, "Concerning the Origin of His Body." This title is best understood as having a double meaning; it refers both to the story of Mani's existence and to the origin of the religious movement he founded. In this respect, "body" refers to the church much as it does in the letters of Paul (Henrichs 1973, 40).

In genre, CMC is best identified as an anthology, collecting "memoirs" of Mani's words and deeds. Like many Manichaean collections, its material consists of several genres: sayings, miracle stories, aretalogies, epiphany stories, revelation dialogue, apocalypses, travelogues, controversy stories, homily, and epistle (Henrichs 1981, 725–26). CMC may also be regarded as religious propaganda, written to persuade its audience toward Manichaeism; at the same time it is also an initiatory text, providing instruction about the practices and theology of Manichaeism for new adherents (Ries 1993, 401). The following divisions in the text may be observed (Henrichs 1981, 725–29; Cameron and Dewey 1979, 3):

1. (pages 2–24) The childhood of Mani, from when he entered the sect of the baptists at the age of four to the age of twelve; miracle stories are prominent in this section, which also contains two conversion narratives.

2. (pages 24–72) Revelation discourses from Mani's first and second revelations by the Syzygos, together with lengthy apologetic sections under the authority of Baraies.

3. (pages 72–99) Mani's separation from the baptists, with controversy stories and dialogue.

4. (pages 99–116) Mani's departure from the baptists, commissioning, and instruction for founding of his sect, presented as revealed dialogue.

5. (pages 116–92) Mani's missionary journey and activities, in which miracle stories and conversion stories are prominent.

The balanced composition of CMC is evident in its ABCB'A' structure, whereby miracle stories and revelatory dialogue form outer and inner frames for the central account of Mani's break with the baptists.

CMC is a rich resource for not only for the history of Manichaeism as a world missionary religion, but also for questions of religious definition and practice in eastern Syria and Mesopotamia in the third century (Koenen 1981; Maier 1986). Mani's origins in a Jewish-Christian baptist group, with affinities to Elchasaites, provides information about the diversity of Christianity in the East, and particularly about the affinities of formative Manichaeism to gnosticism (Bianchi 1983) and later Mandaean practices (Rudolph 1974; Henrichs 1979, 354–67). Because CMC discusses both distinctions in theology and in ritual practice, especially baptism and food laws, it permits more detailed knowledge of religious identity in antiquity (Koenen 1981; Rudolph 1986). The link provided in CMC between the autobiography of Mani and religious practice demonstrates the use of biography as a strategy of religious self-definition and propaganda (Henrichs 1973; Cirillo 1986).

The reliance of *CMC* on Pauline theology is also evident in the quotations from Galatians and 2 Corinthians and in deutero-Pauline concepts seen in Ephesians and Colossians, as well as in Mani's presentation of his apostolic identity, his gospel, and the revelations he received. Mani, as an imitator of Paul, belongs to a trajectory of Pauline theology seen also in Marcion (Henrichs 1973, 32–34; Betz 1986). As a biography of Mani, however, *CMC* may also be compared with the way in which the New Testament gospels employ the biography of a religious movement's founder as a means of self-definition and promotion for the cult (Henrichs 1986, 185). *CMC* also has significant affinities with the Thomas literature, including employing sayings of Mani much as the *Gospel of Thomas* does sayings of Jesus and emphasizing the role of the solitary one (Henrichs 1973, 28, 37–38).

The following selections from *CMC* are translated from the reconstruction in the critical edition (Koenen and Römer 1987); included are excerpts from Mani's description of his call and authorization, his separation from and disputes with the baptists, together with all of pages 99–145, until the text becomes too fragmentary for comprehension. An English translation of all of pages 2–99 is available (Cameron and Dewey 1979).

The Syzygos First Appears to Mani

(17.8) "Well, in the season when my body was completed in its maturity, there immediately flew down and appeared before me that most beautiful and greatest mirror-image of my [person]. (7 lines lacuna) . . . (18.1) [When] I was twenty-[four], in the year when Dariardaxar, the king of Persia subjugated the city of Atra, when the king Shapur, his son, crowned himself with the great diadem, in the month of Pharmouthi, on the eighth day of the (lunar) month, the most blessed Lord was moved with compassion toward me, called (me) into his grace, and sent to me . . . [my] Syzygos, which [was] in great glory. (8 lines lacuna) . . . (19.2), the one who is mindful of and brings to light all the best counsels from our father and from the good, first, right hand far away." And again he (Mani) spoke thus, "When my father was well pleased and rendered both mercy and pity to me in order to ransom (me) from the error of the sectarians, he showed consideration for me through his great many [revelations] and sent [to me] my [Syzygos]. (5 lines lacuna) . . . [and he provided me with the (20.1) best hope], redemption for those who are patient, the truest pledges and intentions, and the laying on of hands of our father.

"Well, when he (the Syzygos) arrived, he loosed me, separated (me), and tore (me) away from the midst of that law in which I was brought up. In this manner, he called me, chose me for himself, drew me, and set me apart from the midst of these ones . . . And after drawing [me to one] side (7 lines lacuna) . . . [he revealed to me] . . . (21.2) and who I am; what my body is; in what manner I have come; how my arrival into this world came about; who I am among those who are most distinguished for preeminence; how I was begotten into this fleshly body; because of what woman I was delivered and brought to birth in this flesh; and from whom . . . I was sown; (7 lines lacuna) . . . (22.1) and how . . . it happened; who my father on high is; and how, separated from him, I was sent forth according to his intent; and what commandment and pledge he presented to me before I put on this instrument, before I went astray in this loathsome flesh, before I put on its drunkenness and guise; and who [it is who] is my [vigilant] Syzygos . . . and the (5 lines lacuna) . . . (23.1) what cannot be spoken, the [thoughts], and the perfections of my father; and concerning me, who I am; and my Syzygos, who is inseparable, who he is; and, moreover, concerning my soul, which is the soul of all the worlds, what it itself is and how it came to be. And he again revealed to me, beyond these matters, the boundless heights and the unsearchable depths. He described to me all that [is] after (7 lines lacuna, after which begins a hymn) . . .

> (24.1) reverently I received as my own possession
> him who is most [trustworthy].
> I believed that he was already mine,
> and is mine, and is a good and gracious counselor.
> I recognized him and understood
> that I am that one from whom I was separated.
> And I have borne witness
> that I am that one himself who is [wholly] equal.
> (8 lines lacuna) . . . (25.1) to him."

And furthermore he (Mani) spoke thus [again], "With greatest ingenuity and skill I went about in that law, guarding carefully this hope in my own understanding, although no one perceived who it was who was with me, whom I myself revealed to no one at all in that time, even though it was very long."

Mani as an Apostle

(62.9) Finally, all the most blessed apostles, saviors, evangelists, and prophets of the truth, each of them saw inasmuch as the living hope was revealed to him for proclamation. And they wrote, left behind, and treasured up in a memoir for the sons (and daughters) of the [Holy] Spirit [who were to be] and were to know (63.1) the sense of his voice.

In this manner, it is attendant upon the apostle most worthy of all praise, through whom and from whom the hope and the inheritance of life have come to us, to write to us and to make a declaration to all who come afterwards, to those who belong to the household of faith, and to those who are spiritual offspring, growing through his brightest waters, so that his rapture and revelation may be made known to them. For we know, brothers (and sisters), how surpassing is the size of wisdom in relation to us with this arrival of the paraclete of the [truth] which [we know] (64.1) he did not receive from humans nor from the hearing of books, as our father (Mani) himself also said in the treatises which he sent to Edessa. For he says thus,

"The truth and the ineffable things that I relate—and the laying on of hands that is mine—I did not receive from humans or fleshly creatures, and neither from the instructions of the scriptures. But when the most blessed [father] who called me into his grace saw me and, because he did not [wish] me and the rest who are [in the] world to perish, had mercy [on me], so that he might extend [his] well-being (65.1) to those who were prepared to be chosen by him out of the sects, even then by his grace he tore me from the council of the multitude who do not know the truth and revealed to me the ineffable things of his and of his undefiled father and of all the world. And he disclosed to me how they were before the foundation of the world, how the groundwork of all works, both good and evil, was laid, and how the things from the mixture [were joined together] during these [seasons and worlds]."

And furthermore he wrote again and (66.1) said in the gospel of his most holy hope, "I, Mani, an apostle of Jesus Christ through the will of God, the father of the truth, from whom I also came to be, who lives and abides forever and ever, who is before all and abides after all things. And everything that is and shall be exists through his might. For from this one himself I was born, and I am also from his will. And from him everything true has been [revealed] to me, and I am from [his] truth. I saw the truth of the ages [which he revealed]. (67.1) And the truth I disclosed to my fellow travelers, but peace I preached to the children of peace, and hope I proclaimed to the immortal race. (The) elect I have chosen, and the path to the height I have shown to those who ascend according to this truth. I have proclaimed hope, revealed this revelation, and written this immortal gospel, putting in it these (secret) rites of the preeminence and disclosing very great works in it, indeed the greatest and most solemn of the strongest works of the [preeminence]. And these things that he revealed, I have shown to those who have life from (68.1) the truest vision, which I have seen, and from the most glorious revelation, which was revealed to me."

Mani's Disputes with the Baptists

(79.13) *Baraies the Teacher* My lord (Mani) said, "I have had enough disputing against each one in that law, when I have sprung up and examined them [concerning the] way of God, the commandments of the savior, (80.1) baptism, the vegetables that they baptize, and their every ordinance and order in which they go.

"When I destroyed and abolished their words and mysteries, showing then that which they followed they had not received from the commandments of the savior, some of them wondered at me, but others grew angry and, being provoked, said, 'He doesn't want to go to the Greeks, does he?' But when I saw their purposes, I said to them kindly, '[This] baptism with which (81.1) you baptize your foods is [nothing]. For this body is defiled and molded from a mold of defilement. And you see that whenever someone purifies his own food and partakes of this, which is now baptized, it appears to us that from it also come blood, bile, gas, and excrement of shame and of the body of defilement. And if someone should keep his mouth from this food for a few days, right away all these offscourings of shame and abomination would be known to be wanting and lacking in the body. If he again partakes of food, (82.1) in the same manner they abound in his body, with the result that it is also evident that from the food itself they overflow. If someone should partake of food that is baptized and purified and then partake of that which is not baptized, it is clear that the beauty and the power of the body becomes known as the same (in either case). Likewise also the foulness and the dregs of both are seen as differing in no way from each other, so that what is baptized, which [it (the body) cast away] and removed, is not at all distinguishable from that [other] which is not baptized.

" 'And the fact that (83.1) you baptize each day in waters is nothing. For if you have been baptized and purified once, why are you baptized again each day? Therefore it is also clear in this that you loathe yourselves each day and that because of foulness you are baptized before being purified. And in this it is very clear that all the pollution is from the body. And behold, even [you] have clothed yourselves in it.

" 'Henceforth, [make an inspection of] yourselves, [what] your purity [is. For] it is (84.1) impossible to purify your bodies completely, since each day the body is moved and stands still through the excretions of nourishment from it, so that the deed happens without a commandment from the savior. Well, this purity, about which was spoken, is that of knowledge, namely, a separation of light from darkness, death from life, and the living waters from those that are stagnant. And that you may know that each is [unequal] to the other, [you will hold fast] the commandments of the savior, [so that] he may redeem your soul from [ruin] and (85.1) destruction. This is truly the most direct purification, which you were entrusted with doing. But you have been gone away from it and bathed and held fast to the purity of the body, which is most defiled and fashioned through foulness; through it (foulness) it (the body) curdled and, having been built up, stood fast.'

"And after I said these things to them and destroyed and rendered useless that which they [sought eagerly], some of them, amazed at me, praised me and regarded me as a leader and teacher. And there was much whispering in that sect (86.1) because of me. Some of them regarded me as a prophet and teacher. Others were saying, 'A living word is sung in him; let us make him a teacher of our sect.' But others were saying, 'Surely a voice has not spoken to him secretly, has it, and he is saying those things that it revealed to him?' And some were saying, 'Something has not appeared to him in a dream, has it, and he is saying what he saw?' But others were saying, 'He is not this one about whom our teachers were prophesying, is he, when they said, "A young man will [arise] from our midst and a new [teacher] (87.1) will come forth to move our whole sect, in the manner in which our ancestral parents spoke concerning the wresting of the garment"?' And others were saying, 'Surely it is not error that speaks in him, is it, and wishes to lead our people astray and divide the sect?' But others of them were filled with envy and anger, of whom some were voting for (my) death. And some were saying, 'This man is the enemy of our [law].' And they were saying, 'He wished to go to the Gentiles and to eat [Greek] bread. . . . For we have [heard] him saying, "It is necessary to partake of [Greek] bread." (88.1) Likewise also this man says that it follows to partake of drink, wheat, vegetables, and fruit, which our ancestors were careful not to eat. Likewise also the baptism with which we baptize he abolishes, and he does not baptize as we do, but neither does he baptize his (midday) meal as we do.'

"So then, because Sita and his [companions] saw that I would not turn toward their [persuasion, but] that little by little I was abolishing and rendering useless their own law and the foods which they set apart and that I was not (89.1) baptizing similarly to them, because they saw that I was opposed to them in all these matters, then Sita and the throng of his companions set up a synod of elders on my account. And they also invited the master of the house, Pattikios, and said to him, 'Your son has turned aside from our law and wishes to go into the world. And we reject and do not eat wheat bread, fruit, and vegetables, but he does not follow these (ordinances) and says that it is necessary to [change] these things. He baptizes in a manner different from [us]. (90.1) And he wishes to eat [Greek] bread.' Because Pattikios saw their very great uproar, he said to them, 'Summon him yourselves and persuade him.'

"And then, when they summoned me and gathered together, they said to me, 'From (your) youth you have been with us, living well in both the ordinances and lifestyles of our law. You have been like a modest bride in our midst. What has happened to you now; what has appeared to you? For you oppose our law and abolish and render useless our sect. You have exchanged (91.1) our way of life for yours. We regard your father with greatest honor. So why do you now abolish the baptism of our law and of our ancestors, in which we have gone about from of old? You have abolished the commandments of the savior, and you wish even to eat wheat bread and vegetables, which we do not eat. Why do you live thus, not assenting to farm the land as we do?'

Then I said to [them], "Far be it from me to [abolish] the commandments of the savior! But if you [reproach] me because of wheat bread, (92.1) because I said, 'It is necessary to eat it,' the savior did this, even as it is written, when, having blessed (it), he offered it to his disciples, 'he said the blessing over the bread and gave (it) to them.' Well, that loaf of bread, was it not from wheat? And it shows that he reclined at table with tax collectors and idolaters (Matt. 9:10–11, and parallels; 11:18–19). And likewise he was invited to the house

of Martha and Mary. When Martha said to him, 'Lord, do you not care about
[me], so as to tell my [sister] to assist me?' the savior said to her, 'Your sister
Mary (93.1) has chosen the [good] part, and it shall not be taken away from
her (Luke 10:38–42).'

"Well, consider how the disciples of the savior ate bread from women and
idolaters, and did not separate bread from bread, nor vegetable from vegetable,
nor did they eat, working with labor and the farming of the land, as you do
today. And likewise, when the savior sent his disciples to preach in each place,
they took with them [neither] mule nor [oven] but . . . taking . . . from. . . ."

(94.1) Za[chias] "Well, if you are accusing me about baptism, behold, again
I show you from your law and from what has been revealed to your leaders
that it is not necessary to baptize. For Elkhasai, the founder of your law, indicates (this): for when he was going to wash in the waters, an image of a man
appeared to him from the spring of water and said to him, 'Is it not sufficient
that your animals [strike] me? But even you [yourself] maltreat [my place]
and profane [my waters].' Therefore Elkhasai [marveled and] said to it, (95.1)
'The fornication, defilement, and impurity of the world are thrown upon you
and you do not refuse (them), but you are grieved at me.' It said to him,
'Although all these people did not know me (and) who I am, you who say that
you are a servant and righteous, why have you not guarded my honor?' And
then, moved, Elkhasai did not wash in the waters.

"And again, after a long time, he wished to wash in the waters and he ordered
his disciples to [look out] for a place that did not [have much] water so that
he might wash. [His] disciples [found] (96.1) the place for him. But when he
[was about to] wash, again for a second time, an image of a man appeared to
him out of that spring and said to him, 'We and those waters that are in the
sea are one. So you have come here too to wrong us and strike us.' Shaking
and moved exceedingly, Elkhasai allowed the mud of his head to dry and so
[shook] it off."

[Again] he (Mani) shows that Elkhasai had plows [laid up in storage] and
went [to] them. The earth cried out and said to him, (97.1), "[Why] do you
make your livelihood from me?" And Elkhasai, after taking soil from that earth
that had spoken to him, wept, kissed (it), and placed (it) on his breast and
began to say, "This is the flesh and blood of my lord."

And once again he said that Elkhasai found his disciples baking loaves of
bread, with the result that the bread spoke with Elkhasai. And he ordered
(them) to bake no longer.

Again he shows that Sabbaios the baptist was bringing the vegetables to the
elder of the city. And that [vegetable began to weep] and (98.1) said to him,
"Are you not righteous? Are you not pure? Why are you leading us away to
the fornicators?" Thus, Sabbaios was moved because of what he heard and
returned the vegetables.

Again he shows that a date-palm spoke with Aianos, the baptist from Kokhe,
and ordered him to say to "my lord," "Do not cut (me) down because my fruit

is stolen, but permit me this year, and in a year I shall give you fruit in proportion to what has been stolen from me in all these years." (99.1) But it also ordered (him) to say to that man who was stealing its fruit, "Do not come at this time to steal my fruit. If you should come, I shall cast you forth from my heights, and you will die."

Mani's Separation from the Baptists and His Mission

(99.10) *Timotheos* Then he said to them, "Consider these renowned men of your law yourselves, those who saw these visions, were moved by them, and proclaimed them as good news to others. Likewise . . . I too practice everything that I was taught [by them]."

When I was saying these things to them, nullifying their words, at once they all became violent out of their anger, with the result that one of them even arose and struck me. They all constrained me in their midst and flogged me. They were also grabbing my hair as though I were an enemy. They were crying out against me with a very great voice, becoming embittered and angry [at] me, as at someone who is superstitious, and wishing to [strangle] me out of the malice that belonged to them. Because of Pattikios, the master of the house, who [begged] them not . . . to be impious toward (101.1) those in their midst, ashamed, they released me. Because this trial had overtaken me, I withdrew to one side and stood at prayer. And I supplicated and begged our Lord to come to my aid.

When I had ceased praying and was altogether grieved, my most blessed Syzygos—that one who is both (my) master and (my) supporter—[appeared] directly opposite me. And he said to me, "Do not grieve or weep aloud." [And I] said to him, "[How] indeed should I not grieve? For those in this [sect], with whom (102.1) I have lived [from my youth], have changed and become enemies to me because I stood apart from their own law. Where then shall I go? For all the sects and parties are antagonistic to the good, and I myself am a stranger and solitary in the world. When in this sect of those who have read about chastity, flagellation of the flesh, and holding fast the resting of the hands, and who all [still know] me by name . . . and the value of the body rather . . . of the sects, for [when] the rearing of my body, (103.1) my nursing, and my lulling to sleep took place in that sect, I used also to have a certain connection with its leaders and elders during the rearing of my body. If these men did not give me room for the reception of the truth, how will the world, its nobles, or its teachings receive me so as to hear these ineffable things and to accept [these] commandments, which are heavy? And how . . . I . . . before the rulers . . . and . . . (104.1) of the world and the leaders of the sects? For, behold, they are extremely great and powerful in their wealth, their boldness, and their possessions, but I am alone and poor in these things."

Well, the most esteemed one himself then said to me, "You were not sent into this sect alone, but into every nation and teaching and every city and place. For [by you] the hope will [now] be made clear and preached in all regions and portions of the [world]. [And] a great many people will [accept] (105.1) your word. Therefore, go forth and go round about, for I myself am with you as an ally and protector in every place where you will speak all that I have revealed. [Thus], do not be distressed or grieved."

Well, very many were the things that he said to me, when he was strengthening (me) and rendering (me) more courageous in his hope. I worshipped before him, and my mind rejoiced at the [remarkable] sight of that most blessed Syzygos of mine, who is both most esteemed and most august. [And I said] to him, ". . . . (106.1) For behold, Pattikios is an old man, and after he saw one struggle come upon me he was moved." Then he said to me, "Go forth and go round about. For behold, two men will come to you from that law, and they will be companions for you. Likewise Pattikios will also be first among your select group, and he will follow along with you."

Well, there [then] came [to me] two young men from the baptists, and they were my neighbors [Simeon] and Abizakhias. And [they came] to me in order to go with me into every place. And they were present as [my] co-workers [where] we [went].

(107.1) Well, I went forth from that law by the will of our master in order to sow his most beautiful seed (cf. Matt. 13:37), to light his brightest lanterns, to ransom the living souls (Gen. 2:7; 1 Cor. 15:45) from their subjection of the rebels, to walk about in the world according to the image of our Lord Jesus, to cast a sword (Matt. 10:34), division (Luke 12:51) and a dagger of the spirit (Eph. 6:17) on the earth, to let [bread] drop (Exod. 16:4) upon [my] people, and to [conquer] the [immeasurable] reproach in the [world], and. . . . (108.1) And I went into foreign parts and into exile like a sheep in the sight of wolves (Matt. 10:16; Luke 10:3), so that through me the faithful might separate (themselves) and be chosen from the unfaithful, the most beautiful wheat from the midst of the weeds, the children of the kingdom from the children of the enemy (Matt. 13:25ff, 38f.; Mark 4:15; Luke 8:12), the descendants of the height from those begotten of the depth, so that through me he separated what is of his household from what is not of his household.

Well, according to the good pleasure of my most blessed father, [I was sent away] into the circuit of the world, so that in me the creation was [sanctified] and [through] me he (109.1) made quite obvious the truth of [his own] knowledge in the midst of the sects and peoples, and in me opposed both the rulers of the earth and the nobles of the world, in order to take what is his own out of all things.

In this manner, I went forth, although none of those of that sect perceived where we went. We walked about [until] we [crossed] first into Ktesiphon. When I did not proceed because the sea [was full, one of the] baptists saw me [staying there]. And indeed when [I left] Pattikios, I did not (110.1) tell him where I was going, with the result that Pattikios was possessed by grief and weeping because of me and went out and went forth visiting the surrounding synods but did not find me; therefore he wept and lamented, and the baptists stood by to comfort him. And that person who saw me went first to them and saw that they were in grief, he said [to] them, "Why are you [grieving?]" And they said [to him], "Because of Mani, because he went out and we do not [know where] he has gone. We are afraid lest somehow [some one] . . . (111.1) him." And he said [to] them, "I myself have seen him crossing at the bridge into the city." And Pattikios, when he heard, rejoiced and went out to me in order to go into Ktesiphon.

When he arrived there, he did not find me, but he went out again and made inquiries. And he came and [found] me outside the city [in] a small village called Nassēr in [the] assembly of the [holy ones]. And immediately when Pattikios [saw me], he [stood by] (me), [kissed] and embraced (me), and [worshipped] before me. And weeping [he said to me], ". . . (112.1) . . . I wept, thinking that you had perished and were no longer to be seen by me. And I was saying, 'Whom shall I call and who will be obedient to me? Or whom would I see before my eyes? And to whom should I utter my sighing? Or to whom should I entrust the mysteries of my heart?' For I myself was hoping to have you as the administrator of everything in this [my] old age. For [whom] am I able to trust better than you? But I see that you [will not be] with me, but I [pray God] not to destroy [you] . . . but I . . . of you . . . (113.1) . . . sad . . . in your friendship, the sighing of my remembrances (Wisd. of Sol. 11:12) will be put into the heart. And perhaps in my sighing for you I shall go out of the world."

Then my lord said to him, "Do not weep or grieve or [be] anxious about me. For you yourself will be with (me). And grace will also be readily accessible to you through me. And what you have gained for yourself until today [was] from the will of [the father] of light (6 lines lacuna) . . . (114.2) is [nothing] to be revealed, since they do not do as it is read to them.

Koustaios, the Son of the Treasure of Life [And again] Pattikios, while he was weeping, said to him, "Son, why do you say [these things]? For now, by making this utterance you have gotten rid of and moved the entire [sect] . . . I . . . of you from the midst . . . and (6 lines lacuna)" . . . (115.1) "And it . . . these things . . . not knowing what had been begotten. For you have built the house, but another has come and lived in it. And you have become a vehicle for that one, but another has begun a war with it, [accomplishing] his intention with it. For you adorned clothing also, but another has donned it. For I, Mani . . . (4 lines lacuna) . . . the whole [world] . . . of someone (4 lines lacuna) . . . (116.3) of that good one. For this one is the one who is my guide, just as he wills and as is fitting for him. Know this, recognizing that I myself do not follow that sect, and neither shall I follow its law.

Timotheos Well, [from] the assembly of [the holy ones] . . . I went out (8 lines lacuna) . . . (117.1) The . . . of [that woman] . . . When we [came first] there in the garden of the . . . village, we [rested]. And when I saw . . ., I said to that woman, "Strange people have [asked us] and [produced] differing and new words about God. . . . And they are (10 lines lacuna) . . . (118.2) all . . . secure . . . of them, the . . ." And she was amazed at [my] wisdom, which . . . not . . . to her. [And likewise] also Pattikios . . . was amazed. [For] he had never heard this speech from [me]. And with prudence he was saying, "When I heard this teaching, [I was moved] . . . (6 lines lacuna) . . . of humility (5 lines lacuna) . . . (119.5) They saw [a vision] in an image of a human being [like] an angel of God, so that they were all moved at what they saw. [After] this, that vision of the human was hidden from [them] and therefore . . . I . . . until (13 lines lacuna) . . . (120.5) [to reveal these things] to me. [And from] the will [of God, I was aware] who it was that [was with] you." And likewise that woman stood and worshipped before me, saying, "I give thanks to God who has made the . . . [You came] here in order that I might see [the magnitude of the power of God. . . ." (10 lines lacuna, including a probable section break).

(121.4) But . . . I did [not] remain. And from [the country] of the Medes, I went [to the brothers (and sisters)] in Ganzak. And there was a stone of tin there. [And] when we went first [into] the [city] of Ganzak, those who with the brothers (and sisters) were anxious about the (11 lines lacuna) . . . (122.4) "Who are you [or what power] do you have?" And I [said to] him, "I am a [physician]." And he answered me, "If you agree, come to my house. For my daughter is being tossed about by an [illness]." And I [went] with him and [found] the girl [stricken] and . . . by an [illness] (7 lines lacuna) . . . (123.1) And, although there were also other . . . men present, he [fell] before [me] and said, "[Ask me] if you want something." [Well, I] said to [him], "I need [nothing] of gold or silver possessions." I took from him only [the day's food] for my brothers (and sisters) [who were with] me.

Ti[motheos] And [again my lord said] (7 lines lacuna) . . . (124.1) he said, "[Inquire] into your [birth] in which [you were begotten] as the body [and] into the truth [which I] have preached as good news [to you. And] thus from your [commandment] ambassadors and [apostles] have been sent forth in every place, and this hope [and the] heralding of peace will be proclaimed [by them] in every city [in which] you wish to go."

[N. N.] (10 lines lacuna) . . . (125.4) And when we were walking [about] . . . in the midst of the mountains and Pattikios was with me, suddenly a wind [blew] so that the sand was stirred up in a storm and [our senses] were thrown into confusion. And I . . . before Pattikios . . . Then that one, my most splendid Syzygos, was beside me [strengthening and encouraging] me. (7 lines lacuna) . . .

(126.2) N. N. the Teacher and N. N. the Bishop Well, the most blessed and shining one (the Syzygos) [then] lifted me up and carried me away into ineffable places which lie unnoticed by these places of humans in which [we spend time]. He showed [me everything] there. And [I saw] in them immense mountains [and] . . . [neighboring] (8 lines lacuna) . . . (127.2) and dissimilar [to those] in these [regions]. And there were also . . . between them and the sweetest, freshest waters. And [he brought me] up onto the [loftiest] mountain, on which I saw [a person], the hair of whose body was a cubit long and [shaggy], adorned with locks of hair. . . . When . . . one of the (8 lines lacuna) . . . (128.2) "Tell [me] the things to do with knowledge; for [this] reason you have come [up] here." And I told him in the . . . so that wisdom rose up into him. I [proclaimed] to him the [resting], the commandments, and the worship of the heavenly lights.

And [again] I said to him, "How did [the hairiness] of [your] body, which [is] different from [all] people [come to be]? . . . Into the (7 lines lacuna) . . . (129.2) my . . . tree . . . and from the [best fruit] I partook, [and] from that [time] this hair has been upon [my] body." And while I was still standing there, he was snatched away from before [me], and he entered into that place, where I saw . . . the people. And he became a herald of [the hope] in that [place], and he [showed the people the] wisdom. (6 lines lacuna) . . . (130.1) I [went] into a place that lay unnoticed and separated from [those] cities. And likewise in it [there was] also a throng of people and a great many cities. And immediately, as I first came into that place, the [heavenly light] of the daytime appeared, and the [ruler] of [that] region [came out] for the hunt. Well, my most splendid governor, the [most trustworthy] Syzygos, then stood [by me and said to] me, (5 lines lacuna) . . . (131.1) but [not far] from the ruler and [his] nobles . . . When [the ruler and his] nobles saw me, they fell into agitation and [wonder] . . . and for me, so . . . to them . . . When I had drawn near to [them], the ruler and his [nobles] dismounted from their [horses]. And [I stood before] him and worshipped (8 lines lacuna) . . . (132.2) to him. and [I uttered] wisdom and [the] commandments before [him], and I [showed] him every deed.

And during the [not] few days that I stayed [there], he sat before [me with] his nobles. [And] I revealed [to them] the difference between [the two] natures [and the matters concerning the beginning] and [middle] and end. (8 lines lacuna) . . . (133.1) he regarded [me as a brother] and received [everything] that he heard . . . [from] me. And [after his] most honored work had been fulfilled in me, immediately, when the [ruler] was seated and his nobles were before [him], this most splendid one flew down and [stood by me, and . . . [to] me. . . . And the ruler and his nobles (8 lines lacuna) . . . (134.2) [And then the] ruler was strengthened in wisdom and was planted [in knowledge] and faith. And likewise [his] nobles also were [filled] with faith. And the ruler accepted [with joy the commandments] that I spoke to him, and [he ordered that they] be [made clear] and [preached] through [his] kingdom. . . . place . . . this and . . . after (8 lines lacuna) . . . (135.3) and from [that] time, this religion was sent out into that place.

Then the most [splendid] one led [me into] that [place], [where] he had separated me from [Pattikios]. When he saw me, he [rejoiced] greatly, [kissed] me, and [said to me], "Where did [you] go . . . alone (10 lines lacuna) . . . (136.2) [for with my own] eyes I have beheld the working of his power, which is beyond [sight and for which] I have waited by my custom. Therefore also . . ." And my master [said] to him, ". . . is your own . . ." He led [him] away [into] very high places and said], "I have done [these things according to the] will [of your father]. And he [sent me] to you."

[N. N.] (7 lines lacuna) . . . (137.3) until . . . [I went] into a [certain] village
called S . . . and I went into the synagogue of the . . . bad . . . of the truth. [And
the] leader of the [sect] spoke [a word to me], "The strictness of the teaching
[of our ancestors] (10 lines lacuna) . . . (138.2) [He made] a dispute with me
[before] the men of his [sect]. In all ways he was [overcome] and [merited]
laughter, with the result that he was filled with [jealousy] and evil. And he sat
down in the manner of [magicians] and [uttered] incantations of his . . . which
. . . they sing over . . . and . . . an incantation . . . to . . . he said, "(6 lines lacuna)
. . . (139.1) in order that . . . Pattikios . . . is healthy." And he thus uttered these
things, singing incantations by . . . evil, so that his intention was [brought to
nought]. For as much as [he used] words of [incantation, my] master undid
[his] evil. [And immediately] that one, my most [trustworthy Syzygos] flew
down and appeared (8 lines lacuna) . . . in a [village] . . . recover . . . into
Pharat, the city near the island of the Mesenians.

[N. N.] the Teacher, (and) Ana the Brother of Zacheas the Disciple [When]
my lord and [Pattikios], the master of his household, had gone into [Pharat,
he preached] in the assembly of the baptists. "(8 lines lacuna) . . . (141.1) [his]
kingdom and power." And we marveled [greatly] at him, astonished at his
words.

When it was the [hour] of prayer, we said [to] Pattikios, "[Let us pray], for
the ordinance of God calls my lord [and us] to prayer. . . ." [Pattikios] begged
us (11 lines lacuna) . . . (142.3) in distinction [to] us.

And again, [in] the hour . . . of fasting . . . he went out and begged for alms
[outside] houses. . . . He did not stand. . . . And I [said to] him, "Why have
you [not] partaken [from our table] . . .?" (12 lines lacuna) . . . (143.2) this
thing . . . ". . . is with your son and the elders and teachers." And [in] him [I]
saw [formerly] that [with all] wisdom, [ingenuity], and the clear truth of the
books, he was a [witness to] us . . . and that . . . distinction . . . of [our] teachers
(10 lines lacuna, including a probable section break) . . .

(144.3) And he was . . . in Pharat, by the name of Og[gias?], a person, [dis-
tinguished] by his [power] and authority of which . . . of men. [And I saw] the
merchants, that they were [sealing] his wares in order to [sail] for Persia and
India, but they were not [getting under way] until he boarded (11 lines lacuna).
. . . (145.3) him . . . to you. Then [he said to] me, "I wish [to board] the ship
and [go] to India [to] . . . receive . . . if this . . ." And I said [to him], "I . . . you
. . ." (12 lines lacuna).

Pages 146–70 are too fragmentary to permit translation.

Bibliography

Betz, Hans Dieter. 1986. "Paul in the Mani Biography (Codex Manichaicus Coloniensis)."
    In *Codex Manichaicus Coloniensis: Atti del Simposio Internazionale (Rende-Amantea 3–7
    settembre 1984)*, ed. Luigi Cirillo, 215–34. Cosenza: Marra.

Bianchi, Ugo. 1983. "Some Reflections on the Greek Origins of Gnostic Ontology, and the Christian Origin of the Gnostic Saviour." In *The New Testament and Gnosis: Essays in Honor of Robert McL. Wilson*, ed. A.H.B. Logan and A.J.M. Wedderburn, 38–45. Edinburgh: T. and T. Clark.

Cameron, Ron, and Arthur J. Dewey, trans. 1979. *The Cologne Mani Codex (P. Colon. inv. nr. 4780: "Concerning the Origin of His Body")*. Society of Biblical Literature Texts and Translations 15, Early Christian Literature Series 3. Missoula, Mont.: Scholars Press.

Cirillo, Luigi. 1986. *Codex Manichaicus Coloniensis: Atti del Simposio Internazionale (Rende-Amantea 3–7 settembre 1984)*. Cosenza: Marra.

———. 1990. *Codex Manichaicus Coloniensis: Atti del Secondo Simposio Internazionale (Consenza 27–28 maggio 1988)*. Cosenza: Marra.

Henrichs, Albert. 1973. "Mani and the Babylonian Baptists: A Historical Confrontation." *Harvard Studies in Classical Philology* 77: 23–59.

———. 1979. "The Cologne Mani Codex Reconsidered. *Harvard Studies in Classical Philology* 83: 339–67.

———. 1981. "Literary Criticism of the Cologne Mani Codex." In *The Rediscovery of Gnosticism*. Vol. 2, *Sethian Gnosticism*, ed. Bentley Layton, 724–33. Leiden: E.J. Brill.

———. 1986. "The Timing of Supernatural Events in the Cologne Mani Codex." In *Codex Manichaicus Coloniensis: Atti del Simposio Internazionale (Rende-Amantea 3–7 settembre 1984)*, ed. Luigi Cirillo, 183–204. Cosenza: Marra.

Henrichs, A., and L. Koenen. 1970. "Ein Griechischer Mani Codex (P. Colon. inv. nr. 4780")." *Zeitschrift für Papyrologie und Epigraphik* 5: 97–216.

———. 1975. "Der Kölner Mani Kodex (P. Colon. inv. nr. 4780) ΠΕΡΙ ΤΗΣ ΓΕΝΝΗΣ ΤΟΥ ΣΩΜΑΤΟΣ ΑΥΤΟΥ, Edition der Seiten 1–72." *Zeitschrift für Papyrologie und Epigraphik* 19: 1–85.

———. 1978. "Der Kölner Mani Kodex (P. Colon. inv. nr. 4780) ΠΕΡΙ ΤΗΣ ΓΕΝΝΗΣ ΤΟΥ ΣΩΜΑΤΟΣ ΑΥΤΟΥ, Edition der Seiten 72, 8–99, 9." *Zeitschrift für Papyrologie und Epigraphik* 32: 87–199.

———. 1981. "Der Kölner Mani Kodex (P. Colon. inv. nr. 4780) ΠΕΡΙ ΤΗΣ ΓΕΝΝΗΣ ΤΟΥ ΣΩΜΑΤΟΣ ΑΥΤΟΥ, Edition der Seiten 99, 10–120." *Zeitschrift für Papyrologie und Epigraphik* 44: 201–318.

———. 1982. "Der Kölner Mani Kodex (P. Colon. inv. nr. 4780) ΠΕΡΙ ΤΗΣ ΓΕΝΝΗΣ ΤΟΥ ΣΩΜΑΤΟΣ ΑΥΤΟΥ, Edition der Seiten 121–192." *Zeitschrift für Papyrologie und Epigraphik* 48: 201–318.

Koenen, Ludwig. 1981. "From Baptism to the Gnosis of Manichaeism." In *The Rediscovery of Gnosticism*. Vol. 2, *Sethian Gnosticism*, ed. Bentley Layton, 734–56. Leiden: E. J. Brill.

Koenen, Ludwig, and Cornelia Römer. 1985. *Der Kölner Mani-Kodex: Abbildungen und Diplomatischer Text*. Bonn: Habelt.

———. 1987. *Der Kölner Mani-Kodex: Über das Werden seines Leibes, Kritische Edition*. Papyrologica Coloniensia 14. Opladen: Westdeutscher Verlag.

Maier, Johann. 1986. "Zum Problem der jüdischen Gemeinden Mesopotamiens im 2. und 3. n. Chr. im Blick auf den CMC." In *Codex Manichaicus Coloniensis: Atti del Simposio Internazionale (Rende-Amantea 3–7 settembre 1984)*, ed. Luigi Cirillo, 37–67. Cosenza: Marra.

Ries, Julien. 1993. "L'Emergence de la figure prophétique de Mani selon le Codex de Cologne." *Studia Patristica* 24: 399–405.

Rudolph, Kurt. 1974. "Die Bedeutung des Kölner Mani-Codex für die Manichäismusforschung: Vorläufige Anmerkungen." In *Mélanges d'histoire des religions offerts à Henri-Charles Puech*, 471–86.

———. 1986. "Jüdische und christliche Täufertraditionen im Spiegel des CMC." In *Codex Manichaicus Coloniensis: Atti del Simposio Internazionale (Rende-Amantea 3–7 settembre 1984)*, ed. Luigi Cirillo, 69–80. Cosenza: Marra.

─── 13 ───

Tales of Holy Fools

Derek Krueger

Holy folly surely ranks as one of the more peculiar forms of Christian ascetic practice in Late Antiquity. Some nuns and monks pretended to be simple or insane as part of their devotion to God. Observers, however, found their behavior embarrassing or scandalous, not understanding that it was a pretense. At its root, the practice of simulated madness cultivated the virtue of humility. Success in more conventional ascetic activities, such as fasting, sexual abstinence, keeping all-night vigils, or living in a forbidding environment often brought fame. Others might shower the ascetic with honor or glory. In order to deflect the praise of others, these holy fools feigned madness and became objects of derision. Thus, although they carried out ascetic professions in private, in the eyes of others they were deemed idiots. They concealed their saintliness behind bizarre and occasionally obscene behavior. Whereas monasticism already involved a rejection of norms of the world, holy folly appeared to involve a rejection of the norms of monasticism itself (Krueger 1996, 43–47).

In looking to explain and perhaps to justify such behavior, Christian authors narrating about holy folly claimed the disguise had biblical inspiration. Paul had written, "If one wishes to be wise in this age, let him be a fool, that he may become wise" (1 Cor. 3:28). He also said of Christians, "We are fools for Christ's sake" (1 Cor. 4:10). While Paul was concerned with the apparent folly of Christian beliefs in the eyes of outsiders, the authors of the tales of holy fools, such as Leontius of Neapolis (Krueger 1996, 65–66), presented holy folly as a literal fulfillment of Paul's command. To some degree, this behavior might also ground itself as an imitation of Christ; many in the Galilee had taken Jesus himself to be a madman, possessed by a demon (Mark 3:21, 30). Furthermore, like Mark's Jesus keeping his Messiahship a secret, the fools concealed their real identity, and often God caused it to be revealed only at their death.

There were many ways to play the fool. The selections translated here attest to the popularity of stories about holy fools between the fourth and the seventh centuries C.E. Nevertheless, these four narratives do not suggest that holy folly had yet developed as a consistent category of practice. Some play the simpleton, others act out. Moreover, the location and character of the strange behavior shift over time. The earliest texts, deriving from the late fourth century, describe fools who remain in monasteries. The nun at Tabennisi (along the banks of the Nile in Upper Egypt) performs menial tasks in the common kitchen, while the monk in the community of Silvanus spends the day in his cell counting pebbles. The two later texts, deriving from the late sixth and early seventh century, tell of the antics of monks who let loose in the city. Mark and Symeon inhabit the urban market-place, where they disrupt commerce, cavort with women and make themselves a public spectacle. Performing works of charity, they are implicit critics of urban life, revealing the folly of the masses.

While folly provides the saint with anonymity, the fool's eventual exposure gives the other characters in the story an opportunity for instruction. The text's audience, also, is invited to learn. The moral point of the story turns on the gap between appearance and reality, the eyes of humans and the eyes of God. Ironically, the holy truth is frequently hidden from church leaders and the laity and must be divinely revealed. And even the identification of holiness in the community is fragile. Shortly after the truth is learned, the nun at Tabennisi disappears; Mark the Fool dies. By classifying holiness as obscure, these tales encourage kindness toward others, particularly those afflicted with mental disorders, since they may be disguised saints. One should treat all as if they were Christ himself. Or to put another spin on it, holiness may be among us, perhaps where we least expect it. At the same time, these didactic tales reveal God's truth through humor. Their Christian authors were not afraid to be funny.

In time the holy fool would become a widely recognized type of saint described by the Greek word *salos* (plural *saloi*). Nevertheless, the term is unattested before the fourth century and is still derogatory slang in these texts, meaning something like "idiot," "madman," or "crazy person" (Grosdidier de Matons 1970, 272–92; Déroche 1995, 154–62; Krueger 1996, 62–66). And although the brief narratives presented here describe monastics in Egypt, Palestine, and Syria, it is unlikely that the practice itself was widespread, since each of the tales assumes that the aberrant asceticism described is a novelty, surprising because unexpected.

The subsequent history of the holy fool demonstrates the popularity of these tales. In the middle of the seventh century, Leontius of Neapolis composed an extended biography of Symeon the Fool (translation in Krueger 1996), where Symeon defecates in public, eats baked beans (bound to make him fart) on fasting days, and eats raw meat. In those episodes, Leontius connects Symeon's behavior with the counter-cultural Greco-Roman Cynic philosophers, particularly Diogenes of Sinope (Krueger 1996). In later centuries, the practice of holy folly and the veneration of holy fools became Christian institutions, particularly among the Eastern Orthodox. The tenth-century Byzantine *Life of Andrew the Fool* (Rydén 1995) circulated widely. And the "Fools for Christ's Sake" played an important part in the development of Russian culture, as can be seen in the colorful, fanciful Cathedral of St. Basil in Red Square in Moscow (dedicated to a sixteenth-century fool), the wise fool who mournfully concludes Moussorgsky's opera *Boris Godunov*, and Dostoyevsky's novel *The Idiot* (Thompson 1987).

The Nun Who Feigned Madness
Palladius, *Lausiac History* 34

Palladius composed the *Lausiac History*, a series of brief accounts of holy people he had encountered, around 419 while a small-town bishop in Asia Minor. Earlier in his life he practiced monasticism in Palestine and in the regions around Alexandria in Egypt, where he became a disciple of Evagrius of Pontus. During the 390s he traveled widely among the solitary hermitages and monastic communities up and down the Nile. Writing more than twenty years after his journeys, Palladius dedicated the work to his patron Lausus, chamberlain of the court of Theodosius II in Constantinople; thus, although the work illustrates the desert of the Egyptian monks and nuns, it was intended for a lay, urban audience. This excerpt is part of a description of a monastery of four hundred women attached to the larger men's foundation of Saint Pachomius at Tabennisi in the Thebaid of Upper Egypt (Vogt 1987; Meyer 1964, 5–7). The Greek contains the earliest extant instance of the term *salos*, here used in the feminine (*salē*) (Krueger 1996, 57–58; Grosdidier de Matons 1970, 283–85). The text translated is *Palladio: La storia lausiaca*, edited by G.J.M. Bartelink, Vite dei Santi 2 (Milan: Mondadori, 1974), 162–67.

The Nun Who Feigned Madness

In this monastery there was another virgin, who feigned madness and demonic possession. And the others were so completely disgusted by her that they never ate with her, which was just as she wanted it. When she wandered into the kitchen she did all the menial chores, and she was, as it is said, "the sponge of the monastery." Thus she truly fulfilled the Scripture, "If any one among you thinks that he is wise in this age, let him become a fool that he may become wise" [1 Cor. 3:18]. She tied a rag around her head—although all the others had cut their hair short and wore cowls. Thus she used to serve. Not one of the other four hundred nuns ever saw her chew food in all the years of her life. She never sat at the table. She never partook of a morsel of bread, but instead was content to sponge the crumbs off the tables and scrub the pots for them. She never insulted anyone, nor did she grumble, neither did she speak either little or much, although she was beaten and insulted, cursed and loathed.

Now an angel appeared to the holy Piteroum, an anchorite who lived on Mount Porphyrites, a most worthy man, and said to him, "Why do you think so much of yourself for being pious and for living in a place such as this? Do you want to see a woman more pious than you are? Go to the women's monastery at Tabennisi, and there you will find one who has a band on her head. She is better than you. Although she is beaten by the whole throng, she has never taken her heart from God. But you, while you dwell here in body, your thoughts are wandering throughout the city." And he, who had never before gone away, left that monastery, and bid the superiors to allow him to enter the women's monastery. They did not fear to lead him in, since he was well regarded and quite old.

Thus he entered and demanded to see everyone. She did not appear. Finally he said to them, "Bring me all of them, for one is still missing." They said to him, "We have one inside in the kitchen who is a fool"—for that is what they call the afflicted. He said to them, "Bring her to me. Let me see her." They went to call her, but she did not answer, perhaps because she perceived what this was about, or because it had been revealed to her. They dragged her out by force and said to her, "The holy Piteroum wishes to see you"—for he was famous. When she came he saw the rag over her brow, and falling before her feet he said to her, "Bless me!" In similar fashion she too fell before his feet and said, "You bless me, lord." All the women were astonished and said to him, "Abba, don't be offended by her insolence, she is a fool." Piteroum said to all of them, "It is you who are fools, for she is our Amma,"—for thus they call the spiritual mothers—"And I pray that I may be found as worthy as she is on the Day of Judgment." When the women heard this, they fell before his feet, each confessing various things: one confessed to pouring slop from her plate on top of her; another to beating her with her fists; another to spreading mustard on her nose. In short they each confessed various outrages. Then after praying over them he left. And after a few days, she could not bear the praise and honor of her sisters, and she was weighed down by their apologies; so she left the monastery. And where she went or where she hid or how she died, no one knows.

A Monk in the Monastery of Abba Silvanus

This story is found in an anonymous fragment of a Greek text concerning the monastery of Abba Silvanus published by F. Nau as an appendix to his edition of John Rufus's *Plerophoriae*. Taking place at the end of the fourth century or beginning of the fifth, it is roughly contemporaneous with the previous story recounted by Palladius. Silvanus had practiced monasticism at Skete in Egypt before taking twelve disciples with him to Mount Sinai around 380. Later he transported his community to Palestine, settling in the region of Gaza. The community described here is not a communal coenobium, but rather a *lavra,* a group of monks dwelling in cells scattered along a pathway. The monks would assemble on Saturdays and Sundays to worship together and share a common meal (Chitty 1966, 71–74). The monk feigning madness actually practices a rigorous mental asceticism, analyzing the moral content of each of his thoughts in a manner similar to that taught by Evagrius of Pontus in his *Praktikos*. As in the previous example, the true identity of the fool is revealed by outside visitors, in this case three men whom the abbot understands to be "holy messengers," like the angels who visited Abraham and Sarah (and the city of Sodom) in Genesis 18–19. The Greek text was published by F. Nau, *Patrologia Orientalis* 8 (1912): 178–79. An English translation of a somewhat different Syriac version is included in Anân Ishô, *The Book of Paradise*, translated by E. A. Wallis Budge (London, 1904), 1:388–90.

A Monk in the Monastery of Abba Silvanus

One of the fathers said that next to the river, near the village where the blessed Silvanus lived in Palestine, dwelt a monk who made a pretense of madness. Whenever other monks met him, he broke into laughter, after which they left him and went away. Once, three fathers came as a group to visit Abba Silvanus. And after saying a prayer, they bid him to send someone with them so that they might behold the monks in their cells. And they said to the abbot, "Have the goodness to tell each monk so that he may meet with us." And the abbot said to the monk who was near them, "Take them to all the fathers." But privately he charged him, saying, "See that you do not take them to that fool, lest they be scandalized."

As they were going about the cells of the monks, the fathers said to their guide, "Have the goodness to take us to everyone." And he said to them, "Okay." But he did not take them to the cell of the fool, in accord with the abbot's orders. When they returned to the abbot, Silvanus said to them, "Have you seen the monks?" They said, "Yes, and we thank you. But we regret that we did not go to all of them." And the abbot said to the one who had taken them around, "Did I not tell you to take them to everyone?" And the monk said, "You did, father." Thus when the fathers were leaving, they said to the abbot, "Truly we are grateful that we saw the monks, but we regret one thing, namely that we did not see all of them." Later the monk told the abbot privately, "To the mad monk I did not take them."

Then after the fathers departed, the abbot thought to himself about what had happened. And he went to visit that monk who feigned madness, and without knocking he gently opened the hideskin door and burst in on the monk. He found him sitting in his cell, with two small baskets, one on his right and one on his left. And when he saw the abbot, true to his manner, he began to laugh. And the abbot said to him, "Stop this right now, and tell me why you sit as you do." But he laughed again. And Abba Silvanus said to him, "You know that except on Saturdays and Sundays I do not come out of my cell. But now I have come in the middle of the week, for God has sent me to you." Then fearing the old man, the monk obeyed and said, "Forgive me, father, but during the morning I sit with these pebbles in front of me. And if a good thought comes to me, I throw the pebble into the basket on the right, but if a wicked thought comes to me, I throw the pebble into the basket on the left. Then in the evening I count the pebbles. And if I find more on the right, I eat. But if I find more on the left, I do not eat. And again the next morning, if a wicked thought comes to me, I say to myself, 'See what you are doing! Again you will not eat.' " When Abba Silvanus heard this, he marveled and said, "Truly, the fathers who visited me were holy messengers who wished to reveal the monk's virtue, for I have received abundant grace and spiritual gladness because of their coming."

Mark the Fool
The Life of Daniel of Skete 3

Daniel was superior of the monks at Skete in Egypt from the middle of the sixth century to around 576. The *Life of Daniel* is less a biography of this Abba than a series of vignettes about the monks, nuns, and lay people that he encountered. Most of the tales contain wondrous and ironic twists, and a number tell of individuals who practiced unusual forms of asceticism, which concealed their sanctity. Daniel and his disciple encounter Mark, who had been a monk—perhaps a hermit—for fifteen years, but who remained a slave to lust. Mark spent the next eight years at the Pempton Monastery, five miles outside of Alexandria, before entering the city to spend eight additional years disguised as a fool. (Grosdidier de Matons 1970, 287–89; Clugnet 1901, 13–14). Altogether Mark had spent thirty years in his monastic profession—the same number of years Jesus had lived, according to Eastern tradition, before he was crucified. Like Jesus, Mark's true identity is revealed only at death. The Greek text translated here is found in *Vie (et récits) de l'Abbé Daniel le Scétiote*, edited by Léon Clugnet, 12–14.

Mark the Fool

This blessed Daniel of Skete had a disciple. And a brother named Sergius lived together with this disciple for a short while before falling asleep in Christ. After Brother Sergius's death, Abba Daniel took his disciple into his confidence, for he loved him very much. Therefore, one day the older monk took his disciple and went to Alexandria, for it was the custom that the superior of Skete would go up to visit the Patriarch of Alexandria for the great Easter festival.

They arrived in the city around the tenth hour, and while they were walking down the avenue they saw a brother naked except for a towel around his loins. But this monk was only pretending that he was a fool. And there were other crazy people also with him. This monk was going around as a fool, uttering nonsense, stealing things in the marketplace and handing them out to the other fools. Now he was called Mark of the Horse, for he hung out at the hippodrome.

It was there that Mark the Fool acted crazy. Everyday he redistributed one hundred copper coins, and it was there that he slept in the bleachers. From the hundred coins he bought himself ten coins' worth of provisions and handed out everything else to the other fools. The whole city knew Mark of the Horse on account of his madness.

Daniel said to his disciple, "Go see where that fool lives." So he went off and asked, and they said to him, "He has gone to the hippodrome, for he is a fool." On the next day, after he had met with the patriarch, in accord with God's plan, Daniel found Mark the Fool in the great Tetrapylon Church. Daniel ran and caught him, and Mark began to cry out, saying, "Men of Alexandria, Help!" Then the fool insulted the old man. A great crowd gathered around them, but the disciple, being wary, stood some distance away. And everyone said to Daniel, "Do not be offended by his insolence; he is a fool." The old monk said to them, "It is you who are fools, for today I have not found a single person in this city who is not a fool except for him." The clergymen of the church rushed to meet Daniel and said to him, "Why in the world did this fool do this to you?" Daniel said to them, "Please take him to the patriarch." So they took him. And Daniel said to the patriarch, "Today in this city there is no vessel of holiness such as this." Now the patriarch knew that Daniel had been fully assured by God concerning the man, and he threw himself at the fool's feet and began to adjure him to reveal himself to them for who he was.

Then coming to himself, Mark confessed, saying that he had been a monk and that the demon of lust had had dominion over him for fifteen years. "So I said to myself, 'Mark, for fifteen years you have been a slave to the Enemy. Now, in like manner, be a slave to Christ.' And I went away to the Pempton Monastery, and remained there eight years. And during the eighth year I said to myself, 'Now go to the city and make yourself a fool for another eight years.' And behold, today my eight years of folly are complete." And they all cried out with one accord.

Mark spent the night in the patriarch's residence with Daniel. And when day came, Daniel said to his disciple, "Brother, please call Abba Mark, so that he might say a prayer for us, before we return to our monastery." And the disciple left and found Mark asleep in the Lord and he went to announce to Daniel that Abba Mark had died. And Daniel told the patriarch, and the patriarch told the military commander, and he ordered there to be a holiday in the city. And Daniel sent his disciple to Skete saying, "Sound the gong, and assemble the fathers and say to them, 'Come and praise the monk.'" And all of Skete went up to Alexandria dressed in white, carrying olive branches and palm fronds, and also the monks of the Enaton and the Cells, and those in the desert of Nitria, and all the lavras in the region of Alexandria, so that the corpse was not buried for five days, and it was necessary for them to embalm the body of the blessed Mark. And the whole of Alexandria, bearing branches and candles and sprinkling the city with tears, turned out to bury the honored remains of the blessed Mark the Fool, extolling and praising the benevolent God who gives such grace and glory to those who love him, now and forever and for all time. Amen.

Symeon the Fool
Evagrius Scholasticus, *Ecclesiastical History* 4.34.

Evagrius Scholasticus, a lawyer who lived in Antioch, wrote his *Ecclesiastical History* in the last decade of the sixth century. While the work is largely concerned with Church politics and the history of the city of Antioch, Evagrius occasionally digresses to relate information about holy men active in his region. Symeon simulated folly in the Syrian city of Emesa near the midpoint of the sixth century. In addition to violating ascetic conventions concerning food, in two of the episodes recounted here, Symeon appears to break rules regarding sex, and thus bears resemblance to tales of other ascetics who converted licentious women and prostitutes after visiting with them (Krueger 1996, 66–71). Evagrius relates that Symeon adopted his guise having "thoroughly stripped off the garment of vainglory," suggesting that he practiced folly not as a tool to gain humility or self-control, but rather after having already achieved such a state. Thus Symeon's folly is a manifestation of his humble virtue. A few decades later, in the 640s, Leontius of Neapolis composed a much longer and even more raucous *Life of Symeon the Fool* (translated in Krueger 1996, 131–71). The text translated here is found in *The Ecclesiastical History of Evagrius with the Scholia,* edited by J. Bidez and L. Parmentier, (1898; reprint New York: AMS, 1979), 182–84.

Life of Symeon the Fool

There was also in Emesa, a man called Symeon who had so thoroughly stripped off the garment of vainglory as to appear insane to those who did not know him, although he was filled with all divine wisdom and grace. For the most part, this Symeon lived by himself, letting absolutely no one know when or how he worshipped the Deity, nor when he was fasting or eating. Often, too, while on the streets in the market, he seemed to be deprived of his composure, and to be utterly senseless or witless. And when he slipped into a tavern, when he was hungry, he ate whatever food he could get his hands on. But if anyone showed him reverence with a nod of the head, he quickly and angrily left the place, for he feared lest his private virtue be discovered by many people. Such was the conduct of Symeon in the public market. But he had certain acquaintances with whom he associated without any dissembling.

Now, one of his friends had a slave girl, who had been corrupted by someone and got pregnant. When she was compelled by her owners to name the man who had run off, she said that Symeon had secretly coupled with her and that she was pregnant by him; and she said that she would swear that this was so, and if necessary, that she would expose him. When Symeon heard this, he conceded, saying that the flesh he bore was frail. And when the story was spread around to everyone, and Symeon, as it seemed, was greatly disgraced, he went into hiding and pretended to be ashamed. When the time came for the woman to give birth, she was set in the usual position, and her labor pains caused great and intolerable suffering and brought her into imminent danger, but the birth made no progress. Therefore, they begged Symeon, who had come out on purpose, to pray for her. He declared openly that the woman would not give birth until she had said who had fathered her child. Once she had done this, and named the real father, the baby came out immediately, midwifed by the truth.

Once he was seen to enter the chamber of a courtesan, and having closed the door, he stayed alone with her for a long time. And when he opened the door again, he went away looking in every direction lest anyone should see him. Suspicion arose so that those who had witnessed it brought the woman out, and inquired why Symeon had come to her and why the visit had lasted so long. She swore that for the past three days, for lack of basic necessities, she had tasted nothing but water, and that Symeon had brought her food and provisions and a jug of wine, and that after he had closed the door, he set a table before her to feed her and bid her to eat until she had had enough to take her fill. She then brought out the leavings of what he had brought her.

Also, just before the earthquake that shook Phoenicia Maritima, and from which Berytus, Byblus, and Tripolis in particular suffered, Symeon raised a whip in his hand, and struck most of the columns in the marketplace, shouting, "Stand still, if you must dance." Now since nothing the man did was meaningless, those who happened to be around remembered which of the columns he passed by without striking. These soon afterwards fell down on account of the earthquake.

He also did many other things, which require a separate treatise.

Bibliography

Chitty, Derwas J. 1966. *The Desert a City: An Introduction to the Study of Egyptian and Palestinian Monasticism under the Christian Empire.* Oxford: Basil Blackwell.

Clugnet, Léon. 1901. *Vie (et récits) de l'Abbé Daniel le Scétiote.* Paris: Picard et Fils.

Déroche, Vincent. 1995. "La spiritualité du *salos*," in Déroche, *Etudes sur Léontios de Néapolis.* Uppsala: Almqvist and Wiksell.

Grosdidier de Matons, José. 1970. "Les Thèmes d'édification dans la Vie d'André Salos." *Travaux et mémoires* 4: 277–329.

Krueger, Derek. 1996. *Symeon the Holy Fool: Leontius's "Life" and the Late Antique City.* Berkeley and Los Angeles: University of California Press.

Robert Meyer. 1964. *Palladius: The Lausiac History.* New York: Newman.

Rydén, Lennart, ed. and trans. 1995. *The Life of St. Andrew the Fool.* 2 vols. Uppsala: Acta Universitatis Upsaliensis.

Saward, John. 1980. *Perfect Fools: Folly for Christ's Sake in Catholic and Orthodox Spirituality.* Oxford: Oxford University Press.

Thompson, Ewa M. 1987. *Understanding Russia: The Holy Fool in Russian Culture.* Lanham, Md.: University Press of America.

Vogt, Kari. 1987. "La Moniale folle du monastère des Tabbenésiotes: Une interprétation du chapitre 34 de l'Historia Lausiaca de Pallade." *Symbolae Osloenses* 62: 95–108.

Locating Religion in Society: Community

— 14 —

Vision for the City

Nisibis in Ephrem's *Hymns on Nicomedia*

David Bundy

The history of Syriac Christianity begins with the cities of Nisibis and Edessa. These cities were on the ancient trade routes that connected Byzantium and Antioch with the East. They were for a time secondary to Palmyra to the South. However, after the rebellion of Queen Zenobia against the Romans, and the resulting destruction of that emporium, Edessa and Nisibis increased in importance as frontier posts and trading centers. During this period any semblance of independence of the border states, such as Osrhoene (with its capital at Edessa), from Byzantine imperial authority, came to an effective end.

The year 359 C.E. was an important year in the city of Nisibis. In the spring of that year, Nisibis endured a siege by the Persians led by Shapur II. In 359 the baptistery attached to the church of Jacob of Nisibis was built. This carefully crafted building, dedicated by Bishop Vologeses, the third bishop of Nisibis recognized by Ephrem of Syria (306–372 C.E.), was replete with its inscription in Greek and still stands (Bundy, forthcoming). The westward vision reflected in the choice of a language for the dedicatory inscription was put into perspective by the *Hymns on Nicomedia*. This collection of sixteen hymns (mēmrē) was ostensibly written about the destruction of the Byzantine imperial summer residence on the western tip of Anatolia by the devastating earthquake of 358 C.E. Hymns one through nine purport to be a description of the social, cultural, and religious situation in Nicomedia before, during, and after the earthquake. However, as far as we know, Ephrem did not visit Nicomedia either before or after the earthquake. The hymns, as was made explicit in hymns ten through sixteen, were actually reflections upon life within the city of Nisibis. To make his argument brief, Ephrem understood the disaster that befell Nicomedia to be a consequence of sin within the city and he urged Nisibis to repent and live justly to avoid the same fate.

The genre of mēmrē is a traditional Syriac literary form. These are discourses, of varying length, that appear in both rhymed and prose forms, characterized by an isosyllabic structure. These were composed by Ephrem in seven syllable form. The *Hymns on Nicomedia* was originally written in Syriac but has survived the vicissitudes of Middle Eastern history, complete, only in an Armenian translation. This Armenian translation was done quite soon after the texts were composed and may be dated, perhaps, to the late fourth or early fifth century. There are only a few fragments in Syriac. In this collection Hymn I is quite short, and Hymn II is missing altogether. The existing texts in Armenian and Syriac were edited by Charles Renoux and accompanied by a French translation. This translation is done on the basis of Renoux's edition. The biblical references identified by Renoux in that text are taken over here and supplemented.

Earlier Records of Christianity and Social Life in Nisibis

The origins of Christianity in Nisibis are lost and it never became important to fabricate a tradition as it did in the major cities of the Byzantine Empire and at Edessa. Ephrem of Syria knew of but four bishops of Nisibis; all of these served during Ephrem's lifetime. If the funerary inscription of Aberkios found in Asia Minor is to be taken at face value, that peripatetic resident of Hieropolis in Phrygia claims to have encountered Christian co-religionists in Nisibis during the period 190–210. He wrote: "My name is Aberkios. I am a disciple of a Holy Shepherd who pastured his sheep on the mountains and the plains. . . . It is he who sent me to teach the faithful Scriptures, . . . It is he who sent me to Rome. . . . I have seen the plain of Syria and all the cities, Nisibis across the Euphrates. Everywhere I have found believers, . . . the faith has led me everywhere" (see Bundy, 1989–1990).

The identity of the Christian believers, their social status, ecclesiastical organization, and belief structures are unknowable. It is only fourth-century texts that begin to provide data regarding this city. Ecclesiastical records, such as they are, begin with Ephrem of Syria.

Ephrem of Syria is the only Christian writer celebrated as saint and/or doctor in all branches of the Christian tradition. He wrote in Syriac, but portions of his oeuvre were translated into Armenian, Coptic, Arabic, Ethiopic (Ge'ez) Chinese, Armenian, Georgian, Greek, Latin, and Paleo-Slavic. According to his own works, he was born into a Christian family at Nisibis, became a member of "The Sons and Daughters of the Covenant" (an ascetic order within the church), and wrote in a variety of genres. He was concerned for the spirituality of the community as well as the divergences within it (cf. McVey, 1989).

In addition to the *Hymns on Nicomedia,* Ephrem wrote many other works, including a collection entitled *Hymns on Nisibis* (see Beck 1961–1963). In some of these, he describes with brilliant rhetoric, but with little historical data, the lives and roles of the first four bishops of Nisibis. As is evident from the texts, Ephrem used these bishops as examples to bolster his mid-fourth-century arguments about church and spirituality; leaving a history to posterity was not one of his goals. The earliest bishop mentioned by Ephrem was Jacob, after whose memory the baptistery built in 358 was named and who, for Ephrem, epitomized in his life and ministry the qualities of a good bishop (Bundy 1991). He attempted to establish ascetic discipline in the Church and had successfully rallied the defenders against the Persians led by Shapur I during the 338 siege. The second bishop, Babu, "by the sword and the law" continued the efforts to discipline and purify the community, but watched helplessly as the church divided over theological issues, probably Arianism. The third bishop, Vologeses, was apparently, to the chagrin of the unordained but ascetic Ephrem, less rigorous in his discipline and more irenic in his approach to the theological factions. Nevertheless, Ephrem, in that context, described the church as "completely formed," and as "peaceful and tranquil (Hymns 15–17)." In the *Hymns on Nicomedia* (Hymn XV), Vologeses was portrayed as a heroic figure in the Persian invasion of 359.

The *Hymns on Nicomedia* would suggest a less idyllic situation. In this work, Ephrem admitted that the discipline of the church is fragile and that the line between "Christians" and "pagans" was difficult to maintain. Ephrem described Nisibis as a wealthy cosmopolitan commercial center on the border of the empires. The *Hymns on Nicomedia* provide an extensive and detailed portrait of a fourth-century city. He describes the fields, gardens, and farms as well as the various occupations, for example artisans, weavers, tailors, weavers, and metal workers. The commercial structures and social life reflected in the *Hymns on Nicomedia* add substance to the description of Nisibis found in another text. A Latin source, written by an unknown Syriac author at about the same time as the *Hymns on Nicomedia,* noted that the citizens of Nisibis "lead a good life."

That source is one of the few non-Christian texts of northern Mesopotamian provenance to have survived: the *Expositio totius mundi et gentium*. It was written ca. 359–360 C.E. by a pagan writer of the Roman province of Mesopotamia, whose native language, Syriac, is reflected in the structure of the extant Latin version. The *Expositio* describes, among others, the city of Nisibis (see Rougé, 1966) as follows:

> After them (the other places) is our land. Thus comes next Mesopotamia and Osrhoene. Mesopotamia itself possesses numerous and diverse cities, of which certain ones, which I shall mention, are remarkable. There are, therefore, Nisibis and Edessa, which possess the best men of all; they are adept in business and good hunters. But especially, they are rich and supplied with all goods. They receive from the Persians that which they sell in all of the lands of the Romans and that which they purchase, they in turn sell to them, except bronze and iron, because it is forbidden to give bronze and iron to the enemies. With regard to these cities, they are still standing thanks to the wisdom of the Gods and the Emperors, their walls are remarkable and they always withstand in battle the valor of the Persians. Bustling with business, they lead a good life as does the entire province. There is also the city of Edessa of Osrhoene, which is also a splendid city.

Although Ephrem's earlier works give hints about life in Nisibis, there is nothing as comprehensive as the *Hymns on Nicomedia* that documents the history of this city of the "good life" in Late Antiquity; indeed, there are few such documents for any city during the period. In these Ephrem gives not only a description of life in a fourth-century northern Mesopotamian city but also a theological analysis and prescription of how life should be lived in the city.

Hymn I

This hymn serves as a theological introduction to the collection. It is probable that the original was longer. This theological framework is essential to understanding the approach Ephrem takes toward the city of Nisibis. For him, the incarnation and hope of future participation in God were the essential realities against which all other realities take form and substance. From this basis comes also the free-will ethic that demands conformity of the will of humans to that of God. Since the goal of life is to be molded to God's will and to return to God, one must live the present life in the city in conformity with the divine model found in the incarnation.

   1. Admirable, Lord, is your divinity,
      for it made you equal with humanity.
   3. Admirable, Lord, is also your humanity,
      for it made us touch your divinity.
   5. It is the more admirable that your majesty
      made you descend toward those below.
   7. Marvelous is also your descent
      that clothes us and makes us rise.
   9. Marvelous, Lord, is your life,
      for it made you participate in death.
 11. Admirable is also your death,
      for it gives life eternal.

Hymn II

Missing in both Armenian and Syriac.

Hymn III

Hymn III begins with an introduction based on the biblical story of Joseph encouraging generosity and giving of alms to the poor. These are exemplary of the virtues on which the well-being of a city and nation depend. They are also the virtues on which the eternal well-being of the individuals who died in the earthquake depend. There are many evils in a city that are displeasing to God, suggests Ephrem. These include disregard for the poor, greed, blasphemy, and dishonesty. Every city, he insists, merits destruction, a catastrophe, which is kept away only by penitential prayer and cultivated habits of benevolent action. The earthquake at Nicomedia was, he opines, a warning to be heeded by other cities as they organize their lives and commerce. Its lessons extend beyond the confines of Nicomedia or Nisibis. Sin, he argues, is a global problem.

The entire text of Hymn III is too lengthy to be translated here. Extracts, with numbering that corresponds to the numbering of the edition, are translated here to provide an abstract of the argument of the Hymn. The text begins with the example of Joseph, on the basis of Genesis 41:51–44:13.

5. Do not sell the life of your brothers,
   for in your granary are their lives.
7. Do not sell for money
   the [fragile] life of the widow.
9. Behold the lives of the Egyptians,
   by the granaries of Joseph, were preserved.
11. He gave to them life
    so that he might not have to answer for their deaths.
13. A second Joseph are you;
    give to the poor their lives,
15. in order that, here below and above, like Joseph,
    you might be lauded in both worlds.
17. See the city that was destroyed;
    only its alms are with it.
19. Its precious things have disappeared below [hell];
    its alms are preserved above [heaven].
21. Its immense wealth has disappeared;
    only its virtues remain.
31. Justice rejoiced there [Nicomedia],
    for its part, it is being done equitably.
33. Grace rejoiced there,
    for its people are decorated with virtue.
35. Chastity rejoiced there,
    for its merchants, with it, are enriched.
37. Faith rejoiced there,
    for the truths have clothed it and have gone.
39. Virginity rejoiced there,
    for those who possessed it acquired the pearl [Matt. 13: 45–46].
41. Holiness [continence] rejoiced there,
    for thanks to it the athletes were crowned [1 Cor. 9:25].
43. The fast rejoiced there,
    it was the life source for the hungry and thirsty one who fasted.

45. Prayer rejoiced in the one who possessed it,
    for it prepared that one's boat for the heavens.

47. Love rejoiced in its brothers [virtues],
    because it became the head [chief or leader] of its friends [the
        other virtues].

65. Death came like a thief [Luke 12:39–40];
    make your treasures depart for above [heaven] [Matt. 6:20].

67. It came suddenly,
    and took both the possessors and the possessed.

69. Their homes became their tombs,
    and their clothing, their burial clothes.

71. One endeavored to prepare burial clothes,
    but in the anger [of earthquake/God] they were buried with the
        clothes.

73. Another constructed and embellished a tomb,
    but in the earthquake, was buried in the home.

75. Another thought to be honored in death,
    but the anger buried him with the dogs.

77. Kings and dogs died together;
    the crowned one became the equal of the despised one.

79. Servant and master died together [Isa. 24:2],
    and death liberated them.

81. The servant it liberated from its yoke;
    and his master from his cares.

83. The servant, as the matron, departed,
    the unhappy with the happy.

85. Thus while among the living they were different,
    in the anguish of death they became equal.

For numerous lines, Ephrem then reflects upon the significance of social, gender, and age barriers being broken during the tragedy of an earthquake. It is interesting, he notes, that the only thing that remains, other than the finality of death, are the virtues of justice, generosity, and love. No element of human greed or lust survives death. The rich who profited and ignored the less fortunate have nothing left. Virtues are to be exercised in the city and become an offering to God in the present and the basis for riches as one stands before God. Throughout the Hymn, Ephrem insists that the events at Nicomedia are a warning to all.

291. The city, mother of kings,
    became the mother of the suffocated.

293. The one in the city
    was in the royal household.

295. He entered in the tomb,
    he who would go there anyway.

297. Do not be careless like persons who are far away
    for, in every place, the anger is near!
299. Be shaken by the warning provided
    lest our land have such an event!

The final strophes of Hymn III (strophes 339–442) graphically reinforce the fact that everyone and everything in the city was destroyed in the earthquake. In structuring this lament, Ephrem provides a vision of an active city full of officials, workers, and goods. It is an energetic animated context for business and "the good life."

339. The abyss of death ensnared them all [Ps. 18:5],
    every male and female, where they were.
341. It touched and seized the buildings . . .
    [line 342 is missing in the text]
343. The travelers died in the public places,
    and the residents in their homes.
345. A stranger enters, and suddenly lives
    in a vast area, without rent.
347. There is no one to make him leave,
    unless some voice be raised at the resurrection.
349. The neighbors who always lived without quarrels
    live in tombs.
351. The one purchased a piece of land [Luke 14:18];
    he went there and found his death.
353. Thus that which he hoped to eat [Gen. 3:19],
    it [the earthquake] suddenly ate it.
355. The vine growers died with their vines,
    and the gardeners [died] with their gardens.
357. The caretaker made them grow,
    and much died in the earthquake.
359. The anger harvested suddenly,
    [both] the harvest and the harvesters.
360. The One who blessed has cursed the earth;
    it has been devastated and has become a terrible place.
369. The prison locked up the prisoners;
    the anger opened it without asking any questions.
371. For a long time they had been incarcerated there,
    and the judges did not judge them.
373. The Judge of judges descended;
    he judged their cases suddenly.
383. The one while laying the foundations [of a house],
    [saw] the collapse of that which he had constructed.
385. Another built a home, decorated and furnished it,
    and trouble was his home.

387. Another saved from his youth
     to establish savings for his old age.
389. Death, suddenly, took him away,
     as it would a slave, from his worries.
403. The lender and the borrower
     are consumed with great cares.
405. The care which suffocated many,
     was suffocated by the anger.
407. The one who fasted went during the fast,
     and the glutton went during the orgy.
409. The prostitute went during her impurity,
     and the one who was pure went in her purity.
411. The judge died at his bench
     with the bribe still in his hand [Micah 3:11].
413. Their debates were extinguished suddenly,
     with their larcenies still in their belts.
415. The young married women disappeared with their bridal
     chambers,
     and the chaste women [disappeared] with their cells.

     . . .

Hymns IV–VI

These Hymns pick up theological themes that were initially addressed in the
earlier Hymns. Again Ephrem asserts (Hymn IV) that a natural catastrophe, such
as that at Nicomedia, is reflective of a restrained exhibition of the anger of God
and can serve as a warning to people in other cities. Each city should repent of
its sins with liturgies that are clear to the entire public, as well as develop the
virtues of prayer, love, and justice. They should establish just and equitable systems for life in the city. This active penitence and intentional transformation of
the city can serve to deflect the anger of God.

Hymn V was written during or after the military threats of the Persian Emperor
Shapur II against Nisibis, during the spring of 359. It argues that one is to live
life in a state of readiness for the judgment of God. That means, insists Ephrem,
that personal and corporate accumulation of wealth and goods should be made
secondary to the development of the virtues. As demonstrated by biblical narratives, there are ways to expedite the development of virtue. One should be detached, as much as possible, from the concerns of wealth and accumulation.
Prayer, fasting, and the giving of alms should take priority. When menaced by
hostile external force, such as Shapur II (lines 255–334), he argues, the fate of
the city partially depends on whether these virtues have been maintained in accordance with the divine priorities for the city. Charles Renoux is certainly correct
in identifying the "anger" mentioned by Ephrem as the invasion of the Persians
in 359 (Renoux, 1975, 71nn. 44–45).

In Hymn VI, the most careful theological essay of the collection, Ephrem struggles with the implications of natural catastrophes for understanding the divine government of the world. He argues that God's actions are not capricious, but characterized by wisdom and grace. Divinely allowed human freedom has allowed divergence from the will of God. Reminders of ultimate human dependence upon God are required if humans are to find their way back to union with God. The earthquake was such a reminder.

Hymn VII

This Hymn begins with a lament about the tragedy of Nicomedia, continues with a description of the disaster, and concludes with theological reflections on the event. The second portion, the portrayal of the earthquake (lines 89–148), is translated here. It is particularly important for its discussion of burial practices.

89. They slept in the evening,
and the roofs fell upon their bodies.

91. They slept at the dawn,
and their houses tumbled on their bodies.

93. That night they were perhaps more vigilant
than during the other nights

95. for the interruption of [their] sleep
indicated [prefigured] the great end of their journeys [through life].

97. Because at the dawn, the city awakened;
all of them returned to their work;

99. the indolent women returned to their toilette,
the working women to their weaving.

101. Each departed to their occupations;
the angel of anger [went to take care of] the destruction.

103. The unfortunate ones did not know
that their death was waiting at the door.

105. The builders departed for their construction work;
the artisans took up their work.

107. The judges entered the chambers;
the visitors went on their visits.

109. At the moment of the third hour,
in the hour of the soft light,

111. the sun set upon the city,
and it became without light.

113. The sick suffocated in their beds;
those who had hoped to rise [from their beds were suffocated].

115. The ceilings collapsed,
and covered the sick and visitors.

117. The sick one was suffocated there,
     and, around him, his visitors.
119. It was at the hour for making visits
     that the anger visited the city.
121. At the hour that the doctors
     went on their rounds;
123. At the same hour went out
     the angels with the orders to destroy.
125. The living were forming a funeral procession for the
     dead;
     the final moment made a funeral procession for all.
127. They themselves became part of the funeral procession with the
     dead,
     for they were buried in place with them.
129. Those who formed a funeral procession for the deceased,
     it [the anger] led them with it to the tomb.
131. People came out to form a funeral procession,
     and they took the path to eternity.
133. The living formed a funeral procession,
     and found themselves among the dead.
135. They themselves came out to form the funeral procession,
     thus, they themselves walked to the tomb.
137. Blessed was the dead one who died a little before that anger,
     for tears were shed by his friends.
139. By his bearers, with honor, he was carried to his tomb,
     and he left the city in peace.
141. He did not see the cruel horror;
     he did not feel the violent shaking of the earth.
143. The undertakers who buried him, returned [to the city];
     they returned and were suffocated in their homes.
145. They buried the dead and returned [to the city]
     to be buried in their places.
147. The city, ancient and established,
     honored and buried its friends.
149. In life it was their nurse;
     in death it was their undertaker.

Hymn VIII

This composition deals again in some detail with themes discussed in Hymn VI. Once again the implications of the event for understanding God are discussed and suggestions made to various groups within the church and city. Each person is instructed to repent, develop virtues, and live a generous life.

The text is a lament for the sin and [potential] devastation of the city. Ephrem develops the lament and instruction using selected Hebrew prophets as models and speakers.

Hymn IX

The next Hymn in this collection is the only text preserved completely in its original language, Syriac. In this text Ephrem discusses the various occupations and finds them illustrative of the central Christian teaching of resurrection. Professions mentioned include: blacksmiths (line 13); tailors (line 37); painters (line 71); artisans (line 401); field workers (line 441); judges (line 467); city bureaucrats (line 467); men of wealth (line 473); women of leisure (lines 191–94) as well as givers and participants in banquets and festivals (lines 199, 201, 413). The passage translated here, from the Syriac original (lines 13–82), references professions in Nisibis; it is also a case study in the comprehensiveness of Ephrem's theological vision. Even the professions and the life in the city are revelatory and confirmatory for him of the divine truths. The quotation in lines 63–64 is clearly a citation according to the text, but it remains unidentified.

13. The blacksmith died while standing
    near the furnace full of symbols.
15. In the furnace, as in combat,
    iron and fire are taken.
17. The fire that masters that which is hard
    is [itself] mastered by the water.
19. That [fire] masters that which is hard
    but the liquid masters it.
21. The natures may be compared to that in the fire,
    one is overcome by the other.
23. All [natures] are overcome by humans,
    the human is overcome by death.
25. At the end, the resurrection triumphs;
    it is that which becomes the crowning glory.
27. The carpenter died while he hammered;
    while building, he was destroyed.
29. From his profession we receive
    an example of the resurrection.
31. For if he learned to build,
    and to hammer [nails] as well as shape;
33. how much more his Lord can build,
    as Creator, members [of the body].

35. He who gave this to humans,
    how much greater is He than His gift!

37. The tailor died upon his clothing,
    while repairing the tears.

39. In his work is hidden his consolation,
    for his work [is] a symbol of the resurrection.

41. For if the tailor was able
    to reunite the separated parts,

43. how more the resurrection can
    reunite the body with the soul.

45. Hidden symbols are represented
    in our work as concerning our resurrection.

47. The Apostle [1 Cor. 15:35–45] also from a seed
    composed a parable of the resurrection.

49. But the source is not misleading for us
    so that we might see the symbols presented to us,

51. for it raises us out from the meaning of the symbols
    and places us among the riches.

53. For sin is the opposite of
    the voice that proclaims the resurrection.

55. For it is known that we are frightened by
    the voice of the judge, and it justifies us.

57. It is known that we are excited by
    the promise and it encourages us.

59. For that reason the Evil One seeded in us
    discouragement concerning the resurrection

61. lest through the promise we might become justified
    and not be frightened by the judge:

63. "Unbind and let go your mouths,
    and take nourishment while you are living."

65. Let us return to the first subject matter,
    For we have wandered from one thing to another.

71. The painter died while he painted;
    upon his work he was destroyed.

73. While he painted images,
    death destroyed his images.

75. His art is a mirror;
    he paints on it the symbol of the resurrection.

77. For if with the colors
    he paints a likeness that did not exist,

79. how much easier [is it] for the Creator of all,
    that, from the earth and the dust,

81. he might paint the likeness that was destroyed. . . .

Hymn X

After a series of Hymns in which Ephrem reflected theologically about the problems of Nisibis, he turns, in Hymn X, to address specific problems. One of these is the use of the traditional sciences of northern Mesopotamia, or as he termed it, "magic." It is clear that he considered practitioners of these arts direct competitors for the minds and souls of the inhabitants of the city. In verse 75 he states his opinion of magic and beginning with verse 193, he exhorts his audience to action. Verses 193–97 are translated from a Syriac fragment.

    75. Incantations, magical rites and divination
           are more serious than all other sins.
  193. Cut off and reject, weak ones,
           the rites and consulting of magicians;
  195. for the anger that is guiding them,
           also us, it carries us away with them.
  197. Let us run, let us take refuge with the chaste
           that we might be saved by their prayers.

The text continues with a discussion of the problems that faith in magicians and astrologers brought upon ancient Egypt, Assyria, Sodom, and Israel, as well as in the personal histories of Lot, Noah, and Achar.

Hymn XI

Ephrem, in Hymn XI, after restating the theological concerns and opportunities for repentance afforded by the earthquake of Nicomedia, continues the argument against the magicians. He is concerned about exploitation of the ignorant and about issues of truthfulness and efficacy.

  167. The city that lost its embellishments
           saw perish also its evil actions.
  169. There, astrology was confounded,
           and there perished divination.
  171. With these and in the middle of these,
           magic was suffocated;
  173. sources [astrology and magic] of bitterness
           which are sweet to bitter men.
  175. There perished also the astrologers
           and their books with them.

179. While their eyes were on the stars,
     and their fingers on the calculations,
181. justice humiliated them
     lest they come to scrutinize the hidden mysteries.
187. The foolish ones despise the truth freely given;
     error they purchase with money.
189. They despise the true science,
     and dispense sums for falsehood.
191. They despise the life freely given,
     and purchase death at a high price.
207. The astrologer reads the horoscopes,
     but justice frees them;
209. There [with the astrologer], [is] that which the error binds,
     there [with justice], the truth frees [them].
211. He read to the poor person: riches;
     and when he [the poor one] wished to rejoice, it came to
        nothing.
213. The anger came suddenly,
     and humiliated them both together.
215. To him whom the lots attributed good,
     evil came suddenly upon him.
217. One read to a sterile woman: conception.
     and she descended suddenly into the tomb.

It is clear that this was not merely a civic problem, but also problem for the church. There are persons in Ephrem's church who have not been able to abandon completely the older regional traditions of healing and transformation for the newer Christian practices.

339. Stop, O foolish women,
     lest you strengthen evil with your divinations.
341. Do not bring anger in the city
     lest it be here like it was there [in Nicomedia],
343. lest your impudent divinations
     humiliate also the honest [women].
345. Because of your mother [Eve], death entered [Rom. 5:12];
     she humiliated the good and the bad at the same time [Gen.
        18:23].
351. Identical for you are
     the doors of the church and those of the diviners.
352. After having entered to pray,
     you run immediately to the sorcerers.

353. The impudent women, thus, hurry along;
    those who appear to be chaste.

355. And they conceal their comings and goings in these
    places,
    but their tracks are left everywhere.

357. They go in disguise,
    but their tracks follow them to these places.

475. What does the foolish diviner give you?
    He sells, at high price, another injury.

477. What does the magician offer?
    He sells, in reality, illusions.

479. What will the astrologer read for you?
    For the fees, in reality, he brings you injury.

481. He takes from you a profit,
    and he gives you a defect.

483. You desire to have children;
    do not suffer a double injury.

485. For your womb is sterile since [your] birth;
    and your design engendered a debt;

487. Let not your sterility engender
    sin and debt instead of children.

489. While you wish to obtain a child,
    you lose your soul.

491. Remember that at the hour of the tribulation [judgment before
    God],
    Your soul is worth more than everything.

Hymn XII

This Hymn presents a remarkable view of the tension between the city dwellers and those from the desert. The text suggests that the daughters of Hagar are Arab women from either tribes in semiresidential status near Nisibis or from tribes that are still nomadic with seasonal visits to Nisibis for trade. The sale of these Arab women to serve as prostitutes or concubines for the men whose wives have joined the Christian community of Ephrem and have accepted its teaching on celibacy as a requirement for baptism (see Beck, 1956 and 1984; Vööbus, 1951) and participation in the community, is causing stress (lines 1–88). Ephrem disapproves and hopes that the Christian women will discipline their husbands and that the Arab women will accept the discipline of the Christian community, receive baptism, become chaste, and achieve heaven [lines 89–118].

Portions of this Hymn are translated here. The deserts in line one refers to the geographical location of Nisibis, which is between the mountainous deserts to the north (later known as the Tur Abdin) and the desert plains to the south (Renoux, 1975, 273n.1).

    1. From the two deserts outside,
       our city is filled with wild beasts.
    3. Savage beasts from the mountains;
       the daughters of Hagar from the desert [Gen. 21:14].
    5. Savage beasts for the cage,
       And savage beasts in the tents.
    7. Savage beasts, ferocious ones,
       enter for the entertainment of the city;
    9. The savage beasts, the daughters of Hagar,
       enter for the loss [destruction] of the city.
  11. Indeed, they lead in [and] release those [women]
       and they embolden [them and] give them freedom.
  13. The savage beasts from the mountains
       scratch [wound] at the most two persons per year.
  15. The savage beasts, the daughters of Hagar,
       tear at everyone who passes by.
  17. The adorned ones from outside cause sin;
       and approach [men] with lascivious gestures.
  19. Whoever sees, lusts, [and] dies secretly [Matt. 5:28];
       whoever approaches [the women], dies visibly.
  21. Oh! Savage beasts, daughters of Hagar,
       who fill our public squares with devastation!
  23. A savage beast flees if it escapes;
       the city, when it sees it, pays attention.
  25. The wild ones slip into the public squares,
       and the city takes pleasure in their rebuff;
  29. They beat with a stick a wild bitch;
       the wild prostitutes they love and respect.
  31. They flee the mouths of the wild beasts;
       and they abandon themselves in the filth of the bitches [Ps. 59:6].
  33. The houses of debauchery are silent
       because [these women] are desired.
  35. The chaste [women] are silent
       because they are not jealous.
  37. Whoever sees the evil ones without reacting
       is complicit in their actions.

The remainder of Hymn XII reflects upon the struggle provoked by the presence of the Arab prostitutes/concubines in the city of Nisibis. Ephrem insists that the sinful activity provoked by their presence would be sufficient to merit an earthquake like that of Nicomedia, and only the repentance of all of the principals in this urban socio-religious drama can bring Nisibis into a positive relation with the universe.

Hymns XIII–XIV

The thirteenth and fourteenth hymns restate the theological issues addressed in the earlier compositions.

Hymn XV

Hymn XV discusses the repentance of Nisibis, in sackcloth, as the Persian Emperor Shapur II besieged the city in the spring of 359. Ephrem recounts the valiant spiritual struggle against personal and social sin that made possible the avoidance of a sack of the city. He insists that, despite the acknowledged vigilance and bravery of the defenders, it was really Bishop Vologeses who effectively led the defense of the city by leading it in repentance, sackcloth and ashes, and prayer. The battle is described as follows:

107. Thanks to it [the sackcloth] our ramparts were honored;
     which the foreigners had defiled.
109. The impure ones defiled [them] and were defiled,
     while this city was honored by the sackcloth.
111. The waters invaded and were vanquished by the sackcloth;
     the dikes were elevated but they were brought down [Ps. 58:7].
113. Elephants arrived and were vanquished
     by the sackcloth, ashes and prayer.
115. Archers came and were wounded,
     for those who were dressed in sackcloth triumphed.
117. Swordsmen came outside [the city walls],
     and they were vanquished by the sackcloth inside.
119. The bow which was strung outside the rampart,
     was vanquished by prayer inside [the city walls] [Ps. 58:7]

Hymn XVI

The earthquake and the siege: God's grace provided warnings for other sinners and sinful cities in the world to repent and return to ways of personal purity and social justice. The slowness to respond to that warning may have led to the punishment of Nisibis. While Nisibis was spared from a sacking by the Persians, Nisibis and every other city needed to be reminded that conformity to the life commanded by God is not optional. Every individual likewise needs to be attentive to the divinely furnished examples of life and the Scriptures. However, Ephrem refuses to go so far as to say that it was specifically because of sin in Nicomedia that Nicomedia was destroyed. They deserved destruction because of their sins, but then all cities do! There is no viable human explanation as to why specifically they were chosen by God to suffer.

Bibliography

Beck, Edmund. 1956. "Le Baptême chez Saint Ephrem." *L'Orient Syrien* 1: 111–36.

————— ed. 1961–1963. "Des Heiligen Ephraem Carmina Nisibena." Corpus Scriptorum Christianorum Orientalium 218–19, 240–41, Syr. 92–93, 102–3; Louvain: Secrétariat du Corpus Scriptorum Christianorum Orientalium.

————— 1984. *Dōrea und Charis. Die Taufe. Zwei Beiträge zur Theologie Ephräms des Syrers.* Corpus Scriptorum Christianorum Orientalium 457, Subsidia 72; Louvain: Peeters.

Bundy, David. 1989–1990. "The *Life of Avercius:* Its Significance for Early Syriac Christianity." *Second Century* 7: 163–76.

—————. 1991. "Jacob of Nisibis as a Model for the Episcopacy." *Le Muséon* 104: 235–49.

—————. 1992. "Christianity in Syria." In *Anchor Bible Dictionary* 1: 970–79. New York: Doubleday.

—————. Forthcoming. "The Baptistery Dedicated to Bishop Jacob at Nisibis: A Case Study in Syriac Religious Architecture and Practice in Fourth Century Northern Mesopotamia."

Drijvers, Han J. W. 1980. "Cults and Beliefs at Edessa." *Etudes préliminaires aux religions orientales dans l'empire romain* 82. Leiden: E. J. Brill.

—————. *East of Antioch* 1984. Collected Studies Series 98. London: Variorum.

—————. 1994. *History and Religion in Late Antique Syria.* Collected Studies Series 464. Aldershot: Variorum.

Fiey, Jean Marie. 1977. "Nisibe: Métropole syriaque orientale et ses suffragants des origins à nos jours." Corpus Scriptorum Christianorum Orientalium 388, Subsidia 54. Louvain: Peeters.

McVey, Kathleen E. 1989. "Hymns." In *Classics of Western Spirituality.* Mahwah, N.J.: Paulist Press.

Renoux, Charles, trans. 1975. "Ephrem de Nisibe, Mēmrē sur Nicomédie. Edition des fragments de l'original Syriaque et de la version Arménienne, traduction Française, introduction et notes." *Patrologia Orientalis* 37, 2–3. Turnhout, Belgium: Brepols.

Rougé, Jean. 1966. "Expositio totius mundi et gentium." Sources chrétiennes 124, §22. Paris: Editions du Cerf.

Vööbus Arthur. 1951. "Celibacy: A Requirement for Admission to Baptism in the Early Syrian Church." *Publication of Estonian Theological Society in Exile* 1. Stockholm: Estonian Theological Society in Exile.

—15—

Acts of Thomas: Scene One

David G. Hunter

The *Acts of Thomas* is one of several early Christian texts, known as apocryphal acts, that describe the legendary journeys and missionary activities of the apostles. The central figure in the *Acts of Thomas* is the apostle Judas Thomas, who is also called Didymus, the Greek word for "twin." He is portrayed as the twin brother of Jesus. This identification is based on a fusion of several New Testament traditions. John 14:22 speaks of a "Judas, not Iscariot" among Jesus' followers; also prominent in John's gospel is the figure of "Thomas, also called the Twin" (John 11:16, 20:24, 21:2). The two were conflated in early Syriac tradition. Moreover, since Mark 6:3 and Matthew 13:55 both mention Judas as a brother of Jesus, Judas Thomas became the twin brother of Jesus. In the *Acts of Thomas* he is Jesus' twin not only in appearance, but also in his work as preacher, healer, and martyr (Gunther 1980, 113–48).

The *Acts of Thomas* exists in early Greek and Syriac versions. Most scholars hold that it was originally composed in Syriac, but the Greek version seems to reflect the more primitive text; the extant Syriac text has been altered to reflect later orthodox perspectives (Attridge 1990, 241–50). The *Acts of Thomas* was translated into several ancient languages: Latin, Coptic, Arabic, Ethiopic, Armenian, Georgian, and Old Slavonic (Geerard 1992, 147–52).

The Syriac original of the *Acts* probably was composed early in the third century, and the Greek version shortly thereafter. The text is clearly a composite, however, and several parts must have circulated independently prior to this time, for example, the Hymn of the Bride (scene one), the famous Hymn of the Pearl (scene nine), and the story of the apostle's martydom (Tissot 1981). It was most likely written at Edessa, where the apostle Thomas was venerated at an early date. The text reflects the milieu of early Syriac Christianity, with its emphasis on radical asceticism, especially sexual renunciation. Several scholars have noted that the *Acts of Thomas* shows affinities with the second-century *Odes of Solomon* and the writings of Tatian the Syrian, the reputed founder of encratite Christianity (Klijn 1965; Winkler 1982). The text also has parallels with other materials associated with the name of Thomas, including the *Gospel of Thomas* and the *Book of Thomas the Contender* from Nag Hammadi (Layton 1987, 359–65; Poirier 1997). The *Acts of Thomas,* along with the other apocryphal acts of apostles, was later adopted as a canonical text by the Manichaeans, who continued to revise and edit the work (Nagel 1973; Kaestli 1977).

The *Acts of Thomas* consists of thirteen scenes or "acts" (*praxeis*), together with an account of Thomas's martyrdom. The opening scenes (1–8) stress the apostle's power as a miracle worker, preacher, and exorcist. He raises several persons from the dead, encounters talking donkeys, and acquires notable converts to Christianity. Thomas also performs sacramental actions throughout the *Acts,* such as baptism, anointing with oil, and Eucharist without wine; the last may have been common in early Syriac Christianity (Rouwhorst 1990, 72–74). The encratite theology of the *Acts* is especially prominent in the second half of the work (scenes 9–13), where Thomas preaches to the wives of several high officials. Some, such as Mygdonia and Tertia, accept the apostle's exhortation to abstain from "sordid intercourse" with their husbands (88). Thomas's ultimate martyrdom results from the opposition of the husbands to his ascetic preaching.

Scene one of the *Acts of Thomas,* which is presented here, contains many features that are typical of the apocryphal literature of the second and third centuries. It begins with an account of the distribution of the apostolic ministry among the apostles, and Thomas is chosen to evangelize India. In his *Ecclesiastical History* (3.1) Eusebius (following Origen) presents a similar tradition, although he says that Thomas was chosen to preach in Parthia. The tradition that places Thomas in Parthia seems to be the earlier one, and the extension of his missionary activity to India may have been a creation of the *Acts* itself (Junod 1981, 245; Dihle 1963). The apostle's initial refusal to accept his mission is reminiscent of the reluctance to respond to the divine call evidenced by other figures in the biblical tradition, such as Moses and Jonah.

When the apostle Thomas eventually accepts his mission, it is only because of the direct intervention of the Lord Jesus: Jesus appears and sells Thomas as a slave to the Indian merchant Abbanes (2). The incident is rich in symbolism, for it serves to recall the parallel between the apostle and Jesus who is described as a slave in the New Testament (cf. John 13:1–17; Phil. 2:5–11). Later in the *Acts,* Thomas will speak of his slavery to Christ as a means to freedom (142, 167), and the fact that Thomas travels to India carrying only the price of his sale (3) also suggests that he remains free, despite being sold into slavery (Klijn 1962, 161–62).

The encratite theology of the *Acts of Thomas* is introduced in section four, the wedding feast hosted by the king of the royal city Andrapolis (the city of man). The theme of the spiritual or heavenly marriage as opposed to the fleshly or earthly marriage was especially dear to Syrian Christians, and the motif is skillfully exploited throughout scene one. For example, the apostle anoints himself at the wedding feast in preparation for his role as groomsman (5). Later, when he is introduced into the bridal chamber, Thomas utters a prayer for the newly married couple and entrusts them into the hands of the Savior, saying "The Lord be with you" (10). The apostle's prayer is fulfilled when the Lord Jesus appears to the couple bearing the appearance of Thomas (11). Jesus proceeds to exhort the couple to renounce "filthy intercourse" and to commit themselves to perpetual celibacy. By renouncing sex, he says, the couple will be able to enter "that true and incorruptible marriage" and will enter "that bridal chamber full of immortality and light" (12). Later, when the bride explains her conversion to her parents, she describes her ascetic resolve in terms of the spiritual marriage: "I have had no intercourse with a temporary husband, which ends only in lust and bitterness of soul, since I have been united with a true husband" (14).

Underlying the ascetic renunciation that the *Acts of Thomas* presents as normative for Christians is an understanding of salvation whose key is found in the famous "Hymn of the Bride," which Thomas sings at the wedding feast (6–7). Unlike the extant Syriac version, which has altered the hymn into one dedicated to the church, the Greek version speaks of a maiden who is a "daughter of light" and who lives in the company of the heavenly king. She leads her attendants into the bridal chamber, where they are enlightened by the vision of the eternal Bridegroom. There they will rejoice forever and glorify "with the living Spirit, the Father of Truth, and the Mother of Wisdom" (7).

In the Greek version, the daughter of light is clearly a heavenly being, similar to the divine Wisdom of Jewish literature, such as the Book of Proverbs and the Wisdom of Solomon. There are also parallels in texts from Qumran (Zur 1993). In the Greek hymn the daughter functions as a bridge between heaven and earth; she mediates entry into the bridal chamber and facilitates revelation of divine mysteries. When read in connection with the later sections of scene one, the Hymn of the Bride presents the encratite teaching that human beings can be restored to their original unity with the divine Spirit by renouncing sexual activity. In the *Acts of Thomas* the bridal chamber, "full of immortality and light," which constitutes the celibate life, is a return to union with the heavenly Father and Mother.

The ascetical exhortations of the *Acts of Thomas,* and especially the language and imagery of the bridal chamber, suggest that the text might fruitfully be read in the light of other religious and cultural texts from Late Antiquity, such as the Hermetic literature and Nag Hammadi documents (Valantasis 1995). Parallels with gnostic writings, for example, are particularly striking. As the groom says after embracing celibacy: "You have shown me how to search for myself and how to know who I was, and who and in what state I am now, so that I might once again become what I was" (15). Nevertheless, the *Acts of Thomas* shows no influence of classic gnostic ideas of a fall in the *Pleroma* (cosmic universe) or a creation by a wicked Demiurge; its themes are closer to those of early Jewish Christianity as it took shape in a Syrian milieu (Klijn 1965; Drijvers 1992, 337).

The Greek text translated here is found in Maximilianus Bonnet's *Acta apostolorum apocrypha.* My translation is adapted and reprinted with permission from *Marriage in the Early Church,* translated and edited by David G. Hunter, © 1992 Augsburg Fortress.

Acts of the Holy Apostle Thomas
Scene One

[1] At that time all of us apostles were in Jerusalem: Simon, who was called Peter, and Andrew his brother; James, the son of Zebedee, and his brother John; Philip and Bartholomew; Thomas and Matthew the tax-collector; James [the son] of Alphaeus and Simon the Canaanean; and Judas [the son] of James. And we divided the regions of the entire world, so that each of us might go to the region which fell to him and to the nation to which the Lord sent him. According to lot, India fell to Judas Thomas, who was also called Didymus [the Twin]. But he did not want to go, saying that he was unable to travel because of the weakness of his flesh. And [he said]: "How can I, a Hebrew man, travel among the Indians to proclaim the truth?" And while he was discussing the matter and talking in this way, the Savior appeared to him during the night and said to him: "Do not be afraid, Thomas! Go to India and proclaim the word there. For my grace is with you." But Thomas would not obey and said: "Send me wherever you wish, as long as it is somewhere else, because I am not going to the Indians."

[2] And as he was saying this and becoming angry, it happened that a certain merchant from India was passing by, whose name was Abbanes. He had been sent by the king Gundaphoros with orders to purchase a carpenter and bring him back to him. Now the Lord, having seen him walking in the marketplace at midday, said to him: "Do you want to buy a carpenter?" And he replied: "Yes." And the Lord said to him: "I have a slave who is a carpenter and I would like to sell him." And after saying this he pointed out Thomas to him from a distance and agreed with him on a price of three pounds of uncoined silver. Then he wrote a bill of sale, saying: "I Jesus, the son of Joseph the carpenter, declare that I have sold my slave, who is called Judas, to you Abbanes, a merchant of Gundaphoros the king of the Indians." When the sale was completed, the Savior took Judas, who is also Thomas, and led him to the merchant Abbanes. When Abbanes saw him, he said to him: "Is this man your master?" And the apostle answered him, saying: "Yes, he is my Lord." Then he replied: "But I have bought you from him." And the apostle was silent.

[3] Early the next morning, after praying and entreating the Lord, the apostle said: "I will go wherever you want, Lord Jesus. Your will be done!" Then he went to Abbanes the merchant, carrying nothing with him but the price of his sale. For the Lord had given it to him, saying: "Let your price be with you, along with my grace, wherever you go." The apostle found Abbanes carrying his baggage onto the ship and, therefore, he began to carry it with him. After they had boarded the ship and sat down, Abbanes questioned the apostle, saying: "What sort of work do you know?" And he replied: "In wood [I can make] ploughs, yokes, and balances, as well as ships, oars for ships, masts, and

pulleys; in stone, pillars, temples, and royal palaces." And Abbanes the merchant said to him: "We have need of such a workman." And so, they began to set sail. They had a favorable wind and sailed quickly until they reached Andrapolis, a royal city.

[4] Leaving the ship they entered the city. Behold, the noise of flutes and water-organs and trumpets sounded around them. The apostle asked: "What festival is going on in this city?" Those who were there said to him: "The gods have indeed led you to make merry in this city. For the king has only one daughter and now he is giving her in marriage to a husband. The festival you have seen today is the rejoicing and assembly for the wedding. The king has sent messengers everywhere to announce that everyone should come to the wedding, rich and poor, slave and free, foreigners and citizens. If anyone refuses and does not attend the wedding, he will have to answer to the king."

When Abbanes heard this, he said to the apostle: "We too should go, so as not to offend the king, especially since we are foreigners." And the apostle said: "Let us go." They found lodging in an inn and, after resting for a little while, they went to the wedding. When the apostle saw everyone reclining, he also lay down in their midst. Everyone looked at him because he was a stranger and from a foreign land. But Abbanes the merchant, since he was a master, reclined in another place.

[5] While the others ate and drank, the apostle tasted nothing. Therefore, those who were nearby said to him: "Why have you come here, neither eating nor drinking?" He answered them in these words: "I have come here for something better than food or drink, that I may fulfill the will of the king. For the messengers announce the king's message, and whoever does not listen to the messengers will be liable to the king's judgment."

So then, after they had eaten and drunk, and after the crowns and ointments had been brought out, each person took some ointment. Some anointed their eyes, others their beards, and others different parts of their bodies. But the apostle anointed the top of his head, and smeared a little on his nose, and dropped some into his ears, and placed some on his teeth, and carefully spread some around his heart. He took the crown that was brought to him, which was woven out of myrtle and other flowers, and placed it on his head. Then he took a branch of a reed and held it in his hands. There was a flute girl who had a flute in her hands, and she went around to all of them and played. When she came to the place where the apostle was, she stood in front of him for a long while, playing over his head. This flute girl was a Hebrew by birth.

[6] As the apostle remained looking at the ground, one of the wine pourers reached out his hand and struck him. The apostle lifted his eyes, looked at the one who struck him, and said: "My God will forgive you this injustice in the age to come, but in this world he will reveal his wonders, and we shall now see this hand that has struck me dragged away by dogs." Having said this he began to sing and chant this song:

The maiden is the daughter of light,
Upon her stands and in her rests the proud glory of kings.
Delightful is the sight of her,
She shines with radiant beauty.
Her garments are like the flowers of spring,
And from them flows a sweet fragrance.
On the crown of her head the king is seated,
And he feeds with his ambrosia those who are seated around him.
Truth is established upon her head,
And with her feet she radiates joy.
Her mouth is open and it well becomes her,
Thirty and two are the number who sing her praises.
Her tongue is like the curtain on the door,
Which waves to those who enter.
Her neck lies like the steps that the first craftsman constructed,
And her two hands make signs and signals.
They announce the dance of the blessed Aeons,
And her fingers reveal the gates of the city.
Her chamber is full of light.
It breathes forth the fragrance of balsam and of every spice.
It gives out the sweet scent of myrrh and leaves.
Within are strewn branches of myrtle and all kinds of sweet-smelling
    flowers.
[7] Surrounding her are the groomsmen, whose number is seven.
She herself has chosen them.
There are eight bridesmaids,
Who form a chorus before her.
Twelve is the number of those who serve her,
Who are her followers.
They gaze upon the Bridegroom,
So that through this vision they may be enlightened.
Forever they will be with him in that eternal joy,
And they will be present at that wedding feast,
Where the great ones will gather,
And where the eternal ones will be counted worthy to rejoice forever.
They shall put on royal robes and wear bright raiment.
In joy and exultation they both shall be,
And they shall glorify the Father of all.
His proud light they have received,
Those who have been enlightened in the vision of their Master.
His ambrosial food they have received,
Which will never run out.
They have drunk of his wine,
Which gives them neither thirst nor desire.

And they have glorified and praised, with the living Spirit,
The Father of Truth, and the Mother of Wisdom.

[8] When the apostle had finished this song, all who were present there gazed at him, but he kept silent. They also saw that his appearance was changed, but they did not understand what he had said, since he was a Hebrew and what he said was spoken in Hebrew. Only the flute girl heard it all, since she was a Hebrew by birth. Moving away from him, she played for the others, but for much of the time she gazed at him, for he was a man of her own country and was more attractive in appearance than the others who were there. When she had finished playing, the flute girl sat down next to him and looked at him intently. But he looked at no one at all and kept his eyes fixed on the ground, waiting for the time when he could depart from there.

But the wine pourer who had struck him went out to the well to draw water. It happened that there was a lion in that place. It killed him and left him lying there with his limbs torn apart. Immediately some dogs came and seized his limbs, and one of them, a black dog, took the right hand in his mouth and carried it into the banquet.

[9] When they saw this, everyone was amazed and asked which of them was missing. It became apparent to all that it was the wine pourer who had struck the apostle. The flute girl then broke her flute and threw it down and went to sit at the feet of the apostle. She said: "This man is either a god or an apostle of God. For I heard him say in Hebrew to the wine pourer: 'We shall now see this hand that has struck me dragged away by dogs.' This is what you have seen, for it has happened just as he said it would." And some of them believed her, but others did not.

When the king heard what had happened, he went to the apostle Thomas and said: "Arise, come with me and pray for my daughter, for she is my only child, and today I am giving her in marriage." The apostle did not want to go with him because the Lord had not yet been revealed to him there. But the king forced him to go to the bridal chamber to pray for them.

[10] Standing there the apostle began to pray in these words: "My Lord and my God, who accompanies his servants on their way, who guides and directs those who trust in him, refuge and resting place of the afflicted, hope of those who mourn and deliverer of captives, healer of sick souls and savior of all creation, who gives life to the world and strength to our souls! You know the future and for our sake you bring all things to completion. You are the Lord, who reveals hidden mysteries and who utters words that are unspeakable. You are the Lord, who plants the good tree and who causes all good things to arise by his own hands. You are the Lord, who is in all things, who came through all things, who exists in all his works, and who reveals himself in the working of all things.

"Jesus Christ, son of compassion and perfect savior, Christ, son of the living God, the undaunted power that has overthrown the enemy, the voice heard by the rulers that has shaken all their powers, the ambassador sent from on high who has gone down even into hell, who has opened the gates and led out from there those who were shut up for many years in the power of darkness, and who has revealed to them the path that leads up on high. I beg you, Lord Jesus, offering you supplication on behalf of these young people, that you make whatever happens to them be for the good." After laying his hands on them and saying, "The Lord be with you," he left them there and departed.

[11] The king ordered the groomsmen to leave the bridal chamber. When everyone had left and the doors were shut, the bridegroom raised the curtain of the bridal chamber in order to take the bride to himself. Then he saw the Lord Jesus conversing with the bride, bearing the appearance of Judas Thomas, the apostle who had just blessed them and departed. And the bridegroom said to him: "Did you not go out before all the others? How is it that you are now here?" But the Lord said to him: "I am not Judas, who is also Thomas, but I am his brother." Then the Lord sat down on the bed and ordered them also to sit down on the couches, and he began to speak to them:

[12] "Remember, my children, what my brother said to you and remember the one to whom he entrusted you. Know that if you refrain from this filthy intercourse, you will become holy temples, pure, free of trials and difficulties, known and unknown, and you will not be drowned in the cares of life and of children, who lead only to ruin. If you produce many children, you will become greedy and avaricious because of them, robbing orphans and defrauding widows, and by doing so you will render yourselves liable to the harshest punishments. For many children become a liability, being harassed by demons, some openly, others covertly. Some become lunatics, other are half-withered or lame or deaf or mute or paralytic or idiots. Even if they are in good health, they will be do-nothings, committing useless and disgusting deeds. They will be caught either in adultery or in murder or in theft or in fornication, and you will be afflicted in all these cases. But if you are persuaded to keep your souls pure for God, living children will be born to you, who will suffer no harm. You will live an untroubled life, free from care and grief, while awaiting that true and incorruptible marriage. At that marriage you will be the attendants of the Bridegroom, as you enter into that bridal chamber full of immortality and light."

[13] When the young people heard this, they believed in the Lord and dedicated themselves to him. They abstained from filthy desire and in this way remained there for the entire night. The Lord departed from them with these words: "The grace of the Lord will be with you." At daybreak the king arrived and, after filling the table, approached the bridegroom and the bride. He found them sitting opposite each other, the bride with her face uncovered and the bridegroom with a joyful look. The mother approached the bride and said: "Why do you sit there so immodestly, child, as if you have been living with your husband for a long time?" Then her father said: "Is it because of your great love for your husband that you are uncovered?" [14] The bride replied:

"Truly, father, I am deeply in love and I pray to my Lord that the love which I have experienced tonight will continue, and I will claim for myself that husband whom I have experienced today. That is why I am no longer covered, since the mirror of shame has been taken from me. No longer am I ashamed or embarrassed, since the work of shame and embarrassment is far away from me. I am not afraid, since fear does not abide in me. I am cheerful and joyful, since the day of joy has not been shaken. I regard as nothing this husband and this marriage that have passed before my eyes, since I have been given in another marriage. I have had no intercourse with a temporary husband, which ends only in lust and bitterness of soul, since I have been united with a true husband."

[15] As the bride was still speaking, the bridegroom answered in these words: "I give thanks to you, O Lord, who have been proclaimed by a stranger and have been found in us. You have put me far from corruption and sown life in me. You have delivered me from this disease, which is hard to heal and difficult to cure and lasts forever, and you have established me in good health. You have shown yourself to me and have revealed to me all that pertains to me and the circumstances of my existence. You have saved me from destruction and led me to a better path. You have freed me from what is temporary and made me worthy of what is immortal and eternal. You have lowered yourself to me and to my smallness, so that you might lift me up to your greatness and unite me to yourself. You did not withhold your compassion from me when I was lost, but you have shown me how to search for myself and how to know who I was, and who and in what state I am now, so that I might once again become what I was. I did not know myself, but you sought me out; I did not understand myself, but you took hold of me, you whom I now experience and cannot forget. Love of you seethes in me, and I cannot speak as I should. Whatever I can say about him turns out to be too brief, too little, and not in proportion to his glory. But he does not find fault with me for not being ashamed to say to him even what I do not know, for it is through his love that I say even this."

[16] When the king heard this from the bridegroom and the bride, he tore his clothing and said to those standing near him: "Go out quickly and search the whole city. Capture and bring to me that man, the magician, who has come to this city to do evil. I led him into my house with my own hands and I told him to pray for my unfortunate daughter. Whoever finds him and brings him to me will receive whatever he asks of me." They went out and searched everywhere for him, but did not find him because he had set sail. They also went into the inn where he had stayed, and there they found the flute girl weeping and upset because he had not taken her with him. But when they told her what had happened to the young couple, she was delighted by the news and put aside her grief, saying: "Now I too have found rest here."

Then she got up and went to them and stayed with them a long time, until they had instructed the king as well. Many of the brothers also gathered there until they heard a report that the apostle had reached the cities of India and was teaching there. And they went away and joined him.

Bibliography

Attridge, Harold. 1990. "The Original Language of the Acts of Thomas." In *Of Scribes and Scrolls,* ed. H. Attridge et al., 241–50. Lanham, Md.: University Press of America.

Bonnet, Maximilianus. 1959. *Acta apostolorum apocrypha.* Vol. 2, part 2, 99–124. Leipzig, 1903. Rpt. Hildesheim: Georg Olms Verlagsbuchhandlung.

Cartlidge, David R. 1986. "Transfigurations of Metamorphosis Traditions in the Acts of John, Thomas, and Peter." In *The Apocryphal Acts of Apostles,* ed. D. R. MacDonald, 53–66. Semeia 38. Atlanta: Scholars Press.

Dihle, Albrecht. 1963. "Neues zur Thomas-Tradition." *Jahrbuch für Antike und Christentum* 6: 54–70.

Drijvers, Han J. W. 1992. "The Acts of Thomas." In *New Testament Apocrypha,* ed. Wilhelm Schneemelcher, trans. R. Mcl. Wilson, 2: 322–411. Louisville, Ky.: Westminster/John Knox Press.

Geerard, M. 1992. *Clavis apocryphorum novi testamenti.* Turnhout: Brepols.

Gunther, John J. 1980. "The Meaning and Origin of the Name 'Judas Thomas.' " *Le Muséon* 93, no. 1–2: 113–48.

Huxley, George L. 1983. "Geography in the Acts of Thomas." *Greek, Roman, and Byzantine Studies* 24, no. 1 (Spring): 71–80.

Junod, Eric. 1981. "Origène, Eusèbe et la tradition sur la répartition des champs de mission des apôtres." In *Les Actes apocryphes des apôtres. Christianisme et monde païen,* ed. François Bovon et al., 233–48. Geneva: Labor et Fides.

Kaestli, Jean-Daniel. 1977. "L'Utilisation des Actes apocryphes des apôtres dans le manichéisme." In *Gnosis and Gnosticism,* ed. Martin Krause, 107–16. Leiden: E. J. Brill.

Klijn, A. F. J. 1962. *The Acts of Thomas. Introduction, Text, Commentary.* Leiden: E. J. Brill.

———. 1965. "The Influence of Jewish Theology on the Odes of Solomon and the Acts of Thomas." In *Aspects du judéo-christianisme. Colloque du Strasbourg 23–25 avril 1964,* 167–79. Paris: Presses Universitaires de France.

Kruse, Heinz. 1984. "Das Brautlied der syrischen Thomas-Akten." *Orientalia Christiana Periodica* 50: 291–330.

La Fargue, J. M. 1985. *Language and Gnosis. The Opening Scenes of the Acts of Thomas.* Harvard Dissertations in Religion 18. Philadelphia: Fortress Press.

Layton, Bentley. 1987. *The Gnostic Scriptures.* New York: Doubleday.

Marcovich, Miroslav. 1981. "The Wedding Hymn of the *Acta Thomae.*" *Illinois Classical Studies* 6, no. 2 (Fall): 367–85.

Nagel, Peter. 1973. "Die apokryphen Apostelakten des 2. und 3. Jahrhunderts in der manichäischen Literatur." In *Gnosis und Neues Testament,* ed. Karl-Wolfgang Tröger, 148–82. Gütersloh: Gütersloher Verlagshaus Gerd Mohn.

Poirier, Paul-Hubert. 1981. *L'Hymne de la Perle des Actes de Thomas.* Louvain-la-Neuve: Université Catholique.

———. 1997. "The Writings Ascribed to Thomas and the Thomas Tradition." In *The Nag*

Hammadi Library after Fifty Years, ed. John D. Turner and Anne McGuire, 295–307. Leiden and New York: E. J. Brill.

Riley, Gregory J. 1990. "Thomas Tradition and the Acts of Thomas." In *Society of Biblical Literature: 1991 Seminar Papers,* ed. E. H. Lovering, 533–42. Atlanta: Scholars Press.

———. 1995. *Resurrection Reconsidered. Thomas and John in Controversy.* Minneapolis: Fortress.

Rouwhorst, Gerard. 1990. "La Célébration de l'eucharistie selon les Actes de Thomas." In *Omnes circumadstantes. Contributions towards a History of the Role of the People in the Liturgy,* ed. Charles Caspers and Marc Schneiders, 51–77. Kampen: J. H. Kok.

Tissot, Yves. 1981. "Les Actes apocryphes de Thomas: Exemple de recueil composite." In *Les Actes apocryphes des apôtres. Christianisme et monde païen,* ed. François Bovon et al., 223–32. Geneva: Labor et Fides.

———. 1988. "L'Encratisme des Actes de Thomas." In *Aufstieg und Niedergang der römischen Welt,* 2.25.6, ed. W. Haase, 4,415–30. Berlin and New York: Walter de Gruyter.

Valantasis, Richard. 1995. "The Nuptial Chamber Revisited: The Acts of Thomas and Cultural Intertextuality." In *Society of Biblical Literature: 1995 Seminar Papers,* ed. Eugene H. Lovering, Jr., 380–93. Atlanta: Scholars Press.

Winkler, Gabriele. 1982. "The Origins and Idiosyncrasies of the Earliest Form of Asceticism." In *The Continuing Quest for God. Monastic Spirituality in Tradition and Transition,* ed. William Skudlarek, O.S.B., 9–43. Collegeville, Minn.: Liturgical Press.

Zur, Yiphtah. 1993. "Parallels between Acts of Thomas 6–7 and 4Q184." *Revue de Qumran* 16, no. 61 (September): 103–7.

—16—

An Anonymous Letter to a Woman Named Susanna

Maureen A. Tilley

This sermon displays the attitude of Christians of Late Antiquity toward women who vowed virginity and later reneged on that promise. For many years this work was attributed to Ambrose, Bishop of Milan (ca. 339–397), who had written several works celebrating virginity; scholars of the twentieth century dispute the attribution. Some believe it was written by Nicetas of Remisiana along the Danube (now Bela Palanka in Serbia), a bishop active from about 370 to his death in 414. At any rate, it illustrates the mores of the late fourth century and provides insight into similar views expressed in the present toward pre-marital sex and rape.

A narrative found in the Greek version of the Book of Daniel (13:1–63) forms the background for this sermon. It is devoted to Susanna, for whom the addressee of the sermon was named. The biblical Susanna was a beautiful and virtuous young Jewish matron living in Babylon during the Exile in the sixth century B.C.E. Susanna was pressured by two respected Jewish judges: if she failed to submit to rape by them, they threatened that both would testify in court that she committed adultery with a younger man. She did refuse and was unjustly convicted. She was sentenced to be stoned, but at the critical moment she was vindicated by the prophet Daniel, who exposed the duplicity of her accusers' testimony.

She became the paradigm for chaste women accused of illicit sexual activity. The irony her chaste image provides will be obvious.

The text is translated from *Incerti auctoris "De lapsu Susannae"* (*"De lapsu virginis consecratae"*), edited by Ignatius Cazzaniga (Turin: G. B. Paraviae, 1948). Translation © Maureen A. Tilley, 1998.

An Anonymous Letter to a Woman Named Susanna

[I.1] Why are you silent, O my soul? Why are you troubled in your thoughts? Why don't you let your voice break forth and lay bare the ardent desire of your mind so that you might have some relief? This surely, this will be like a remedy for your trouble, if you would open up your mouth and set out to explain what the crime is. Similarly, lancing and draining a boil, however swollen it has been, offers relief from the festering.

[I.2] Hear me now, you who are near, you who are far away, you who fear the Lord, and you who rejoice in the joy of his Church and grieve in its sadness; for so it is written: "Rejoice with those who are rejoicing and grieve with those who are grieving" [Rom. 12:15]. I call on you, I say, you who hold fast to the most genuine love of Christ, and who do not rejoice over iniquity, but rather weep over it. Pay attention to what I say; judge what issues from justified sorrow. Tremble along with me at the nature of this crime, which has been uncovered.

[I.3] A noble virgin, consecrated to Christ, wise and learned, tumbled down into the ditch of disgrace. She conceived sorrow and gave birth to iniquity [cf. Ps. 7:14]. She ruined herself and stained the Church. Because of this, the entire soul of Christianity suffers a grave wound, for what is holy was given to the dogs and pearls were cast before swine [Matt. 7:6]. The precious name of propriety has been mutilated by the lustful persons, and by filthy and vile people has the precious way of the life of chastity been treated with contempt.

[I.4] This is why there is seething in my mind; this is why there is an incurable sorrow, because no evil deed drags so much good away with it! The little cloud of one sinful woman obscures almost the entire light of the Church. Therefore, I will raise a prophetic voice and with tears in my eyes declare: "Hear me, all you peoples, and see my sorrow," [Lam. 1:12]. My virgins and young men have gone away into captivity. And surely this is captivity when souls captive to sin are led to death and are held by diabolical domination; surely, this is captivity.

[II.5] I want to speak to you directly since *you* are the source of these things and the cause of these evils. You are wretched many times over because you have lost even the title of virgin, along with its glory. It was not right for Susanna to be called unchaste and no one should be allowed to call you what you are not. Where should I begin? What should I say first, or last? Should I mention the good things you have lost? Or should I bewail the evils you have found?

[II.6] You were a virgin in the garden [*paradisium*] of God. By all accounts you were among the flowers of the Church. You were a bride of Christ. You were the temple of the Lord. You were the dwelling place of the Holy Spirit [1 Cor. 3:16]. As many times as I say "you were," it is just that often you must weep because you are *not* what you were. You advanced in the Church just like that dove about whom it is written: "The feathers of the dove are made of silver and the tail feathers look like gold" [Ps. 67:13]. You shone like silver, you glistened like gold, when you advanced with a pure conscience. You were just like a shining star in the hand of the Lord; you were not afraid of any wind or any clouds of war.

[II.7] What is this sudden shift? What is this instantaneous change? You are transformed from a virgin of God to a spoil of Satan, from a bride of Christ to a repulsive prostitute, from a dwelling place of the Holy Spirit to a shack of the devil, from a temple of God to a sanctuary of slime. You who advanced in fidelity like a dove now hide in darkness like a stellion [a kind of common lizard]. You who shone like gold because of the honor of your virginity now have become lower than the dirt in the streets, so that you should be trampled underfoot even by the feet of shameless people. You were once a shining star in the hand of God. Just as if you fell from high in heaven, your light has gone out and you are changed into dead coals.

[III.8] Woe to you, you wretch, and woe again! You have lost so much good for the sake of the licentiousness of such a short moment! How much hope in Christ the Lord have you lost for yourself! You who have taken a member of his body and made it into a member of the body of a whore [cf. 1 Cor. 6:15]! How will the Holy Spirit visit you when you have repudiated the Spirit, which keeps clear of even impure thoughts?

[III.9] But let us proceed to human exemplars, so that through them we may come to understand the divine. Consider who among the holy men, who among the holy women would not shudder to come near you? Open your eyes, if you can! Lift up your eyes, if you dare! Look any of the saints in the eye confidently! Knowledge of your transgression depresses you and weighs you down like a lead weight, doesn't it? Will not the dread darkness of night remain before your eyes? Will not fear and trembling shake your soul and body [Ps. 55:5]?

[III.10] So if you are not able to look into the eyes of people made of flesh and subject to some transgression of their own, buried as you are in such great confusion, how will you show your face before the chaste apostles? How will you show your face before Elijah, Daniel, and the army of such great prophets? How will you show your face before John? How will you show your face before Mary, Thecla, Agnes, and the unspotted chorus of purity? Finally then, how will you show your face before the holy angels? Will you not be scorched by the splendor and the brightness of those who have no sin as if you were struck by lightning?

[III.11] But perhaps you have to say: "I could not hold out against him because I am embodied in an all too frail flesh." Blessed Thecla with her innumerable associates will answer you: "We were clothed with the same flesh. Nevertheless, the fragility of flesh was not able to diminish our solid determination for chastity nor could the savagery of tyrants rob us of our chastity by their diverse torments." Truly the flesh cannot be corrupted unless the soul were corrupted first. Therefore, the soul preceded the flesh in its delight and will remain mired in its offense.

[III.12] But you say: "I did not will this evil; I suffered violence." That most brave Susanna, whose name you falsely wear, will answer you: "Placed between two elders, there between two judges of the people, set there alone between the trees of the garden [Dan. 13:20ff.], I could not be conquered; because I did not will to be." Could you not have shown some resistance against an inexperienced adolescent, there in the middle of the city, if you had not already wished to be corrupted? Then who heard your cries? Who observed your struggle? [See Deut. 22:23–27] So that I might say nothing about these things, surely after the violence to which you were exposed you should have revealed the wicked deed to your parents or to your sisters, if not to others. There might have been some excuse for this misfortune; there might have been a complete cleansing of your conscience, if you had publicly revealed the enemy of your modesty.

[III.13] But perhaps you would have blushed, lest so many people know that you had been dishonored. But why were you afraid when there was nothing to be afraid of, except perhaps that you might more likely connect the charge with adultery by keeping silent? Granted however, shame keeps you from admitting this. What do you have to say about the second time you had sex? What about the third time? What about this repeated traffic in immorality? Shut up, shut up about this charade of violence. You have to shut up about this excuse of shame since you are constantly offering to most abominable fornication those very members of your body consecrated to Christ but now contaminated even in their inmost parts.

[III.14] The soul shudders, yes it does, the mind melts away when it comes to raising the issue of this crime. It is like when a doctor, however brave in spirit, cuts deeply into a wound, I think that he will suffer dread to some degree. Alas, lost one, do you not understand already that all avenues of excuse are closed to you? Do you not already feel how much evil impious desire has brought you in both your soul and your flesh?

[III.15] Your father had not anticipated this dishonor from you, he who counted you as his singular point of pride. Your mother would not have believed that this mourning and these tears would be born to her from you, she who was consoled by your virginity for the pain of her having given birth. Neither your brothers nor your sisters anticipated this disgrace from you. You have seriously wounded all of them with the single sword of your crime.

[III.16] If you had died of natural causes, your parents would have wept a bit for you on account of their love; but they had rejoiced exceedingly because they had sent forth an immaculate virgin, a living offering to the Lord, one who would surely atone for their own transgressions. But now they weep for you as dead, but not dead; they weep for you living and not living, dead surely to the glory of your virginity, alive in the dishonor of disgrace.

[III.17] Your father is mad at the part of his own body with which he begot you. Your mother curses her uterus from which you unhappily came forth into the light of day. Nevertheless, they do not find any limit for their sorrow except that they clearly seem to have this as their only consolation: your father did not compel you nor did your mother force you to profess virginity. You later declared of your own will. For I know when your father explained its many difficulties to you, when he kept saying that the virgin's way of life was difficult, not only did you obstinately oppose him, but you called the disclosures given to you frightful.

[III.18] They placed their hope of some little reward for themselves, therefore, in the fact that they did not resist your plan. Understand, O wretch, that the onus of judgment grows in this: you have not fulfilled what you promised. By what coils did that good for nothing Serpent bind you? With what venom did he who deceived Eve inject you so that he might strike you with such blindness, so that he might produce such forgetfulness in your soul?

[V.19] Don't you remember that holy day, the day of the resurrection of the Lord, on which you offered yourself to be veiled at the divine altar? In such a solemn assembly of the Church of God, you advanced amidst the shining light of the neophytes, among the candidates for the Kingdom of Heaven, just like a new bride of the King. Don't you remember the sermon preached to you on that day: "Look, daughter. See, O virgin. Forget your people and your father's house; [the King will desire your beauty] because he is the Lord your God" [Ps. 44:10–11]? Remember how many people assembled for the glory of the marriage of you and your Lord. You should have kept the vow you made before such witnesses, and you should have always thought about the One to whom you vowed virginity. You should have found it easier to pour out your blood with your soul than to lose your chastity.

[V.20] On that day of your consecration, with these words and with many praises for your chastity, you were clothed with the holy veil. Then all the people signed as witnesses to your marriage, not in ink but in the Spirit [2 Cor. 3:3], as they all cried out "Amen." I am overcome with tears when I remember these things; I am pricked by these goads when I consider these human parallels. Normally, a marriage is contracted before ten witnesses, and once the marriage is consummated, any woman joined to a mortal husband does not commit adultery without grave risk. So how can the spiritual bond made before the innumerable witnesses of the Church, before the angels and the armies of heaven be dissolved by adultery? I don't know whether it is possible to come up with a suitable death or penalty for this offense.

[V.21] A person might say: "It is better to marry than to burn" [1 Cor. 7:9]. This saying applies to one who is not yet vowed, to one who has not yet taken the veil. On the other hand, she who responded to Christ and accepted the holy veil, she is already married, she is already joined to the heavenly man. If a woman had already vowed to be wedded to her spouse in the ordinary manner and committed adultery, she becomes the handmaid of death. If this is so, what do we have to say about her, this one who was debauched in hidden and clandestine disgrace and pretends that she is what she is not? She may be dressed like a virgin, but she has not acted like one. She is an adulteress twice over, both in deed and in appearance.

[VI.22] But I return to you now, you who put up with forgetting so many good things and became the repository of so many evils. How is it that virginal behavior, advancement in the Church among the chorus of virgins, did not enter your mind in the course of this ignominious action? How is that the light of vigils did not caress your eyes? How is it that the melody of spiritual songs did not penetrate your ears? How is that the excellence of heavenly texts did not inflame your mind? How can this be when the Apostle cries out regarding this: "Avoid fornication; because every sin a person commits is outside the body; but a person who commits fornication sins against their own body." [1 Cor. 6:18]? And when he says "against their own body," he points out that according to Christ they are sinning against [the body of] Christ. For he added: "Do you not know that your members are the temple of the Holy Spirit, which you have from the Lord, and that you are not your own; you have been bought for a great price, glorify and carry the Lord in your body" [1 Cor. 6:19–20]. And again he says: "Let not fornication or any impurity be named among you, as befits the saints" [Eph. 5:3]. And, setting aside all flattery, the Apostle framed this adage, "Know this and understand that no fornicator or impure or greedy person will be heir in the kingdom of Christ and God" [Eph. 5:5].

[VI.23] Didn't these things, and such terrible things at that, enter your mind when your body was pursued for that nefarious deed? No, deadly forgetfulness drowned you in the deepest abyss and raging desire led you like a captive.

[VI.24] Now you have to remember, don't you, that place where you stood in the Church separated by boards [in a special place in the church] and how pious and noble women earnestly ran there, seeking your kiss, women who were holier and more worthy than you? You have to remember, don't you, those precepts, which the inscribed wall itself flung at your eyes: "The married woman and the virgin differ: the one who is not married thinks about the affairs of the Lord, how she might be holy in body and in soul" [1 Cor. 7:34]. You, however, turned the saying on its head, acting in such a way, thinking in such a way, that you might be holy neither in your body nor in your soul: in your body, in fact, by fornicating; and in your spirit, on the other hand, by giving the lie to your virginity.

[VI.25] O, how horrible! Rumor usually follows a deed, but in your case rumor actually preceded your evil deed. For when there had been, in fact, rumor and whispering about you for three years already, you pretended to be pure and in the Church you publicly demanded compensation for the imprecations. What trouble did I put up with! What burdens did your father bear on account of your reputation, asking about people one by one, putting them under oath one by one, so that we might discover the author of the slander! It was onerous for us and intolerable for all good people that anything shameful should be said or even believed about a virgin of God.

[VI.26] You had no fear in all this. It did not impinge on your consciousness when you appeared joyful before your enemies and you kept enraged those who were laboring on behalf of your reputation! What presumption, what impudence that your conscience should not haunt you! But you with your pretend virginity, you thought that you could deceive the Lord himself! But he is the one who said: "There is nothing hidden which will not be revealed" [Matt. 10:26] and "You," he says, "you did it in secret: I, however, will reveal it in the open" [2 Sam. 12:12]. The One who does not lie revealed your secret crime in public, and in the sight of his sun he stripped your works of their shadows.

[VI.27] O whatever Rumor alleged, coarser things actually occurred. Although Rumor wanted to be moderate, she did not find a way. You have forgotten your way of life. You have forgotten your parents. You have forgotten the whole Church. You have forgotten the glory of virginity. You have forgotten the honor of your dignity. You have forgotten the promise of the Kingdom. You have forgotten terrible judgment. You have embraced corruption. You have brought forth the fruit of corruption. In truth, you have brought forth cruelest death and eternal damnation.

[VII.28] And surely you do not have anything to complain about regarding any oversight on our part. Neither you nor anyone else has been denied pastoral care. Spiritual affection was employed; holy admonition was not lacking. You have forgotten your father's house, just as scripture says [Ps. 45:10]. You passed on to the monastery of virgins. Placed among them as you are, not only do I say that you should have been safe, if you had wanted to be, but you should even have been able to distinguish yourself beyond the others. But in vain these and other things were provided for.

[VII.29] In vain have I expounded the hymn of virginity, in which you have sung equally of the glory of your way of life and of its observance. I have sown on the roadway, I have sown among the thorns, I have sown in a rocky place. The birds, that is the demons, have snatched my words from your heart. My words were choked by your evil thoughts and withered by the excess heat of passion [cf. Luke 8:5–8]. Alas, when I thought I was building with gold, silver, and precious stones, I was found to be working with wood, hay, stubble, kindling material [1 Cor. 3:12]! I quote the Prophet: "Alas! I have become like one who collects stubble at the harvest [cf. Micah 7:1]."

[VII.30] In fact, if you had injured yourself alone, it would have been truly sad, but in a sense tolerable. But how many souls have you wounded by your offense! How many souls have I made do penance on account of you and your way of life! How many lips of the faithful have been defiled by blaspheming the way of the Lord! Paganism has opened its mouth among us: because of your dishonor, the Synagogue of the Jews has boasted against the holy Church.

[VII.31] If the one who scandalized a single person ought to have a millstone hung around the neck and be thrown into the sea [Matt. 18:6], what should I say about you, by whose transgression every soul is wounded and the name of the Lord blasphemed among unbelievers? As often as the word 'virgins' is mentioned, isn't that just how often the abundance of your iniquity torments you? Look, you lie there wounded. Look, you lie there thrown to the ground.

[VIII.32] I want to do good, but I cannot be helpful because "my whole head is in pain and my whole heart is in sorrow; from head to foot"—so says Isaiah—"there is nothing to ease the pain" [Isa. 1:5–6]. Your sickness resists the help of every human medicine. It is permitted that good people and even evil people should be upset by a just indignation and judge you worthy of destruction, torment by every kind of torture, maltreatment in death, and worthy to be burned in flames. Nevertheless, since I know how greater tortures are reserved for transgressors and that impious souls remain tormented not only for a limited time but for all eternity, I wish you to be afflicted with other torments, beneficial ones, not ones that will promote the loss of your soul.

[VIII.33] Therefore, I am going to give you advice in accord with divine judgment; this is the one and only remedy to try, which the divine voice granted to the wretched through Ezekiel. He says: "I do not want the death of the sinner, but that the sinner be converted and live" [Ezek. 33:11]. And a little later the Lord speaks again: "I said: 'Turn to me. Is there no balm in Gilead; is there no doctor there? Why hasn't the health of the daughter of my people improved?' " [Jer. 8:22]. Surely these sayings inspire penance; these words of God call sinners to repentance. Just as medicine is necessary for those who have been wounded so penance is necessary for those who have lapsed.

[VIII.34] So now, how much and what sort of penance do you think is necessary? What equals the transgressions or, in fact, goes beyond them? See whether this sin of adultery is an uncomplicated one or perhaps it may be doubly weighty on account of that ruin that is said to have been accomplished in secret. Then the magnitude of the penalty must be set in proportion to the quantity of guilt. However, penance is not accomplished in words but in deeds. So you have to do this when you envision how far you have fallen from glory and how your name has been erased from the Book of Life. This is especially so if you believe that you have been placed in the outer darkness where there is the weeping of eyes and the gnashing of teeth without end [Matt. 8:12]. The duplicitous soul must be handed over to infernal punishments and the fires of Gehenna. There is no other remedy established after a single Baptism than the consolation of repentance. When you accept this in your mind as a matter of firm faith, as it is, then be content with however much affliction, however much suffering you undergo, because all the while you are being freed from eternal punishments.

[VIII.35] Then, while you are mulling these things over within yourself and withdrawing into your mind, be a very strict judge of your deeds. First, you must take all of your medicine in the midst of this life. Thinking of yourself as if you were dead, and, in a sense, you are, consider how you might be able to be restored to life. Then you must wear mourning dress and you must punish your mind and every member of your body deserving correction. You should cut off the curls that were responsible for the opportunity for licentiousness through vainglory. Your eyes should pour forth tears, for it was your eyes which gazed on a man in a less than upright manner. Your face should grow pale, that face, which used to blush shamelessly. Finally, your entire body should be bowed down and tormented with fasting. It should tremble, sprinkled with ashes and clothed in a hair shirt because it has wrongly been pleased with itself on account of its beauty. Your heart must truly melt like wax, worrying itself with fasting and stirring itself up with thoughts about the reason it might be ruined by the Enemy. Even the senses must be tormented, because once they gain dominion over the members of the body, they yield their power only with difficulty.

[VIII.36] Such a life, such performance of penance, if you are perseverant, will dare to give you hope, if not of glory, perhaps of exemption from punishment. As God says: "Turn to me, and I will turn to you. Turn with your whole heart, in fasting, in weeping, and in mourning. Tear your hearts, and not your clothes; for he is kind and merciful" [Joel 2:12–13]. In that way the great King David was converted and forgiven [2 Sam. 12:13]; in that way that sinful city of Nineveh escaped the damnation that threatened it [Jonah 3:5]. Therefore, if a sinner does not spare herself, she will be spared by God. And if she will have made up for future eternal punishment in Gehenna in the short run of this life, she will free herself from eternal judgment.

[VIII.37] Intense affliction needs thorough and deep-acting medicine; a great crime requires great repayment. For there is no doubt that it is a less serious offense when a person voluntarily confesses her sin and does penance. But when she hides her evil deeds, she is revealed involuntarily and she is exposed against her will: that crime is all the more serious. You cannot deny that this is what happened to you. Therefore, you must lament all the more, because your sin is more serious.

[VIII.38] If sinners would perceive in their minds the kind of judgment God passes on the world, and the fact that human sensation is not distributed at random by the vanity of this world, they would not be burdened by infidelity. However much, whatever sort of torment they might freely suffer in the present, they would suffer willingly—even if their life were prolonged—if it meant that they would not incur the punishment of eternal fire. But you who have now entered into the combat of penitence, press on, you wretch. Hold on tightly, you shipwreck of the boards, [a reference to penance as a plank to which sinners cling] hoping that through it you might be freed from the depths of your faults. Hold onto penance to the end of your life and do not presume to grant yourself any pardon in this life because anyone who wants to promise you this is deceiving you. You who have sinned of your own will against the Lord, from him alone is it proper for you to wait for a relief on the day of judgment.

[IX.39] Now what should I to say about you, son of the Serpent, minister of the Devil, violator of the temple of God? In one evil deed you committed two crimes, both adultery and sacrilege. And sacrilege it was when you with your insane rashness polluted the vessel offered to Christ, dedicated to the Lord. Belshazzar, the king of the Persians, made use of the Lord's vessels which had been taken from the Temple at Jerusalem by his father to drink with his friends and concubines. That very night he was punished by the hand of an angel, cut down by a cruel death [Dan. 5:1–30]. What should I think about you, you who are ruined as much as you are a ruiner, you who impiously polluted the human vessel consecrated to Christ, sanctified by the Holy Spirit? You defiled her sacrilegiously, unmindful of your way of life, contemptuous of divine judgment. On the whole, it would have been better if you had not been born, but since you were born, that Gehenna should claim you for itself as its own son.

[IX.40] The very awareness of the crime is allowed to push you to the crisis point in various ways. For "the impious man has fled with no one to follow him" [Prov. 28:1]. Dreadful phantoms of sin are allowed to terrorize you when you are sleeping and not only when you are awake. Nevertheless, since a shepherd should never deny medicine to a sick sheep much less to one dying, I am giving you some advice. You should ask voluntarily for the prison of penance; you should bind your innermost parts with chains; you should torment your soul with groaning and fasting; you should seek the help of the saints; you should cast yourself at the feet of the elect; so that your unrepentant heart should not store up wrath for itself on the day of wrath and day of the just judgment of God who renders to each according to his works [Rom. 2:5–6]. May you not stand among the number of those whom Paul mourns: those who sinned before and have not done penance for their impurity and their fornication and the passionate deeds which they have committed [2 Cor. 12:21].

[IX.41] You should not delude yourself about the multitude of similar sins, nor should you say, "I have not done this by myself; I have plenty of companions." But realize that plenty of companions don't provide you with immunity for your offenses. For countless people lived even in Sodom and Gomorrah and in all of the five cities, and all alike who treated their own bodies licentiously burned in a rainstorm of fire [Gen. 19:24]. But only Lot escaped from that inevitable conflagration, because he showed himself opposed to that disgrace.

[IX.42] Now then, O wretch, with mourning and continual tears drive from your heart the flattery of the Serpent. While your soul full of darkness is upset within your impure body, acquire for yourself a remedy for that inevitable day, always holding before your eyes the words of the Apostle: "we must all appear before the judgment seat of Christ so that each one may account for what belongs to him in his own body, according to what he has done, whether good or bad" [cf. 2 Cor. 5:10].

[X.43] "Who may console you, virgin daughter Zion, now that your contrition has become as great as the sea. Pour out your heart like water in the presence of the Lord. Raise your hands to him" [Lam. 2:19] as a remedy for your sins. Then take up a lament. First, do not give up reciting the fiftieth psalm for even a single day. For it is recited under these circumstances, all the way down to the verse: "God does not despise a contrite and humble heart" [Ps. 51:17] when it runs to him with tears and groaning.

[X.44] In addition, with compunction pour out this lamentation in the sight of God the judge, "Who will give water to my head and a fountain of tears to my eyes [Jer. 9:1]" so that I might weep for the wounds of my soul? "My feast days have been turned into mourning and my songs into lamentations [Amos 8:10]." The sound of hymns and the happiness of psalms gave way, and the grinding of teeth and the weeping of eyes approached [cf. Matt. 22:13]. "I became speechless, I was humbled, I did not speak about anything good, and my sorrow was redoubled. My heart grew hot within me and fire burned in

my thoughts [Ps. 39:3]." "Fear and trembling came upon me and darkness
covered me [Ps. 54:5]." "The abyss surrounded me. Finally my head sank in
the clefts of the mountains [Jonah 2:5–6]."

[X.45] Alas! I became like Sodom and I was burnt like Gomorrah [Gen.
19:24]. Who will take pity on my ashes? I have transgressed more severely
than Sodom because it did not know the law when it did wrong, but I, even
after receiving grace, I sinned against the Lord. "If one person sins against
another, there will be some one to intervene. I have sinned against the Lord.
What intercessor will I find [1 Sam. 2:25]?" I conceived sorrow; I gave birth
to iniquity; I opened a pit and dug it out and I fell into the hole which I had
made. Therefore, my sorrow whirled round in my head and iniquity has descended from my head [Ps. 7:14–16]. My impurity was right in front of me. I
was not mindful of my end and I have fallen wretchedly.

[X.46] "There is no one to console me. O how sour is the fruit of licentiousness, more bitter than gall, more cruel than the sword! How have I gotten into
such a desolate state? Suddenly I fell; I perished on account of my iniquity as
if I were rising from sleep. Therefore my appearance was despised in the city
of God [Ps. 72:20, Vulgate only]." My name was erased from the Book of Life
[cf. Rev. 3:5]. I have become like a night owl in a house, like a single sparrow
in a building [Ps. 101:7–8 Vulgate]. There is no one to console me. Look
toward the right and see that there is no one who knows me. Escape eludes
me and there is no one who will care for my soul [Ps. 142:4]. I have become
like a broken vessel. I have heard all my neighbors blaming me [Ps. 30:12].
Woe for the day on which my unfortunate mother gave birth to me and that
cruel light received me! It would have been better had I never been born than
that I should be made a laughing stock among the people [Job 3:3; Jer. 20:14;
1 Kings 9:7]. Confusion has come upon all the servants of God because of me
and on all who worship him worthily [Dan. 3:33, Vulgate only].

[X.47] Mourn for me, mountains and hills, mourn for me, O springs and
rivers, because I am the daughter of weeping. Mourn for me, beasts of the
woods, reptiles of the earth, birds of the sky, and every spirit which has life.
You are blessed, beasts and birds, for you are not afraid of the netherworld and
you don't have to give an account after death. The penalty of cruel Tartarus
hangs over us because we have taken leave of our senses; so there is no peace
for sinners.

[X.48] My sin and my iniquity are not like the offenses of other people; they
are a sacrilege. When I promised that my flesh would serve as a virgin and I
publicly professed chastity, I lied to the Lord. Now I have no confidence in
invoking the Lord most high, because my mouth is blocked by transgressions.
The Prophet proclaims my evil deed saying: "Those who distance themselves
from the Lord will perish; he scatters every fornicator from him" [Ps. 73:27];
and elsewhere he says: "My tongue sticks to my mouth and I am brought down
into the dust of death [Ps. 22:15]."

[X.49] Nevertheless, I shall cry out to the Lord while there is still time, as long as there is still time; because there is no remembrance in death and there is no praise in the netherworld [Isa. 38:18]. "Lord, do not reprove me in your anger, nor in your rage reproach me. For your arrows have struck me. There is no health in my flesh because of the wound of your anger. There is no peace in my bones because of my sins. For my iniquities hang heavily on my head and they weigh me down like a huge burden. My wounds fester and grow even worse because of my foolishness. I am afflicted with troubles and I am bent all the way down. I cry out with a moan from my heart. My heart reels within me, my strength has left me and there is no light in my eyes" [Ps. 38:1–10]. God, you have rejected me and you have ruined me. You have been hard on me, you have given me the wine of compunction to drink [Ps. 60:3]. I have been removed from your sight. Now I am not cast down so that I should rise again to your holy temple, but I have been destroyed.

[X.50] "What good is there in your blood when I go down into corruption" [cf. Ps. 30:9]? You don't perform miracles for the dead, do you? Will the doctors raise them from the dead [cf. Ps. 88:10]? It is your word, it is your promise: I do not prefer the death of a sinner, but rather conversion that she may live [Ezek. 33:11]. My conversion is to you, my God: because you alone can make all things new; you can call back souls from the netherworld. You release those bound; you, O God, raise those struck down, you give light to the blind, you raise the dead [cf. Ps. 146:8].

[X.51] "I have wandered astray like a lost sheep" [Ps. 119:176]. Watch out for your servant [Ps. 119:176] so that the cruel wolf does not swallow me. Many people say to my soul: "There is no safety for her in her God [Ps. 3:2]." But your plan is your own. How long will your servant live; when will you pass judgment on my behalf [Ps. 119:84]? But do not enter into judgment against your servant [Ps. 143:2]. My soul grows faint without your salvation; my eyes are worn out with tears; my reputation is spread over the earth [Ps. 119:81–83]. When will you turn to me and restore my soul [cf. Ps. 35:17]? You have reproached me on account of my iniquity, and you have made my soul waste away like a spider [Ps. 39:12 Vulgate]. Remember me, O Lord, for I am dust: see my humiliation and my suffering and forgive all my sins [Ps. 25:18]. Forgive me, so I may be refreshed before I depart and no longer exist [Ps. 39:13], for there will be no praise in the netherworld [Isa. 38:18].

[X.52] You are able, O Lord, to tear off my sackcloth and clothe me in joy [Ps. 30:11]. Break my bonds with which I have been tied and fettered, you who did not reject unclean Rahab [Josh. 6:17]. Remove your anger from me, O Lord [for I have sinned against you terribly] while you vindicate me and lead me into the light. God of all power, grant that my penance may be effective and my confession steadfast so that the deceiver of the soul may not trip me up. Grant me this gift. I desire to receive grace from your fountain so that I may confess you forever, you who live and reign in Trinity for ever and ever. Amen.

——17——

A Plea to a Local God for a Husband's Attentions

David Frankfurter

Letters to deceased family members complaining of misfortunes and injustices in this life had long provided a means for ordinary Egyptians to negotiate supernatural forces outside the walls of the temple cult. (Gardiner and Sethe 1928, 1–12; Wente 1990, 210–20). A scribe might be called upon to write out the letter on papyrus and then, according to one example, to read it aloud before the tomb before depositing it nearby; but the sentiments written seem to have been authentic voices of individuals.

Papyrus Schmidt, from about 100 C.E., is a rather late example of this ancient tradition, and it is among a small number of such letters that are written to local gods, not deceased family members. Osiris of Hasroe is probably a mortuary god, the highest authority among the deceased and thus the ultimate recourse for a woman desperate to carry on her lineage (cf. Hughes 1958). P. Schmidt is also unique among such letters because it is written, not in the traditional Hieratic or demotic Egyptian writing in which texts of a ritual nature were normally inscribed, but rather in Old Coptic, a combination of Greek letters and hybrid characters that allowed the Egyptian language to be more easily vocalized (Satzinger 1984). This fact raises some interesting questions about Esrmpe herself and/or the scribe who prepared this letter: was she, in fact, able to read these characters herself, but not Hieratic or demotic writing? Or, if her Egyptian name implies illiteracy in Greek as well as Egyptian, was the scribe able only to write in this hybrid assortment of characters, or was he somehow committed to vocalizing the precise sounds of Esrmpe's appeal for ritual effect (Frankfurter 1998, 251–52)?

Above all, the Schmidt Papyrus provides an intimate reflection of the supernatural world available to, and ritual acts conducted by, ordinary Egyptians of the Roman period. Local gods like Osiris of Hasroe, as well as ancient popular gods like Hathor, provide the objects of appeal, not grand syncretistic gods (Frankfurter 1998, chap. 3). Eventually, with Christianization, the locus of such appeals would become the martyrial sanctuary; yet the realities of life would still dominate the sense of the supernatural world.

The following translation is Helmut Satzinger's, reprinted with permission from *Journal of the American Research Center in Egypt* (Satzinger 1975). To maintain the intimate tone of Esrmpe's plea, I have changed Satzinger's translation of Old Coptic *nagg* (from Egyptian *nk:* see Satzinger 1975, 42n.n) from "cohabit with" to "make love with."

A Plea to a Local God for a Husband's Attentions

It is Esrmpe, the [daughter] of Kllaouč, who is complaining about Hor, the [son] of Tanesneou.

My lord Osiris, [Lord] of Hasro! I complain to you, do justice to me and Hor, the [son] of Tanesneou, concerning what I have done to him and what he has done to me. Namely, he does not make love with me, I having no power, I having no protector-son. I am unable to help [myself], I am childless [?]. There is no one who could complain concerning me before you [lit. him] because of Hor.

. . . I complain to [you . . .] . . . Osiris, listen to my calls! . . . what he has done to me. Open the way for [lit. give way to] your [messengers(?)] . . . Osiris, [lord] of Abydos, Osiris [. . .] Isis, . . . Ophois[?], Hathor[?], nurse [of] Anubis the Osiride, the cowherd of . . . do justice to me!

Bibliography

Frankfurter, David. 1998. *Religion in Roman Egypt: Assimilation and Resistance.* Princeton: Princeton University Press.

Gardiner, Alan H., and Kurt Sethe. 1928. *Egyptian Letters to the Dead.* London: Egypt Exploration Society.

Hughes, George R. 1958. "A Demotic Letter to Thoth." *Journal of Near Eastern Studies* 17: 1–12.

Satzinger, Helmut. 1975. "The Old Coptic Schmidt Papyrus," *Journal of the American Research Center in Egypt* 12: 37–50.

———. 1984. "Die altkoptischen Texte als Zeugnisse der Beziehungen zwischen Ägypten und Griechen." In *Graeco-Coptica: Griechen und Kopten im byzantinischen Ägypten,* ed. Peter Nagel, 137–46. Halle: Martin-Luther-Universität.

Wente, Edward. 1990. *Letters from Ancient Egypt.* Atlanta: Scholars Press.

——18——

Bishop Avitus of Vienne to His Excellency Ansmundus

Maureen A. Tilley

This letter is a companion piece to the previous sermon to Susanna. It addresses the issue of fornication under the aspect of male responsibility rather than female guilt.

It was written by Alcimus Ecdicius Avitus, bishop of Vienne in France from 490 to his death ca. 519. In this letter he addresses a man named Ansmundus, the patron of a man accused of impregnating a virgin who, despite her vow of chastity, had not been chaste even previous to her relationship with the unnamed subject of the letter. Apparently, this man had persuaded Ansmundus that he was innocent. He then requested that his patron ask Avitus to protect him from charges of sexual crimes. Not knowing all of the circumstances, Avitus assented. But when the good bishop learned that the man really was guilty, he was chagrined at being placed in a position of defending him. In this letter Avitus tries to enlist Ansmundus's assistance in reforming the sinner by whatever means necessary, including a threat of castration.

According to some medieval canonists, Matthew 19:9 ("Whoever divorces his wife, except for fornication, and marries another commits adultery") provided grounds for allowing that a man separated from his wife because of her adultery might remarry without penalty. (See *Marriage in the Catholic Church*, vol. 3: *Divorce and Remarriage,* pages 232–34 and 236, by Theodore Mackin [New York and Ramsey, N.J.: 1984]; and *Medieval Handbooks of Penance: A Translation of the Principal "Libri Poenitentiales,"* pages 85, 208, edited by John T. McNeill and Helena M. Gamer. New York: Columbia University, 1990).

The Latin text is found in PL 59.266–267. Translation © Maureen A. Tilley, 1998.

Bishop Avitus of Vienne to His Excellency Ansmundus

When I was at Lyon, the person for whom you considered me worthy to intercede denied to me the accusation that the whole world was shouting. I am really amazed that after he came to his senses and admitted it, he should have asked you for this favor. That he seeks it so unreservedly proves that this man should acknowledge his place among the ranks of the guilty.

But because of the honor you pay me, I would not have the freedom to do anything other than what you prescribe. Nevertheless, because of your opinions, I cannot resign from the task unless I explain what I am complaining about.

Your Piety knows and has heard read out frequently in church how the Scriptures differentiate many degrees in the evil of adultery. In the first case, a man sins by falling into fornication when he is inflamed by passion and desires a woman to whom he is not married. In the second and worse case, he violates the honor of the innocent marriage bed by his foul theft. Although the human mind might think nothing more serious than this outrage, consider just how the chastity of heavenly justice might be offended if a man were to look wantonly on a bride dedicated to Christ and vowed by consecration at the bridal chamber of the holy altar. I need not say more.

Now I can hear that particular young man saying that it was not a 'virgin' he has disgraced since her body has already been used improperly and shamefully. His own guilt in this affair is obvious. Unless he repents and your intercession frees me, one cannot tell how much misery there may be. He cannot confess the crimes of third party in place of his own reconciliation.

In this affair I accuse the negligence of the clergy of our era since we do not investigate these things carefully. But then offenses of such magnitude offer themselves to us without our having to make any investigation. Who goes looking about for his own companions' evils? Who gets involved in other people's sins? Would that his obscenity would moderate itself so that it would lie hidden!

In the end, he should chose whichever of these two alternatives he wishes. First, if he has sinned in the flesh with the young woman, he should await what the Apostle foretells: "If anyone profanes the temple of God, God will bring him to ruin" [1 Cor. 3:17]. On the other hand, if he simply added to the seduction that he himself had not begun, what could you consider more disgusting, what could be more horrible than that he could not keep himself away from a prostitute. (It is only because of this situation that God permits a man to be separated from his wife.)

Consider this: at this point I am not the only one upset. Her pious parents bewail the crime he committed. They mourn as if they had lost their child; they declare themselves childless in their lamentations.

What should I say about the grief of the [woman who has become a] mother? A shameful life worse than any death has deprived her of her promised spouse long before any death might have? Although her partner had gotten used to being aroused in intercourse, now he has to bear patiently having a son without filial duties, being a spouse without progeny, being a father without anyone to inherit from him. Besides, although the child is supported by his efforts and is being raised from such a well-known evil of this eminent adulterer, nevertheless, in the birth of this desired little monstrosity, there is no evidence of his lineage but proof of his disgrace.

In fact, except for the defense, which God provides me in you, I would fear the aforementioned crime more than its repentance. But I ask that this man not be angry because I have said these things: I am the lookout; I hold the trumpet; I am not allowed to be silent. Would that the sinner had a human heart accustomed to yielding good-naturedly, to repenting by making amends. Otherwise his anger would grow, his pride swell and his bullish lewdness stink. Though he may vomit out contradictory flames against me and cry out for a hearing by perhaps even the Church at Rome, and if it were still his pleasure, say that I have children, I will neither respond to his threats with flattery nor will fear that he wear me down along the way [cf. Matt. 5:25]. I am not wearied any more by civil suits in my own territory nor will I deny that I have many children—I already regret that I have begotten one of them. But this misdeed has demanded little from me.

However, you have a greater capacity for correcting him by the prerogative of your most eminent power. So you must censure this man vigorously. Declare my inclination to him. Declare to him that I will take care so that this wrong-doing will not be brought up again either in a legal action or an injunction. But if he does not mend his ways of his own accord or if he is not restrained in custody at the very least, his capacity for misdeed will be cut away from him, if the power of penance is not able to persuade him.

—19—

Chrysostom's Catecheses: A Hermeneutic
of Social Institutions

Arthur B. Shippee

John Chrysostom came from a fairly wealthy family of Antioch, a great city in the Empire. An apt student, he received an excellent education worthy of an honorable and remunerative career. He responded, however, first to the allure of the desert, living with the Christian monks outside Antioch before returning to the city and a church career, itself an honorable profession. He was ordained a priest in 386, quickly assuming an extensive preaching schedule. He was more or less kidnapped to be consecrated bishop of Constantinople in 398. His work to centralize the authority and raise the discipline of the Church earned him a range of enemies, a prime cause of his exile, which led to his death in 407.

John, the leading preacher of his day, used his rhetorical and pastoral skills to find a workable way to live out in the city the essential virtues of the monks' ascetic life. While the city could not be a copy of the monks' world, the two were not to be separate worlds. The city was to be like the monks' community not so much in fasting from food as in fasting from vices. John did not seek from Christians extraordinary achievements, but he did seek a consistent moral attentiveness, so that they would pursue their Christian life as vigorously as they pursued other important activities.

Catechesis is the preparation of candidates for baptism, especially in the final period before Easter. While ancient catecheses have been studied extensively, practices varied more than is often realized. John's catecheses show a different process from those of Cyril of Jerusalem or Theodore of Mopsuestia, who also wrote catechetical sermons. He provided less information than either of these, for his goal was to provide the proper frame of mind in which the catechumens ought to be baptized.

John's catecheses are usually presented as twelve in number, making three "series" from different years. At enrollment candidates were registered to be baptized at the Easter vigil; teaching and exorcism took place on Holy Wednesday and Thursday. Most of John's catecheses are in sermons delivered on the two holy days. Other sermons addressed the congregation, often with passages of moral exhortation for the newly baptized.

The texts chosen for this book shed light on a particular question of community formation: how did John present Christianity to members of a society where the population was becoming more and more Christian and the government was becoming more and more centralized in the imperial hierarchy? John did not oppose social institutions to Christianity, instead he wove the forms of social institutions into a Christian understanding of God and humanity. He spoke to the integration of society and kingdom.

John's goal was to evoke an emotional response and a commitment from his catechumens by invoking what was familiar and attractive to them already. He began with the traditional catechetical imagery of the Christian coming before God in baptism, becoming a soldier of Christ, and becoming betrothed to Christ, but he developed these images using contemporary culture. Baptism is like an imperial audience, with all its opportunities. Becoming a soldier of Christ is like an appointment to a high rank in one of the services of the imperial government, either the military or the civil service. (Such an appointment was one of the chief means of social and financial advancement, and so a central ambition.) Becoming a bride of Christ is like a brilliant marriage, here to a great king— another road to wealth, an object of ambition of fourth-century people in the empire.

By filling out the traditional catechetical imagery with these familiar ambitions, John achieved several things. He was able to draw on the emotional energy already invested in these conventional ambitions and transfer it to the catechumens' appreciation of Christianity. Christianity is exciting because it is a brilliant marriage, a great promotion, and an imperial audience; as one applies oneself diligently to gain ambitions like these, so too one should apply oneself diligently to gain standing in God's kingdom. John wanted his catechumens to enjoy their new religion and apply to it the zeal that they would apply to important social goals.

John made Christianity palatable by showing the connections between social institutions and the kingdom of God, and this linkage also allowed him to mold society into greater conformity with the kingdom. After all, the imperium is a type of God's rule, illustrative of heaven and ultimately responsible to it as well.

The sermons are full of the language of benefaction, but translation hides the specific shadings. For example, I have represented the Greek word, *philanthropia* as "philanthropy," but it also meant an imperial virtue marking the emperor's care for his realm and subjects.

The translations here come from originals found in editions by Migne, Piédagnel, Wenger, and Kaczynski. Citations follow the standard set forth in my review of Kaczynski in the *Journal of Early Christian Studies* 3 (1995): 72–75. I use the numbering of the editions used, followed by Harkin's numbering.

Sermon Delivered Wednesday of Holy Week, 387, to a Mixed Congregation of Catechumens and Baptized Christians [M.2]

[4] ... Let us scrutinize the name of this great gift. As ignorance of the greatness of a dignity makes those honored become lazy, so the knowledge renders them grateful and makes them more earnest. Besides this, it seems ridiculously shameful for those who enjoy such fame and honor from God's hand not to know what in the world the names profess to show. ...

[2.15] Since you know all this, beloved, repay your benefactor by virtuous conduct, and, bearing in mind the greatness of the sacrifice, adorn the members of your body. Bear in mind what you receive in your hand: never lift it up to beat someone, nor shame with the sin of a blow what was honored by such a gift. Bear in mind what you receive in your hand and keep it clean of all greed and theft. [16] Consider that you not only receive it in your hand, but also that you place it into your mouth, and keep your tongue clean of shameful and insolent language like blasphemy, perjury, and all other similar things. It is ruinous to take what serves such most terrible mysteries, reddened by such blood and made a gilded sword, and turn it towards abuse and insolence and ribaldry. Respect the honor God bestows on it and do not reduce it to the mean state of sin. [17] Consider also that after your hand and mouth, your heart receives this terrible mystery, so do not devise any trick against your neighbor, but keep your mind clean from any evil deed. In this way you will be able to keep your eyes and ears safe. Isn't it wicked, after the mystic and heaven-sent voice—I mean that of the Cherubim—to defile the hearing with lewd lyrics and feeble melodies? [18] Don't you deserve the most dire punishment for using the eyes with which you have looked upon the ineffable and awesome mysteries to look upon whores and imagine adultery?

You are called to a wedding, beloved. Do not go in wearing stained clothing, but take the proper apparel. [19] People invited to a wedding, however poor, will often borrow or buy clean clothing before going to meet those who invited them. But as you are called to a spiritual wedding and an imperial feast, bear in mind that the clothes you buy should be extraordinarily proper. There is, however, no need to shop for them. The host himself gives them to you as a gift, so that you will not have poverty as an excuse. [20] Guard then the clothing you received, since, if you ruin it, you will not be able to borrow or buy it again, for it is not for sale anywhere. ...

[3.29] Notice that it is the same with grace [as with virtue]. If anyone is lame, if he has lost his eyes, if he is disabled in body, if he has fallen into a debilitating chronic illness, by none of these is grace hindered from coming upon the soul, for grace seeks only the soul eager to receive, and neglects all such outer things.

[30] In the case of earthly soldiers, those about to induct them into the army examine both their bodily size and physical health, and not only these are required of the recruit, but he must be free as well. If anyone is a slave, he is thrown out. The King of heaven, however, does not examine such criteria, but will accept into his army without shame slaves and the aged and those feeble in limb. [31] What could be more philanthropic than this? What more beneficial? He seeks only what is in our control, while they seek what is not in our control. To be slave or free is not our decision, nor again is it in our control to be tall or short, nor old nor young, nor such things. To be gentle or good, however, and things like these, belong to our will.

God asks of us only these things over which we are master, [32] which stands to reason, because it is not from any need of his, but from beneficence that he calls us to his grace. Yet kings recruit for the service rendered them; and while they lead into a physical war, God leads into a spiritual battle.

[33] One can see the same analogy not only in the case of worldly wars, but also in the case of the games. Those who are about to be led into that arena do not immediately go down to the events until the announcer takes them and leads them before everyone's eyes, calling out, "Does anyone accuse this one?" Yet indeed these are not bouts involving the soul, but bodies. Why then do you demand an account of his lineage?

[34] Here, however, there is none of this, but everything is different, the bouts not involving wrestling grips with the hands, but involving philosophy of the soul and virtue of the will. The commissioner acts differently, too: he does not take him and lead him around and say, "Does anyone accuse this one?" Instead he calls out, "If all people—if all demons arrayed with the Devil himself accuse him of the most unspeakably dire crimes, I will never dismiss him nor disdain him. Instead, delivering him from the accusations and freeing him from this base condition, in this way do I lead him unto the events!" [35] This also stands to reason. There the commissioner does not help the contestants to victory, but stands in the middle. Here, however, the commissioner of the contests of piety is an ally and aid, joining with them in the fight against the Devil.

[4.36] That God forgives our sins is not the only amazing point, but also that he does not disclose them nor make them plain and clear, nor require a public appearance to confess one's offenses. To himself alone he requires an accounting, and before him a confession. Among the secular judges, indeed, if anyone offered to some captured thief or tomb-robber that he could admit his offenses and be forgiven the penalty, he would certainly admit it eagerly, discounting the shame in his desire for safety. But here there is none of this. Instead, he forgives the sins and does not require that they be paraded before others. One thing only he always seeks, that the person who himself enjoys the forgiveness might know the greatness of the gift. . . .

Sermon Delivered on Wednesday of Holy Week to Catechumens [W.1]

[1] The present season is one of joy and spiritual gladness. Behold, the longed-for and beloved days of the spiritual marriages are close at hand. Nor does one err to call what takes place today a marriage, and not only a marriage, but even a marvelous and unexpected type of military enlistment. And let him not consider these things to be contradictory. Let him rather listen to the blessed Paul, the universal teacher, who has used both these examples. . . .

[3] So let us speak as to a bride about to be led into the sacred marriage chamber, to indicate to you the groom's exceeding wealth and the indescribable philanthropy that he shows for her. Let us show her what she who has left so much is about to enjoy. If we may, we shall first examine her case and see what state she is in and how the groom receives her, for this will show best the boundless philanthropy of the common Master of all. He has not admitted her because of her beauty or her desirability or the sight of her body, but she whom he has brought into the nuptial chamber is deformed and ugly, wholly and shamefully sordid, and, one might say, wallowing in the very mire of her sins. . . .

[5] With this precisely understood, let us learn clearly the soul's prior deformity, so that we may marvel at the Master's philanthropy. What could be uglier than one forsaking her high rank and forgetting her exalted birth, or than one practicing the worship of stone and wood and beasts and things even more dishonorable, even adding to her ugliness with burning fat and defiling blood and smoke? From such, furthermore, comes the manifold swarm of pleasures: the revels; drinking bouts; outrageous deeds; and all those shameful pursuits enjoyed by the demons they worship.

[6] When he saw her in such a state, swept naked into the very abyss of evil and disgracing herself, the good Master did not consider her ugliness nor her extreme poverty nor the great extent of her evils, but showing his own extraordinary philanthropy, he received her with favor. He reveals this very disposition when he says through the prophet, "Hear, O daughter, consider and incline your ear; forget your people and your father's house, and the king will desire your beauty" [Ps. 45:10–11]. . . .

[44] I beg you, do not deliberate concerning your own salvation negligently. Consider your worth and blush. If someone prides himself on a human rank, he is always declining to engage in some activity or another so that it will not inflict any outrage on the rank. You who are about to acquire so high a rank, ought you not now to render yourself venerable? Your rank is so great that it coextends with the present age and it accompanies you into the life to come. What is this, then? From now on, by the philanthropy of God, you are called "Christian" and "Faithful." Look! It's not one rank but two. You are about to

put on Christ in a little while, and it beseems you to act and consider everything as if he is always present with you.

[45] Look at those who administer governmental activities. Do you see how, whenever they are wearing clothing bearing the imperial images, they take pride in themselves and therefore they expect to be counted worthy of more honor and they enjoy an armed escort? If indeed these expect to be venerable because they have the image lying on their robe, how much more does this hold for you who are about to put on Christ himself! As it says, "I will live in you and walk among you, and I will be your God" [2 Cor. 6:16, quoting Lev. 26:12].

Sermon Delivered Thursday of Holy Week to Catechumens [W.2]

[1] Well, then, let me again preach some few words to those enlisted into Christ's own special troop, showing to them the power of the weapons they are about to take up and the indescribable goodness of the philanthropic God that he displays to the human family, so that, coming forward with a certain trust, they may enjoy his most liberal munificence. Consider, beloved, the extravagance of his goodness from the onset. If he counts worthy of such a gift those who have never toiled nor shown any excellence (and he forgives all the sins ever committed), and if you, being well disposed after such munificence, are willing to contribute what is yours, then how generous a compensation from the philanthropic God is likely to be approved for you! . . .

[29] But since you are close by the imperial entrance and you are about to draw near to the throne itself where sits the King who distributes gifts, demonstrate great ambition in regard to your demands—nothing worldly, nothing human, but make a demand worthy of the one who provides them.

Upon coming up from these divine streams, demonstrating in the ascent from them a symbol of the resurrection, demand his alliance so that you can demonstrate good custody over what has been given to you, so that you can be unconquered by the contrivances of the Evil One. Call for the peace of the churches, raise supplications for those who still err, beg for those who are in sin, so that we might be thought fit for some mercy. He has, after all, given you complete freedom of speech, and he has written you into the list of the first of his friends, and he has promoted to adopted children you who were before captives and slaves and silenced, and he will not deny your demands but will grant you everything, in this also imitating his own goodness.

[30] And by this especially you will draw him into greater good will. When he sees you showing such great solicitude to your fellow members and concerned with the salvation of others, he will indeed count you worthy of great freedom of speech. Nothing delights him so much as our sympathy towards our own fellow members and our affection for our brothers and our great care for the salvation of our neighbors. . . .

Sermon Delivered to the Congregation at the Entrance of the Neophytes, Addressing Now One, Now the Other [W.4]

[1] I see that today the assembly is brighter than usual, the church of God taking delight in her own offspring. As an affectionate mother seeing her children surrounding her is pleased and leaps and flies with the pleasure, so in the same way this spiritual mother rejoices at beholding her own offspring and exults in seeing herself a fertile field with amber waves of this spiritual grain [cf. Homeric Hymn to Demeter 450–55]. . . .

[3] These who yesterday and the day before were slaves of sin, silenced under the tyranny of the Devil and like captives ordered about here and there, behold, today they are received into the order of children, having shed the heavy load of sins and clothed themselves in the royal robe. They nearly outshine heaven itself; displaying a light brighter than those stars, they shine upon the eyes of those who behold them. Those stars appear only at night, never appearing in daytime, but these shine equally both night and day, for they are spiritual stars, and they vie in light with the sun itself, or rather they even outshine it by a large amount. If the Master Christ used this image to show the brilliance of the righteous in the age to come, saying, "Then the righteous will shine like the sun" [Matt. 13:43], it was not because they shine only so much, but because there is not to be found another physical example so bright as this. On this account did he compare the lot of the just to this image. . . .

[5] Such a person, even if he goes about the earth, will be as if residing in heaven, thinking of things above, picturing the things above, no longer fearing the treacheries of the evil demon. When the Devil sees such a change, with those who were formerly under his mastery exalted to such a height and judged worthy of such philanthropy from the Master, he departs in shame, not daring to face them. He cannot bear the sparkles glinting thenceforth, but blinded by the beam of light, he turns his back and departs.

[6] You, however—the new soldiers of Christ, those entered as citizens in heaven today, those summoned to this spiritual banquet and about to enjoy the imperial table—show an eagerness worthy of the greatness of the gift so that you might gain even greater grace from above. Since our Master is philanthropic, whenever he sees those who are grateful for what has already come to them and who show careful custody over the greatness of the gifts, he is lavish with grace and, if we ever contribute some little bit he himself will present us with great gifts. . . .

[16] Let us listen, I beg you, both those initiated of old and those just lately enjoying the Master's bounty, to the apostolic exhortation, "everything old has passed away; see, everything has become new," [2 Cor. 5:17] and so, forgetting all that had gone before, like citizens in a new life thus let us amend our lives, keeping in mind the worthiness of the one who dwells within us in everything we say and do.

[17] People who take up secular public services carry a portrait of the imperial images on the clothing they usually wear, and because of this they appear to everyone else to be trustworthy. They would certainly refuse to do anything that might be unworthy of this clothing that bears the imperial portraits. Furthermore, should they themselves attempt this, they have many who would prevent them, and should some others desire to treat them badly, they have the covering of the clothing as sufficient security against suffering anything odious. Given all this, consider those who have Christ himself, not on the robe but dwelling in their soul, along with the Father and the reception of the Holy Spirit: all the more are they duty-bound to show great circumspection and in everything to make manifest, through strict conduct and diligent attention to their manner of life, that they do bear the imperial image.

[18] As they who display the imperial likenesses on their clothes over their breast stand out clearly to all, so also, if we should wish it, we who have put on Christ permanently and are worthy to have him dwell within, we are able wordlessly to demonstrate to all the power of the one who dwells within us through a strict way of life. As now the covering of your clothes and the brilliance of your robes attract everybody's eyes, so also, if you will it, by preserving the brightness of the imperial garment even more strictly than now through your strict conduct under God, you are able continuously to attract all who behold you to similar zeal and to the praise of the Master. . . .

[23] Let us keep in mind the saying of the Lord, "I tell you, on the day of judgment you will have to give an account for every careless word you utter" [Matt. 12:36]. [24] Let there no longer be among us any discussion that is worldly and useless, providing no gain. We have chosen a new and wholly different conduct, and it befits us to practice what follows from this conduct, so that we may not be unworthy of it. Don't you know, among worldly dignities, how those who are eager to be accepted into what they call the Senate are hindered by human laws from practicing some things which are freely conceded to others? In the same manner we, both you who are just now initiated and those formerly found worthy of this grace, also ought to have the duty, since we have been permanently inscribed into the spiritual Senate, not to pursue such things as others do, but rather to demonstrate a strictness in speech and a high purity of mind, and to train each of our faculties to pursue no work that will not be engaged in much profit for the soul. . . .

[29] Therefore, being Christ's and having put him on and being worthy of his spiritual food and drink, let us compose ourselves so as to have nothing in common with the affairs of the present life. And indeed we have been enrolled into another citizenry, into that of the Jerusalem above. Therefore, I exhort you, let us demonstrate works worthy of that citizenry, so that, through those things in which we pursue virtue and through those things by which we call others to glorify the Master, we may attract great good favor from above. Whenever our Master is glorified, he himself pours out his own gifts very liberally

to us, inasmuch as he has accepted our gratitude and seen that he is not granting his own benefactions to the thankless and ungrateful.

[30] I know that I have given a long talk: please excuse me.

Sermon Delivered to the Catechumens at Their Enrollment for Baptism, Thirty Days before Easter [P.-K.1]

[1.1] How longed for and beloved is this class of our new brothers! I address you as brothers already before your birth, and before labor, I rejoice at your kinship with us. For I know, I know quite well how great are the honor and the office you are about to receive, and so I do now what all do who seek to honor those about to assume an office even before they enter in on it, who thus store up for themselves future good will by such service. Nor is it just any office you are about to receive, but a royal office—or rather not just royal, but of the very kingdom of heaven! [1.2] On this account, I beseech you that you remember me when you enter in upon that royal office. . . .

[2.3] The initiated know the strength of this cup, but you will know it too a little while later. Remember me, therefore, when you come into that kingdom, when you receive the royal robe, when you don the purple, dyed by the Master's blood, when you are crowned with a diadem sparkling every which way with flashes brighter than the rays of the sun. Such are the Groom's wedding gifts, beyond our worth, but worthy of his philanthropy. [2(4)]: Therefore, already now I bless you even before your holy marriage chambers. . . .

[11.18] For he did not only say, "You were washed," but also, "you were sanctified" and "you were justified" [I Cor. 6:11]. [11.19] What could be more unexpected than when one sees righteousness born without toil and sweat and good works? Such indeed is the grace of the divine gift that it makes people righteous without sweat! If an emperor's letter, bearing just a few words, can release free some who are liable to a myriad of charges, and also lead others to the highest honor, in much greater measure the all-accomplishing Holy Spirit of God will deliver us from every evil as well as grant us much righteousness and fill us with great freedom of speech. As a little spark falling into the wide ocean is immediately extinguished and disappears, drowned in the vastness of the waters, so too every human evil, when it falls into the bath of the divine streams, is drowned and disappears faster and more easily than that spark. . . .

[15.27] But it is out of season for you to hear a lecture about repentance, and may it never be in season for you to need such remedies, but may you maintain the beauty and brightness that you are about to receive now, keeping it uncontaminated. [16.27] That you may remain so forever, let us address you briefly concerning ethical duties.

[16.28] In the gym, errors do not harm athletes, since they wrestle with their fellows and practice everything on the bodies of their teachers. When the time for the matches arrives, however, and when the stadium is open and the crowd is seated above, and when the commissioner arrives, it comes time for the negligent to fall and leave in great shame and for the eager to win crowns and prizes. [16.29] So too among you, these thirty days are like a gym with exercises and practice. Let us start to learn to prevail over that evil demon, for it is against him that we are about to strip following baptism, against him to box and to fight. Let us then start to learn his grips, the source of his strength and the way he can easily injure us, so that when the matches begin we may not be unprepared or confused when we see new moves. Instead, practicing among ourselves and learning all his wiles, let us courageously lay hold of him. . . .

Sermon Delivered on Wednesday of Holy Week to the Catechumens [P.-K.2]

[3.5] . . . I want to remind you of a debt that I promised in the previous sermon but that I did not pay, since the development compelled us to more necessary things. What was the debt? I was investigating for you why our fathers, passing by every time in the year, legislated that your souls would be initiated in this season, and I was saying that the observance of the season was neither super-ficial nor pointless. While it is ever the same grace and it does not depend on the time, for the grace is divine, yet the observance of the season has a certain mystic side. Why then did the fathers legislate this festival at this time?

Now our King is victorious in the war against the barbarians! For barbarians, and even more savage than barbarians, are all the demons. Now he has deposed sin, now he has quelled death and subdued the Devil and taken captives. [6] Indeed, we celebrate the memorials of those victories on the present day.

The fathers legislated that the royal gifts be distributed now, because this is the law of conquerors. Thus even secular kings do, conferring many honors on the days of their victories. But that way of honor is rife with dishonor, for what sort of honor are the shows and the things done and said in the shows? Aren't they filled with every kind of shame and abundant crude humor? [7] But the honor here is worthy of the munificence of the one who dispenses the honors.

They legislated this to take place now, so that by the season they might remind you of the victory of the Master, and so that there would be in these victory parades some dressed in splendid robes who are entering in upon the King's honor. Yet not only for these reasons, but also so that throughout the season you might be a partner to the Master. It is recorded that he was crucified with wood; be crucified yourself by baptism, for baptism is a cross and a death—but the death of sin, but the cross of the old person [Rom. 6:6]. [John goes on to link baptism and the cross, to show how baptism is both a burial and a resurrection.]

[6.14] By what has just been said, I would say that we have sufficiently established for you the reasons why the fathers ordained that initiation take place in this season. Now I want to repay you another debt, if you are not weary of listening, and say why we send you off next to the formulas of the exorcists naked and barefoot. Indeed, the same reason appears here again, since the King, victorious in war, has taken prisoners. This is the appearance of prisoners. Hear, for instance, what God said to the Jews. "Just as my servant Isaiah has walked naked and barefoot," thus will the children of Israel walk into captivity naked and barefoot [Isa. 20:3 confused with Ezek. 12:11]. Wanting, then, to remind you of the former tyranny of the Devil through your appearance, God sends you off so as to remind you of the old state of low birth. And you stand not only naked and barefoot, but even with hands upturned, so that you confess God's future sovereignty, which you now come under.

Sermon Delivered Monday Morning of Easter Week, from §5 Addressed to Neophytes [IpA 1]

John begins by noting the drop in attendance from Easter's crowds, but in his opinion these zealous few, mostly from the working poor, are worth more than the crowd; Elijah and Elisha, poor, were friends of God (Heb. 11:37–38). But John grieves that those absent prefer the shame of the theater to the church, saying more on the problem of poor attendance. John then turns to the Book of Acts and the importance of the titles of books.

[5] . . . I intend to direct the rest of the lecture to the neophytes. Now, by neophyte I don't mean only those baptized two or three days, or ten days [i.e., from Easter vigil to Monday, and to the following Sunday], but also those baptized last year, and even longer ago, for even they deserve this address. If we show great zeal for our soul, it is possible to be neophytes even after ten years, if we should maintain the newness granted by baptism. For it is not time that makes a neophyte, but a pure life. . . .

Your affairs are a war and a contest. No slave contends; no servant soldiers. But should one who is a slave be caught, he is, after vengeance is extracted, thrown out of the catalogue of soldiers. Not only in warfare, but also in the Olympic games this self-same custom prevails. After the thirty days' residence, they take them up and lead them to the suburb [of Daphne]. When the whole theater has been settled, the announcer calls out, "Does any accuse this one?" Once he has been cleared of the charge of slavery, he enters the games. Now, if the Devil won't allow slaves into his own games, how could you dare, being a slave of sin, enter Christ's contests?

There the announcer says, "Is there anyone to accuse this one?" But herein Christ does not speak so. "Even if everybody accuses a person before his baptism," he says, "I will receive him, and I shall clear him of slavery, and having freed him, I shall lead him to the contests." Do you see the philanthropy of the commissioner? He does not seek out prior deeds, but rather he asks one to account for what happens afterwards. When you were a slave, you had countless accusers, a guilty conscience, sins, all sorts of demons. Not one of these, he says, arouses me against you, nor rules you unworthy of my contests. Rather I have received you into the events, not by your worthiness, but by my philanthropy. Remain so and fight, should you need to run or box or wrestle. But not hazily nor foolishly nor randomly. . . .

Bibliography

Baur, C. 1959. *John Chrysostom*. Westminster, Md.: Newman.

Cameron, A. 1993. *The Mediterranean World in Late Antiquity: AD 395–600*. London: Routledge.

Dujarier, M. 1979. *A History of the Catechumenate: The First Six Centuries*. New York: Sadlier.

Harkins, P. 1963. *St. John Chrysostom: Baptismal Instructions* (*Ancient Christian Writers* 31). Westminster, Md.: Newman.

Jones, A.H.M. 1964. *Later Roman Empire 284–602*. Oxford: Basil Blackwell.

Kaczynski, R. 1992. *Chrysostomus: Catecheses Baptismales*. Freiburg: Herder. (Reprints the *Sources chrétiennes* and *Patrologia Graeca* texts.)

Kelly, J.N.D. 1995. *Golden Mouth: The Story of John Chrysostom—Ascetic, Preacher, Bishop*. London: Duckworth.

Liebeschuetz, J.H.W.G. 1972. *Antioch. City and Imperial Administration*. Oxford: Oxford University Press.

———. 1990. *Barbarians and Bishops*. Oxford: Oxford University Press.

Matthews, J. 1989. *The Roman Empire of Ammianus*. Baltimore: Johns Hopkins University Press.

Migne, J. P. *Patrologia Graeca* 49 for M.2; 51 for *IpA* 1.

Paverd, F. van de. 1991. *St. John Chrysostom, the Homilies on the Statues*. *Orientalia Christiana analecta* 239. Rome: Pontifical Institute.

Piédagnel, A. 1990. *Trois catéchèses baptismales* (*Sources chrétiennes* 366). Paris: Editions du Cerf. For P.-K. 1–3.

Shippee, A. 1995. *Journal of Early Christian Studies* 3: 72–75.

———. 1996. "The Known Syriac Witnesses to John Chrysostom's Catecheses." *Le Muséon* 109, no. 1–2: 87–111.

Treggiari, S. 1991. *Roman Marriage*. Oxford: Oxford University Press.

Wenger, A. 1957. *Huit catéchèses baptismales* (*Sources chrétiennes* 50). Paris: Editions du Cerf. For W. 1–2, 4–8, and P.-K. 4.

—20—

John Chrysostom
Sermons on City Life

Blake Leyerle

The name "Chrysostom" or "Golden-tongued" was bestowed upon John post-humously in recognition of his enormous talent as a preacher. From his ordination to the priesthood in 386 C.E., he preached tirelessly in Antioch and Constantinople until his exile in 404. While not all of his sermons have been preserved, those that have fill eighteen volumes of Migne's double-columned *Patrologia Graeca*. After Augustine, Chrysostom is our best-represented father of the early Church.

Even more impressive than the sheer quantity of these sermons, however, is their contribution to social history. Chrysostom's habit of illustrating his homilies with contemporary scenes has preserved for us a wealth of information on Late Antique urban life. Sometimes fragments of social data are mentioned only in passing, but at other times scenes are developed in great detail, adorned, and embellished. Such descriptive interludes were not only restful for his congregation, allowing them a pause in instruction or rebuke, but also extremely enjoyable. Transported by his words, they admired his ability to conjure up familiar objects and situations. The passage of centuries has only sharpened this enjoyment, as it is only through descriptions such as these that we can hope to "see," for example, the standard furnishings of a rich man's house in Late Antiquity.

Yet Chrysostom's reputation as a preacher rests on far more than a tendency to sketch aspects of daily life. As Peter Brown has remarked, he seems to have identified with the concerns of his congregation "with almost mediumistic sensitivity (Brown 1988)." No where is this gift more apparent than in his habit of inserting into his homilies imagined objections. Although a standard device in ancient rhetoric, this technique takes on a freshness in Chrysostom's hands, lending to his words a strikingly contemporary feel. For extended passages it is easy to forget that we are listening to a homily and not to a debate. If these imagined ripostes represent actual, voiced objections within the community—as would seem likely given Chrysostom's renown as a preacher—they provide us with an exceptionally clear window onto the dominant values, assumptions, and prejudices of fourth-century Antioch.

These imagined objections, as well as contemporary scenarios, can never be divorced from Chrysostom's rhetorical strategy. Both serve his moral agenda, which was to extend the ways and values of monasticism to the life of every Christian. With the zeal of a reformer, he attacked traditional institutions and assumptions. Particularly abhorrent to him was the system of public benefaction in which wealthy individuals undertook the funding of civic institutions such as the baths, the circus, the hippodrome, and the theater. Such displays of open-handedness were praised as appropriate and indeed laudable expression of "honor," or what we might call in our own day self-respect and a sense of social responsibility. But to Chrysostom, they were exhibitions of and enticements to vainglory.

Our first selection, therefore, describes the behavior and social genesis of the honor-loving man. Intent on correcting this behavior, Chrysostom focuses on the evanescence of worldly honor, the jealousy occasioned by displays, and the true financial hardship that follows. His moral agenda, however, emerges particularly clearly at the end, where he attacks the notion that human dignity depends upon appearances. Here the forcefulness of his argument is particularly hard to capture in English, since the word translated as "dignity" is exactly the same as "appearances."

This pervasive cultural tendency towards display continues in the second selection, excerpted from one of Chrysostom's many tirades against the theater. So zealous was he in this condemnation that he is now, ironically, our best source on the Late Antique stage. For him, the theater summed up everything he hated most: a primary venue for encouraging vainglorious display, it was also responsible for subverting morality. Not only were actors in antiquity notorious for their loose-living ways, theatrical conventions demanded their flagrant violation of gender expectations. Most plots, moreover, rang the changes on sexual misconduct. Yet the theater's propensity towards subversion had still another aspect. As one of the primary places where citizens gathered en masse and political dignitaries were welcomed by acclamation, the theater exerted considerable political influence. A group of men who had initially been hired by the actors to applaud their efforts gradually assumed wider powers. At the end of this selection, Chrysostom harshly criticizes this theatrical claque for fomenting urban riots. But despite his fulminations against theatrical professionals, Chrysostom remains remarkably clearsighted about who is ultimately responsible for these immoral displays. Were there no audience to applaud, he observes, there would be neither actors nor spectacles.

Theatrical themes appear also in the third selection on urban poverty as we glimpse people driven to desperate measures to attract revenue. The plight of the poor and the absolute duty of almsgiving are undoubtedly among the major themes of Chrysostom's preaching. Again we see how Chrysostom holds the theater responsible for inculcating a callous disregard for the sufferings of others, as the wealthy are condemned for their unwillingness to part with money without first being entertained. To these men, he stresses the obligation of our common humanity, but he is also willing to appeal to their self-interest: by almsgiving the rich can buy for themselves a secure place in heaven.

The last selection in the section on "Public Life" describes the judicial proceedings after the Riot of the Statues. In 386, when a new tax levy was imposed, rioting erupted in Antioch. During the frenzy, the statues of the imperial family were pulled down from their pedestals and broken. This was a treasonous offense. As soon as the disturbance settled down, a huge fear of imperial reprisal gripped the city. Conciliatory embassies were sent to Constantinople, but in the interim, arrests were made and judicial executions ordered in the hope of placating the emperor's wrath. The process described by Chrysostom is one in which cross-examination, torture, appeal, judgment, and execution are all public. The intent behind this judicial spectacle was, as a couple of short selections from Chrysostom's homilies on Lazarus make clear, to shame the malefactors and their families as well as to discourage similar behavior from others.

Domestic matters also exercised Chrysostom. Of these none was more pressing than the establishment of correct gender relations. Our first selection on marriage customs, therefore, not only describes in rich detail the process of betrothal and the appurtenances of a respectable wedding, but also articulates the roles and duties appropriate for men and women. Particularly striking is the concern over finances as young men are shown consulting lawyers on issues familiar to us from prenuptial agreements. Repeatedly Chrysostom warns men against trying to get rich through marriage. Prompting this advice is, once again, a concern to maintain the gender hierarchy. For, in the words of a common adage repeated elsewhere by Chrysostom, to marry a rich woman is to acquire a master rather than a bride.

The topic of social hierarchy extends into the next section, which describes the punishment of slaves. Here, as in the earlier section on urban poverty, we see the limits of Chrysostom's reforming vision. Though he counsels lenience in punishment, by appealing to the self-concept of the master, he does not question the institution of slavery.

Our final selection describes a few of the many superstitions and omens regulating the lives of Late Antique men and women. In this passage, Chrysostom is scornful of these fears and practices, but elsewhere he tries to substitute Christian for pagan amulets.

The end of Chrysostom's life was tragic. Because of his huge reputation as a preacher, he was whisked against his will to Constantinople in 397, where he was installed as bishop. In this position, he did not fare well. Within just a few years, through a series of mistimed reforms, incautious interference, and impolitic rhetoric, he managed to alienate neighboring bishops, his own clergy, the leaders of the local monastic communities, the new aristocracy of the city, and finally also the imperial family. His own congregation rallied behind him, but they were not able to save him from deposition. He died in exile on September 14, 407.

English translations of Chrysostom's works are available in several series. *The Nicene and Post Nicene Fathers* has the most extensive collection, but it is also the least readable. Better translations of some texts can be found in the *Fathers of the Church* and *The Ancient Christian Writers* series. For those wishing to consult the original Greek, critical editions continue to appear in the *Sources Chrétiennes* series. For many of Chrysostom's works, however, Migne's *Patrologia Graeca* remains our only source. This translation relies on the latter two works.

PUBLIC LIFE

CIVIC MUNIFICENCE

On Vainglory 4–6, 13–14

Sources chrétiennes 188.74–80, 90–94

The theater is full and all the people, sitting right up to the top, present a brilliant spectacle composed of so many faces that even the roof and the undergirding rafters are largely obscured by bodies. Neither roof tiles nor stone seats are visible, but as far as the eye can see, human faces and bodies.

In the sight of all these people enters the man who has gathered them together out of the love of honor. Immediately, they spring to their feet and raise a shout as though from a single mouth. In unison they call him "Guardian" and "Patron" of their common city, stretching out their hands. Then, in the midst of all these cries, they compare him to the Great River, likening the mighty outpouring of his benefactions to the unstinting waters of the Nile. He himself, they say, is the "Nile of gifts." Others, flattering him even more, deem this comparison—that of the Nile!—too meager. Dismissing rivers and seas, they introduce the ocean and say that he is this: that as the Ocean is in waters, so is he in benefactions. In short, they leave no form of praise unsung. . . . Then, having bowed low to the people and thus in turn honored them, the great man sits down amidst the congratulations of his peers, each of whom prays that he too may have this experience and then straightway die.

An enormous outlay of gold and silver, horses, garments, slaves, and all such things follows. After many fortunes have been expended, the people escort their benefactor out again with great acclamation—but there are no longer quite so many of them, as once the show is over each man hastens home. Then at the great man's house there is sumptuous feasting and great good cheer: the day is brilliant. In the afternoon, the same events unfold. And thus it continues for two or three days. Only when all his resources, even ten thousand talents of gold, have been depleted does it become clear that these cries of praise are nothing but dust, ashes, and soot. For whenever the great man scrutinizes his household accounts and considers the extravagance of his outlay, he goes into mourning. But in the midst of satisfying his desire for vainglory, he acts just like a drunkard: he would spend even himself without the slightest perception of loss. . . .

But let us turn to another kind of vainglory. "Which one?" you ask. The one that pertains to many and not just to one or two. Namely, that we are delighted whenever we are praised—even for matters in which we have not been the least involved. Even a poor man bends every effort to wear beautiful clothing for no other reason than to be praised by others. Often, although he is able to look after himself, he buys a slave, not because he needs one but so that he may avoid disgrace in the eyes of others for attending to his own needs. Tell me why, after having looked after yourself with your own hands for so long, you are now wanting to be served by another? Or why does a person, who subsequently acquires some additional gold, buy silver furnishings and an imposing house? None of these things are necessary. . . .

If someone were to ask the people who have acquired silver, "Why ever do you want this stuff? Tell me the reason. What use is it?" The owner could say nothing other than, "Honor from the public." "I have acquired it in order to be admired and not despised; but I hide it again to avoid being envied and threatened abusively." What could be worse than this foolishness? If you have something in order to be honored by the public, show it to everyone. But if you are afraid of envy, it is not good to acquire it at all.

I will tell you another bit of foolishness. Many times people, who have deprived themselves of necessary things and are suffering hunger, are still concerned about their furnishings. If you ask them why, they answer, "I must keep up appearances." What appearances? The dignity of a person does not consist in appearances. . . . There is only one thing that is disgraceful—to acquire many things—and this is indeed extremely disgraceful. For by it, one gains a reputation of cruelty, effeminacy, stupidity, vanity, vainglory, and brutality. Dignity is not about wearing beautiful clothing; dignity is about being clad in good works.

THE THEATER

Homily 37 on Matthew 5–7

Patrologia Graeca 57.425–27

If the songs of the theater are not disgusting, go down onto the stage yourself and emulate what you praise. Or go for a walk with the one who excites your laughter. Of course, you could not endure it. Why then do you shower him with such honor? Whereas secular laws deem actors to be "people without honor," you welcome them along with the whole city as if they were ambassadors and generals. . . .

What is this applause? What is this clamor? What are these satanic cries and diabolical gestures? One man, while still young and wearing his hair long, assumes female gender traits: in look and gesture, in clothing and in every other way, he strives to seem just like a young girl. Another man, but this time elderly, has shaved his head with a razor and belted heavy padding around his sides. Having cut off his self-respect long before his hair, he stands ready to be struck with the slapstick: all set to say or do anything. Even the women stand bare-headed in public without blushing to speak their lines—such a study have they made of shamelessness. Into the souls of their audience these actors pour the last word in licentiousness and effrontery. Their sole intent is to overturn modesty from its foundations: to shame nature and satisfy the lust of the wicked demon. For in that place are disgraceful expressions and yet more disgraceful gestures: depilation and a suggestive gait, garment, and voice, as well as broken melodies, roving eyes, pipes, flutes, and plots. Everything there is filled to the brim with lasciviousness.

So tell me, when will you come to your senses? Given that the devil is even now mixing great cups of licentiousness and pouring out the undiluted wine of adultery for you. For adulteries and stolen marriages are at the theater. There are female prostitutes, male "companions," and pleasure boys: in short, everything that is illegal, monstrous, and full of shame. At sights such as these, the people sitting in the audience should not laugh, but rather weep and groan bitterly.

"What then?" one of you objects, "are we to lock up the stage and at your word turn everything upside down?"

To the contrary, it is the current state of affairs that is upside down. Tell me, for instance, from where do those who plot against marriages come? Is it not from this theater? From where do those who undermine bedrooms come? Is it not from that stage? Is it not from there that husbands become burdensome to their wives? Is it not from there that wives become easily despised by their husbands? Is it not from there that most people are adulterers? The person who is turning everything upside down is, therefore, the one who goes to the theater; he is the one who is introducing a harsh tyranny. . . .

"Who," you ask, "has been made an adulterer by theatrical shows?" Rather, who has not been made an adulterer? If it were possible now to call out their names, I would show just how many men those prostitutes have separated from their wives—how many prisoners they have taken—dragging some from the marriage bed itself while holding others back from even venturing upon marriage.

"What then? Tell me! Are we to turn all our customs upside down?"

Goodness! Only illegality is turned upside down by disbanding these theatrical spectacles. For they are the source of those who treat our cities with contempt. From there stem insurrections and riots. It is the men maintained by the dancers, who sell their voices for the sake of their stomachs and whose work is to shout and do every crazy thing, who enflame the people most of all; it is they who fill our cities with riots.

URBAN POVERTY

Homily 21 on 1 Corinthians 5–6

Patrologia Graeca 61.176–79

Clearly it is madness and utter derangement to be so intent on stuffing chests full of clothing that we overlook a human being, made in the image and likeness of God, who is naked, trembling and scarcely able to stand from the cold.

"But he's faking," one of you protests, "this trembling and weakness."

. . . If indeed he is acting, he does so out of necessity and need. It is your cruelty and lack of empathy that require such pretenses—and your disinclination to pity. For who is so miserably wretched that he would disgrace himself to this extent without pressing need? Who would maim himself and endure such punishment for a single loaf of bread? His acting thus proclaims far and wide your inhumanity. Since he cannot obtain even subsistence fare by going about all day begging, entreating, uttering pitiable words, keening and crying, he has devised this technique for which the blame and disgrace fall not so much on him as on you. . . .

But why do I speak of nakedness and trembling? I can tell you about something far more horrifying. In order to move our hardened hearts, some people have been driven to maim their children while very young. For when they went about naked but able to see, neither their age nor their misfortune swayed the pitiless. To such great sufferings they added another more frightful misfortune to relieve their dire hunger. They thought that it would be easier for their children to be deprived of the sunlight that shines on us all than for them to struggle continuously with starvation and suffer a miserable death. Because you have not learned to pity penury but, to the contrary, rejoice only in misfortunes, they satisfy this insatiable desire of yours, thereby kindling a hotter blaze in Hell for you as well as for themselves. So that you may understand that it is your hardheartedness that is the cause of these and other such abuses, I will set forth indisputable and iron-clad proof.

There are other poor people of unstable and excitable disposition who cannot bear hunger and would suffer anything rather than endure it. With pitiable gestures and words they often appealed to you, but after receiving nothing they ceased their supplications. From then on, they have outstripped even your wonder-workers: some chew the leather of old worn-out shoes; some pierce their heads with sharp nails; others lie with their bare stomachs immersed in water frozen by the cold; yet others endure even more senseless things in order to gather around themselves a wretched audience.

And you, while all these things are going on, stand there laughing and marveling—making a parade out of the sufferings of others—while our common nature is disgraced. Could a savage demon behave worse? And then, so that he may do these things more readily, you shower him with money. Whereas you deem worthy of neither an answer nor a glance the man who prays and calls on God and approaches you reasonably. Indeed, whenever he seems to have been pestering you relentlessly, you unburden yourself of even these gross expressions: "Must this fellow live?" "Is it really necessary that he breathe and see the sun?" But to those others, you are cheerful and generous. . . .

"But I am not compelling them," you say.

Explain to me how you are not compelling them, when you cannot bear even to listen to the more seemly people who weep and call on God, but to those who behave disgracefully, you freely supply money while gathering many others to marvel at them.

"Let's stop pitying them," someone objects.

And you, do you also order this? You are quite right that there is no pity, man, in demanding such punishment in return for a few coins, in ordering mutilation for subsistence fare—in cutting their scalp in so many places so sharply and pitifully.

"Speak gently," you reply, "we are not the ones driving nails into those heads."

Would that you were. For then the horror would not be so great. It is a much graver crime to command a person to cut his own throat—which is precisely your situation with regard to these poor men—than to cut it yourself. The pains they endure are far more bitter when they are commanded to inflict these wretched orders upon themselves. . . .

As things stand now, you would hand over your children for charioteers; for theatrical dancers, you would give your very souls. But for Christ dying of hunger, you part with not the tiniest bit of your possessions. Or if you do give a little silver, you act as though you had handed over everything. Don't you know that true almsgiving is not simply giving, but giving freely. . . .

What is the greatest rationalization of all? "The poor have the church's fund." And what benefit is that to you? If I give, you will not come through safely; nor, if the church provides for the poor, have you wiped away your sins.

THE LEGAL SYSTEM

Homily 13 on the Statues 1–2

Patrologia Graeca 49.134–39

On that day, the fearful court of justice was set up in the city, and shook the hearts of all and made the day seem no better than night, not by extinguishing the sun's rays, but by dimming your eyes with despondency and fear. . . .

The majority of the city had fled to the wilderness and settled in ravines and secret hollows from fear of that threatening situation. Terror gripped them on all sides. The houses were empty of women and the marketplace of men. Scarcely two or three men were seen walking together in public and even these skulked about like spiritless corpses.

I went off to the court of justice intending to see the outcome of these events.

Seeing there the remnants of the city clustered together, I marveled most of all at this: that with such a crowd about the doors, the silence was as deep as if no one were present. Everyone was scanning each other's face but no one dared to question the person standing beside him or hear his answer. Each suspected his neighbor because of the multitude that had already been dragged off by force—against every hope—from the midst of the marketplace and imprisoned. . . .

This was the situation in front of the doors. But when I went inside the courtyard, I saw other things more fearful than these: soldiers armed to the hilt with swords and clubs keeping the peace for the judges within. For all the relatives of those who had been arrested—wives, mothers, daughters, and fathers—were standing before the doors of the court of justice. The soldiers, although maintaining a distance, terrified everybody. They instilled an anticipatory dread so that no one in the crowd would so utterly lose control that he would cause an uproar and rioting, if disaster occurred and one of his relatives were seen being led away on the road to death.

The most pitiful of all was the mother and sister of one of the men being tried inside. They had settled before the door of the court of justice and were rolling on the ground, a common spectacle to all bystanders. Covering their eyes, they dishonored themselves only to the extent demanded by the duress of this disaster. There was no maidservant with them, nor neighbor, nor acquaintance, nor any other close friend. But all alone in public, hemmed in by so many soldiers, wrapped in cheap clothing, they crawled in the dirt before the doors themselves. They suffered more pitifully than those under trial inside, hearing the voice of the public executioners, the smack of the whips, the shriek of those being flogged and the fearful threats of the judges. At each blow, they themselves endured sharper pains than those being beaten. For in the confessions of others, there was risk of future accusations. If ever they heard someone screaming while being flogged to furnish the names of those responsible for the riot, they looked up to heaven and pleaded with God to give that man strength and endurance so that the safety of their own relatives not be betrayed by the weaknesses of others unable to bear the sharp anguish of the blows. . . .

As the day was hastening to its end and the shadows of evening falling, all the people were in great anguish, anticipating the verdict. . . . At last, the judges sent out the prisoners bound in chains and shackled with iron. Men who were accustomed to rearing horses and adjudicating athletic games were sent to prison through the middle of the marketplace. Men who could list ten thousand notable acts of civic munificence had their possessions confiscated by the state and seals placed prominently on their doors. The wives of these men, having been cast out from their fathers' house, each had to play the part of Job's wife. For they went from house to house and place to place seeking refuge [Job 2:9 LXX]. But this was not easy for them to find, since everyone was afraid and shrank from taking in or aiding in any way the relatives of those held responsible for the riot.

Homily 4 on Lazarus 1, 3

Patrologia Graeca 48.1,007–8, 1,010

When a ruler has led a condemned man into the midst of the marketplace and gathered public executioners and is beginning to cross-examine the suspect, everyone runs up with great eagerness wanting to hear what the judge asks and the condemned man answers. . . .

In the courtrooms of the world, when people are accused of robbery or murder, the laws dictate that they stand far from the sight of the judge and are not allowed to hear his voice. In this matter, as in others, they are dishonored. An intermediary transmits the questions of the judge and the answers of those under judgment. . . .

The law courts are clearly visible and every day we hear that some poor wretch has been thrown into prison and his possessions confiscated, that someone else has been condemned to work in the mines, another has been executed by fire, and still another has died by a different type of punishment or torture. But despite hearing these things, criminals, magicians, and evil men do not mend their ways. But what am I saying—that those who have never been caught in these crimes do not come to their senses? Oftentimes many of those who have been apprehended, yet escaped punishment by digging their way out of prison and taking to their heels, have returned to their old way of life and even gone on to commit much worse crimes than before.

PRIVATE LIFE

MARRIAGE CUSTOMS AND GENDER RELATIONS

On the Kind of Women That Make Good Wives 1–5

Patrologia Graeca 51.226–35

Today I intend to speak to you on the same subject so that those intending to enter into marriage will give this undertaking careful forethought. For when we are planning to buy houses or slaves we go to endless trouble ferreting out from the vendors as well as from the previous owners the condition of those being sold: both the health of their bodies and the disposition of their souls. When planning to get married, we ought to demonstrate far more of this kind of forethought. For it is possible, after all, to return a house that is inadequate and to send back to the seller a slave who proves to be all thumbs. But once a wife has been taken, it is not possible to return her to those who gave her. We must keep her in our house till death. . . .

But when you're planning to get married, you run as quickly as you can to the secular lawyers. Sitting at their side, you question them on every minute detail. "What will happen if my wife dies without children?" "What if she does have a child—or two or three?" "How much control will she exercise over her own affairs if her father is still living, or if he is not?" "What portion of the inheritance will go to her brothers and what to her husband?" "When will he have such control over everything that no one will be able to wrest away any part of it?" "Under what circumstances will he be deprived of everything?" Demanding from them answers to many other similar questions, you go to endless trouble. You sift and scrutinize every detail so that there is no chance that any part of your wife's resources will go to any of her relatives. Although, as I have already pointed out, if anything unanticipated should happen, only money is at stake. But all the same you cannot bear to overlook any eventuality. Isn't this ridiculous? When it is a matter of losing anticipated money we show such intense concern, but when we are endangering our souls and the judgment hereafter we don't give it a thought. . . .

Do not search for deep pockets when you are thinking of marrying a woman. Marriage is not to be thought of as a retail venture, but as a life in common. I have heard many of you saying, "That lucky devil got rich from his marriage, although he was poor before. Ever since he married a woman with plenty of the ready, he's been living in wealth and luxury." What are you saying, man? Do you want to profit from your wife? Doesn't that make you ashamed? Aren't you blushing? Wouldn't you sink into the earth, desiring to turn a profit through such means? Where are the sentiments of a husband? A wife has only one task: to guard the goods that have been collected, to keep a close watch over income, to take care of the house. For this purpose God gave her: that she might help us in these matters and in all others.

It is customary to understand our life as made up of two parts: political affairs and private matters. When God made this division, he apportioned to the woman management of the household, but to men all the affairs of the city: the business of the marketplace, the courts, the Council, the military, and everything else. A woman cannot throw a spear or hurl a missile, but she can grasp a distaff, work at the loom, and effectively manage all other domestic matters. She cannot register an opinion in the Council, but she can do so in the house. Indeed, whatever her husband knows about household affairs, she often knows better. She is not able to manage public matters well, but she is expert at raising children, our most important possession. She is able to take in at a glance the mistakes of the slave girls, and to cultivate prudence in the servants. She can provide complete freedom from care for her husband, lifting from him every worry about the house, the storerooms, wool-working, meal preparation, and the routine care of clothing. She takes care of all the other tasks that a man could not undertake appropriately or easily, even if he were determined to try ten thousand times. . . .

When you are intending, therefore, to marry, do not turn to humans for help. Do not look to women who make a business out of the misfortunes of others and are interested in only one thing: how they will receive their payment. Turn rather to God. God will not be ashamed to become your matchmaker. . . .

Homily 12 on Colossians 7

Patrologia Graeca 62.390

. . . When you are making preparations for a wedding, do not run from house to house, borrowing mirrors and clothing. This event is not a show, nor are you leading your daughter in a parade. Instead, make your house festive with what you already have and invite your neighbors, friends, and relatives. Invite as many people as you know who are moderate, and ask them to be satisfied with what is provided. Let no one from the theater be present, since that involves excessive and unseemly expense. Before all others, invite Christ. Do you know how to invite him? As he says, "Whatever you do to one of the least of these, you do to me." Don't consider it annoying to invite the poor for Christ's sake. It's annoying to invite prostitutes. To invite the poor is the beginning of wealth; the others, the beginning of ruin.

Adorn the bride not with ornaments made of gold, but with moderation and modesty and her usual clothes. In place of every golden ornament and elaborate hairstyle, clothe her in ready blushes and a sense of shame—and the strong desire to avoid both of these. Let there be no uproar nor confusion. Let the groom be called; let him receive his bride. Let the midday and the evening feasting be filled not with drunkenness but with spiritual pleasure. From a marriage such as this, ten thousand blessings and assurances of a secure life will come. But from marriages such as are celebrated now—if they can even be called marriages and not parades—see how many evils arise. As soon as the banquet hall is dismantled, cares and fear follow. Pleasure gives way to intolerable despondency, as the mother-in-law frets lest any of the borrowed things has gone missing.

THE TREATMENT OF SLAVES

Homily 15 on Ephesians 3

Patrologia Graeca 62.109–10

When women get angry with their female slaves, they fill the whole house with their shouting. Many times if the house happens to be situated on a narrow street, even passers-by can hear the woman's shouts and the slave's outcry. What could be more unseemly than this? To hear this wailing?

Immediately all the neighboring women pry into the situation and ask, "What's going on in there?" "That harridan," one replies, "is beating her slave." What could be more disgraceful than this?

"What then? Is there to be no beating?"

I do not say this. For it is necessary—but not continuously, nor immoderately, nor, as I am always saying, on account of some mistake of your own, or because she has omitted some detail of her duties—but only if she is harming her own soul. If you beat her for this reason, everyone will praise you and no one will find fault. But if for your own mistakes, everyone will condemn you for harshness and cruelty.

Yet there is something still more shameful. There are women so fierce and savage that the welts from their floggings do not stop bleeding within the same day. For they strip their slave girls, often even tying them to their beds, and call their husband for this purpose. Dear God, but does no thought of Gehenna come to you in that moment? That you would strip the girl and expose her to your husband? Are you not ashamed that he might condemn you? To the contrary, you urge him on even more. After reviling the wretched woman ten thousand times, calling her a faithless Thessalonian, a runaway, and a prostitute, you threaten her with imprisonment. . . . Should these things happen in the houses of Christians?

"But slaves," one of you objects, "are a wicked, headstrong, shameless, and incorrigible bunch."

I know this too. But there are other means of exercising control: terrors, threats, and words. These can, in fact, bite her more deeply, even while sparing you disgrace.

OMENS AND SUPERSTITIONS

Homily 12 on Ephesians 3

Patrologia Graeca 62.92

A superstitious person is like a man who has been plunged in darkness and sees nothing lying in plain view. Seeing a piece of rope, he believes it to be a live serpent; or snagged by a fence, he suspects that some person or demon holds him back. Great is his alarm and huge his distress. . . .

You might see a superstitious person purifying himself from touching a dead body, but from dead works, never. Another labors assiduously for money but considers it all lost at a single cockcrow. Thus is their reasoning plunged in darkness. Their soul is filled with many terrors. For example, "So and so was the first person I met when I left my house: at least ten thousand evils must surely follow." Or, "When my damned slave was handing me my sandals, he held out the left one first: now frightful disasters and gross insults threaten." Or, "When I was leaving home, I extended my left foot first: a sure sign of misfortunes. . . ." Women also take it as a sign when they press down the threads of the woof with the comb so zealously that the toggles strike against the long beam of the loom and fly upwards under the impact of the blow. And there are ten thousand other things equally ridiculous. If a donkey brays, if a rooster crows, if a person sneezes—if anything at all happens—they act as though they were bound with ten thousand chains or, as I said before, as though held in darkness. They are suspicious of everything and more servile than ten thousand slaves.

Bibliography

Baur, Chrysostomus. 1959. *John Chrysostom and His Time.* 2 vols. Trans. Sr. M. Gonzaga. Westminster, Md.: Newman.

Brown, Peter R. L. 1988. *The Body and Society: Men, Women, and Sexual Renunciation in Early Christianity.* New York: Columbia University Press.

Clark, Elizabeth A. 1979. *Jerome, Chrysostom and Friends: Essays and Translations.* New York: Edwin Mellen.

Dagron, Gilbert. 1970. "Les Moines et la ville. Le Monachisme à Constantinople jusqu'au concile de Chalcédoine (451)." *Travaux et Mémoires* 4: 229–76.

Hunter, David G. 1988. *John Chrysostom, A Comparison between a King and a Monk / Against the Opponents of the Monastic Life.* Lewiston and Queenston: Edwin Mellen.

Leyerle, Blake. 1994. "John Chrysostom on Almsgiving and the Use of Money." *Harvard Theological Review* 87: 29–47.

———. 1997. "Appealing to Children." *Journal of Early Christian Studies* 5: 243–70.

Liebeschuetz, J.H.W.G. 1972. *Antioch: City and Imperial Administration in the Later Roman Empire.* Oxford: Clarendon.

Stark, Rodney. 1996. *The Rise of Christianity: A Sociologist Reconsiders History.* Princeton: Princeton University Press.

Regulating Religious Expression: Law

—21—

Laws on Religion from the *Theodosian* and *Justinianic Codes*

Matthew C. Mirow and Kathleen A. Kelley

The *Theodosian* and *Justinianic Codes* have long been considered useful historical sources. That they contain important data concerning religious practices in Late Antiquity has been overshadowed by their essential place in the history of Roman law. Nonetheless, they contain much material concerning religious practice and belief, as well as the relationship between political policy and religious orthodoxy. Due to the surplus of material available on religion in the codes, selecting representative laws is a difficult task. Our guiding principle has been to select, edit, and translate those laws that shed light on religious practice rather than on institutional structure or on particular legal or social privileges associated with religious status. The codes, however, are not silent about these concerns.

We have grouped laws from both codes together under three categories. This organization seems appropriate because the laws of each code overlap; in other words, laws from different dates and in the same code may address the same subject matter. This overlap can be noticed even though the compilers tried to edit out laws that were no longer in force or that had been superseded, thereby producing a code presenting the current state of the law (Sirks 1993, 57–58). This method was applied even more stringently in the *Justinianic Code* (Honoré 1998, 153). Where established dates are available we have included them after the law. Where not, we have given the name of the ruling emperor. We have assigned each selection a consecutive number for ease of reference.

In addition, many of the laws found in the *Theodosian Code* are repeated in the *Justinianic Code*. Where the codes address religion, they both provide a chronological presentation of laws. For example, the changing policy towards pagan temples can be traced from tolerance to destruction in the selection presented here. Nonetheless, a sense of unidirectional development or change may be a false construction, as times of greater religious toleration and plurality were present during the period (Boyd 1905, 29). For legal purposes, the most recent provision would provide the guiding principle for application, but as students of religious practice we are fortunate that the codes present rich archeological layers of official thought. Honoré sees the chapter on religion in the *Theodosian Code* as exceptional in its inclusion of contradictory laws from different dates (Honoré 1998, 146).

It is tempting to read the selections as part of a process of "Christianizing the Roman Empire." Nonetheless, we are inclined to agree with David Hunt who writes, "The concept is certainly a snare, and very probably a delusion as well. It is so big an aspect of Late Antiquity as to be all but beyond the control of the historian, and admits of so many layers of meaning and varieties of interpretation that it is in danger of becoming meaning*less*" (Hunt 1993, 143). In the same essay, Hunt addresses directly the temptations to which these selections may give rise:

> Roman emperors from Constantine onwards issued very many laws which condemned all forms of religious allegiance other than officially sanctioned Christianity. But laws, of course, "do not a Christian make." The relationship between official discrimination and actual religious commitment is inevitably complex, but Christianisation, whatever it may be, was not to be achieved simply by making paganism and heresy *illegal*. (Hunt 1993, 143–44)

Although some scholars disagree, the *Theodosian Code* "was not conceived as part of a campaign against paganism" (Honoré 1998, 124). Justinian's desire, however, to create a Christian state is clearer (Honoré 1978, 30).

The extent to which Romans complied with laws is uncertain. It is most likely that the laws were made known when decreed, either by announcing or posting the text, or sometimes by having the law engraved on bronze or marble (Matthews 1993, 42). Nonetheless, there is evidence that the prohibited conduct of pagans and heretics often continued despite decrees (Hunt 1993, 157). "[W]hile legislation regarding heresy is abundant, information regarding its execution is meager" (Boyd 1905, 57). Furthermore, difficulties of interpretation abound.

The decrees of Arian emperors concerning heresy were excluded from compilations (Boyd 1905, 13). Nonetheless, the occasional privilege granted to such groups may find its way into the works. A well-known example from the *Theodosian Code* (No. 24) contains Valentinian II's law granting free assembly to Arian Christians from 386 (Honoré 1998, 145, 182–83). Apart from Arianism, numerous other heresies are addressed in the codes (Boyd 1905, 33–70). "Laws concerning heresies and other church matters read as if the emperor had thought of the idea himself, but presumably the proposals came from bishops or holy men, perhaps filtered through pious imperial ladies" (Honoré 1998, 133). A usual sanction against heretics was the loss of certain rights associated with Roman citizenship, notably the right to leave property by testament (Honoré 1998, 249).

Although the laws are stated in general terms, and certainly one aspect of codification is to provide "general" law, they were frequently responses to specific situations (Honoré 1998, 128–36, 161). For example, the provisions forbidding public debate of religion (Nos. 25 and 26) stem from an Arian uprising in Constantinople in 387 (Boyd 1905, 49–50). Likewise, Constantius's decree forbidding "nocturnal sacrifices" (No. 36) is aimed at the rebel Magnentius's toleration of such practices (Boyd 1905, 22). When reading these selections it is best to remember the characterization by Jill Harries of the *Theodosian Code* (which applies equally to those of the *Justinianic Code*) as "a compendium of imperial responses to stimuli which were largely external" (Harries 1993, 15).

The *Theodosian Code* dates from the first half of the fifth century and the *Justinianic Code* from the first half of the sixth century. They contain laws given usually by imperial letter in response to particular situations. The laws they contain were usually drafted by an official called a quaestor who might be a lawyer or nonlawyer, a Christian or pagan. Nonetheless, Justinian himself might draft a law when it concerned Christian dogma (Honoré 1978, 25). Both codes aim to compile materials from the time of Constantine to their present day. In each code the laws dealing with religion are grouped together; in the *Theodosian Code,* they are found at the end of the code in book 16; and in the *Justinianic Code,* they are found in the first book. Both were compiled in Constantinople and are products of the eastern court (Honoré 1998, 124).

The *Theodosian Code* was the product of two commissions, one from 427 and another from 434, under the eastern emperor Theodosius II. One underlying goal of the *Theodosian Code* was to resolve conflicts between the eastern and western empires through a unified text of laws (Honoré 1998, 129). Furthering this goal, the *Theodosian Code* came into force in the east and west in 439, but the eastern and western aspects of the laws are complex (Honoré 1998, 130–32, 136–48, 214, 256–57). The compilation of the *Theodosian Code* was directed by Quaestor Antiochus Chuzon, who himself had drafted decrees from 427 to 430 (Honoré 1998, 112–18). In the east, the *Theodosian Code* was soon supplanted by the *Justinianic Code;* in the west, many of its provisions were to continue as a fundamental source of laws for the Visigothic king, Alaric II, who in 506 promulgated the *Lex Romana Visigothorum,* also know as the *Breviary of Alaric* (Wood 1993, 159). This work, or the *Code* itself, influenced greatly the sixth- and seventh-century codes of Merovingian Gaul (Wood 1993, 161–77).

The *Justinianic Code* was compiled during the first few years of Justinian's reign. In 528, John of Cappadocia led a commission to restate the laws, including those issued since the *Theodosian Code,* into a practical handbook (Honoré 1978, 13, 48). The work was completed by 529 and a second edition of the *Code,* prepared under Tribonian, was promulgated in 534 (Honoré 1978, 57, 212). With Justinian's *Digest,* the *Institutes,* and the *Novels,* the *Code* is one part of the *Corpus Iuris Civilis,* a foundational text in the history of Roman and European law and, in turn, in the intellectual history of the west.

The reasons behind codification in this era are complex, but certainly one important aspect of codification was an attempt to centralize power and unify legal rules and practice over large areas. For our purposes, the now well-established distinction between the legal, political, social, and religious arenas are anachronistic; to codify legal rules was also to attempt to define and structure political, social, and religious practices. It is noteworthy that although such codifications sought to centralize power, both codes were written during a time of imperial disintegration. One scholar has viewed the *Theodosian Code* as reflecting "desperate efforts to make the system work" (Williams 1952, xvii).

These laws reflect how the Empire came to terms with Christianity. Religious orthodoxy and political stability went hand in hand. Reading these selections, one imagines a world in which every religious act could be viewed as a political act, for or against imperial authorities. Read as overlapping texts, these laws provide insight into the practices and status of pagans, the unique position of the Jews, and the myriad forms of heresy addressed by law during the period. Thus, these selections seek not only to demonstrate the way these laws draw lines between Christian and other religious practices and belief, but also to reveal the way imperial policy sought to establish doctrinal uniformity in the church. Caution in drawing firm conclusions is warranted; as one scholar of the *Theodosian Code* has written, "Behind the Code was a world of social fluidity and diversity, of tradition interacting with change and of complexities which could not be encompassed by 'general' rules. The contents of the Code provide details from the canvas but are an unreliable guide, in isolation, to the character of the picture as a whole" (Harries 1993, 96).

The selections here are translated from the texts as found in the *Palingenesia* of Honoré 1998 if therein, and we have included his citation number (e.g., E309). If not, they are from the text of T. Mommsen and P. M. Meyer, eds., *Codex Theodosianus* (1905), or D. Godefroy ed., *Codex Iustinianus* (1663).

One Holy, Catholic, Christian Church

[1] We should believe in one deity of the Father, Son, and Holy Spirit equal in majesty in the Holy Trinity. We order that those following this law embrace the name of Catholic Christians; considering the rest fools and madmen we order that they bear the disgrace of heresy. (*CJ* 1.1.1, 380 C.E.)

[2] Let no one sell, let no one buy relics of the saints. (*CJ* 1.2.3, 386 C.E.)

[3] We forbid unlawful meetings to be held even outside the Church in private houses under penalty of confiscation of the house, if the owner of the house allowed clergy in it to hold new and uproar-causing meetings outside the Church. (*CJ* 1.3.15, 404 C.E.)

[4] By this faithful and pious order we decree that no one be allowed to remove those who have taken refuge in holy Churches, so that under this order if anyone seeks to violate this law he shall be arrested for the crime of treason. (*CJ* 1.12.2, 414 C.E.)

[5] We specially order that it is not lawful for anyone to carve or paint an image of Christ the Savior either on the earth, in stone, or in marble placed in the earth, but an image shall be destroyed wherever it is found; if anyone tries to do so against our laws he shall be punished with the severest penalty. (*CJ* 1.8.1 [E846], 427 C.E.)

[6] Henceforth let no one, whether he be a member of the clergy, the military, or of any other position whatsoever, try to discuss the Christian faith publicly with a gathered and listening crowd, seeking to cause an uproar and an opportunity for treachery. . . . Therefore, if one who has dared to discuss religion publicly is of the clergy he shall be removed from the community of clergy; if he is a member of the army he shall be stripped of his rank; others guilty of this offense, if they are free men shall suffer the appropriate punishments under the law and be banished from this most sacred city; if they are slaves they shall suffer the most severe chastisements. (*CJ* 1.1.3, 459 C.E.)

[7] We decree that no one is allowed either to sell, mortgage, or pawn the most holy and sacred vessels, vestments, or other offerings, which are necessary for the divine religion (since even the old laws did not permit those things that were of divine law to be entangled in human affairs) . . . (*CJ* 1.2.17, 528 C.E.)

Status and Privileges of Clergy

[8] The Emperor Constantine greets the clergy: Pursuant to that decree that you formerly deserved and under which no one can burden you or your slaves with new taxes, you shall continue to enjoy the exemption, and, in addition, you shall not have to provide quarters for guests. (*CJ* 1.3.1, 343 C.E.)

[9] . . . this exemption we grant also to your wives and children and servants, to males and females equally, whom we also decree shall remain exempt from taxation. (*CTh* 16.2.10, 353 C.E.)

[10] Generally, whoever has been ordained a member of any clerical rank and returns to the secular life, he shall be stripped of his [clerical] rank and returned to his former status as a citizen. (*CJ* 1.3.4, 361 C.E.)

[11] We order that priests, deacons, sub-deacons, and also exorcists, lectors, porters, and acolytes shall be exempt from the personal duty of public service. (*CJ* 1.3.6, 377 C.E.)

[12] Let no one think the burial of human bodies is allowed [in churches] of the Apostles and martyrs. (*CJ* 1.2.2, 381 C.E.)

[13] Women who, contrary to divine and human laws, cut off their hair through an impulse to make a public declaration shall be kept away from the doors of the Church. It shall not be lawful for them to attend the Lord's Supper nor shall they be entitled by any public prayer to visit the altars, which are revered by all; furthermore, if a bishop should allow a woman with cut hair to enter he himself shall be thrown out and barred from his office. . . . (*CTh* 16.2.27 [E309], 390 C.E.)

[14] Whoever professes to be a monk shall be ordered to go to and dwell in deserted places and empty wilderness. (*CTh* 16.3.1 [E314], 390 C.E.)

[15] In accordance with the order of the Apostle [Paul] no woman shall be admitted to the rank of deaconess unless she has reached the age of fifty.

We do not permit anyone under thirty-five to become a priest; nor anyone under twenty-five to become a deacon or sub-deacon, nor anyone under eighteen to become a lector. Also we forbid anyone under thirty-five to be ordained a bishop.

We order that no woman who is under forty or who has married a second time shall be ordained a deaconess in the holy Church. (CJ 1.3.9, 390 C.E.)

[16] Whoever has been registered in the lists [as a serf] let him refrain from every clerical office against the will of the master of the land. (CJ 1.3.16 [E654], 409 C.E.)

[17] It pleases our majesty that the clergy have nothing to do with public acts or political affairs. . . .

We forbid consecrated bishops, priests, deacons, subdeacons, lectors, and all other members of any religious rank or order, to play at the [gaming] boards or to participate in or attend any other games or to attend any other show for the sake of seeing it. (CJ 1.3.17, 416 C.E.)

[18] Those who out of piety have granted freedom to their deserving slaves in the bosom of the Church are deemed to have granted it pursuant to the law by which the Roman state customarily granted it with the formalities completed. (CJ 1.13.2, 425 C.E.)

[19] We decree that henceforth no monk nor anyone else of any rank or status whatsoever shall attempt unlawfully to carry the holy cross or relics of the martyrs into a public building or into any place built for the enjoyment of the people, nor shall they dare to occupy those places that have been built either for public purposes or for the amusement of the people. For, since religious buildings are available, after consulting the holy bishops (as is necessary), they can place there the relics of the holy martyrs, not through exploitation by anyone but through the authority of the bishops. (CJ 1.3.26, Emperor Leo.)

[20] No one shall buy the position of priest with a bribe of money, but rather each one shall be judged not by how much he can give but by how much he deserves. For what place will be safe and what cause will be justified if the holy temples of God are stormed by the force of money? What defense of honesty will we provide, what fortress for faith, if the hunger for gold creeps into our sacred sanctuaries? Finally what can be safe or secure if incorruptible holiness is corrupted? (CJ 1.3.29, Emperors Leo and Anthenius.)

[21] We decree that those who rape virgins, widows, or deaconesses who have been consecrated to God, committing the worst of crimes, shall be subject to the penalty of death because the injury done is not just to man but is also an insult to almighty God himself.

If this [crime] has been committed against a holy virgin who is living either in a hermitage or monastery, whether she has been ordained a deaconess or not, the property of the offender shall be forfeited to the hermitage or monastery, so that meeting her needs she might have compensation from his property while she lives; and the hermitage or monastery shall have complete ownership of all the property. (CJ 1.3.41, Emperor Justinian.)

[22] Actresses and prostitutes who profit through the wantonness of their bodies shall not wear the habit of those virgins dedicated to God. (*CJ* 1.4.5, Emperors Theodosius, Arcadius, and Honorius.)

Heretics, Pagans, and Jews

[23] We think unworthy of his priestly office a bishop who by unlawful exploitation of authority has repeated the sacred rite of baptism. For we condemn the error of those who trample on the teachings of the Apostles and who do not purify by a second baptism but rather defile and pollute in the name of cleansing those who have received the sacraments of Christian faith. (*CJ* 1.6.1, 377 C.E.)

[24] We grant the right of assembly to those who believe in accordance with those doctrines established to endure forever in the time of holy Constantius, when the priests were called together from the whole Roman world and the faith was set forth at the Council of Ariminum [359 C.E.] by those very people who now are known to disagree, doctrines that were also confirmed by the Council at Constantinople [381 C.E.]. The right to assemble shall also remain available to those to whom we have already granted it. (*CTh* 16.1.4 [W58], 386 C.E.)

[25] We have learned that some of the Arians offer such a version of our orders that they can exploit those which seem to suit their purposes. They should know that no order of the sort that they offer has issued from our sanctuary. Therefore, if anyone henceforth should circulate such an order offered by them for their own purposes he shall be judged guilty of fraud. (*CTh* 16.5.16 [E255], 387/88 C.E.)

[26] No one shall have the opportunity to go to the public and debate concerning religion or to discuss it or give any advice about it. If anyone hereafter should think, with great and culpable daring, that he can go against a law of this kind or if he dares to pursue a course of destructive obstinacy he shall be restrained with suitable punishment and fitting penalty. (*CTh* 16.4.2 [E264], 388 C.E.)

[27] We order that the Apollinarians and other followers of different heresies be barred from all places, from the confines of cities, from the company of honest men, from the communion of the saints; they shall not have the authority to ordain clergy; they shall be cut off from the opportunity to assemble congregations either in public or in private churches. No authority to ordain bishops shall be afforded to them and those bishops shall lose the title and rank of this office. They shall go to places that will cut them off from human contact most thoroughly as though by a wall. (*CTh* 16.5.14 [E258–59], 388 C.E.)

[28] Those who have betrayed the holy faith and desecrated holy baptism by heretical superstition shall be barred from the company of all, barred from

testifying against another, and barred from the ability to make a will (as we have already decreed). Nor shall they inherit anything from anyone. (*CJ* 1.7.3, 391 C.E.)

[29] Let all heretics know without doubt that all their places are to be taken from them, whether they call those places churches, property of a deacon or of a church, whether they provide a place for meetings in private houses or places of any sort; those houses and private places will be transferred to the Catholic Church. It shall be forbidden to all to assemble by night or day to perform prayers in unholy assemblies. . . . (*CJ* 1.5.3, 396 C.E.)

[30] By the authority of this decree we provide that the enemies of the Catholic faith be rooted out. Therefore, by this new constitution, we particularly decree that the sect which has preferred to be called a schism rather than a heresy must perish. For these whom they call Donatists are said to have gone to such a point of wickedness that they repeat holy baptism, renewing the rites with criminal rashness and they have tainted with the infection of unholy repetition those cleansed by the gift of divinity. Thus it happened that a heresy was born from a schism. (*CTh* 16.6.4 [W328], 405 C.E.)

[31] We prosecute Manichaeans and Donatists with deserved severity. Thus let them have nothing in common with others of the human race, either in customs or in laws. First, we desire that this [belief] be a public crime because whatever is done against divine religion brings injury to all. We prosecute them by the confiscation of their property. Also, we wish them to be barred from receiving any gift or inheritance of any kind. Furthermore, to anyone convicted [of these heresies] we allow no ability to give, to buy, to sell, even to make a contract. (*CJ* 1.5.4, 407 C.E.)

[32] Arians, Macedonians, Pneumatomachians, Apollinarians, Novatians, Sabatians, Eunomians, Tetradites, Tessarecaedecadites, Valentinians, Paulians, Papianists, Montanists, Priscillians, Phrygians, Pepuzites, Marcionists, Borborites, Messalians, Euchites, Enthusiasts, Donatists, Audians, Hydroparastetes, Tascodrogites, Batracites, Hermogenians, Photinians, Paulinists, Marcellians, Ophites, Encratitians, Carpocratitians, Saccophores, and Manichaeans, who have sunk to the worst depravity of crimes, shall never be allowed to assemble or dwell in a Roman place. The Manichaeans are to be driven out of cities and subject to severe penalty, for no place should be allowed to them in which to do harm even to the elements themselves. Also, all laws enacted at different times against them and others who resist our faith, shall remain in force always as if brand new, whether those laws concern donations for the assemblies of heretics (which they boldly try to call churches), property bequeathed in a last will in any way whatsoever, or private buildings in which they assemble with the permission or connivance of the owner (which shall be confiscated for the benefit of the holy Church). . . . So that they may not be able to assemble in a public place or build what they call churches for themselves, or design anything at all to circumvent the laws, they shall also be deprived of all aid, whether military or civil, of the law courts, the defenders and judges. . . . (*CJ* 1.5.5, 428 C.E.)

[33] Therefore we forbid the Eutychians and Apollinarians to ordain and have bishops, priests, or other clergy. For those Eutychians and Apollinarians who have dared to appoint anyone bishop, priest, or clergy, as well as those who have allowed a clerical title to be given to them and who retain the title, shall suffer the penalty of loss of their property.

Furthermore, no Eutychians or Apollinarians shall have the opportunity to assemble a congregation whether publicly or privately, or to draw together private meetings to discuss their heretical error and assert the perversity of their criminal beliefs. Nor shall it be lawful for them to say, write, publish or put forth anything against the holy Chalcedonian Synod, or to publish the sayings or writings of others on this same topic. Let no one dare to possess or preserve books of this sort or sacrilegious memorials of these writers. Those convicted of such crimes shall be punished with perpetual banishment.

Therefore all papers and books of this sort which contain the deadly beliefs of Eutyches and Apollinaris shall be burned so that the traces of their criminal perversity may perish, consumed by flames. (*CJ* 1.5.8, 457 C.E.)

[34] If it should happen that a part of our palace or other public building has been touched by lightning, the custom of the former observance shall be retained and inquiry shall be made of the soothsayers what it may portend. These [portents] shall be carefully collected and recorded and brought to our attention. Permission shall be granted to others to make use of this custom, provided that they refrain from domestic sacrifices which have been specifically forbidden. (*CTh* 16.10.1, 320/21 C.E.)

[35] Because we have learned that some clergy and other followers of the Catholic sect have been forced by men of different religions to conduct pagan sacrifices, we hereby decree that if anyone believes that those who follow divine law can be forced to perform a rite of pagan superstition, he shall be publicly beaten with clubs, if his rank permits, but if his rank protects him from such punishment, he shall pay a heavy fine, which shall go to public works. (*CTh* 16.2.5, 325 C.E.)

[36] Nocturnal sacrifices formerly allowed by the authority of Magnentius are forbidden and henceforth this criminal freedom is repealed. (*CTh* 16.10.5, 353 C.E.)

[37] By the authority of the emperors' council, we decree that the building formerly dedicated to crowded assemblies and now open to the people, in which images have reportedly been placed (which should be measured by the value of their art rather than by their divinity), shall always be open. And we allow no secret imperial order to hinder this.

In order that it may be seen by the multitudes of the city, your experience shall preserve every celebration of festivals and by the authority of our order the temple shall be allowed to remain open, but in such a way that people do not believe the observance of prohibited sacrifices is allowed by this access. (*CTh* 16.10.8, 382 C.E.)

[38] Let no mortal dare to make a sacrifice, that by inspection of the liver and the foretelling of the entrails he might obtain the hope of empty promise

or learn the future by accursed inquiry, which is worse. He who seeks to find the truth of the present or the future, contrary to what has been forbidden, shall be subject to severe punishment. (*CJ* 1.11.2, 385 C.E.)

[39] No person at all, from whatever class or order of men or office, whether currently in power or having completed an office, whether powerful by the chance of birth, or humble in class, legal status, and wealth, shall sacrifice an innocent victim to senseless images in any place or in any city; nor shall any one by more private sacrifice worship his [household] *lar* with fire, his [personal] *genius* with wine, or his [household] *penates* by kindling lights, burning incense, or hanging wreaths for them.

But if anyone dares to dedicate a victim in sacrifice or to consult the living entrails, he shall merit, as one guilty of treason, an accusation open to all and a suitable punishment, even though he has asked nothing contrary to or about the welfare of the emperors. For it is enough to constitute a serious crime that anyone wish to break the laws of nature herself, to examine forbidden things, to disclose the hidden, to attempt the proscribed, to find out the limit of another's life, to promise the expectation of another's death.

But if anyone worships with incense those images made by human hands and destined to endure time, if anyone in a laughable way, suddenly fearing the empty images that he himself has created, seeks to honor them either by adorning a tree with sacrificial bands, by building an altar with dug-up sod, or by an offering however small (though it is still an insult to religion), since he is guilty of the violation of religion he shall forfeit that house or holding in which he is proved to have been a slave to heathen superstition. For we decree that all places that prove to have reeked with the smell of incense shall be united with our treasury, if they are shown to have belonged by law to those burning incense. (*CTh* 16.10.12 [E366], 392 C.E.)

[40] Inasmuch as we have forbidden the temple sacrifices, we nonetheless desire the ornaments of public works to be preserved. And, lest those who seek to destroy [these buildings] flatter themselves with their supposed authority, if any law or imperial decree is held out as a pretext [for such authority], let the documents of such sort be seized from their hands and brought to our attention. (*CJ* 1.11.3, 399 C.E.)

[41] Images, if any even now stand in temples and shrines, which have received or do receive any worship of pagans, shall be torn from their foundations, since we know that this has been very often decreed by repeated ordinance.

The buildings themselves of the temples, which are in cities or towns or outside of towns, shall be dedicated to public use. Altars in all places shall be destroyed and all temples within our holdings shall be dedicated to public use. The proprietors shall be forced to destroy them.

It shall not be lawful at all to hold banquets in places polluted with blood in order to honor sacrilegious rites or to celebrate any sort of ritual. (*CTh* 16.10.19 [W356], 408 C.E.)

[42] We decree that astrologers be expelled not only from the city of Rome but also from all cities, unless they are ready to burn the books containing their errors under the eyes of the bishops and convert to belief in the Catholic religion, never to return to their original error. If they do not do this and are found in any city in violation of our wholesome decree, or if they teach the secrets of their error and belief, they shall merit the punishment of deportation. (CJ 1.4.11, 409 C.E.)

[43] Let no one reopen for worship or veneration the shrines that have already been closed. Let there be no return in our age to the honor formerly given to forbidden and accursed images. It is sacrilege rather than religion to wreath the unholy doors of temples, to burn pagan fires or incense on an altar, to sacrifice victims, and to pour libations of wine. (CJ 1.11.7, 451 C.E.)

[44] It shall be unlawful for the Jews to bother any man who has converted from Judaism to Christianity or to injure him in any way . . . (CTh 16.8.5, 336 C.E.)

[45] If anyone converts from Christianity to Judaism and joins their sacrilegious assemblies, when the accusation has been proved, we order his property forfeited to our treasury. (CJ 1.7.1, 357 C.E.)

[46] No Jew shall marry a Christian woman, nor shall any Christian marry a Jewish woman, for if anyone is guilty of such a marriage he shall suffer as if guilty of the crime of adultery . . . (CJ 1.9.5, 388 C.E.)

[47] No Jew shall keep his own law regarding marriage nor shall he obtain a marriage according to his law nor shall he marry in separate marriages at the same time. (CJ 1.9.7 [E433], 393 C.E.)

[48] The Jews shall be bound by their own religious ceremonies . . . (CTh 16.8.13 [E534], 397 C.E.)

[49] The governors of the provinces shall prohibit Jews from lighting with fire the rites of their festival in remembrance of the crucifixion [of Haman] or burning a representation of the Holy Cross in sacrilegious contempt of the Christian faith. Nor shall they affix the symbol of our faith upon their buildings, but they may observe their rites without contempt toward Christian law and they shall without doubt lose what has been previously permitted them unless they refrain from what is forbidden them. (CJ 1.9.10, 408 C.E.)

[50] On the Sabbath day and other days when the Jews observe the worship of their faith, we order that no one either do anything [to them] or summon them to court on any matter; nor can they summon orthodox Christians to court on that day, so that Christians shall not suffer any harm from a court summons on those days, since it appears that the remaining days will be sufficient for the need of our treasury and the suits of private parties. (CJ 1.9.12, 409 C.E.)

[51] No innocent Jew shall be trampled on, nor shall any religion expose a Jew to abuse, nor shall their synagogues or dwellings be burned, nor shall they be wrongly injured without reason; for when one of them is accused of crimes, the power of the judges and the protection of public law have been established

to prevent anyone from exacting vengeance himself on his own behalf. But since we wish to provide this for the Jews, we think they ought to be warned, lest they become arrogant and, carried away with their protection, rashly commit any act of vengeance upon the Christian religion. (*CJ* 1.9.13, 412 C.E.)

[52] It is our pleasure that in the future none at all of the synagogues of the Jews be taken away or consumed by flames and if, after this law, there are any synagogues which have been recently seized or claimed by churches or, in fact, dedicated to holy rites, in their place shall be afforded to the Jews locations where they may build synagogues commensurate with those taken away.

For the rest, in the future no synagogues shall be built and old synagogues shall remain as they are. (*CTh* 16.8.25 [E783], 423 C.E.)

[53] If it appears that Jews have circumcised a man of our faith or have ordered it done, they shall be punished with confiscation of their property and perpetual banishment. (*CJ* 1.9.15, 439 C.E.)

Bibliography

Boyd, William K. 1905. *The Ecclesiastical Edicts of the Theodosian Code*. New York: Columbia University Press.

Harries, Jill, and Ian Wood. 1993. *The Theodosian Code*. Ithaca: Cornell University Press.

Honoré, Tony. 1978. *Tribonian*. Ithaca: Cornell University Press.

———. 1998. *Law in the Crisis of Empire 379–455 A.D.* Oxford: Clarendon.

Hunt, David. 1993. "Christianizing the Roman Empire: The Evidence of the Code." In Harries and Wood 1993, 143–58.

Matthews, John. 1993. "The Making of the Text." In Harries and Wood 1993, 19–44.

Pharr, C., ed. and trans. 1952. *The Theodosian Code and the Sirmondian Constitutions*. Princeton: Princeton University Press.

Scott, S. P. 1932. *The Civil Law: The Code of Justinian*. Cincinnati: Central Trust.

Sirks, Boudewijn. 1993. "The Sources of the Code." In Harries and Wood 1993, 45–67.

Williams, C. Dickerman. 1952. "Introduction." In *The Theodosian Code and the Sirmondian Constitutions*. Ed. and trans. C. Pharr. xvii–xxii. Princeton: Princeton University Press.

Wood, Ian. 1993. "The Code in Merovingian Gaul." In Harries and Wood 1993, 161–77.

— 22 —

The Acts of the Council of Aquileia (381 C.E.)

Kenneth B. Steinhauser

From the Acts of the Council of Aquileia emerges a sketch of the Christian Arian theological stance current in Italy and Illyricum toward the end of the fourth century. Acknowledging the danger of oversimplification, one may nevertheless legitimately identify four different kinds, categories, or sects of Arianism in antiquity. First, Arius and traditional Arians asserted that the Son has a beginning in time and there was a time when the Son did not exist. In other words, the Son is a creature of the Father. Second, the homoiousians take their cue from the homoousians. The homoousians asserted that the Father, Son, and Holy Spirit are equal and coeternal and of the same (*homos*) being (*ousia*). The word *homoousios,* meaning "one in being" or "of the same substance" and later rendered *consubstantialis* in Latin, was actually adopted in the Creed of Nicea (325) and became equated with orthodox Christianity. The homoiousians, later called semi-Arians, attempted a mediating position by substituting the word similar (*homoios*) for same (*homos*). They distinguished "similar" from "same." If the Father, Son, and Holy Spirit were not of the "same" being but of "similar" being, the pitfall of monarchianism, also called Sabellianism, could be avoided because the distinction of persons is preserved through the use of this formula. In substituting "similar" for "same," the word "similar" is actually indicating a certain dissimilarity. Paradoxically, in this context "similar" means "different." Though ultimately rejected as heretical, even Hilary of Poitiers was willing to accept the word *homoiousios* as equivalent to *homoousios.* In other words, he had no problem with the designation if it were properly understood as a synonym. Third, the anomoians, also called Eunomians, maintained a distinction among the Father, Son, and Holy Spirit insisting that the three persons are radically dissimilar or unalike (*anomoios*). Fourth, the homoians, like all Arian positions, rejected *homoousios* but maintained the Son was like (*homoios*) the Father. The so-called Arians in attendance at the Council of Aquileia were actually homoians, of whom Palladius of Ratiaria was the most vocal. The Acts of the Council of Aquileia record the events that took place on September 3, 381. Three concrete references to the Acts themselves enable one to draw a picture of the historical, theological, and political situation in northern Italy and Illyricum at the end of the fourth century.

Palladius dixit, "Ego Arrium non novi."

Gesta concili aquileiensis 25; Corpus Scriptorum
Ecclesiasticorum Latinorum 82, 3, 341

Palladius insisted that he did not know Arius. Commentators all too frequently describe this and other similar comments as a subterfuge based on the temporal and geographical distance of the historical Arius from contemporary debates. However, a close examination of the text of the Acts within the historical context of the debate must of necessity lead one to conclude that Palladius's protests were absolutely genuine. Though accused of Arianism by their opponents and labeled Arian without hesitancy, Latin homoian bishops in no way regarded their theological position as Arian. How is this possible? The homoian position had already been made abundantly clear in the Council of Rimini (359). Both Arians and homoians alike firmly rejected the Nicene *homoousios* as non-biblical and Sabellian. Yet, unlike Arius and the Arians, in asserting that the Son was begotten, the homoians denied that the Son was created. Therefore, they could logically distance themselves from Arius and publicly disavow the presence of Arianism in their teaching. In fact, a harbinger of the Latin homoian position may be found even earlier than Rimini in Lucian of Antioch, whose moderate subordinationism in the Origenist tradition could have been considered orthodox. Although Latin homoians refused to see themselves as the direct theological descendants of Arius, they seem to have accepted an association with Arius's teacher, Lucian, without reservation. One text in particular, namely the anonymous commentary on Job, specifically mentions Lucian of Antioch, praising his life, his faith, and his martyrdom of which the suffering Job was a precursor and a type. (PG 17, 470–71) Lucian was generally considered to have been the author of the creed, which, after his martyrdom, was adopted by the Council of Antioch (341) and Lucian's position closely approximates the position of the homoians. Although scholars concede that the text of the Creed of Antioch has been so modified that it may be difficult to determine exactly what Lucian wrote, Athanasius's *De Synodis* 23 (AW 2, 1, 249–50) offers a reasonably accurate rendition of the text. The Creed of Antioch appears to steer a middle course in utilizing the word *ousia* while avoiding the word *homoousios*. More importantly, what would subsequently become a favorite expression of the homoians appears there, namely "only begotten God," which is attested in John 1:18. Thus, the intellectual heritage of the homoians should more appropriately be traced back to Lucian rather than to Arius.

Palladius dixit, "Verus filius dei est."

Gesta consili aquileiensis 19; Corpus Scriptorum
Ecclesiasticorum Latinorum 82, 3, 337

Neither the word *ousia* nor its Latin equivalent entered into the debates at Aquileia. Instead the discussion centered on *verus*. Palladius was quite content to called Christ *verus filius*, true Son, but he refused to call Christ *verus deus*, true God. Totally devoid of references to the Greco-Roman classical tradition, Arian or homoian Latin literature of the West was biblically based to the exclusion of subtle philosophical distinctions. The homoian bishops were essentially biblicists, whose philosophically unsophisticated teaching frustrated Ambrose and the other pro-Nicene bishops at the Council of Aquileia. Especially fond of Johannine literature, the homoians present at Aquileia made three significant assertions: (1) The Father is unbegotten; (2) The Son is only begotten; and (3) The Father is greater than the Son. Throughout the debates Palladius and his colleagues deny—or at least refuse to assert—that the Son is true God because any such assertion would fundamentally obliterate the distinction between the Father and the Son and fall into monarchianism, which appears at this time to have been a more distressing problem to them than the danger of tritheism. The Father alone is true God. However, the homoian bishops have no difficulty in referring to the "true Son of God" so that Christ may be called true Son but not true God. The homoian bishops also have no difficulty in referring to the Son as "only begotten God," which is biblically attested, while reserving "unbegotten God" and "true God" to the Father alone. The final characteristic of the homoian theological teaching is an unabashed subordinationism. Palladius explicitly states that the Father is greater than the Son because in John's gospel Jesus himself states, "The Father is greater than I (John 14:28)."

Palladius dixit, "Iam dixi, non vobis respondeo usque ad plenum concilium."

Gesta consili aquileiensis 29; Corpus Scriptorum
Ecclesiasticorum Latinorum 82, 3, 343

Palladius and the other homoian bishops suddenly found themselves defendants in a kangaroo court rather than delegates in an ecclesiastical council. During the council Palladius's nemesis is Ambrose, Bishop of Milan. Earlier Ambrose had been on the defensive because in 378 at the behest of the emperor Gratian, he was required to explain his faith. He responded with books one and two of *De fide*, essentially accusing his opponents of teaching that the Father was *dissimilis* from the Son. In other words, he accused the homoians of radical anomoianism.

Palladius rejected this as preposterous and took great offense at Ambrose's inaccurate characterization of the homoian position. In 380 Ambrose continued his assault on his opponents by writing books three and four of *De fide*. By the time Ambrose wrote *De spiritu sancto* in 381, he is praising Gratian for his intervention in returning the basilica, which had been sequestered for the use of the homoians some three years earlier. In 378 Gratian, in spite of his pro-Nicene tendencies, had attempted to maintain a religious neutrality. However, by 381 Gratian seems to have drifted toward the pro-Nicene camp and developed a personal friendship with Ambrose. At Aquileia, Ambrose had clearly stacked the deck against the homoian bishops. He had convinced Gratian not to invite the eastern bishops supposedly because the travel would have been too great a hardship for them, particularly the elderly and infirm bishops. This left a small band of homoian bishops isolated at the council and opposed by a larger group of pro-Nicene bishops, who near the end of the proceedings issued a condemnation of Palladius and Secundianus of Singidunum and anathematized them. Palladius insisted that the entire proceeding was invalid because the easterners were not present, although the emperor Gratian himself had guaranteed their invitation. Furthermore, the stenographers were not recording his comments. He demanded that *auditores* be summoned. Apparently he wanted to submit the case to impartial arbiters. The pro-Nicene forces insisted that lay *auditores* should not sit in judgment of clergy. Procedurally the homoians were overwhelmed. Occasionally all Palladius could do was refuse to respond. Contrary to the popular hagiographic tradition surrounding Ambrose that the Council of Aquileia definitively destroyed Arianism in the West, the decisions of the council did not go unchallenged and a homoian revival took place in Milan soon after the council. Palladius wrote a vigorous apology sharply critical of the council and its decisions and of Ambrose personally. With the support of the emperor's mother Justina, Auxentius of Durostorum arrived in Milan in 384 and, assuming the role of local homoian bishop, he was soon looking to take over a basilica for his community. In fact, homoianism remained strong in the West until the death of Magnus Maximus and the entrance into Milan of the emperor Theodosius, whose occupation of the western provinces marked its demise.

The critical edition of the *Gesta concili aquileiensis* is that of Michaela Zelzer (*Corpus scriptorum ecclesiasticorum latinorum* 82). Paris, Bibliothèque Nationale, lat. 8907 contains contemporary scholia written by Palladius himself and possibly other homoian participants at the council. These have been edited by Roger Gryson (*Corpus christianorum* 87), who published the *Gesta* and scholia with a French translation (*Sources chrétiennes* 267). Regarding my translation of the *Gesta*, I consulted both editions and, where there were variants, I judged on a case by case basis, always preferring the text of Zelzer to that of Gryson. There is also an Italian translation of the *Gesta* by Giuseppe Cuscito. Peter Heather and John Matthews (Translated Texts for Historians 11) published an English translation of the life of Ulfila contained in the scholia. To my knowledge the *Gesta* have not been translated into English. From the *Acts of the Council of Aquileia*—a total of seventy-five paragraphs—the passage below contains approximately half the text uninterrupted from paragraph 12 to paragraph 43.

The Acts of the Council of Aquileia

[12] [Addressing Palladius and his companions] Bishop Ambrose said, "You yourselves insisted that we should be seated here today. For today you yourselves said because we as Christians come to Christians, you regard us as Christians. You promised that you would enter into discussion. You promised that you would offer and accept logic. Therefore, we gladly accept your explanation, but we wished that you had come as a Christian. I offered you the letter of Arius, which Arius wrote, from whose name you say you frequently sustain injury. You say that you do not follow Arius. Today your opinion ought to be open. Either condemn him or defend him using whatever evidence you wish." And he added, "Therefore, according to the letter of Arius is not Christ the Son of God eternal?"

Palladius said, "We said that we will prove ourselves Christians only in a plenary council. We are absolutely not responding to you in order not to prejudice a future council."

Bishop Eusebius said, "You ought to express the profession of your faith without deceit."

Palladius said, "And what do we reserve for the council?"

[13] Bishop Ambrose said, "In every mouth the condemnation was announced against him who denies that the Son of God is eternal. Arius denied this. Palladius, who does not wish to condemn Arius, follows him. Therefore, consider whether this opinion of his ought to be tested. Consider whether he is speaking according to the scriptures or whether he is thinking contrary to the scriptures. For it was read, 'Eternal is the power of God and divinity' [Rom. 1:20]. Christ is the power of God. Therefore, if the power of God is eternal, then Christ is clearly eternal because Christ is the power of God."

Bishop Eusebius said, "This is our faith. This is the catholic understanding. Whoever would not say this is anathema."

All the bishops said, "Anathema."

[14] Bishop Eusebius said, "In particular he [Arius] says that only the Father is eternal and the Son began at some time."

Palladius said, "Neither have I seen Arius nor do I know who he is."

Bishop Eusebius said, "The blasphemy of Arius is expressed when he denies that the Son of God is eternal. Do you condemn this perfidy with its author or do you assert it?"

Palladius said, "Where there is no authority for a plenary council, I am not speaking."

[15] Bishop Ambrose said, "Do you hesitate to condemn Arius after divine judgment since he burst forth in our midst?" And he added, "The holy men, the legates of the Gauls, should also speak."

Bishop Constantius, legate of the Gauls, said, "We have always condemned the impiety of this man and now we condemn not only Arius but also anyone who would not say that the Son of God is eternal."

Bishop Ambrose said, "What does my lord Justus say?"

Bishop Justus, legate of the Gauls, said, "Whoever does not confess that the Son of God is coeternal with the Father should be held anathema."

All the bishops said, "Anathema!"

[16] Bishop Ambrose said, "The legates of the Africans, who have brought here the opinions of all their citizens, should speak."

Bishop Felix, legate, said, "If anyone would deny that the Son of God is forever eternal and if anyone would deny that he is coeternal, not only do I, legate of the entire African province, condemn him, but also the entire priestly choir itself, which sent me to this most holy gathering, has already condemned him."

Bishop Anemius said, "The capital of Illyricum is none other than the city of Sirmium and I am bishop of that city. Therefore, I declare him anathema, who does not confess that the Son of God is eternal and coeternal with the Father because the Father is forever eternal, and I also condemn those men who do not confess the same."

[17] Bishop Ambrose said, "Listen to the following."

And this was read: "Only eternal, only without beginning, only true, only having immortality."

Bishop Ambrose said, "And on this point also, condemn him who denies that the Son is true God. Since he himself is truth, how is he not true God?" And he added, "What do you say to this?"

Palladius said, "Who does not say that the Son is true?"

Bishop Ambrose said, "Arius denied it."

Palladius said, "When the apostle says that Christ is God above all, can anyone deny that he is the true Son of God?"

[18] Bishop Ambrose said, "You should know that the truth is required of us without reserve. Indeed, I speak as you speak, but I consider it a half truth. When you speak in this way, you seem to deny that the Son is true God. However, if you are going to confess without reserve that the Son of God is true God, add these words in the order that I myself propose."

Palladius said, "I speak to you according to the scriptures, I declare the true Son of God God."

Bishop Ambrose said, "Do you declare that the Son of God is true God?"

Palladius said, "When I declare the Son true, what more can I say?"

Bishop Ambrose said, "I not only ask whether you declare the Son true, but also whether you declare the Son of God true God."

[19] Bishop Eusebius said, "Christ is true God according to the faith of all and according to catholic belief."

Palladius said, "He is the true Son of God."

Bishop Eusebius said, "Indeed we are also sons through adoption but he is Son according to the specific attribute of divine generation." And he added, "Therefore, do you confess that the true Son of God is true God according to birth and specific attribute?"

Palladius said, "I declare that the true Son of God is only begotten."

Bishop Eusebius said, "Therefore, do you think it contrary to the scriptures if one would declare Christ to be true God?"

[20] And when Palladius remained silent, Bishop Ambrose said, "Whoever says 'true Son of God' only and does not wish to say 'true God' seems to deny the latter. Nevertheless, if Palladius professes his faith, then he should profess it using the appropriate word order and he should say whether he would declare the Son of God true God."

Palladius said, "When the Son says, 'That they may know you the one true God and Jesus Christ whom you sent' [John 17:3], is it feigned or is it sincere?"

Bishop Ambrose said, "John declared in his letter, 'He is true God' [1 John 5:20]. Do you deny this?"

Palladius said, "When I tell you true Son, I also profess true divinity."

Bishop Ambrose said, "In this there is deceit. For you are accustomed to say 'one and true divinity' only of the Father but you would not say 'one and true divinity' also of the Son. Therefore, since you refer me to the scriptures, if you wish to speak openly, affirm what the evangelist John said 'He is true God' [1 John 5:20] or deny the statement.

Palladius said, "Apart from the Son no other has been generated."

[21] Bishop Eusebius said, "In your opinion is Christ true God according to the faith of all and according to catholic belief or is he not true God?"

Palladius said, "He is the goodness of our God."

Bishop Ambrose said, "You are not at liberty to profess this and consequently anathema upon him who does not confess that the Son of God is true God."

All the bishops said, "Whoever would not say that Christ the Son of God is true God should be held anathema."

[22] Likewise the reading continued, "Only true, only havir̦ ̦mortality."

Bishop Ambrose said, "Does the Son of God have immortality or does he not have it according to divinity?"

Palladius said, "Do you accept the apostle or not? 'The king of kings who alone has immortality' [1 Tim. 6:15–16]."

Bishop Ambrose said, "What do you say concerning Christ the Son of God?"

Palladius said, "Is Christ a divine or human name?"

[23] Bishop Eusebius said, "Certainly according to the mystery of the flesh he is called Christ, but this same Christ is God and man."

Palladius said, "Is Christ the name of flesh? Is Christ a human name? You answer me."

Bishop Eusebius said, "Why do you delay interminably? When the impiety of Arius was read, who declares this concerning the Father because 'he alone has immortality' [1 Tim. 6:16], you advanced testimony to support the impiety of Arius from the apostle saying, 'Who alone has immortality and dwells in inaccessible light' [1 Tim. 6:16]. But you should understand that by the noun 'God' the apostle expressed the dignity of the entire nature in as much as both the Father and the Son are designated by the noun 'God.' "

Palladius said, "And when I asked you, you did not wish to respond."

[24] Bishop Ambrose said, "From you I openly ask your opinion: Does the Son of God have immortality according to divine generation or does he not have it?"

Palladius said, "According to divine generation he is incorruptible, through flesh he died."

Bishop Ambrose said, "Divinity did not die, but flesh died."

Palladius said, "First you respond to me."

Bishop Ambrose said, "Does the Son of God have immortality according to divinity or does he not have it? Did you also report that your insidious and perverse statements were not in agreement with the profession of Arius?" And he added, "Arius denies that the Son of God has immortality, what do you think?" All the bishops said, "He should be held anathema."

[25] Palladius said, "Divine nature is immortal."

Bishop Ambrose said, "Clever that you should say this so that you may express nothing clearly concerning the Son of God. And I say: The Son of God has immortality according to divinity. Either affirm or deny that he has immortality."

Palladius said, "Did Christ die or not?"

Bishop Ambrose said, "According to flesh he died, but our soul does not die, for it is written, 'Be unwilling to fear those who can kill the flesh, but cannot kill the soul' [1 Pet. 4:1]. Since, therefore, our soul cannot die, do you think that Christ died according to divinity?"

Palladius said, "Why do you fear the mention of death?"

Bishop Ambrose said, "In no way do I fear but I confess according to my flesh through which it is that I am bound to the chains of death."

Palladius said, "The separation of the spirit causes death; for Christ the Son of God assumed flesh and through flesh died."

Bishop Ambrose said, "It is written that Christ suffered. Therefore, he suffered according to the flesh, according to divinity he has immortality. Whoever denies this is the devil."

Palladius said, "I did not know Arius."

[26] Bishop Ambrose said, "Therefore, Arius spoke wrongly, since the Son of God has immortality according to divinity as well." And he added, "Did he speak rightly or wrongly?"

Palladius said, "I do not agree."

Bishop Ambrose said, "With whom do you not agree? Anathema upon him who does not display the freedom of his faith."

All the bishops said, "Anathema."

Palladius said, "Say what you wish; his divinity is immortal."

Bishop Ambrose said, "Whose? The Father's or the Son's?" And he added, "Arius amassed many impieties. Let us go on to others."

[27] And this was read, "Only wisdom."

Palladius said, "The Father is wise of himself. However, the Son is not wise."

Bishop Ambrose said, "Is, therefore, the Son not wise since he himself is wisdom? For indeed we say that the Son was born from the Father."

Bishop Eusebius said, "Is anything more impious and more profane than to deny that the Son of God is wise?"

Palladius said, "He is called wisdom. Who can deny that he is wisdom?"

Bishop Ambrose said, "Is he wise or not?"

Palladius said, "He is wisdom."

Bishop Ambrose said, "Therefore, he is wise since he is wisdom."

Palladius said, "We respond to you according to the scriptures."

Bishop Ambrose said, "From what I see, Palladius is now known to deny that the Son of God is wise."

Bishop Eusebius said, "Let him be anathema who denies that the Son of God is wise."

All the bishops said, "Anathema."

[28] Bishop Eusebius said, "Let Secundianus also reply to this."

And when Secundianus remained silent, Bishop Ambrose said, "Because he is silent, he wishes to obtain a separate judgment." And he added, "Did he confess or did he deny the Son when he calls the Father alone good?"

Palladius said, "Do we read 'I am the good shepherd' [John 10:11], and do we deny this? Who would not say that the Son of God is good?"

Bishop Ambrose said, "Therefore, Christ is good."

Palladius said, "Good."

Bishop Ambrose said, "Therefore, Arius spoke wrongly concerning the Father alone, since the Son of God is also God in all."

Palladius said, "Whoever does not say that Christ is good speaks wrongly."

[29] Bishop Eusebius said, "Do you confess that Christ is good God? For I am good, he said to me, 'It goes well, good servant' [Matt. 25:21], and 'A good man brings forth from his storehouse good things' [Luke 6:45]."

Palladius said, "I already said that I am not going to respond to you until the plenary council."

Bishop Ambrose said, "The Jews said 'He is good' [John 7:12], and Arius denies that the Son of God is good."

Palladius said, "Who can deny this?"

Bishop Eusebius said, "Therefore, the Son of God is good God."

Palladius said, "The good Father generated the good Son."

[30] Bishop Ambrose said, "And he generated us good but not according to divinity. Do you declare the Son of God good God?"

Palladius said, "The Son of God is good."

Bishop Ambrose said, "Therefore, because you declare Christ good Son and not good God, you see what is asked of you." And he added, "Anathema upon him who does not confess that the Son of God is good God."

All the bishops said, "Anathema."

[31] And this was read, "Alone powerful."

Bishop Ambrose said, "Is the Son of God powerful or not?"

Palladius said, "Is he who made all things not powerful? Is he who made all things less mighty?"

Bishop Ambrose said, "Therefore, Arius spoke wrongly." And he added, "In this respect do you condemn Arius?"

Palladius said, "How should I know who he is? I respond to you for myself."

Bishop Ambrose said, "Is the Son of God powerful God?"

Palladius said, "Powerful."

Ambrosius said, "Is God good?"

Palladius said, "I already said that the only begotten Son of God is powerful."

Bishop Ambrose said, "Powerful God?"

Palladius said, "The powerful Son of God."

[32] Bishop Ambrose said, "Men are also powerful. It is written, 'Why do you glory in evil you who are powerful in iniquity' [Ps. 51:3]? And elsewhere, 'When I am weak, then I am strong' [2 Cor. 12:10]. I ask this of you that you confess that Christ the Son of God is powerful God or, if you deny this, prove it. For I, who speak of the single power of the Father and of the Son, call the Son of God just as powerful as the Father. Therefore, do you hesitate to confess that the Son of God is powerful God?"

Palladius said, "In this discussion I already stated, we respond to you to the extent that we can. For you wish to be litigants and you wish to be judges at the same time. We are not going to respond to you now, but we are going to respond to you in a general and plenary council."

Bishop Ambrose said, "Anathema upon him who denies that Christ is powerful God."

All the bishops said, "Anathema."

[33] And this was read, "Alone powerful, judge of all."

Palladius said, "The Son of God is judge of all, it is he who gives, it is he who receives."

Bishop Ambrose said, "Did he give through grace or through nature? And judgment is also given to men."

Palladius said, "Do you call the Father greater or not?"

Bishop Ambrose said, "I am going to respond to you later."

Palladius said, "I am not responding to you if you do not respond to me."

Bishop Eusebius said, "Unless you have damned the impiety of Arius point by point, we will not give you the authority to question us."

Palladius said, "I am not responding to you."

Bishop Ambrose said, "As it was read, is the Son of God judge or not?"

Palladius said, "If you do not respond to me, I am not responding to you because you are impious."

[34] Bishop Ambrose said, "You have my profession by which I responded to you. Meanwhile let the letter of Arius be read to the end." And he added, "In the letter of Arius you will find this sacrilege which you prepare."

Palladius said, "Why do you not respond to what I ask?"

Bishop Eusebius said, "We declare that the Son of God is equal to God."

Palladius said, "You are the judge, here are your stenographers."

Bishop Ambrose said, "Your associates, who so desired, were also writing."

[35] Palladius said, "Is the Father greater or not?"

Bishop Eusebius said, "According to divinity the Son is equal to the Father. You have in the gospel that the Jews persecuted him, 'because he not only broke the sabbath but also called God his Father, making himself equal to God' [John 5:18]. Therefore, what the impious persecutors confessed, we believers cannot deny."

Bishop Ambrose said, "And elsewhere you have, 'Who, although he was in the form of God, did not judge his being equal to God a theft, but he emptied himself, accepting the form of a slave, having been made similar to men, obedient unto death' [Phil. 2:6–8]." And he added, "Do you see why 'in the form of God' means equal? And, he said, he accepted the 'form of a slave.' In what way, therefore, is he less? Certainly according to the form of a slave not according to the form of God."

Bishop Eusebius said, "Just as he was not found in the form of a slave inferior to a slave, so also he could not have been found in the form of God inferior to God."

[36] Bishop Ambrose said, "Tell us whether the Son of God is inferior according to divinity."

Palladius said, "The Father is greater."

Bishop Ambrose said, "According to flesh."

Palladius said, " 'He who sent me is greater than I' [John 6:44 and 14:28]. Was flesh sent from God or the Son of God?"

Bishop Ambrose said, "Today we prove that the divine scriptures are falsified by you. For thus it is written, 'My peace I give you, my peace I leave with you, do not let your heart be troubled, for not as this world gives, do I give to you. If you loved me, you would rejoice because I said: I go to the Father because the Father is greater than I' [John 14:27–28]. He did not say, 'He who sent me is greater than me.' "

Palladius said, "The Father is greater."

Bishop Ambrose said, "Anathema upon him who adds anything to divine scriptures or subtracts anything from them."

All the bishops said, "Anathema."

[37] Palladius said, "The Father is greater than the Son."

Bishop Ambrose said, "According to flesh the Son is less than the Father, according to divinity he is equal to the Father. Therefore, as the evidence already brought forth attests, I read that the Son of God is equal to the Father. However, why are you amazed that he is less according to flesh, since he called himself a slave, since he called himself a stone, since he called himself a worm, since he called himself less than the angels because it is written, 'You count him little less than angels' [Ps. 8:6]."

Palladius said, "I see you are making impious assertion. We are not going to respond to you without arbiters."

Bishop Sabinus said, "No one requires an opinion from him who already blasphemed in so many innumerable opinions."

Palladius said, "We are not answering you."

[38] Bishop Sabinus said, "By all these assertions Palladius has already been condemned. The blasphemies of Arius are much less than those of Palladius." And when Palladius had risen and wished to leave, Bishop Sabinus continued, "For that reason Palladius stands because he perceives that he will necessarily be refuted by the explicit testimonies of the scriptures as he has already been refuted. For he knows, as it has been read, that according to divinity the Son is equal to the Father. He should also agree that the Son of God has none greater according to divinity. It is written, 'When God made the promise to Abraham, because he had none greater by whom he could swear, he swore by himself' [Heb. 6:13]. Therefore, you see the scripture passage 'he had none greater by whom he could swear.' However, the Son is the one concerning whom it is said that he himself had been seen by Abraham, and thus he said, 'Abraham saw my day and rejoiced' [John 8:56]."

Palladius said, "The Father is greater."

Bishop Eusebius said, "When he spoke as God, he had none greater; when he spoke as man, he had a greater."

[39] Palladius said, "The Father generated the Son, the Father sent the Son."

Bishop Ambrose said, "Anathema upon him, who denies that according to divinity the Son is equal to the Father."

All the bishops said, "Anathema."

Palladius said, "The Son is subjected to the Father, the Son keeps the precepts of the Father."

Bishop Ambrose said, "He is subjected by reason of the flesh. And you remember the rest because you yourself read, 'No one comes to me unless the Father has drawn him' [John 6:44]."

Bishop Sabinus said, "Let him say whether the Son is subjected to the Father according to divinity or according to incarnation."

[40] Palladius said, "Therefore, the Father is greater."

Bishop Ambrose said, "And elsewhere it is written, 'God is faithful, through whom you have been called into the communion of his Son' [1 Cor. 1:9]. I say that the Father is greater according to the assumption of flesh, which the Son of God received, but not according to divinity."

Palladius said, "What comparison is there to the Son of God? Flesh can say: God is greater than me. Was flesh or divinity speaking, because flesh was there?"

Bishop Ambrose said, "Flesh without a soul does not speak."

Bishop Eusebius said, "God in the flesh was speaking according to the flesh when he said, 'Why are you persecuting me, a man' [John 8:40]? Who said this?"

Palladius said, "The Son of God."

Bishop Ambrose said, "Therefore, the Son of God is God according to divinity and he is man according to flesh."

Palladius said, "He accepted flesh."

Bishop Eusebius said, "Therefore, he used human words."

Palladius said, "He received human flesh."

[41] Bishop Ambrose said, "Let him explain why the apostle said that he was subjected not according to divinity but according to flesh; for it is written, 'He humbled himself having been made obedient unto death' [Phil. 2:8]. In what way, therefore, did he taste death?"

Palladius said, "Because he humbled himself."

Bishop Ambrose said, "Not divinity but flesh was humbled and subjected." And he added, "Did Arius say 'perfect creature' rightly or did he say it wrongly?"

Palladius said, "I am not answering you who do not have authority."

Bishop Ambrose said, "Profess what you wish."

Palladius said, "I am not answering you."

[42] Bishop Sabinus said, "Do you not respond on behalf of Arius? Do you not respond to the questions?"

Palladius said, "I did not respond on behalf of Arius."

Bishop Sabinus said, "Thus far you have responded that you deny the Son of God power and you deny that he is true God."

Palladius said, "I do not allow you, whom I accuse of impiety, to be a judge."

Bishop Sabinus said, "You yourself assembled us to be seated together."

Palladius said, "I ordered that you be seated in order to confront you. Why did you steal the ear of the emperor? You insisted that there should not be a plenary council."

Bishop Ambrose said, "When the impieties of Arius were read, your impiety, which agreed with the Arian impiety, was condemned at the same time. In the midst of the letter it suited you to propose the passage which you wished. You were answered how the Son of God called the Father greater, namely that regarding the acceptance of flesh the Son called the Father greater. You also proposed that the Son of God was subjected. Regarding this you were answered that the Son of God was subjected according to the flesh and not according to divinity. You have our profession, now hear the rest. Since you were answered, respond to that which was read."

[43] Palladius said, "I am not answering you because whatever I said has not been recorded. Since only your words were recorded, I am not answering you."

Bishop Ambrose said, "You see that everything is recorded. Indeed what was recorded is sufficient to prove your impiety." And he added, "Do you call Christ a creature or do you deny this?"

Palladius said, "I am not answering."

Bishop Ambrose said, "Less than an hour ago when it was read that Arius called Christ a creature, you denied it. When the option of condemning this perfidy was offered to you, you refused. Now tell us whether Christ was born of the Father or whether he was created."

Palladius said, "If you wish, our scribes could come and the entire discussion could be written down."

Bishop Sabinus said, "Let him lead in his scribes."

Palladius said, "We will respond to you in a plenary council."

Bibliography

Bindley, T. Herbert, and F. W. Green. 1950. *The Oecumenical Documents of the Faith.* London: Methuen.

Cuscito, Giuseppe. 1982. "Il concilio di Aquileia del 381 e le sue fonti." In *Aquileia nel IV secolo,* Antichità altoadriatiche 22, vol. 1, 189–253. Udine: Arti grafiche Friulane.

De la Rue, Charles, and Charles Vincent de la Rue, eds. 1860. Anonymous (pseudo-Origen). *Commentarius in Job.* In Origen, *Opera omnia.* Patrologia Graeca 17, 371–522. Paris: J. P. Migne.

Gryson, Roger. 1980. *Scolies ariennes sur le concile d'Aquilée,* Sources chrétiennes 267. Paris: Editions du Cerf.

Hanson, R.P.C. 1988. *The Search for the Doctrine of God: The Arian Controversy 318–381.* Edinburgh: T and T Clark.

Heather, Peter, and John Matthews. 1991. *The Goths of the Fourth Century.* Translated Texts for Historians 11. Liverpool: Liverpool University Press.

Hort, Fenton John Anthony. 1876. "On the Words μονογενὴς θεός in Scripture and Tradition." In Hort, *Two Dissertations,* 1–72. Cambridge: Macmillan.

McLynn, Neil B. 1994. *Ambrose of Milan: Church and Court in a Christian Capital.* Berkeley and Los Angeles: University of California Press.

Meslin, Michel. 1967. *Les Ariens d'occident 335–430,* Patristica sorbonensia 8. Paris: Editions du Seuil.

Opitz, Hans Georg. 1934. *De synodis.* In *Athanasius Werke* 2, 1, 231–78. Berlin: Walter de Gruyter.

Simonetti, Manlio. 1975. *La Crisi ariana nel IV secolo.* Studia ephemeridis "Augustinianum" 11. Rome: Institutum Patristicum Augustinianum.

Williams, Daniel H. 1995. *Ambrose of Milan and the End of the Nicene-Arian Conflicts.* Oxford: Clarendon.

Zelzer, Michaela, ed. 1982. *Gesta concili aquileiensis.* In *Ambrose. "Opera."* Corpus Scriptorum Ecclesiasticorum Latinorum 82, 3, 313–68. Vienna: Hoelder-Pichler-Tempsky.

Canons of the Council in Trullo (692 C.E.)

James C. Skedros

The Council in Trullo was held sometime in the capital of the Roman empire, Constantinople. Although the dates of the Council are often given as 691–692 C.E., it is most likely that the Council gathered "between the 1st of September and the 31st of December, probably in October 691" (Joannou 1962, 98). The Council met in the same domed room (*trullo* is Latin for dome) of the imperial palace where the Sixth Ecumenical Council (680 C.E.) had been held. This was considered an ecumenical council, that is, a gathering of bishops or their representatives from the five main centers of Christianity—Rome, Constantinople, Alexandria, Antioch, and Jerusalem—as well as other bishops throughout the Mediterranean. In practice, however, these ecumenical councils remained largely a Greek enterprise, in that they were held in the Eastern part of the Roman empire and consisted mainly of Greek-speaking bishops. The Council in Trullo was no exception.

The ecumenical councils, an expanded version of the local and regional councils of the early Church, were convened in order to render decisions concerning the practice and content of the Christian faith. In addition to doctrinal statements and definitions, these councils produced decrees of a legal nature. These decrees, known as canons, offered practical, liturgical, pastoral, and ethical guidelines on how clergy and laity ought to live a Christian life. These canons, coupled with imperial legislation, became the basis of ecclesiastical law for the Greek and Latin churches.

Not all ecumenical councils, however, issued decisions of a canonical nature. The Fifth and Sixth Ecumenical Councils, held in Constantinople in 553 and 680, respectively, did not issue any canons. Recognizing that no canonical definitions had been produced by the council convened by his father in 680, the Emperor Justinian II (685–695 and 705–711) convened the Council in Trullo. An intensely religious man who was the first emperor to put an image of Christ on imperial coins, Justinian took the lead in formulating Byzantine ecclesiastical legislation. Although the official acts of the Seventh Ecumenical Council held in

Nicaea in 787 refer to the Council of 691 as "the Holy and Ecumenical Sixth Council" (Dura 1995, 12–13), Byzantine canonists of the twelfth century gave the appellation *Penthekte* or "Fifth-Sixth" to the Council (Dura 1995, 15), implying that this council issued the canonical legislation that the fifth and sixth ecumenical councils failed to produce. Thus, in addition to its name as the Council in Trullo, the Council of 691 is often referred to as the Fifth-Sixth (*Quinisext* in Latin, *Penthekte* in Greek) Council.

The Council issued 102 canons that focus specifically on ecclesiastical and liturgical practices of the Greek-speaking Church. The manuscript tradition divides the canons into three general groups: canons 3–39 deal with the ordained clergy, canons 40–49 with monastics and their monasteries, and canons 50–102 deal with general issues concerning the laity. The first two canons of the collection offer traditional affirmations recognizing the decisions of earlier councils and enumerate canonical collections of previous councils that are to be given ecclesiastical approval.

Several themes recur throughout the canons of the Council in Trullo. Some thirty-two canons deal directly with liturgical issues; several canons refer to liturgical and ecclesiastical practices of the Roman Church (canons 2, 13, 36, 55) and the Armenian Church (canons 32, 33, 56, and 99) (Calivas 1995, 126). In particular, the Roman practices of clerical celibacy and fasting on Saturdays during the forty days of Lent are rejected, as well as the Armenian practice of not mixing water and wine in the communion chalice. These canons should not be seen as anti-Roman or anti-Armenian but rather reflect a view of the Church in which Byzantine and eastern practices are considered normative. Also prominent are issues regarding marriage laws and, in particular, the prohibition against second marriages for clergy and mandatory celibacy for bishops. Several canons attempt to regulate monastic practices, whereas certain canons are concerned with eradicating pagan practices that were being followed in provincial areas. The prohibitions of the Council in Trullo provide a unique glimpse into the ecclesiastical, religious, and secular life of Christians in the eastern Mediterranean at the end of the seventh century.

The Church of Rome eventually refused to recognize the authority of the canons of the Council in Trullo. Pope Sergius (687–701) repudiated the signatures of the papal legates appended to the decisions of the Council. Sergius refused to accept canonical decisions that were in direct opposition to established Roman practices. It seems that a compromise was reached by Pope Constantine in 711, when he appears to have accepted those canons that did not directly oppose Roman practice, although he had never formally signed the decisions of the Council of 691. To this day, however, the Roman Catholic Church has not officially recognized the decisions of the Council in Trullo.

The penalties associated with nonadherence to the canons are basically the same for most of the canons. Clergy are to be deposed while, in general, the penalty of excommunication is placed upon the layperson who fails to follow the canonical norms. Exactly what is meant by "deposed" and "excommunicated" varied over time. In general, deposition implied that a cleric was to be removed from all his priestly responsibilities and was to cease from participating in any liturgical duties. There were several types or levels of excommunication, ranging from complete removal from the Church to a temporary deprival of Communion. The canons of the Council in Trullo fail to make any distinction. What follows is a selection from the 102 Canons of the Council in Trullo.

CANONS OF THE ONE-HUNDRED AND SIXTY-FIVE HOLY FATHERS ASSEMBLED AT CONSTANTINOPLE IN THE ROOM OF THE DOME OF THE IMPERIAL PALACE UNDER JUSTINIAN, OUR PIOUS AND CHRIST-LOVING EMPEROR

CANON 3

Our pious and Christ-loving emperor has addressed this holy and ecumenical council in order that those who are enrolled in the ranks of the clergy and who share divine things with others, who are blameless celebrants of the liturgy and are worthy of the spiritual sacrifice of the great God, who is both that which is offered and the high priest, ought to be purified from the soil of unlawful marriages. Seeing that those of the most holy Roman Church propose to maintain the rule of strict discipline, while those under the see of this divinely guarded and imperial city propose to maintain the rule of mercy and sympathy, we have brought both practices together in a fatherly and God-loving way, so that neither leniency falls into license, nor sternness turns into harshness. Therefore, since the fault of ignorance has reached a considerable number of men, we decree that a priest who is involved in a second marriage up to the fifteenth of the past month of January of the fourth Indiction commencing in the year 619, and who remains a slave to sin and does not intend to turn away from this, is to be put under canonical deposition.

For those who have fallen into this passion of a second marriage, but, before this gathering of ours, have acknowledged the spiritual advantage of cutting off the evil within them and have banished this strange and unnatural union; as well as for those whose wives from a second marriage are already dead; or for those who have repented on their own accord, re-learning chastity and having quickly forgotten their past transgressions; whether they are priests, deacons, or sub-deacons, it has been decided that they are to terminate all sacramental duties and other priestly functions and should be placed under penance for a specified time. However, they are to retain the honor of their seat and the place occupied by those of their rank being content with their position and mourning before the Lord to forgive them for their transgressions committed out of ignorance. For it is inconsistent for someone who is taking care of his own wounds to bless another.

Those who are married to a woman who happens to have been a widow, as well as those who after ordination have lawlessly entered into a marriage, whether they are priests, deacons, or sub-deacons, they are to be suspended from priestly duties for a short time. After they have been rebuked, they are to be restored to their proper rank but in no way are they to advance to a higher ecclesiastical rank and their unlawful marriage is to be openly dissolved.

On account of our episcopal authority, we have decreed these things to apply only to those who have been participating in the aforesaid errors up to the fifteenth of the month of January of the fourth Indiction, reaffirming at the present time and renewing the canon that says, "He who after baptism has married for a second time or keeps a mistress cannot become a bishop, priest, deacon or any other rank of the clergy" [Apostolic Canons, 17]. Likewise, "He who marries a widow, or a divorced woman, or a harlot, or a slave, or an actress, cannot become a bishop, priest, deacon or any other rank of the clergy" [Apostolic Canons, 18].

CANON 9

It is not lawful for a cleric to operate a tavern. For if it is not allowed for a clergyman even to enter into a tavern, how much more is it forbidden for him to serve others in such a place and to undertake tasks which are not customary for him? If he has done such a thing, he is to cease or he will be deposed.

CANON 11

No one among those who are enrolled in the ranks of the clergy or are laypersons are allowed to eat unleavened bread used by the Jews, nor to live among them, nor to call upon them in sickness and to receive medical treatment from them. Neither is one allowed to bathe together with Jews in the public baths. If anyone attempts to do these things, if a cleric, let him be deposed; if a layperson, let him be excommunicated.

CANON 14

Let the canon of our holy and God-bearing fathers be upheld that states that "a presbyter is not to be ordained before the age of thirty. Although he may be worthy, he is still to wait since the Lord, Jesus Christ was thirty years old when he was baptized and began his ministry." Likewise, "neither is a deacon to be ordained before the age of twenty-five, nor a deaconess before the age of forty."

CANON 23

No one among those who are bishops, priests, or deacons administering holy communion are to require money or any kind of fee from those receiving holy communion. For the grace of God is not for sale, nor do we hand over the sanctification of the Spirit by means of money. Those worthy of the gift must be given their share without deceit. If anyone among the members of the clergy demands any kind of a fee from those to whom he administers holy communion, he is to be deposed as an imitator of the error and wickedness of Simon the magician.

CANON 24

It is not permitted for a monk or anyone from among the ranks of the clergy to enter into the hippodrome or to be present at theatrical games. When a cleric has been invited to a wedding and the games start to become deceitful, "he is to rise from his seat and depart immediately" [Council of Laodicia, canon 54], as is the teaching commanded to us by the fathers. If someone commits these offenses he is either to cease or he will be deposed.

CANON 32

It has come to our attention that in the land of the Armenians wine alone is brought to the holy altar, and those who celebrate the bloodless sacrifice do not mix water with it. In their defense they bring forth John Chrysostom, the teacher of the Church, who states the following in his commentary on the Gospel of Matthew: "Why, after his resurrection, did he not drink water but wine? Clearly, to pull up by its roots another perverse heresy which uses only water in the holy mysteries. When Christ instituted the mysteries he offered wine, and when, after his resurrection, he set up a plain and simple table not for the mysteries, Christ used wine, 'the fruit' he says, 'of the vine.' For the vine produces wine not water." On account of this these heretics suppose that our teacher abolishes the offering of water during the holy sacrifice.

So that they may not remain in ignorance any longer, we now reveal the orthodox thinking of our father. The perverse and ancient heresy of the *Hydroparastatae* used water and not wine in their sacrifice. However, our God-bearing father dismantles the lawless teaching of this heresy and shows that it stands in opposition to the apostolic tradition, as shown by that which has just been quoted. Each time he celebrated the bloodless sacrifice in his own church where he had undertaken pastoral responsibilities, he offered water mixed with wine. This commingling represents the mixture of blood and water that came out of the sacred side of our redeemer and savior Christ our God and which was poured out for the life of the entire world and for the forgiveness of sins. Therefore, in every church where spiritual luminaries have sinned, this God-given practice remains in force. For both James, the brother of Christ our God according to the flesh, who was the first one entrusted with the seat of the Church of Jerusalem, and Basil, archbishop of Caesarea, whose fame runs throughout the entire inhabited earth, have passed on to us in their writings dealing with the mystical sacrifice that we are to offer the holy chalice with water and wine to be consecrated during the divine liturgy. Even the holy fathers assembled at Carthage have expressed this: "during the holy mysteries, as the Lord himself has taught, nothing is to be offered except the body and blood of the Lord, that is, bread and wine mixed with water." If then a bishop or priest does not act according to the order handed down by the apostles and does not offer the undefiled sacrifice with water and wine, let him be deposed since he inadequately reveals the mystery and offers innovations to the tradition.

CANON 34

This holy canon clearly declares that since the crime of a secret society or fraternity is already forbidden by civil law, the more so ought it to be forbidden within the Church of God. We ourselves earnestly keep watch so that if clerics or monks are found either in secret societies, in fraternities, or are found participating in intrigues against bishops or their colleagues among the clergy, they are to be deprived completely of their rank.

CANON 42

Those who are called hermits, that is, those who are dressed in black and wear their hair long, have been found roaming throughout the cities and coming into contact with lay men and women thereby insulting their own profession. We have therefore determined that if they cut their hair and receive the habit of other monks they may join a monastery and be enlisted there among the brotherhood; but if they do not want to do this, they are to be removed altogether from the cities and resettled in the desert, the place from where they derive their name.

CANON 45

We have learned that in certain women's monasteries those who are about to put on the holy habit are first adorned in silk and all kinds of garments by those who are presenting them at the altar. After being adorned with gold and precious stones, they approach the altar where they are then stripped of these material adornments and are immediately given the blessing of the monastic habit and are clothed with a black robe. We therefore decree that from this time forward this practice is no longer to occur since it is not done on account of piety. The woman has on her own accord shunned all the delights of this life and has embraced the way of life according to God. Since she has already confirmed this choice through her steadfast thoughts and her entrance into the monastery, it is unlawful for her to remember those things, which are corruptible and pass away—those very things that she has already left behind. From these things doubts arise and the soul is disturbed, being tossed to and fro like the waves of the ocean, and she will not have one tear left to shed in order to show through her physical body the compunction of her heart. But if, as is likely, a small tear escapes her, those who see this will consider this not as an expression of her desire for the ascetic struggle, but rather as the result of her abandonment of the world and those things that are found in it.

CANON 48

The wife of one who is being promoted to the episcopal office is to separate from her husband by mutual consent and is to enter, after his consecration as a bishop, into a monastery located at a great distance from his episcopal residence. She is to receive financial assistance from him, and if she is found to be worthy, she may advance to the rank of deaconess.

CANON 50

No one from among the laity or the clergy is, from this time forward, to play dice. If anyone is caught doing so, if he is a cleric let him be deposed, if a layman, let him be excommunicated.

CANON 51

This holy and ecumenical council absolutely forbids the performances of those who are called mimes and of their antics, and especially animal hunts performed in the theater, as well as dances on stage. If anyone refuses to follow this canon and participates in that which is forbidden, if he is a cleric, let him be deposed, if a layman, let him be excommunicated.

CANON 53

The relationship according to the spirit is greater than the physical union of the bodies. Therefore, since we have learned that in certain regions there are those who, after having undertaken the responsibility of sponsoring children at the holy and salvific mystery of baptism, have entered into marriage with the widowed mothers of these children, we decree that from this time forward this practice is to cease. But, if after the publication of this canon, some are found doing this, they are to be separated immediately from such a lawless marriage and then subjected to the canonical penalties of fornicators.

CANON 55

Since we have learned that in the city of Rome, contrary to ecclesiastical tradition, fasting is observed on the Saturdays of Holy Lent, the holy council has determined that the following canon should apply likewise to the Church of Rome: "If a cleric is found fasting on Sunday or Saturday, with the one and only exception of Holy Saturday, let him be deposed, if he is a layman, let him be excommunicated."

CANON 57

One must not offer honey and milk at the altar.

CANON 61

Those who seek the advice of fortune tellers, the so-called *hecatontarches*, or other similar individuals in order to learn from them that which they want revealed about themselves, let them, according to the recent decisions of the fathers, be placed under the canon of six years. Further, let those who keep bears and other animals on leashes for the entertainment and harm of the simple-minded be subjected to the same canonical penalty. The same goes for those who speak of destiny, fate, genealogies, and a multitude of meaningless talk that stems from error, as well as for those who are called the dispersers of clouds, those who practice witchcraft, those who distribute amulets, and sooth-sayers. We have decided that those who continue to participate in such activities and do not change their ways nor flee from these destructive practices and Greek customs, are to be thrown out completely from the Church, just as the divine canon declares: "For how is it possible for light to have communion with dark or for the Church of God to have concord with idols, or belief to be part of disbelief, or for Christ to be in agreement with Beliar?"

CANON 62

We have determined that the rituals known as the "Calends," the "Bota," the "Broumalia," and the festival celebrated on the first day of the month of March, are to be removed completely from the life of the faithful. Further, we reject both the public dances of women that cause much disgrace and harm as well as the dances and rites performed by men or women in the name of those falsely called gods of the Greeks, according to an ancient custom foreign to the life of Christians. We have also decided that no man is to dress in the clothes of a woman, nor is a woman to dress in clothes suitable for a man. Likewise, one is not permitted to wear comic, satirical, or tragic masks, to invoke the name of the abhorrent Dionysus while crushing grapes in wine presses, nor to arouse laughter while pouring wine into wine jars acting out of ignorance or frivolousness like those who are possessed by the error of the pagan demons. Therefore, those who from this time forward commit any of the above-mentioned acts while having knowledge of what we have said about them, if they are clerics, we order them to be deposed, if laity, they are to be excommunicated.

CANON 63

We have determined that the stories of the martyrs that have been fabricated by the enemies of the truth in order to discredit the martyrs of Christ and to lead to unbelief those who hear them read, are not to be read publicly in the churches but are to be handed over and burned. Those who accept them and acknowledge them as being true, we anathematize.

CANON 65

Those who light fires in front of their businesses and homes on the new moons, and, behaving foolishly and following an ancient custom, jump over them, we order from this time forward to desist from this practice. Whoever continues to follow such practices, if he is a cleric, let him be deposed, if a layman, let him be excommunicated. For it is written in the fourth book of Kings: "Manasseh erected an altar for all the hosts of heaven in the two courtyards of the temple of the Lord, and he passed his children through the fire; and he practiced astrology and divination, and employed ventriloquists and soothsayers. He did not cease doing evil in front of the Lord, provoking the Lord to anger" [2 Kings 21:5–6].

CANON 69

It is not allowed for those who are enlisted among the ranks of the laity to enter into the altar. However, according to a very ancient custom, the emperor is in no way prohibited from doing this whenever he desires to offer gifts to the Creator.

CANON 70

Women are not allowed to speak during the Divine Liturgy. According to the teaching of the Apostle Paul, "Let them be silent. For they are not allowed to speak, but they should be subordinate, even as the law says. But if they want to learn something, let them inquire of their own husbands at home" [1 Cor. 14:34–35].

CANON 74

One must not hold the so-called "agape" meal in houses belonging to the Lord nor in churches in general. Nor is it allowed to spread out couches and eat a meal inside a church. Those who continue to do this are to cease or be excommunicated.

CANON 77

Higher clergy, simple clerics, and ascetics are not allowed to bathe in the public baths in the company of women, nor is this allowed for any Christian man, since this practice is condemned even among the pagans. If someone is discovered doing such a thing, if he is a cleric, let him be deposed, if he is a layman, let him be excommunicated.

CANON 79

Because we confess that the birth of the divine child from the Virgin was without the pains of childbirth and that the conception was without seed, and we preach this to the entire flock, we want those to be corrected who, out of ignorance, practice things that are not proper. Therefore, since some on the day after the holy birth of Christ our God are found boiling wheat and giving this to others, on the pretense that they show honor to the childbirth of the spotless Virgin Mother, such a thing is no longer to be done by the faithful. For it does not bring honor to the Virgin who bore in the flesh the incompressible Word in a manner that is beyond reason and explanation. It is wrong to define and delineate her inexpressible childbirth through things that are common to ourselves. Therefore, if, from this time forward, someone is detected practicing such a thing, if he is a cleric, let him be deposed, if a layman, let him be excommunicated.

CANON 82

In some holy icons one finds depicted a lamb to which the Forerunner, John the Baptist, points his finger. The lamb has been received as a *typos* of divine grace, prefiguring the true Lamb, Christ our God, who has been revealed to us through the law. Although in the Church we recognize these ancient types and shadows as symbols and representations of the Truth, we prefer the grace and the truth that we received as the fulfillment of the law. In order for that which is perfect to be seen by the eyes of all, we decree that he who is the lamb who takes away the sin of the world, Christ our God, is, from this time forward, to be depicted in icons according to his human form instead of the ancient lamb. Through him we have come to know the great humility of God the Word, and by this we may be led to the memory of his life in the flesh, his passion, his salvific death, and the redemption that came to the entire world.

CANON 83

No one is to administer the Eucharist to a dead person. For it is written, "Take, eat" [Matt. 26:26]; dead bodies are not able to take or to eat.

CANON 88

No one is to bring an animal into church, except a traveler who, being in great need and unable to secure a shed or resting-place, may rest his animal in church. For, if the animal had not been brought indoors it might have perished and, due to the loss of his animal, the traveler would be left without means for his journey and would be in danger of dying. We have been taught that, "the Sabbath was made for man" [Mark 2:27] and that we are to prefer above everything else the salvation and preservation of humanity. But if someone is found bringing his animal into a church without the needs described above, if he is a cleric, let him be deposed, if a layman, let him be excommunicated.

CANON 91

Those who give drugs to induce abortions and those who take poisons to kill the fetus are to be subjected to the punishment of a murderer.

CANON 96

Those who have put on Christ through baptism have promised to imitate his life in the flesh. Therefore, those who by offering bait for easily agitated souls arrange and fix their hair in highly skillful braids to the detriment of those who see them, we paternally offer the appropriate rebuke, guiding them and teaching them to live in moderation in order to lay aside the deceit and vanity of material things. They are continuously to raise their minds to the imperishable and blessed life, to live a pure life in the fear of God, to draw near to God as close as a pure life allows, and to adorn the interior person rather than the exterior one with virtues and with good and blameless morals so that they may not leave any traces in themselves of the wickedness of the enemy. If anyone acts contrary to the present canon, let him or her be excommunicated.

CANON 99

We have learned that in the land of the Armenians the following practice is being observed. Certain men bearing pieces of meat offer them at the holy altars reserving the best pieces for the priests as in the manner of the Jews. So that we may safeguard the purity of the Church, we decree that it is not lawful for any priest to receive a specified piece of meat from those who are offering them, but they are to be content with those pieces that the one offering chooses to give him, as long as the offering is done outside the church. If anyone does not do these things in this way, let him be excommunicated.

CANON 102

For those who have received from God the power to loose and to bind, it is necessary for them to examine the character of the sin and the readiness of the sinner for conversion and to apply the appropriate remedy to the illness so that, by using the appropriate measure according to each case, they might not err in the salvation of one who is ill. For the malady of sin is not a simple thing. Rather, it is complex and varied and produces many offspring out of which much evil extends and progresses until it is stopped by the power of the physician. First, the practitioner of spiritual medicine is to examine the disposition of the sinner in order to determine whether the sinner desires health, or if, on the contrary, by his conduct, the sinner provokes his own illness. Then, the practitioner is to see how the sinner conducts himself during the period of his recovery. If he does not oppose the techniques of the practitioner but, nevertheless, the ulcer of the soul grows by reason of the remedies applied to it, let the practitioner show mercy according to the worthiness of the sinner. The entire matter is between God and the one who has been entrusted with the pastoral duty of bringing back the lost sheep and of completely curing the wounds inflicted by the serpent. He is not to push them over the precipice of despair nor is he to loosen the bridle that could lead towards a weakening of and disdain for life. Whether through austere and bitter remedies or through more gentle and milder ones, the goal is to resist the malady and to struggle for the healing of the ulcer by judging the fruits of repentance and by wisely guiding the one who is called to illumination from above. "Therefore, it is necessary for us to know both methods, that of the strict application of the commandments and that of customary practice, and for those who do not choose to follow the more stringent path, the traditional method," as St. Basil has taught us.

Bibliography

Calivas, Alkiviadis C. 1995. "The Penthekte Synod and Liturgical Reform." *Greek Orthodox Theological Review* 40, nos. 1–2 (Spring-Summer): 125–47.

Dura, Ioan. 1995. "Some Specifications with Regard to the Date and Names of the Second Session of the Sixth Ecumenical Synod." *Greek Orthodox Theological Review* 40, nos. 1–2 (Spring-Summer): 11–16.

Hefele, C. J., and H. Leclercq. 1907. *Histoire des conciles.* Vol. 3. Paris: Letouzey.

Joannou, Périclès-Pierre. 1962. *Les Canons des conciles oecuméniques.* Rome: Pontifical Commission on the Codification of Eastern Canon Law.

Laurent, V. 1965. "L'Oeuvre canonique du concile in Trullo (691–92), source primaire du droit de l'église orientale." *Revue des études byzantines* 23: 7–14.

Mansi, J. D. 1759. *Sacrorum Conciliorum nova et amplissima collectio.* Florence.

Ohme, Heinz. 1990. *Das Concilium Quinisextum und seine Bischofsliste. Studien zum Konstantinopeler Konzil von 692.* Vol. 56 of *Arbeiten zur Kirchengeschichte.* Berlin: Walter de Gruyter.

Percival, Henry R. 1900. *The Seven Ecumenical Councils.* Vol. 14 of *Nicene and Post-Nicene Fathers.* New York: Charles Scribner's Sons.

Ralles, G., and M. Potles. 1852. *A Collection of the Holy and Divine Canons* (Σύνταγμα τῶν θείων καὶ ἱερῶν κανόνων). Athens.

Creating Religious Ceremonial: Ritual

— 24 —

The Mithras Liturgy and *Sepher Ha-Razim*

Kimberly B. Stratton

The two texts presented in this chapter, the Mithras Liturgy and *Sepher Ha-Razim* (The book of secrets), contribute to our understanding of magic in the ancient world by confounding the very term "magic." For the ancients, magic—in the way that we might conceive of it as something nefarious and illegal—applied only to certain types of ritual actions that sought to harm or bind another member of society (Segal 1987; Graf 1997, 20–60). Other ritual actions, namely those that sought health, protection, or salvation, did not constitute "magic" (*goetia*) as the ancients understood it. In fact, much of what we would today label magic fell under the rubric of legitimate science and medicine. Other areas of religious practice, which we might also today designate as magic, such as divination or questioning an oracle, belonged to the highest, most solemn, and respected aspects of ancient religion, including the Delphic oracle, the Jewish temple, and the Roman auspices. We also discover, in the following two texts, that goals traditionally associated with religion, such as immortality, salvation, and devotion, merge easily with supposedly magical aims such as protection, success, and healing. To further undermine the distinction between magic and religion, many accepted religions of the ancient world granted or ensured practical success and well-being for their adherents—something typically associated with magic. Thus, we need only think of our contemporaries praying to God or to a favorite saint for health, success, and well-being to comprehend the difficulties inherent in the designation "magic."

Nature of the Texts

Both the Mithras Liturgy and *Sepher Ha-Razim* reflect a genre of literature common in the ancient world, namely, the ascension text (Johnston 1997). This type of literature documents the ascent to heaven of a hero and his experiences and visions there. Such visionary ascents constitute the core of Jewish apocalyptic writings, many gnostic writings, and the Hermetic corpus, and inform Philo of Alexandria's understanding of Moses as the greatest philosopher (Segal 1980). These texts all presume a Neo-Platonic cosmology, according to which the heavens are arranged in descending order, emanating from a supreme Godhead—experience of whom is the main object of the philosopher, mystic, or gnostic. Thus, in these texts, a person who is appropriately wise and pure is able to ascend to heaven and learn the secrets of the cosmos. Such visionary literature serves to legitimate beliefs and expectations about the world concerning important issues like the fate of the soul after death, punishment of evil-doers, rewards for the righteous, and the coming end of time (ibid.). Through his experiences, the visionary confirms that the cosmos follows a pre-ordained plan and that, contrary to human perception, the universe and people's lives have meaning and follow divine providence. Such visionary literature arises most often in times of crisis among people who seek confirmation of their worth and purpose in the cosmic scheme of things.

Another outstanding feature in many of the ascension texts is the role played by angels or daemons who, once placated by pronunciation of their names and possession of the proper amulet, can be made to serve and abet the visionary in his ascent toward the highest heaven. Concomitantly, the mystic's power over such angels enables him to gain favors of a more mundane and pragmatic nature; hence we see a natural partnership between magic and mystical ascent, further obfuscating the distinction between magic and religion.

The Mithras Liturgy, which forms part of a magical recipe book from Egypt, combines elements of visionary ascent with those of magical praxis. As in ascent literature, the magician in this text encounters opposing gods who attempt to prevent his ascension. After silencing them and uttering a special prayer (logos), the mystic gains their assistance and is able to proceed upward toward his encounter with the Great God, Helios Mithras, and his ultimate goal—immortalization. The Mithras Liturgy also incorporates elements of magic, such as preparing special concoctions (of crushed beetles and obscure plants) for use as an unction of immortality, with devotional prayers and language typical of Hellenistic mystery religions (mysterion, epopteuo). Furthermore, the goal of this magical ritual is one typical of mystery religions and shared by ancient Christians: communion with the divine and the promise of immortality (Segal 1990, 58–71). Like ancient Christians undergoing initiation through baptism, the magician in this text is reborn and receives, as a pledge of his new status, a newly fashioned horoscope.

Sepher Ha-Razim shares many features with Jewish ascent texts of the late rabbinic period—the so-called Hekhalot literature—and appears to have emerged from the same milieu. This text presumes, for example, the seven-heaven cosmology of Hekhalot mysticism and requires possessing names of the guardian angels for permission to ascend through each heavenly palace. Sepher Ha-Razim also shares with Hekhalot literature its final goal—a vision of God's Merkavah (glorious throned chariot), whose description derives from Ezekiel's vision (Ezek. 1). In this document, good Mishnaic Hebrew and knowledge of rabbinic purity laws combine with pagan magical operations, involving the eating of blood and pouring of oblations to foreign deities (Helios, Aphrodite). Such actions transgress rabbinic law as codified in the early third century C.E. These magical praxes (or practices), however, are imbedded in a cosmological narrative that shows a close relationship with Jewish mystical literature and piety. Although the rabbinic establishment eschewed mystical speculation and magical practice, the Talmud contains ample references to such phenomena, attesting to rabbinic involvement in these practices (Scholem 1960; 1974, 40–79). *Sepher Ha-Razim* further underscores the difficulty in clearly defining normative Jewish practice in the ancient world by exemplifying the crossover between Jewish piety grounded in Torah, monotheism, and observance of Jewish law, with magic and pagan syncretism.

It is possible that for ancient Jews such juxtapositions were not perceived to be incongruous. In *Sepher Ha-Razim,* the description of the seventh heaven and abode of God attests to the piety of this mystical text despite its inclusion of illegal magic praxes and foreign gods. Vision of the throne in the seventh heaven inspires pages of *hallel* (exalted praise) in which every imaginable acclamation for God is quoted from the Bible, demonstrating the firm foundation this document has in Torah. The author of *Sepher Ha-Razim* displays sound Biblical education and firm monotheistic piety. Perhaps by this time, these deities—regarded as mere angels or daemons, populating the lower heavens and subject to control through invocation of their names—were no longer perceived to be a threat to monotheism or to Jewish piety. For the author of *Sepher Ha-Razim,* apparently, pagan gods bear no more resemblance to the Great God of Israel than servants bear to their master. Confusion of the two is unthinkable.

History of the Texts

The Mithras Liturgy represents lines IV. 475–829 of the *Greek Magical Papyri* (*PGM*) published by Preisendanz in 1928. The PGM collection is an ancient magical library or recipe book, containing diverse materials compiled over a period of 700 years from the second century B.C.E. to the fifth century C.E. Spell books, such as PGM, represent only a small portion of the material evidence for ancient magic, which includes over 1500 published spells preserved on metal tablets, ostraka, and bowls (Gager 1992; Naveh 1987). Such magic books were frequently banned in the ancient world and, as the New Testament recounts, were sometimes objects of systematic destruction (Acts 19:19). This and similar outbreaks of violence may have contributed to the frequent admonishings for secrecy found in these books since, especially with the rise of Christianity, magical literature was increasingly forced underground.

The Mithras Liturgy acquired its name in 1903 when Albrecht Dieterich proposed that these lines from PGM constituted a Mithraic initiation ritual that had been appropriated by magicians and incorporated into a spell book (Meyer 1976, xii). Soon after Dieterich published his article "Eine Mithrasliturgie," scholars

(Cumont and Reitzenstein) challenged this proposition on the grounds that it lacked certain essential features of a Mithraic ritual (ibid., viii). Yet despite these objections, the so-called Mithras Liturgy in PGM does display many Mithraic themes, such as a pronounced reverence for the solar deity, the centrality of astrology and the four cardinal elements, and Persian-style descriptions of Helios Mithras and the Highest God. Whatever the origin of this text, it presents an ascension ritual leading to divine transformation, showing strong similarities with mystery initiations (language) and with magical operations (praxis).

In 1963 Mordecai Margalioth, a rabbinic scholar, researching *Geniza* fragments at Cambridge University, discovered among them a magic spell. He recalled seeing elsewhere other similar spells in fragments from the same *Geniza* (storeroom for retired Torah scrolls and other sacred literature) and postulated that these fragments derived from a common source, which he presumed to be a magical handbook (Margalioth 1966, ix). He began to reconstruct this text from the fragments he found and, in 1966, published *Sepher Ha-Razim*. The text dates to the late third or early fourth century C.E., as witnessed by, among other things, its composition in elegant Mishnaic Hebrew (Morgan 1983, 8). *Sepher Ha-Razim* provides an important resource for understanding popular Jewish religion in the early rabbinic period. The document raises questions concerning the extent of rabbinic influence both because it violates certain rabbinic prohibitions and because it displays clear knowledge of rabbinic purity laws. In this way, *Sepher Ha-Razim* forces us to consider that adherence to rabbinic legislation was not necessarily an all-or-nothing phenomenon. Rather, rabbinic influence may have been wide and very influential, but it was not absolute, and syncretism with pagan practices coexisted with monotheistic devotion and purity observances.

The structure of *Sepher Ha-Razim* mirrors the cosmology it describes. The book is divided into seven sections, one for each heaven, plus a preface, describing the book's transmission and thereby attempting to establish its authenticity. Each chapter describes a particular heaven, providing a list of angelic names and a corresponding magical praxis that enables the magician to control the angels inhabiting that heaven. With this information, the mystic is able to ascend to the next heaven and he can also achieve practical benefits on the way, such as turning the opinion of a king or minister toward his favor.

Both *Sepher Ha-Razim* and the Mithras Liturgy demonstrate that magic in the ancient world crossed boundaries. It crossed the boundaries of language and culture, combining elements from diverse religions and ethnic communities. It crossed boundaries of literary genre, combining magical recipes with devotional hymns. Thus magic is representative of the syncretism that characterizes the Hellenistic period. Magic bridges the cultural fissures that separated the distinct communities of the ancient world by addressing the common concerns, experiences, and aspirations that united them all. Magic demonstrates the existence of a shared cosmology and world view, constituting a type of cultural *lingua franca* that unified the ancient Mediterranean.

I have tried to preserve, as much as possible, the punctuation of the original texts in order to convey the often rambling style of these rituals. I have also tried to retain the original language even when it renders the prose awkward or unwieldy in its use of technical terms or constructions. This approach, I think, best captures the deliberately esoteric and highly ritualized style of the texts that enhanced the mystery of the rite.

Sepher Ha-Razim contains lists upon lists of angelic names, which, because of the lack of voweling in rabbinic Hebrew, are difficult to translate. Rather than present these names as strings of consonants, rendering them difficult to pronounce and awkward to read, I have tried to preserve their resemblance to names whose invocation constituted the central aspect of the ascension ritual. In this endeavor, I guessed at many of the pronunciations and, no doubt, some scholars will disagree with these pronunciations.

One final note: both texts contain *voces mysticae* (special nonsense language), which play an important function in ancient magic (Gager 1992, 5–10). Many of these incomprehensible words derive from real languages but, as the magical texts were copied and passed down over the centuries, these words became garbled—especially by people who did not know the original language and could not, therefore, understand the words. In other cases, the nonsense passages are deliberately cryptic utterances—strings of vowels or consonants—that lack manifest linguistic content. These nonsense passages serve to make the texts more obscure and mysterious as well as mark the transition from mundane into sacred reality. No doubt, *voces mysticae* were regarded as comprehensible to the angels and daemons to whom they were addressed, distinguishing their higher level of comprehension from human ones, their mystical discourse from our limited human language (Cox Miller 1986; Tambiah 1968, 177–78). Nonsense language, like ritual purity or sacred space, separates ritual from profane reality, transporting the practitioner into a higher realm of awareness and sacrality.

Mithras Liturgy

[475] Be merciful to me, O Providence and Psyche, who am here writing these things that cannot be sold, being transmitted mysteries, for I deem immortality worthy for an only child, O initiates of this our power . . . [483] which the great god Helios Mithras commanded to be transmitted to me by his archangel, in order that I alone ascend to heaven as a petitioner and observe all.

[485] This is the invocation for the spell:

"First genesis of my genesis: AEEIIOUO, first principle [*archē*] of my first principle PPP SSS PHR[E], breath of breath, first of the breath in me MMM, fire, divinely given to my mixture of the mixtures in me, first of the fire in me EIY EIIA EEI, water of water, first of the water in me OOO AAA EEE, [495] first earthy substance of the earthy substance in me UEI UOEI, perfect body of me, so and so, [whose mother is] so and so, having been molded by a noble arm and by an immortal right hand in a dark yet radiant world, both lifeless

and animated with soul UEII AYI EYOIE. [500] If it is in your judgment MET-
ERTA PHOTH, [in another place METHARTHA PHEIRIEI] IEREZATH hand
me over to immortal birth and subsequently to my underlying nature; so that,
after the exceedingly urgent need which is upon me, I will behold [*epopteusō*]
the immortal [505] first principle with the immortal breath ANKHREPHRE-
NESOUPHIRIGKH; with the immortal water ERONOUI PARAKOUNEITH,
with the most stable air EIOAEI PSENABOTH, in order to be born again in
knowledge KRAOKHRAX R OIM ENARKHOMAI, [510] and the holy breath
may be breathed in me NEKHTHEN APOTOU NEKHTHIN ARPI EITH, so
that I will marvel at the sacred fire KUPHE, so that I may wonder at the awe-
inspiring boundless water of the dawn NUO [515] THESO EKHO OUKHIEK-
HOA, and the all-embracing generative Aether may hear me ARNOMEITHPH,
since today, I am destined to behold with immortal eyes, born from a mortal
womb, yet changed for the better by a mighty power and an immortal right
hand, with immortal breath the [520] undying Aeon and ruler of the fiery
diadems, made holy by sacred consecrations, while, sustained in holiness, for
a short time, by the human [525] spiritual power in me, which I will again
receive after the undiminished bitter necessity [*ananke*] that has blocked me
and pressures me, I so and so, whose mother is so and so, according to the
unalterable decision of God EYEI UIA EEII AO EIAY [530] IYA IEW. Since, it
is not possible for me, having been born an impure mortal, to ascend with the
golden gleaming immortal brilliance OEIY AEO EIYA EOEI UAE OIAE, stand,
O perishable nature of mortal man, and immediately take me safe and sound
from the implacable and pressing [535] need. For I am the son PSUKHON
DĒMOU PROKHO PROA, I am MAKHARPH[.]N MOU PROPSUKHON
PROE."

Draw in breath from the rays, three times sucking up as much as you are
able, and you shall see yourself being raised up and [540] passing over to the
summit, so that you seem to be in mid-air. You will hear nothing of men nor
of another living being; neither shall you see anything of the mortal world in
that hour, rather, you shall see everything immortal: for that day and that hour
[545] you shall see the presiding planetary gods ascending in heaven while
others are descending, according to divine arrangement.

[556] And you shall see the gods looking intently at you and charging at
you. So, immediately put your right finger to your mouth and say: "silence,
silence, silence, symbol of the eternal living god! [560] Protect me, silence
VEKHTHEIR THANMELOU." Thereupon, whistle a long shrill piping sound,
after that smack the lips saying: "PROPROPHEGGEI MORIOS PROPHUR
PROPHEGGEI NEMETHIRE ARPSENTEN PITEITMI MEOU ENARTH
PHURKEKHO [565] PSURIDARIO TUREI PHILBA" and now you shall see the
gods looking at you kindly and no longer charging at you, but instead proceeding in their own order of affairs. So, whenever you shall see the world on
high clear and [570] wheeling about and none of the gods or angels charging
at you, expect a crash of great thunder to be heard, so as to strike you with

panic. And again say: "silence, silence [prayer], [575] I am a star wandering about with you, and from the height shining out OXU O XERTHEUTH."

[621] Upon saying these things, you will hear thunder and turmoil from the enveloping sphere. Likewise, you will perceive yourself being agitated. But, say again: "Silence" [prayer], then open your eyes and you should see the doors [625] opened and the world of the gods, which is inside the doors, so that, from the pleasure and delight of the spectacle, your spirit gathers itself and ascends. Then, coming to a standstill, immediately draw from the god into yourself the spirit while you gaze earnestly. After that, [630] when your soul has been recovered say: "Come, O Lord, ARKHANDARA PHOTAZA PURI-PHOTA ZABUTHIX ETIMENMERO PHORATHEIN ERIEI PROTHRI PHOR-ATHI." Having said this, the rays will turn toward you. [Look] into the middle of them, since, [635] when you shall do this, you shall see a youthful god, handsome, with fiery hair, in a white tunic and a red soldier's mantle, wearing a fiery crown. Immediately salute him with the fire salutation.

[640] "Greetings O Lord, Great Power, Far-Ruler, King, Mightiest of gods, Helios, the lord of heaven and earth, O God of Gods, mighty is your breath, mighty is your strength, O Lord: if it be in your judgment, announce me to the supreme deity, to the one who begat and made you, so that a human being—I, so and so [whose mother is] so and so [645], born from the mortal womb of so and so and from seminal fluid—this man, having been reborn today from you, out of so many myriads, deified in this hour according to the judgment of God, the exceedingly good, [650] deems it worthy to worship you and requests according to his human power, in order that you shall take with you the day today and the ascendant hour [of my new horoscope] in the name THRAPSIARI MORIROK, so that appearing, he shall give oracles during the good hours: EORO RORE ORRI ORIOR ROR ROI [655] OR REORORI EOR EOR EOR EORE!"

[661] Having said all this, you shall see doors being pulled back and coming out from the depth seven virgins in linen garments, having faces of asps. They are called Fates of heaven, brandishing golden batons.

[692] And when they shall array themselves here and there in order, look intently into the air and you shall see flashes of lightning descending and lights sparking [695] and the earth quaking and an exceedingly awesome god descending, having a shining countenance, youthful, golden-haired, in a white tunic and with a golden crown and Persian trousers, holding in his right hand a golden shoulder [700] of a young bull, who is Ursa Major the one who sets in motion and turns heaven about, moving upwards and downwards in an orbit according to the hour. Thereupon, you shall see lightning bolts leaping from his eyes and stars from his body. Then, immediately, [705] emit a great bellow, straining your stomach so that you activate the five senses, bellow long again until exhausting your storage of air, and, kissing the amulet, say: "MOK-RIMO PHERIMOPHERERI life of me, so and so, stay, inhabit [710] my soul, do not abandon me, for ENTHO PHENEN THROPIOTH commands you."

Then look intently at the god while bellowing long and salute him: "Hail O Lord, master of water, hail O Ruler of the earth, hail O Lord of breath, brightly [715] shining one PROPROPHEGGEI, EMETHIRI ARTENTEPI: THEITH: MIMEO UENARO PHURKHEKHO PSEIRI DARIO PHREI PHREILBA! Give an oracle, O Lord, regarding the matter concerning so and so. O Lord, while being born again I am falling away, while increasing in power and having increased in power [720] I am coming to an end, while being born from a life-giving birth, I cross over, having been released to death, as you established, as you ordained and made a mystery. I am PHEROURA MIOURI." Having said all this, immediately [725] he will prophesy.

[750] Instruction for the magical operation: taking a solar dung-beetle having twelve rays, let it fall into a deep turquoise cup during a dark moon, toss in together with it a seed from the fruit pulp of a Nile water lily [755] and honey, after grinding it smooth, make a little cake and immediately you shall see it [the beetle] approaching and eating, and when he shall eat it, immediately he dies.

[767] And on the seventh day, after taking up the beetle and conducting funerary rites for it with myrrh, Mendesian wine, and a linen [shroud], stow it away in a flourishing bean field. Then, after entertaining and feasting together, store in a pure manner [770] the ointment for the immortalization.

[778] And this is the introduction to the great god: after acquiring the prescribed [780] plant, *kentritis,* during the conjunction [i.e., new moon] that falls in the constellation Leo take the juice and, mixing it with honey and myrrh, write on a leaf of the persea tree the eight-letter name as given below and, keeping yourself pure for three days, come early in the morning to face the direction of sunrise, [785] lick off the leaf, showing it to the sun and he will pay perfect attention to you. So, begin to perform it during the new moon, according to god, which occurs in Leo.

Sepher Ha-Razim (The Book of Secrets)
Preface

This is a book from the books of mysteries that were given to Noah, son of Lamech, son of Methuselah, son of Enoch, son of Jared, son of Mehallalel, son of Kenan, son of Enosh, son of Seth, son of Adam, by the angel Raziel, in the year that he went into the ark, before his entrance. And Noah wrote it very clearly on sapphire stone and from it he learned miraculous works and secrets of knowledge and orders of wisdom and thoughts of humility [5] and plans of counsel, to understand inquiry into the ascending levels of heaven, to roam about in all that is in the seven [heavenly] dwellings and to gaze upon all the planets and to determine the way of the sun and to elucidate inquiry into understanding and knowledge of the paths of Ursa Major, Orion, and the Pleiades and to state the names of the overseers of each and every heavenly strata and [to know] their area of sovereignty and by what means [they can be made] to cause success for anything [requested] and what are the names of their attendants and what to offer them as libation and if it is the proper time to get [10] them to hear and to fulfill each desire of every one who approaches them in purity. [Noah acquired] from it knowledge of how to cause death and how to give life, to understand the evil and the good, to inquire into hours and minutes, to know the time to give birth and the time to die, the time to strike and the time to heal, to decipher dreams and visions, to incite battle and to quiet wars and to control spirits and evil daemons so as to dispatch them and they will go [obediently] like slaves, to gaze upon the four winds of the earth, to be wise in the [15] sound of thunder claps, to [be able] to explain the meaning of lightning strikes, to foretell what will happen in each and every month, to understand the business of each and every year, if for plenitude or for famine, if for ample provisions or for dearth, if for peace or for war, to be like one among the terrible ones and to be wise in the songs of heaven.

[29] [S]o, many books were delivered into his hand and this was found to be most valuable and worthy and difficult of them all. Enriched is the eye that gazes upon it, enriched is the ear that anticipates its wisdom because in it are the seven levels of heaven and all that is in them. From their camps one learns to be wise in everything and to succeed in every undertaking, to think and to act from the wisdom of this book.

The First Heavenly Strata

The name of the first heavenly strata is called *Shamayim,* within it are camps filled with fury and seven thrones arranged there and on them seven overseers sit and surrounding them are camps [of angelic forces] here and there and they listen to human beings at the hour they practice [magic]—to every one who has learned to stand and offer libation to their names and to invoke them by their symbols at the hour in which they hear [requests] so as to gain success [5] for a [magical] endeavor; over all the camps of these angels, these seven overseers rule so as to dispatch them to hasten and confer success for every desire.

These are the names of the seven overseers that sit on the seven thrones: the first name is Orphaniel, and the second name is Tigrah, and the third name is Danahel, and the fourth name is Kalmiyah, the fifth is Asimor, the sixth is Pesacher, the seventh is Boel. And all of them were created [10] from fire and their appearance is like fire and their fire glows because from fire they emerged. And [their attendants] do not go out without their authorization to carry out a magical action until the command comes to them from the seven overseers sitting on the thrones ruling over them because they are subject to their will and under their authority in all their [comings and] goings.

[107] These are the names of the angels who serve in the fourth camp under

Kalmiyah: Avriyah, Imrahi, Demanay, Emanaher, Yemanoch, Patachiyah, To-
viel, Goliel, Ophri, Gamati, Orniel, Perichihu, Yeran, Latmiel, Orit, Timogo,
Enamri, Elaminiel, Yichmatu, Setartu, Tzevakani, Bortiyas, Resaput, Kerason,
Amaph, Vepatna, Achel, Seviel, Belakir, Pekahor, Haseter, Seteriel, Elisas, Chal-
isiel, Tersapu, Kristos, Malachiel, Ardok, Chasidiel, Echasaph, Amiel, Parnos,
Gadiel, Sevivel.

These are the angels who bring around the opinion of the king and the will
of great men and heads and [115] the directors of the kingdom and leaders
and confer grace and mercy on all those standing [before them] to petition
something from them in purity. Perform this scrupulously and you will succeed.

If you desire to make the opinion of the king incline toward you or [that]
of the minister of the army or of a rich man or an officer or a city judge or
all the inhabitants of the country or the heart of a prominent or rich woman
or the heart of a beautiful woman take a lion cub and slaughter it with a
copper knife and collect its blood and [120] tear out its heart and put the
blood into the midst of it and write the names of these angels in blood on
the skin that is in the middle of its face and blot it out with wine that is three
years old and combine it with the blood. Then, take three principle spices,
styrax [istorkon] and myrrh and a measure of musk, and stand before the
planet Venus clean and pure and put the spices on the fire and take in your
hand the cup that has the blood and wine in it and say [the following spell]
and invoke the name of the overseer and the names of the angels of his camp
[125] twenty-one times over the blood and over the wine and, facing the
planet Venus, say the name which is Aphrodite three hundred times and that
of the angel Chasidiel: "I adjure you by the name of the angels of the fourth
camp who serve Kalmiyah to turn the king so and so toward me and [to
deliver] the heart of his army and the heart of his attendants into my hand,
I, so and so son of so and so, so that I may find grace and mercy before him
and he shall fulfill my will whenever I request [something] and in the hour
that I request [it] from him."

[133] And if you wish to come into the presence of the king or any man or
a judge, bathe yourself in living water and take from the blood and from the
wine and rub it over your skin and place the [lion's] heart over your heart.

[160] If you desire to speak with the moon or with the planets about dealing
with any matter, take a white cock and finely sifted flour and slaughter the
cock in living water. Then, knead the flour into the blood and water and make
three cakes and put them in the sun and write on them in blood the name[s
of the angels] of the fifth camp and the name of the overseer and put the three
of them on a myrtle wood table and stand facing the moon or facing the planets
[165] and say: "I adjure you to make conjunct the horoscope of so and so and
his [ruling] planets with the planet of so and so and his horoscope so as to be
his lover joined in the heart of so and so son of so and so." Or say: "Put fire of
your fire into the heart of this man, so and so, or woman, so and so, so that

she shall abandon the house of her father and mother for love of this man, so and so, son of the woman, so and so."

[174] Then blow into the wind and wash your face each dawn for nine days with the wine and with the cake which is crumbled in it.

The Second Heavenly Strata

The second heavenly strata is called "heaven of heavens;" in it are frost and haze and storehouses of snow and storehouses of hail and angels of fire and angels of vapor and spirits of fear and spirits of awe. The heaven is full of dread because within it are angels, beyond comprehension, constituting armies of armies and above them are ministers and overseers.

[160] If you wish to raise up to his [former] social status a king or minister or officer or judge that fell from his position, take oil and honey and finely sifted flour and put them in a new glass phial. Then, purify yourself of all ritual impurity and abstain from eating *nevelah* [meat from an animal that has not been ritually slaughtered] and do not touch the couch of a woman for seven days and on the seventh day stand beneath the moon, in its fourteenth or fifteenth or sixteenth day, and take the phial [165] in your hand and write on it [the names of the angels of] this camp that is on high and, facing the moon, invoke over it the names of the angels seven times.

The Seventh Heavenly Strata

And the seventh heavenly strata is entirely sevenfold light and from its light all the heavenly dwellings shine and in it the throne of glory rests on the four creatures [*chayot*] of glory.

[6] For he alone sits in the heaven of his holiness, expounding law, dividing justice, judging according to truth, and speaking righteously and before him books of fire open and from before him flow rivers of fire and when he raises himself up the mighty are afraid and when he bellows the columns shake and from his voice the doorsills tremble and his soldiers stand before him but do not gaze directly upon his likeness because [10] he is hidden from all eyes and no one can see him and live.

[13] And [the four] creatures [*chayot*] and [throned-chariot] wheels [*ophanim*] lift him up as they fly on their wings and they each have six wings and in their wings they conceal their faces and beneath them they present their faces and to the four of them they [15] turn their faces but they do not lift their faces up toward heaven on account of their fear and awe. And one above the other, before him, stand troops and troops and they immerse themselves in rivers of purity and wrap themselves in garments of white fire and together they sing with humility in a strong voice: "Holy, Holy, Holy is the Lord of

Hosts. All the world is filled with his glory." He is prior to all the acts [of creation] and he was when earth and heaven were not yet. He is alone and there is no other with him. By his strength, he suspends the heavenly dwellings and in all the heavens he is feared and [20] among all the angels he is revered for by the breath of his mouth they were formed and to glorify his power they were established. For he is one and who can dissuade him? And if he commands there is none who can rescind. Because he is the king of kings of kings, he rules over all the kings of the earth and is exalted among the heavenly angels. He examines hearts when they are still uncreated and he knows thoughts before they come to pass. Blessed is his name, and blessed is the eminence of his glory forever and forever, and for an eternity of eternities and beyond then because, apart from him, there is no god and [25] there are no gods beneath him.

[38] Blessed is his name alone on his throne and blessed is the place of his majesty. Blessed is his name in the mouths of all living souls and blessed in song by all his creation. Blessed is the Lord forever, Amen, Amen, Hallelujah.

Bibliography

Betz, Hans Dieter, ed. 1992. *The Greek Magical Papyri in Translation Including the Demotic Spells.* 2d ed. Chicago and London: University of Chicago Press.

Cox Miller, Patricia. 1986. "In Praise of Nonsense." In *Classical Mediterranean Spirituality*, ed. A. H. Armstrong, 481–505. New York: Crossroad.

Frankfurter, David. 1997. "Ritual Expertise in Roman Egypt and the Problem of the Category 'Magician.'" In *Envisioning Magic: A Princeton Seminar and Symposium*, ed. Peter Schäfer and Hans Kippenberg, 115–35. Leiden, New York and Cologne: E. J. Brill.

Gager, John G. 1992. *Curse Tablets and Binding Spells from the Ancient World.* New York and Oxford: Oxford University Press.

Graf, Fritz. 1997. *Magic in the Ancient World.* Trans. Franklin Philip. Cambridge and London: Harvard University Press.

Johnston, Sarah Iles. 1997. "Rising to the Occasion: Theurgic Ascent in Its Cultural Milieu." In *Envisioning Magic: A Princeton Seminar and Symposium*, ed. Peter Schäfer and Hans Kippenberg, 165–94. Leiden, New York and Cologne: E. J. Brill.

Margalioth, Mordecai. 1966. *Sepher Ha-Razim: A Newly Recovered Book of Magic from the Talmudic Period.* Jerusalem: Yediot Achronot.

Meyer, Marvin, ed. and trans. 1976. *The "Mithras Liturgy."* Missoula, Mont.: Scholars Press.

Morgan, Michael, trans. 1983. *Sepher Ha-Razim: The Book of the Mysteries.* Chico, Calif.: Scholars Press.

Naveh, Joseph, and Shaul Shaked. 1987. *Amulets and Magic Bowls: Aramaic Incantations of Late Antiquity.* 2d ed. Jerusalem: Magnes Press, Hebrew University.

Preisendanz, Karl, ed. and trans. 1928. *Papyri Graecae Magicae: Die Griechischen Zauberpapyri.* Stuttgart: B. G. Teubner.

Scholem, Gershom G. 1960. *Jewish Gnosticism, Merkabah Mysticism, and Talmudic Tradition.* New York: Jewish Theological Seminary.

———. 1974 [1941]. *Major Trends in Jewish Mysticism.* New York: Schocken Books.

Segal, Alan. 1980. "Heavenly Ascent in Hellenistic Judaism, Early Christianity and Their

Environment." In *Aufstieg und Niedergang der römischen Welt 2.23.1,* ed. Hildegard Temporini and Wolfgang Haase, 1,334–94. Berlin and New York: Walter de Gruyter.

———. 1987. "Hellenistic Magic: Some Questions of Definition." In *The Other Judaisms of Late Antiquity,* ed. Alan Segal, 79–108. Atlanta: Scholars Press.

———. 1990. *Paul the Convert: The Apostolate and Apostasy of Saul the Pharisee.* New Haven and London: Yale University Press.

Tambiah, S. J. 1968. "The Magical Power of Words." *Man* 3: 175–208.

— 25 —

Manichaean Ritual

Jason David BeDuhn

Coptic Manichaean Psalm-Book, Psalm 222: A Bema Psalm
Psalm-Book, Part II, 7.1–9.1

The annual Bema festival was the high point of the Manichaean liturgical year. The festival commemorated the apotheosis of Mani at his death in the dungeons of Bahram I of Persia. It took its name from a judgment seat set up on a platform in the assembly, upon which Mani's presence was both symbolized and invoked. Mani was thought to occupy the position of judge in lieu of Jesus, who would take his place upon the judgment seat at the end of time. Until then, Mani offered an annual renewal of the community through a general amnesty for sins, comparable in certain respects to the Jewish Day of Atonement.

We possess a considerable number of liturgical compositions for the Bema festival, in Middle Iranian dialects as well as in Coptic. The example translated here comes from the fourth-century Egyptian Coptic Manichaean Psalm Book and falls into three parts, with a total of fourteen stanzas. The first seven stanzas are addressed to the individual soul of the believer. In stanza eight, the believer is instructed to speak to the Bema, and the remainder of the psalm consists of the words to be directed to it. The final stanza is a closing benediction on Mani and his Bema, with a single-line prayer on behalf of the ubiquitous Mary appended.

This Bema psalm makes much of the springtime setting of the Bema festival, drawing analogies between the release of plants from the bonds of winter and the hoped-for liberation of the Manichaean from the fetters of sin. The judgment seat is characterized as a visible reminder of impending judgment and at the same time a promise of forgiveness. But, more than that, it stands as a symbol for the entire system of the Manichaean faith. The individual's approach to it, to "walk on these holy steps," which led up to the platform on which the seat was placed, was a manifest commitment to the faith. Another psalm from the same collection

(Psalm 227) suggests that Manichaeans placed roses on the Bema when they walked up to it. Stanza nine perhaps contains an allusion to the practice of placing Mani's writings on the judgment seat, in this way making him present through his teachings.

The introduction of stanza numbers to this and some of the other Coptic Manichaean psalms in this collection is based primarily upon the layout of their texts on the manuscript page, which shows clear signs of such divisions through marginal placement and enlarged first letters. The stanza numbers do not correspond with the text line numbers of Allberry's edition.

Psalm 222: A Bema Psalm

1. [O] soul, know this great sign, that this is the sign of the remission of your sins:

2. this visible Bema, which the Word set before you so that he might plant in you through what is visible the remembrance of the hidden judgment which you have forgotten since the day when you drank the water of madness, O soul.

3. Behold, the gift has come to you of the day of joy: for your part reveal today without fear all of your sins, and remember your end; and prepare yourself in your deeds: for the Bema of wisdom moves you concerning it.

4. Paul, the glorious one, bears witness, saying unto you: "The Bema of Christ, there is no respect of persons in it; whether we wish or not we shall all [stand before] it." This is what the Bema also silently proclaims.

5. Take power over the corrupt roots (?) of wickedness, the [. . .] and that of defiled lust; and [. . .] of wrath and envy and sadness. The bitter [. . .] of wickedness, also, dissolve them today.

6. [May] the judge see you keeping these commandments and [may he] honor [you] and give you life. The forgiveness of all sins will he bestow upon you. Come, therefore, and walk on these holy steps.

7. May the Bema become for you a harbor of your existence, a place of cleansing of your life, a chest filled with teaching, a ladder to the height, a scale of your deeds. And as you see the likeness of these things in the Bema, bless it.

8. Say unto it: "You are blessed, great instrument of the Word, upright Bema of the great judge, the seat of the Fathers of Light who are far from error: the foundation of the sweet victory, full of wisdom."

9. "Hail, Bema of victory, great sign of our city, joyous shining garland of the victorious souls, but the judgment and condemnation of sinners. Hail, Bema of the Mind—the holy Scriptures."

10. "Behold, all trees on this day have become new again. Behold, the roses have spread their beauty, since the bond that does harm to their leaves has been cut. Do you also cut the chains and bonds of our sins."

11. "The whole air is luminous, the sphere glows today, the earth itself is resplendent also; the waves of the sea are still, since the gloomy winter, full of trouble, has passed. Let us, too, be released from the iniquity of wickedness."

12. "Forgive the sins of those that know your mystery, the ones to whom has been revealed the knowledge of the secrets of the Exalted One, through the holy wisdom—in which there is no error—of the holy church of the Paraclete, our Father."

13. "The joy-filled treasure of the glorious spirit: give it to us as a present and distribute it to us all, and wash us in joy and [. . .] its drops also, which will wash the [. . .]."

14. Glory to you, our Father Manichaios, the glorious one, [the great] God, the savior. [You are the] forgiveness of all sins, the preaching of life, the envoy of those [on high]. Glory to your Bema, your seat that gives (?) [. . .]. May [the] soul of Mary also gain access to your mercy, my Lord.

Coptic Manichaean Psalm-Book, Psalm 240: A Bema Psalm
Psalm-Book, Part II, 41.8–29

This short Bema psalm provides key evidence for the modern reconstruction of the festival. In the first place, discussing the timing of the festival, this psalm tells us that it took place on the third day following the end of a month (actually twenty-six days) of fasting that marked the days of Mani's imprisonment (stanza 5). The transition from death to apotheosis was conceived to last three days, as in the Zoroastrian and other Near Eastern traditions. Secondly, this day corresponded to the day of the full moon in the lunar calendar observed by the Manichaeans (stanza 8). Thirdly, the festival day was preceded by a vigil through the previous night (stanza 4). The psalm is tied together by a simple, repeating refrain.

Psalm 240: A Bema Psalm

1. We praise, we sing to you, our Father Manichaios, [our] savior, O glorious one.

2. You are the one to whom we call, father, king, immortal god: hear the prayer of your sheepfold, O glorious one.

3. [You have] come (?), the one whom the Father sent forth from on high that he might release the souls that are apportioned to him, O glorious one.

4. We now therefore make festival, fulfilling your [holy] day, keeping a vigil with your happiness, O glorious one.

5. You are an immortal creature on this third day. You are an envoy; another has sent you to us, O glorious one.

6. Wash us now, therefore, in the dew drops of your joy, for we are ordained to the service of the holy Bema, O glorious one.

7. Open to us the passage of the vaults of the skies, and [walk] before us to the happiness of your kingdom, O glorious one.

8. We are accustomed to worshipping the sign of your chair when you set it up on the day of the full [moon)], which is hidden today, O glorious one.

9. Glory to you, Manichaios, glorious one. Victory to your praised Bema, O glorious one, and to the soul of the blessed Mary.

Coptic Manichaean Psalm-Book: A Psalm of the Vagabonds
Psalm-Book, Part II, 162.21–163.32 and 177.31–179.6

The subject matter of this composition is the Living Soul, the personification of the Light trapped in mixture with Darkness. Although many phrases remind one of the funeral psalms from the same collection, the words of encouragement and triumph are not directed here to the individual human soul, but to particles of light gathered by the Catechumens in the food they have brought to the ritual meal of the Elect. These particles are also "souls" and, like the liberated souls of human beings, ascend to heaven with the help of Manichaean practices. This psalm most likely represents a Manichaean meal hymn sung by the Elect in the setting of the ritual meal. The meal was the principal daily ritual of the Manichaeans. By partaking of food brought to them by laypersons (called Catechumens in this psalm), the Elect were believed to extract the Light, or "soul" bound in the food, and be able to liberate it back to the realm of light from which it originally came.

The soul addressed is envisioned to be female, the "daughter of the Father of Lights," and is implicitly identified with the Maiden of Light, who acts as warrior and weapon against Darkness, both in this psalm and in Manichaean literature in general. Another character in the Manichaean pantheon appears in this psalm: the Mind of Light, the personification of correct belief and behavior endowed upon every Manichaean, particularly the Elect. He is invoked not only as an essential agent in the ritual, but also as a sort of Muse for the singer.

This psalm appears in two recensions in the Coptic Manichaean *Psalm-Book,* suggesting that the book is an original compilation made up of material from a number of sources. The two versions differ only in minor points: one additional verse in each version, one instance of inverted stanzas, a few phrases transposed from one stanza to another, and a half-dozen grammatical differences. The content is scarcely affected.

A Psalm of the Vagabonds

1. [With] our holy voice we give glory to the Mind, for when he dwells with us we give fruit that is holy.

2. [O] Father, O Mind of Light, come: wear me until I have produced the weeping of the Son of Man.

3. [My] lord Jesus, come: wear me until I purify the body of the First Man.

4. O alms of glory, daughter of the Father of Lights, [. . .] all; no one knows your honor.

5. [. . .] make music, [the] only sons of the Paraclete, the ones who [. . .] you, [. . .] weeping daily for your wounds.

6. You are the two-edged axe with which the bitter root was cut.

7. You are the [. . .] that is in the hand of the Maiden, the one which was thrust into the heart of the enemy [Psalm-Book 178.9 reads: "the one which *she* thrust . . ."].

8. You [are] the first ship of the first hero [literally, "giant"], the one in which was caught the robbers that had sprung forth.

9. You are the first weapon of the first warrior, the one that he cast at the foe that rose up.

10. You are [the] church of the Father, the First Man; you are the vineyard of the first cultivator [Psalm-Book 178.15–16 reads differently: "You are the church of *my* Father, the First Man; you are the vineyard of *my father, the Living Spirit*"].

11. You are the eye of the fullness that came with the abundance, until it had closed the eyes to these malignant ones [Psalm-Book 178.17–18 reads differently: "You are the eye of the fullness, the one that came from *the place of* abundance until it had closed the eyes of *this malignant one*"].

12. How great is your strength, O daughter of wisdom: for you have not yet wearied, while you serve as guard over the enemy.

13. You are the one for whom the ships wait on high that they may draw you up and take you to the Light [Psalm-Book 178.22 reads: ". . . take you to *your kingdom*"].

14. Behold the Perfect Man is stretched out in the midst [of] the world, so that you may walk in him [and] receive your unfading [wreaths] [Psalm-Book 178.26 reads: ". . . and be taken to the Light." Stanzas 14 and 15 are transposed relative to one another in the two recensions.].

15. Behold, the five Porters are spread over the world, so that your heart may not suffer [and that] you may cast the burden from off you.

16. Behold, the righteous will illumine you; behold, the forgiveness of sins of the Catechumens of the faith [Psalm-Book 178.27–28 reads: "behold the knowledge and the wisdom will put your clothes upon you"].

17. [Behold], the medicine-chest of the physician will heal your wounds; behold, the knowledge and the wisdom will put your clothes upon you [Psalm-Book 178.29–30 reads: "behold, the forgiveness of sins of the Catechumens of the faith"].

18. Walk, therefore, joyfully, drawn to the land of the Light, sealed with your seal [Psalm-Book 178.32 reads: "sealed with your seals."] and your wreaths that do not fade.

19. Walk also happily: your sufferings have passed today; behold, the harbor of peace—you have docked at it.

20. When you go to the height [. . .] the Darkness [. . . the forgiveness] of sins of the Catechumens of [the] faith [This stanza appears only in Psalm-Book 179.3–4].

21. Glory to this alms-offering and [to] the ones who purify it and [to] the ones who save it, the Catechumens of the faith [Psalm-Book 178.5 reads: "Glory to this alms-offering, and [to] *the one who will* purify [it . . ."].

22. May there be peace and rest for the soul of the blessed Mary, Theona [Psalm-Book 178.5–6 reads: "(. . . and [to] the) soul of Plousiane, (and) the blessed (Mary)"].

Bibliography

BeDuhn, Jason David. 1996. "The Manichaean Sacred Meal." In *Turfan, Khotan and Dunhuang,* ed. R. E. Emmerick et al., 1–17. Berlin: Akademie Verlag.

———. 1999. *The Manichaean Body in Discipline and Ritual.* Baltimore: Johns Hopkins University Press.

Puech, Henri-Charles. 1979. "Liturgie et pratiques rituelles dans le manichaisme." In Puech, *Sur le manichéisme et autres essais,* 235–394. Paris: Flammarion.

Wurst, Gregor. 1995. *Das Bemafest der ägyptischen Manichäer.* Altenberge: Oros Verlag.

—26—

The Seal of the Merkavah

Michael D. Swartz

The principal intellectuals and religious leaders of Judaism in Late Antiquity were the rabbis, scholars who held that devotion to Torah and performance of the commandments would bring reward in the world to come. At the same time, a small group of mystics, while accepting much of the essentials of Rabbinic Judaism, told stories of early rabbis who were supposed to have traveled to heaven to see God seated on his glorious throne and to participate in the angelic liturgy. These mystics wrote a remarkable corpus of texts known as the *Hekhalot* literature. These texts, written between the fifth and eighth centuries C.E., describe this journey in great detail. They tell how two of the greatest rabbis of the second century, Rabbi Akiba and Rabbi Ishmael, traveled through the seven layers of heaven, called palaces or *Hekhalot,* fought off fierce angels who guard the gates of those palaces, and eventually arrived at the throne room of God, where they had the privilege of listening to the magnificent praise of God by the angelic hosts. There too, they experienced a vision of God seated on his Merkavah, the divine chariot-throne described in chapter 1 of Ezekiel and chapter 6 of Isaiah. Although this journey involves an ascent to heaven, it is paradoxically called a "descent" in some texts. Its practitioners are called the "Descenders to the Chariot," or *Yorde Merkavah.*

These texts were written centuries after those early rabbis died and could not have been written by them. Exactly who wrote them is under debate, but they were probably written by Jews who lived in the rabbinic milieu but who did not participate in the central circles or rabbinic leadership. Although there are some indications that the Merkavah tradition began in Palestine sometime after the compilation of the Mishnah in 200 C.E., the texts seem to have taken shape largely in the Jewish communities of Babylonia (present-day Iraq). Eventually these texts were compiled into collections by the Jewish pietists (*Ḥaside Ashkenaz*) of medieval Germany. The textual tradition also made its way to the Eastern Mediterranean in the Middle Ages, where some of these texts were placed in a Fustat (Old Cairo), Egypt depository, which has come to be known as the Cairo Genizah.

The text translated here comes from that depository. It is important as a unique expression of the Merkavah tradition, as a testimony to the unusual sensibilities of its author, and as an indication of the influence of the Merkavah tradition. Because it mentions "a certain sage in Babylonia," we can suppose that it was written in Jewish Babylonia somewhat between the time of the completion of the Talmud in the sixth century C.E. and the time when the manuscript was written in the eleventh century. The text bears the influence of one of the central Hekhalot texts, *Hekhalot Rabbati*, which details the ascent to heaven and presents elaborate prayers for recitation in the heavenly court. This text, however, is distinguished by its narrative quality.

This text is a fragment of a larger work that consisted of several subdivisions, such as a text for acquiring the secrets of Torah and memory through the cultivation of an angel known as the *Sar-Torah* and one describing the colossal size of the divine body (*Shi'ur Qomah*). As we can see from a subscription at the end of the text, the subdivision translated here was entitled *Ḥotam ha-Merkavah*, "the Seal of the Merkavah." The text was apparently the record of a revelation given by the angel Ozhaya to Rabbi Ishmael regarding how to make the journey to the Merkavah by taking the proper path and by warding off the hostile angels using a special seal, which authorizes the traveler to pass through the gates.

The top of the fragment is torn and leaves many gaps. It is difficult to tell what is going on at the beginning, but we can suppose the following: the main narrator of the text is Rabbi Ishmael, who reports his conversations with an angel named Ozhaya regarding how to ascend (or descend) to the Merkavah and obtain the secrets of wisdom. As we can see from section II below, the text supposes the angel instructed the rabbi, who writes down the angel's instructions and receives several other aids to the journey from him: a scroll, a seal, and a path. He describes the dangers of the journey in frightening detail, warns him about how to avoid them, and tells him his reward: he will be seated in the divine throne room along with other visitors.

The extant fragment begins in the middle of an excursus, in which Ozhaya has been telling Rabbi Ishmael about a powerful name, Tandrael, which is reserved not for any angel, but for a certain "master" (or rabbi) in Babylonia. This passage apparently describes the role of this esoteric name and that of the angel Ozhaya in creation. This description is difficult because of its fragmentary nature and its esoteric ideas, but it probably alludes to two esoteric myths of prehistory. One is the idea that the firmament is suspended as a tent from a particular point, indicated here by a tent stake. The second apparently has to do with how the waters were beaten back after the flood (cf. Gen. 7:10; 1 Enoch 6 and 65; and Schäfer's note [Schäfer 1983, 110] to this passage). Because the destruction of the world at the flood leads to a better one, the angel rebukes his heavenly colleagues: "And you, why are you crying out? The Creator was destroying a clay vessel, which was in his hand, and wished to make it into another vessel!"

At this point, Ozhaya continues, God announced that the name Tandrael was to be prepared not even for the most exalted of angels, such as the Angel of the

Presence, but for a scion of the "house of the Master in Babylonia." We do not know who this person is, but it is apparent that the author had someone specific in mind and wished to single him out as an extraordinary, perhaps messianic figure. At the same time, his six-letter name has apparently been distinguished from Tanrael, a divine name of five letters, so as not to confuse the name of that man with that of God himself. Other Hekhalot texts, notably 3 Enoch, warn of the dangers of confusing an archangel figure with that of God.

In the next section, the angel returns to what he has been doing before the excursus, that is, instructing Rabbi Ishmael how to "descend to the Merkavah." At this point we learn valuable information about how this text validates its authority and sanctity. It presents itself as the result of a process by which the mystic, here Rabbi Ishmael, acts as a kind of amanuensis, writing down the details of the procedure dictated by the angel. This process of revelation is akin to that of several apocalyptic books of the second-temple period, such as Jubilees, in which the "angel of the Presence" reveals divine secrets to the writer. This text is one of several gifts that the practitioner (and by implication the community of readers who will receive this text) acquire from heaven. The angel also gives him a seal and a path. In the Hekhalot tradition, a seal is a specific magical divine name— analogous to the signets used in ancient Near Eastern administration—that is recited by the traveler to the Merkavah in order to authorize him to enter the heavenly gates. The path consists of instructions on how to avoid the zealous and terrifying angels eager to defend the divine presence against intruders.

One detail among these details is particularly striking for what it reveals about the world-view of the author. At the sixth Hekhal, the angelic array and the roaring fires cause such a tumult that they could cause the mystic to faint. Therefore, he must dig his fingernails into the "ground of the firmament" and plug up his orifices so that his breath does not escape. This is probably an indication that the mystical circle responsible for this text did not distinguish sharply between body and soul. It is not only an immaterial soul that ascends to heaven in this narrative, but, somehow, some aspect of the physical person himself (cf. the deposition of Rabbi Neḥuniah from heaven in *Hekhalot Rabbati,* described by Scholem 1965, 9–13; cf. Gruenwald 1980, 241–44); likewise, the author apparently thinks of heaven as a physically real place.

The fragment resumes at the top of folio 2b, which is badly damaged. It is difficult to make out the meaning of the first five lines, but they probably refer to the resuscitation and renewed strength that will result from the technique for ascent that has just been described and from the rescue of the traveler by the angel. The speaker here seems to be God himself. The text proceeds with a description of the culmination of the journey, the seventh Hekhal. There the mystic is rewarded for his efforts by being welcomed by an attending angel (an archangel known in Hekhalot terminology as the "youth") and seated along with the angelic hosts and earthly visitors in the throne room of God. The text concludes with a testimony to the effectiveness of the procedure. It could be performed even by the most inferior student in the group, and be effective. The instructions in the text are therefore valid for any virtuous person who wants to make the journey to the divine world.

The Seal of the Merkavah can be read as a kind of mystical novella. It is a remarkable portrait of a mystical tradition in evolution. The extant text does not tell the reader how to cultivate a mystical state that might result in such a vision of travel to the heavens, but the author clearly believed that such travel was possible—if not in his time, than in a heroic age of early rabbis. It weaves apocalyptic elements such as the revelatory angel and a messianic hero into a saga of history, quest, triumph, and theophany.

This text comes from the Taylor-Schechter Genizah collection of the Cambridge University Library and bears the classmark TS K1.21.95.C. It was first published by Ithamar Gruenwald (1969a and 1969b) and subsequently by Peter Schäfer (1983, 97–111; there it is designated text G8). The most extensive translation of the text to date is Halperin 1988, 368–69; cf. also Himmelfarb 1988. For discussions of this text see those works as well as Gruenwald 1980, 188–90; Swartz 1996, 125–26; and Wolfson 1993, 19–26, and 1994, 82–85. For a translation and discussion of another text from the same fragment, see Swartz 1996, 126–30. This translation is based on Schäfer's edition, supplemented by Gruenwald's critical notes and drawing on insights from the translations cited above. Words in curly brackets { } indicate emendations or restorations suggested by Gruenwald, Schäfer, or this translator.

I. Tanrael and His Role in Prehistory

[. . .] and pious, and upright, and pure [. . .] at the time when Tandrael YH [Ṣvaot, God of Israel, seated upon the cheru[bim] from within [. . .] every day to his servants [. . .] this [name . . .] that he does not even give to me—I, Ozhaya, who [. . .]. I heard him when it [is said] according to his way, when he would look through it into many generations and would arrange what he adorned [. . .], when the [. . .] to the stake, to the beginning of which the embroidery of the world is tied; the point of the stake strikes the fabric of the curtain, on which the completion of the world and its ornamentation and its surface stands. And immediately [. . .] all the wells of the great deep opened up and there was a flood over the world and the upper and lower [wat]ers [. . .]; and {I} was pulverized until I took a whip from before him whose length was 8,000 myriad parasangs and the measure of whose thickness was as 1,000 {whips, and [he] would beat} the upper and lower [waters] continuously. Lightning bolts went forth from its height and embers from its lashes. Flashing balls burst forth from it and clouds of smoke from when I struck it, until the flood became the arrows of the wrath of the King of the universe, and his anger—not to say that the King was beating.

And you, why are you crying out? The Creator was destroying a clay vessel, which was in his hand, and wished to make it into another vessel—why are you crying out?

He beat until I had subdued the entire world for him. Then I heard him when he said: Tandrael, the {angel}: Let this name be prepared and reserved (not) for the prince, or for any of my servants and not even for the Angel of my Presence, but for a certain sage, who is yet to appear in the end of years in the house of the master in Babylonia, and who will be established before me in Babylonia, by this house, which will appear in the time to come in Babylonia. For you will tie two crowns: one from the six days of creation and one for the end of years. For I bequeath this name to that sage who will be established before me in Babylonia in the house of the master. And I called him, I and all creation, So-and-So Tanrael, for the number of the letters of his name is equal to those of this name. For this name is five letters, and that name is five letters. Ozhaya, the Prince of his Presence, deferred all the generations from the six days of creation and {added} to it an extra letter. And what was the letter by which he called him? Tandrael. I did so for my reasons and he for his reasons— {so that you would not} say that my name had six letters and the name of the sage who will be established before me in Babylonia in the house of the master that I govern {had six le}tters. As this house is established, so he is established, and the number of the letters in his name is five and the number of my name is five, so that it be measure for measure. For I, Ozhaya, am appointed over one of them, whose name is Magog, like his name, and Tanr[ael Y]HWH God of Israel is appointed over one of them, to exalt him in the eyes of the supreme assembly.

II. Instructions for Descending to the Merkavah

So return, O companion, to the study of the descent to the Merkavah, that I was setting it out before you in order and teaching you: How one descends, and how one ascends, the nature of the first Hekhal, how one compels {the angels}, what their adjuration is. But I have interrupted you—write.

Here is the seal of the descent to the Merkavah for the inhabitants of the world, for you and for whoever wishes to descend and to gaze at the King and his beauty. Now take this path, and descend, and see, and you will not be harmed. For I have placed it on a scroll for you and seen it. Afterward you descended and tested it, and you were not harmed. For I have placed the paths of the Merkavah for you like light, and the byways of the firmament like the sun—not like those before you who found great disgrace. For they are like someone who is lost in a great desert, and took a path, and as he walked it thrust him into a populated forest, and he found there dens of lions and cubs, lairs of tigers and dwellings of wolves. He comes and stands among them and does not know what to do. Then one of them strikes him, tears him, and drags him. So too your colleague who descended before you. To you, O companion, I swear [by] this glory, that they dragged Ben Zoma one hundred times at the first Hekhal—and I am a witness, for I counted how many times he was dragged, he and his comrades, whether they saved him or not, whether he was saved or harmed—two hundred times at the second Hekhal, and four hundred at the third, and eight hundred at the fourth Hekhal, and sixteen hundred at the fifth Hekhal, and thirty-two hundred at the sixth Hekhal, sixty-four hundred at the seventh Hekhal. But you will not suffer even one scratch from the princes, from the guards of the Hekhalot, or from one of the angels of destruction.

Then you arrive at the sixth Hekhal. There are troops of princes and of battalions, who were at the gate of the second one pushing and repelling and ejecting—myriads and camps and attendants, all at once—but there is no delay and you are not harmed. For you hold a great seal, and all the supernal angels recoil from it.

Return, O companion, to the warning signs of the sixth Hekhal, that are held for you, like its counterparts, and you will not be destroyed. See the tumultuous fires going forth from the seventh Hekhal to the sixth Hekhal, a coal-like fire and a gushing fire, and a blazing fire, and a sweet fire. They go in and out like arrows. For this reason I have told you not to stand between them in the gate of the sixth Hekhal, but to the side. When they go out from the seventh Hekhal to go into the sixth Hekhal, it is a dangerous sign. Let it be known to you and do not be afraid. For there is a distance of eighty million parasangs from the gate of the seventh Hekhal to the place where you are standing. And when they let forth sound, one in another, you stood. And if you are standing, {sit}. And if you are seated, recline. If you were reclining, lie down on your neck. And if you are lying down on your neck, lie down on your face. If you are lying down on your face, dig your fingernails and toenails into the ground of the firmament, and put cotton in your ears and cotton in your nostrils and cotton in your anus, so that your breath will remain and will not escape, until I reach you and resuscitate you and your spirit returns and your soul lives.

For thus I have commanded you when you wish to descend to the Merkavah to see the King and his beauty, you and all who wish to descend to the Merkavah, whether in your generation or other generations. Over each and every Hekhal he shall pronounce my name and call me in a low voice. Immediately, no creature will harm him or catch him, and he will see the wondrous exaltation and the rarefied beauty. And let this be a sign for you: even though you are lying on your face against the tumult of the fires of [. . .] that approach that place where you are lying, your ears. . . .
[end of folio 2a]

[folio 2b]
It is [. . . wounding] and healing for you, so that you [{do not} . . .] like clay,

...] you were lying down. Be firm and strong, [. . .] in the paths of fire in the Hekh[al . . .] for you, we have no path for the descenders to the Merkavah, [. . .] fear and trembling are mine. And in the Hekhal [. . .] and fear and dread are mine, and war and din are mine. [   ] If he does not do it, you have no [. . .] Hekhalot [. . .] and they are strong and great and mighty. Immediately they seal [. . .] and close and obstruct the way against the descenders to the Merkavah [. . .]; and one by my authority, and another by my authority. And at once he stood [at . . . the gate of the six]th Hekhal, the light of this tumult. He cools the fires for you, [. . .] to the paths before you. The gate of the seventh Hekhal, [. . . nature] of the sixth Hekhal, to warn and teach the descenders to the Merkavah so that they can descend and not be harmed.

The Nature of the Seventh Hekhal:

[. . .] open, and {their} swords are hanging, their bows are drawn, and spears are at their {arms} and lances are at their [. . .], and warriors [. . .] . They are [. . .] and terrified and hide their faces and great silence is on their faces. A two-fold wheel hovers like a bird and the horn is held by its two ends, and a horn-blast sounds. This Hekhal is like six Hekhalot; these guards do not [. . .] Ozhaya, my servant. For I am a [. . .] king, a resplendent king, an upright king. Whoever knows that he is pure of transgression and bloodshed and possesses Torah, let him enter and be seated before me. And so three times a day the herald announces. Now see the youth who goes out to greet you from behind the Throne of Glory. Do not bow down to him, for his crown is like the crown of his King, and the shoes on his feet are like the shoes of his King, and the cloak he wears is like the cloak of his King, and a cloak {inlaid with precious stones} is bound on his loins. The sun goes forth from the belt that is before him, and the moon from the knots that are behind him. His eyes burn like torches, his eyeballs burn like lamps. His radiance is like the radiance of his King, and his splendor is like the splendor of his Creator. Zehuvadiah is his name, and behold, he seizes you and seats you [. . .]—Not only because you alone have come, but he seats others on a seat that has been reserved before the Throne of Glory.

This is the nature of the sign of the seventh Hekhal: Rabbi Ishmael said: I did this from the first Hekhal to the seventh Hekhal, and I [{looked}] and saw the King in His beauty. Rabbi Ishmael said: I did not move from that spot until I had completed and ornamented it for descent and ascent [. . . he] revealed for the generations, for the wise to descend and ascend. So I wrote it, concerning the Hekhal and its princes, and its interpretations, those one hundred and nineteen—{are they not} written at the beginning of this book?

Rabbi Ishmael said: this praxis was performed by me and I did not believe it, until this praxis was performed by one student, the least of all of us in the company, and he descended [. . .] and he said to me, ascend, and bear witness in the company, for four times it is written that the testimony of the seal of the Merkavah is seen, to descend by it, and to see the King in his beauty. Immediately the world was redeemed. These are they, O friend and his student: Behold, they are many years at the end of years, the years in the days of the house of the master, and at once redemption will come to Israel. Thus far the Seal of the Merkavah.

Bibliography

Alexander, P. 1983. "3 (Hebrew Apocalypse of) Enoch." In *The Old Testament Pseudepigrapha,* ed. James H. Charlesworth, 223–315. Garden City, N.Y.: Doubleday.

Cohen, Martin Samuel. 1983. *The Shi'ur Qomah: Liturgy and Theurgy in Pre-Kabbalistic Jewish Mysticism.* Lanham, Md.: University Press of America.

Gruenwald, Ithamar. 1969a. *Qeṭa'im Ḥadashim Mi-Sifrut ha-Hekhalot. Tarbiz* 38: 354–72.

———. 1969b. "Tiqqunim ve-He'arot le-'Qeṭa'im Ḥadashim mi-Sifrut ha-Hekahlot.'" *Tarbiz* 39: 216–17.

———. 1980. *Apocalyptic and Merkavah Mysticism.* Leiden: E. J. Brill.

Halperin, David J. 1988. *Faces of the Chariot: Early Jewish Responses to Ezekiel's Vision.* Tübingen: Mohr.

Himmelfarb, Martha. 1988. "Heavenly Ascent and the Relationship of the Apocalypses and the *Hekhalot* Literature." *Hebrew Union College Annual* 59, 73–100.

———. 1993. *Ascent to Heaven in Jewish and Christian Apocalypses.* New York and Oxford: Oxford University Press.

Martin, Dale B. 1995. *The Corinthian Body.* New Haven: Yale University Press.

Schäfer, Peter. 1981. *Synopse zur Hekhalot-Literatur.* Tübingen: Mohr.

———. 1983. *Geniza-Fragmente zur Hekhalot-Literatur.* Tübingen: Mohr.

———. 1987–1995. *Übersetzung der Hekhalot-Literatur.* 4 vols. Tübingen: Mohr.

———. 1992. *The Hidden and Manifest God: Some Major Themes in Early Jewish Mysticism.* Albany: State University of New York Press.

Scholem, Gershom, 1954. *Major Trends in Jewish Mysticism.* New York: Schocken.

———. 1965. *Jewish Gnosticism, Merkavah Mysticism, and Talmudic Tradition.* New York: Jewish Theological Seminary of America.

Segal, Alan. 1980. "Heavenly Ascent in Hellenistic Judaism, Early Christianity and Their Environment." *Aufstieg und Niedergang der römischen Welt* II.23.2, 1,333–94.

Smith, Morton, 1963. "Observations on Hekhalot Rabbati." In *Biblical and Other Studies,* ed. Alexander Altmann, 142–60. Cambridge: Harvard University Press.

Swartz, Michael D. 1992. *Mystical Prayer in Ancient Judaism: An Analysis of Ma'aseh Merkavah.* Tübingen: Mohr.

———. 1996. *Scholastic Magic: Ritual and Revelation in Early Jewish Mysticism.* Princeton: Princeton University Press.

Wolfson, Elliot. 1993. "Yeridah la-Merkavah: Typology of Ecstasy and Enthronement in Ancient Jewish Mysticism." In *Mystics of the Book,* ed. R. A. Herrera, 13–44. New York: Peter Lang.

———. 1994. *Through a Speculum That Shines: Vision and Imagination in Medieval Jewish Mysticism.* Princeton: Princeton University Press.

—— 27 ——

Anonymous Spanish Correspondence; or
the Letter of the "She-ass"

Virginia Burrus and Tracy Keefer

A late eighth- or early ninth-century manuscript from the monastery of Saint-Gall in France—the *Codex Sangallensis* 190—contains the only extant copy of two intriguing letters. The first bears no heading in the body of the manuscript, but the second is labeled "another" letter to Marcella and identified in the concluding line as a work of Jerome; the index that appears at the beginning of the manuscript lists them as "two letters of the presbyter Jerome." However, in 1928, G. Morin demonstrated that Jerome is unlikely to have authored either letter, since the first was clearly written by a woman; he considered this probable in the case of the second as well, given the author's artful self-representation as a she-ass (*asina*) and other indications of a female perspective, such as interest in pregnancy and childbirth. Indeed, Morin thought it likely that both letters were written by the same woman (Morin 1928, 290–91). Both letters are addressed to female correspondents.

It has been suggested that the letters might have been produced within a sixth-century Gallic convent, since they follow a fragment of Baudonivia's preface to the *Life of Radegund* in the Saint-Gall manuscript (Thiébaux 1987, 57). However, the Baudonivia fragment, together with a fragment of Jerome's *Commentary on St. Paul's Letter to the Ephesians* (which might, by a similar logic, have been invoked on behalf of the earlier attribution to Jerome), fills a blank space at the end of one bound section, or quaternion, while the letters, written in a different hand, begin another quaternion. There is thus no evidence of an original connection between the two sections, which may not have been joined until relatively late in the process of the manuscript's compilation.

Morin's placement of the letters' author (or authors) in the neighborhood of the Spanish Pyrenees ca. 400 appears better founded, even if his hypothesis cannot be accepted in all of its particulars. For assigning both date and provenance, Morin relied on two arguments. First, he suggested that the fourth canon of the

Spanish Council of Saragossa (380) might have been drafted in order to combat the ascetic practices specified in the second of the anonymous letters (Morin 1928, 303–4): "On the twenty-one continuous days from December 17th to Epiphany, which is the 6th of January, let no one be allowed to be absent from the church: they are not to be concealed in houses, nor to remain on rural estates, nor to head for the mountains, nor to walk with bare feet, but to flock to the church." The parallel between the three-week pre-Epiphanal retreat promoted by the letter and the three-week withdrawal here prohibited by the Saragossan Council is quite close, and the custom is otherwise unattested, although there is much general discussion of Epiphanal observances in contemporaneous Latin literature (see also Burrus 1995, 37–38; Talley 1986, 141–55).

Second, Morin argued that the letters contained striking echoes of the language of Bachiarius, a late-fourth-century Spanish ascetic (Morin 1928, 304–7). This observation, however, did not easily harmonize with his theory of female authorship. Morin thus appealed to the analogy of Jerome's *Epistle* 46—addressed to Marcella on behalf of Paula and Eustochium—and reinvoked a comparison that had seemingly once led to the attribution of the two Saint-Gall letters to Jerome; however, he then speculated that Bachiarius, not Jerome, had had a hand in drafting the letters, and he further specified that Bachiarius was not actually their author but merely their original scribe or "secretary" (Morin 1928, 307). Morin's secretarial hypothesis has not persuaded all scholars, and there are serious difficulties with his claim to detect traces of both (female) authorial and (male) scribal voices in the texts. To the degree that his identification of significant similarities of word usage between the letters and Bachiarius's relatively meager extant textual corpus proves persuasive, it seems better accounted for by reference to a literary-theological milieu common to the letters' authors and Bachiarius (and perhaps also other Spanish ascetics like Priscillian). Contrary to Morin's theory, the two letters do not appear to be the work of one writer (or, by the same token, of one heavily editorializing "secretary"), as their language and syntax differ notably. Consequently, the sex of the author of the second letter is still an open question.

While Spain remains the most probable place of origin for the letters, a Gallic provenance for their recipients (if not also their authors) should not be ruled out, given the inclusion of the letters in a collection of material that can be localized to Aquitania (part of modern France), together with the widely acknowledged frequency of communication between members of the Spanish and Gallic elites. The core of the Saint-Gall manuscript seems to represent the family archives of Ruricius, Bishop of Limoges (ca. 485–ca. 508), and his probable relative, Desiderius, Bishop of Cahors (630–655). Perhaps these texts became a part of the library of Ruricius and passed along with the family letters to Desiderius.

The second of the two letters (*Quamlibet sciam sacerdotali*) is here translated into English, the first (*Nisi tanti seminis*) having already been published in an English translation (Thiébaux 1987, 57–62). The central theme of the second letter—the necessity for observing a period of ascetic discipline during the three weeks encompassing the festivals of Christ's Nativity and his Epiphany—renders this text particularly valuable for the study of the varied Late Antique religious practices by which time itself was Christianized and a distinctly Christian year produced, in evident competition and tension with the ongoing annual festivals of the "gentiles," namely, the Saturnalia and Kalends of January (see Markus 1990, 85–135; Salzman 1990, 235–46). Renarrating the sequence of the seasons, the letter also maps onto the space of every Christian's life both the sacralized solitude of the "desert" and the pressing distraction of the sociality of "Egypt." If any place can be a desert, any person can be an ascetic, when the time is right: practices like prayer, fasting, and above all solitude (and thus by implication sexual continence) are not seen as the particular prerogatives of a spiritual elite of virgins or monks but rather are enthusiastically appropriated by married lay people—in this case, perhaps more specifically by married laywomen (cf. Cooper 1996, 92–115).

The letter's explicit resistance to an exclusive idealization of virginity offers a striking contrast to the better-known and ultimately more influential view of the contemporaneous Ambrose of Milan, and it produces a somewhat unorthodox Mariology, (the theology regarding Mary, the mother of Jesus) (see Morin 1928, 308). Whereas Ambrose repeatedly describes Mary as giving birth without pain or groans, the Mary of the second letter is held up as a model of the "groans and sighs" of labor required of anyone who would give birth to her (or his) salvation (Burrus 1994, 40–41, 48–50). In the letter, the preparatory quiet of the final period—or tenth lunar month—of Mary's gestation, her painful labor and birthing, and the subsequent manifestation of the Word, her Son, all serve to articulate a restructuring of both time and space. The ripening of Mary's pregnancy parallels the gradual maturing of the year, even as the birth and divine manifestation of her child marks the ritual opening of a new age; similarly, Mary's womb—or, alternatively, the solitude that the author is certain she would have sought in her time of birth-giving—represents the inner space of calm and rest that constitutes a sacred "desert" potentially accessible to even the most worldly Christian.

The exegetical practices enacted in the letter are as intriguing as the ascetic practices therein described, identifying the text as an artifact of a distinctively scriptural literary culture emerging in the Latin West. The author whom Morin refers to as *l'incorrigible allégoriseuse* (an incorrigible allegorizing woman) (Morin 1928, 292) expertly interweaves biblical citations and allusions with a self-conscious virtuosity that verges on the playful; an unusual degree of familiarity with the Latin Pentateuch is particularly notable. The writer initially takes on the scriptural persona of the she-ass, whose inferior offspring—the letter itself—might (it is hoped) be redeemed by the sacrificial lamb of its author's pure intentions and exalted topic, in accordance with the priestly law of the Old Testament. This suggestion, however, is quickly modified by a proposal that the she-ass's progeny might after all substitute for the preferred offspring of the sheep, much as Balaam's unlikely she-ass was transformed into a vehicle of divine revelation. Continuing this line of interpretation, the writer notes humorously in closing that even unredeemed asses have demonstrated their usefulness to no less a personage than Christ himself, thereby implying that the incarnation eliminates the Levitical distinction between the pure and the impure, making all offerings worthy.

The foot of the wandering Balaam, pressed against the vineyard walls by the balky ass, becomes a figure for the extremity of a year, the end of which should (it is urged) be observed not in the frenetic motion of pagan festivities but with a Marian withdrawal into the stillness of solitude. The brooding figure of Mary—a veritable temple of the Lord—is superseded by the image of the ark, enclosed and at rest amidst the teeming floods, which is in turn reconfigured as the temple of Solomon's silent fabrication. Daniel's three weeks of fasting and prayer at the end of the tenth month—December—locates the self-mastery of the "man of desires" in time, while the prophecy of Zechariah aligns the scripturally swaddled birth of the new age (Jesus) from the old (Joshua) with both the rebuilding of the destroyed temple and Ezra's re-inscription of the divine word. The restless slide of images—as one scriptural figure is repeatedly exchanged for another, in a fluid and seemingly endless labor of significatory redemption—may finally be understood to produce a center of calm and a moment of silent readiness, preparing even the most asinine reader for the Epiphany of Christ.

The translation is from the Latin text *Quamlibet sciam sacerdotali* in the *Codex Sangallensis* 190, 55–66, first edited by G. Morin, "Pages inédites de deux pseudo-Jérômes des environs de l'an 400," and reprinted in Adalbert Hamman, ed., *Patrologiae Latinae Supplementum 1* (1958), cols. 1,038–44. Thanks are owed to Paul Harvey, Ralph Mathisen, Danuta Shanzer, and Mark Vessey, who generously offered advice on the rendering of the letter's frequently obscure Latin.

Anonymous Spanish Correspondence; or the Letter of the "She-ass"

However well I may know that only choice sacrifices of words are to be offered to a priestly family, nevertheless, because I did not find anything worthy to offer you when I looked back over the flock of my thoughts, I have taken refuge in these sole words of defense, so that I may redeem the offspring of the she-ass with a sheep [cf. Exod. 13:13, 34:20]—that is, defend the brute expression of my foolish mind with the simplicity of Christian innocence, according to the apostle, who says: "It is not in earthly wisdom that we abide" [2 Cor. 1:12]. And because the utterance of a foolish beast is of less value than the offspring of an impure animal, this may serve for the balance of the ransom: that we speak with you not of earthly but of heavenly matters. Thus we ask that you, a woman trained in priestly doctrine to discern and distinguish between the pure and the impure, accept our plodding words, like the offspring of the she-ass, in exchange for the sheep, since these words tell of things divine and holy; and we ask that you not drive them from the temple of your heart. For the discipline of the law put in place by the angels [Gal. 3:19] provided for the weakness of human beings in such a way that extravagance of gifts should not be sought so much as the longing for an abundant and simple will in these who, poor in understanding, had nothing choice to be sacrificed to God—that is, to the spirit. This is clearly shown in the book of Numbers [sic; cf. Lev. 27:8], where it says that if someone wants to have his redemption effected by a priest and does not have the price, the priest should place him before the Lord, and the price of redemption should be reckoned for him in accordance with his wish. Knowing this, we ask that you accept what is intended in our words, not what is actually accomplished; for a poor understanding has more will than ability.

Because we made mention above of the she-ass, we must therefore also produce examples of her work, which can present us with patterns for improving the life of learning. For we read that that she-ass of the soothsayer Balaam trembled so at the sight of the angel that she is said to have fallen to her knees [Num. 22:21–27]. We must imitate this, if ever the spirit of the world incites our she-ass—that is, the indolent nature of the flesh—with the goads of its temptation and spurs us toward those blandishments of the age that Balak promises [Num. 22:17], so that the angel may be in her path—that is, the precepts of spiritual eloquence may return to her memory, concerning which the blessed Moses says, "They shall come to you at every movement of your eyes" [Deut. 6:8]—and she may bend her knees to the Father of our Lord Jesus Christ [Eph. 3:14]. For we know from the teaching of the apostle, who said, "If one of you suffers evil, pray" [James 5:13], that nothing is as effective against the goads of temptations as the protection of prayer. Let us press Balaam's foot between the vineyard walls—that is, let us choke the wandering freedom of the worldly spirit according to the utterances of the divine books, once the desires to wander have been resisted. For the foot of Balaam is the vice of restless and ever-wandering movement. In truth, what are the walls of the vineyards if not the fortifications of books, which defend the fruits of the branches—that is, the work of the souls—from the attack of wild animals—that is, from the longing for vices?

And the appropriate time draws near for us to restrain and destroy the foot of the soothsayer Balaam [Num. 22:25]—that is, either the desire to wander or the final heel of the year, as the gentiles seem to observe it. For unless I am mistaken, the sacred festival of the tenth month [December] approaches, which we ought to celebrate with the examination of a more careful life; indeed, when "the Spirit of the Lord filled the world" [Wisd. of Sol. 1:7]—that is, "the Word was made flesh" [John 1:14]—and "when the silent calm contained all things, and night had run half its course" [Wisd. of Sol. 18:14]—that is, ignorance prevailed among mortals—"a word, leaping from the royal throne, a stern conqueror, leapt forth into the midst of the doomed land, and touched heaven, filling all things powerfully" [cf. Wisd. of Sol. 8:1]. Are not the oracles of this prophecy proven for us in this month, when a word from the royal throne— that is, the Word and Son of God—has entered the doomed land—that is, the mortal members and night of the flesh? Moreover, because he said "and when the silent calm contained all things," I believe he wanted to show that all were mute before they knew and perceived the Word of God.

We know therefore that the sacrament of this mystery is completed in the tenth month—that is, on the three-hundredth day—when we are to imitate the groans of the holy Mary as she labors, so that just as within the concealed matrix of the womb, so within the private cell of the monastery, something may take shape in us that advances salvation, and in the tenth month a new work may appear from our fruits, at which the world may wonder. For if that incorrupt and holy Mary did not pour forth the hope of her salvation without groans and sighs, how do you think that we, whom the serpent's counsels have deceived, must strive so that we may be capable of imitating some such thing [cf. Gen. 3:16, 1 Tim. 2:14–15]? But perhaps you may say: "Why do you trick me with the promise of a vain hope? Virgins alone are allowed to give birth to Christ." Truly, I am not willing for you to enclose the grace of God within the boundaries of one person. For consider where the apostle says to sinners and transgressors, "Until Christ may be formed in you" [Gal. 4:19].

But remember that holy Mary, when she performed this labor, desired an especially private and solitary place: no one is said to have been her attendant, no one her companion; even if blessed Joseph offered the companionship that was his duty, nevertheless what may be believed except that he was absent during the groans of her laboring? Moreover, judge from this how the one who desires to give birth to Christ ought to choose a private and quiet place, since even he who was the preacher of Christ's coming is said to have announced these things only in the desert. Perhaps you despair of salvation because in these regions there is no desert. But remember that it [this region] is akin to Egypt; and when you begin to dwell not far from the society of human beings in the retirement of a monastery, what may you be said to be, if not near Egypt in the desert?

Therefore, if you please, let the ark of your body stay fixed in the flood of the stormy age in the tenth month—that is, do not go out in public; and thus close the door that is made from the side of the ark [Gen. 6:16]—that is, the entrances or exits of your ears—lest some droplet of the worldly tales, which are like water running in different directions, should reach the inner chambers of your heart, and soon you should have to cry out, "The waters have entered my soul" [Ps. 69:2]. And thus let the inundation of the waters cease for you who toil—that is, let the flow of clamoring and disparaging words be dried up. Then there will be revealed to you the peaks of mountains [Gen. 8:5]— that is, of the opposing virtues—covered by the waters; that is, strength, al- though overwhelmed by the crowd, will be revealed. When you were among the waves—that is, when you were borne by human sociality—you were un- able to contemplate these things. For the peaks of the mountains lie concealed from us as long as our ark is set squarely—that is, borne by the elemental formation of the flesh—among the waters—that is, among the crowds; when indeed it begins to settle—that is, to repose in retirement and solitude—then, as the waves of idle tales dry up, the dominions of total evil cannot lie concealed. Or, considered otherwise, you yourself are the peak of the mountain, which you cannot surmount so long as you converse and live among people. And do not let the retirements of solitude terrify you, for your inner person will have with him his spouse, concerning whom Solomon says, "I decided to take her to me in marriage" [Wisd. of Sol. 8:9]. You will also have sons with their wives—that is, the fruits of good work, joined with the arts of knowledge [Gen. 7:7]. Nor will the origin of all beasts and flying things be lacking, among which you will recognize the pure and the impure [Gen. 7:8]; for just as we experience spiritual disturbances, through which we are often tempted, so the mental virtues through which we are corrected from depraved thoughts are not lacking. Nor will the very dove of the Holy Spirit be lacking for your consolation; and if sometime she may perhaps depart, on account of external concerns, nevertheless, when she does not find rest elsewhere, without doubt she will return to you with all haste, frequently bearing to you in her mouth the fruit of the Mount of Olives as well, whence our Lord ascended to heaven after his resurrection. And then you may know that, if you have done these things, the kingdom of heaven is to be bestowed upon you.

And because I know that the imitation of Solomonic work delights you, so that you may construct a temple for the Lord where he may dwell and rest, do this, so that you may complete the entire preparation of the temple in the tenth month, just as you read that he did [cf. 1 Kings 6:38]. May you have seventy thousand burden carriers and eighty thousand stone cutters [1 Kings 5:15], so that the sevenfold Spirit may bear the burdens of sins, and the number eight of the circumcision may give order to a formless and unperfected carnality. Let the voice of the hammer not be heard in the construction of your temple, nor let there be the blow of an axe in that transformation [1 Kings 6:7]. That is, let none of these hammerers approach you; by making harsh and disparaging remarks, they are accustomed to strike the patience of their neighbors as they would a stationary anvil, and then, by making noise with many tales, like hammers, they break into the silence of the sacred resting place. Indeed the very sound of words delights the ears of a restless person; but you, a woman who is proceeding elsewhere, should despise such things. Nor let the axe be heard—that is, an evil tongue—that habitually prepares a trap for its neighbor; for "upon whom shall the Lord rest, if not on the one who is humble and calm?" [Isa. 66:2].

And if by chance it is hard to grasp a work of unfamiliar habit, and your spirit desires to be engaged in its customary social interactions, let the blessed Daniel, "man of desires" [Dan. 10:11], come to mind as an aid; so that just as he deserved this name because of the virtue of his deed, so we might merit being—and being called—"powerful men" in respect to all our desires and pleasures. For just as a woman obedient to her husband is said to be subjugated and subjected to him [cf. Eph. 5:22; Col. 3:18], so also when we know that we have subdued our own wives—that is, our desires—what do we acknowledge that we are, if not men, or husbands, of desires? And just as he is described as praying and fasting for three weeks between the tenth and the eleventh visions [cf. Dan. 10:2ff.], so let us unite prayer with fasting at the conjunction of the tenth and eleventh months; not only so that we may cure our brothers' bondage—that is, our body's members—but also so that through the announcement of the angel—that is, the revelation of the spirit—the secrets of the future may be revealed to us.

Let the blessed Joseph be born at the end of the tenth month—that is, after the tenth patriarch [cf. Gen. 30:22–24]—because "Christ is the end of the law for justice" [Rom. 10:4], on the grounds, however, that he is not the eleventh, but the first from the tenth [January]. And although our own Joseph, who is "made under the law" [Gal. 4:4], made from flesh, arises within the tenth month, nevertheless let the eastern magi—that is, the understanding of our mind—find him in the eleventh; now they are not restrained by the chain of the law, but just like the sons of Abraham, beholding the stars of heaven in the night—that is, closely studying the testimonies in the obscure tales of the books of prophecy—they recognize the seed of the promised blessing. And between the tenth, Haggai, and the eleventh, Zechariah, let the fabric of the destroyed temple be restored, and the bondage of the Israelite people be ended; and just as in the eleventh month Zechariah was found [cf. Zech. 1:7]—because he himself is found to be the eleventh [book of the minor prophets]— let us deserve to find our Jesus placed in the manger of prophecy itself and wrapped in dirty rags, as it were [Zech. 3:3]—that is, with the obscurity of letters. For where, if not in the memory, could the Word of God be disclosed, as well as guarded faithfully, and, when it is seasonable, made manifest? For the blessed Zechariah himself signifies "memory." Therefore let there be born in the tenth number—that is, the Old Testament—the blessed name, Jesus [Joshua: cf. Zech. 3:3], and in the eleventh—that is, in the New—let him be manifested and made known. The day of Epiphany itself is said to mean "manifestation" in Latin. Let Ezra—that is, the memory of the scriptures [cf. 2 Esd. 14:40]—labor in this month, so that, with the approach of the eleventh month, to which he, who is called the "door" [ianua] in the gospel, gives his name, no woman coming from foreign stock [cf. 1 Esd. 9ff.]—that is, gentile faithlessness and doubt—may be found in the Israelite people; so that, like Gideon's companions [Judges 7:6], we may spend the three-hundredth day not bending the knee to Baal [1 Kings 19:18; Rom. 11:4], but that, like the Israelite soldiers, serving for three weeks in fasts and prayers, we might through a careful investigation arrive at the knowledge of the very cherubim of the Lord, who is contained in this number [cf. Ps. 80:1]. Let there rise in our hearts the true morning star in this time of the month, whereby the concealed poisons of all serpents are made sluggish in their caves, whereby the cold of continence dulls the bud of all trees—that is, the charms of wanton flesh—so that we can say, "Who survives before the face of his cold?" [cf. Ps. 147:17]. And when our visible aspects are infertile, then let our invisible aspects give birth; and let the solemn rite, which the world has introduced publicly between the two adjacent festivals of holy days, be abolished, and, just as when the two columns—that is, the end and beginning of the gentile year—have been pulled down by the Nazarite man, let the whole crowd that has gathered for dissipation die [cf. Judg. 16:29ff.].

"Let your flight not be in winter or on the Sabbath" [Matt. 24:20]. For what is flight if not the vice of running about and wandering? For while we dread the disparagements of tongues and the people of this age, we flee the blessed calm of a more attentive life. Moreover, you will find without any trouble that the tenth month is called the month of the Sabbath in the scriptures, whether in the prophecy of the blessed Zechariah, where the first speech of the Lord is directed to him [Zech. 1:7], or in Maccabees, where Simeon is said to have been killed [1 Macc. 16:14]. Nor is it without reason that it is called the month of the Sabbath, in which the repose of our salvation is revealed to us: while, as we said above, no other besides she who shall be giving birth to the male may be found in the refuge of the monastery, so that there may be nothing else besides the manger, which is an analogy, in which our true food—that is, the word of God—is wrapped in rags—that is, rolled in the leaves of parchment. Let even Joseph himself accept being separated for this time without difficulty: for as a reward for the separation of a few days' abstinence, sadness will give birth to the fruit of doubled joy. And if someone perhaps should object, saying that what the ordinances of the elders do not teach ought not be done, let him hear that in Maccabees in the very month in which, Simeon, the last, is said to have been killed [1 Macc. 16:14], the entire generation of fathers and priests, along with their observances, came to an end, so that we may understand that we are not to be deterred from the observance of a novel custom, either by the precedent of law or by the teaching of the fathers; and let him understand that, for Simeon himself, the impulse to wander through the cities caused his death—he who would not have been vulnerable at all to the plots of his enemies if in this month he had kept to the solitude of his own property.

And since I have been presumptuous, I beg your pardon, if perchance I have been making much out of little while I have been speaking to you: remember that I have offered the offspring of the she-ass, whence I have been hesitant to speak. And if your benevolence shall have accepted this gift in place of the sheep, I give thanks; but if in truth it cannot be redeemed, I am not terribly afraid, for, because Christ was born according to the flesh, an ass was also needed to serve in the passion, since "God chooses what is the world's foolishness" [1 Cor. 1:27]. He will attribute what I have presumed to say concerning such lofty matters to your praying and not just to my folly.

Bibliography

Burrus, Virginia. 1994. "Word and Flesh: The Bodies and Sexuality of Ascetic Women in Christian Antiquity." *Journal of Feminist Studies in Religion* 10, 27–51.

————. 1995. *The Making of a Heretic: Gender, Authority and the Priscillianist Controversy.* Berkeley and Los Angeles: University of California Press.

Cooper, Kate. 1996. *The Virgin and the Bride: Idealized Womanhood in Late Antiquity.* Cambridge: Harvard University Press.

Markus, Robert. 1990. *The End of Ancient Christianity.* Cambridge: Cambridge University Press.

Morin, G. 1928. "Pages inédites de deux pseudo-Jérômes des environs de l'an 400." *Revue Bénédictine* 40, 289–318.

Salzman, Michele. 1990. *On Roman Time: The Codex-Calendar of 354 and the Rhythms of Urban Life in Late Antiquity.* Berkeley and Los Angeles: University of California Press.

Talley, Thomas J. 1986. *The Origins of the Liturgical Year.* New York: Pueblo.

Thiébaux, Marcelle, trans. 1987. *The Writings of Medieval Women.* New York: Garland.

— 28 —

Amuletic Invocations of Christ for Health and Fortune

David Frankfurter

The following four texts, inscribed in varying levels of Greek, in different media, and in different parts of the Late Antique Christian world, show the ways that ordinary Christians made use of the new god Christ and his stories and attributes to negotiate the misfortunes and hopes of life.

Text A, a papyrus amulet from fifth/sixth-century Egypt, seeks to heal a woman from illness through allusion to the healing acts of Christ and the intercession of the Virgin Mary. Text B, another amulet from the fifth-century Egyptian city of Oxyrhynchus, renders Christ as a pursuer of demons—the "God of the sheep-baths" dedicated to the alleviation of ills. Text C, from fifth/sixth-century Sicily, was inscribed on limestone to invoke Christ's fructifying powers for the benefit of a vineyard. Text D, a silver amulet from third/fourth-century Pisidia in Asia Minor, protects a man from demonic attack by invoking the combined powers of "the right hand of God and the blood of Christ and all his angels and Church."

Although the fourth and subsequent centuries saw ecclesiastical authorities making various degrees of effort to define and root out "magic" in Christendom, their focus tended to be ritual acts used in secret or ostensibly subversive circumstances (see Brown 1970; Kippenberg 1997). The preparation of amulets, meanwhile, became among the dominant functions of Christian shrines, holy men, and ecclesiastical scribes throughout the Roman empire. In this way the authority and efficacy of Christian "power" spread far and wide, while at the same time local peoples could find practical benefits in the new institution. There is no evidence that these texts, or any of their analogues in the various amulet collections or ritual manuals from around the Late Antique world, were composed in secret, or subversively, or with an awareness that they might involve a "magic" separate from the Christian religion (see, on Gaul: Flint 1991; on Britain: Jolly 1996; on Egypt: Meyer and Smith 1994, Frankfurter 1998, 214–17, 257–64, 267–72; on the Mediterranean world in general: Vikan 1984).

Indeed, to the extent that Christian evangelists actually proffered the Church as a panacea for misfortune and a bulwark against demons, these texts may provide a glimpse of Late Antique ecclesiastical practice as important as that offered in sermons. Where text B, for example, was commissioned to combat an illness-demon in particular, and thus was found "tightly folded and tied with a string" (Preisendanz 1973/74, II:212), text D seems to have been presented as part of an exorcism conducted in the baptismal liturgy. The silver lamella, rolled into a small tube to be worn around the neck, would seal the baptism and protect the initiate henceforth from all manner of evil powers (see Kotansky 1994, 174–80; 1995). The wording of texts A and B suggests the work of ecclesiastical scribes rather than of freelance wizards, with references to the "holy Gospels" and the intercession of the Theotokos, a quotation from the prologue of the Gospel of John, scriptural titles for Christ, and even the list of local saints from the region of Oxyrhynchus. Such features of the spells reflect an earnest attempt to remain orthodox while calling the Christian pantheon into service for human affliction.

But this endeavor to keep the wording of spells based in official tradition in no way diminishes the concrete efficacy—the magic—attributed in these texts to Christ's mythical accomplishments. The ritual pattern of recounting a mythical event in order to reconcile a similar situation in the here-and-now has great antiquity in the Mediterranean world. Scholars have labeled the form *historiola*: a brief story recounted in a ritual context—often radically abbreviated—in order to transfer supernatural power from a mythical dimension, in which mythical figures complete an action or resolve a problem, to a human dimension where action is open-ended or a similar problem lies unresolved. As a creative form of synthesis between official symbols and everyday life through the medium of narrative, the *historiola* involves a creative analogizing—from the condition of the client to the endlessly malleable heroes and narratives of the Christian tradition (see Frankfurter 1995). Whether composed by monk, ecclesiastical scribe, or stone-carver, *historiolae* reflect the practical life of religious lore.

Text C is reprinted with permission from an article by D. R. Jordan in *Greek, Roman, and Byzantine Studies* 25 (1984).

TEXT A

Florence, Istituto Papirologico "G. Vitelli," inv. 365,
ed. Preisendanz 1973/74, II:227 (= *Papyri Graecae Magicae* P18)

✝ Holy Holy Holy Lord

. . .

. . . and the one who healed again, who raised Lazarus from the dead already on the fourth day, who healed Peter's mother-in-law, who also performed many untold healings—beyond what are recounted in the holy Gospels, heal the bearer of this divine amulet from the illness crushing her, by prayers and intercession of the ever-virgin Mother, the Theotokos, and all . . .

TEXT B

Papyrus Oxyrhynchus VIII.1151, ed. Preisendanz
1973/74, II:212–13 (= *Papyri Graecae Magicae* P5b)

✝ Flee, polluting spirit! Christ pursues you! The Son of God seizes you—and the holy spirit! O God of the sheep-baths, deliver your servant Joannia, whom Anastasia bore—also known as Euphemia—from every evil!

✝ "In the beginning was the Word, and the Word was with God and the Word was God. All things came into being through him, and without him not one thing came into being." [John 1:1–3]

Lord ✝ Christ, Son and Word of the living God, who heals every sickness and every weakness, also heal and watch over your servant Joannia, whom Anastasia bore—also known as Euphemia—and chase away and banish from her every fever and every kind of chill—daily, tertian, quartian—and every evil. Implore, through the intercession of our mistress the *Theotokos,* and of the esteemed archangels, and of the holy and esteemed apostle and evangelist and theologian John, and of Saint Serenus and Saint Philoxenus and Saint Victor and Saint Justus and all the saints, for your name, Lord God, I have invoked: the miraculous and highly revered (name), (the name) that terrifies enemies. Amen! ✝

TEXT C

Inscribed Christian Prayer, Sicily, ed. Jordan 1984, 298

Amēl . . . Christ, who has multiplied stars in the sky and the water in the sea, multiply also the fruits in the vineyard of Paul.

TEXT D

Silver lamella, Antiochia Caesarea, Pisidia,
ed. Kotansky 1994, 169–80 (= Papyrologica Colonensia 22.35)

Against spirits: PHŌ ATHPHRO! Leave Basileios! By the right hand of God and the blood of Christ and all his angels and Church!

Bibliography

Brown, Peter. 1970. "Sorcery, Demons, and the Rise of Christianity from Late Antiquity into the Middle Ages." In *Witchcraft Confessions and Accusations,* ed. Mary Douglas, 17–45. London and New York: Tavistock.

Flint, Valerie I. J. 1991. *The Rise of Magic in Early Medieval Europe.* Princeton: Princeton University Press.

Frankfurter, David. 1995. "Narrating Power: The Theory and Practice of the Magical *Historiola* in Ritual Spells." In *Ancient Magic and Ritual Power,* ed. Marvin Meyer and Paul Mirecki, 451–70. Religions of the Graeco-Roman World 129. Leiden: E. J. Brill.

———. 1998. *Religion in Roman Egypt: Assimilation and Resistance.* Princeton: Princeton University Press.

Jolly, Karen Louise. 1996. *Popular Religion in Late Saxon England: Elf Charms in Context.* Chapel Hill and London: University of North Carolina Press.

Jordan, D. R. 1984. "Two Christian Prayers from Southeastern Sicily." *Greek, Roman, and Byzantine Studies* 25, 3: 297–302.

Kippenberg, Hans G. 1997. "Magic in Roman Civil Discourse: Why Rituals Could Be Illegal." In *Envisioning Magic: A Princeton Seminar and Symposium,* ed. Peter Schäfer and Hans G. Kippenberg, 137–63. Leiden: E. J. Brill.

Kotansky, Roy. 1994. *Greek Magical Amulets: The Inscribed Gold, Silver, Copper, and Bronze Lamellae, Part 1: Published Texts of Known Provenance.* Papyrologica Coloniensia 22.1. Opladen: Westdeutscher Verlag.

———. 1995. "Greek Exorcistic Amulets." In *Ancient Magic and Ritual Power,* ed. Marvin Meyer and Paul Mirecki, 243–77. Religions of the Graeco-Roman World 129. Leiden: E. J. Brill.

Meyer, Marvin, and Richard Smith, eds. 1994. *Ancient Christian Magic: Coptic Texts of Ritual Power.* San Francisco: Harper.

Preisendanz, Karl. 1973–1974. *Papyri Graecae Magicae: Die griechischen Zauberpapyri.* 2d ed. 2 vols., ed. Albert Henrichs. Stuttgart: Teubner.

Vikan, Gary. 1984. "Art, Medicine, and Magic in Early Byzantium." *Dumbarton Oaks Papers* 38: 65–86.

Singing Divine Praises: Hymnody

— 29 —

The Hymns of Ambrose

Carl P. E. Springer

Ambrose, bishop of Milan from 374–97 C.E., was the most successful Latin Christian hymn writer in Late Antiquity. Ambrose's hymns are unlike those of his early contemporary, Hilary of Poitiers, who introduced the congregations in Gaul to hymn singing after his return from exile in 360, but whose compositions were long and somewhat obscure. Ambrose's hymns differ from those of his own protégé, Augustine, who wrote a *Psalmus contra partem Donati* in trochaic tetrameters for his flock in north Africa. Ambrose composed hymns that were well received not only in his own lifetime but long thereafter. Their use spread rapidly from Milan to other Latin-speaking congregations and Ambrose's success inspired a host of later imitators to write hymns in the same manner. Eventually "Ambrosian" became a term that was used to describe any hymn written in iambic dimeter quatrains, no matter who the author (Walpole 1922, 18).

Perhaps the single greatest advantage of Ambrose's hymns was the fact that everyone could sing them, a quality that Ambrose himself (*Sermo contra Auxentium,* 34) called "a great charm" (*grande carmen*). The Ambrosian hymn was simple, short, and memorable. These compositions were clearly not intended for the private delectation of religious literati or for the solo performance of a trained virtuoso, but rather for group singing in a liturgical context. Even though not so ambitious as the longer hymns of Hilary and Augustine's *Psalmus* or as sophisticated as the later literary masterpieces of Prudentius's *Cathemerinon*, these tersely written hymns had their own powerful effect on Ambrose's contemporaries (see, for example, Augustine's emotional reactions as recounted in *Confessions* 9.6). Ambrose's hymns continued to be sung in Latin all over western Europe throughout the Middle Ages and many of them were incorporated into the liturgy.

Among Ambrose's most important contributions to Christian Latin hymnody was the introduction of the practice of antiphony to the churches in the West. In the early spring of 386, during the siege of the Portian basilica in Milan by the troops of Valentinian II (see Augustine's *Confessions* 9.7), Ambrose adopted the practice common in the East of having the congregation sing hymns antiphonally.

Instead of simply listening in silence to a choir or soloist, or singing responsively with a worship leader, the congregation divided into two groups and sang hymns alternately. In this instance, as in so many other areas of artistic expression, form followed function. As students of the Ambrosian hymn have frequently noted, every hymn has an even number of stanzas and every stanza, furthermore, is a self-contained unit, with little or no enjambment between stanzas. The potential benefits for antiphonal singing are obvious. The first stanza was apparently intended to be sung by one half of the congregation, the second stanza by the other half, the third stanza by the first half, and so on. It is probably no accident, then, that most Ambrosian hymns can also be broken down into four smaller structural units, consisting of two stanzas each. Stanzas 1 and 2 form a unit of thought, as do 3 and 4, 5 and 6, and 7 and 8.

What has not been so widely observed, however, is how thoroughly the principle of antiphony affects both the structure and meaning of the Ambrosian hymn. If we examine, for example, the first two stanzas of the first hymn translated below, *Veni redemptor gentium,* it is apparent at once that they are alike in a number of respects. Both begin with a command, as the author calls on God to manifest himself. In fact, the imperative mood dominates in these two stanzas as it does nowhere else in the hymn; there are six commands in only eight lines. Especially striking is Ambrose's repetition of the exhortation "come" (*veni*), a command that helps to link the two stanzas even more closely; the first ends with "*veni,*" while the second begins with the same word. When sung antiphonally such a repetition must have been quite dramatic, as the echo of the first *veni* sung by one half of the congregation would still have been reverberating in the church when the second half of the congregation began the second stanza by singing the very same word. Despite the compelling parallels between the two stanzas, however, there are also some obvious differences. The second group of singers does not simply repeat what the first half of the congregation has just sung. The first stanza uses language and imagery rooted in the Old Testament, taken almost verbatim from Psalm 80:1ff. Ambrose prays in the first stanza to the God who is the ruler of Israel, the powerful "Lord God of hosts" of the Old Testament who sits above the cherubim. He is to appear not to the entire world, but to a single Israelite tribe, Ephraem. In the second stanza, by contrast, the request for divine manifestation is addressed to the redeemer of all the nations, not just Israel. The whole world will wonder now, not at the power of God, but rather at his lowliness (cf. Phil. 2:6–11). The divine has become mortal, a New Testament emphasis. God is no longer above the cherubim, but has descended to earth to be born as a baby. The contrast as well as the connection between the Old and New Testament is reflected in the antiphonal structure of the two stanzas.

The pattern established in the first two stanzas continues throughout the hymn as the double-stanza units trace a powerfully simple line of thought that gathers momentum over the course of this short hymn's thirty-two lines. Each pair of stanzas presents us with a new idea and each pair (with the exception, of course, of the first) builds on the preceding pair of stanzas as the hymn moves from the invocation, to the fact of the incarnation, to the salvific life of Christ, and finally to the application to the believer's faith-life. At the same time, the individual stanzas that make up each paired unit present contrasting sub-points of view. The structure of the hymn provides, therefore, a sense not only of direction and movement from beginning to end, but also of antithesis and balance within that larger development. It is clear that this hymn possesses the qualities of *"Einfalt"* (Simplicity) and "simplicity" so prized by nineteenth-century critics of the Ambrosian hymn, but it would be unfortunate if the attention paid to these readily recognizable features of *Veni redemptor gentium* would lead us to overlook the hymn's rather complex and artfully constructed literary structure.

Another one of the most important, but often overlooked, structural features of Ambrose's hymns is the fixed number of stanzas (eight) in each hymn. Before the fourth century we find very few examples in Latin verse of compositions of set rather than indeterminate length. By contrast, the restriction of Ambrose's hymns to eight stanzas is so characteristic that it is used as one of the internal criteria to distinguish the hymns that Ambrose is likely to have written himself from those attributed to him by later generations.

It does indeed seem likely that Ambrose's decision to use eight stanzas was more than arbitrary. Not only does this format lend itself readily to the kind of binary composition suited for antiphonal singing, but the number eight itself would certainly have had a profound spiritual significance for the bishop of Milan and his flock. For early Christians, the cube of two assumed special importance as a symbol of *stabilitas, plenitudo,* and *perfectio.* As the number that represents Sunday, the "eighth" day of the week, the day when Jesus rose from the dead, eight symbolized the entire plan and promise of salvation history, as Ambrose himself observes (see *CSEL* 64, 347). That eight souls were preserved from the flood in the ark (cf. 1 Pet. 3:20–21 and 2 Pet. 2:5) or that Jesus was circumcised on the eighth day after his birth seemed more than mere coincidence to early Christians, and the number came to be connected especially with the ideas of baptism, the new life of faith, and eternal life.

This distinctive eight-stanza structure helps us to understand another specific characteristic of the Ambrosian hymn; its unemphatic sense of closure. *Deus creator omnium* comes the closest of Ambrose's hymns to concluding with what could be called a doxology, although it is hardly formulaic. More typical of Ambrose's practice is the last stanza of *Agnes beatae virginis* or the last stanza of *Veni redemptor gentium.* In neither of these hymns do we find the Trinitarian formulae or expressions of praise and thanksgiving so commonly associated with the final stanzas of many later hymns (e.g. *Veni creator Spiritus*). While the lack of a doxology was certainly felt (and often supplied) in the later tradition, it may have been clearer to Ambrose himself and his contemporaries that the eight-stanza structure itself has the same kind of internal dynamic that also occurs in alphabetic hymns. The first stanza of Sedulius's *A solis ortus cardine,* for instance, begins with A, while the last begins with Z, so the first letter of the last stanza is, in and of itself, a clear indication that we have reached the end of the hymn (Springer 1987, 74). No other formal signal of closure is necessary. So too, when early Christians sang the last line of the eighth stanza of an Ambrosian hymn, the very number of stanzas that they had sung—regardless of whether the last stanza contained a doxologic element—conveyed powerfully the sense of conclusion.

We may apply this consideration to the second of the hymns translated below, one that has not always been considered one of Ambrose's stellar (or even genuine) compositions, *Inluminans altissimus*. While it must certainly be granted that this hymn could have been more "tightly" connected and neatly concluded (the regular antiphonal structure of *Veni redemptor gentium* is noticeably absent), it should be said that there is something fitting about its "open-endedness," especially if, as seems quite possible, it was intended only to be one element of the larger liturgy, rather than a self-contained and independent literary entity. In a certain sense, for believers like Ambrose and his congregation, the activity of praising God is never actually completed on earth, but only interrupted temporarily, to be continued in the unending song of "angels, archangels, and all the company of heaven." There is an anagogical flavor to the eucharistic description of the feeding of the five thousand in the concluding stanzas of the hymn. (The eucharist itself was commonly seen by early Christians as an anticipation of the heavenly feast.) Just as this hymn begins in heaven, therefore, where the stars shine in their glory, so also, one might suggest, it ends in heaven, where believers will join in the marriage feast of the Lamb. This said, however, it also seems important that we entertain in our evaluation of this hymn the serious possibility that it does possess a degree of concinnity, a sense of unity and closure, which is determined in great measure by an eight-stanza structure that organizes and unifies its diverse elements, tying together the baptism of Jesus, his other "epiphanies," and the Eucharist with its significance for the new life of faith now miraculously possible for the believer—an eight-stanza structure whose symbolic significance was probably more transparently obvious to their first audience than it has proved to be to more recent critics.

While in no way meant to detract from the remarkable simplicity for which critics have so often (and justly) praised the hymns of Ambrose, I hope that these observations may lead to a greater appreciation of the sophisticated artistry of these hymns' poetic structures, which reflect and reinforce their theological meaning. It is this inspired artistry—united inseparably with the Ambrosian hymn's straightforward but profound message—which, I suggest, may well have helped to save these hymns from the fate of other "simple" but less thoughtfully constructed or aesthetically satisfying compositions whose banality condemned them long ago to well-deserved obscurity.

The following is based on the Latin text in Fontaine's edition and is indebted to the translations and commentary in Walpole.

Veni redemptor gentium

Pay attention, you who rule Israel,
you who sit above the cherubim;

make your appearance to Ephraem;
stir up your power and come.

Come, savior of the nations;
show them the birth of a virgin.
Let all the world marvel;
such a birth is fitting for God.

Not from human seed,
but by the mysterious Spirit
is the Word of God made flesh,
and the fruit of the womb made to blossom.

The belly of a virgin swells,
but the barrier of chastity remains intact.
The banners of her virtue gleam forth;
God is dwelling in his temple.

Let him come forth from his bridal chamber,
the royal court of chastity,
the giant of a two-fold nature;
let him swiftly enter upon his course.

His progress is from the Father;
his regress is to the Father.
His detour is all the way to hell;
his return is to the throne of God.

Equal to the eternal Father,
you gird yourself with the trophy of flesh,
strengthening the weakness of our body
with your unfailing power.

Now your crib shines
and the night exhales an unusual light.
May night never interrupt it
and may it shine with continual faith!

Inluminans altissimus

O highest one, you who shed your light
on the spheres of the shining stars,
peace, life, light, truth,
O Jesus, listen with favor to our prayers.

Whether by your mysterious baptism
you did once on this very day

sanctify the waters of the Jordan
turned back for the third time,

or the star shining in heaven
showed the birth of the virgin
and led the magi on this day
to your manger to worship you,

or you infused jugs full of water
with the flavor of wine;
the servant drew out what he knew
he himself had not filled;

seeing the waters change color,
the rivers grow intoxicating,
he was amazed that the elements had been changed,
adapted for a different purpose.

Thus also for five thousand men,
when you divided five loaves of bread,
the food was growing in their mouth,
between their teeth, even as they ate it.

The amount of bread was increased
the more it was dispensed.
Who is there, seeing this, who will be surprised
at the never failing courses of springs?

In the hands of those who break it
the bread is poured out in plenty;
the leftovers which they had not broken
are piling up on the men.

Aeterne rerum conditor

O eternal founder of the world,
you who govern night and day
and establish the times of the seasons
to relieve our monotony,

the herald of the day now sounds,
after watching through the deep night,
a nocturnal light for wanderers,
dividing one part of night from the other.

At this sound, awakened, the morning star
releases the sky from gloom;

at this sound, every band of prowlers
abandons the way of violence;

at this sound, the sailor gathers strength
and the swelling waves of the sea subside;
at this sound, the church's Rock himself
washes away his guilt.

Let us, then, arise with vigor;
the cock arouses the slug-a-beds
and upbraids the drowsy;
the cock rebukes the unwilling.

Hope returns at the song of the cock;
health is restored to the sick;
the sword of the robber is sheathed;
confidence returns to the fallen.

O Jesus, look back at those who waver,
and correct us with your glance.
If you look back, our backslidings vanish,
and our guilt is washed away with our weeping.

Shine, O light, into our thoughts,
and shake off the sleep of the soul.
May our voices sing your praises early
and may we discharge our vows to you.

Splendor paternae gloriae

O splendor of the Father's glory,
bringing forth light from light,
light of light and source of lumination,
enlightening day of days;

O true sun, steal into our souls,
shining with eternal brightness,
and shed the ray of the Holy Spirit
into our hearts.

Let us call upon the Father, too,
the Father of eternal glory,
the Father of powerful grace,
to banish far from us slippery guilt,

to make our actions energetic,
to blunt the tooth of the malignant one,

to change harsh events for the better,
to give us grace to act well,

to direct and rule our souls
in pure and loyal bodies;
let faith burn warmly
and know nothing of the poison of deceit.

And may Christ be our food,
and our faith our drink;
let us drink joyfully
of the sober intoxication of the Spirit.

May this day pass happily!
With our chastity like the twilight,
and our faith as the noonday,
may our soul know no dusk!

The dawn proceeds on its course;
let him who is the dawn come forth entirely,
the entire Son in the Father,
and the entire Father in the word.

Deus creator omnium

O God, creator of all things,
ruler of the heavens,
clothing the day with beautiful light,
and the night with the gracious gift of sleep,

that rest might repair limbs relaxed in sleep
for the service of work,
relieve our fatigued souls,
and disperse our fretful grief;

now that the day is over
and at the beginning of night, bound to our vow,
we pay our thanks and prayers,
singing in hymns that you might help us.

You, let the depth of our heart magnify,
you, let tuneful voice celebrate,
you, let our chaste love cherish,
you, let our clear-headed mind adore:

so that when the deep darkness of night
has encompassed the day,

our faith may know no shadows
and night may be illumined with faith.

Do not let the soul sleep—
guilt knows how to sleep!
May faith, cooling the chaste,
dissipate the hot fumes of sleep.

Casting off treacherous thoughts
may our deepest heart dream of you;
nor let dread of the evil foe's craft
disturb us as we lie quiet in sleep.

We pray to Christ and the Father
and the Spirit of Christ and the Father,
one God, all powerful,
protect us as we call on you, O Trinity!

Bibliography

Sections of the introduction have been adapted and excerpted from articles on the Ambrosian hymn published by the author in 1991 and 1995. For fuller details see the bibliographical entries below.

Bernt, G. 1983. "Ambrosius von Mailand: *Hic Est Dies Verus Dei.* Ein patristischer Paschahymnus." In *Liturgie und Dichtung: Ein interdisziplinäres Kompendium* 1: 509–46. St. Ottilien: Eos Verlag.

Beyenka, M. M. 1957. "St. Augustine and the Hymns of St. Ambrose." *American Benedictine Review* 8: 121–32.

Corpus Scriptorum Ecclesiasticorum Latinorum. 1866ff. Vienna: Hoelder-Pichler-Tempsky.

Cunningham, M. P. 1955. "The Place of the Hymns of St. Ambrose in the Latin Poetic Tradition." *Studies in Philology* 52: 509ff.

Den Boeft, J. 1991. "*Vetusta Saecula Vidimus:* Ambrose's Hymn on Protasius and Gervasius." In *Eulogia: mélanges offerts à Anton A. R. Bastiaensen,* ed. G. J. M. Bartelink, A. Hilhorst, and C. H. Kneepkens, 65–75. Turnhout: Brepols.

Diehl, P. 1985. *The Medieval European Religious Lyric.* Berkeley and Los Angeles: University of California Press.

Dreves, G. M. 1893. *Aurelius Ambrosius, der Vater des Kirchengesanges: Eine hymnologische Studie.* Freiburg: Herder.

Dudden, F. H. 1935. *The Life and Times of St. Ambrose.* Oxford: Clarendon.

Fontaine, J. 1974. "L'Apport de la tradition poétique romaine à la formation de l'hymnodie latine chrétienne." *Revue des études latines* 52: 318–55.

———. 1992. *Ambroise de Milane, Hymnes, Texte établi, traduit et annoté.* Paris: Editions du cerf.

Henry, H. 1948. *The Hymns of the Breviary and Missal.* New York: Benziger Brothers.

Julian, J. 1957 [1907]. *A Dictionary of Hymnology.* Rpt. 2d rev. ed. New York: Dover.

Jullien, M.-H. 1989. "Les Sources de la tradition ancienne des hymnes attribuées à Saint Ambroise." *Revue d'histoire des textes* 19: 57ff.

Paredi, A. 1964. *Saint Ambrose: His Life and Times*. South Bend, Ind.: University of Notre Dame Press.

St. Laurent, G. E. 1968. "St. Ambrose's Contribution to Latin Liturgical Hymnography." Ph.D. dissertation, Catholic University of America.

Simonetti, M. 1952. "Studi sull'innologia popolare cristiana dei primi secoli." *Atti della Accademia Nazionale dei Lincei. Memorie della classe di scienze morali, storiche, e filologiche*, Ser. 8, 4.6: 341–485.

Springer, C. P. E. 1985. "The Artistry of Augustine's Psalmus contra Partem Donati." *Augustinian Studies* 16: 65–74.

———. 1987. "Sedulius' *A Solis Ortus Cardine:* The Hymn and Its Tradition." *Ephemerides Liturgicae* 101: 69–75.

———. 1991. "Ambrose's *Veni Redemptor Gentium:* The Aesthetics of Antiphony." *Jahrbuch für Antike und Christentum* 34: 76–87.

———. 1995. "The Concinnity of Ambrose's *Illuminans Altissimus*." In *Panchaia: Festschrift für Professor Klaus Thraede*, 228–37. Münster: Aschendorffsche Verlagsbuchhandlung.

Steier, A. 1903. "Untersuchungen über die Echtheit der Hymnen des Ambrosius." *Jahrbücher für klassische Philologie*, Supplbd. 28: 549–662.

Szövérffy, J. 1964. *Die Annalen der lateinischen Hymnendichtung. Ein Handbuch*. Berlin: E. Schmidt.

———. 1989. *Latin Hymns*. Turnhout: Brepols.

Thraede, K. 1990. "Und alsbald krähte der Hahn—Der Morgenhymnus des Ambrosius von Mailand." In Thraede, *Hauptwerke der Literatur* 17: 35–47. Regensburg: Regensburg University Press.

Trench, R. 1874. *Sacred Latin Poetry*. 3d ed. London: Macmillan.

Walpole, A. S. 1922. *Early Latin Hymns with Introduction and Notes*. Cambridge: Cambridge University Press.

—30—

Hymns to Mary, the Mother of God,
the Theotokos

Vasiliki Limberis

Proclus of Constantinople

Proclus of Constantinople (388–446 C.E.) is one of the least studied but most important bishops of the Christian Church. There are three reasons for this: he was instrumental in the institutional development of the cult of the Theotokos; he strengthened and extended the power of the See of Constantinople; and his contributions to the elaborations of liturgical hymnography were immense. In fact, he has the great accomplishment of being the author of the *Trisagion* (Thrice-Holy) Hymn. The church historian, Socrates (ca. 380–450), mentions that Proclus studied rhetoric and was an excellent orator (*Church History* 7.28.41.43).

Proclus lived during the tumultuous period of the early fifth century. In 428, because of political machinations, he was unable to assume his position in Cyzicus, where he was the bishop. Consequently he lived in his natal city, Constantinople. There he became a theological and political confidant of Empress Pulcheria, who was more powerful than her brother, Emperor Theodosius II. Through their alliance and her persuasion, not only did he write panegyrics to the Empress praising her for her devotion to the faith, he began preaching rousing sermons extolling Jesus' mother, the holy Virgin Mary, the Theotokos (God-bearer). Nestorius, the bishop of Constantinople, was no friend of Pulcheria; he soon began preaching rival sermons both against the Empress and against the use of the title "Theotokos" for the Virgin Mary.

On December 26, 428, at Pulcheria's request for the occasion of her Virginity Festival, Proclus delivered a famous sermon in praise of Mary Theotokos and all dedicated virgins. Proclus went on to write several Marian hymns, based on encomiastic panegyric, that are embedded in larger sermons. Although he makes liberal use of Biblical imagery, Proclus is unique among Marian hymnographers for two reasons. First, he reinterprets Biblical events in such a way that Mary's submission to the divine conception redeems all the Biblical events in which women have had detrimental roles, such as those featuring Eve, Delilah, and Jezebel. Second, he uses verbal imagery reminiscent of pagan hymns to Olympian goddesses, blending them into the identity of Mary Theotokos. Rather than eliciting Mary's qualities of humility and long-suffering, Proclus's hymns create a Mary who is beneficent, wise, and—above all—powerful.

Proclus's hymns are the earliest example of high Mariology in the Church. Only later hymns of the ninth through twelfth centuries elaborate more fully on the exuberant language. His most famous hymns were written and delivered during the period before he became bishop of Constantinople, between the deposition of Nestorius and the Council of Ephesus, when Maximian was bishop. Proclus assumed the episcopal office of Constantinople in 434. During his tenure, he extended the geographical area of Constantinople's authority. The See would now rule the area from Cappadocia to Ilyricum.

Proclus's hymns to the Virgin display all the characteristics of ceremonial, liturgical reenactment. He was one of the earliest to incorporate the repetition of the acclamations. Through the use of lofty praise, startling metaphors, and repetitions of acclamation used as refrain, the congregation could easily participate in the drama. Because Proclus was bishop of the capital during the time when the See's power and influence were eclipsing the ecclesiastical importance of both Alexandria and Ephesus, encomiastic hymns to the Theotokos, brimming with high Mariology, spread all over the Levant. We see this in the hymns of Chrysippus of Jerusalem and Basil of Seleucia.

These translations are based on the texts found in the *Patrologia Graeca.*

Hymn to the Theotokos
From "Oration to the Theotokos," Patrologia Graeca 65.680–81

For this reason we now call the Holy Virgin Mary, "Theotokos,"
She is the unstained treasure of virginity, the expression of paradise of
   the second Adam,
She is the workshop of the union of the natures, the festival of the
   covenant of salvation.
She is the bridal chamber in which the Logos wedded the flesh,
She is the living bramble bush of nature that the fire of divine birth
   pangs did not consume.
She is truly the delicate cloud, the producer of His body, above the
   Cherubim,
The purest fleece of the heavenly rain from which the shepherd clothed
   the sheep.
Mary, the servant and mother, the Virgin and heaven, the only bridge
   from God to humanity,

She is the awe-inspiring loom of the divine economy on which the
  garment of unity was woven, inexpressibly,
The weaver of which is the Holy Spirit, the overshadowing power from
  above, the woolworker.

Hymn to the Theotokos
From Chrysostom spuria Patrologia Graeca 61.737–38

Hail, full of grace, untilled soil of heavenly grain,
Hail, full of grace, undeceitful virgin mother of the true vine,
Hail, full of grace, unfailing net of the immutable Godhead,
Hail, full of grace, wide open field of the undivided nature,
Hail, full of grace, unstained bearer, bride of the widowed world.
Hail, full of grace, you who weaves without hands the crown for
  creation,
Hail, full of grace, you are the return for those who fled the world,
Hail, full of grace, you are the undepletable treasury of the starving
  world,
Hail, full of grace, the joy from you, holy Virgin, is infinite,
Hail, full of grace, you are adorned with virtues, bearing light, and
  inextinguishable light brighter than the sun,
Hail, full of grace, you are the bait of the eager intellect,
Hail, full of grace, O coffer, noetic one of glory,
Hail, full of grace, golden jar containing the heavenly manna,
Hail, full of grace, you always replenish the sweet drink of the ever-
  flowing spring for the thirsty,
Hail, full of grace, you contain the noetic sea and the heavenly pearl,
  Christ,
Hail, full of grace, O bright heaven, you are the one who contains God,
  who is undivided and unconfined.
Hail, full of grace, pillar of cloud, containing God who guided Israel in
  the desert.
What do I say and what will I speak?
How can I bless the utter glory?
That, except for God alone, you are higher than all.

Chrysippus of Jerusalem

Little is known of the life of Chrysippus. He was born in Cappadocia around 395.
Along with his two brothers, Cosmas and Gabriel, he traveled to Palestine, seeking
out the monastic life. There they founded what eventually became known as the
famous *lavra* (a loose association of hermits living in the same place) of St. Eu-

thymius. In 466 the great honor of becoming the *stavrophylax* (the keeper of the cross) at the Church of the Holy Sepulchre in Jerusalem was bestowed upon him.

Four of his panegyrics survive, but he is most famous for the "Oration to the Theotokos." Chrysippus's style, images, and florid language reflect his Chalcedonian Christology and his central role in helping to spread the cult of the Theotokos. This excerpted hymn gives an example of the encomiastic hymn as the ideal conveyance for Mariological veneration.

Hymn to the Theotokos
From the "Ninth Oration to the Theotokos," Patrologia Orientalis *19.218–19*

And the voice of the Archangel still delineates the borders of salvation.
    It is now the time for us to add praises to the archangel's prediction:
Hail, thus always,
Hail, full of grace,
Hail, one to whom by chance befell the motherhood of nature, and
    who is wider than the heavens themselves.
Even if indeed the heavens were unable to contain him, you [God]
    made space for him through her.
Hail, the spring of light that enlightens every person.
Hail, the eastern source of the sun that is ever unable to set.
Hail, dispenser of life,
Hail, the garden of the Father,
Hail, the field of all the fragrance of the Spirit,
Hail, the root of all goodness,
Hail, the stone of the pearl, surpassing all other honor.
Hail, vine, beautifully clustered,
Hail, cloud full of rain that waters the souls of the saints,
Hail, cistern ever filled with the water of life,
Hail, bramble bush, burning with noetic fire, yet never consumed,
Hail, closed gate, open only to the king,
Hail, mountain, whence the cornerstone is severed without hands.

Basil of Seleucia

What one can learn of Basil of Seleucia's life is rather sketchy. He served as bishop of Seleucia in Isauria from 440 to 448. He too was caught in the drama of the Nestorian controversy. Between the councils of Ephesus and Chalcedon, he first sided with the Monophysites, but changed his allegiance at the Robber Council in 449. After Chalcedon he wrote a commentary on the *Formula of Union* of 433, authored by Cyril of Alexandria.

Fifty homilies of his survive, although some scholars dispute whether Basil authored all of them. B. Marx is one who claims that the "Hymn to the Virgin" from the Thirty-ninth Oration (included here) belongs to Proclus, but his thesis has not convinced the majority of scholars. Basil's hymns are less flowery than Proclus's, but they still bear witness to the spread of the style of encomiastic panegyric throughout the Eastern Empire. In addition, they reflect the growth of the cult of the Theotokos, sanctioned by the bishops, incorporated into the liturgical cycle of the year.

Hymn to the Theotokos
From "Thirty-ninth Oration on the Annunciation of the all-holy Theotokos,"
Patrologia Graeca 85.441–44.

O Virginity, through whom the angels rightly are glorified, while they just now diverted our own race to be sent out for the service of humanity, and Gabriel rejoiced, believing the message of the divine conception.
Wherefore, from joy and grace of the appellation, the angel begins:
Hail, full of grace, the Lord is with you.
Hail, full of grace, brightness fills your face.
Out of you all is born, and the ancient curse of all is stopped, and the rule of death is destroyed, and hope of the resurrection is presented to all.
Hail, full of grace, O unfading flower of pure paradise, whence the tree of life grows and shoots forth the fruit of salvation for everyone, whence comes the spring of the four mouths of the Gospel.
It will flow like the rivers of compassion for the faithful.
Hail, full of grace, you are the mediator between God and humanity, in order to destroy the partition of hate, and to unite the earthly with the heavenly.

Bibliography

Abineau, Michel. 1985. "Emprunts de Proclus de Constantinople à Cyrille d'Alexandrie, dans son Homélie XXII In illud: 'Et postquam consummati sunt dies octo' (Lc 2:21)." In *After Chalcedon: Studies in Theology and Church History*, ed. C. Laga, J. Munitiz, and L. Van Rompay, 23–34. *Orientalia Lovaniensia analecta* 18. Leuven: Peeters.

———. 1988. *Chrysostome, Severien, Proclus, Hesychius et alii: Patristique et hagiographie grecques*. London: Variorum.

———. 1989. "Ps-Chrysostome In S Stephamun (*Patrologia Graeca* 63.933–34): Proclus de Constantinople, l'impératrice Pulchérie et saint Etienne." In *Fructus centesimus*, ed. A. Bastiaensen, 1–16. Dordrecht: Kluwer.

————. 1991. "Citations de L'Homélie de Proclus. In Nativitatem Salvatoris (CPG 5068), Dans un florilège Christologique des IVᵉ et Vᵉ siècles." *Vigiliae Christianae* 45: 209–21.

————. ed. 1972. *Les Homélies pascales.* Sources chrétiennes 187. Paris: Editions du Cerf.

Barkhuizen, J. H. 1994. "Proclus of Constantinople Homily I: A Perspective on His Christology." *Patristic and Byzantine Review* 13: 49–63.

Basil of Seleucia. *Patrologia Graeca* 85.27–444.

Caro, R. 1971. *La homiletica mariana griega. Marian Library Studies,* 3. Dayton, Ohio: University of Dayton Press.

Capelle, B. 1943. "La Fête de la Vierge à Jerusalem au Vᵉ siècle." *Le Muséon* 56: 1–33.

Chrysippus of Jerusalem. *Patrologia Graeca* 111.6705–8; *Patrologia Orientalis* 19.336–43.

Constas, N. 1995. "Weaving the Body of God: Proclus of Constantinople, the Theotokos, and the Loom of the Flesh." *Journal of Early Christian Studies* 3: 169–94.

Esbroeck, M. van. 1987. "Jalons pour l'histoire de la transmission manuscrite de l'homélie de Proclus sur la Vierge (BHG 1129) [texts in Greek, Armenian, Georgian, Ethiopic, Latin]." In *Texte und Textkritik: eine Aufsatzsammlung,* ed. J. Dummer, 149–60. Berlin: Akademie Verlag.

Galot, J. 1989. "Une Seule Personne, une seule hypostase: Origine et sens de la formule de Chalcedoine." *Gregorianum* 70: 251–76.

Hevia-Ballina, A. 1972. "Salvacion y Pascua." In *Genethliakon Isidorianum,* ed. A. Ortega and G. Andres, 267–88. Salamanca: Universidad Pontificia.

Leroy, F. 1963. "Une Homélie mariale de Proclus de Constantinople et le pseudo-Gregoire le Thaumaturge." In *Hommage à Bruno Lavagnini,* ed. A Pertusi, 357–84. Brussels: Fondation Byzantine.

————. 1967. *L'Homiletique de Proclus de Constantinople. Studia theologica* 247.

Limberis, V. 1994. *Divine Heiress: The Virgin Mary and the Creation of Christian Constantinople.* London: Routledge.

Lucchesi, E. "L'Oratio I 'De laudibus S Mariae' de Proclus de Constantinople: Version syriaque inédite [Syriac text of Sachav 220; Latin text of Proclus]." *In Memorial A-J Festugière,* Cahiers d'orientalisme 10, ed. E. Lucchesi and H. Saffrey, 187–98. Geneva: P. Cramer.

Maas, P. 1910. "Das Kontakion." *Byzantinische Zeitschrift* 285–306.

Martin, C. 1939. "Mélanges d'homiletique byzantine, I, Hesychius et Chrysippe de Jérusalem." *Revue des études historiques* 35: 54–60.

Marx, B. 1941. "Der homiletische Nachlass des Basileios von Selukia." *Orientalia Christiana Periodica* 7: 329–69.

Mitsakis, K. 1971. "The Hymnography of the Greek Church in the Early Christian Centuries." *Jahrbuch der Österreichischen Byzantinistik* 20: 31–49.

Parys, M. van. 1971. "L'Évolution de la doctrine christologique de Basile de Seleucie." *Irenikon* 44: 493–514.

Perrone, L. 1980. *La Chiesa di Palestina e le controversie cristologiche: dal consilio di Efeso (431) al secondo Concilio di Constantinopoli (553).* Brescia: Paedeia Editrice.

Proclus of Constantinople. *Patrologia Graeca* 65.68–57, 841–50; and under Pseudo-Chrysostom *Patrologia Graeca* 61.737–38.

Richard, M. 1942. "Proclus de Constantinople et le théopaschism." *Revue d'histoire ecclésiastique* 38: 303–31.

Rohan-Chabot, C. de. 1989. "Exégèse de Job 2:6 dans une homélie inédite de Basie de Seleucie." In *Studia Patristica* 20, ed. E. Livingstone, 197–201. Leuven: Peeters.

Rompay, L. van. 1985. "Proclus of Constantinople, 'Tomus ad Armenios' in the Post-

Chalcedonian Tradition." In *After Chalcedon: Studies in Theology and Church History,* ed. C. Laga, J. Munitiz, L. Van Rompay, 425–49. *Orientalia Lovaniensia Analecta* 18 Leuven: Peeters.

Tevel, J. M. 1989. "The Manuscript Tradition of Basilius of Seleucia and Some Deductions Concerning the Early Development of Liturgical Collections." In *Studia Patristica* 20, ed. E. Livingstone, 396–401. Leuven: Peeters.

Vailhe, S. 1905. "Chrysippe Prêtre de Jérusalem." *Revue de l'Orient Chrétien* 10: 96–99.

Voss, B. R. 1970. "Berührungen von Hagiographie und Historiographie in der Spätantike." In *Frühmittelalterliche Studien,* vol. 4, ed. K. Hauck, 53–69. Berlin: Walter de Gruyter.

— 31 —

Manichaean Hymnody

Jason David BeDuhn

Coptic Manichaean Psalm-Book, Psalm 246: A Funeral Psalm
Psalm-Book, Part II, 54.7–55.15

Death, according to the Manichaeans, is the moment when a perfected soul can rise to heaven and be liberated forever. Since the individual soul is a fragment of a single primordial soul, the Living Soul, its liberation is the culmination of a long saga of imprisonment and endurance. The individual soul, once it reaches sufficient unity and consciousness, can speak as the Living Soul, as happens in this funeral psalm, which was found in the Coptic Manichaean Psalm-Book produced in fourth-century C.E. Egypt.

The chorus gives encouragement in stanza 1, and again in stanzas 13 and 14. The soul speaks as the Living Soul in stanzas 2 through 12, relating its tale of suffering and survival, of subjection and ultimate triumph. In this section, the psalm strongly resembles the *Hymns of the Living Self* known in Middle Iranian. The language approaches pantheism; but for the Manichaeans the life force is only temporarily mixed into this world and yearns for its original home. The matriarch of its imprisonment is called *Hyle* here; but it would be a mistake to translate this Greek term as "matter." Manichaean dualism is more complex than a simple spirit/matter opposition. *Hyle* is used as a personal name of this evil being in western Manichaean literature, just as Az (literally, "greed") is used for it in eastern Manichaean texts.

Bit by bit, the Living Soul works its way free. A portion is ready for liberation when it coalesces as the soul of a Manichaean Elect. This psalm celebrates the good death of such an Elect. It closes with a benediction on Mani and on the community of the Elect that Mani created as the instrument of the Living Soul's ascent.

Psalm 246: A Funeral Psalm

1. [Come to] me, my kinsman, the Light, my guide. [O] soul, endure, you have the savior. Christ is your strength, for he will receive you into his kingdom.

2. Since I came forth to the Darkness I have been given a water to drink which [intoxicates] me. I endure under a burden which is not my own.

3. I am in the midst of my enemies, the beasts surrounding me. The burden under which I endure is that of the rulers and the authorities.

4. They burned in their wrath; they rose up against me; they ran to [scatter] me, like sheep that have no shepherd.

5. Hyle and her sons divided me among them; they burnt (?) me in their fire; they gave me a bitter likeness.

6. The strangers with whom I mixed, me they do not know, [but] they tasted my sweetness, [and] they desired to keep me with them.

7. I was life to them, but they, they were death to me. I endured beneath them; they wore me as a garment upon them.

8. I am in all things; I bear the skies, I am [their] foundation; I support the earths; I am the Light that shines forth, that gives joy to the souls.

9. I am the life of the world; I am the milk that is in all trees; I am the sweet water that is beneath the sons of Hyle.

10. [. . .] I came forth to the [. . .] the Aeons [. . .], they sent me forth to the [. . .]

11. [I] endured these things until I had fulfilled the will [of my father; the] First Man is my father whose [will] I have fulfilled.

12. [Behold], the Darkness I have subdued, behold, the fire of the fountains [I have extinguished], while the sphere turns diligently, as [the sun receives] the purified [portion] of Life.

13. [O] soul, raise your eyes to the height and examine your bond; [. . .] you have reached it. Behold, your fathers are calling [you].

14. [Now] board the ships of the Light and receive your [garland of glory], and go to your kingdom, and rejoice with all [the Aeons].

15. Glory and honor to our lord Manichaios [and his] holy Elect, and the soul of the blessed [Mary].

Coptic Manichaean Psalm-Book, Psalm 264: A Funeral Psalm
Psalm-Book, Part II, 80.27–81.18

As a fragment of the Living Soul, the individual soul aspires ultimately to reunification with its source and rest from the turmoil of its isolated existence mixed with the forces of Darkness. This aspiration is well represented in this funeral psalm, built around the refrain of "take me in to you." The soul stands at the moment of ascent, with the path to the heights laid bare before it. The Maiden of Light has arrived to accompany the soul, along with the three angels who will attire the soul in its rewards of victory: a robe, a garland, and a crown (only the robe is mentioned specifically in this psalm).

Psalm 264: A Funeral Psalm

1. O firstborn, take me in to you.

2. Behold, the path of the Light has stretched before me into my first city, the place [. . .]

3. [. . .] to which I look, which [. . .] the destruction [. . .] aeon. The image of the savior has come to me. O firstborn, take me in to you.

4. [Behold, the] Light of the Maiden has shone on me, the glorious likeness [of the truth], with her three angels, the gift-[givers]. O firstborn, take me in to you.

5. [The gates] of the skies have opened before me through the rays of [my] savior and his glorious likeness of light.

6. [I have left] the garment upon the earth, the oldness of diseases that was with me. The immortal robe I have put upon myself.

7. Ferry me to the sun and the moon, O ferry of the Light that is at rest above these three [earths (?)]. O firstborn, take me in to you.

8. [I] have become a holy bride in the bridal chambers [of] the Light that are at rest; I have received the gifts of the victory. O firstborn, take me in to you.

9. O wonderful toil in which I have toiled! O my end that has become fortunate! O my eternal possession! O firstborn, take me in to you.

10. Glory and victory to our lord Manichaios and his holy Elect, and the soul of the blessed Mary.

Coptic Manichaean Psalm-Book: A Psalm of the Vagabonds
Psalm-Book, Part II, 183.19–185.2

The refrain of this psalm commemorates the apotheosis of Mani. The focus of the composition is on the commitment of the speaker to Mani and to the life required of the Manichaean Elect. The latter received five virtues from the Mind of Light, which they were to incorporate into their personalities: Love, Faith, Perfection, Patience, and Wisdom. The Elect were to wear these virtues like garments and never to be found naked of them. The speaker has searched the world for happiness, for security, for hope, but has found none of those things. Only in the Manichaean community does this search come to a satisfying conclusion, and that is the reason, the speaker tells us, that he has made the commitment of love to Mani.

A Psalm of the Vagabonds

1. I loved you as you were drawn to the skies at the time of the joy of the angels. My lord, when I call you answer me.

Since I loved you, I became beloved; I loved the things that are lovable. At the time of the joy of the angels.

2. [I] loved the Love that does not change, the church of my spirit. At the time of the joy of the angels.

I found the Faith that does not become foolish, the heart of the Father that is gathered in. At the time of the joy of the angels.

[Perfection]: let us perfect it, [and] bring our toil to the shore. At the time of the joy of the angels.

[Patience]: we bear every labor that comes with it. At the time of the joy of the angels.

[Wisdom: . . .] and we cut (?) [. . .]. At the time of the joy of the angels.

3. This is our clothing [. . .] wear (?) it. At the time of the joy of the angels.

The holy spirit has come to us; [we] have found five [holy (?)] garments. At the time of the joy of the angels.

He has [brought] the cup of water; he has given it to his church, too. At the time of the joy of the angels.

We have [found] love, we have found mercy, we have found faith, we have found [. . .]. At the time of the joy of the angels.

4. The [. . .] today, the cold water, the [. . .]. At the time of the joy of the angels.

[. . .] the new wine; we rejoice, we are drunk with [it].

[. . .] is sweet honey, burning (?) pepper [. . .] being perfect. At the time of the joy of the angels.

But the provisions of the holy spirit are these prayers, these songs, and these psalms. At the time of the joy of the angels.

5. Where is he that hungers for this love? [Where is he that] thirsts for this wisdom? At the time of the joy of the angels.

They all sought the things of the body: but perhaps the spirit is not in them. At the time of the joy of the angels.

6. But I loved you as you were drawn to the skies at the time of the joy of the angels.

I trusted in your hope; I did not trust in gold and silver. At the time of the joy of the angels.

I looked out in the whole world, I found no harbor except your harbor. At the time of the joy of the angels.

I found no trust except your trust; I found no hope except your hope. At the time of the joy of the angels.

I found no joy except your joy, I found no rest except your rest. At the time of the joy of the angels.

I found no rejoicing except your rejoicing: may it continue for us forever and ever.

7. Glory, victory to the Paraclete, our lord, our [light], Manichaios. May there [be] salvation and rest for the soul of the blessed Mary.

Bibliography

Boyce, Mary. 1954. *The Manichaean Hymn Cycles in Parthian.* London: Oxford University Press.

Brunner, C. J. 1980. "Liturgical Chant and Hymnody among the Manichaeans of Central Asia." In *Zeitschrift der deutschen morgenländischen Gesellschaft* 130: 342–68.

Puech, Henri-Charles. 1979. "Musique et hymnologie manichéennes." In Puech, *Sur le manichéisme et autres essais,* 179–233. Paris: Flammarion.

Säve-Söderbergh, Torgny. 1949. *Studies in the Coptic Manichaean Psalm-Book.* Uppsala: Almquist and Wiksells.

— 32 —

An Isis Aretalogy from Kyme in Asia Minor, First Century B.C.E.

Gail Corrington Streete

The Worship of Isis in the Greco-Roman World

The Greco-Roman goddess Isis was first worshiped in Egypt as 'Aset, the personification of the throne that was believed to "give birth" to the pharaoh, the incarnation of Osiris (later known as Sarapis), god of vegetation and of the afterlife. According to varying versions of the myth of Isis and Osiris, the most well-known of which was recounted by the Greek author Plutarch in his treatise, *On Isis and Osiris* (50–120 C.E.), it was Isis who searched for, put back together, embalmed, and then raised the dead and dismembered body of Osiris, then magically conceived the infant Horus, who was "reborn" in the person of each Egyptian pharaoh. For this reason, beginning in Egypt and eventually throughout the Greco-Roman world in which she was widely worshipped, Isis was considered the goddess who had supreme control over the powers of the cosmos, including life and death, and most especially fate.

The spread of the worship of Isis outside of Egypt began even before its conquest by the Greeks and later the Romans. As early as the fifth century B.C.E., the Greek historian and ethnographer Herodotus described the worship of Isis in Egypt, at Cyrene, Bubastis, Sais, and Memphis. In his *Histories* Herodotus claims that "Isis is Demeter in the Greek language (2.59.156)," and that the "mysteries" known as the Thesmophoria in Greece, which celebrated the goddess Demeter, had their origin in the worship of Isis at Sais (2.171). In mainland Greece, Isis was also being worshipped in Piraeus, the port of Athens, by Egyptian merchants as early as the fifth century B.C.E. (Turcan 1996, 81). By the beginning of the second century B.C.E., the worship of Isis, with or without her associated deities—Sarapis, Horus, and her assistant, the jackal-headed god Anubis—was known throughout the Hellenistic world, from Sicily to the shores of the Black Sea. It appears probable that most of the spread of this cult is attributable to merchants, sailors, and the trade in slaves from Egypt. Nevertheless, judging from the aretalogies (or hymns of praise) to Isis, found in the Mediterranean world from about the first century B.C.E., there seems also to have been a conscious attempt on the part of officials of her cult to win proselytes to the faith. For example, the earliest datable hymns, the related aretalogies of Kyme in Asia Minor, Andros, and Maroneia in Thrace, emphasize Isis's sovereignty over "every land" and reinforce her identification with goddesses like Artemis and Demeter, the Roman Ceres.

Isis's worship also spread through the Greek-speaking colonies of southern Italy, until it reached Rome. According to the second-century C.E. author Apuleius of Madauros, who may have become an upper-level initiate (*pastophoros*) in the cult of Isis and Osiris, the cult was founded in the time of the dictatorship of the Roman general Sulla, ca. 88 B.C.E. Within the city of Rome itself, however, the worship of Egyptian deities, particularly Isis, seems to have had a difficult time achieving legal recognition by the Senate. Much of the distrust of the Isis religion seems to have been the result of the traditional Roman senatorial prejudice against any "new" or "foreign" religion, particularly ones that seemed to involve numbers of adherents who were slaves, members of the lower classes, or women of any rank. The severe persecution of the worship of Isis by the emperor Tiberius in 19 C.E. seems to have been the result of the involvement of foreign and lower-class clergy and worshippers of Isis in the seduction of a matron of senatorial rank, Paulina, by a knight, Decius Mundus (Josephus *Jewish Antiquities* 18.65–80). The cult of Isis proved to be resilient, however, and revived under several emperors and was even sponsored with enthusiasm by some, including Caligula, the Flavian emperors, the Antonine Commodus, and the Severan Caracalla. Until the end of the fourth century C.E., the worship of Isis still continued to draw from both the "noblest and most distinguished" and the "lower classes" among Roman pagans, and the great Isis festival, the *Navigium Isidis,* was still celebrated in Italy as late as 416 C.E. (Heyob 1975, 35). The worship of Isis in Egypt was not effectively suppressed by Christian authorities until the sixth century.

Traces of the worship of Isis, "the goddess of many names," remain in numerous inscriptions, votive articles, and remains of temples, but the most complete witnesses of the formal practice of the religion are the hymns to Isis in manuscript and on stone and an entire chapter of a second-century novel, the *Metamorphoses,* by Apuleius of Madauros, who relates an initiation into the cult of Isis and Sarapis at the Greek seaport town of Cenchreae in the eleventh and final chapter of his novel. He describes in some detail the procession of worshippers at Isis's greatest festival, the *Navigium Isidis,* which opened the shipping season in March, and of the daily ritual in her temples at Cenchreae and at Rome. Details of Isis's more solemn autumn festival, the Finding of Osiris, are found in Plutarch (*On Isis and Osiris*) and the Christian writer Firmicus Maternus (*The Error of Profane Religions*). Roman pagan authors like the elegists Tibullus (1.3.23–32) and Propertius (2.33.1–4) and the satirists Juvenal (*Satires* 6.522–41) and Martial (*Epigrams* 10.48.1) also give us glimpses into the worship of Isis, particularly the requirements of chastity and periods of sexual abstinence (cf. Apuleius *Metamorphoses* 11.19).

The daily worship of Isis, open to all worshipers, even those not initiated into the mysteries, is described by Apuleius (*Metamorphoses* 11.20) and by Tibullus (1.3.29–32). At dawn, the white curtains of the inner shrine of the temple were drawn apart to reveal the goddess's statue, which had been ritually prepared by being washed, dressed in a robe of black, white, or multi-colored linen, and having its hair combed. The priest of Isis then made the rounds of the altars throughout the temple with prayers and libations of holy water, presumably from the Nile (cf. Juvenal *Satires* 6.522). According to Tibullus, whose mistress Delia was devoted to the goddess, her linen-clad worshippers chanted hymns in her honor twice daily, perhaps to the accompaniment of Isis's characteristic instrument, the bronze rattle or *sistrum*. According to Chaeremon, the Stoic writer of the first century C.E., the priests of Egyptian gods recited hymns of praise three or four times daily, at dawn, midday, sunset, and evening, the exact time of which was regulated by water-clocks (Chaeremon *fr.* 10; Porphyry *Abstinence* 4.6, 8; cf. Fowden 1986, 55; Turcan 1996, 113). The ritually animated statue was adored by the goddess's worshippers (*Metamorphoses* 11.17), until "she" retired for the night. On the days of festivals, according to Apuleius, the temple ritual would include a reading by a scribe, perhaps from a sacred text in hieroglyphics, in front of the assembly of the minor clergy (*pastophoroi*) and the other faithful. Some hymns and chants seem to have been especially composed for festivals. Apuleius mentions songs sung in the procession of the *Navigium Isidis*, including a "charming hymn . . . by a talented poet," preludes to a part of the ritual known as "the Great Vows," and a tune to "the great Sarapis" played on pipes (*Metamorphoses* 11.8–12).

Of these hymns Françoise Dunand remarks, "There exists in Egyptian religious literature a whole collection of hymns inserted into the daily ritual or reserved for festivals, which are essentially chants of praise, some having an actual liturgical function, others being mainly, or so it appears, literary creations." Dunand finds both types of hymn "a collective praise of the powers and benefits of the deity (Dunand 1973, 213)." The hymns chanted in procession, at festivals, and in the daily worship of Isis, consistent with what we find in the evidence, inscriptional and literary, are mainly aretalogies, litanies or recitations (*logoi*) of praise of the virtues (*aretai*) of the deity, her names, her sanctuaries, her attributes. As Apuleius puts it, they are lists of "by whatever name, whatever rite, whatever aspect" the worshipper may call upon Isis, the universal "goddess of the thousand names" (*Metamorphoses* 11.2.18–20). Most often, the aretalogies are cast in the form of self-revelations by the deity, each "virtue" beginning, like the Kyme-Memphis aretalogy, with the formulaic "I am. . . ." Others are praise of Isis and her *aretai* in the second person. The survival of so many of these texts and their variants testifies to the prominence of the goddess in the ancient Mediterranean and to the efficient organization of her cult.

Texts of Isis: Aretalogies, Hymns, and Related Materials

The most complete, widely disseminated and well-known Isis aretalogy, translated below, is that known as the aretalogy of Kyme-Memphis. According to R. E. Witt, this "stereotyped litany for worshippers" survived "in half a dozen variant forms" outside of Egypt, its presumed place of origin (Witt 1971, 102). His view is supported by Dunand (Dunand 1973, map 2), Fowden (Fowden 1986, 55), Totti (Totti 1985, 1), and Grandjean (Grandjean 1975, 8–9). This aretalogy, discovered in 1925 and dating from the first or second century B.C.E., claims to have been "transcribed" from one engraved on a stele at the temple of Hephaestus in Memphis (Kyme-Memphis aretalogy, verse 2) and so is assumed by nearly all commentators to have derived from a Memphite original. Five other versions of the aretalogy are known: the Hymn to Isis from Andros, the first-discovered of the Isis hymns (1838), dating from about the first century B.C.E., being a poetic expansion of the Kyme aretalogy in the Doric dialect; the Isis aretalogy from Thessalonica, dating from the first to second century C.E.; the aretalogy from Ios, composed in the second or third century C.E.; the recently discovered (1969) Isis aretalogy from Maroneia in Thrace, written in the second person; and the Isis aretalogy of Cyrene, dating from about 103 C.E. An extract that appears to be taken from the Kyme-Memphis aretalogy is recorded by the first-century B.C.E. historian, Diodorus Siculus, in his *Bibliotheca Historia* 1.27.4 (Grandjean 1975, 8–9). All of these texts are found in Maria Totti, *Ausgewählte Texte der Isis-und Sarapis-Religion* (1985).

Related to, and possibly influenced by, the Kyme-Memphis aretalogy or one like it, are the fragmentary *Papyrus Oxyrhynchus* 1380, dating from the second century C.E., which lists the many names, sanctuaries, and attributes of Isis, and four hymns composed by Isidorus to Isis-Hermuthis, also known as the Egyptian harvest-goddess Renenunet, found at Medinet-Madi (Narmuthis) in the Fayyum in Egypt, and dating from the first century B.C.E. (Fowden 1986, 49; Totti 1985, 62, 76). Other hymns to Isis include a fragmentary text in hexameters from the third century C.E., an invocation to Isis in a magical papyrus, also from the third century C.E. (*Papyri Graecae Magicae* [PGM] II, *Papyrus* VII), a hymn by Mesomedes, written in the time of Hadrian, and a "demotic invocation of Isis," *Papyrus Tebtunis Tait* 14 (Fowden 1986, 49n.12). Aretalogies, hymns, appearances, and healings by the goddess are contained in two extensive literary works. The so-called *Life of Aesop* contains two versions of a folktale about the storyteller, at first unable to speak, who is healed by Isis through the intervention of her priestess. The previously mentioned *Metamorphoses* by Apuleius is a picaresque novel about a young man, Lucius, whose youthful misadventures and experiments with magic turn him into an ass that can only be transformed back into a human with the assistance of Isis. Chapter XI of the *Metamorphoses* contains both an aretalogy in the form of a self-revelation by Isis (11.5) and an aretalogy in the form of a hymn of praise to the goddess by the newly initiated Lucius (11.25). The *Kore Kosmou,* a revelation dialogue between Isis and her son Horus, containing what seem to be references to earlier aretalogies, appears in the third-century collection of esoteric philosophical texts known as the *Corpus Hermeticum.* The *Kore Kosmou* plays upon the supposed relationship between Isis and Hermes, which is mentioned in many of her aretalogies (e.g., *Kyme-Memphis,* verse 3). There are other related hymns, a first-century C.E. hymn from Kios in Bithynia in honor of Anubis, the frequent companion-god of Isis, and a hymn from Chalcis, dating from the end of the third century C.E., in honor of Karpocrates, or Harpocrates, another name for Isis's son, Horus, whose representation in iconography with his finger to his lips was believed to be the symbol for the secrecy required by the mysteries (Grandjean 1975, 10–11). Although Apuleius, Isidorus, and the Kyme and Andros aretalogies mention the existence of "sacred writings" in the Egyptian hieroglyphics, all of these aretalogies and hymns, except for Apuleius's *Metamorphoses,* written in Latin, and the demotic invocation of Isis from the Tebtunis papyrus, are written in Greek, the common language of the Greco-Roman world, perhaps for the purposes of more effective religious propaganda.

An Isis Aretalogy: Text with Commentary

The Greek text of this aretalogy (the only complete text extant) is taken from the most complete collection of longer texts relating to the Greco-Roman worship of Isis (Totti 1985, 1–4). Other works containing this text are listed by Totti on page one of her anthology. The text of the aretalogy from Kyme will be compared in the commentary with other, similar texts, including the extract of Diodorus Siculus in his *Bibliotheca Historia* 1.27.4, the poetic variants in the hymn to Isis from Andros and the hymn from Cyrene, the aretalogy from Maroneia, the hymns of Isidorus, the praises of Isis from *Papyrus Oxyrhynchus* 1380, Apuleius's *Metamorphoses* 11, and the *Kore Kosmou* from the *Corpus Hermeticum.* The numbered "paragraphs" of Totti's recension appear as numbered verses in the translation.

The Isis Aretalogy of Kyme-Memphis

[1] Demetrius son of Artemidorus and Thraseas the Magnesian from Meander [offer] an invocation to Isis:

[2] These lines are transcribed from the stele in Memphis that stands in front of the sanctuary of Hephaestus.

[3] I am Isis, the sovereign of every land; and I was educated by Hermes and with Hermes I invented letters, both sacred and common, so that all things would not be written with the same letters.

[4] I established ordinances for mortals, and I framed laws that none can change.

[5] I am the eldest daughter of Kronos.

[6] I am wife and sister of King Osiris.

[7] I am she who discovered fruit for mortals.

[8] I am mother of King Horus.

[9] I am she who rises in the Dog-Star.

[10] I am she who is called god by women.

[11] For me was the city of Boubastis built.

[12] I separated earth from heaven.

[13] I indicated the pathways of the stars.

[14] I established the orbit of the sun and the moon.

[15] I invented seafaring.

[16] I made the right mighty.

[17] I drew man and woman together.

[18] I ordained that a woman bring forth her infant at ten months.

[19] I ordained that parents be dearly loved by their children.

[20] I established retribution for parents without natural affection.

[21] I, with my brother Osiris, put an end to cannibalism.

[22] I demonstrated mysteries to mortals.

[23] I taught them to honor the images of the gods.

[24] I set up sanctuaries of the gods.

[25] I put an end to the dominion of tyrants.

[26] I put an end to murder.

[27] I compelled women to be loved by men.

[28] I made justice stronger than gold and silver.

[29] I ordained that truth be considered lovely.

[30] I invented marriage contracts.

[31] I established different languages for Greeks and barbarians.

[32] I caused the good and the shameful to be distinguished by their nature.

[33] I made nothing more to be feared than an oath.

[34] I delivered the one who plots harm against others to the power of the one plotted against.

[35] I established retribution for those who practice injustice.

[36] I ordained pity for suppliants.

[37] I honor those who defend themselves justly.

[38] With me justice is mighty.

[39] I am mistress of the rivers and the winds and the sea.

[40] No one is honored without my judgment.

[41] I am mistress of warfare.

[42] I am mistress of the thunderbolt.

[43] I calm and I agitate the sea.

[44] I am she who is in the rays of the sun.

[45] I sit beside the sun in its course.

[46] What seems good to me will also be brought to pass.

[47] To me everything is possible.

[48] I release those who are in chains.

[49] I am mistress of seafaring.

[50] I make the navigable unnavigable, when it seems good to me.

[51] I established the walls of cities.

[52] I am she who is called the lawgiver.

[53] I brought the islands from the depths of the sea to the light.

[54] I am mistress of rainstorms.

[55] I conquer Fate.

[56] Fate obeys me.

[57] Farewell, Egypt, who fostered me.

Commentary

[1] ". . . an invocation to Isis." As with the hymn to Isis from Maroneia and the hymns composed by Isidorus, the "authors" may intend this as a prayer for the

goddess to bestow her benefits or to thank her for favors received. On the other hand, the fact that they say they have transcribed this aretalogy from the stele in Memphis indicates that they may be priests, scribes, *pastophoroi,* or wealthy patrons of the sanctuary of the goddess at Kyme. It was not unusual for sacred writings and sacred objects of the cult to be brought from the "holy land," Egypt (Apuleius *Metamorphoses* 11.20.4; Juvenal *Satires* 10.522–23; Turcan 1996, 111–14).

[2] ". . . the stele in Memphis that stands in front of the sanctuary of Hephaestus." Diodorus Siculus (*Bibliotheca Historia* 1.22.2–6) says that Isis is "buried" in Memphis, where in his day one could visit her "tomb" in the sanctuary of Hephaestus, the Egyptian Ptah. Diodorus nonetheless takes his excerpt of the Isis aretalogy from that of "some scribes," who say that they took it from her sanctuary at Nysa, in Arabia (1.27.4). Herodotus (*Histories* 2.176) mentions "the great and most marvelous sanctuary of Isis" at the Hephaistion in Memphis. *Papyrus Oxyrhynchus* (hereafter *P. Oxy.*) 1380, a fragmentary listing of all the titles and sanctuaries of the goddess, mentions one title as coming "from the house [sanctuary] of Hephaestus" (*P. Oxy.* 1380.2), and also addresses the goddess as having "your sanctuary in Memphis" (*P. Oxy.* 1380.249). These data seem to confirm the claim of the Kyme aretalogy that the original was in Memphis.

Hephaestus, the Greek god of craft and the forge, was the Greek equivalent to the Egyptian god Ptah (Witt 1971, 102). Regarded in the theology of the priests of Memphis as the creator god, Ptah later became identified with Osiris, brother and spouse of Isis.

[3] ". . . the sovereign of every land . . ." The Greek uses the feminine definite article before the masculine noun *tyrannos,* or "sole ruler." In Diodorus's extract of the aretalogy (1.27.4), he uses the title *basilissa* (queen) (cf. *P. Oxy.* 1380.32). Analogous feminine terms expressing Isis's supreme power are found in *Kyme-Memphis* (verses 41, 42, 49, 54) and *Andros* 6. *Papyrus Oxyrhynchus* 1380 echoes the Kyme-Memphis aretalogy in calling her "queen and mistress of every land" (23–24), "queen of the inhabited world" (121; cf. 218–19), and "ruler over diadems" (193–94), while Isidorus (1.1–2) calls her also "queen, almighty ruler (*pantokrateira;* cf. *P. Oxy.* 1380.20–21)." Apuleius's hero Lucius addresses her as "queen of heaven" (*Metamorphoses* 11.2.2), and in a vision, she tells him that the Egyptians, who celebrate her with her proper rituals, also call her by her "true" name, "Isis the queen" (11.5.19–21).

". . . and I was educated by Hermes. . . ." Isis's education by Hermes (cf. Diodorus 1.27.4) creates an association later exploited in the *Kore Kosmou,* in which Isis learns secret wisdom from Hermes, which she communicates to Horus (*Kore Kosmou* 67). Hermes is the Greek equivalent of the Egyptian Thoth, the ibis-headed scribe of the gods who invented writing and was associated with arcane wisdom and magic.

". . . I invented letters, both sacred and common. . . ." This accomplishment, lacking in Diodorus's excerpt, is found in most variants and derivatives of the Kyme-Memphis aretalogy (*Andros* 10–12; *Kore Kosmou* 66; *Isidorus* 4.18). According to *Cyrene* (10–11), it is Isis alone who invents writing (cf. *P. Oxy.* 1380.123–24). The aretalogy of Maroneia (23–24) connects Isis's discovery of writing with her invention of the mysteries. The "sacred" letters were the hieroglyphics ("holy writings") that were the exclusive province of the Egyptian priests and scribes belonging to the sanctuaries of the gods. "Common" or "demotic" letters were for nonsacred writings and were not the province of a priestly elite.

[4] "I established ordinances . . . and I framed laws . . ." (Cf. verses 18, 19, 20, 29 and 52; cf. also *Andros* 20; *Cyrene* 20; *P. Oxy.* 1380.204–5; *Isidorus* 1.6; *Kore Kosmou* 65.) *Papyrus Oxyrhynchus* 1380 refers to various numbers of "commandments" of Isis: either "ten in all" or "fifteen" in line 120 and "the grace of two commandments" in lines 156–57.

[5] ". . . eldest daughter of Kronos." (Cf. *Andros* 15.) Diodorus 27.4 has "eldest daughter of Kronos, the youngest god." In the aretalogy of Maroneia, Isis is the daughter of the Earth (16–17). Kronos, the Greek god who was son of Ouranos (Heaven) and Gaia (Earth) and father of the twelve Olympians, known as Saturn to the Romans, was also identified with the Egyptian sun-god Re or Ra.

[6] ". . . wife and sister of King Osiris." One of the foremost characteristics of Isis, this is found in Diodorus 1.27.4; *Andros* 16–17; *Maroneia* 17; *Papyrus Oxyrhynchus* 1380.186–89. *Papyrus Oxyrhynchus* 1380.242–43 also refers to a central feature of the myth of Isis and Osiris, Isis's resurrection of Osiris from the dead.

[7] ". . . discovered fruit for mortals." (Cf. verses 22 and 52; Diodorus 1.27.4; *Andros* 84–87; *Cyrene* 12, 18; *P. Oxy.* 1380.170–71; Apuleius *Metamorphoses* 11.4.1; *Isidorus* 1.8, 13; 2.3.) *Karpos,* the Greek for fruit, can also be translated "grain" or "harvest." An alternative translation would read, "I am she who invented the harvest for mortals." Herodotus, like other Greeks, identified Isis with Demeter, the Roman Ceres, goddess of grain, produce, and the harvest par excellence (Herodotus *Histories* 2.59, 123). Like Demeter, Isis was also regarded as inventor of the mysteries, which celebrated the triumph of life over death as expressed by the return of vegetation. In Apuleius's *Metamorphoses* 11.2.1–4, Isis is identified with Ceres/Demeter. In the aretalogy of Maroneia (36), the invention of the harvest connects Isis with Demeter, Kore, and Triptolemus and the founding of the mysteries at Eleusis.

[8] ". . . mother of King Horus." (Cf. Diodorus 1.27.4.) One of the most widespread images of Isis in the Greco-Roman world portrays her suckling or carrying her son, the infant Horus (Cf. Tran Tam Tinh 1973). According to the mythology of Isis, she protected the infant Horus, whom she conceived after raising Osiris from the dead, from Seth/Typhon, his father's murderer (Plutarch, *On Isis and Osiris* 355–58). In the Egyptian worship of Isis, upon his enthronement, the

pharaoh was "born" from Isis as Horus. *Papyrus Oxyrhynchus* 1380.220–23 mentions Isis's establishment of her son, Horus Apollo, as the "new master of the whole world."

[9] ". . . she who rises in the Dog-Star." (Cf. *Andros* 23; Diodorus 1.27.4.) The rising of Sirius, the Dog-Star, known as Sothis or Io-Sothis in Egypt (*P. Oxy.* 1380.143–44), signaled the day that the Nile flooded. Some representations of Isis, including the tympanum over the entrance to the temple of Isis on the Campus Martius in Rome, depict her riding upon a heavenly dog. (Turcan 1996, 80, 91, Plate II.)

[10] ". . . called god by women." (Cf. verses 17, 27.) The masculine, *theos* (god), rather than the available feminine form, *thea* (goddess), is used here (*Andros* 10; *Cyrene* 7; *P. Oxy.* 1380.130–31). Also note the use of the masculine *tyrannos* in verse 3.

[11] ". . . the city of Boubastis . . ." (Cf. Diodorus, 1.27.4; *Andros*, 25; *P. Oxy.* 1380.4, 37–38.) Boubastis (or Bubastis) in Lower Egypt was the center of worship for the cat-headed goddess Bastet (or Bubastis), whom the Greeks identified with Artemis, but with whom Isis was also identified by Greeks and Egyptians alike (Herodotus *Histories* 2.59, 137, 156; cf. Witt 1971, 101).

[12] ". . . separated earth from heaven." (Cf. *Andros* 26–27; Isidorus 2.11.)

[13] ". . . the pathways of the stars." (Cf. verse 14; *Andros* 28; *Cyrene* 16–17; *P. Oxy.* 1380.159–60; Apuleius *Metamorphoses* 11.3–4, 22.10, 12.)

[14] ". . . the orbit of the sun and moon." (Cf. verse 13; Apuleius *Metamorphoses* 11.22.11.) Isis was most often identified in Greco-Roman syncretism with the moon, probably because she was depicted in Egyptian iconography wearing the horns of the cow-goddess, Hathor, which represented the crescent moon. For this reason, Isis is also identified with the goddesses Artemis—Roman Diana— (cf. *P. Oxy.* 1380.84–85), and Selene or Luna (cf. *P. Oxy.* 1380.103–4). She is identified with the sun (cf. verses 44 and 45, below; *P. Oxy.* 1380.112–13) through her relationship with her son Horus, also called Helios. (Cf. *Andros* 29–31; *Maroneia* 18–19; *P. Oxy.* 1380.221–22; Isidorus 1.9–10.)

[15] ". . . seafaring." (Cf. verses 39, 43, 49; *Andros* 34–35.) Some of Isis's well-known titles were "Lady of the Lighthouse" (cf. Tibullus 1.3.31) and "Lady of the Seas." The goddess is often mentioned in her aretalogies by titles that call attention to her protection of seafarers (cf. *P. Oxy.* 1380.8–9, "fleet-commanding"; 15–16, "safe-harboring"; 69–70, "pilot"; 73–74, "bringer-to-harbor"; 98–99, "Fair Voyage"). Isis mythically "invented" seafaring when she set sail in search of the body of the murdered Osiris (cf. *P. Oxy.* 1380.186–88). This sailing was commemorated ritually by her worshippers in a carnival-like festival, the *Navigium Isidis*, or vessel of Isis, which Apuleius chronicles at some length in the *Metamorphoses*

(11.8–17). This major festival, held in early March, signified the opening of the shipping and sailing season, the *Ploiaphesia* (Turcan 1996, 114).

[16] "... the right mighty." Isis's championship of right, justice, and truth, especially as protector of the oppressed, is a constant theme in her aretalogies. (Cf. verses 28, 35, 37, 38; *Andros* 36; *Maroneia* 24; *Kore Kosmou* 67.)

[17] "... woman and man together." (Cf. verses 10, 27, 30.) This phrase, which may also be translated, "wife and husband," reflects the belief that Isis was patroness of marriage. (Cf. *Andros* 36–37, 41–42.) *Papyrus Oxyrhynchus* 1380.146–48 has the interesting variant: "You draw healthy women into mooring with men."

[18] "... bring forth an infant at ten months." (Cf. *Andros* 37–39; *P. Oxy.* 1380.194–96.)

[19] "... parents be dearly loved by their children." (Cf. verse 20; *Andros* 39–41.) In *Maroneia* 32–33, Isis ordains that parents should be loved "as gods" by their children.

[20] "... parents without natural affection." (Cf. verse 19; *Andros* 41–44.)

[21] "... an end to cannibalism." (Cf. verse 26; *Andros* 44–47.) Isis and Osiris were considered bringers and patrons of civilization, unlike the disruptive brother and enemy of Osiris, Seth or Typhon, who, according to the myth, tricked, killed, and dismembered Osiris and scattered the pieces of his body, which Isis later found and gathered.

[22] "... demonstrated mysteries . . ." (Cf. *Kore Kosmou* 68, Mesomedes, "To Isis," 5.) Like Demeter, Isis was believed to have "invented" the mysteries through her conquest of death. As Demeter, the goddess of grain, wandered in search of her daughter Kore, the grain-maiden, and with the finding of Kore eventually brought the dead vegetation back to life, so Isis wandered in search of Osiris, the god of vegetation, and magically brought him back to life as their son, Horus. Herodotus identifies Isis with Demeter (*Histories* 2.59; cf. Apuleius *Metamorphoses* 11.5.13–14), and equates the mystery-deities of the Greeks, Demeter and Dionysus, the "rulers of the lower world," with Isis and Osiris (2.123). He also alludes to a celebration of "mysteries" at Sais, which he equates with the Greek Thesmophoria, a women's festival in honor of Demeter that the Danaids brought to Greece (2.171). Presumably these mysteries are related to the "Finding of Osiris," the solemn festival celebrated at the end of October. *Papyrus Oxyrhynchus* 1380.111 says that "at the Hellespont," Isis' title is "*mystis*," which may mean either a participant or a leader in the mysteries. The aretalogy of Maroneia, which refers to Isis's invention of hieroglyphics specifically for the mysteries (23), credits Isis with having "honored Athens above all Hellas" by bringing to it the Eleusinian mysteries (35–40). In Apuleius' *Metamorphoses*, Isis is also identified with Demeter, the Roman Ceres, and with her mysteries (11.5.13–14). Summoned by Isis herself, who promises him protection while he lives and the reward of a blessed

afterlife (11.6.22–28), Lucius undergoes initiation (11.22–25), in the course of which he approaches "the threshold of death" and is joyfully reborn. Like the Eleusinian mysteries, the Isiac mysteries seem to involve the ritual conquest of death and fate, with the assurance of a "blessed life" in the present and the promise of its continuing after death. Unlike the Eleusinian mysteries, which were fixed at Eleusis and open to Greek speakers only, those of Isis were not geographically fixed and were potentially open to all who were summoned by the goddess. Even poverty need not necessarily be a drawback (cf. *Metamorphoses* 11.28.13–16).

[23] ". . . the images of the gods." (Cf. verse 24; *Andros* 94–96; Apuleius *Metamorphoses* 11.24.5.) Turcan claims that the daily adoration of the deity in the form of his or her image was a "form of piety" introduced to the West by the Isis religion (Turcan 1996, 112–13).

[24] ". . . sanctuaries of the gods." (Cf. verse 23; *Andros* 95–96; *Kore Kosmou* 65.) According to *Papyrus Oxyrhynchus* 1380, Isis is responsible for introducing *all* forms of divine worship, including the images, sacred animals, and appropriate liturgies (139–42, 179–83).

[25] ". . . the dominion of tyrants." (Cf. verse 1; *Andros* 96–97; *P. Oxy.* 1380.193–94; 240–42.)

[26] ". . . an end to murder." (Cf. verse 21; *Andros* 97–98; *Kore Kosmou* 65.)

[27] ". . . women to be loved by men." (Cf. verses 10, 17, 30; *Andros* 101–2.) As in verse 17, an alternative translation of this verse would be, "I compelled wives to be loved by husbands." *Papyrus Oxyrhynchus* 1380.214–16 has the variant, "You made the power of men equal to [that of] women."

[28] ". . . justice stronger than gold and silver." (Cf. verses 16, 35; *Andros* 104–5.)

[29] ". . . truth be considered lovely." (Cf. *Andros* 105–8.)

[30] ". . . marriage contracts." (Cf. verses 17, 27; *Andros* 108–11.)

[31] ". . . languages for Greeks and barbarians." (Cf. verse 3, *Andros* 112–13; *Maroneia* 26–27.) Here is another indication of Isis's power over the world and her invention of different letters for writing.

[32] ". . . good and shameful . . ." (Cf. Plato *Symposium* 208c–12c; *Andros* 114–15; Isidorus 3.27.) Another possible translation would be "beautiful and ugly," since moral beauty and physical beauty were usually considered to be the same.

[33] ". . . than an oath." (Cf. *Andros* 116–17; *Kore Kosmou* 67.) According to the Greeks, even the gods had to abide by oaths they swore by the Underworld's River Styx.

[34] "I delivered the one who plots harm. . . ." (Cf. verses 16, 20, 28, 35, 37, 38; *Andros* 119–20.) Isis's reputation for justice included the idea that she presided over its implementation.

[35] ". . . retribution for those who practice injustice." (Cf. preceding verse and verses 16, 20, 34, 37, 38.)

[36] ". . . pity for suppliants." (Cf. *Andros* 121–26; Totti 1985, 8; Isidorus 2.30; 3.19, 34.) Apuleius's Lucius is a literary example of Isis's own pity for suppliants (*Metamorphoses* 11.5.1, 25.3).

[37] "I honor those who defend themselves justly." (Cf. verses 16, 20, 28, 34, 35, 37, 38.)

[38] ". . . justice is mighty." (Cf. verses 20, 28, 34, 35, 37, 38.) An almost exact repetition of verse 16.

[39] . . . "mistress of the rivers and the winds and the sea." (Cf. verses 15, 43, 49; *Andros* 127–28; *P. Oxy.* 1380.61–62 ["At Heraklion, mistress of the sea"], 122–23, 222–23, 237–39; Isidorus 1.10–11; 2.12; 4.11–13; Apuleius *Metamorphoses* 11.25.6.)

[40] ". . . honored without my judgment." (Cf. *Andros* 39–41.)

[41] ". . . mistress of warfare." (Cf. Isidorus 1.27; 3.16–17.) In *Papyrus Oxyrhynchus* 1380, the title "warlike" is applied to Isis in the cities of Menouphis (71) and Rome (83), and appropriately enough, among the Amazons (102–3). Lines 239–40 address her as "mistress of warfare and of dominion."

[42] ". . . the thunderbolt." (Cf. *Andros* 129, 168–71; *P. Oxy.* 1380.237–39; Apuleius *Metamorphoses* 11.25.14.)

[43] ". . . the sea." (Cf. verses 15, 29, 49; *Andros* 130–33; *P. Oxy.* 1380.98–99 ["At Gaza, Fair Voyage"]; Apuleius *Metamorphoses* 11.5.25–26; 7.23–25; 25.6–7).

[44] ". . . in the rays of the sun." (Cf. verse 45; *Andros* 139–40; *P. Oxy.* 1380.112–13 ["At Tenedos, eye of the sun"]; Isidorus 1.11; 2.14; 4.13–14; Apuleius *Metamorphoses* 25.11.) The Egyptian sun-god was called by various names (Ra, Amun, Amon-Ra, Aton) and was a complex figure, combining not only the names, but also the functions and iconography of many of the deities of Egypt. In some hymns and texts, the sun was reborn daily, either from the sky or the "divine cow," Hathor, who also became identified with Isis. The life-giving rays of the sun were often depicted as ending in an *ankh* that was also adopted widely as a symbol of Isis's life-giving power and an equivalent of the "Isis-knot," part of her distinctive dress. As one of the most "syncretistic" of the Greco-Roman deities, "Isis of the thousand names" seems to have absorbed the functions of many previously existing deities (Apuleius *Metamorphoses* 11.5.4–5).

[45] ". . . sit beside the sun . . ." (Cf. verse 44; *Andros* 139–40; *P. Oxy.* 1380.157.) In some of the Egyptian myths, the sun was envisioned as sailing through the sky by day and by night through the underworld, conducting a nightly battle with Apophis, the serpent of darkness. To win this battle, the sun needed the assistance of other gods (cf. Frankfort 1948, 18–19). Although Isis was not originally envisioned as one of these gods, her assimilation to other deities connected with the sun (Hathor, for example) probably associated this function with her as well.

[46] ". . . brought to pass." (Cf. verse 47; *Andros* 141–42; *Cyrene* 15; *P. Oxy.* 1380.194–96; Isidorus 4.16.)

[47] ". . . everything is possible." (Cf. verse 46; *Andros* 141–44.)

[48] ". . . in chains." (Cf. *Andros* 144–45.) In Apuleius's *Metamorphoses* 11.15.29–31, Lucius, released from his donkey skin through the intervention of Isis, is told by her priest to dedicate himself to the goddess's service, and then he will never be enslaved.

[49] ". . . seafaring." (Cf. verses 15 [and commentary], 39, 43, 50; *Andros* 145–48.)

[50] ". . . navigable unnavigable . . ." (Cf. verses 15, 39, 43, 49; *Andros* 148–57.) Most probably this claim refers to the *Ploiaphesia,* the opening of the shipping season, at the time of the *Navigium Isidis* festival. In the hymn of Andros this verse and the verse above are poetically expanded with numerous mythological allusions.

[51] ". . . walls of cities." (Cf. *Andros* 158–59; *Cyrene* 13–14; *Maroneia* 30–31; *P. Oxy.* 1380.57–58 ["queen of cities"]; Isidorus 2.2.) Isis's establishment and protection of cities is celebrated in many hymns.

[52] ". . . the lawgiver." Isis's functions as giver of "laws and ordinances" and dispenser of justice, retribution, and mercy occupy a prominent, if not the preeminent, place in this aretalogy (verses 4, 16, 19, 20, 25, 26, 28, 29, 33, 34, 35, 36, 37, 38, 40). This title is also prominent in other hymns and aretalogies. (Cf. *Andros* 20, 159–60; *Maroneia* 29; *P. Oxy.* 1380.119–21; Isidorus 4.4; *Kore Kosmou* 68.) *Thesmophoros* (lawgiver) is also an important epithet of Demeter, whose festival, the Thesmophoria, took place in Greece in late October, was celebrated by married women, and apparently involved ritual reenactment of the myth of Demeter and her search for and finding of Kore. Herodotus (*Histories* 2.59, 171) connects the Thesmophoria with the mysteries of the Egyptian "Demeter," Isis. The Kyme-Memphis aretalogy and its variants have also drawn parallels, sometimes consciously, between the two goddesses, their attributes, and their mysteries (see verses 7, 22), but usually it is the Eleusinian mysteries, not the Thesmophoria, that Isis is supposed to have influenced.

[53] ". . . islands from the depths . . ." (Cf. *Andros* 160–61.

[54] ". . . rainstorms." (Cf. verses 39, 43; *Andros* 57; *P. Oxy.* 1380.227–31; Apuleius *Metamorphoses* 11.25.14; Mesomedes, "To Isis," 7–8.)

[55] "I conquer Fate." (Cf. verse 56; *Andros* 171–72; *Cyrene* 1 [addressed "To Good Fortune"].) The speech of the Isis priest in Apuleius's *Metamorphoses* 11.15 is largely an encomium to Isis for helping Lucius overcome the vicissitudes of Fortune.

[56] "Fate obeys me." (Cf. verse 55; *Andros* 172–75 [very fragmentary].) Isis's promise to Lucius in the *Metamorphoses* is that, if he is initiated, she will help to prolong his life "beyond the limits decreed by your fate (11.6.31–32)."

[57] "Farewell Egypt . . ." (Cf. Diodorus 1.27.4; *Andros* 176–78, which substitutes "the Nile" for "Egypt" as Isis's nurse.) It would seem as though the world-ruling Isis, who is "worshipped under many forms, with various rites, and with many names (Apuleius *Metamorphoses* 11.5.7–8)," is destined, like this aretalogy, to be taken from Egypt, where she was "born" and "raised."

Bibliography

Bergmann, J. 1968. *Ich bin Isis: Studien zum memphitischen Hintergrund der greichischen Isisaretalogien.* Stockholm: Almqvist and Wiksell.

Dunand, Françoise, 1971–1973. *Le Culte d'Isis dans le bassin oriental de la Méditeranée. Etudes préliminaires aux religions orientales dans l'empire romain* 24–26. 3 vols. Leiden: E. J. Brill.

Fowden, Garth. 1986. *The Egyptian Hermes: A Historical Approach to the Late Pagan Mind.* Cambridge: Cambridge University Press.

Frankfort, Henri. 1948. *Ancient Egyptian Religion: An Interpretation.* New York: Columbia University Press.

Grandjean, Yves. 1975. *Une Nouvelle Arétalogie d'Isis à Maronée. Etudes préliminaires aux religions orientales dans l'empire romain* 49. Leiden: E. J. Brill.

Heyob, Sharon Kelly. 1975. *The Cult of Isis among Women in the Graeco-Roman World. Etudes préliminaires aux religions orientales dans l'empire romain* 51. Leiden: E. J. Brill.

Leclant, Jean. 1972–74. *Inventaire bibliographique des Isiaca (IBIS). Etudes préliminaires aux religions orientales dans l'empire romain* 18. Leiden: E. J. Brill.

Peek, W. 1930. *Der Isishymnus von Andros und verwandte Texte.* Berlin: Weidmann.

Takács, Sarolta A. 1995. *Isis and Sarapis in the Roman World.* Religions in the Graeco-Roman World 124. Leiden: E. J. Brill.

Totti, Maria. 1985. *Ausgewählte Texte der Isis- und Sarapis-Religion.* Subsidia Epigraphica 12. Hildesheim: Georg Olms.

Tran Tam Tinh, Victor. 1973. *Isis lactans. Etudes préliminaires aux religions orientales dans l'empire romain* 26. Leiden: E. J. Brill.

Turcan, Robert. 1996. *The Cults of the Roman Empire.* Trans. Antonia Nevill. The Ancient World. Oxford, U. K. and Cambridge, Mass.: Basil Blackwell.

Vidman, Ladislas. 1969. *Sylloge inscriptionum religionis Isiacae et Sarapicae.* Berlin: Walter de Gruyter.

Witt, R. E. 1971. *Isis in the Graeco-Roman World.* London: Thames and Hudson; Ithaca: Cornell University Press.

Sacrificing Self to God: Martyrology

The Passion of Saints Perpetua and Felicity

Maureen A. Tilley

The Passion of Perpetua and Felicity is the oldest surviving Christian material one may attribute to a definite historical woman. It records events of the persecution of Christians in Carthage, near modern Tunis in Tunisia in the year 203.

The text consists of five parts:

I.1–II.3	An introduction written by an unknown editor
III.1–X.15	The prison diary of Perpetua
XI.1	The editor's linking verse
XI.2–XIII.8	The dream of Saturus, one of her companions, taken from his prison diary
XIV.1–XXI.11	The story of Felicity and the deaths of the martyrs, probably written by the editor.

The account focuses on the deaths of two women, one a respectably well-off young married woman, and the other a pregnant slave. The narrative and visions provide models of behavior during persecution, the justification of the power of martyrs, and a variety of role models, especially for women. In the course of the narrative family relationships are eclipsed by relationships within the Christian community, the "family of faith." The more Perpetua separates herself from her natural family, the easier it becomes for her to take her place as the head of the Christian family in prison.

A number of details make this text particularly interesting. At III.6 it is necessary to understand that prisoners were not normally provided with food, water, and bedding by the prison authorities, but by their visitors. Absent visitors, guards supplemented their wages by selling provisions to prisoners.

Many commentators see the eating of the cheese at IV.9 as a reflection of the North African ritual of offering the newly baptized milk and honey to drink. Given Perpetua's status as a recent convert and her social and educational status, it is just as likely—or more likely—that the accent ought to be placed on eating food in another world as a way of insuring one's link to the world; for instance, Persephone/Proserpina eating pomegranate seeds in the Underworld linking her to her new home.

Although not a part of modern judicial practice, torture (VI.2) was very common in the Roman Empire as a part of judicial investigation. In this case, what they confess is that they are Christians.

Perpetua's sexual transformation at X.7 has been the subject of many commentaries. Given the gender roles of antiquity, it is not surprising that she is transformed. It would have been unthinkable for her to have fought in the arena in a woman's body. Note that immediately upon her victory she is addressed as "daughter." Once the reason for her masculine body no longer exists, she returns to her previous identity.

At XIII.3 the text affirms that the martyrs enjoyed a higher authority than members of the clergy. This authority would remain unchallenged in North Africa until the epsicopate of Cyprian of Carthage in the 250s.

The highly stylized apologetic introduction gives way quickly to the diaries of the martyrs. This translation and the enumeration of the sections are based on the critical edition published by Cornelius Ioannes Maria Van Beek (Nijmegen: Dekkers and Van de Vegt, 1936). Translation © Maureen A. Tilley, 1997. For an extended commentary on the text see Maureen A. Tilley, *The Passion of Perpetua and Felicity* in *Searching the Scriptures*, vol. 2: *A Feminist Commentary*, ed. Elisabeth Schüssler Fiorenza (New York: Crossroad, 1994), 829–58.

The Passion of Saints Perpetua and Felicity

[I.1] If we have recorded earlier accounts of faith testifying to God's grace and promoting popular edification in order to honor God and to comfort the reader by a recreation of the past events, why shouldn't we consider more recent examples equally appropriate to faith? [I.2] Perhaps these later stories may someday become ancient history, indispensable for those who are our successors, even though in our day they are accorded less authority out of some prejudicial deference to antiquity. [I.3] People who would like to limit the Holy Spirit to a single pattern for perfection for all time should consider this: these more recent events should be considered greater since they are closer to the end of time and to the fullness of grace allotted to the final days. [I.4] For " 'in the last days,' says the Lord, 'I shall pour out my Spirit on all of humanity and their sons and daughters will prophesy. I shall pour out my Spirit on my men servants and women servants. Young people will see visions and the old will dream dreams' " [Acts 2:17–18; cf. Joel 2:28]. [I.5] So we who consider these new visions promised just as much as those prophecies acknowledge the rest of the virtues of the Holy Spirit as provisions for the Church to whom the same Spirit is sent to direct all the gifts for all the people, as the Lord distributes them to each person [1 Cor. 7:17; Rom. 12:3]. Therefore, we judge it imperative to place in order and produce these written accounts for the glory of God. In this way people weak in faith and those on the verge of despair will not regard the grace of close association with the Divine as present or sent only in ancient times to those worthy of martyrdom or visions. They will realize that God always accomplishes what God promised not only for people who might be converted by such testimony but also for those who already believe in God's favor. [I.6] So brethren and dear children, we "announce to you what we heard and felt" so that you who are present now may recall the glory of the Lord, and those who now understand by hearing "may be in communion with" the holy martyrs, and through them with our Lord "Jesus Christ," to whom is "glory and honor for ever and ever. Amen" [1 John 1:1, 3].

[II.1] Some young catechumens were arrested: Revocatus and Felicity (his companion in service), Saturninus and Secundulus. Among them was Vibia Perpetua, nobly born, well educated, respectably married. [II.2] Her mother and father were still living, as well as two brothers, one a catechumen with her. She also had an infant son she was breast-feeding. She herself was about twenty-two years old. [II.3] She narrated this whole affair of the martyrdom herself. She has written it in her own hand and she leaves us her own impressions.

[III.1] "Then," she says, "while we were with the prison guards, my father wanted to dissuade me by arguing with me. He kept trying to shake my resolve because of his own love for me. I said, 'Father, do you see this vase lying here, which for the sake of a name we call "pitcher" or whatever?' And he said, 'I see it.' [III.2] Then I said to him, 'Can it be called by any other name than what it is?' And he said, 'No.' 'So too I cannot be called anything else except what I am, a Christian.' [III.3] Enraged by my words, my father pulled me toward himself, like he was going to gouge out my eyes. But he only shook me, and defeated, he left along with his diabolical arguments.

[III.4] "For a few days my father did not visit me. I thanked God, and I was comforted by his absence. [III.5] During this time we were baptized. The Spirit told me not to ask anything from the water except for patient endurance in the flesh.

"A few days later we were taken to prison and I was terrified because I had never experienced such darkness before. [III.6] What a rough time we had between the intense heat resulting from overcrowding and extortion by the soldiers! Then I was tormented with a brand new concern—my child. [III.7] At that point Tertius and Pomponius, the blessed deacons who ministered to us, made arrangements to bribe the guards so that we might be moved out to a better part of the prison. That way we could refresh ourselves. [III.8] Then we left the dungeon and everybody refreshed themselves. I breast-fed my son who had already lost weight from not eating. Since I was worried about him, I spoke to my mother. I also tried to comfort my brother. I asked them to take care of my son. I kept growing weaker because I saw them pining away for my sake. [III.9] I suffered such worries for several days and I insisted that my child remain in the prison with me. Immediately I regained my strength and I was relieved of fatigue and of my worry about my child. Then all of a sudden the prison became a palace for me, so much so that I preferred to be there over anywhere else.

[IV.1] "Then my brother said to me: 'Noble sister, you already have such a great reputation that you could ask for a vision and it would be revealed to you whether we will be martyred or released.' I knew that I could discuss these things with the Lord, whose favors I had already experienced, so I promised him faithfully: 'Tomorrow I shall report to you.'

[IV.2] "I did ask and this is what I was shown: I saw a bronze ladder of great height reaching all the way up to heaven [cf. Gen. 28:12]. It was so narrow, you couldn't climb up unless you went single file. All sorts of weapons were attached to the sides of the ladder. [IV.3] There were swords, lances, hooks, daggers, and javelins, so that if someone were careless or not paying attention as they were ascending, they would be cut to pieces, and bits of their flesh would get caught on the weapons. [IV.4] There was a huge dragon lying under that same ladder. It threatened to attack those who were ascending, frightening them so they would not climb up. [IV.5] However, Saturus went up first. He was our inspiration. He had voluntarily handed himself over for our sake so he was not with us when we were arrested. [IV.6] When he came to the top of the ladder, he turned toward me and said, 'Perpetua, pull yourself together. Watch out so the dragon doesn't bite you.' I replied, 'In the name of Jesus Christ, it will not harm me.' [IV.7] It slowly stuck its head out from under the ladder as if it were afraid of me, and as if I were using its head for the first step I mounted the ladder, and I ascended [cf. Gen. 3:15].

[IV.8] "Next I saw the broad expanse of a garden and a grey-haired man sitting in the middle of it, dressed like a shepherd, a tall man milking a sheep. Standing around him were many thousands of people dressed in white. [IV.9] He raised his head and looked at me. Then he said to me: 'Welcome, child.' He called me over and gave me the cheese he milked, just about enough for a small mouthful. I took it in my cupped hands and ate it, and everyone standing around said: 'Amen.'

[IV.10] "I woke up at the sound of their voices, still tasting something sweet, which I could not identify. I immediately reported this to my brother and we understood that we would undergo martyrdom and we began to put no hope in this world.

[V.1] "After a few days the rumor went around that we would be granted a hearing. However, my father, all consumed with anxiety, arrived unexpectedly from the city. [V.2] He came up to me to persuade me saying: 'Take pity on my grey hair, daughter. Take pity on your father, if I am worthy to be called your father. Haven't I raised you up to this point in your life? Haven't I favored you over all your brothers? Don't disgrace me in front of everybody. [V.3] Consider your brothers. Consider your mother and your aunt. Consider your son who will not be able to live once you are gone. [V.4] Lay aside your pride; do not destroy all of us. None of us will ever be able to speak freely again if you suffer any of this.' [V.5] He said these things just like a father doing the utmost of his duty, kissing my hands, and throwing himself at my feet. In his weeping he did not call me 'daughter,' but 'madam.' [V.6] I felt sorry for my father's situation because he alone of all my relatives did not rejoice in my martyrdom. I tried to comfort him saying: 'What happens on this prisoners' platform is whatever God has willed. You must realize that we are not in our own power but in God's.' This made him terribly sad so he left.

[VI.1] "The next day while we were eating breakfast, all of a sudden we were bound over for trial. We arrived at the forum and immediately the report circulated through the neighborhood of the forum and a huge crowd assembled. [VI.2] We ascended the prisoners' platform. Several people were questioned under torture and confessed. Then they came to me. My father appeared there with my son and he pulled me down the step saying: 'Offer the sacrifice. Take pity on your son.'

[VI.3] "Hilarianus, the procurator who had assumed the power to enforce the death penalty, succeeding the late proconsul Minucus Timinianus, said, 'Take pity on your father's grey hair. Take pity on the tender age of your boy. [VI.4] Perform the sacrifice for the welfare of the Emperors.' I responded, 'I will not do it.' Hilarianus asked: 'Are you a Christian?' I responded, 'I am a Christian.' [VI.5] When my father kept trying to pull me down, Hilarianus ordered him thrown out and beaten with a rod. My father's situation made me sad, as if I myself had been beaten, and so I was upset because of his miserable old age.

[VI.6] "Then Hilarianus passed sentence on all of us and he condemned us to the beasts. Then we went back to the prison full of joy. [VI.7] Since my son had gotten used to breast-feeding and to staying with me in prison, I immediately sent the deacon Pomponius to my father, asking for him. [VI.8] But my father would not hand him over. Then as God willed it, my son no longer desired my breasts nor were my breasts swollen. Consequently, I did not wither away with worry about my child or about any pain in my breasts.

[VII.1] "A few days later while we were all praying, all of a sudden in the middle of prayer, a word sprang from my lips and I spoke the name 'Dinocrates.' And I was flabbergasted because he had never entered my mind until now, and I felt sorry for him when I remembered his predicament. [VII.2] Instantly I recognized that I had a right and an obligation to pray for him. And I began to pray a lot about him and cry out to the Lord. [VII.3] Right away, that very same night, I saw this vision. [VII.4] I saw Dinocrates coming up out of a very dark place, where there were a lot of people. I saw that he was really hot and thirsty. His clothes were dirty, he was pale, and he had the wound on his face that he had when he was dying. [VII.5] This Dinocrates was my brother according to the flesh. He was seven years old and he died from a tumor on his face so that his death was disgusting to everyone. [VII.6] So I prayed about him; but there was a great gulf between him and me, so that neither one of us could come near the other [Luke 16:26]. [VII.7] There where Dinocrates was, there was a pool full of water but its rim was taller than the boy. Dinocrates kept stretching up to drink from it. [VII.8] I was very upset because although the pool contained water, he could not drink, because the rim was too high.

[VII.9] "I woke up and I knew that my brother was suffering but I was confident that I could help him. So I prayed for him every day until we went to the military prison, for we were to fight in the military games since it was the birthday of Geta Caesar. [VII.10] I prayed for my brother day and night groaning and crying, so that my prayer might be answered.

[VIII.1] "On the day we were kept in chains I had this vision: I saw the place I had seen before, and I saw Dinocrates all cleaned up and well dressed, re-freshed. Where the wound had been, I saw only a scar. [VIII.2] I saw the pool which I had seen before with its edge dropped down as low as the boy's navel. He gulped water from it continually. [VIII.3] On its rim was a golden bowl full of water. Dinocrates came up and began to drink from it, yet the bowl was never drained dry. [VIII.4] Once he was satisfied, he stopped in order to play in the water, having fun the way little children do. Then I woke up. At that point I realized that he had been relieved of his pain.

[IX.1] "Finally a few days later, Pudens, the centurion in charge of the prison, began to praise us. He realized that we had a lot of courage. He let several people in to see us so that we might comfort each other. [IX.2] However, when the day of the games approached, my father came to me consumed with wear-iness and he began to tear out the hair from his beard and to throw the hairs on the ground. He cursed his years and said such things as would move all creation. [IX.3] I felt sorry for his unhappy old age.

[X.1] "The day before we were to fight the beasts, I had a vision in which Pomponius the deacon came to the prison gate and was knocking hard. [X.2] I went out and opened up for him. He was dressed in white and wore fancy sandals. [X.3] And he said to me, 'Perpetua, we are waiting for you. Come on.' He held my hand, and we began to go through rough and tortuous places. [X.4] When we finally arrived all out of breath at the amphitheater, he led me into the middle of the arena, and said to me, 'Don't be afraid: I am here with you and fighting alongside you.' Then he left.

[X.5] "Next I saw a huge crowd of bewildered people. I could not understand why no beasts had been let loose against me, since I knew that I had been condemned to fight the beasts. [X.6] However, a particular Egyptian, a really ugly one, came out against me, with his seconds, to fight with me. Good-looking young men came toward me, my seconds, and my cheering section. [X.7] I was stripped and I had become a man! My trainers began to rub me down with oil, as they do in competition. I saw the Egyptian on the other side rolling in the dust.

[X.8] "Then some man came out, so wondrously tall that he was even taller than the top row of the amphitheater. He was wearing a tunic without a belt and it was purple on the center of his chest with white stripes on both sides. He was wearing fancy sandals made of silver and gold. He carried a rod, like a person who trains gladiators, and a green branch with golden apples on it. [X.9] He called for silence and said, 'If the Egyptian wins, he will kill her with the sword; if she wins, she will receive this branch.' Then he stepped back.

[X.10] "Next we approached each other and began to throw a few jabs. He tried to grab my feet, but I bashed his face with my heels. Then I was lifted up into the air and I began to attack him but it was like my feet were not touching the ground. [X.11] When I noticed his delaying tactics, I put my hands together so I could intertwine my fingers, and I caught his head between my hands. He fell on his face and I stepped on his head [cf. Gen. 3:15]. [X.12] The people began to shout and my trainers began to sing. I stepped up to the trainer and accepted the branch. [X.13] He kissed me and said to me: 'Peace be with you, daughter.' And I began to proceed in triumph to the gate of the victors.

[X.14] "Then I woke up and I realized that I would not have to fight against the beasts but against the devil, and I knew that victory was mine. [X.15] I have written what happened up to the day before the games. Anyone who wishes to write about what happened on that day should do so."

[XI.1] The blessed Saturus also related his vision, which he himself wrote down. [XI.2] He said: "As we were suffering, we left our bodies, and we began to be carried eastward by four angels whose hands did not touch us. [XI.3] However, we were proceeding not backward but turned face forward as if we were going up a gradual slope. [XI.4] When we were freed from this world, we saw an intense light, and since Perpetua was there at my side, I said to her, 'This is what the Lord promised us. Now we understand the promise.'

[XI.5] "While we were being carried by the four angels, there appeared to us a broad expanse, which was something like a garden. It had rose trees and all kinds of flowers. [XI.6] The trees were as tall as cypresses, and their leaves were falling all the time. [XI.7] In the garden were four more angels even more glorious than the others. When they saw us, they greeted us with respect and they said to the other angels with admiration, 'They're here, they're here.' The four angels who were carrying us began to tremble and they put us down. [XI.8] We crossed an open expanse on our own by a broad pathway. [XI.9] Here we came upon Jocundus and Saturninus and Artaxius who had been burnt alive in the same persecution, and Quintus who had already died a martyr in prison and we asked them where the others were. [XI.10] But the angels said to us: 'Step right up. Come in and greet the Lord.'

[XII.1] "We approached a place where the walls looked like they were made of light. Four angels stood in front of the entrance to this place, and dressed those who were entering in white stoles. [XII.2] We went in and we heard one united voice saying: 'Holy, holy, holy' without ceasing (Isa. 6:3). Then we saw someone sitting there who looked like an old man. He had grey hair but a youthful face. We could not see his feet. [XII.4] At his right and left were four elders and behind them stood several other elders. [XII.5] We went in and stood in amazement before the throne. Four angels lifted us up, and we kissed him, and he stroked our faces with his hand. [XII.6] The other elders said to us: 'Let us stand.' So we stood up and gave the kiss of peace. Then the elders said to us, 'Go and play.' [XII.7] And I said to Perpetua, 'You have your wish.' And she said to me, 'Thanks be to God. However happy I was in the flesh, I am happier here and now.'

[XIII.1] "Then we went out and outside the gates I saw Optatus, the bishop, on the right and Aspasius, the presbyter and teacher, on the left, separated from one another and sad. [XIII.2] They threw themselves at our feet, and they said: 'Make peace between us because you died and left us this way.' [XIII.3] We said to them, 'Aren't you our bishop, and you our presbyter? How can you throw yourselves at our feet?' We were moved and we embraced them. [XIII.4] Then Perpetua began to speak to them in Greek, and we took them over to one side in the garden under a rose tree. [XIII.5] While we were speaking with them, the angels said to them, 'Let them relax. If you have disagreements between you, forgive each other.' [XIII.6] This upset Optatus and Aspasius. Next the angels said to Optatus, 'Correct your people, because they come to you just like they're coming back from the circus fighting about their favorite teams.' [XIII.7] It seemed to us that the angels wanted to close the gates. [XIII.8] But then we began to recognize many brothers and sisters, even some martyrs. We all felt as if we were nourished by an indescribable scent, which satisfied us. Then I woke up filled with joy."

[XIV.1] These are the remarkable visions of the blessed martyrs Saturus and Perpetua, which they themselves have written. [XIV.2] God called Secundulus to a speedy departure from the world while he was in prison, so that by God's grace he might not have to fight the beasts. [XIV.3] Nevertheless even if he did not experience the sword in his spirit, he at least knew it in the flesh.

[XV.1] About Felicity now, the grace of the Lord touched her in this way. [XV.2] She was already pregnant when she was arrested. She was now in her eighth month. As the day of the exhibition games approached, she was terribly distressed that she might be separated from us on account of her pregnancy, since pregnant women were not allowed to be executed. She was afraid that she might have to pour out her holy and innocent blood at a later date along with criminals. [XV.3] Her co-martyrs were terribly saddened that they might have to leave such a good companion as their associate there alone on the road to her hope.

[XV.4] Therefore, two days before the games they poured out their prayer to the Lord with a single united cry. [XV.5] Immediately after their prayer, her labor pains arrived. While she was in labor she was in great pain due to the natural difficulty of a birth in the eighth month. One of the prison guards said to her, "You're crying now. What will you do when you are thrown to the beasts, whom you scorned when you didn't want to sacrifice?" [XV.6] She responded, "What I suffer now, I suffer; but there will be someone within me who will suffer for me because I will be suffering for him." [XV.7] She gave birth to a girl and one of the sisters brought her up as her own daughter.

[XVI.1] Therefore, the Holy Spirit permitted and by permitting willed that the order of events at the games be written down. Even if we are unworthy to add anything to such a glorious account, nevertheless, we carry out our charge as if it were a command from the most holy Perpetua. Thus we add one more proof of her constancy and the sublimity of her soul.

[XVI.2] The tribune treated the prisoners most severely. Because of warnings from deluded persons he feared that they might contrive to escape through some magical incantations; Perpetua responded to this directly, [XVI.3] "Why don't you even let us refresh ourselves since we are the most distinguished of your criminals? After all, we are the ones who are going to fight on Caesar's birthday. Or wouldn't it be to your credit if we were brought out to him all spruced up?" [XVI.4] The tribune bristled at this and then blushed. Later he ordered that they be treated more humanely. Consequently, permission was given for the brothers and sisters and for others to come in and comfort them. At that time the centurion in charge of the prison was a believer.

[XVII.1] The day before the games the prisoners were having their last meal which they call a *libera* or free meal. But they ate not a free meal but an agape or love feast.

They sent word to the public with the same firm perseverance, warning of the judgment of God, witnessing to their happiness about their martyrdom, joking about the curiosity of the bystanders. Saturus said, [XVII.2] "Won't tomorrow be enough for you? Why do you stare so eagerly at those you hate? Friends today, enemies tomorrow. Nevertheless, notice our faces well, so that you will recognize us on that day." [XVII.3] So the people all went away bewildered and many of them came to believe.

[XVIII.1] The day of their victory dawned. They filed out of the prison into the amphitheater as if into heaven, joyful, their faces radiant, trembling with joy not fear. [XVIII.2] Perpetua was following them with shining face and peaceful pace, like a bride of Christ, the delight of God, strong enough to stare down all the spectators. Felicity was there too, rejoicing that by giving birth she had been freed so she could fight the beasts. [XVIII.3] She could go from one kind of bleeding to another, from the midwife to the games, ready to be washed after childbirth by a second baptism.

[XVIII.4] When they had been led out through the gate, they were forced to put on costumes. The men were decked out like priests of Saturn and the women as those dedicated to Ceres. But noble perseverance fought back even to the last minute. [XVIII.5] Perpetua said, "Now we came here of our own will, so our freedom might not be constrained. We were ready to forfeit our lives so that we would not have to do anything like this. You agreed with us on this." [XVIII.6] Even Injustice recognized justice. So the tribune relented and they were led in just as they were.

[XVIII.7] Perpetua was singing as if she were already stepping on the head of the Egyptian. Revocatus and Saturninus and Saturus started to reproach the spectators. [XVIII.8] Then when they came before Hilarianus, they began to say to him through their gestures and nodding, "What you do to us, God will do to you." [XVIII.9] In response the people became infuriated and they demanded that they be scourged in front of a line of gladiators who usually fought with animals. Revocatus and Saturninus and Saturus gave thanks to God that they might imitate the passion of the Lord at least in this way.

[XIX.1] But the One who said, "Ask and you shall receive," gave to those who asked the death each one desired. [XIX.2] For when they were discussing among themselves their desire for martyrdom, Saturninus specifically confessed that he wished to be thrown to all the beasts, so that he might wear an exceptionally glorious crown. [XIX.3] Therefore, at the start of the spectacle, he and Revocatus contended with a leopard and then they were set on a platform and maimed by a bear. [XIX.4] However, Saturus dreaded nothing more than the bear. He had anticipated being dispatched by a single bite of the leopard. [XIX.5] Then he was paired up with a boar. He was not gored by it, but rather the gladiator who had tied him to the boar was gouged by the same beast and died a couple of days after the games. Saturus was only dragged around. [XIX.6] When he was tied to a bridge for the bear, the bear didn't want to come out of its cage. So Saturus was called back to the sidelines unharmed one more time.

[XX.1] However, the devil prepared a most ferocious cow for the young women. It was not an animal·usually employed in the games but it was intended to match their sex. [XX.2] They were brought out, stripped naked, and covered with nets. The people recoiled at seeing the one delicate young woman, and the other immediately post partum with milk still leaking from her breasts. [XX.3] So they were called back and carelessly dressed. [XX.4] First Perpetua was tossed by the cow and fell on her hip. When she sat up, she pulled her torn tunic from her side to cover her thigh, thinking more of her modesty that of her pain. [XX.5] After looking for her hair pin, she pinned up her disheveled hair. It was not appropriate that the martyr suffer with her hair disheveled. She wouldn't want to look like she was in mourning in the hour of her glory. [XX.6] When she got up and she saw Felicity thrown to the ground, she went over to her, gave her a hand and pulled her to her feet. [XX.7] Both of them stood together. The insensitivity of the people was finally exhausted and the women were recalled through the gate of victors.

[XX.8] There Perpetua was taken care of by a man by the name of Rusticus who was then a catechumen. He stayed close to her. Then she woke up as if she had been dreaming—she was actually caught up in the Spirit and in ecstasy. She began to look around and to the astonishment of all she asked, "When are we going to be brought out to fight this cow or whatever it is?" [XX.9] When she had heard what had just happened, at first she did not believe it until she recognized the marks of torture on her body and on her clothing. [XX.10] She called for her brother and the catechumen and said to them, "Stand firm in faith. Love one another, all of you, and do not be tempted to give up because of our suffering" [Acts 14:22].

[XXI.1] Meanwhile at another gate Saturus was trying to convert the soldier

Pudens. He said, "Up to this point, it has been just as I imagined and predicted. As yet no beast has hurt me. Now believe with your whole heart. I am going out there and I am going to be devoured by the leopard in one bite."

[XXI.2] Then just as the spectacle was ending the leopard was let loose and in one bite Saturus was covered with blood, so that as he was being brought back the people cried out to him a testimony to his second baptism, "Well washed, well washed." [XXI.3] For surely anyone who was washed that way was saved. [XXI.4] Then he said to Pudens the soldier, "Goodbye and remember the faith. Don't let these things upset you, but let them strengthen you." [XXI.5] At the same time he asked Pudens for the little ring from his finger. He dipped it in the blood of his own wound and gave it to him as a keepsake. He left him a token, a memento of his death. [XXI.6] After that he fell lifeless and was thrown in the usual place for people who were going to have their throats slit. [XXI.7] Then the people called for the others to be brought into the center of the arena, so that through their own eyes the spectators might be accessories in their murder as the sword penetrated the bodies of the martyrs. So the martyrs all got up and on their own went to the place the people wanted them to go. But first they kissed each other so they might bring their martyrdom to completion with the kiss of peace. [XXI.8] Some including Saturus were decapitated calmly and in silence. He had gone up the ladder first and now he gave up his spirit first. He was the one who encouraged Perpetua. [XXI.9] However, Perpetua had to experience more pain and she cried out when she was pierced between the collar bones, and she herself guided the faltering right hand of the novice gladiator to her throat. [XXI.10] Perhaps such a woman, one feared by an impure world, could not be killed in any other way than the way she herself wished to be.

[XXI.11] O bravest and most blessed martyrs, truly called and chosen for the glory of our Lord, Jesus Christ! Anyone who exalts, honors, and adores that glory should read these illustrations no less than those of the past for the edification of the Church. In that way new examples of virtue will effectively bear witness to the same Holy Spirit and God, the almighty Father and his son Jesus Christ our Lord, to whom be glory and boundless power for ever and ever. Amen.

— 34 —

The Martyrs of Lyons

Frederick W. Weidmann

The ancient work often called "The Martyrs of Lyons and Vienne," or more briefly, "The Martyrs of Lyons" (*M. Lyons*), bears no title in our only source for it. It is embedded within the fourth-century C.E. *Church History* of Eusebius of Caesarea, which contains many earlier documents quoted in full or in part. In the introductory remarks to Book 5 of the *Church History*, Eusebius refers to, and treats, *M. Lyons* as a work that has its own integrity and dates from the time of the persecution, which it reflects: "The document has been handed down for posterity. . . ." He then proceeds to quote most of it, adding an occasional editorial remark. Interestingly, Eusebius also states that he has preserved the document in its entirety in a "Collection of Martyrdoms," which, unfortunately, has not been preserved from antiquity.

The original form of *M. Lyons* was a letter sent from Christian communities in Lugdunum and Vienna, two cities in Roman Gaul about 15 miles apart from each other (modern-day Lyons and Vienne, France), to fellow believers in Asia Minor and Phrygia (Roman provinces that, on today's map, cover significant portions of western and central Turkey). As such, it conveys several consistencies with what is perhaps the earliest known martyrdom, *The Martyrdom of Polycarp*, which was also written as a letter soon after the persecution it reflects, a decade or two prior to *M. Lyons*. Interestingly, that work was sent from a city in Asia Minor to a city very close to the Phrygian border. These consistencies are likely no coincidence.

The experience of the Christian communities in Lyons and Vienne in 177 C.E. is part of a larger story of the development and expansion of Christianity within the Roman empire. It is very possible that the first community of Christians in Lyons and/or Vienne was founded by immigrants from Asia Minor. Such mobility as this existed within the empire and is part of the Christian story from early on, as can be observed, for example, within the letters of Paul in the New Testament. Individuals from Asia Minor and Phrygia figure prominently in *M. Lyons* and, by extension, within the communities at Lyons and Vienne (see for example, 1.17 and 1.49; for further discussion see Frend 1965, 3–5); the prominent Christian writer and administrator Irenaeus, who was named Bishop of Lyons following the persecution, came from Asia Minor. The very fact that the letter is written in Greek and was sent to Greek-speaking areas is telling, since the Greek language was not commonly used in western parts of the empire, including Gaul. Further, and consistent with the matters both of language and of ties to Asia Minor and Phrygia, one wonders if the very foreignness of at least some of the Christians in these communities in Gaul might have fueled popular feelings of distrust and disgust toward them (see 1.63).

For Christians, Asia Minor and Phrygia might have presumed certain proclivities. For example, a movement called the New Prophecy (or Montanism, a reference to one of its founders, Montanus), which developed in Phrygia in the second half of the second century, was associated with a heightened enthusiasm for martyrdom. The traditions of Asia Minor included such great personages as the martyr Polycarp (a beloved local bishop) and the martyr Ignatius (a Syrian bishop who had met and corresponded with several Christian individuals and communities in Asia Minor). Besides personal memories and stories handed down, writings by and about them would have been available and familiar to many Christians, as were various letters of Paul (who founded several Christian communities in Asia Minor), the Book of the Revelation (whose seven cities of the apocalypse are located in Asia Minor), and at least some of the letters and the Gospel of John (who was said to have lived in and around Asia Minor). That Christians mined such significant personages and works in developing their understandings of martyrdom is to be expected and is evident in documents such as M. Lyons.

Perhaps the obvious fascination with a document such as M. Lyons is the occasion it provides for viewing the interplay—"collision" might be a better word—of Christianity and its agendas with the imperial government and its agendas. To consider the document this way is fair enough. But, to quote two old sayings, "the truth is in details" and "all politics is local."

At the time of the persecution of Christians in Lyons and Vienne, there was no imperial persecution against Christianity. Such did not exist until at least the middle of the third century under Decian, and much more likely not until a few generations later, under Diocletian. That is not to say that Christians were not persecuted; they were—in particular places, at particular times, in particular ways.

What precipitated the persecution of Christians in Lyons in 177 C.E.? It was likely a combination of several factors. From the standpoint of the drafters of the text, what occurred was religious and cosmic: an instance of the ongoing struggle pitting God and God's forces, in the form of these local Christians, against the Devil and the demonic forces, in the form of the provincial governor, the local authorities, the non-Christian citizenry, the torturers, and the beasts of the arena. Such occurrences were bound to happen in anticipation of the final cosmic battle (see, for example, 1.5 and the Book of Revelation in the New Testament).

On another level there may be a significant factor, which is as mundane as it is gruesome and inhumane. In an important article written several decades ago, a team of scholars concludes that the persecution in Lyons occurred as it did, "because the imperial government had just created for the Three Gauls a special privilege which enabled the priests of the imperial cult to acquire cheaply and use instead of gladiators prisoners condemned to death." How did these scholars come to this conclusion? Because of the existence of a "smoking gun": an inscription of an act of the Roman senate, ratified just prior to the time of the persecution of the Lyons and Vienne communities, in which "Emperors and Senate co-operated to reduce for the upper class the burdens imposed by spectacles in the amphitheatres" (Oliver and Palmer 1955, 321, 325).

Still, the Senate's act only provides motive for finding a supply of persons condemnable to death. Why the Christians? The same team of scholars has a suggestion: "The plague which began at Seleuceia on the Tigris in the Fall of A.D. 165 and for ten years swept back and forth across the entire empire together with the cruel raids and miseries of war convinced many that the old gods had been alienated by neglect. Under the circumstances the attitude of the Christians became more noticeable and offensive" (Oliver and Palmer 1955, 327). That rings true with much of what we know about the empire generally, and the practice of religion in the empire specifically, and it also rings true with that issue of "foreignness" raised above.

Christians, given their worship of a different god and—more importantly—their refusal to acknowledge and make sacrifice before those gods generally recognized within the Empire, posed a threat. The gods needed to be appeased if the Empire was to thrive. A generation or so following the persecution in Lyons, Tertullian, a prominent Christian from North Africa, penned the following well-known phrase with his characteristic bravado: "they think the Christians the cause of every public disaster, of every affliction with which the people are visited. If the Tiber rises as high as the city walls, if the Nile does not send its waters up over the fields, if the heavens give no rain, if there is an earthquake, if there is famine or pestilence, straightway the cry is, 'Away with the Christians to the lion!' " (Tertullian "Apology," 40).

It is no surprise that among the charges leveled, or presumed to be leveled, against the Christians are those of atheism and impiety (1.9). Both strongly imply that the ones so charged despise or (at least) ignore the generally acknowledged gods. Though it may be counterintuitive for today's readers to think of Christians as atheists, in the Roman context it makes sense. These Christians did not act appropriately toward the recognized gods. The other charges stated or implied within the text (1.14, 1.26, 1.52), including such things as unacceptable sexual acts and cannibalism, are familiar from other sources and presume ignorance and/or polemical intent on the part of those making the charge (for further discussion, see Benko 1984, 54–78).

Another detail notable in M. Lyon is the different treatment afforded those who are Roman citizens (1.44, 1.47). In point of fact, citizens were treated differently and, for the most part, better (MacMullen 1990, 204, 211, 215). But then why is

Attalus, a citizen (1.44), treated so miserably (1.52)? Part of the answer, as summarized in a standard article on the subject, is that in the Roman empire "governors had a right to freedom of action, they did a great deal more than mechanically apply some rule-book" (MacMullen, 1990, 206). The other part of the answer is supplied by the narrative: "the governor, by way of pleasing the crowed, brought out Attalus again to the beasts . . ." (1.50). All politics is local.

Returning to the senatorial loophole allowing for condemned prisoners to be used in place of gladiators, notice the detail in 1.37: "The day of beast-fights was given by design on our account." The term used, "beast-fights," does not approximate the Latin word standardly used for gladiatorial displays. In theory, a gladiatorial display (*munus*) and a staged animal hunt or beast-fight (*venatio*) were two separate things. However, the lines become increasingly blurred in the imperial period. A standard scholarly account of Roman gladiatorial displays describes "the morning massacre" in which "criminals of both sexes and all ages, who by reason of their villainy—real or supposed—and their humble status had been condemned *ad bestias,* were dragged . . . into the arena to be mauled by the wild animals" (Carcopino 1964, 243; a more recent work, Ville 1981, 387, confirms the "progressive integration" of gladiatorial and beast games). So, the detail in M. *Lyons* may indicate several things, among them: consistent with the senatorial act, Christians were indeed substituting for, or supplementing the action of, gladiators; the apparent integration of beast-fights and gladiatorial combat is consistent with recognized trends at the time; these horrible beast-fights accounted for no little break from the regular action, or even for a whole morning of activity, but, extraordinarily, took up the entire day!

In their own horrible ways, the spectacles of the Roman amphitheater were all about excess and drama, two things also amply provided within M. *Lyons*. According to one scholar, martyrdoms "are documents that are driven by the forces of conflict inherent in the life and spectacle of the Roman world" (Potter 1993, 71). Throughout M. *Lyons* such conflict is evident in many excessive and dramatic ways, perhaps no way more so than in the narrative's use of irony and reversal.

One of the heroes, if not *the* (human) hero, of M. *Lyons* is Blandina. Notice how she is introduced; not exactly a compliment—or is it? Through Blandina, "Christ illustrated that the things which are cheap, unseemly, and readily despised . . . are deemed worthy of great glory by God . . ." (1.17). All the reader knows for sure about Blandina at this point is that she is female. Perhaps, given the social-historical context, that is enough (for a discussion about ancient views of women and the feminine and their presumed inherent inferiority, see Laqueur 1990). But there is more. One sentence later we find out that she is a slave; her status sinks lower.

The reversal is clear and stated from the top. This most lowly of humans (according to accepted norms within that culture) is "deemed worthy of glory by God." The irony goes deeper. We know Blandina's name; we do not know her mistress's name! Further, she is introduced first, and indeed the mistress is defined and located in terms of Blandina (1.18).

That is not all. The image painted by the narrative of Blandina "being suspended, so far as one saw, in the shape of a cross" and calling forth this reaction from the others—"they . . . saw through their sister the one who was crucified on their behalf"—is charged with Christian symbolism and is fascinating in and of itself (1.41). But the narrative goes on to mine the symbolism of the Roman arena to enhance the image: "The small, weak, and easily despised one had put on the great and unconquerable athlete, Christ, and having forced out the opponent through many lots and through contests, she was crowned with the crown of incorruptibility" (1.42). What irony! In the Empire, "the criminal was not on a par with the great figures who won fame and fortune as athletes or gladiators. The condemned was a prop, deprived of self . . ." (Potter 1993, 65). And yet in this document, in the parallel universe (to that of Roman life and spectacle) that it presumes and promotes, the condemned does have identity and is victorious and does receive the crown (the ancient equivalent of our "trophy").

Shortly after these descriptions of Blandina the reader is told about the recanting of those who had previously denied. That is, ones who had earlier denied their Christianity were now claiming it again, thereby assuring their own execution. Notice the prose: "there was great joy for the virgin mother who was recovering those living ones whom she had aborted as dead" (1.45). Within the narrative of M. Lyons and the reasoning it presumes and promotes, those who had earlier denied their Christianity had at that time been "aborted" from "virgin mother" (probably a metaphor for the Christian community; notice too the implicit paradox of a virgin aborting). These same ones, who had now assured themselves a place on death row by reclaiming their Christianity, were accepted back as "living ones." Indeed, the narrative goes on to say that they "were being conceived again and coming alive again" (1.46).

At Blandina's death, she is heralded not only as a "mother" of her "children," the martyrs, but is further called "well-born"—remember, she is a slave. Further, while she and those with her have just been gruesomely executed before the governor, the narrative maintains that in fact they are "victorious" and are on their way to the (true) King, their God (1.55). In a borrowing of biblical imagery, M. Lyons repeatedly refers to martyrdom as an "exodus" (1.36, 1.55) and even as a "wedding feast" (1.55; see also 1.35).

Perhaps by this point it should not surprise readers that it is not only women about whom birthing imagery can be used. Alexander, who is introduced into the text with several details and accolades, was "encouraging" others to make "their confession." That is, on the one hand, he was encouraging them to confess Christianity and thereby bring on their own punishment and death; on the other hand, he was encouraging them to affirm their rebirth into the victory of martyrdom. Consistent with the latter, "he appeared as though in labor" (1.49).

Thus, there are a number of candidates for "ultimate irony" within this text, which honors, celebrates, and recounts with literary verve the suffering of various forms of oppression and gruesome execution. Perhaps the most obvious candidate is the simple statement at 1.58: "They [i.e., the ones doing the torturing and executing] had been defeated." Another place to look might be the particular terms used of the torturers' observations and comments vis-a-vis their victims. For example, at the end of Blandina's first torture session, her tormentors "confess" that they have been defeated (that is, they were unable to break her), and "make testimony" that their torture should have killed her (1.18). These are, of course, the same terms used to define, locate, and glorify the Christian actions of boldly confessing their belief in God and making testimony to that fact through their martyrdom.

In Greek, "testimony" and "martyrdom" are derived from the same root. All uses of "martyrdom" and "testimony" in this translation presume these very closely related Greek words. Also in Greek, the word that refers generically to "nations" is the same word that, in specific contexts, refers to "gentiles." Christians adopted—some might say "co-opted"—many terms and notions of self-definition from Judaism, and from the texts they shared with Judaism. Like "exodus," "wedding feast," and other terms, I believe the use of "gentiles" here, for the most part, reflects biblical idiom. In one case I opt for "nations."

The word traditionally translated as "brothers" in Christian literature and scholarship about Christianity derives from a Greek term that could be, and was, used to refer to siblings of both sexes. Since the term as used in M. Lyons presumes both men and women, I use "siblings" throughout. The word generally translated as "father" derives from a word that could be, and was, used to refer a parent of either sex. Since in M. Lyons there is a juxtaposition of "mother" and "father" imagery (see especially 2.6), it seems to me that the narrative presumes the meaning "father." Though the masculine imagery of the ancient text has been retained, I have not employed the masculine personal pronoun in reference to God.

For purposes of clarity and efficiency, I have left out all of Eusebius' editorial comments. Of the many allusions to and quotations from biblical literature, I note only the most direct quotations by including the biblical reference in brackets. This translation is based upon the Kirsopp Lake's Eusebius: Ecclesiastical History; I also consulted Herbert Musurillo's The Acts of the Christian Martyrs.

The Martyrs of Lyons

[1.3] The slaves of Christ sojourning in Vienne and Lyons of Gaul to the siblings throughout Asia and Phrygia who hold our same faith and hope regarding redemption. Peace and grace and glory from God our Father and from our Lord Jesus Christ.

[1.4] . . . The magnitude of the oppression here, both the extent of the anger of the gentiles against the saints as well as how much the blessed martyrs endured, we are not able to say accurately, nor is it possible to be encompassed in a writing. [1.5] The opponent attacked with full force, giving a prelude to his imminent final coming, and preparing and training his own against the slaves of God, so that not only were we cut off from houses, and baths, and marketplaces, but also any one of us was forbidden to be seen generally by them in any place.

[1.6] But the grace of God countered: on the one hand it saved the weak, on the other it set up steady pillars who were able, through endurance, to draw to themselves the whole assault of the Evil One. They advanced together, bearing up against every kind of abuse and punishment. Considering many to be a few, they were pressing on toward Christ, becoming ones who illustrate that "the sufferings of the present time are not worthy to be compared to the coming glory which will be revealed for us" [Rom. 8:18].

[1.7] First, they nobly endured all that was brought on them in heaps by the crowd: jeers, blows, dragging, plunder, stoning, confinement, and all such things that are apt to occur when an enraged mob acts as though against enemies and foes. [1.8] They were brought up into the marketplace and, after being questioned by the military tribune and the foremost authorities of the city in the presence of the whole mob, they confessed and were confined to prison until the arrival of the governor.

[1.9] Next, after they had been brought before the governor and while he was employing every cruelty against us, there advanced one Vettius Epagathus, one of the siblings, filled with love for God and for others, whose citizenship was perfected to such a degree that, although being a youth, he was equal to the testimony regarding the elder Zechariah: he has walked "in all the commandments and ordinances of the Lord blameless" [Luke 1:6], and in every service to others untired, having great zeal toward God, and bubbling over with the Spirit. Being such a one as this, he did not tolerate the unreasonable judgment coming against us, but got very angry. He even demanded to be heard, making a defense on behalf of the siblings that neither atheism nor impiety was to be found among us. [1.10] But after those around the governor's judgment seat shouted him down (because he was notable), and after the governor would not tolerate the just demands put forth thusly by him but asked only if he also might be a Christian, he confessed in the most brilliant phraseology, and himself took up the martyrs' lot. He bears the title, "Advocate of the Christians," even having the advocate in him, the spirit of Zechariah, which he exemplified through the fullness of love, deeming it appropriate to lay down his own life, making a defense on behalf of the siblings. He was and is a genuine disciple of Christ, "following the lamb wherever he might go" [Rev. 14.4].

[1.11] Thereupon, those remaining became distinguished from each other: the first martyrs who were clearly ready and who were fulfilling the confession of martyrdom with all enthusiasm, and those who appeared unready, untrained, and still weak, not being able to bear a straining of a great contest, of whom about ten in number even aborted. These effected in us great grief and immeasurable sorrow, and cut off the enthusiasm of the others who had not been arrested, who despite acutely suffering all things had nevertheless remained with the martyrs and had not abandoned them. [1.12] But then, all became very scared because of the uncertainty of the confession, not fearing the coming punishments, but focusing on the goal and dreading that a given individual would fall away.

[1.13] And so day after day the worthy ones were being arrested, filling up their number, so that all the zealous ones (especially those through whom things have been established here) were collected from out of the two Christian communities. [1.14] Even some of our gentile household slaves were being seized, since the governor ordered publicly that all of us be investigated. These, also consistent with Satan's ambush, feared the tortures that they saw the saints suffering, and when the soldiers urged them thusly they falsely alleged against us Thyestean feasts and Oedipean sexual intercourse and such things as for us it is neither appropriate to speak about or to think about, or even to believe might ever happen among human beings. [1.15] When these [allegations] had been spread around, all became like beasts against us, so that even if certain ones previously were controlled due to familiarity, then they became greatly enraged and gnashed their teeth against us. Thus was fulfilled that which was spoken by our Lord: "The time will come in which anyone who has killed you will presume to be doing a service for God" [John 16.2].

[1.16] Next, by way of continuing, the holy martyrs endured punishments beyond all description, while Satan was endeavoring that something blasphemous be uttered by them. [1.17] All the anger of the crowd, the governor, and the soldiers, which had exceeded all bounds, was mounted against Sanctus, the deacon from Vienne, and against Maturus, a novice but a noble contestant, and against Attalus, who was of Pergamene descent and had always been a pillar and foundation of those there, and against Blandina, through whom Christ illustrated that the things which are cheap, unseemly, and readily despised among human beings are deemed worthy of great glory by God on account of the God-directed love, which is illustrated with power and not bragged about through appearance.

[1.18] For while we were dreading everything, and while Blandina's earthly mistress, who was herself one contender among the martyrs, was contending [within herself] lest she not be able to make the bold confession on account of the weakness of the body, Blandina became filled with such power that those who were torturing her, successively and in every way, from morning until evening, gave up and were exhausted, and themselves confessed that they were defeated, having nothing which they might further do to her, and they marveled even that she remained breathing. Her whole body being broken and opened, they even made testimony that one kind of wrenching torture was sufficient to make the soul depart, let alone such things to such an extent. [1.19] But the blessed woman, like a noble athlete, became reinvigorated through her confession to such an extent that her refreshment, rest, and relief from that which was happening to her came in saying, "I am a Christian, and among us there is nothing petty."

[1.20] Sanctus himself also went beyond the mark, enduring nobly beyond any human being all the assaults from the lawless ones who were hoping,

through the persistence and extent of the tortures, that something unfit might
be heard from him. He resisted them with such certainty that he did not declare
his own name or nationality or from which city he came, not even whether he
might be slave or free, but to all the questions he responded in Latin: "I am a
Christian." This he confessed in place of name, city, ethnicity, and everything
otherwise. The gentiles did not hear another phrase from him. [1.21] Consequently, a great contentiousness arose from the governor and the torturers
against him, so that by the time they no longer had anything which they might
do to him, last of all they were applying red-hot metal plates to the most delicate
parts of his body. [1.22] These were burning, but he was persisting unbending
and unyielding, firm in the confession, being sprinkled and empowered by the
heavenly fountain of the water of life, which comes from the belly of Christ.
[1.23] His body was a testimony about the things that had been happening,
completely a wound and a bruise, having been pulled and thrown out of human
shape. In him Christ, while suffering, was achieving great glory, rendering the
opponent idle and showing, for the example of others, that there is nothing
fearful where the Father's love is, neither is there anything painful where the
glory of Christ is.

[1.24] Days later, while the lawless ones were torturing the martyr, they
were thinking that when his body parts were swollen and inflamed they might
overcome him should the same correctional instruments be used, since he
could not bear the touch of hands, or that while dying from the tortures he
might produce fear among the rest. Not only did no such thing happen concerning him, but even beyond all glory of human beings he emerged. His body
was even straightened out in the subsequent tortures, and he assumed his
former look and the use of his body parts, so that not punishment but cure
was what, though the grace of Christ, the second torture became for him.

[1.25] As for Biblis (one of the those who had denied), the Devil, who was
thinking to have put her in check already and was further wishing to condemn
her through blasphemy, led her to punishment, necessitating that she say the
ungodly about us, as though she were an easily broken and now cowardly
thing. [1.26] But through the torture she regained her senses and awakened
(as if to say she awakened out of a deep sleep, having been reminded by these
temporary torments about the eternal punishment in Gehenna) so that she
directly contradicted the blasphemers by saying, "How could such ones eat
children when for them it is out of bounds to eat animal's blood?" From then
on she was confessing that she was a Christian and was added to the lot of
martyrs.

[1.27] When the punishments of the tyrant had been rendered idle by Christ
through the endurance of the martyrs, the Devil thought up other instruments—confinement in prison in the darkest and harshest place, stretching of
feet on the stocks hyperextended to the fifth hole, and other assaults as many
as attendants, being angry and filled with the things of the Devil, are accustomed to dispatch on the confined—so that most were strangled in prison (as

many as the Lord, who was illustrating the self-originating glory, wished to depart thusly). [1.28] Some, who had been tortured so cruelly that it seemed that not even having obtained every healing would they be able to live, persisted in prison, destitute from the care of human beings but strengthened by the Lord and empowered both in body and spirit, even looking after and encouraging the rest. But the young ones who had just now been arrested, whose bodies had not been tortured before, were not bearing the burden of confinement but were dying in there.

[1.29] The blessed Pothinus, who had been entrusted with the administration of the Church in Lyons, was over 90 years of age and was quite weak in his body; though barely breathing on account of the bodily weakness affecting him, he was being strengthened by the enthusiasm of the Spirit, through the pressing desire for martyrdom. He also was dragged to the governor's judgment seat, and although his body had been undone by old age and disease, nevertheless his soul was kept in him in order that through it Christ might triumph. [1.30] After he was carried to the judgment seat by the soldiers, with the local authorities and the whole mob flanking him and making all kinds of screams as though he himself were Christ, he rendered a fine testimony. [1.31] While being examined closely by the governor regarding who might be the god of the Christians, he said: "Should you be worthy, you will know." Then he was dragged harshly and suffered many blows, while those nearby were insulting him in every way with their hands and feet (not honoring his age), and those more distant were hurling at him whatever they had at hand. All were thinking it an offense and an impiety should anyone cut off the brutality against him, for thusly they were supposing to avenge their gods. So, scarcely breathing, he was thrown in prison. Two days later he stopped breathing.

[1.32] Next, a particularly great dispensation of God occurred and the measureless mercy of Jesus was manifested in a way which has seldom occurred among the community of siblings but which is not lacking from the means of Christ. [1.33] Those who became deniers at the first arrest were themselves confined and shared in the terrors. At this time denial was no advantage. Rather, the ones confessing that which they were, were confined as Christians (no other charge being forwarded against them), while the others were held as murderers and foul creatures, being punished twice as much as the rest. [1.34] The joy of the testimony lifted up the former, as well their hope for the promised things and their love for Christ and for the spirit of the Father. As for the latter, conscience took revenge in a big way, so that when they passed by their look was distinguishable from all the others. [1.35] The former went ahead cheerfully, glory and great grace having blended together in their looks so that even their chains were draped around like a fitting ornament, as on a bride adorned with dappled gold brocade, and altogether they were smelling of the sweet smell of Christ so that to some it seemed that they had even been anointed with worldly perfume. The latter were downcast, humiliated, ugly, and filled with disgrace, and beyond that they were derided by the gentiles as being ignoble and cowardly. Holding the charge of murderers, they had let go of the honorable, glorified, and life-giving title. The others, seeing these things, were strengthened, and the ones being arrested were confessing without any doubt, giving no thought to the Devil's reasonings.

[1.36] . . . After this, their martyrdoms of exodus separate out into every kind. For weaving one crown from different colors and various flowers they offered it to the Father. Therefore it was necessary that the noble athletes, having endured various contests and having been greatly victorious, receive the great crown of incorruptibility. [1.37] Marturus, Sanctus, Blandina, and Attalus were led to the beasts, into the gentiles' public and common spectacle of inhumanity. The day of beast-fights was given by design on our account.

[1.38] Marturus and Sanctus again went through all the punishments in the amphitheater as though they had previously suffered not at all, but were rather as ones who had already forced out the competitor by lots and were engaging in contests for the crown itself. Again they bore up under the gauntlet of whips (customary there), the mauling by beasts, everything as much as the maddened public, variously located, were shouting and demanding, and after everything the iron chair, on which the bodies roasting filled them with the odor of roasting meat. [1.39] But the torturers did not stop. On the contrary, they grew still more mad, wishing to conquer the endurance of these ones. Yet as from Sanctus they heard nothing other than that which from the beginning he was accustomed to say; his statement of confession. [1.40] As for these, then, their soul persisting in much through great contest, in the end they were sacrificed, having been made a spectacle for the world through this day in place of the various events of the beast-fights.

[1.41] Blandina, having been suspended from a post, was exposed to the beasts, which were being herded in. Being suspended, so far as one saw, in the shape of a cross, through her vigorous prayer she affected great enthusiasm in the contestants who, while they were watching from within the contest and with eyes from some distance away, saw through their sister the one who was crucified on their behalf in order that he might persuade those believing in him that any one who suffers on behalf of the glory of Christ has communion with the living God always. [1.42] Then, after none of the beasts had touched her and she had been taken down from the post, she was taken up again into the prison to be held for another contest, in order that being victorious through more exercises she might make the judgment against the crooked serpent conclusive, and might encourage the siblings. The small, weak, and easily despised one had put on the great and unconquerable athlete, Christ, and having forced out the opponent through many lots and through contests, she was crowned with the crown of incorruptibility.

[1.43] Attalus himself was demanded loudly by the crowd (for he even had a name). He entered a prepared contestant because of his good conscience since, having been genuinely trained in Christian organization, he had always been a testimony of truth among us. [1.44] He was led around the amphitheater with a placard carried before him on which had been written in Latin: "this is Attalus the Christian." While the people were becoming violently worked up against him, the governor, learning that Attalus was a Roman, ordered him to be taken up again with the rest of those in prison about whom he had written to the emperor and was awaiting the latter's response.

[1.45] The intervening time was neither idle nor fruitless. Rather, the mercy of Christ was manifested immeasurably through their endurance, because through the living the dead were being made alive. The martyrs were supplying grace to those who did not make testimony, and there was great joy for the virgin mother, who was recovering those living ones whom she had aborted as dead. [1.46] For it is by the martyrs that most of the deniers were measuring themselves, and were conceiving again and coming alive again, and were learning to confess. And now living and braced up, they proceeded to the governor's judgment seat cheered by a God who does not wish for the death of a sinner but is kind with regard to repentance, in order that they might again be questioned by the governor.

[1.47] The emperor had written that they were to be beaten to death, but if particular ones were to deny, these were to be let go. And now that the festival there (which is crowded by many from all nations who come to it) had begun, the governor led the blessed ones to the judgment seat, making of them a spectacle before the crowd. For this reason he examined them again, and as for those who seemed to have had Roman citizenship, he cut off their heads, but the rest he was sending to the beasts.

[1.48] Christ was greatly glorified by those who had formerly denied but then made their confession contrary to the supposition of the gentiles, for they had been examined separately so that they actually might be let go. Making their confession they were added to the lot of the martyrs. There remained those outside who never had a trace of faith, a perception of the bridal garment, or a concept of the fear of God, but rather were blaspheming the Way through their manner of life; so it is with the children of destruction [John 17:12]. But, all of the rest were added to the church.

[1.49] While they were being examined a certain Alexander, a Phrygian by race and a physician by profession, having lived in Gaul for many years and being known to nearly everyone on account of his love for God and his boldness of speech (for he was not without a share of the apostolic charisma), was advancing to the judgment seat and by signals encouraging them in their confession. He appeared as though in labor to those standing around the judgment seat. [1.50] The crowd, irritated since those who had previously denied again confessed, shouted down Alexander as though the one making this happen. The governor, feeling assured, examined him too as to who he might be. But when he said, "a Christian," the governor, becoming enraged, condemned him to the beasts.

On the next day he went in with Attalus (for the governor, by way of pleasing the crowd, brought out Attalus again to the beasts). [1.51] In the amphitheater, after passing through all the instruments devised for punishment, and after enduring great contests, finally they too were sacrificed. Alexander neither moaned nor groaned anything whatsoever, but was conversing with God in his heart. [1.52] Attalus, when he was placed on the iron seat and was being burned, at which time the odor of roasting meat was rising from his body, said to the mob in Latin: "Behold, what you are doing is eating people, but we neither eat people, nor do anything else which is evil." When he was asked what name God has, he answered, "God does not have a name as does a person."

[1.53] Beyond all this, on the last day of the beast-fights, again Blandina was brought in with Ponticus, a youngster of about fifteen years old. These two were being led in every day to see the punishment of the others and were being compelled to swear by the idols. On account of their remaining steadfast and their contempt, the mob became enraged at them, so that there was neither pity for the age of the young one, nor regard for the woman. [1.54] They exposed these two to all the terrors and led them around through all the punishments by way of compelling a swearing, but were unable to accomplish it. As for Ponticus, he was encouraged by his sister, so that even the gentiles saw that she was comforting and strengthening him, who having nobly endured every punishment, gave up his spirit.

[1.55] As for the blessed Blandina, last of all just like a well-born mother who had encouraged her children and sent them as victorious ones to the King, while also having measured out to her all the contests of her children, she sped after them, rejoicing and glorying in her exodus, as though having been called to a wedding feast rather than having been thrown to the beasts. [1.56] After the whippings, after the beasts, and the griddle, she was at last thrown in a net and exposed to a bull. After being thrown about sufficiently by the beast, she no longer had an awareness of what was happening to her because of her hope and hold on the things believed and her converse with Christ. And so she was sacrificed, and the gentiles were confessing that never among them had a woman suffered such things for such a time.

[1.57] But not so was their madness and cruelty towards the saints satisfied (a wild and barbarous tribe stirred up by a wild beast is hard to appease). And again, their wanton violence on the bodies began. [1.58] That they had been defeated did not shame them since they did not possess human reason. On the contrary, their madness burned just like a beast, with the governor and the public likewise displaying unjust hatred against us, in order that the scripture might be fulfilled, "Let the lawless be lawless still, and let the just one be just still" [Rev. 22:11]. [1.59] Those strangled in prison were exposed to the dogs and guarded carefully night and day lest any corpse be attended to by us. Then having added the remains from the wild beasts and from the fires, the former torn so, the latter charred so, and the heads of those remaining with their severed parts, they guarded the unburied thusly with military care for many days. [1.60] Some were rebuking them and gnashing their teeth, seeking to receive some further justice from them, while others were laughing and mocking, exalting their idols together and attributing to them the punishments. Still others, more moderate ones who even seemed to sympathize to varying degrees, were giving much reproach saying, "Where is their God and what benefit to them was their religion which they even chose over their own life?" [1.61] Things on their side varied like so, while among us things were set within a great sorrow on account of not being able to bury the bodies in the ground; for night was not contributing on our behalf regarding this matter, neither was money persuading nor was entreaty bringing about shame, but in every way they were keeping guard as though they were making a certain great profit should burial not happen.

[1.62] . . . The bodies of the martyrs, having been made an example of and exposed in every way for six days, were next burned and turned into ashes by the lawless ones, and then swept into the Rhone River, which flows nearby, so that no remains of them might still appear on the earth. [1.63] They were doing these things as though they were able to conquer God and take away the martyrs' rebirth in order, so they were saying, "that they might have no hope of resurrection, since, convinced about that, they brought in new and foreign religions among us and despised the terrors, going as ones prepared, even with joy, to death; now let us see if they will rise again and if their God will be able to help them and take them out of our hands."

[2.1] . . . The martyrs . . . [2.2] became emulators and imitators of Christ (who "though being in the form of God did not think that equality with God was something to be seized" [Phil. 2:6]) so that though being in such a state of glory and though making testimony not once, or even twice, but many times, and though brought back again from the beasts having burns, scars, and bruises all around, they neither pronounced themselves martyrs, nor did they leave it to us to address them by this label; on the contrary, if any one of us ever in a letter or in speech called them martyrs, they rebuked that one severely. [2.3] Gladly did they concede the title of martyr to Christ, the trustworthy and true martyr, firstborn from among the dead and beginning of the life of God. They would also remember the martyrs who had already gone before, and say, "These are already martyrs whom Christ deemed worthy to be taken up at their confession, sealing their martyrdom through their exodus, but we are common and humble confessors." And with tears they would summon the siblings, begging the latter for intense prayers for the perfection of their martyrdom. [2.4] They were displaying the power of their martyrdom in deed, conveying much boldness to the gentiles, and making clear their nobility through their endurance, fearlessness, and dauntlessness. Nevertheless, they were declining the title of martyr among the siblings, being filled with the fear of God.

[2.5] . . . They were humbling themselves under the strong hand by which now they are being greatly exalted. They were making a defense for all, but accusing none. They were releasing all, but binding none. They were even praying on behalf of those who were applying the tortures, just like Stephen, the perfect martyr: "Lord, do not set this sin against them" [Acts 7:60]. And if on behalf of those who were stoning him he was making entreaty, how much more so on behalf of the siblings?

[2.6] . . . Indeed this was the greatest battle for them, on account of the genuineness of their love, that the beast, having choked on those whom it had earlier thought to have swallowed down, might vomit up living beings. For they did not boast with regard to those who had fallen but were themselves acting out of abundance, providing help for those in need in this manner: having motherly feelings and shedding many tears on behalf of the latter in front of the Father, [2.7] they asked for life and that one gave it to them; in turn they divided this life among others, thereby departing to God as victors in everything. Having ever loved peace and having commended peace to us, they traveled to God with peace. They left behind no affliction for their mother and no strife or battle for their siblings, but rather joy, peace, harmony, and love.

Bibliography

Benko, Stephen. 1984. *Pagan Rome and the Early Christians.* Bloomington: Indiana University Press.

Carcopino, Jerome. 1964 [1940]. *Daily Life in Ancient Rome: The People and the City at the Height of the Empire,* ed. Henry T. Rowell and tr. E. O. Lormer. New Haven: Yale University Press.

Frend, W.H.C. 1965. *Martyrdom and Persecution in the Early Church: A Study of a Conflict from the Maccabees to Donatus.* Oxford: Basil Blackwell.

Hall, Stuart G. 1993. "Women among the Early Martyrs." In *Martyrs and Martyrologies: Papers Read at the 1992 Summer Meeting and the 1993 Winter Meeting of the Ecclesiastical History Society,* ed. Diana Wood, 1–21. Oxford: Basil Blackwell.

Lake, Kirsopp. 1980 [1926]. *Eusebius: Ecclesiastical History.* Vol. 1, Books 1–5. Cambridge: Harvard University Press.

Laqueur, Thomas. 1990. *Making Sex: Body and Gender from the Greeks to Freud.* Cambridge: Harvard University Press.

Les Martyrs de Lyon (177). 1978. Colloques Internationaux du Centre National de la Recherche Scientifique Series 575. Paris: Editions du Centre National de la Recherche Scientifique. Includes several articles written in English.

MacMullen, Ramsey. 1990. "Judicial Savagery in the Roman Empire." In MacMullen, *Changes in the Roman Empire: Essays in the Ordinary,* 204–17. Princeton: Princeton University Press. Essay originally published in *Chiron* 1986.

Musurillo, Herbert. 1972. *The Acts of the Christian Martyrs.* Oxford: Clarendon.

Oliver, James H., and Robert E. A. Palmer. 1955. "Minutes of an Act of the Roman Senate." *Hesperia* 24: 320–49.

Potter, David. 1993. "Martyrdom as Spectacle." In *Theater and Society in the Classical World,* ed. Ruth Scodel, 53–88. Ann Arbor: University of Michigan Press.

Tertullian. 1995 [1885]. "Apology." In *Latin Christianity: Its Founder, Tertullian,* ed. A. Cleveland Coxe, 17–60. Anti-Nicene Fathers Series 3. Peabody, Mass.: Hendrickson.

Ville, Georges. 1981. *La Gladiature en occident des origines à la mort de Domitien.* Rome: Ecole Française de Rome.

— 35 —

The Martyrdom of Habbib the Deacon

Robert Doran

Habbib, as well as the other two martyrs mentioned at the end of the narrative, *The Martyrdom of Shemona and Guria,* appears in the Syriac Martyrology (ca. 411 C.E.) where it is noted that he was martyred by fire. Ephrem of Edessa (d.373 C.E.) mentions the three martyrs as patrons of Edessa whose festival is celebrated there, and they are the only ones said to have been martyred at Edessa during the Diocletian persecution. The *Acts of Shemona and Guria* and the *Acts of Habbib* are both said to have been written by Theophilus, who claims to have witnessed the execution. Theophilus may in fact have been the author of a trilogy, *The Martyrdom of Shemona and Guria, The Martyrdom of Habbib the Deacon,* and the story of Euphemia and the Goth, as Burkitt argues (Burkitt 1913). The text evidences a good knowledge of the geography of Edessa, but the problems of dating and naming officials suggest that the text was written some time after the events themselves.

The Social Situation in Edessa

These martyrdoms are often used to explore the situation of Christianity in Edessa at the beginning of the fourth century. Eusebius of Caesarea in his *Ecclesiastical History* (1.13) provides an account of a correspondence between Jesus and King Abgar of Edessa, and the *Doctrine of Addai* builds on that fiction by having a portrait of Jesus painted and sent back to Edessa. These remarkable fictions reflect the importance of Edessa (today a small town, Urfa, in eastern Turkey) as a major city on the Armenia-Syria caravan route in antiquity. Because Edessa boasted, at least by the end of the fourth century, that it possessed the bones of the apostle Thomas, it has been suggested that writings associated with Thomas, the *Gospel of Thomas* and the *Acts of Thomas,* were composed there. The *Odes of Solomon* have also been linked to Edessa, as well as the *Diatessaron* of Tatian. It was in Edessa that the early Christian writer Bardaisan worked. Edessa thus had a fascinating Christian lineage, which makes it all the more remarkable that the martyrs who are celebrated by Ephrem are people of low social status from the villages around Edessa. By the beginning of the fifth century, the *Acts of Sharbel and Barsamya* spoke of the conversion and martyrdom of high officials in Edessa during the reign of Trajan, but these *Acts* are spurious. There are Christians in Edessa, among them Bishop Kona, who built a Christian church in Edessa in 313, as well as those mentioned in *The Martyrdom of Habbib the Deacon* (38), who take care of the burial of Habbib. Yet they are not persecuted, even though sections four and five emphasize that anyone who did not sacrifice was to be punished. Rather than inferring that Christianity in Edessa was primarily found in the villages, one might suggest that action was taken against Habbib, as against Shemona and Guria, because he prominently went against the imperial edict. The actions of Theotekna (8–10), as well as the widespread sympathy for Habbib even among Jews and pagans, suggest that the persecution was not very popular. The cry is not for Christians to sacrifice to the local gods, Bel and Astarte; the Roman governor wants Habbib to sacrifice to Zeus, the imported god. Habbib, as a minister of the Christian community and one who was known for his resistance to the decree, gains his wish for martyrdom.

The Date of the Martyrdom

The precise date of the martyrdoms remains in doubt. Burkitt, by using draconian measures with the transmitted text (Burkitt 1913, 29–34), argued that the date for Habbib's persecution was 310, while Shemona and Guria would have been martyred a year earlier. There are clear problems with the dates in the present text. The opening sentence places the martyrdom in the year 620 according to the Greeks, which would be 308 C.E. Yet Constantine and Licinius were first together as consuls in 312. Another problem arises because Licinius is described as instituting the persecution, yet he signed (with Constantine) the Edict of Toleration in 313, and it is only in 320 that he began a rather mild persecution. I suggest that the best point of departure to determine the date lies in the mention that Habbib was executed on the second of Elul, the day it was heard that Constantine had begun to leave the interior of Spain to go to Rome to attack Licinius (39). Burkitt tries to save the reference to Licinius by suggesting that *qrb 'm* might mean "to fight 'with' Licinius (the present Emperor of the East) *against the persecutors*" (Burkitt 1913, 31). But the phrase means "to do battle with." One must accept that Licinius is consistently portrayed as the villain in the present text. However, the reference to Constantine's moving on Italy, even if he came from the Rhineland rather than from Spain, would place the events in 312. During the summer of 312, Constantine crossed into Italy to move against Maxentius in Rome, no persecutor of Christians. The famous battle at the Milvian Bridge on October 28, 312, left Constantine master of the Western Roman Empire. Licinius and Constantine were consuls in 312. In the Eastern Roman Empire, the Edict of Toleration issued by the Emperor Galerius on April 30, 311, shortly before his death, had been slowly but steadily countermanded by Maximin Daia from October/November 311 through June 312. However, the victory of Constantine led Maximin to check the persecution against the Christians and he grudgingly followed the injunctions of the Edict of Toleration issued by Constantine and Licinius in February 313. If one places the martyrdoms of Shemona and Guria toward the end of 311 and that of Habbib in September 312, they fit nicely into the known chronology of the persecutions. One must still acknowledge that the date of 620 according to the Greeks is wrong and that the narrative is set up to contrast the good Constantine and the evil Licinius, which may be the result of the later conflict between the two rulers. One inference is that the author did not write the martyrdom narrative immediately after the event. Yet it must be borne in mind that the text displays none of the technical post-Nicene and post-Nestorian terminology to describe Jesus—"I worship and praise the God who put on a body and became a human being" (25)—as is found in the Acts of Sharbel. Burkitt (Burkitt 1913, 23) suggests that the term n'sh' 'lmy' (men of the world) (38), refers to sympathizers of the Christians, rather than its later technical referent, laypersons.

The Structure of the Trial

The text purports to be a compilation of the records of the trial, but it is interesting to see how the questions posed to Habbib fall into five categories. First, the discussion in 15–18 centers around the question of idols. It then moves in 19 to a question of whether Christ will deliver Habbib, and Habbib's insistence that there is another world to which Christ belongs. In 20–24, Habbib goes on the offensive by claiming that the governor does not obey the emperor's orders. At 25–29, the question is why the Christians worship a human being, and in 30–33 the view that the Christians hate their own bodies surfaces. In these last two sections, scripture is quoted to ground Habbib's position. The first discussion on idols parallels the fourth where Christians are said to worship a human being; the second and fifth both discuss the notion that Christians look to another world. The third is a hinge section, whereby the governor is criticized for dragging out the tortures. The trial thus gives the impression of being neatly organized, and not quite so spontaneous as a trial record might be.

The Text

This translation is of the one Syriac manuscript of the Martyrdom of Habbib found in British Museum (Add 14645, folios 238b–245a). The text was first edited by Cureton and later by Burkitt; Von Dobschutz edited the Greek traditions about the martyrdom. The Syriac manuscript is dated to 936. Doubts were raised about the historicity of the martyrdom, but Burkitt gave a sound defense of its authenticity. There are some problems in the present text. Burkitt (Burkitt 1913, 175) has noted how the governor's name was probably Ausonius rather than the name Lysanias found in the present Syriac text. The reference to the dust collected from the martyr's footsteps seems to be a later, clumsy addition.

In my translation, I have followed the enumeration used by Von Dobschutz and followed by Burkitt.

The Martyrdom of Habbib the Deacon

[1] In the month of Ab of the year 620 of the kingdom of Alexander the Macedonian, in the consulship of Licinius and Constantine, [which is the year in which he was born,] in the magistracy of Julius and Barak, in the days of Kona, bishop of Edessa, the aforesaid Licinius persecuted the church and all the Christian people after the earlier persecution that the Emperor Diocletian had made. The Emperor Licinius commanded that sacrifices and oblations be made and altars restored in every place, incense and frankincense be burnt before Zeus. As many were being persecuted, they were crying out of their own accord, "We are Christians!" They were not fearing the persecution because those who were persecuted were more numerous than the persecutors.

[2] Now Habbib, who was from the village Tel-zeha and had been appointed a deacon, was secretly entering and leaving the churches in the villages, ministering and reciting the scriptures. He was heartening and strengthening many by his word. He cautioned them to be firmly set in the certainty of their belief and not to fear the persecutors, and he charged them. Many were strengthened by his words and lovingly received his commands, being cautioned not to deny the covenant in which they stood. [3] When the city informers who had been appointed for this purpose heard of this affair, they went and made it known to Ausonius the governor who was in the city of Edessa. They said to him, "Habbib, a deacon in the village of Tel-zeha, is going around and ministering secretly in every place. He stands opposed to the command of the Emperor and is not afraid." [4] When the governor heard these things, he was filled with rage against Habbib. He made a petition and sent and made known to Emperor Licinius everything that Habbib had done, so that he might learn and see what command would be issued concerning him and those who were not willing to sacrifice. For although a command had been issued that everyone should sacrifice, it had not been commanded what should happen to those who did not sacrifice, because they had heard that Constantine, (emperor in) Italy, Gaul, and Spain, was a Christian and was not sacrificing. [5] The Emperor Licinius commanded the governor Ausonius, "We, the Emperor, command that the one who so dares to transgress our command be burnt by fire, and let the rest of those who are not persuaded to sacrifice perish by the death of the sword."

[6] When this decree came to the city of Edessa, Habbib, on whose account

the petition had happened, crossed over to the region of Zeugma to minister there also in secret. When the governor had sent and was seeking him in his own village and in all the surrounding region and he was not found, he had ordered that his family and his fellow villagers be seized. They seized them and put them in fetters, his mother and the rest of his family and also some of the villagers. They brought them to the city and locked them up in prison. [7] When Habbib heard what had happened, he reasoned in his intellect and reflected in his mind, "It is better for me to go and show myself to the judge of the region rather than that I remain in hiding and others advance and be crowned because of me and I find myself in great disgrace. For how does the name of Christianity help one who flees from the acknowledgment of Christianity? Behold, if he flees from this [death], a natural death is ahead of him wherever he goes; he cannot escape it because this is decreed upon all humans."

[8] Habbib rose up and went to Edessa in secret. His back was ready for the scourges and his sides for the iron combs and his body for the burning of the fire. He went into the courtyard to Theotekna, a veteran who was chief of the governor's guards and said, "I am Habbib of Tel-zeha whom you seek." [9] Theotekna said to him, "If in fact no one saw that you came to me, hearken to what I say to you and leave. Go to wherever you were and stay there for now. Let no one know and be aware that you came to me and spoke with me and I advised you in this way. Do not worry at all about your family and your villagers, for no one is doing them any harm. They will be in prison for a few days and the governor will send them away because the emperors ordered nothing cruel and terrible concerning them. But if I do not persuade you by what I am saying to you, I am innocent of your blood because, if indeed you show yourself to the judge of the region, you will not escape from a death by fire according to the order that the emperors have ordered upon you."

[10] Habbib answered Theotekna, "I am not worrying myself about my family and villagers but about my life lest it be lost. I was indeed very grieved that I was not in my village on the day the governor sought me and so on my account many were placed in fetters and I seemed to him like a fugitive. Wherefore, if you will not consent to my wish that you bring me before the governor, I myself will go alone and appear before him." [11] When Theotekna heard him speak to him in this way, he held him fast and handed him over to his servants and they led him accompanied by [Theotekna] to the courthouse of the governor. Theotekna entered and informed the governor and said to him, "Habbib from Tel-zeha has come, the one whom your Lordship was seeking." The governor said, "Who is it who brought him? Where did they find him? What was he doing where he was?" Theotekna said to him, "He himself came of his own free will without human compulsion as no one was aware of him."

[12] When the governor heard, he was very bitter against him so he said, "This person who acted so has truly scorned me and treated me with contempt and regarded me as no judge. Because he acted in this way, it is not right that any mercy be shown him, and also that I not be in a hurry to order his death

as ordered upon him by the Emperors, but it is right that I protract with him so that his torments and cruel punishments be increased the more and that through him I make many afraid so that they will not ever dare to flee."

[13] Many gathered and were standing near him at the door of the court-house, some of the officials and some of the townspeople. Some of them were saying to him, "You acted wickedly in that, without the compulsion of the judge, you came and showed yourself to those seeking you." But others were there who were saying to him, "You acted well in that of your own free will you came and showed yourself rather than the compulsion of the judge should bring you. For now it is known that your confession of Christ is of your own free will and not by the compulsion of humans." [13a] These are what the city informers had heard from those speaking to him while standing at the door of the courthouse, and also it had been told to the city informers that he had gone secretly to Theotekna and he did not want to uncover him. They made known to the judge everything that they had heard. The judge was furious against those who were saying to Habbib, "Why did you come and show yourself to the judge without the compulsion of the judge?" He said to Theotekna, "It was not right for a man who was made chief of his comrades to act so treacherously against his own leader and void the order of the Emperors issued against the insolent Habbib that he be burnt by fire." Theotekna said, "I did not act treach-erously against my comrades and also I did not look to void the order issued by the Emperors. For what am I before your Eminence that I would dare to do this? For I interrogated him fully as·to what your Eminence was seeking through me so that I might know and see whether indeed he came here of his own free will or whether the compulsion of your Eminence had not brought him by means of others. When I had heard from him that he had come of his own will, I diligently brought him to the honorable door of the courthouse of your Uprightness."

[14] The governor immediately commanded and they brought Habbib before him. The official said, "Behold, he is standing before your Eminence." He began to interrogate him in this fashion and said to him, "What is your name and where do you come from and what are you?" He said to him, "My name is Habbib, and I come from the village of Tel-she, and I was made a deacon." [15] The prefect said, "Why did you violate the command of the Emperors and you ministered in your ministry, something that was not commanded to you by the Emperors, and you are not willing to sacrifice to Zeus whom the Em-perors worship?" Habbib said, "We are Christians. We do not worship what is made by humans, those that are nothing and also those making them are noth-ing. But we worship the God who made humans." [16] The governor said, "Do not remain in that insolent mind in which you came to me, dishonoring Zeus, the great glory of the Emperors." Habbib said, "But this Zeus is an idol, the work of humans. You say rightly that I am dishonoring it. For if the carving of him out of wood and the fastening of him with nails shout out about him that he is something made, how do you say to me that I am dishonoring him

because behold! his dishonor is from himself and is upon him." [17] The governor said, "By this very thing that you are not willing to worship him, you dishonor him." Habbib said, "If I dishonor him because I do not worship him, truly how much dishonor did the carpenter do to him who carved him with an iron axe and the smith who struck him and fastened him with nails?"

[18] When the governor heard that he spoke in this way, he ordered that he be beaten mercilessly. When he had been beaten by five, he said to him, "Do you obey the Emperors now? For if you do not obey, I will surely lacerate you with combs and torture you with all kinds of tortures and then at the end I will command that you be burnt with fire." Habbib said, "These threats with which you threatened me are much fewer and lesser than those that I had previously placed in my mind to endure. Therefore I came and showed myself to you. [18a] The governor said, "Throw him in the iron restraint for murderers and let him be beaten as he deserves." As he was being beaten, they were saying to him, "Sacrifice to the gods!" and he was crying out and saying, "Your idols are accursed, and like you are those who worship them with you." The governor commanded and they brought him up to the prison. They did not allow him to speak with his family and villagers in accordance with the judge's order. Now that day was the festival of the Emperors.

[19] On the second day of Elul, the prefect commanded and they brought him out of the prison, and he said to him, "Do you deny what you profess and obey the order the Emperors issued? If you do not obey, I will pass over you with cruel combs so that you will obey them." Habbib said, "I have not obeyed them, and also I am determined in my mind not to obey them, not even if you condemn me to punishments that are even crueler than those the Emperors commanded." [19a] The governor said, "I swear by the gods that if you do not sacrifice I will not exclude anything severe and bitter that I will not inflict on you, and we will see if the Christ whom you worship delivers you." Habbib said, "All who worship Christ are delivered because it is through Christ that they have not worshipped creatures along with the creator of creatures." [19b] The governor said, "Let him be stretched out and beaten with whips until no place is left on his body on which he has not been beaten." Habbib said, "From these afflictions that you consider cruel in their scourgings are woven crowns of victory to those who endure them." [19c] The governor said, "How do you [plural] call afflictions relief? and how do you [plural] reckon the sufferings of your [plural] bodies a crown of victory?" Habbib said, "It is not for you to ask me about these things, for your impiety does not deserve to hear the explanation of these. I said and I say that I do not sacrifice." [19d] The governor said, "I place you in these punishments because you deserve them. I myself will put out your eyes that look on this Zeus and do not fear him. I will block up your ears that hear the ordinances of the Emperors and do not tremble." Habbib said, "God, whom you here deny, has another world, and there you will confess him with scourges after you have denied him further." [19e] The governor said, "Let go of that world about which you speak and pay heed now

to this trial in which indeed you are standing, because there is no one who is able to deliver you from it except the gods deliver you if you sacrifice to them." Habbib said, "Those who die for the name of Christ and do not worship things made and creatures are alive in God's presence. Those who love the life of the present age more than this, their torment is forever."

The governor commanded and they hung him up and they combed him. [20] As they were combing him, they were pulling on him, and he was hanging a long time until his shoulder blades creaked. [21] The governor said to him, "Are you persuaded now to place incense before this Zeus?" Habbib said, "Before these pains I did not obey you. Now that indeed I suffer them, how do you think that I will be persuaded by you so that I should lose by them anything I attained by them?" [22] The governor said, "In accordance with the command of the Emperors, I am ready with more bitter and cruel punishments than these to make you pay attention until you do their will." Habbib said, "You are sentencing me because I do not obey the command of the Emperors, and look! even you, whom the Emperors have raised to honor and made a judge, you transgress their command in that you do not do to me what the Emperors commanded you." [23] The governor said, "Because I was patient with you, you speak in this way like someone bringing a complaint." Habbib said, "If you had not scourged me and imprisoned me and combed me and put my feet into stocks, one could suppose that you were patient with me. But if these happened, where is this patience towards me that you talk about?" [24] The governor said, "These things that you said will not help you because all of them are not in your interest and they bring upon you afflictions even more bitter than those the Emperors commanded." Habbib said, "If I was not aware of the things that help me, I would certainly not speak about them in your presence." [24a] The governor said, "I myself will silence these words of yours in a minute, and I will appease through you the gods whom you do not worship, and I will assuage through you the Emperors because you defied their commands." Habbib said, "I do not fear the death with which you threaten me. For if I had feared it, I would not have gone around from house to house and ministered. This [death] is why I ministered in this way." [25] The governor said, "Why do you worship and glorify a human being, yet you are not willing to worship and glorify this Zeus?" Habbib said, "I do not worship a human being because it is written for me, 'Cursed is everyone who puts his trust in a human being' [Jer. 17:5]. For I worship and praise the God who put on a body and became a human being." [26] The governor said, "Do what the Emperors order. What is in your mind is your affair, whether you are willing to renounce it or whether you are not willing not to leave it?" Habbib said, "It is not possible for both things to be because lying is contrary to truth. It is not possible that I be taken away from this understanding that is fixed in my mind." [27] The governor said, "I will act on you with bitter and cruel afflictions so that you depart from your understanding that you said 'It is fixed in my mind.' " Habbib said, "These afflictions through which you think that I will be uprooted from my understanding, by them my understanding grows strong within as a tree that bears fruit." [28] The governor said, "Why do scourgings and lacerations help your tree? Especially when I order fire against it for its complete burning?" Habbib said, "I do not see in these things what you see, because in them I observe hidden things, and therefore I do the will of God the Maker and not that of a made idol that does not feel anything."

[29] The governor said, "Because he so denies the gods whom the Emperors worship, let lacerations be added upon his former lacerations, for he has forgotten those former lacerations by the many questions that I was patient with him to ask him." As they were lacerating him, he was crying out and saying, "The sufferings of this time are not equal to the glorious praise that is prepared that will be revealed in those who love Christ [cf. Rom. 8:18]." [30] When the governor saw that not even by these afflictions was he willing to sacrifice, he said to him, "Does your doctrine teach you so that you hate your bodies?" Habbib said, "It is not that we hate our bodies. This scripture was written for us, 'Whoever loses his life will find it' [Matt. 10:39] but also another saying for us 'Do not give holy things to dogs, and do not throw pearls before swine.'" [Matt. 7:6] [31] The governor said, "I know that you are saying all this in this way so that my anger and the fury of my mind will rise up and I will hastily order death upon you. Therefore, I do not hasten to what you desire, but I will be patient. It is not for your relief, but so that the affliction of your torments might be multiplied and that you see your flesh as it falls before you by the combs that come upon your sides." Habbib said, "I also look for this that you abundantly inflict torture on me as you said." [32] The governor said, "Obey the Emperors who have authority so that whatever they wish they do!" Habbib said, "It does not belong to humans that they do whatever they want, but only God whose authority is over heaven and over all the inhabitants on earth. There is no one who finds fault with his power and says to him, 'What are you doing?'" [33] The governor said, "For this effrontery of yours death by the sword is too lenient. So I am prepared to order upon you a death that is harsher than the sword." Habbib said, "I myself look forward to that death whose duration is lengthier than that of the sword, and which you will order upon me whenever you want."

[34] After this the governor began to pronounce against him the sentence of death and he spoke loudly before his officials and also the nobles of the city and he said as they listened to him, "As for this Habbib who denied the gods as also you heard him and who also reviled the Emperors, it is fitting that his life be denied under this venerable sun and he should not see this light, the companion of the gods. If it were not ordered by former emperors that the corpses of murderers be buried, it was not even fitting that this fellow's corpse be buried because he was so presumptuous. I order that a leather strap be put upon his mouth as upon a murderer's mouth and that he be burnt with a slow fire, one whose duration is long so that the torment of his death be increased."

[35] He went out from the presence of the governor as the strap was placed

on his mouth. Very many of the inhabitants of the city ran after him. For the Christians were rejoicing that he had not changed and had not turned away from his covenant, and the pagans were threatening him because he was not willing to sacrifice. They led him from the arched western gate opposite the cemetery, the entrance built for Abshelama, the son of Abgar. Now his mother was dressed in white and she went out with him.

[36] When he arrived at the place where they were to burn him, he stood and he and all those who went out with him prayed and he said, "King Christ, to whom this world and the world to come belong, look and see that when I was able to flee from these afflictions I did not flee so that I might not fall into the hands of your righteousness. May this fire with which I burn be for me retribution before you so that I may be delivered from that fire, which is unquenchable. Accept my spirit before you through the spirit of your divinity, glorious son of the adorable Father."

When he had prayed he turned and blessed them and they gave him "Peace," while men and women were weeping and saying to him, "Pray for us in the presence of your Lord so that he make his peace among his people and restoration for the churches that are uprooted." [36a] While Habbib was standing, they had dug a place and they brought him and made him stand within it and they had thrust in with him a stake. They came to bind him onto that stake and he said to them, "I will not depart from this place where you are setting me on fire." [37]. They brought pieces of wood and they arranged and placed them all around him. When a fire was raging and its blaze shot up sharply they cried out to him, "Open your mouth!" The moment he opened his mouth he died.

[38] The men and women wailed with the sound of weeping and they dragged and pulled him out of the fire, as they were laying upon him fine linen [garments] and choice ointments and perfumes. They were snatching some of the pieces of wood from his burning and the brethren and men of the world lifted him up and they prepared and buried him near the martyrs Guria and Shemona in the same grave in which they were placed, on the hill that is called Beth Alah Kikla, as they were saying over him psalms and hymns and they were lovingly and reverentially escorting his burnt body. [38a] Even some Jews and pagans took part with the Christian brethren in shrouding and burying his body. At the very time of his burning and even while they were burying him, one spectacle of mournfulness was appointed upon those who belonged and those who were outsiders. For tears were flowing from all eyes while everyone gave praise to God for whose name's sake he had given his body to the burning of the fire.

[39] Now the day on which he was burnt was the Friday of the second day of the month of Elul. On that day it was heard that Constantine the Great had begun to leave the interior of Spain to go to Rome, the city of Italy, so that he might make war with Licinius, who is now ruling in the eastern parts of the Roman Empire. Behold! the regions on all sides are disquieted because no one

knows which of them will conquer and will remain in his imperial power. By this news, the persecution abated a little from the churches.

[39a] Now the notaries were writing down whatever they heard from the judge, and the city informers were writing the remaining other things said outside the door of the courthouse and, as is the custom, they informed the judge of all that they heard and saw and the determinations of the trial were written in their acts.

[40] I, Theophilus, who had renounced the evil portion of my ancestors and believed in Christ, diligently wrote a copy of these acts of Habbib as I had formerly written [those] of his fellow martyrs, Guria and Shemona. He who deemed them blessed in their death by the sword was himself likened to them by the fire of the burning of his crowning. I wrote the year and the month and the day of the crowning of these martyrs not for the sake of those who like me saw the deed but for the sake of those who come after us so that they might learn what was the time of these martyrs and who they were and also by the acts of the earlier martyrs who [were] in the days of the Emperor Domitian and the remaining other Emperors who also made persecution to the church, and they also executed many with scourges and with combs and with cruel afflictions and with sharp swords and with burning fire and by the fearsome sea and in the merciless mine and all of these [afflictions] and those like them upon the expectation of the reward that is to come. For the afflictions of these martyrs and those about whom I heard opened my eyes, I Theophilus, and enlightened my mind and I believed in Christ who is the son of God and is God (and the dust of the feet of these martyrs, which I received when I ran after them at the time that their being crowned took place). May he whom I denied forgive me and may he acknowledge me before those who worship him, I who acknowledge him now.

At the twenty-seventh cross-examination which the judge questioned Habbib, he handed down the sentence of death by burning by fire.

The martyrdom of Habbib the Deacon is ended.

Bibliography

Burkitt, F. C. 1913. *Euphemia and the Goth with the Acts of Martyrdom of the Confessors of Edessa.* London: Williams and Norgate.

Cureton, William. 1864. *Ancient Syriac Documents Relative to the Earliest Establishment of Christianity in Edessa and the Neighboring Countries from the Year after Our Lord's Ascension to the Beginning of the Fourth Century.* London: Williams and Norgate.

Drijvers, Hans J. W. 1982. "Facts and Problems in Early Syriac-Speaking Christianity." *Second Century* 2: 157–75.

———. 1984. *East of Antioch: Studies in Early Syriac Christianity.* London: Variorum.

Segal, Judah Benzion. 1970. *Edessa "The Blessed City."* Oxford: Clarendon.

Von Dobschutz, Ernst. 1911. *Die Akten der edessenischen Bekenner Gurjas, Samonas und Abibos aus dem Nachlass von Oscar von Gebhardt.* Leipzig: Hinrich.

—36—

4 Maccabees

Clayton N. Jefford

Our primary witnesses for the text of 4 Maccabees include the two early uncial manuscripts of Sinaiticus and Alexandrinus, the ninth-century Codex Venetus (minus 5:11–12:1), and various collected writings of Flavius Josephus. Eusebius of Caesarea and Jerome assumed Josephus to be the author of 4 Maccabees, but this view is no longer widely accepted. Instead, for most scholars, our writer remains an unknown Hellenistic Jew who lived sometime around the first century C.E., most likely before the fall of the Temple in the year 70. While some researchers believe the origins of the text to have been in Alexandria or the region of northern Egypt, a more likely setting is Antioch in Syria. A clear knowledge of 4 Maccabees by the early Antiochean bishop Ignatius suggests a probable Syrian origin, as does a strong reverence for the Maccabean tradition that has persisted in popular local culture. Our text was first composed in Greek and bears numerous terms that are unique to the author. Popular usage soon required, however, that the text be translated into Syriac.

The purpose of 4 Maccabees is specifically identified in the opening lines of the text: to demonstrate the superiority of pious reason over desires or passions. In this effort our author has borrowed from the so-called martyrs sequence of 2 Maccabees 6:18–7:42, a passage that serves as a demonstration of the power of reason. These materials, a series of vivid tortures, are developed and inserted into a philosophical framework that praises both fidelity to the Jewish law and pious resolution in the face of persecution.

Elements of Stoicism, universalism, and devotion to faith tradition abound throughout the text. The author demonstrates a deep respect for the history of pious suffering as seen through the history of Israel. The afflictions of the Jews are viewed, not only as an inspiration for the people of God, but as a vehicle of salvation for the world. On the one hand, those who die at the hands of their Greek conquerors are portrayed as a sacrificial offering on behalf of their own people. At the same time, these victims of destructive greed and power are offered as a model of endurance for the enemy soldiers themselves. The rudiments of this

faith perspective are clearly evident in the rise of later Christian theology, especially among the second- and third-century theologians of Eastern Christendom.
The original used for this translation is from Alfred Rahlfs's *Septuaginta*.

4 Maccabees

[1.1] Since I am about to offer a philosophical discourse about whether pious
reason can master desires, I advise you to give special care to philosophy, [2]
because good judgment is the ultimate virtue and is basic to the pursuit of
knowledge. [3] So, if reason seems to conquer desires that frustrate self-control,
that is, gluttony and lust, [4] it would also appear to dominate desires that
thwart justice, like hate, and that hinder courage, like anger, fear, and pain.
[5] But perhaps one may ask, "If reason foils desires, why does it not master
forgetfulness and ignorance?" To suggest this is absurd. [6] Reason does not
curb its own desires, but those that oppose justice, courage, and self-control.
It does not nullify them, but helps us to confront them. [7] I can show you
many times in many cases where reason was master over desires, [8] but I can
illustrate it best from the bravery of those who died for virtue—Eleazar, the
seven brothers, and their mother. [9] All of these showed that reason controls
desire by their rejection of death's pains. [10] I am now compelled to praise
the virtue of those who, with their mother, died for what is noble and good,
and who moreover were blessed by honor. [11] Everyone, even the torturers,
marveled at the courage and endurance of these who tore down the tyranny
over their people, conquering the tyrant through endurance and serving as the
means to cleanse their homeland. [12] I will address this after I make my point,
as is my way. At that time I shall turn to their story, giving glory to all-knowing
God.

[13] Let us consider, then, whether reason is master over desires. [14] Here
we distinguish between reason and desire, as well as desire's many forms, and
whether reason conquers all of these. [15] Clearly, reason is a mind of true
logic that prefers a life of wisdom. [16] Likewise, wisdom is the knowledge of
divine and human affairs, and of their causes. [17] This, then, is what the law
offers, a way to learn respect for divine matters and profit from human affairs.
[18] Forms of wisdom include orderly judgment, justice, courage, and self-
control. [19] Dominant over all of these is good judgment, by which reason
conquers desire. [20] Pleasure and pain are the principal stems of desire. Each
comes naturally both to body and soul. [21] Many results derive from the
desires of pleasure and pain. [22] Thus, lust precedes pleasure, followed by
joy. [23] Fear precedes pain, followed by grief. [24] Anger is a desire that
includes both pleasure and pain, as can be seen upon reflection. [25] A malicious element exists within pleasure, the most complex of all desires. [26] It
appears as arrogance, greed, ambition, contentiousness, and envy within the
soul; [27] in the body, as swinish eating, gluttony, and devouring food in

private. [28] Just as pleasure and pain are two plants sprung from the body and soul, many branches sprout on these plants. [29] Reason serves as the chief gardener for each, weeding, pruning, staking, watering, and drenching all parts in order to reclaim the forest of habits and desires, [30] because reason is a guide of virtues, but master of desires.

Observe, first, that reason is master of desires through the restraining works of self-control. [31] Self-control rules over lust. [32] There are both mental and physical lusts, and reason clearly conquers both. [33] How else could we resist the enticing pleasure of forbidden foods? Is it not because reason can conquer longing? I should say so! [34] When we crave seafood, fowl, animals, or various foods forbidden to us by the law, we resist through the conquest of reason. [35] The longings of desire are checked by the rational mind, and all the body's urges are harnessed by reason.

[2.1] Yet why should we be surprised if the soul's craving to possess beauty is suppressed? [2] The rational Joseph is praised exactly for this—that his intellect persuaded him to avoid indulgence. [3] Though young and in his sexual prime, he curbed the urgency of his desires by reason. [4] Reason clearly dominates frantic indulgence, but also every craving. [5] The law specifies, "You shall not covet your neighbor's wife nor anything that is your neighbor's [Exod. 20:17]." [6] While the law has told us not to covet, I could argue further that reason can control any craving.

So it is with any desire that thwarts justice. [7] How else can those who devour food in private, are gluttons or drunks change their ways, unless reason is clearly lord of desires? [8] Even people who are misers, if they conform to the law, are immediately forced to change and to loan money to the needy without interest, canceling the debt during the seventh year. [9] Stingy people are swayed by the law, through reason, neither to harvest their fields bare nor to strip their grapevines clean.

We also see that reason dominates desires in other ways. [10] For example, the law dominates affection for parents, to avoid any temptation to betray virtue. [11] It conquers love of wife, to permit rebuke when she breaks a rule. [12] It dominates love of children, to allow punishment for misbehavior. [13] It masters love of friends, to permit correction of their misdeeds. [14] It makes sense that reason can conquer hostility through the law and yet not destroy the fruitful plants of its enemy. The plants of the enemy are preserved, and what falls is gathered.

[15] Reason even seems to dominate the most savage desires—ambition, vanity, pretension, arrogance, and envy. [16] A rational mind rejects each of these malicious desires. It even masters anger. [17] When Moses was angry with Dathan and Abiram, he did not respond in anger but controlled his anger through reason. [18] As I have said, the rational mind can overcome desires, changing some and neutralizing others. [19] How else could wise father Jacob condemn the families of Simeon and Levi for the senseless slaughter of the Shechemites, saying, "Cursed be their anger" [Gen. 49:7]? [20] If reason could

not dominate anger, he would not have spoken this way. [21] When God created people, they were given desire and disposition. [22] At that time the mind was enthroned as a sacred ruler over all things by means of the senses. [23] A way was given here by which people could conduct themselves along a rational, just, good, and courageous path.

[24] Why then, we may ask, does reason not manage ignorance and forget-fulness, if it is master of desires? [3.1] The question is truly absurd, for reason does not seek to overcome its own desires, but those of the body. [2] We cannot ignore lust, but reason helps us to avoid enslavement to it. [3] We cannot ignore buried anger, but reason helps us to be rescued from it. [4] We cannot stop bad habits, but reason is an ally so that they do not subdue us. [5] Reason does not uproot desire, but opposes it.

[6] This is clearly illustrated by the story of King David's thirst. [7] During a long day's battle, David and his warrior comrades killed many foreign invad-ers. [8] That evening he came sweating and exhausted to the royal tent around which our ancestors' army was encamped. [9] The others were at dinner, [10] but the king had an incredible thirst. Springs were plentiful, yet none could satisfy him. [11] Instead, an irrational lust for water from enemy territory tore and gnawed at him. [12] When the guards complained about his dilemma, two brave young soldiers, in response to the king's lust, armed themselves and scaled the enemy's perimeter with a pitcher. [13] Avoiding the gate watchmen, they moved in search throughout the camp. [14] They found the spring and boldly returned to the king with his drink. [15] Though he had an irrational burning thirst, he saw this as a spiritual danger, equal to a drink of blood. [16] So he put reason over lust and poured it out as a drink offering to God. [17] A rational mind thus can conquer the drives of desire and soothe the sting of inflammation. [18] It overwhelms bodily pain, even though extreme, and by noble reason resists the powers of lust.

[19] I now offer some narrative support for rational reason.

[20] After our ancestors had enjoyed such profound peace and prosperity that even Seleucus Nicanor, king of Asia, had placed funds in their Temple and accepted their situation, [21] certain people revolted, bringing disaster against the general welfare.

[4.1] There was a certain Simon who was a political opponent of Onias, a worthy and good man who held priesthood for life at the time. After his failure to slander Onias before the people, Simon fled his homeland in order to betray it. [2] When he arrived before Apollonius, governor of Syria, Phoenicia, and Cilicia, he said, [3] "I support the king and have come to reveal that a large sum in private funds is in the Jerusalem treasury, which does not belong to the Temple but to King Seleucus." [4] Once Apollonius had learned the details, he commended Simon for his fidelity to the king and went to tell Seleucus of the treasures. [5] When he had received the necessary authority, he came quickly to our homeland with the accursed Simon and a considerable army. [6] He announced that he came by royal order to take the private funds of the treasury. [7] The people, in bitter protest, responded that it was dreadful that those who entrusted their holdings to the sacred treasures in good faith should be robbed! Therefore, they resisted. [8] Nevertheless, Apollonius proceeded with threats to the Temple [9] where the priests, with women and children, pleaded for God to shield the sanctuary from dishonor. [10] As Apollonius and his army approached to seize the funds, angels on horseback appeared from heaven flashing their weapons and spreading great fear and trembling. [11] Apollonius then collapsed in the outer courtyard of the Temple, stretched his hands toward heaven, and tearfully asked the Hebrews to pray for the heavenly army to be calmed. [12] He admitted that he had sinned in a manner worthy of death, yet he would bless the holy place if he were spared. [13] The high priest Onias heard these words and, though skeptical that King Seleucus would think that Apollonius was turned by human treachery and not divine justice, prayed for him. [14] Saved to his surprise, Apollonius went to explain all to the king.

[15] With the death of King Seleucus, power shifted to his son, Antiochus Epiphanes, an arrogant and awful man. [16] He removed Onias as high priest and installed his brother Jason, [17] who agreed, if given the office, to pay a yearly tribute of 3660 talents. [18] So Antiochus permitted him to be high priest and ruler of the people. [19] He changed their lives and government contrary to the law, [20] so that a gymnasium was built near our national citadel and the Temple workers were disbanded. [21] Angered by this, divine justice led Antiochus to wage battle against them, [22] for after his wars against Ptolemy in Egypt, he heard that a rumor about his death had been received with great joy in Jerusalem. He marched quickly against them, [23] and after the destruction he decreed that anyone who followed ancestral traditions would die. [24] Yet he was unable to stop the popular observance of the law through his decrees, but saw that each threat and punishment came to nothing. [25] For instance, even fully aware of the danger that they and their infants would be thrown to their death, women still circumcised their sons! [26] So, since the people ignored his decrees, he himself used torture to force them to eat impure food and abandon Judaism.

[5.1] Seated on a high place with his counsel and encircled by his armed soldiers, the tyrant Antiochus [2] instructed the guards to catch and force each Hebrew to eat pork and food sacrificed to idols. [3] Those who refused were to be broken on the wheel. [4] When many were gathered, a leader who was named Eleazar, of priestly family and elderly, prominent in the law and widely known by the tyrant's counsel, was brought to him.

[5] Antiochus saw him and said, [6] "Old man, to avoid your torture, I suggest that you eat pork and save yourself. [7] I pity your old age and gray hair. But, though you are advanced in years, I cannot think of you as a seeker of wisdom since you honor Jewish rituals. [8] Why do you recoil at the fine meat of this animal that nature provides? [9] It is foolish not to enjoy shameless foods, and wrong to reject nature's gifts. [10] You would be a fool if, in devotion

to some vanity, you should cross me at your own expense. [11] Wake up to your senseless views, drop your silly logic, be mature in your thought, think reasonably, [12] and respect your old age by heeding my kind invitation. [13] Indeed, if some power actually does steer your faith, surely it will excuse any misdeed that is forced on you."

[14] When the tyrant had urged him about the forbidden meat, Eleazar asked to speak. [15] Receiving permission, he spoke to the assembly in this way: [16] "Antiochus, having resolved to be ruled by divine law, we know of no other compelling force that we wish to obey. [17] Thus, we can think of no reason to break it. [18] Even if our law were not truly divine, as you suggest, though we hold it to be, it would be impossible to dismiss our religious views. [19] Do not think that it would be a minor sin if I were to eat impure food. [20] It is the same to break the law in small or great ways, [21] for the law is violated in either case. [22] You mock our view of wisdom as though we live like fools. [23] Yet it instructs us in self-control so that we can control pleasures and lusts. It teaches courage so that we can freely endure any pain. [24] It prescribes justice so that there is equality in every situation. And it requires faith so that we can approach the one living God properly. [25] Thus, we do not eat impure food because, in our belief that God established the law, we realize that the cosmic Creator naturally made the law out of pity for us. [26] He has made it possible for us to eat whatever is well-suited for our lives, but forbids us to eat meat that is unacceptable. [27] It would be tyrannical to make us break the law, moreover to have us eat such hateful meat for your amusement. [28] But you will have no chance to laugh at me, [29] nor will I relax the sacred oaths of our ancestors law, [30] not even if you cut out my eyes or disembowel me. [31] I am not so old or cowardly that I do not have youthful sense about faith. [32] Prepare the wheel and stoke the flames eagerly! [33] I am not so concerned about my age that I will break ancestral law. [34] I will not betray you, guiding law, nor abandon you, dear self-control, [35] nor disgrace you, voice of wisdom, nor deny you, honorable priesthood and wise legislation. [36] Nor, Antiochus, will you tarnish my solemn old mouth, nor my dutifully lived years. [37] The ancestors will accept me as pure, unafraid of your fatal violence. [38] Though you tyrannize the ungodly, you will not master my pious reason, neither by word nor by deed."

[6.1] Having finished this rebuttal to the tyrant's words of comfort, the guards cruelly dragged Eleazar to the tools of torture. [2] First, they stripped the old man, though he remained robed in pious splendor. [3] After binding each arm, they whipped him brutally. [4] "Heed the king's commands," a herald yelled from the side. [5] In true spirit, the proud and noble Eleazar was unshaken, as if tortured in a dream. [6] But looking to heaven, his flesh was whipped to shreds, his blood gushed and his sides were gashed. [7] And sinking to the floor because his body could not stand the pain, his reasoning remained straight and sober. [8] A guard rushed over and cruelly kicked him in the ribs to make him get up. [9] But he took the blows, ignored the pain, and endured the torture. [10] Like a true athlete, the old man held firm before his torturers. [11] As he gasped through the sweat, they actually were impressed by his resilience.

[12] Then, feeling pity for his age, [13] sympathy because they knew him, and wonder at his bravery, some of the king's men drew near and said, [14] "Why kill yourself with these unreasonable torments, Eleazar? [15] Save yourself. We will serve you some kind of meat that you can pretend to eat as pork."

[16] Eleazar, seething in torment at this suggestion, yelled, [17] "Children of Abraham, let us not so degrade ourselves that we carelessly pretend to fulfill some disgusting task. [18] For it would be foolish if, having lived in truth and respected the law our entire lives, we should change [19] and actually become an ungodly standard for our youth by our example of eating impure food. [20] What a shame that we should live a few years only to be ridiculed as cowards [21] and despised by the tyrant as fearful because we did not defend our divine law till death. [22] For this reason, O children of Abraham, die nobly for your beliefs. [23] Guards of the tyrant, why do you wait?"

[24] Seeing that he proudly weathered the suffering and was unaffected by their offer, they led him to the fire. [25] There they threw him down, searing him with horrible devices, and plugged his nose with foul solutions. [26] As his bones broke and he neared death, he looked for God and said, [27] "God, you know that I choose not to save myself but die from fiery tortures for the law. [28] Have mercy on your people and let my suffering spare them. [29] Let my blood be their sacrifice and take my life for theirs." [30] Having said this, the holy man died nobly from his tortures, resisting them to the death by reason of the law.

[31] Surely, then, pious reason is master of desires, [32] for if desire had dominated reason, we would have seen the victory. [33] But now, with reason's conquest of desire, we must accept its controlling power. [34] It is appropriate to concede reason's dominance, since it conquers external forces. Even better! [35] I have shown how reason not only dominated suffering, but also did not yield to pleasure.

[7.1] So, like a true helmsman, the reasoning of our father Eleazar steered the ship of faith through a sea of desires. [2] And, though abused by the tyrant's threats and overwhelmed by waves of torture, [3] in no sense did his faith stray before he sailed into the harbor of immortal victory. [4] No city ever withstood a siege of such varied weapons as did that holy man. Though his sacred spirit was twisted and burned, he defeated the tortures through a defense of pious reason. [5] Father Eleazar stretched his mind like a precipitous peak to surround the waves of foaming desire. [6] O worthy man, true priest! You did not permit forbidden meat to stain your sacred teeth or upset your reverent and pure belly. [7] O, to be in tune with the law and the wisdom of divine life! [8] Those who craft the law should defend it by their own blood and sweat, suffering till death. [9] Father, you directed us by your glorious submission, endorsed holiness through your solemn speech, and confirmed the divine wisdom of your words in action. [10] O Eleazar, old man who defeats torture, elder who overpowers fire, great king over desires! [11] Just as father Aaron ran through the crowd with the censer to defeat the fiery angel, [12] so his descendant, Eleazar, while melting in the fire, did not abandon reason. [13] And amazingly, though old, wrinkled, and out of shape, with soft flesh and weak muscles, he was restored [14] in spirit by reason and, by the intellect of Isaac, he neutralized the multi-headed rack. [15] O blessed old man of white-headed dignity and innocent life, whom the reliable seal of death has finished!

[16] So, if an old man can snub death by torture through faith, surely pious reason is ruler over emotions. [17] People may say, "Not everyone has control over desires, because some do not have steady reasoning." [18] But only those who discern with their whole heart can conquer the desires of the flesh, [19] since they, like the patriarchs Abraham, Isaac, and Jacob, believe that through God they do not die, but live. [20] Thus, there is no contradiction when certain people with weak reasoning are driven by passion. [21] What philosopher, driven by wisdom, trusting in God, [22] and aware that each pain endured for virtue is blessed, would not master desire out of devotion? [23] For only a wise and brave person is master over desires.

[8.1] By wisdom of pious reason, even youth have conquered bitter tortures. [2] For when the tyrant had clearly failed in his first attempt to force an old man to eat impure food, he ordered in a fit of rage for other Hebrews to come forward. Any who ate would be released; any who refused would be cruelly tortured. [3] After these words, seven brothers—handsome, modest, noble, pleasing in all ways—were led forward with their elderly mother. [4] When the tyrant saw them grouped around their mother like a choir, he was touched. Stunned by their appearance and dignity, he smiled and called them nearer, saying, [5] "O young men, I am pleasantly amazed at each of you. Out of pity for so many fine brothers, I suggest you not follow in the madness of that tortured old man, but join me and enjoy my friendship. [6] Just as I can punish those who disobey my orders, I am kind to those who obey me. [7] Trust me, then, and after you renounce the traditional law of your ancestors, you will receive positions of power in my realm. [8] After you convert to a Greek life-style, you will enjoy your youth! [9] But if you anger me by disobedience, you will force me to destroy each of you by nasty tortures. [10] Do yourselves a favor then. Even I, your enemy, pity your youth and virility. [11] Will you not consider that if you disobey, you will die on the rack?"

[12] After saying this, he called for the torture equipment to be set before them in order to scare them into eating impure food. [13] As the guards ar-ranged a wheel, joint-spreader, rack, bone-breaker, catapult, caldron, broilers, thumbscrews, iron claws, wedges, and bellows, the tyrant went on to say, [14] "Take care, little boys! Will the law that you revere be kind to you when you are forced to break it?"

[15] But hearing the seduction and seeing the danger, they not only were unafraid, but countered the tyrant and dismissed his tyranny through prudent

argument. [16] Imagine, if some had been timid or cowardly, would they not have said something like, [17] "What pathetic fools we are! The king has kindly encouraged us to obey him, [18] so why hold on to stupid ways and be killed by disobedience? [19] Brothers, should we not fear the torture devices and consider the pain of torment, and abandon this vanity and destructive pretension? [20] Let us pity our youth and have compassion on our elderly mother. [21] Remember that we will die if we disobey. [22] And divine justice will pardon us for our fear of the king's power. [23] Why should we rob ourselves of a pleasant life and sweet world? [24] Let us neither face violence nor needlessly endure the rack. [25] The law itself would not condemn us for our fear of torture. [26] Why should we anguish over this or be eager to die, when to obey the king means a carefree life?" [27] But, facing torture, the youths did not say or even consider such, [28] for they shunned desire and were masters over pain. So, when the tyrant finished his advice to eat impure food, they said in one voice and in full agreement,

[9.1] "Why wait, O tyrant? We would rather die than break a commandment of our ancestors, [2] for we would clearly dishonor those who came before us if we disobeyed the law or counselor Moses. [3] But you, lawless counselor and tyrant, do not pity us while hating us, [4] for we prefer a violent death to safety under your random pity. [5] You try to scare us with a painful death as if you learned nothing just now from Eleazar. [6] If older Hebrews endured torture through devotion to their faith, it is only fair that we younger men not worry about a torturous death, much like our old teacher. [7] So try us, tyrant! Though you kill us for our faith, do not think that you actually torture us, [8] for we will gain the prize of virtue through patient suffering and will be with God for whom we suffer. [9] But you will endure deserved eternal pain from fire as divine justice for our murder."

[10] With this said, the tyrant was not only angered by their disobedience but enraged by their rudeness. [11] By his order, the guards then brought the eldest forward, tore off his clothes, and bound his hands and arms to his sides with straps. [12] After beating him to exhaustion with whips, they put him on the wheel [13] and stretched the noble youth until he was pulled apart. [14] With each stretch the youth scoffed and said, [15] "Murderous tyrant, vicious enemy of divine justice, you do not disfigure me like this because I am a murderer or ungodly, but because I embrace divine law." [16] And when the guards said, "Agree to eat so that you can be released from the tortures," [17] he answered, "O disgusting slaves, your wheel is not strong enough to bend my reasoning. Sever my limbs, burn my flesh, and wrench each joint, [18] for I will show you with each torture that Hebrew children alone are victorious in virtue." [19] As he spoke, they tightened the wheel and fanned a fire which they spread under him. [20] The wheel was completely covered in blood, and the mound of coals was quenched by the dripping fluids. Bits of flesh fell around the machine's axles. [21] Though the tendons between his bones already had been torn, this proud child of Abraham did not moan. [22] But, as

if transformed into immortality by the fire, he nobly endured the wrenching. [23] "Imitate me, brothers," he said. "Do not abandon me in this struggle or cut me off from our strong family bonds. [24] Fight the holy and noble war for faith, so that the righteous providence of our ancestors will be gracious to the people and bring vengeance on the accursed tyrant." [25] With this, the revered youth died.

[26] While everyone marveled at his fierce spirit, the guards led forward the second oldest and, putting on sharp iron claws, tied him to the torture machine and catapult. [27] First, however, they asked if he wished to eat, and witnessed his noble resolve. [28] Ripping his tendons with their iron hands, these leopard beasts stripped his scalp and all the flesh up to his chin. But enduring the pain of this misery, he said, [29] "How sweet is any death that is suffered for our ancestors' faith!" He said to the tyrant, [30] "Does it not seem, most savage tyrant, that you are tortured more than I as you see your tyranny beaten by glorious reason through the endurance of our faith? [31] I am elated by the pleasure of virtue, [32] but you are tortured by vulgar gloating. You cannot escape the God's angry judgment, miserable tyrant."

[10.1] After this remarkable death, the third brother was led forward. Many pleaded for him to eat the meat and be saved, [2] but he called out, "Do you not realize that I have the same father and mother as these who died and that I was trained the same? [3] I will not reject my noble family bonds". . . . [5] Enraged by his speech, the men cruelly dismembered his hands and feet with their machines. Skillfully forcing the joints apart, [6] they broke his fingers, arms, legs, and elbows. [7] Unable to subdue him with power, they scalped him with their fingers like Scythians, [8] then took him to the wheel. As his spine was torn apart, he saw his body rip all around and blood drip from his abdomen. [9] And nearing death, he said, [10] "O disgusting tyrant, we suffer for our training and divine virtue, [11] but you will continually suffer for your ungodly and disgusting nature!"

[12] When this one died like his brothers, they went for the fourth, saying, [13] "Do not follow in your brothers' madness, but obey the king and save yourself." [14] But he told them, "Your fire is not hot enough to intimidate me. [15] No, neither the death of my sacred brothers, nor the tyrant's endless slaughter, nor the eternal life of the pious can make me break my noble family bonds. [16] Tyrant, devise torments by which to discover that I am a brother of these who were tortured." [17] Hearing this, the bloodthirsty, murderous, abominable Antiochus called for his tongue to be clipped. [18] But he replied, "Even if you stop me from talking, God hears those who are silent. [19] See, my tongue is ready. Take it, because to do so will not silence my thought. [20] We gladly let our bodies be mutilated for God's sake. [21] But God will soon pursue you, because you mutilate a mouth that is melodious with divine hymns."

[11.1] When this one also had died from disfigurement, the fifth sprang forward, saying, [2] "Tyrant, I can hardly wait to be tortured on behalf of virtue.

[3] I offer myself so that, by murdering me, heavenly justice will take vengeance on you for even more crimes. [4] O you who hate virtue and humanity! Why do you destroy us like this? [5] Is it because we worship the Creator of all things and live according to virtuous law? [6] These things are worthy of honor, not torture!". . . . [9] As he spoke, the guards bound and pulled him to the catapult, [10] where they tied him on his knees with iron clamps around his hips. They stretched him over the edge of the wheel until he was wrenched backward like a scorpion. [11] In this way, his spirit gasping and his body strained, [12] he said, "What fine gifts you give us, O tyrant, these noble ways to show our brave endurance for the law!"

[13] After he died, the sixth was led forward, only a boy. When the tyrant asked if he would eat in order to be freed, he said, [14] "Though younger than my brothers, I believe the same. [15] Born and trained in these beliefs, we ought to die in like manner. [16] So if you intend to torture me if I do not eat impure food, then go ahead." [17] When he finished, they took him to the wheel [18] where his spine was slowly pulled apart while he was roasted. [19] They shoved sharp, heated stakes into his back, pierced his ribs, and burned his insides. [20] During the torture he said, "O blessed struggle in whose harsh arena we brothers were called by faith but are not defeated! [21] O tyrant, pious insight cannot be defeated! [22] I will die with my brothers, clothed in nobility and integrity. [23] I myself will be a great avenger against you, inventor of tortures and enemy of the truly pious. [24] Six boys have destroyed your tyranny, [25] for you were unable to change our minds or force us to eat impure food. Is this not your destruction? [26] Your fire chills us, your catapult is no bother, your violence is limp. [27] Divine law directs us, not the tyrant's guards. Thus, we hold reason to be victorious."

[12.1] After he died in exaltation after being lowered into the caldron, the youngest of the seven came forward. [2] Though the brothers had roundly insulted the tyrant, he felt sorry for this one when he saw him already in chains. He called him and, in comfort, said, [3] "You saw your brothers' foolish death. They were tortured to death for their disobedience. [4] If you do not obey, you also will suffer torture and die young. [5] Obey me, and become a friend and leader of the kingdom." [6] Having said this, he summoned the boy's mother to comfort her for the loss of so many sons and to have her urge the last to obey and be saved. [7] But after she prompted him in Hebrew, as we shall see in a moment, [8] he said, "Release me. Let me speak to the king and all his friends." [9] And quite pleased by the boy's words, they quickly released him. [10] Running to the closest broiler, [11] he said, "Wicked tyrant, most profane of all who are evil, having received good things and a kingdom from God, are you not ashamed to kill his servants and put to the wheel those who act piously? [12] For this, justice has saved vicious, eternal fire and torture for you that can never be stopped. [13] You brutish animal, were you not ashamed as a man to cut out the tongues of those who have feelings like you, and to mistreat and torture them like this? [14] Their noble deaths completed their service to God, but you will cry in agony, because you killed these who in-nocently fought for virtue." [15] Then, about to die, he said, [16] "I shall not forsake my brothers' heroism. [17] I call for the God of our ancestors to have pity on our people. [18] But God will punish you in life and in death." [19] After shouting this, he threw himself onto the broiler and died.

[13.1] Since the seven brothers held no concern for painful death, all must agree that pious reason is master over desire. [2] If, as slaves to their desires, they had eaten impure food, we would admit they were defeated. [3] But, to the contrary, they overcame desire through divinely sanctioned reason. [4] The power of the mind should not be overlooked, because they held firm against desire and pain. [5] How, then, can one deny true reason's power over desire based upon these who were not dissuaded by the incentive of fire? [6] Like harbor shoals that calm the threat of swelling waves so that ships may enter for refuge, [7] these seven human walls of reason conquered extreme desire through the firm barriers of faith. [8] Standing like a holy choir, they supported each other, saying, [9] "Brothers, let us die as family for the law. Let us imitate the three young men of Assyria who were unconcerned for similar fires. [10] Let us show our faith boldly." [11] One said, "Courage, brother," while another said, "Endure nobly." [12] One counseled, "Remember your roots, the father who would have sacrificed Isaac for faith." [13] They all said with cheerful confidence, "Let our whole heart be purified by God who gave us our souls, and let our bodies stand as guardians for the law. [14] Do not fear our intended killer, [15] for the soul is a good guide and the danger of eternal torment lies before whoever rejects God's commandment. [16] Let us arm ourselves with divine reasoning against desire [17] so that, if we should die, Abraham, Isaac, and Jacob will receive us and all our ancestors will praise us." [18] As each was taken, the remaining brothers said, "Do not shame us, brother, or betray our brothers who have died already." [19] You are aware of the strong family bonds that divine, all-knowing Providence distributes through a father's de-scendants and a mother's womb. [20] Each brother spent much time and for-mation there, being formed from the same blood and life. [21] Each developed for the same period of time and fed from the same source. Close loving lives are nourished like this. [22] Solid maturity comes from being nurtured and living together daily, from broad education and our training in God's law. [23] So, since they typically had sympathetic bonds as siblings, the seven brothers felt close to one another. [24] Educated under the same law, trained in the same virtue, and raised in a proper setting, they loved each other all the more. [25] A common zeal for decency and nobility raised the good will and unity among them, [26] since they maintained their brotherly bonds in faith. [27] Even though nature, custom, and virtuous habits had welded them together in brotherhood, those who watched their brothers be disfigured and tortured to death were sustained by faith. [14.1] Furthermore, they incited the atrocities, both as scorn for the pain and as a way to show the bonds of brotherly love.

[2] O reason, ruler of kings and most unfettered of freedoms! [3] O sacred

and harmonious symphony of the seven brothers' faith! [4] None of the seven boys was a coward or wavered before death, [5] but all sought a torturous death as though running an immortal path. [6] Much as hands and feet act together on command, so these holy boys met death as directed by the immortal will of faith. [7] O revered symphony of seven brothers! Just as the seven days of creation encircled faith, [8] so the boys formed a circle of seven to break the fear of torture. [9] When we hear of the affliction of those youths, we shudder. They not only saw and heard the threats directly, but patiently endured the suffering, and even the pain of fire. [10] What could be more awful? Since the power of fire is piercing and swift, it quickly devoured their bodies.

[11] Yet, though it is fantastic that reason's power took control of these men during the torture, a woman's mind shunned multiple agonies! [12] The mother of the seven youths endured the wrenching of each child. [13] See how complex a love for children is as it draws all feelings inward. [14] As with people, even dumb beasts feel desire and affection for their young. [15] Some birds protect their young under the eaves of houses, [16] while others deliver and defend their young in mountaintops, steep ravines, and holes at the top of trees. [17] If they can offer no defense, they fly in circles calling in love's distress, doing what they can to save their little ones. [18] But why limit ourselves to dumb beasts to illustrate sympathy for children, [19] since even bees at honey time defend against threats. As with iron needles, they sting those who approach their hive, defending it to the death. [20] But, as with Abraham, sympathy for her children did not dissuade the mother of the young men.

[15.1] O reason of children, tyrant of desire! O faith of a mother, more desirable than children! [2] Two options were set before that mother: faith, or the temporary safety of seven sons as promised by the tyrant. [3] She loved faith more, which God had promised would save them into eternal life. [4] How may I portray the love for a child? We impress the likeness of life and form upon a small child's wonderful character. A mother has a special feeling because of her role in the pains of birth. [5] As mothers are delicate by nature and have many babies, the love for their children is greater. [6] The mother of the seven boys had the most love for her children, since she had loved them through seven pregnancies. [7] She had a strong bond with each because of the labor pains that she had endured, [8] but from fear of God, she looked past the momentary safety of the children. [9] She held an even greater affection for the sons because of their decency, nobility, and respect for the law. [10] They were righteous and modest, brave and magnanimous, loving toward one another and their mother so that they obeyed her, keeping the law until the end. [11] Yet, despite the mother's affection for each child, none of the various tortures was strong enough to sway her views for any of them. [12] She urged each and every one to die for the sake of faith. [13] O sacred nature and love of parents! O affection for offspring! O nourishment and unbroken desire of mothers! [14] Though seeing them tortured and burned, this mother did not turn her back on faith. [15] She saw the fire melt her children's flesh, their toes and fingers twitching on the ground, and the flesh of their heads to their chins displayed like masks. [16] O pain that is more intense than that of a mother in labor! [17] O woman who alone brought forth perfect faith! [18] You did not yield when the firstborn expired, nor as the second gazed at you in pity during torture, nor when the third died. [19] Nor did you mourn when you saw the eyes of each who remained, staring wildly at the torture, each outrage the same, or at their nostrils that foretold death. [20] Seeing the flesh of children burned off onto the flesh of other children, hands cut off onto hands, heads beheaded onto heads, corpses piled onto corpses, and the crowd that gathered there to see the tortures, you did not cry. [21] Neither melodious sirens nor swans pull a hearer as strongly as do the cries of tortured children to a mother. [22] How extensive then were the mother's own tortures as her sons were broken with the wheel and blazing irons. [23] But pious reason compelled her to stout courage and to disregard her momentary feelings for the children. [24] Though she saw the complexities of the torture and the destruction of seven children, the noble mother was led through everything by her faith in God. [25] As she weighed the values of nature, family, love of children, and danger to children as resourceful advisors in the council chamber of her own soul, [26] this mother held two options for her children: death or safety. [27] She did not choose to save the seven sons for a mere temporary salvation, [28] but this daughter of devout Abraham was patient. [29] O mother of a nation, avenger of the law and protector of faith, who takes home the emotional trophy from the contest! [30] O to be more patient and courageous in endurance than any man! [31] For as the ark of Noah carried the world and survived the waves in the cataclysmic flood, [32] so you, guardian of the law, with the wind and waves of emotion emerging from all sides as your sons were tortured, nobly endured and survived the storms against faith.

[16.1] If an old woman, mother of seven sons, endured while she saw her children tortured to death, one must admit that pious reason is master over desires. [2] I have thus shown that, not only have men dominated desires, but a woman has snubbed great tortures. [3] The lions around Daniel were not so fierce and the fiery oven around Mishael was not so hot as were the flames of her motherly love when she saw the various tortures of her seven sons. [4] Yet, the mother was able to smother those raging desires by pious reason.

[5] Consider that if this woman, though a mother, were timid, she would have wept for them and probably said, [6] "O, I am at a loss and inconsolably grieved that, having brought forth seven boys, I now am the mother of none! [7] O seven vain childbirths! O seven empty pregnancies, barren nurturings, and laborious nursings! [8] O sons, I endured many labor pains and difficult anxieties in your development, for nothing! [9] O my boys, some unmarried, some married but childless! I will not see your children or be blessed by their tiny voices. [10] O, a woman with many beautiful children, I am now widowed, alone, and pitiful! [11] No sons will bury me when I die."

[12] But this holy, God-fearing woman did not moan in tears like this, nor

did she prevent any of their deaths, nor did she grieve when they died. [13] But having a resolve of steel and elevating all her sons toward immortality, she called out and urged them to die for their faith. [14] O mother, elderly female soldier of God for faith! Through patience you even defeated a tyrant. Your actions and words proved you to be more capable than a man. [15] When you were gathered with your sons, you saw the torture of Eleazar and said to them in Hebrew, [16] "O sons, when serving as witnesses for a people, it is noble to fight eagerly for our ancestors' law. [17] How shameful for you young men to show fear at torture, while such an old man endures agony for the faith. [18] Remember that you are alive and in the world because of God, [19] and, for this reason, you can endure any situation through God. [20] It was for God that our father Abraham ran to sacrifice his son Isaac, ancestor of our people. Seeing his father's hand and the knife coming toward him, Isaac did not flinch. [21] Righteous Daniel was thrown to the lions. Hananiah, Azariah, and Mishael were slung into an oven. Yet each survived because of God. [22] You, therefore, having the same faith in God, must not be upset. [23] Steeped in faith, it only makes sense to withstand pain."

[24] The mother of the seven used these words to induce and convince each son to die rather than to break God's commandment. [25] They knew that those who die for God also live for God, just like Abraham, Isaac, Jacob, and all the patriarchs.

[17.1] Some guards reported that, as she waited to be taken to her death, she threw herself into the fire so that her body would not be touched.

[2] O mother, who with your seven children destroyed the tyrant's violence, cancelled his evil schemes, and revealed faith's possibilities! [3] You stood over your sons like a roof upon pillars, standing firm and riding out the earthquake of tortures. [4] So take heart, O holy-minded mother, and remain firm in your enduring hope in God! [5] Heaven's moon does not shine as brightly among the stars as you shine in honor before God and your sons in heaven, those seven stars whom your light guided to faith. [6] You truly brought forth children worthy of your father Abraham.

[7] If the history of faith could be painted, would not those who view it shudder when they see this mother and seven children submit to various deadly tortures for faith? [8] It would seem best to offer this epitaph as a reminder to our people: [9] "Here lies an aged priest, elderly woman, and seven sons because of the violence of a tyrant who wanted to destroy the Hebrew way of life. [10] They avenged their people by looking toward God and enduring tortures until death."

[11] Surely their struggle was divine, [12] for virtue was the judge, testing their endurance. The prize was immortality in eternal life. [13] Eleazar led the way, the mother of the seven sons entered, and the brothers contended. [14] The tyrant served as opponent. The world and humanity were spectators. [15] Fear of God won and crowned its own athletes. [16] Who would not marvel at the athletes of the divine law? Who would not be impressed?

[17] The tyrant himself and the whole assembly marveled at their endurance, [18] for which they now stand before God's throne and live in eternal blessing. [19] For Moses said, "All the holy ones are in your hands [Deut. 33:3]." [20] These holy ones are honored through God, but not for this reason only. Because of them, our people were not conquered by the enemy, [21] the tyrant was punished, and our country was cleansed. It is as if their lives were given for the people's sins. [22] Because of the blood of these who endured and their atoning death, God's will saved Israel from misery. [23] When their bold virtue and endurance under torture was revealed, the tyrant Antiochus offered them to his soldiers as models of endurance. [24] This made them noble and brave in battle and siege, so that he conquered every city by such fearlessness.

[18.1] O descendants of Abraham's seed, children of Israel, obey this law and be pious in all ways! [2] Know that pious reason is master of desires, both of internal and external struggles.

[3] These who gave up their bodies to pain on behalf of faith received both human admiration and the honor of divine credit.

[4] They brought peace to the people and ravaged the enemy by reviving order at home. [5] Vengeance came to the tyrant Antiochus on earth, but now he is punished in death. Since he was unable to force the Israelites to adopt foreign ways and abandon their tribal heritage, he left Jerusalem to fight the Persians.

[6] The mother of the seven sons also passed these values to her children: [7] "I was a modest young woman who stayed at home, taking care of the house. [8] A seducer in some barren wilderness did not defile me, nor did the snake, that deviant trickster, rob me of my chaste virginity. [9] After I was grown, I stayed with my husband. After our sons were raised, their father passed away. That man was happy because his life was rich with good children and he never saw any of them die. [10] During his time he taught you the scriptures. [11] He told you about Cain's murder of Abel, Isaac as a sacrifice, and Joseph in prison. [12] He spoke to you about the zeal of Phinehas, and taught you about Hananiah, Azariah, and Mishael in flames. [13] He praised Daniel in the den of lions and blessed him. [14] He recalled the text of Isaiah that reads, 'Even going through the fire, the flames will not devour you' [Isa. 43:2]. [15] He sang the tunes of David, saying, 'The righteous have many troubles' [Ps. 34:19]. [16] He shared with you the parable of Solomon that says, 'There is a tree of life for anyone who does God's will' [Prov. 3:18]. [17] He affirmed Ezekiel's question, 'Can these dry bones live?' [Ezek. 37:2–3]. [18] And he did not forget to teach the song that Moses himself taught, which says, [19] 'I kill and bring to life. This is your life and longevity' [Deut. 32:39]."

[20] O bittersweet was the day when that egregious Greek tyrant heaped fire upon fire in the caldrons, and with cruel hostility led these seven sons of Abraham to the catapult and then to his other tortures! [21] He punctured their pupils, pulled out their tongues, and killed them through many tortures. [22] Divine justice has and will take revenge on the evil tyrant for all of this.

[23] But Abraham's sons are gathered with their victorious mother into the chorus of their ancestors, having received a holy and immortal existence from God. [24] Glory be to God forever. Amen.

Bibliography

Anderson, Hugh. 1985. "4 Maccabees: A New Translation and Introduction." In *The Old Testament Pseudepigrapha,* ed. James H. Charlesworth, vol. 2, 531–64. Garden City, N.Y.: Doubleday.

Bickermann, E. J. 1945. "The Date of IV Maccabees." In *Noah, Daniel, and Job,* ed. Shalom Spiegel, 105–12. New York: American Academy for Jewish Research.

Hadas, Moses. 1953. *The Third and Fourth Book of Maccabees.* New York: Harper.

Henten, Jan Willem van. 1997. *The Maccabean Martyrs as Saviours of the Jewish People.* Leiden: E. J. Brill.

Rahlfs, Alfred. 1935. *Septuaginta.* Stuttgart: Deutsche Bibelgesellschaft.

Enlivening Thought:
Philosophy and Theology

37

Gregory Nazianzen
Homily on the Nativity of Christ

Nonna Verna Harrison

Gregory Nazianzen (ca. 329–ca. 391 C.E.) was one of the three great Cappadocian theologians who articulated the doctrine of the Trinity in its classic form and sought to transform and incorporate the Greek philosophical and literary heritage into the emerging Christian culture. Though by temperament a reclusive contemplative and man of letters, Gregory became a bishop renowned for his preaching and teaching. The apex of his career came when he served for about two and a half years as bishop of Constantinople at a crucial turning point in church history. In 379, when the city was in the hands of the Arians, he was invited to lead a small Nicene house church. When he left in 381, the emperor Theodosius had convened the Council of Constantinople, which reaffirmed the teachings of the Council held at Nicea in 325 and established the creed considered definitive by the mainstream Eastern and Western churches throughout subsequent history. Gregory built on the work of Athanasius of Alexandria and his Cappadocian colleague Basil of Caesarea in affirming that Christ, who assumed a full humanity in his incarnation, is from all eternity fully God as the Father is fully God. Gregory likewise held that the Holy Spirit is fully God, and that the three persons are one God, the Holy Trinity. He formulated his teachings on the Trinity and sought to refute his Arian and Neo-Arian opponents, who denied the full divinity of Christ, in a series of brilliant sermons at Constantinople, most notably the *Five Theological Orations*.

The text translated here is *Oration* 38, presented in Constantinople on December 25, 379 or 380. From the beginning of the fourth century, the birth of Christ was celebrated in Rome on December 25 to provide Christians with an alternative to the popular festival of the Unconquered Sun. In the eastern Mediterranean at that time, the birth of Christ, together with the adoration of the Magi and his baptism in the Jordan, were celebrated together on January 6, at a feast known as Epiphany or Theophany. In the late fourth century the separate celebration of

Christmas on December 25 was adopted throughout the empire as a way of affirming, against the Arians, that Christ is truly God incarnate and that, therefore, his birth itself is a great theophany. When Gregory preached *Oration* 38, this feast had recently been introduced in Constantinople, so he explains its name and meaning. This changing liturgical practice lies behind our text's confusing title, *On the Theophany.* The next homily in the collection was preached soon after on January 6 and celebrates the baptism of Christ, which is still commemorated on this day in the Byzantine rite.

In Late Antiquity rhetoric was pre-eminent both as a literary form and as a performing art, and Gregory was one of its great masters. He was also a theological poet and his prose has a poetic character. So it is best read slowly with attention to the meaning of each word. He often encapsulates profound theological insights in lapidary phrases. In *Oration* 38 he narrates the birth, life, death, and resurrection of Christ, summarizes the doctrines of the Trinity and the Incarnation and argues against his Arian opponents. Moreover, in sections 7–14 he outlines his systematic theology, discussing the nature of God, the creation of the angelic and material worlds, the creation, the identity and fall of humans, and God's remedy for humankind in Israel's salvation history and in Christ. His account of God and creation reveals a Platonic Christian world view. He believes that the human person is created to unite the spiritual and material worlds with each other and with the transcendent God. The homily is filled with Biblical citations and allusions, only a few of which are noted in this translation. Gregory's understanding of the human condition, expressed in his interpretation of Genesis 2 and 3, is particularly interesting.

Through its liturgical setting and in other ways, this text discloses important links between theological reflection and religious practice. Gregory asks his audience of Christians who worship the divine Word or Logos—the principle of rationality, order, and meaning in the universe—to celebrate his birth as a human being in a fitting manner. They should avoid the revelry and excess commonly associated with winter holidays at the time and instead enjoy a feast of sacred words. The event of Christ's birth is made present in its liturgical celebration, and the congregation is invited to join the angels, shepherds, and Magi in worshipping him. Gregory further exhorts them to honor God by accepting a truthful account of God's being and activity. Finally, he appeals to them to act on their beliefs by inscribing the life and sufferings of Christ in their own lives through imitation of him and thereby share through grace in his saving death and resurrection.

This text is translated from Claudio Moreschini's *Grégoire de Nazianze. Discours 38–41,* 101–48.

Oration 38, On the Theophany

[1] Christ is born, give glory; Christ is from the heavens, go to meet him; Christ is on earth, rise up. "Sing to the Lord, all the earth" [Ps. 92:1], and, to

say both together, "Let the heavens be glad and let the earth rejoice" [Ps. 96:11], for the heavenly one is now earthly. Christ is in the flesh, exult with trembling and joy; trembling because of sin, joy because of hope. Christ comes from a Virgin; women, practice virginity, that you may become mothers of Christ. Who would not worship the one "from the beginning" [1 John 1:1]? Who would not glorify "the Last" [Rev. 1:17, 2:8]?

[2] Again the darkness is dissolved, again the light is established [Gen. 1:3–4], again Egypt is punished by darkness [Exod. 10:11], Again Israel is illumined by a pillar [Exod. 13:21]. Let the people sitting in the darkness of ignorance see a great light of knowledge. "The old things have passed; behold, all things have become new" [2 Cor. 5:17]. The letter withdraws, the spirit advances; the shadows have been surpassed, the truth has entered after them. Melchizedek is completed, the motherless one becomes fatherless; he was motherless first, fatherless second [Heb. 7:3]. The laws of nature are dissolved. The world above must be filled. Christ commands, let us not resist. "All nations, clap your hands" [Ps. 47:1], "for to us a child is born, and to us a son is given, the power is on his shoulder," for he is lifted up along with the Cross, and he is called by the name "angel of great counsel," that of the Father [Isa. 9:6]. Let John proclaim, "Prepare the way of the Lord" [Matt. 3:3]. I myself will proclaim the power of this day. The fleshless one takes flesh, the Word is made dense, the invisible one is seen, the impalpable one is touched, the timeless one makes a beginning, the Son of God becomes Son of Man, "Jesus Christ, the same yesterday and today and for the ages" [Heb. 13:8]. Let Jews be scandalized, let Greeks mock, let heretics talk till their tongues ache. They will believe when they see him ascend into heaven, and if not then, at least when they see him coming from heaven and sitting as judge.

[3] These things come later. Now is the feast of the Theophany, and thus of the Nativity; for it is called both, since two names are ascribed to one reality. For God appeared to human beings through birth. On the one hand, he is and is eternally from the eternal Being, above cause and principle, for there was no principle higher than the Principle. On the other hand, for us he later comes into being, that the one who has given us being might also grant us well-being; or rather that, as we fell from well-being through evil, he might bring us back again to himself through incarnation. The name is Theophany, since he has appeared, and Nativity, since he has been born.

[4] This is our festival, this is the feast we celebrate today, in which God comes to live with human beings, that we may journey toward God, or return (for to speak thus is more exact), that laying aside the old human being we may be clothed with the new, and that as in Adam we have died so we may live in Christ, being born with Christ and crucified with him, being buried with him and rising with him. For it is necessary for me to undergo the good turnaround, and as painful things came from more pleasant things, so out of painful things more pleasant things must return. "For where sin abounded, grace superabounded" [Rom. 5:10], and if the taste [of forbidden fruit] con-

demned, how much more does the Passion of Christ justify? Therefore we celebrate the feast not like a pagan festival but in a godly manner, not in a worldly way but in a manner above the world. We celebrate not our own concerns but the one who is ours, or rather what concerns our Master, things pertaining not to sickness but to health, not to the creation but to the new creation.

[5] And how will this be? Let us not put wreaths on our front doors, or assemble troupes of dancers, or decorate the streets. Let us not feast the eyes, or mesmerize the sense of hearing, or make effeminate the sense of smell, or prostitute the sense of taste, or gratify the sense of touch. These are ready paths to evil, and entrances of sin. Let us not be softened by delicate and extravagant clothing, whose only beauty is its inutility, or by the transparency of stones, or the brilliance of gold, or the artificiality of colors that falsify natural beauty and are invented in opposition to the [divine] image; nor by "revelries and drunkenness," to which I know "debauchery and licentiousness" are linked [Rom. 13:13], since from bad teachers come bad teachings, or rather from evil seeds come evil harvests. Let us not build high beds of straw, making shelters for the debauchery of the stomach. Let us not assess the bouquet of wines, the concoctions of chefs, the great cost of perfumes. Let earth and sea not bring us as gifts the valued dung, for this is how I know to evaluate luxury. Let us not strive to conquer each other in dissoluteness. For to me all that is superfluous and beyond need is dissoluteness, particularly when others are hungry and in want, who are of the same clay and the same composition as ourselves [Gen. 2:7].

[6] But let us leave these things to the Greeks and to Greek pomp and festivals. They name as gods those who enjoy the steam rising from the fat of sacrificed animals and correspondingly serve the divine with their stomachs, and they become evil fashioners and initiators and initiates of evil demons. But if we, for whom the Word is an object of worship, must somehow have luxury, let us have as our luxury the word and the divine law and narratives, especially those that form the basis of the present feast, that our luxury may be akin and not foreign to the one who has called us.

Would you like me—for I am your host today—to set before you, my good guests, a discourse as abundant and lavish as possible, that you may know how a stranger can feed the local inhabitants, and a rustic the city dwellers, and one without luxury the luxurious, and one poor and homeless those brilliant in wealth? I will begin from this point, and let me ask that you purify your mind and hearing and thoughts, you who enjoy luxuries of this kind, since the discourse about God is also divine, that you may depart having truly received the luxuries that are not empty. This discourse will be at the same time very full and very concise, so as neither to sadden you by its poverty nor cause distaste through satiety.

[7] God always was and is and will be, or rather always "is," for "was" and "will be" belong to our divided time and transitory nature; but he is always "he

who is," and he gave himself this name when he consulted with Moses on the mountain [Exod. 3:14]. For holding everything together in himself, he possesses being, neither beginning nor ending. He is like a kind of boundless and limitless sea of being, surpassing all thought and time and nature. He is sketched only by the mind, and this in a very indistinct and mediocre way, not from things pertaining to himself but from things around him. Impressions are gathered from here and there into one particular representation of the truth, which flees before it is grasped and escapes before it is understood. It illumines the directive faculty in us, when indeed we have been purified, and its appearance is like a swift bolt of lightning that does not remain. It seems to me that insofar as it is graspable, the divine draws [us] toward itself, for what is completely ungraspable is unhoped for and unsought. Yet one wonders at the ungraspable, and one desires more intensely the object of wonder, and being desired it purifies, and purifying it makes deiform, and with those who have become such he converses as with those close to him—I speak with vehement boldness—God is united with gods, and he is thus known, perhaps as much as he already knows those who are known to him [1 Cor. 13:12].

For the divine is without limits and difficult to contemplate, and this alone is entirely graspable in it, namely, that it is without limits, whether one supposes that to be a simple nature is to be wholly ungraspable or perfectly graspable. For what is a being whose nature is simple? Let us inquire further, for simplicity is clearly not the nature of this being, just as composition alone is clearly not the nature of composite entities.

[8] The absence of limit is contemplated in two ways, with regard to the beginning and to the end, for that which is above both and is not contained between them is without limit. When the mind gazes steadfastly into the depth above, not having a place to stand and relying on the representations it has of God, from this perspective it names as "without beginning" that which is without limit and without outlet. Yet when it gazes at what is below and what is subsequent, it names it "immortal" and "indestructible"; and when it views the whole together, "eternal." For eternity is neither time nor some part of time, nor is it measurable, but what is time for us measured by the movement of the sun is for everlasting beings eternity, since it is coextensive with these beings, as if it were a kind of movement and interval of time.

For me this is enough philosophizing about God at present. For it is not the time to go beyond these things, since our concern here is not "theology" [i.e., discussion of God in Godself] but "economy" [i.e., discussion of God's relations with the created world]. When I say "God," I mean Father and Son and Holy Spirit. The divinity is not diffused beyond these, lest we introduce a crowd of gods, but nor is it limited to fewer than these, lest we be condemned to a poverty of divinity, either Judaizing because of the monarchy or Hellenizing because of the abundance. For the evil is alike in both cases, though it is found in opposites. This then is the Holy of Holies, which is veiled by the Seraphim and glorified with a threefold "Holy" [Isa. 6:2–3], converging in one Lordship and divinity, which another who preceded us has explained in a most beautiful and exalted way.

[9] Yet it was not sufficient for goodness to be moved only in contemplation of itself, but it was necessary that the good be poured forth and given paths to travel, so that there would be more recipients of its benevolent activity, for this was the summit of goodness. Therefore, it first thought of the angelic and heavenly powers, and the thought was action, accomplished by the Word and perfected by the Spirit. And thus were created the second splendors, the servants of the first Splendor, which are either intelligent spirits, or a kind of immaterial or bodiless fire, or some other nature as close to this as possible. I would like to say that they are unmoved toward evil and have only the movement toward the good, since they are around God and are the first to be illumined by God; for things here below are illumined second. Yet I am persuaded to consider and say that they are not immovable but only difficult to move on account of the one who was called Lucifer [i.e., Light-Bearer] because of his splendor [Isa. 14:12–15] but both became and is called darkness because of his pride, and the rebellious powers under him, who are fashioners of evil through their flight from the good and who incite evil in us.

[10] So, therefore, for these reasons the intelligible world was created by God, at least as far as I can investigate these matters, estimating great things by my small discourse. And since the first world was beautiful to him, he thought a second material and visible world, that which is composed of heaven and earth and the system and composite of realities existing between them. It is praiseworthy because of the good disposition of each thing, but more praiseworthy because of the good connectedness and harmony of the whole, as each thing is well adapted to another and all to all, into the full realization of one world. Thus God has shown that he was able to create not only a nature akin to himself but also what is entirely foreign to him. For the spiritual natures and those apprehended only by the mind are akin to the divine, but those apprehended by the senses are entirely foreign to it, and those that are entirely without life or movement are still farther removed.

Yet perhaps one who is excessively ardent and devoted to feasts may ask, "What are these things to us? Spur on your pony toward the goal post. Investigate for us what concerns the feast and the reasons why we are seated here today." Truly I will do this, even if I have begun with things a bit exalted, since my desire and my discourse have constrained me.

[11] Thus far mind and sense perception, distinguished from each other in this way, remained within their own limits and bore in themselves the magnificence of the Creator Word. They silently praised the greatness of his works and were heralds sounding afar [Ps. 19:3–4]. But there was not yet a blending out of both, nor a mixing of opposites, which is the distinctive sign of a greater wisdom and of divine superabundance concerning created natures, nor was the full wealth of goodness yet made known. So then wishing to manifest this, the Creator Word also makes one living creature out of both, I mean invisible

and visible natures, that is, the human being. And having taken the body from the matter already created, he breathed in breath from himself [Gen. 2:7], which is surely the intelligent soul and the image of God of which Scripture speaks [Gen. 1:26–27]. The human being is a kind of second world, great in smallness, placed on the earth, another angel, a composite worshipper, a beholder of the visible creation, an initiate into the intelligible, king of things on earth, subject to what is above, earthly and heavenly, transitory and immortal, visible and intelligible, a mean between greatness and lowliness. He is at once spirit and flesh, spirit on account of grace, flesh on account of pride, the one that he might remain and glorify his Benefactor, the other that he might suffer and in suffering remember and be corrected if he has ambition for greatness. He is a living creature trained here and transferred elsewhere, and, to perfect the mystery, deified through inclination toward God. For the light and the truth present in measure here bear me toward this end, to see and experience the splendor of God, which is worthy of the one who has bound me [to flesh] and will release me and hereafter will bind me in a higher manner.

[12] This being was placed in paradise, whatever that paradise was then, honored with self-determination so that the good would belong to the one who chose it no less than to the one who provided its seeds. The human being was a cultivator of immortal plants [Gen. 2:15], that is perhaps divine thoughts, both the simpler and the more complete. He was naked because of his simplicity and life, free from artifice and far from any covering or screen, for such a condition befitted the one who existed at the beginning. God gave him a law as material on which his free choice could work, and the law was a commandment indicating which plants he could possess and which one he was not to touch. And that was the tree of knowledge, which was neither planted from the beginning in an evil way nor forbidden through envy—let the enemies of God not wag their tongues in that direction, nor imitate the serpent—but it would be good if possessed at the right time. For the tree is contemplation, according to my own contemplation, which is only safe for those of perfect disposition to undertake; but it is not good for those who are still simpler and those greedy in their desire, just as adult food is not useful for those who are still tender and in need of milk. But after the devil's envy and the woman's spiteful treatment, both what she underwent as more tender and what she set before [the man] as more persuasive—alas for my weakness, for that of the first father is mine!—he forgot the commandment given him and yielded to the bitter taste. And at once he came to be banished from the tree of life and from paradise and from God because of the evil, and was clothed in the tunics of skin [Gen. 3:21], that is perhaps the more dense and mortal and rebellious flesh, and for the first time he knew his own shame and hid from God. He gained a certain advantage from this; death is also the cutting off of sin, that evil might not be immortal, so the punishment becomes love for humankind. For thus, I am persuaded, God punishes.

[13] The human being was first educated in many ways corresponding to

the many sins that sprouted from the root of evil for different reasons and at different times; by word, law, prophets, benefits, threats, blows, floods, conflagrations, wars, victories, defeats; signs from heaven, signs from the air, from earth, from sea; unexpected changes in men, cities, nations; by all this God sought zealously to wipe out evil. At the end a stronger remedy was necessary for more dreadful diseases: murders of each other, adulteries, false oaths, lusts for men, and the last and first of all evils, idolatry and the transfer of worship from the Creator to the creature [Rom. 1:25]. Since these things required a greater help, they also obtained something greater. It was the Word of God himself, the one who is before the ages, the invisible, the ungraspable, the incorporeal, the Principle from the Principle, the light from the light, the source of life and immortality, the imprint of the archetypal beauty, the immutable seal, the undistorted image, the definition and explanation of his Father. He approaches his own image and bears flesh because of my flesh and mingles himself with a rational soul because of my soul, purifying like by like. And in all things he becomes a human being, except sin. He was conceived by the Virgin, who was purified beforehand in both soul and flesh by the Spirit, for it was necessary that procreation be honored and that virginity be honored more. He comes forth, God with what he has assumed, one from two opposites, flesh and spirit, the one deifying and the other deified. O the new mixture! O the paradoxical blending! He who is comes into being, and the uncreated is created, and the uncontained is contained, through the intervention of the rational soul, which mediates between the divinity and the denseness of flesh. The one who makes rich becomes poor; he is made poor in my flesh, that I might be enriched through his divinity. The full one empties himself; for he empties himself of his own glory for a short time, that I may participate in his fullness. What is the wealth of his goodness? What is this mystery concerning me? I participated in the image [of God], and I did not keep it; he participates in my flesh both to save the image and to make the flesh immortal. He shares with us a second communion, much more paradoxical than the first; then he gave us a share in what is superior, now he shares in what is inferior. This is more godlike than the first; this, to those who can understand, is more exalted.

[14] In regard to these things, what do the slanderers say to us, the bitter calculators of divinity, the accusers of praiseworthy things, the dark ones speaking of the light, the uneducated speaking of wisdom, for whom "Christ died in vain" [Gal. 2:21], the unthankful creatures, fashioned by the Evil One? Do you bring as a charge against God his good deed? Is he small because he is humble for your sake? Do you accuse the Good Shepherd because he went to the one who strayed, he who laid down his life for the sheep, to find the stray "on the mountains and the hills where you offered sacrifice" [Hos. 4:13], and having found it, took it on his shoulder, on which also he carried the Cross, and having taken it, brought it back to the life on high, and having brought it on high counted it again among those who remained there? Do you accuse him because he lit a lamp, his own flesh, and swept the house, cleansing

the world of sin, and searched for the coin, the royal image covered with a heap of passions, then calls together his friends, the [angelic] powers, once he has found the coin, and makes participants in his joy those [angels] initiated into the mystery of his saving plan [Luke 15:8–9]? Do you accuse him because the most radiant Light follows the lamp, his forerunner John [the Baptist], and the Word follows the voice, and the bridegroom follows the friend of the bridegroom, who prepares for the Lord a chosen people and through water purifies them beforehand for the Spirit? Do you bring these charges against God? Do you also suppose that he is inferior for these reasons, that he girds himself with a towel and washes the feet of his disciples, and shows that the best way to be exalted is lowliness, since he lowers himself because of the soul bent down to the ground, so as also to lift up with himself those leaning downward because of sin? But how do you not accuse him because he also eats with tax collectors and at the homes of tax collectors and makes tax collectors his disciples, that he also may make some profit for himself? What profit? The salvation of sinners. If so, one must also blame the physician for bending over one who is ill and enduring the stench to give health to the sick; or one who through compassion leans over a pit to rescue, according to the law [Deut. 22:4], the animal that has fallen into it.

[15] He was sent, but as human, for he was twofold. For he was tired and hungry and thirsty and endured agony and wept through the law of the body, but if he underwent these things also as God, what of it? Consider the good will of the Father to be sent forth, and to it the Son ascribes his own activities, both as honoring the timeless Beginning and so as not to seem to be a rival god. For indeed [Scripture] says that he was given up [Rom. 4:25; 1 Cor. 11:23], but it is also written that he gave himself up [Gal. 2:20; Eph. 5:2, 25]; and he was raised and taken up to heaven by the Father [Acts 17:31; Rom. 4:24; Mark 16:19], but he also resurrected himself and ascended there again [Matt. 22:6, Mark 16:9, 19]. For one is the Father's good will, the other is his own power. You speak of what belittles him, but you overlook what exalts him; you recognize that he suffered, but you do not add that it was voluntary. It is as if the Word still suffers now! By some he is honored as God but confused with the Father; by others he is dishonored as flesh and separated from him. Against which is one more angry? Rather, whom must one pardon more? Those who unite Father and Son wrongly or those who divide them? For the former would need to distinguish and the latter would need to conjoin; the ones in regard to number, the others in regard to divinity. Do you take offense at the flesh? So did the Jews. Do you also call him a Samaritan [John 8:48]? I will be silent about the rest. Do you disbelieve in his divinity? This even the demons do not do. O you who are more unbelieving than demons and more senseless than Jews! The latter regarded "Son" as a term denoting equality of honor [John 5:18], the former knew that God drove them out, for they were persuaded by what they suffered. But you neither accept the equality nor confess the divinity. It would have been better for you to be circumcised and possessed by a demon,

if I may say something ridiculous, rather than in uncircumcision and good health to be in a state of wickedness and atheism.

[16] So shortly you will also see the purification of Jesus in the Jordan for my purification; or rather he is cleansed for the purification of the waters, for he indeed did not need purification, he who takes away the sin of the world. The heavens are parted and he receives the testimony of the Spirit, who is akin to him. He is tempted and conquers the tempter and is served by angels. He heals every sickness and every infirmity, and gives life to the dead. (Would that he would give life to you who are dead through your false doctrine). He drives out demons, some by himself and others through his disciples. With a few loaves he feeds tens of thousands, and he walks on the sea. He is betrayed and crucified and crucifies my sin with himself. He is offered as a lamb and offers as a priest, he is buried as a human being, raised as God, then also ascends, and he will return with his own glory. How many celebrations there are for me corresponding to each of the mysteries of Christ! Yet they all have one completion, my perfection and refashioning and restoration to the state of the first Adam.

[17] Now welcome for me his conception and leap for joy, if not indeed like John in the womb [Luke 1:41], then like David when the ark came to rest [2 Sam. 6:14]. Be awed at the census list through which you have been recorded in heaven, and revere the birth through which you have been released from the bonds of birth, and honor little Bethlehem, which has brought you back to paradise, and bow before the manger through which you who were without reason have been fed by the Word. Know, like the ox, your owner—Isaiah exhorts you [Isa. 1:3]—and like the ass, know your master's crib, whether you are among those who are pure and under the law and chew the cud of the Word and are prepared for sacrifice, or whether up to now you are among the impure and unfit for food or sacrifice and belong to the Gentiles. Run after the star, and bring gifts with the Magi, gold and frankincense and myrrh, as to a king and a God and one dead for your sake. With the shepherds give glory, with the angels sing hymns, with the archangels dance. Let there be a common celebration of the heavenly and earthly powers. For I am persuaded that they rejoice and celebrate together today, if indeed they love humankind and love God, just as David represents them ascending with Christ after his Passion as they come to meet him and exhort each other to lift up the gates [Ps. 24:7–10].

[18] You should hate only one of the events surrounding the birth of Christ, Herod's murder of children; but rather, revere this sacrifice of those of the same age as Christ, who are sacrificed before the new victim. If he flees to Egypt, be willingly banished with him. It is good to flee with the persecuted Christ. If Christ delays in Egypt, call him forth from Egypt, where he is worshipped well. Travel blamelessly through all the stages of Christ's life and all his powers, as a disciple of Christ. Be purified, be circumcised, that is, remove the veil that has surrounded you since birth. After this teach in the temple, drive out the

traders in divine things [Matt. 21:12], be stoned if it is necessary that you suffer this; you will escape from those throwing the stones, I know well, and you will flee through the midst of them like God [John 8:59, Luke 4:30]. For the Word is not stoned. If you are brought before Herod, do not answer for the most part. He will revere your silence more than the long discourses of others. If you are scourged, seek the other tortures. Taste the gall because of the taste [of the forbidden fruit]. Drink the vinegar, seek the spittings, accept the blows, the beatings; be crowned with thorns through the harshness of a life in accord with God. Put on the scarlet robe, accept the reed and the worship of those who mock the truth. Finally, be crucified with him, die with him, be buried with him willingly, so as also to be resurrected with him and glorified with him and reign with him, seeing God as far as is possible and being seen by him, who is worshipped and glorified in the Trinity, whom even now we pray to be manifest to us as clearly as is possible to prisoners of the flesh, in Christ Jesus our Lord, to whom be glory and dominion unto the ages of ages. Amen.

Bibliography

Browne, Charles Gordon, and James Edward Swallow, trans. 1983. *S. Gregory Nazianzen: Select Orations and Letters.* Nicene and Post-Nicene Fathers, ser. 2, vol. 7. Grand Rapids, Mich.: Wm. B. Eerdmans.

Moreschini, Claudio, ed. 1990. *Grégoire de Nazianze. Discours 38–41.* Sources chrétiennes 358. Paris: Editions du Cerf.

Moreschini, Claudio, and D. A. Sykes. 1997. *St. Gregory of Nazianzus, "Poemata arcana."* Oxford: Clarendon.

Norris, Frederick W. 1991. *Faith Gives Fullness to Reasoning: The Five Theological Orations of Gregory Nazianzen.* Trans. Lionel Wickham and Frederick Williams. Leiden: E. J. Brill.

Studer, Basil. 1993. *Trinity and Incarnation: The Faith of the Early Church.* Collegeville, Minn.: Liturgical Press.

Winslow, Donald F. 1979. *The Dynamics of Salvation: A Study in Gregory of Nazianzus.* Cambridge, Mass.: Philadelphia Patristic Foundation.

—38—

Texts on Iconoclasm: John of Damascus
and the Council of Hiereia

David Vila

I saw the human shape of God

and my soul found its salvation.

—John of Damascus, *First Treatise in Defense of the Icons*
(Migne 1860, 1256)

Yuhanna b. Mansur b. Sargun (ca. 655–ca. 749 C.E.), better known as John of Damascus, lived through the cultural transition from Late Antiquity to Early Islam and thus offers an important window into the practice of Late Antique Christian faith in a changing cultural milieu.

John's family is traceable to at least two generations of prominent Arab Christians. His grandfather, Mansur b. Sargun, and his father, Sargun b. Mansur, were both among the educated elite of Damascus and participated in the Umayyad Muslim government that was then headquartered at Damascus (Sahas 1992, 187). It is thought that John's grandfather played an important role in the capitulation of Damascus to Khalid b. al-Walid and the Muslim armies in the year 635 (Sahas 1972, 17). Although Mansur seems to have held a position of authority even before the Muslim invasion, it is likely that his part in the capitulation of the city helped assure him a high position in the new Muslim caliphate. Sargun b. Mansur followed in his father's footsteps and, according to both Christian and Muslim sources, was a high government official during the caliphate of ʿAbd al-Malik (r. 684–705). John is thus situated firmly within an Arab and Muslim milieu.

In spite of the prominence of his family, information on John's life is particularly scarce. The date of John's death must have been before the iconoclastic Council of Hiereia, (754), which condemned him and presumed him dead. The date of his birth is somewhat more conjectural but can generally be placed between 650 and 660, a dating necessary for John to have been a friend of the future Caliph Yazid I (b. 644), as we are told in several sources.

It seems that up until he was twelve, John underwent a traditional Muslim education. We are also told in one of the vitae that Sargun b. Mansur wanted a Greek tutor for his son so that he could learn "not only the books of the Muslims, but those of the Greeks as well (Sahas 1972, 38–39)." John grew up as a bilingual and bicultural person, standing at the threshold of the transition from Late Antiquity to Early Islam.

John's role in the Muslim government of Damascus was one of financial administration, as we are told in the Acts of the Seventh Ecumenical Council of 787, where he was compared to the evangelist Matthew, a tax collector. After a time in that office, John retired to the Monastery of Mar Saba near Jerusalem. Although the dates for this move are somewhat uncertain, it is generally agreed that the reforms of the Caliph 'Abd al-Malik and his successors toward a more thoroughly Islamic government likely influenced his retirement from public office. From the nature of his earliest writings at Mar Saba, it also seems clear that John wanted to move into a vocation that was more properly ecclesiastical and devotional. His earliest treatises, written around the year 726 were decidedly practical and devotional in tone. It is, therefore, rather certain that by 726 John was already at the monastery of Mar Saba, where he remained until his death around 749.

Many scholars argue that the issues involved in the iconoclastic controversy were primarily Christological controversies in material form. In other words, the basic opposition to the use of icons, particularly those of Christ, was that the iconic depiction of Christ necessarily led to the humanizing of the God-man. According to this reconstruction, the Divine is necessarily undepictable and since in Christ the divine and the human have been united perfectly, the depiction of a Christ in bodily form necessarily robs him of his divinity. Furthermore, those who adore such a human Christ are not worshippers of the God-man Christ, but of a merely human Christ. In the Acts of the iconoclast Council of Hiereia we find the following articulation of the iconoclast argument:

> For [the iconophile] has made an icon which he has called 'Christ.' But 'Christ' is a name of God as well as man. Consequently, along with describing created flesh, he has either circumscribed the uncircumscribable character of the Godhead . . . or he has confused that unconfused union, falling into the iniquity of confusion. Thus, in two ways, with the circumscription and the confusion, he has blasphemed the Godhead. (Sahas 1986, 83)

This separation of the human nature from the divine nature was, according to the iconoclasts, the heresy of Nestorius and so was to be rejected (Sahas 1986, 77).

A second iconoclast argument proceeds from the liturgy of the Church. In this case it is argued that the only proper icon of Christ is that one instituted by Christ himself; the Eucharist. Again in the Acts of the Council of Hiereia we read with reference to Christ,

> For when He was about to offer Himself voluntarily to his ever memorable and life-giving death, taking the bread He blessed it and . . . Similarly, passing on the cup, He said: This is my blood; do this in remembrance of me. He did so, because there was no other kind or form under the sun selected by Him which could depict his incarnation. Here is, therefore, the icon of his body. . . . (Sahas 1986, 92–93)

Properly speaking, the iconoclasts, according to this statement, were not entirely iconoclast. They merely rejected any icon that they believed was not instituted by Christ himself. The Eucharist, being such an authorized icon of Christ, was the only legitimate icon for use in Christian worship.

A third iconoclast argument is also based on the practice of the Christian faith, as it was understood by those who opposed icons. "On the contrary, the ill name of the falsely called 'icon' neither has its existence in the tradition of Christ, or the Apostles, or the Fathers, nor is there any prayer of consecration for it to transpose it from the state of being common to the state of being sacred" (Sahas 1986, 97). Whereas in the previous argument it is the practice of Christ that is mentioned in opposition to the iconography of Christ, here it is the practice of the Church that is opposed to the depiction of Christ and especially in light of the fact that there is, according to tradition, no "anaphora" or prayer of consecration that transposes the icon from a common state to a holy state of being.

A fourth argument against icons is directed against icons of Mary, and the prophets, apostles, and martyrs of the Church. The council declares merely that since the use of icons of Christ has been abolished, a fortiori images of other beings are certainly forbidden (Sahas 1986, 100).

A fifth form of argument has to do with the medium employed in the creation of icons: "How do they also dare to depict through the vulgar art of the pagans the all-praised mother of God, upon whom the fullness of the Godhead cast His shadow . . . or again those who will reign with Christ and sit along with Him to judge the world? . . . Are they not ashamed to depict them through a pagan art? For it is not lawful for Christians . . . to use the customs of nations that worship demons" (Sahas 1986, 105). It is the very medium of the iconophile that is rejected, as it is based on pagan models. The Council stated that the Christian Church had no business imitating the ways of the pagans because, ". . . the catholic Church of us Christians stands in the middle between Judaism and paganism" (Sahas 1986, 101).

A sixth argument looks to the Scriptures for direct refutations to the use of icons in worship. In support of their beliefs the iconoclasts quote from John 4:24, "God is spirit, and those who worship him must worship him in spirit and truth"; from Deuteronomy 4:12, "Thou shalt not make to thyself an idol, nor likeness of any thing, whatever things are in heaven above, and whatever are in the earth beneath"; and Romans 1:23 and 25, "And, they exchanged the glory of God, who is incorruptible, with the likeness of an image of man who is corruptible . . . and they paid respect to and worshipped the creature rather than the Creator . . ." among numerous other Scripture passages (Sahas 1986, 107–11). In concluding their arguments against the iconophiles, the Council of Hiereia declared:

> Therefore, having collected the biblical and patristic testimonies, we have put together in this present Definition of ours only a few of them out of the many, so that this may not become too long. For, although there are many more, we wittingly left out an infinite number of them . . . and having fixed our feet with certainty on the stone of worshipping in spirit and in truth . . . decree . . . that every icon, made of any matter and of any kind of gaudiness of colours by painters, is objectionable, alien, and repugnant to the Church of the Christians. (Sahas 1986, 143–44)

These were the main arguments of iconoclast Christians, less than a decade after the death of John of Damascus.

An important distinction that John makes is that between absolute worship (*latreia*) and relative worship (*proskynēsis*). As examples of the latter John mentions Daniel bowing before an angel, David venerating the holy places, Jacob bowing before his brother Esau, Joseph's brothers prostrating themselves before him in Egypt, among others (Anderson 1997, 21–22). The former type of worship is to be given to God alone.

As John approaches his defense of icons he turns first to a theological argument from the Christian doctrine of creation. For John, God is the first iconophile because God made human beings in the *imago dei* (image of God). For human beings to pay honor to other human beings is no less than to honor the image of God in them. Basil of Cappadocia (d. 379) is used as support, quoting from his *On the Holy Spirit* where he says "the honor (*timē*) paid to the image (*eikonos*) is passed on (*diabanei*) to the prototype." John seems to be saying that honor is actually not given to an image nor the non-divine figure represented by an image, but rather only to God through the image. Continued support for this is found in the example of Moses and the children of Israel. God instructed Moses to build the tabernacle according to the pattern shown to him on the mountain; that pattern included images of cherubim. God not only creates icons but also commands humans to follow the divine example in creating their own icons for use in worship. As another example, John mentions the temple in Jerusalem, again built according to divine instructions. Certainly if God ordains the use of images, who are we, according to John, to say that God is wrong. Thus in one short paragraph John argues from the theological principle of the *imago dei*, from a prominent early Christian writer (Basil) and from the practice of the Jews in favor of icons.

John then admits that the Scriptures condemn those who adore (*proskynountōn*) "carved things" (*glyptois*) and those who sacrifice to the demons. In this case the translation "carved things" is probably better translated as "statues." John's context here is to the practice of the Greeks, for whom sacred statuary was relatively common. According to John, even the relative worship of carved images is forbidden. Regrettably, while referring the matter as "according to the Scriptures,"

John does not mention any specific scriptural passages that he might have in mind.

Continuing on this theme, John reminds his readers of the impiety of attempting to portray an image of the invisible God. He makes the great distinction between practice under the "old [testament]" and under the new; that is, God in Christ became visibly human and thus it is possible to depict this "visible" God through the use of images. Expanding on the matter, John reminds his readers that Christ became human not merely in appearance (*en eidei*), but according to true substance (*kat˙ ousian*). Thus in this radical incarnation God took on the very substance of humanity: a truly physical body. For John, this state of affairs came because of the depth of God's mercy and for humankind's salvation. John ties the justification for a Christian iconography to the fact of human redemption: it was for humankind's redemption that God took on the substance of humanity; a denial of the use of icons in worship may even be a denial of the reality of human redemption in Christ.

The incarnation was not just an event in time past. The life, death, and resurrection of Christ were also recorded in the Scriptures so that people not then present could still hear and believe in the incarnate God. And since some are illiterate, and others do not have the time to read, the Fathers agreed that the life of Christ could be depicted. Icons serve a pedagogic purpose in the life of the Church to instruct those who have no other access the basic Christian teachings. Interestingly, John mentions not only those who are not able to read, but also those who simply fail to make time for reading. Icons are even justified to compensate for human laziness.

John then turns to another practical argument: when Christians, failing to be mindful of the passion of Christ, sometimes find themselves imagining in their minds the events of the passion they are moved to adore him. Persons in such a state do not adore the image in the mind but rather that which the image represents, Christ himself. Similarly says John, when one worships (*proskynein*) the cross or the Gospel (i.e., an actual book), it is not these physical things that are worshipped but rather what they represent.

As John turns to the honor paid to the "Mother of God," he argues that such honor is passed on to the One who became incarnate from her. For John, honor is not really given to Mary but rather to Christ through Mary. Likewise honor paid to the saints is passed on to God, as "the honor paid to the image is passed on to the prototype," John quotes from Basil of Cappadocia. In concluding this section John asserts that the use of icons in Christian worship is part of the "written" tradition of the Church. Other examples are worshipping toward the east and worshipping the cross. But John also turns to oral tradition to bolster his story.

John refers to a "certain story" (*tis historia*) about Abgar King of Edessa. Abgar is first mentioned in Eusebius's *Ecclesiastical History* (1.13) and was ruler of Edessa from ca. 13–50 C.E. According to the earliest legends, Abgar sent a letter to Jesus asking to be healed of a deadly disease. In a letter of response, Jesus promises that after he ascends to heaven, he will send one of his disciples to cure Abgar. According to the story, this happens through a disciple named Thaddaeus. Later expansions on this story relate that a messenger from Abgar painted a portrait of Jesus and that the portrait protected the city of Edessa from all sorts of maladies. It is a variation on this story to which John refers even though it seems clear from the way he couches the story in rather tentative language that he is not altogether convinced that the events described actually took place; he uses them nonetheless because they serve his purposes.

Significantly in John's telling of the story, it is Christ himself who makes the image of his own face for Abgar. Therefore, who can argue that images of Christ are forbidden if Christ himself made an image of himself for human use? In spite of the rather tentative language of the story, John seems to be arguing as though the story were true. This seems even clearer as we move to the final paragraph where he attempts to ward off the challenges of those who deny that the events surrounding Abgar ever took place. John argues that it should not be surprising that the Abgar story is true even though it is not found in the canonical Gospels, because there are many things that were handed down orally as we are told in 2 Thessalonians (2:15) and in 1 Corinthians (11:12).

The text of "On the Orthodox Faith" translated here is that of the critical edition published in *Die Schriften des Johannes von Damaskos,* vol. 12, edited by Boniface Kotter, O.S.B., 206–8.

John of Damascus, Concerning Icons

Since there are certain people who find great fault with us for adoring and honoring the image of the Savior and that of our Lady, as well as those of the rest of the saints and servants of Christ, let them hear how from the beginning God formed humans according to his own image. Why then, do we adore one another, except as the image of the God who formed us? For as Basil, who is inspired and rich in theological insight, says: "the honor paid to the image is passed on to the original." And the original is the thing imaged out of which the copy comes into being. Why then did the people of Moses gather around the tabernacle to adore the image and pattern of heavenly things, or rather, of all creation that it bore? Indeed, God told Moses: "See that you make everything according to the pattern which was shown to you on the mountain." And were not the cherubim that overshadowed the place of propitiation also the work of human hands? And what about the magnificent temple in Jerusalem? Was it not built and furnished by human skill?

Now, Holy Scripture condemns those who adore graven things and also those who sacrifice to the demons. Both the Greeks and the Jews used to sacrifice—the Greeks to the demons and the Jews to God. And the sacrifice of the Greeks was rejected, but that of the just was acceptable to God. Thus, Noah sacrificed "and God smelled a sweet aroma" of the good intention and accepted the fragrance of the gift offered to him. And so the statues of the Greeks, being representations of demons, are rejected and condemned.

Moreover, who can represent the invisible, incorporeal, uncircumscribed, and unportrayable God? It is, then, crazy and impious to portray the divinity. This is why it was not the custom in ancient times to use images. But God, on account of his great mercy, became truly human for our salvation. And not merely in human appearance as was seen by Abraham and the prophets, but truly and substantially he became human. And as a human he spent time on earth, and living among humanity he worked miracles, suffered, was crucified, rose from the dead and ascended; and all these things really happened and were seen by humanity, and indeed were written down to remind and instruct us, who were not present then, in order that, although we have not seen, yet hearing and believing we may attain to the blessedness of the Lord.

Since, however, some are illiterate and others do not have leisure to read, the Fathers deemed it proper that certain of these worthy events should be depicted as a concise reminder. It certainly happens often that not having the Lord's Passion in mind and seeing the image of his crucifixion, we are reminded of his saving passion and, falling down we adore, not the material but that which is represented. Likewise it is not the material of the Gospel or that of the cross that we adore, but what they typify. For what distinguishes a cross which does not typify the Lord from one which does? So also with the Mother of God: for the honor paid to her is passed on to the One who was incarnated from her. Likewise, we are moved to bravery, zeal, imitation, and the glory of God by the virtues of holy people. For, as we have said, the honor expressed indulgently toward fellow servants gives proof of good will toward the common Master, and the honor paid to the image is passed on to the original. This is the written tradition, just as is worshipping toward the east, worshipping the cross, and so many other similar things.

Furthermore, there is a certain story about when Abgar was ruling of the city of the Edessenes, he sent an artist to make a likeness of the image of the Lord. But he was unable to do so on account of the brilliant radiance of his face, so the Lord, pressing a cloth to his own life-giving face, impressed on the cloth his own likeness and so sent this to Abgar who had so yearned for it.

And Paul, the apostle of the Gentiles, writes that the Apostles handed down many things unwritten: "Therefore, brethren, stand firm and hold fast to our traditions which you have learned, whether by word or by our epistle"; and to the Corinthians: "Now I praise you, brethren, that in all things you remember me and keep the traditions as I have delivered them to you."

The Council of Hiereia

The following material is taken from the *Definition* of the Council of Hiereia in 754 C.E. as it is reproduced in the Acts of the Second Council of Nicea in 787

C.E. The text translated here is taken from selections found on columns 208–345 of Giovanni Momenico Mansi's *Sacrorum Conciliorum nova et amplissima Collectio,* vol. 13.

The *Definition* of the Holy, Great and Seventh Ecumenical Council

The holy and ecumenical council, which was convened by God's grace and the most pious decree of our God-fearing and orthodox kings, Constantine and Leo, having been gathered in this God-guarded and royal city, in the sacred church of our holy, immaculate Lady Theotokos and ever-virgin Mary . . . defined the following:

The Divinity, cause and accomplisher of everything, who in goodness brought all things out of nonbeing into being, commanded people to live in a determined and orderly way. God did so in order that they might properly manifest in their lives that which was gifted to them by grace, and in this way preserve in their journey steadfast and unwavering, inclining towards neither side from the path of truth.

But darkness resulted from the rebellious power of that one who because of his previous brilliance had his dwelling near God and yet by his own thinking challenged his Creator. Having fallen by his own choice from the most brilliant, light-giving divine order, he became dark and proved himself to be the doer, inventor, and teacher of every evil. He could not bear seeing humanity, having been created by God, being introduced instead of him into his former glory so he unleashed all his evil against humanity, and with deception he alienated them from the glory and brilliance of God by suggesting that they could worship the creature rather than the Creator.

And since humanity was unable to restore their previous relationship with God—the one who forms, and since God did not want to see the work of his hands end in total destruction—after he had provided the Law and the Prophets for the salvation of humanity, God deemed it worthy to send his own Son and Word to earth, in the final and predetermined times. . . .

He [Christ] removed us from the destructive teaching of the demons, which is the error of worshipping idols, and he handed over to us a worship that is in spirit and truth. Afterwards he was raised into heaven in that which he had assumed, having left behind his holy disciples and apostles as teachers of this redemptive faith. They, having adorned our church as his bride with various brilliant doctrines of godliness, raised her to be all beautiful and exceedingly bright, surrounded by and decorated with golden tassels. It is this beauty of hers that our illustrious Fathers and teachers, and the six holy and Ecumenical Councils, have received and guarded relentlessly.

But again, the previously mentioned creator of evil, not wishing to see her beautiful, employed at different times various means of wicked scheming in order to put humanity under his hand. So under the name of Christianity he brought back idolatry imperceptibly by convincing with his sophistries those who had their eyes turned to him. Thus they did not put aside creation but rather worshipped it, adored it, honored it, and considered as divine that which was made, calling it with the name "Christ."

And just as in the past, Jesus—the author and perfecter of our salvation—who sent out his most wise disciples and Apostles in the power of the most holy Spirit to abolish all such things, so also now he has raised his servants, our faithful kings. And they who are comparable to the Apostles have been made wise by the power of the same Spirit—in order to equip and teach us, as well as to break down the demonic strongholds that are opposed to the knowledge of God, and to refute diabolic pursuit and error.

Moved by the divine zeal that was in them, and not tolerating the ravaging of the Church of the faithful by the treachery of demons, they called together the entire priestly assembly of God-loving bishops, so that, being assembled as a council, and they might search the Scriptures together about the deceptions of painted likenesses, which bring down the human mind from the high worship due to God to a base and material creature-worship. Thus, set in motion by God, this assembly will pronounce that which seems proper, knowing what was written in the Prophets: "The lips of priests ought to guard knowledge and they should seek the law at their mouth: for they are messengers of the all-powerful Lord. . . ."

Having looked into these matters with great care and consideration, under the inspiration of the all-holy Spirit, we have also judged that by the unlawful art of the painters they have blasphemed against this very fundamental doctrine of our salvation; that is, against the dispensation in Christ, and that they have overturned these most holy and Ecumenical six councils, convened by God. . . .

We thought it right, therefore, to expose in detail, through our *Definition* here, the error of those who make and of those who honor images.

All the God-bearing Fathers and the holy and Ecumenical Councils have handed down the pure, untarnished and God-tested faith and confession that no contrivance should be made to divide or confuse what is above reason and understanding, the unspeakable and unknowable unique hypostatic union of the two natures of a person who is in truth absolutely one. Therefore, what is this pointless work of the painter of likenesses who, for the sake of easy money, tries to do what cannot be done, that is, forming with dirty hands things that are believed with the heart and confessed with the mouth? . . .

Let no one dare to do so godless and unholy a thing. From this day forward, anyone who makes, venerates, or sets up an icon in a church or their own home, or who hides one, if a bishop, presbyter, or deacon, let him be removed from office; if monk or layperson, let them be anathematized and subjected to the royal laws, as one who opposes the commandments of God and is an enemy of the teachings of the Fathers.

If anyone tries to comprehend the divine incarnate character of God the

Word through material colors, and so does not offer adoration with spiritual eyes and fully from the heart to the One who is beyond the brightness of the sun and is at God's right side in the highest, sitting on a glorious throne—let them be anathema.

If anyone tries to express fully the inexpressible essence and hypostasis of God the Word, on account of the incarnation, with material colors in icons and in an anthropomorphic way they thus fail to treat him as God (because even after the incarnation he is still inexpressible)—let them be anathema.

If anyone tries to set up likenesses of the saints in soulless and speechless icons made of material colors, which bring no benefit, instead of imitating their virtues from what has been written (and thus becoming themselves ensouled icons), being zealous to imitate them as our God-inspired Fathers have said— let them be anathema.

Bibliography

John of Damascus. 1860. "First Treatise in Defense of the Icons." In *Patrologiae Cursus Completus, Series Graeca* 94. Ed. J. P. Migne. Paris.

———. 1958. *Writings*. Trans. Frederic H. Chase, Jr. New York: Fathers of the Church.

———. 1973. *Die Schriften des Johannes von Damaskos* 12. Ed. Boniface Kotter, O.S.B. Berlin: Walter de Gruyter.

———. 1997. *On the Divine Images*. Trans. David Anderson. Crestwood, N.Y.: St. Vladimir's Seminary Press.

Mango, Cyril A. 1986. *The Art of the Byzantine Empire 312–1453: Sources and Documents*. Toronto: University of Toronto Press.

Mansi, Giovanni Momenico. 1902. *Sacrorum Conciliorum nova et amplissima Collectio* 13. Paris: H. Welter.

Nasrallah, Joseph. 1950. *Saint Jean de Damas, son époque, sa vie, son oeuvre*. Harissa, Lebanon: St. Paul Press.

Núñez, Jacinto González. 1995. *La Leyenda del Rey Abgar y Jesús: Orígenes del cristianismo en Edesa*. Madrid: Editorial Cuidad Nueva.

Sahas, Daniel. 1972. *John of Damascus on Islam: The "Heresy of the Ishmaelites."* Leiden: E. J. Brill.

———, ed. and trans. 1986. *Icon and Logos: Sources in Eighth-Century Iconoclasm*. Toronto: University of Toronto Press.

———. 1992. "The Arab Character of the Christian Disputation with Islam: The Case of John of Damascus (ca. 655–ca. 749)." In *Religionsgespräche im Mittelalter*. Ed. B. Lewis et al., 186–205. Weisbaden: Harrassowitz.

Schick, Robert. 1995. *The Christian Communities of Palestine from Byzantine to Islamic Rule: a Historical and Archaeological Study*. Princeton, N.J.: Darwin.

39

Asterius of Amasea

Ekphrasis on the Holy Martyr Euphemia

Elizabeth A. Castelli

St. Euphemia of Chalcedon died as a Christian martyr in 303, the first year of the Great Persecution under the Roman emperor Diocletian. Very little is known about her life and death; indeed, apart from the date of her martyrdom, recorded in the fifth-century *Martyrologium Hieronymianum* and the *Fasti Vindobonenses* (a liturgical document compiled from the fourth through the sixth centuries), there is virtually no historically verifiable information about her at all. The *Fasti Vindobonenses* offers only this brief record of Euphemia's martyrdom:

> Diocletiano VII et Maximiano V. His cons. ecclesiae demolitae sunt et libri dominici combusti sunt et passa est sancta Eufemia XVI kal. octobris.

> In the consulships of Diocletian VII and Maximian V, churches were destroyed, holy books burned, and Saint Euphemia died on the 16th of October.

Despite the absence of significant historical information about the virgin martyr, she enjoyed considerable veneration during Late Antiquity and in the Middle Ages. For example, the famous pilgrim Egeria remarks that the city of Chalcedon is the site of a martyrium of Euphemia in her diary narrating her trip, which probably took place 381–384 C.E. (23.7), and a fantastical account of her martyrdom appears in the medieval *Golden Legend* (Voragine 1993, 2: 181–83). Moreover, Euphemia played the important role of patron saint over the Council of Chalcedon, the ecumenical council held in 451 in a church named for her; and at least one story of her miraculous intervention on behalf of orthodoxy circulated as part of her cult. According to the story, preserved in the *Synaxarion of Constantinople* (cols. 811–13), two professions of faith—one, orthodox, and the other, Eutychian (monophysite)—were both placed inside the saint's tomb, on the breast of her corpse. The tomb was then carefully sealed. When it was re-opened some days later, the orthodox text was found in the saint's hands while the heretical text lay under her feet (Lucchesi 1964, 154; Schneider 1951, 291–302).

There are three separate Late Antique traditions concerning Euphemia's death: a well-known Greek passion thought to have been composed for the Council of Chalcedon in 451 (Halkin 1965), a collection of testimonia associated with the transfer of her relics from Milan to Rouen (Schrier 1984), and a much less well known sermon composed in the late fourth century by Asterius, bishop of Amasea, the text translated here (Datema, 1970, 153–55). These three traditions cannot be reconciled since they include radically different accounts of the death of Euphemia: in Asterius's version, she dies by fire; in the tradition linked to Milan and Rouen, she dies by the sword; in the later passion, she dies in the arena. The passion has been dismissed as highly legendary by most, if not all, scholars. There remains considerable debate over the authenticity of the two remaining traditions.

Asterius's less well-known text is translated here because of its particular interest, not only to students of Christian martyrdom, but also as a source for considering the artistic production of Late Antique Christianity. In the sermon, Asterius describes the martyrdom of Euphemia as it is captured in a large painting in a church near the tomb of the saint.

What is one to make of this lively description by Asterius? Did the painting really exist, or should one read Asterius's *ekphrasis* (a verbally artistic description of a work of art) as an elaborate and imaginative rhetorical exercise? If the painting did exist, was it based on an historical account of the martyrdom of Euphemia, or did the artist engage in a form of visual rhetoric in portraying the death of this virgin saint? These are questions that scholars have debated for years, and they are unlikely to be answered definitively. For the purposes of this translation, the historical reliability of Asterius's account of Euphemia's martyrdom is a less important question than others that might be posed to the text.

Whether or not Euphemia died in the way Asterius describes, his description offers some insight into the values that circulated around the notion of martyrdom in Asterius's world and the manner in which martyrs were commemorated in the early church—in Euphemia's case, by an annual festival during which the priests make a speech describing the martyrdom. Moreover, whether or not the painting he describes ever actually existed, that he chose to make his point concerning Euphemia's death through a description of a vivid visual image is intriguing. Through his description, Asterius seeks to help his audience see the martyrdom of Euphemia. His description is hardly neutral, and the starkly dualistic struggle between purity and profanity that one encounters frequently in martyrologies is certainly recapitulated in this *ekphrasis*. And the text implies that the description itself will have a salutary effect on Asterius's audience, an effect that both ancient Christians and modern scholars have noted. Asterius's *ekphrasis* was read into the official record of the Seventh Ecumenical Council of Nicea in 787 in the midst of a theological debate over the use of images. More recently, at least one scholar has argued that Asterius's text would have most likely been composed as a missionary text in order to appeal to non-Christians (Speyer 1971). This argument is based primarily on the vocabulary of Asterius's description of the church as a temple (*temenos*), the priests as "hierophants of the mysteries of God" (language taken from the ancient mysteries), and the explanation of the festival practices, which presumably Christians would already know.

Those who have some knowledge of the martyrological tradition will recognize many familiar elements in Asterius's account of Euphemia's death: the cruelty of the persecutors, the combined virtues of modesty and bravery displayed by the Christian virgin, the graphic quality of the violence described, the miraculous intervention of a sign. Whether or not Asterius's *ekphrasis* is a historically accurate description of Euphemia's death, it clearly belongs in a tradition where the graphic narration of martyrs' deaths are used for the spiritual elevation of an audience.

This translation is based on the Greek text established by Datema, who reviews the manuscript tradition associated with this text and thirteen other sermons written by Asterius (Datema 1970, 149–55).

Ekphrasis on the Holy Martyr Euphemia

[1.1] O men, the day before yesterday, I had in my hand the clever Demosthenes at the place where Demosthenes casts sharp arguments at Aischines. Having spent a long time with the argument and feeling weighted down by its meaning, I needed relaxation and a walk so that I might release my soul a little from my labor. Departing from my little house and these notable men, walking slowly toward the agora, thence I arrived in the temple (*temenos*) of God offering prayers in a leisurely way. [2] And by chance I walked on the public passageway under the roof, and saw there a painting the sight of which overtook me completely. You might say that this masterpiece is more pleasurable than some of those of the ancients, whose efforts raised the picture to great animation with minimal propriety. Here, if you please—for there is leisure now for a narrative—I will describe the painting for you. For not even we, the children of the muses, have an altogether simpler remedy against painters.

[2.1] A certain holy woman, a pure virgin who had dedicated her chastity [*sōphrosynē*] to God—they call her Euphemia—chose for herself a fatal venture when a tyrant was very zealously persecuting the pious. The citizens and the community members completed the religious ceremony on her behalf, honoring the virgin who was equally courageous [*andreia*] and holy; having built her tomb near the temple [*hieron*] and buried her coffin, they perform honors for her and they make an annual public festival and common assembly. [2] So the priests of the mysteries of God [*hierophantai tōn tou Theou mystēriōn*] always honor her memory with a speech and with the intention to teach the comprehending people thoroughly in what manner she diligently completed her struggle of steadfastness. So the pious painter through the full power of his art placed the story on a linen canvas near the holy tomb; the masterpiece is like this.

[3.1] The judge sits high on his throne looking cruelly and hostilely at the virgin. For art, when it wants, grows angry even on inanimate material. There are the spear-bearing bodyguards of the ruler and many soldiers, and the scribes who record the minutes of the trial bearing writing-tablets and styluses. One of the scribes, hanging his hand on the wax table, looks impetuously at the condemned prisoner with his face turned fully toward her as if exhorting her to speak louder in order that he not err in listening and recording the proceedings. [2] The virgin stood in a dark tunic and cloak, the sign of philosophy, as it seemed to the painter, and refined in appearance. It seemed to me that her soul was adorned with virtues. Two soldiers led her to the ruler, one dragging her forward, the other urging her on from behind. The virgin's figure blended modesty and enormous strength. For, on the one hand, she bows her head toward the earth [an ambiguous gesture signifying both modesty and aggression, as when soldiers bow their heads to charge] just as she blushed before men's eyes; on the other hand, she stood fearing nothing she suffered in the wretched struggle. [3] As for myself, at other times I would compliment the painter publicly, as if I were contemplating the drama of that Colchian woman [Medea], how just when she is about to inflict the sword on her children her countenance divides between pity and anger. One of her eyes manifests wrath, the other reveals a mother who restains herself and bristles [at the crime]. Now I have reported my admiration for the painting about which I speak; I was astonished by the talent of the painter who, mixing feelings better than colors, balanced modesty and courage, which seem to be virtues which are by their nature contrary to one another.

[4.1] Advancing further along in the representation [mimēsis], some executioners scantily clad in short garments had already begun their work. One of them laying hold of her head and leaning it back holds it in readiness for the other who is prepared to punish the virgin's face; the one standing beside her knocked out all her teeth. The tools of this punishment appear to be a hammer and a borer. From this point, I weep and the suffering cut short my discourse. For the painter had smeared drops of blood so manifestly that it seemed to pour truly from the lips and you would depart singing a dirge.

[2] Thereupon the prison: and again the holy virgin sits alone in grey clothes stretching out her arms toward heaven and calling God as her ally against sufferings. While she prays, over her head appears the sign, which clearly is the custom for Christians to worship and inscribe; I imagine it to be the symbol of the very suffering that awaited her.

[3] Immediately, at any rate, the painter lit a violent fire elsewhere, consolidating the flame with red color shining on this side and that. She is standing in the midst of it, and she unfolded her arms toward heaven. She revealed no burden on her face, but quite the contrary, she rejoiced that she was on her journey toward a bodiless and blessed life.

[4] At this point, the painter stopped his hand and I my speech; it is the

time for you and she, if you please, to finish the picture, so that you might judge very closely the effects of this interpretation.

Bibliography

Datema, C. 1970. *Asterius of Amasea, Homilies I–XIV: Text, Introduction and Notes*. Leiden: E. J. Brill.

Halkin, François. 1965. *Euphémie de Chalcédoine: Légendes byzantines*. Subsidia Hagiographica 41. Brussels: Société des Bollandistes.

Leclercq, Henri. 1922. "Euphémie (Sainte)." *Dictionnaire d'archéologie chrétienne et de liturgie* 5.1: 745–46.

Lucchesi, Giovanni. 1964. "Eufemia di Calcedonia." *Bibliotheca Sanctorum* 5: 154–60.

Schneider, Alfons M. 1951. "Sankt Euphemia und das Konzil von Chalkedon." In *Das Konzil von Chalkedon: Geschichte und Gegenwart,* ed. Aloys Grillmeier and Heinrich Bacht, 1: 291–302. Würzburg: Echter-Verlag.

Schrier, O. J. 1984. "A propos d'une donnée négligée sur la mort de Ste. Euphémie." *Analecta Bollandiana* 102: 329–53.

Speyer, Wolfgang. 1971. "Die Euphemia-Rede des Asterios von Amaseia: Eine Missionschrift für gebildete Heiden." *Jahrbuch für Antike und Christentum* 14: 39–47.

Voragine, Jacobus de. 1993. *The Golden Legend: Readings on the Saints*. 2 vols. Trans. William Granger Ryan. Princeton: Princeton University Press.

— 40 —

Christian Oracle Shrines

David Frankfurter

The following six texts, from the sixth and seventh centuries and all but the last in Greek, represent queries to Egyptian Christian oracle shrines, presented according to a procedure recorded in Egypt as early as the New Kingdom (1550–1070 B.C.E.). The procedure involved presenting a written query to the shrine worded in both positive and negative forms ("If I will give birth"; "If I will not give birth"); the shrine-god would send back the part of the query written in the appropriate form. The query formula would either include or imply the request to return the appropriate ticket: thus, "If I will give birth, then return this ticket" (Stewart 1985; Černý 1962; McDowell 1990, chap. 4; Ryholt 1993).

This procedure was already widespread in Egypt by the Ptolemaic period, and oracle tickets in Demotic Egyptian and then exclusively Greek (called *pittakion*) abound through the third century C.E. (Schubart 1931; Frankfurter 1998, 159–62), requesting all manner of mundane and existential answers from a diversity of gods.

The continuity of this procedure in Late Antique Egypt and under the aegis of Christian saints sheds further light on Christianization in Egypt (and elsewhere) as a process of assimilating indigenous religious forms. The six texts, and the large hordes of similar ones that have been discovered in the last century, show an exact replication of the classical form of oracle-ticket: the use of *pittakion* in A and the "if . . ." clauses expressed or implied in each (apparently mixed with another interrogative form in A). (See Papini 1985; Papaconstantinou 1994; Frankfurter 1998; 193–95). Texts C and D, in fact, belong to the same piece of papyrus cut in half (Youtie 1975); and the last words of texts B and E likewise suggest corresponding "negative" tickets.

The crosses and sacred figures on A–C and F are not for decoration but rather indicate the amuletic potential of the chosen ticket. In the Persian and Ptolemaic periods Egyptian temples would provide amuletic "decrees" from the god, which could be worn in a tube around the neck for protection against ghosts, demons, and misfortune (Edwards 1960; with Ptolemaic-era analogues discussed in

Thompson 1938). A Greek astrological forecast likewise instructs the preparation of a protective amulet (*Papyrus Oxyrhynchus* 2554). So also in the Christian cases, the divinely chosen "ticket" would thereafter constitute the saint's promise of fortune in following the oracle's instruction.

Little can be reconstructed of the cults of Saints Philoxenus and Leontius. But another Christian oracle shrine using the "ticket-exchange" procedure, that of St. Colluthus at Antinoë, gained a reputation throughout Egypt for its healing and oracular powers (Papini 1985, 1998). Other polemical witnesses refer to oracles sought regularly at Christian martyrial shrines, e.g., Athanasius in his *Festal Letter* 42. These divination practices were obviously not restricted to isolated pockets of "demi-Christians" but rather typified the Christianity embraced and used by a populace anxious to turn an institutional worldview into social guidance. Concerns for business (texts C–D), location of residence (A), marriage (E), and fertility (F) recall the queries of earlier times, as well as those made to diviners and shrines throughout the history of religions.

Finally, one should note St. Philoxenus's title as "protector [prostatēs]" in texts B–D. "Protector" during the fourth and fifth centuries designated a form of muscled regional patronage not unlike a boss or overlord that had come to gain much power in the countrysides, as Libanius of Antioch laments (*Epistle* 47; see Frankfurter 1998, 77–82). Calling Philoxenus "protector," if only to distinguish his status from that of God, gives some indication of how saints were imagined in rural Egypt.

Translations are from the following texts:

A: *Papyrus Oxyrhynchus* 925, ed. Preisendanz 1973/74, II:209 (*Papyri Graecae Magicae* P1).

B: *Papyrus Oxyrhynchus* 1150, ed. Preisendanz 1973/74, II:216 (*Papyri Graecae Magicae* P8b).

C: *Papyrus Oxyrhynchus* 1926, ed. Preisendanz 1973/74, II:216 (*Papyri Graecae Magicae* P8a).

D: *Papyrus Harris* 54, ed. Preisendanz 1973/74, II:232 (*Papyri Graecae Magicae* P24).

E: *Papyrus Berlin* 21269, ed. Treu 1986, 29–30.

F: Rylands Coptic 100, ed. Crum 1909, 52.

CHRISTIAN ORACLE SHRINES

A

✠ O God almighty, holy, truthful, lover of humanity and creator, O Father of the Lord and our savior Jesus Christ, reveal to me the truth in you: If you wish me to go up to Chiout or do I find that you are with me as helper and benefactor. Let it be so. Amen!

B

✝ O God of our protector [*prostatēs*] Saint Philoxenus, if you command to bring Anoup in to your hospital, show [your power] and let the ticket come forth.

C (recto)

✝ My Lord, God almighty, and Saint Philoxenus my protector [*prostatēs*], I beseech you in the great name of the Lord God, if it is not your will that I speak either about the bank or about the weighing, advise that I may learn— that I not speak.

C (verso)

✝ X M G   ✝ X M G   ✝ X M G

D

My Lord, God almighty, and Saint Philoxenus my protector [*prostatēs*], I beseech you in the great name of the Lord God, if it is your wish and you join with me to get the bank-business, I beseech [you] to advise that I may learn and speak.

E

O God of the Christians, that your will is that we give your servant Theodora to Joseph—Yes

F

✝   ✝   ✝

O God of Saint Leontius, if I stay in the house that I am in, and remain within with my mother, my heart will be at rest and I will give birth to a living child . . . [the rest is obscure].

Bibliography

Černý, Jaroslav. 1962. "Egyptian Oracles." In Richard A. Parker, *A Saite Oracle Papyrus from Thebes in the Brooklyn Museum*, 35–48. Providence, R.I.: Brown University Press.

Crum, W. E. 1909. *Catalogue of the Coptic Manuscripts in the Collection of the John Rylands Library, Manchester*. Manchester: Manchester University Press.

Edwards, I.E.S. 1960. *Oracular Amuletic Decrees of the Late New Kingdom*. 2 vols. Hieratic Papyri in the British Museum 4. London: British Museum.

Frankfurter, David. 1998. *Religion in Roman Egypt: Assimilation and Resistance*. Princeton: Princeton University Press.

McDowell, A.G. 1990. *Jurisdiction in the Workmen's Community of Deir El-Medina*. Leiden: Nederlands Instituut voor het Nabije Oosten.

Papaconstantinou, Arietta. 1994. "Oracles chrétiens dans l'Egypte byzantine: Le Témoignage des papyrus." *Zeitschrift für Papyrologie und Epigraphik* 104: 281–66.

Papini, Lucia. 1985. "Biglietti oracolari in copto dalla necropoli nord di Antinoe." In *Acts of the Second International Congress of Coptic Study,* ed. Tito Orlandi and Frederik Wisse, 245–55. Rome: C.I.M.

—————. 1998. "Fragments of the *Sortes Sanctorum* From the Shrine of St. Colluthus." In *Pilgrimage and Holy Space in Late Antique Egypt,* ed. David Frankfurter. Religions of the Graeco-Roman World. Leiden: E.J. Brill.

Preisendanz, Karl. 1973–1974. *Papyri Graecae Magicae: Die griechischen Zauberpapyri.* 2 vols. 2d ed. Ed. Albert Henrichs. Stuttgart: Teubner.

Ryholt, Kim. 1993. "A Pair of Oracle Petitions Addressed to Horus-of-the-Camp." *Journal of Egyptian Archaeology* 79: 189–98.

Schubart, W. 1931. "Orakelfragen." *Zeitschrift für Ägyptische Sprache* 67: 110–15.

Stewart, Randall. 1985. "The Oracular εἰ." *Greek, Roman, and Byzantine Studies* 26: 67–73.

Thompson, Herbert. 1938. "Self-Dedications." In *Actes du Vᵉ Congrès international de papyrologie,* 497–504. Brussels: Fondation égyptologique Reine Elisabeth.

Treu, Kurt. 1986. "Varia Christiana II." *Archiv für Papyrusforschung* 32: 23–31.

Youtie, Herbert C. 1975. "Questions to a Christian Oracle." *Zeitschrift für Papyrologie und Epigraphik* 18: 253–57.

— 41 —

Popular Religious Practices in Fifth-Century Egypt

David Frankfurter

Numerous sermons and saints' lives bear witness to continuing forms of traditional Egyptian religious practices through the Arab conquest, and Shenoute of Atripe, formidable abbot of a monastery outside the upper Egyptian city Panopolis, is one of the most acerbic critics and destroyers of such ongoing practices. But the following texts show that the ritual eclecticism outside the monastery walls was not paganism. The popular Christianity of the fourth and subsequent centuries was a synthesis of Christian and local materials and involved the creative contributions of local monks, minor ecclesiastical authorities, and ritual experts and healers unaffiliated with the church.

The passage by Shenoute is part of a protracted sermon against the use of extracanonical books by rival Christian leaders of uncertain identity (see Orlandi 1985). Shenoute's style tends to be dramatically oral and does not reproduce easily on the page. The second passage is part of a sermon promoting the cult of the martyrs. Although carrying a manuscript attribution to Athanasius of Alexandria, it comes from a later epoch.

Both texts show the importance of healing in the popular assimilation of Christianity in the Coptic world (see Frankfurter 1998, 46–52, 214–17, 267–72). Both also show that healing ritual combined sanctuaries, expert *nrefmoute* [enchanters] from within and without the church, and amulets, composed of traditional materials and blessed by someone with authority.

In addition, Text A alludes to the use of healing and oracle sanctuaries. With multiple Christian oracle and healing shrines by this period, like Apa Mena in the western desert, Saints Cyrus and John east of Alexandria, and sanctuaries of Saints Philoxenus and Colluthus to the south, it is unlikely that Shenoute is criticizing native Egyptian shrines, but rather local Christian ones, a subject to which he refers in other sermons. In these sentiments he echoes the scripturalist attitudes of the fourth-century Bishop Athanasius of Alexandria, who criticized the popular cult of martyrs (see Lefort 1954; Baumeister 1972, 63–73; Brakke 1998). And yet practices of the popular Christian shrines of the fourth and fifth centuries—incubation, healing waters, oracle rites—clearly reflect traditions maintained in Egyptian sanctuaries like Dendarah, Abydos, Soknopaiou Nesos, and Tebtunis, all of which were active through the third century C.E. (see Frankfurter 1998, 46–52, 267–72).

Text B's reference to the poetic forms of demons seems to denote traditional Egyptian deities, still invoked by name. It is likely that some people maintained an eclectic variety of powerful names to invoke alongside their eclectic variety of religious practices.

Text A is translated from Orlandi's edition; Text B from Lefort's.

Text A: Shenoute's *Against the Origenists*

[255] But at the time of suffering, those fallen into poverty or in sickness or indeed some other trial [*peirasmos*] abandon God and run after enchanters or diviners or indeed seek other acts of deception, [256] just as I myself have seen: the snake's head tied on someone's hand, another one with the crocodile's tooth tied to his arm, and another with fox claws tied to his legs—[257] especially since it was an official [*archōn*] who told him that it was wise to do so! Indeed, when I demanded whether the fox claws would heal him, he answered, "It was a great monk who gave them to me, saying 'Tie them on you [and] you will find relief.' "

[258] Listen to this impiety! Fox claws! Snakes' heads! Crocodiles' teeth! And many other vanities that men put on themselves for their own relief, while others deceive them.

[259] Moreover, this is the manner that they annoint themselves with oil or that they pour over themselves water while receiving [ministrations] from enchanters or drug-makers, with every deceptive kind of relief. . . . Still again, they pour water over themselves or annoint themselves with oil from elders of the church, or even from monks!

[260] It is about them that the Prophet Elijah blamed Israel in that time, saying, "How long will you limp on two legs? If the Lord is God, follow him, but if Baal, then follow him!" [cf. 1 Kings 18:21].

[261] Thus also, those [of you] who do these things or who put these things on themselves, how long will you limp on two legs? If the oracle sanctuary of demons is useful to you—and enchanters and drug-makers and all the other things that thus work for lawlessness—then go to them, so that you will receive their curse on earth and eternal punishment on the day of judgment!

[262] But if it is the house of God, the Church, that is useful to you, go to it. . . .

Text B: Ps.-Athanasius's *Homily on Virginity*

. . . There are among us today those who worship the poetic forms of demons—[forms] contrived from the beginning in their deceitfulness and deluding people as healing cults; . . . some of them practice abominations in city and village. For it is said that some of them ablute their children in polluted water and water from the arena, from the theater, and moreover they pour all over themselves water with incantations [spoken over it], and they break their clay pots claiming it repels the evil eye. Some tie amulets on their children, hand-crafted by men—those [men] who provide a place for the dwelling of demons—while others anoint themselves with oil that is evil and incantations and such things that they tie on their heads and necks.

Bibliography

Baumeister, Theofried. 1972. *Martyr Invictus: Der Martyrer als Sinnbild der Erlösung in der Legende und im Kult der frühen koptischen Kirche.* Forschungen zur Volkskunde 46. Münster: Regensberg.

Brakke, David. 1998. " 'Outside the Places, Within the Truth': Athanasius of Alexandria and the Localization of the Holy." In *Pilgrimage and Holy Space in Late Antique Egypt,* ed. David Frankfurter. Religions of the Graeco-Roman World. Leiden: E. J. Brill.

Frankfurter, David. 1998. *Religion in Roman Egypt: Assimilation and Resistance.* Princeton: Princeton University Press.

Lefort, L.-Th. 1954. "La Chasse aux reliques des martyrs en Egypte au IVᵉ siècle," *La Nouvelle Clio* 6: 225–30.

———. 1958. "L'Homélie de S. Athanase des papyrus de Turin." *Le muséon* 71: 5–50, 209–39.

Orlandi, Tito. 1982. "A Catechesis against Apocryphal Texts by Shenute and the Gnostic Texts of Nag Hammadi." *Harvard Theological Review* 75: 85–95.

———. 1985. *Shenute: Contra Origenistas.* Rome: C.I.M.

— 42 —

The Zenith and Destruction of

a Native Egyptian Oracle in 359 C.E.

David Frankfurter

The fourth-century pagan historian Ammianus Marcellinus offers a critical account of the uprooting of a long-established and renowned Egyptian oracle. His
account, written twenty years or so after the events, is invaluable both for showing
the continuing prominence of native cult sites through the fourth century and for
offering a close look at what could happen when Roman anxieties about subversive powers encountered the formal divination rites of indigenous Mediterranean
cultures.

The history of the Abydos Bes oracle is amply documented from the early
Ptolemaic period to beyond the fourth century, through pilgrims' graffiti, divination manuals, and a Coptic saint's life. The temple was a prominent shrine of
Osiris in Pharaonic times; an incubation oracle of the god Sarapis—a Hellenistic
hybrid of Osiris—began there in the beginning of the Ptolemaic period. At this
stage, people would make pilgrimage to Abydos to sleep somewhere in the vicinity
of the sacred precinct and thereby receive dreams from the god. There may also
have been a "speaking" oracle such as existed in other oracular shrines in the Late
Antique Mediterranean world: a priest would utter the words of the god into the
incubation chamber from some secret location. A convenient crypt for the priest
actually exists in the Abydos Memnonion immediately behind much of the outer
wall's graffiti.

But how this voice, and the priestly enterprise involved in promoting it,
changed from Sarapis to Bes in the Roman period is unclear. Bes himself, as
portrayed on myriad terracottas, amulets, stone stelae, and even ritual manuals
from the Roman period, governed safety in conception, childbirth, and home—
a god of immense popularity, even with an Alexandrian intellectual like Demetrius
in this passage (12). There may well have been a traditional association between
Bes and sleep, especially the divinatory sleep involved in incubation. Although
there were no major temples of Bes, he remained a popular figure, one associated

with other gods. Given Bes's traditional profile in Egyptian culture, then, it is striking to see in Ammianus's report the extent of the scribal apparatus that had developed by the fourth century to support the oracle and to solicit inquiries from around the Mediterranean world (4–5). By this time the Abydos cult was evidently much more than a native Egyptian oracle shrine; it was an advice center for the politically ambitious everywhere. (On the history of the Abydos Bes oracle, see Dunand 1997; Frankfurter 1998, 169–74. For further material on Egyptian oracles in Roman period: Frankfurter 1998, chap. 4. Further on Bes: Michailidis 1963/64; Malaise 1990; Frankfurter 1998, 124–31.)

It was precisely the use of this native shrine for political ambition that brought it into the emperor's view and consequently led to its immediate closure, with torture for those of elite rank involved with the cult or even wearing amulets or visiting cemeteries (14). But why this response to a native oracle? Roman culture, of course, had no less of a repertoire of popular rituals for divination or for binding people and situations than any other ancient culture. But Roman legal and administrative culture had a chronic fear of the secret and subversive, which motivated innumerable purges and religious edicts over the course of the empire— particularly after Constantine (see Maurice 1927; Brown 1970; Kippenberg 1997). However violent or widespread these purges might be, however, none carried lasting effect at the local level, for subversion was always elusive and the religious groups and rites that occasionally fell under scrutiny were themselves perennial.

Along with binding rites, which were often viewed in Roman culture as an unfair, supernatural advantage over situations—from love to politics—already fraught with tension, divination practices were especially feared, especially those ancient and authoritative ones promulgated in places like Egypt. "One can readily see what was targeted" by purges during the time of the Abydos cult's demise, the historian Pierre Chuvin observes; "the political dangers of a science capable of indicating, however obscurely, who would succeed a reigning emperor and when" (Chuvin 1990, 40). In 199 C.E., a Roman prefect tried, out of concern for social welfare and concord, to condemn traditional oracles in Egypt, whether "in writings as it were divinely delivered or through the processions of images"— practices so deeply ingrained in the functioning of temples that the edict could and did have little effect (P. Coll. Youtie I.30 = P. Yale inv. 299, ed. Rea 1977). Abydos, however, was another story, for its very archives had revealed just the sort of inquiries—just the sort of secret ritual involvement in political affairs— that the imperium found terrifying. Abydos demonstrated "pagan superstition" in its most corrosive form to an emperor already consumed with the extirpation of sorcery and divination (Chuvin 1990, 38–41). Hence the purge struck not only at the oracle's clients but at anybody using any form of divination (14–15).

One assumes the closure of the oracle was decisive, even though there are no descriptions of its shutting down nor any indications of its modified functioning over the rest of the fourth century. But in the fifth century, we learn from the *Life of Apa Moses of Abydos,* the god Bes reappears as a dwarfish demon haunting the Abydos temple. He is finally exorcized from the place and his priests destroyed, through the militant prayers of Moses and his fellow monks (in Till 1936, 46–81; see Frankfurter 1998, 129–31).

The following translation is by Walter Hamilton, printed with permission from Penguin Books Ltd. from Ammianus Marcellinus *Histories* 19.12.3–16.

AMMIANUS MARCELLINUS'S ACCOUNT OF ABYDOS

[Book 19.12.3] In the furthest part of the Thebaid there is a town called Abydos, where a god locally called Besa used to reveal the future through an oracle and was worshipped with traditional rites by the inhabitants of the surrounding regions. [4] Some of those who consulted the oracle did so in person, others sent a letter by an intermediary containing an explicit statement of their requests. In consequence, records of their petitions on paper or parchment sometimes remained in the temple even after the replies had been given. [5] Some of these documents were sent to the emperor [Constantius II] out of malice. His small mind made him deaf to other matters, however serious, but on this point he was more sensitive than the proverbial ear-lobe, suspicious and petty. He burst into furious anger and ordered [his *notarius*] Paul to proceed at once to the East, conferring on him, as on an experienced commander of great distinction, authority to have cases brought to court as he saw fit. . . .

[7] In obedience to his orders Paul went panting off, full of deadly spite. The way was open to false accusations on a large scale, and people were brought from all over the world, gentle and simple alike. Some were crushed by the weight of their chains, other succumbed to the rigours of close confinement. [8] The town of Scythopolis in Palestine was chosen to witness these cruel tortures. Two reasons made it seem particularly suitable: it was comparatively secluded, and it was also midway between Antioch and Alexandria, from which most of the victims were brought to be tried.

[9] Among the first to be prosecuted was Simplicius, son of the former prefect and consul Philip. He was accused of having consulted the oracle about his chances of the empire. Constantius, who in such circumstances never allowed loyal service to atone for a fault or a mistake, expressly commanded that he should be put to the torture, but by some special providence he escaped with a whole skin and was condemned to exile in a specified place. [10] Next was Parnasius, formerly prefect of Egypt, a man without guile; though he had to face a capital charge, he also was banished. He had often been heard to say that when he left his birthplace and home at Patras in Achaea to obtain an official post he dreamed that he was escorted by a number of figures dressed like tragic actors. [11] Then Andronicus, the celebrated scholar and poet, was brought to the bar, but, since nothing suspicious could be proved against him and he defended himself calmly and confidently, he was acquitted. [12] The philosopher Demetrius also, nicknamed Cythras, a man of great age but sound in body and mind, was shown to have offered sacrifice to Besa on several

occasions. He could not deny it, but maintained that, though he had observed this practice from early youth, his purpose was simply to propitiate the deity, not to inquire into his own prospects of advancement; nor did he know of anybody who made this his aim. So after a long time on the rack, during which he boldly and confidently adhered to his plea without the slightest variation, he was allowed to depart to his native city of Alexandria without further injury.

[13] These, then, and a few others were saved from the last extremity by the justice of fate, which came to the aid of truth. But, as such charges spread more widely and there seemed no end to the complicated web, some people died on the rack and others suffered the further penalty of confiscation. Paul was the prompter in this theatre of cruelty, continually producing fresh material from his reserves of lies and mischief; one might almost say that the lives of all involved depended on this nod. [14] Anyone who wore round his neck a charm against the quartan ague or some other complaint, or was accused by his ill-wishers of visiting a grave in the evening, was found guilty and executed as a sorcerer or as an inquirer into the horrors of men's tombs and the empty phantoms of the spirits which haunt them. [15] The matter was treated as seriously as if a host of people had consulted Claros or the oaks of Dodona or the once famous oracle of Delphi with a view to the emperor's death. [16] So the palace clique ingeniously contrived a foul form of flattery; they asserted that the emperor would be exempt from the ills common to humanity, and loudly declared that the never-failing providence which protected him had manifested itself in the destruction of those who plotted against him.

Bibliography

Brown, Peter. 1970. "Sorcery, Demons, and the Rise of Christianity from Late Antiquity into the Middle Ages." In *Witchcraft Confessions and Accusations*, ed. Mary Douglas, 17–45. London and New York: Tavistock.

Chuvin, Pierre. 1990. *A Chronicle of the Last Pagans*. Trans. B. A. Archer. Revealing Antiquity 4. Cambridge: Harvard University Press.

Dunand, Françoise. 1997. "La Consultation oraculaire en Egypte tardive: l'oracle de Bès à Abydos." In *Oracles et Prophéties dans l'antiquité: Actes du Colloque de Strasbourg, 15–17 juin 1995*, ed. Jean-Georges Heintz, 65–84. Paris: De Boccard.

Frankfurter, David. 1998. *Religion in Roman Egypt: Assimilation and Resistance*. Princeton: Princeton University Press.

Hamilton, Walter, trans. 1986. *Ammianus Marcellinus: The Later Roman Empire*. Harmondsworth: Penguin.

Kippenberg, Hans G. 1997. "Magic in Roman Civil Discourse: Why Rituals Could Be Illegal." In *Envisioning Magic: A Princeton Seminar and Symposium*, ed. Peter Schäfer and Hans G. Kippenberg, 137–63. Leiden: E. J. Brill.

Malaise, Michel. 1990. "Bès et les croyances solaires." In *Studies in Egyptology Presented to Miriam Lichtheim*, ed. Sarah Israelit-Groll, vol. 2, 680–729. Jerusalem: Magnes.

Maurice, Jules. 1927. "La Terreur de la magie au IVᵉ siècle." *Revue historique de droit français et étranger* 6: 108–20.

Michailidis, Georges. 1963/64. "Bès aux divers aspects," *Bulletin de l'Institut d'Egypte* 45: 53–93, Plates I–XX.

Rea, John. 1977. "A New Version of P. Yale inv. 299." *Zeitschrift für Papyrologie und Epigraphik* 27: 151–56.

Till, Walter. 1936. *Koptische Heiligen- und Martyrerlegenden.* Orientalia Christiana Analecta 108. Rome: Pontifical Institute for Oriental Studies.

Manichaean Theology

Jason David BeDuhn

Coptic Manichaean Psalm-Book, Psalm 223: A Bema Psalm
Psalm-Book, Part II, 9.2–11.32

Manichaeans claim that Mani (a third-century Persian) was the Paraclete promised by Jesus in the Gospel of John. As such, it was Mani's role to perfect the Christian community and complete its instruction in the truth. This psalm both asserts the identification of Mani with the Paraclete and summarizes the basic theogony, cosmogony, and eschatology of the Manichaean cosmos. This is "the knowledge of Manichaios," summed up in the "two natures" (stanza 3) and the three times of "the beginning, the middle, and the end" (stanza 21). The psalm appears to be composed of quotes from Mani's writings, and exact parallels can be found for nearly every phrase in other surviving fragments of Manichaean literature from as far afield as China.

The first three stanzas introduce Mani, his status, and authority. His teaching about "the beginning" is then covered in stanzas 4 through 13. God resists the assault of Darkness by means of a series of emanations that become the principal pantheon of Manichaeism and that establish the cosmos in its present order. "The middle" of the cosmic drama gets the shortest treatment, really only a transition from past to future in stanzas 14 and 15, which describe the ongoing purification of the world through the operations of sun and moon while a new world is being prepared for the liberated Light. Finally, Mani's teaching about "the end" comes in stanzas 16 through 19, which describe the dissolution of this world and the final separation of Light and Darkness into their respective eternal domains. The psalm closes with a two-stanza benediction on Mani and those fortunate enough to believe in his teachings.

Psalm 223: A Bema Psalm

1. Let us worship the spirit of the Paraclete.

2. Let us bless our Lord Jesus who sent to us the Spirit of Truth. He came; he separated us from the error of the world. He brought us a mirror. We looked; [we] saw this universe in it.

3. When the Holy Spirit came, he revealed to us the way of truth. He taught us that there are two natures, that of the Light and that of the Darkness, [separate] from one another from the beginning.

4. [The] kingdom of the Light existed in five greatnesses, which are: the Father, and his twelve aeons, and the aeons of the aeons, the living air, the land of light—as the great spirit breathes in them, nourishing them with his light.

5. But the kingdom of the Darkness exists in five storehouses, which are: smoke, and fire, and wind, and water, and darkness—as their counsel creeps in them, moving them and [inciting(?)] them to make war with one another.

6. As they were making war with one another, therefore, they dared to make an attempt upon the land of Light, thinking to themselves that they would be able to conquer it. But they do not know that that which they thought [to do] they will bring down upon their [own] heads.

7. Now there was a multitude of angels in the land of Light, having the power to go forth to subdue the enemy of the Father, whom it pleased that by his Word which [he would] send he would subdue the rebels, the ones who desired to exalt themselves above that which was more exalted than they.

8. It is just as when a shepherd sees a lion coming to destroy his sheepfold: he makes a strategy; he takes a lamb; he sets it as a snare so that he may catch him by means of it. By a single lamb he saves his sheepfold; after these things he heals the lamb that has been wounded by the lion.

9. This, too, is the way of the Father, who sent his strong son; the latter from himself gave birth to his Maiden, equipped with five powers, so that she might fight against the five pits of the Darkness.

10. When the guardian stood at the borders [of the] Light, he showed to them his Maiden, who is his soul. They stirred in their pit, desiring to exalt themselves over her; they opened their mouth, desiring to swallow her.

11. He held on to her head, he spread her over them, like nets over fish. He caused her to rain down upon them like purified clouds of water. She thrust herself into them [in the manner of] a piercing lightning. She crept into their inner parts; she bound them all, though they did not know it.

12. When the First Man had finished his war, the Father sent his second son. He came; he helped his brother out of the pit. He established [this] whole world out of the mixture that existed of the Light and the Darkness.

13. All of the powers of the pit he scattered to ten heavens and eight earths; he shut them up into this world at one time. He made it, indeed, a prison for all the powers [of the] Darkness; while it is also a place of purification of the soul that was swallowed in them.

14. The sun and [the] moon were established; they were placed on high [to] purify [the] soul. Daily they take up the purified part to the height; this sediment, however, they scrape [off and cast it below; and the] mixed [portion] they rotate, now above and now below.

15. This whole world stands for a time, [while a] great building is being built outside [of this] world. At the time when the builder will finish, the whole world will be destroyed and set on fire so that the fire may melt it away.

16. All life, the remnant of the Light which is in every place, [he will] gather to himself and fashion of it a statue. The counsel of death, however, all the Darkness, he will [gather] together and fashion of it its own [. . .] ruler (?).

17. In an instant, the Living Spirit will come [. . .]; he will assist the Light. The counsel of death and the Darkness, [however], he will imprison in the storehouse that was established for it, so that it might be bound in it forever.

18. There is no other means by which to bind the enemy except this means, since he will not be accepted by the Light because he is a stranger to it; nor again will he be left in his land of Darkness, that he may not make a war greater than the first.

19. A new aeon will be built in the place [of this] world which will be destroyed, so that in [it] the powers of the Light may reign, because they have done, they have fulfilled [the] entire will of the Father. They have subdued the hated one; they have [. . .] over him forever.

20. This is the knowledge of Manichaios: let us worship him [and] bless him. Fortunate is everyone who shall believe [in him], for that is the one who shall live with all the righteous.

21. Glory and victory to our Lord Manichaios, the Spirit of [Truth] who is from the Father, the one who revealed to us the beginning, the middle, and the end. Victory to the soul of the [blessed] Mary, Theona, Pshaijmnoute (or: Pshai, Jmnoute).

Kephalaion 59: The Chapter of the Elements that Wept
Kephalaia 148.21–151.4

This chapter well represents the tragic element in the Manichaean view of the universe and of salvation history. Because Manichaeism gives full weight to the reality of evil, it sees the struggle between good and evil as a bitter battle with no easy resolution. The ultimate victory of good is a long process, with several moments in which a substantial portion of the divine substance is trapped in the grasp of evil. That entangled portion is identified as the five children or garments of the First Man, who accompany him into the primordial battle to defend the realm of light from the aggression of darkness. They are the principal characters of this chapter, the "elements that wept."

When these five elements looked upon Darkness rushing to attack them, they understood the fate that awaited them and they wept (148.29–149.3). When they saw their father, the First Man, rise successfully from the battle and return to the realm of Light without them, they wept (149.4–13). When the Living Spirit assembled the cosmos from the mixture of good and evil and let the five elements know that they would have to struggle through to their own liberation, they wept (149.14–28). There will come yet a fourth occasion of weeping, when all of the divine substance that will be able to free itself from Darkness will have done so— the final portion forming the Last Statue,—the remaining amount will be unredeemable. At this final, tragic moment, both the residual "souls" left behind will weep, and so too will the liberated elements, who mourn for their lost comrades (149.29–150.23).

This account provides a much reduced summary of the Manichaean narrative of cosmogony, salvation history, and eschatology also treated in the previous selection from the Psalm-Book. There is a play on words lost in translation: the elements are repeatedly said to be "heartbroken," literally "divided" or "rent of heart"; but when they resolve to stop weeping and work their way up through the earths to liberation, they are said to "turn their heart to the heights," and to "become of one heart," thus healing the damage of their suffering and grief. As the chapter closes, Mani speaks of all the work of all the prophets of history as a response to this fundamental story of the weeping elements and the tragedy of their loss. The gods and apostles, too, weep over them. He urges his listeners to keep the tale always in mind.

The Chapter of the Elements that Wept

[148.24] Once again he speaks to his disciples: the garments, the sons of the First Man, wept bitterly on three occasions. Afterwards, they were silent. There is another fourth time of weeping, in which they will weep at the end. And [then] they will cease weeping and they will not set themselves to weeping from this time.

[148.29] Now the first weeping in which they wept is the occasion when they saw the darkness, the enemy being about to burst out against them. They understood everything that would happen to them. They were aware of the one that would rise to them and come upon them, but because of necessity they hastened towards it and [fought] with it. They mastered it, they seized it. [They] bound it with their body and their limbs, they seized its death and its fire and its darkness.

[149.4] [The] second occasion in which they wept is [the occasion when] their father, the First Man, came up from the [abyss] of darkness [and] left them; that is the occasion when he stripped [them off from] him [and] left them below. The occasion, then when [they] saw the First Man, that he came up out of the abyss [and] left them, [and] they remained behind him in the enmity, they wept [and] were heartbroken. But what could they do, wishing [. . .] their heart to every affliction? They [stayed] behind, growing sick under the pressure of the heavy burden of all things until the end of time.

[149.14] [The] third occasion that they wept is the occasion when the Living Spirit stripped off the three garments of activity [Gardner's suggested translation of *mntashire*. Gardner 1995, 157], [and] placed them beneath all things. He beckoned to them to lift their heads and come to the heights from that place; and to pass and journey through all the earths until they should reach the land of tranquility and peace, the place of rest, which is prepared for them. On the occasion, then, when they saw him, that he separated himself from them, while they themselves stayed behind him [and] did not come up, at that moment when they stayed behind him, these three garments wept. After their crying, they turned their [heart] to every height that was concealed from them. They became of one heart so that [they might] raise themselves up and come to the height, and pass over all things until the time that was ordained for them all [. . .] at the end of the worlds.

[149.29] The fourth occasion when they will weep is the occasion when the Statue will be taken up on the last day, and they will weep [for] the souls of the liars and blasphemers. For they may give [. . .] since their limbs were severed from [. . .] of the darkness. Those [other] souls, however, [on] the occasion when the Statue will go [up and] they are left alone, they will weep because they will stay behind in affliction forever, since they will [be cut off] and separated from the Last Statue. These souls become by necessity prepared for loss in accordance with the retribution for the deeds that they have done—the ones who go in [to] this [darkness] and are bound with the darkness, just as they desired it, [and] loved it, [and] placed their treasure with it. At that very moment in which the Last Statue goes up, they will weep. Afterwards, they will give a great cry because they will be severed from the company of this great Statue; and they will stay behind forever. This great weeping [. . .] is bitter. It occurs in front of the souls and [. . .] who are ready for loss in accordance with their deeds. Yet they [will] weep with that crying, they will never be silent in it, since they will not attain rest from this time.

[150.17] Now they themselves are the garments of these elements. This fourth weeping is heartbreaking for them. It is much worse for them than these other three first weepings. This [fourth] weeping is not for themselves [literally, "is not theirs"]. But they weep and are heartbroken for these souls who will be cut off from rest, since rest will not occur for them, to cause them to rest from torment forever.

[150.23] Indeed, with a view to the end of the loss of souls, all the apostles and the fathers, the revealers of the good, the true prophets, cause [themselves] to do every labor and every bitter necessity, so that they [i.e., the souls] might be saved from the second death. Not a single one of all the apostles wished to receive his reward on the earth, but spent all their time existing in affliction, receiving pain, and being crucified in their body, so that they might redeem their souls from that lost [and] go up to this rest forever. [. . . in the] new aeon. But it is not proper to [. . .]. The one who is a wise person causes himself to reflect at all times on this subject, since it is heartbreaking and sad for the gods and the apostles.

Coptic Manichaean Psalm-Book: A Psalm of the Vagabonds
Psalm-Book, Part II, 155.16–42

This psalm is devoted to the manifestation of the imprisoned Light known as the Living Soul, here praised as the foundation of the cosmos as well as the source of salvation. The Manichaean concept of the Living Soul is the epitome of the redeemed-redeemer theme. The psalm consists primarily of characterizations of the Living Soul in the form of identifications, metaphors, and paradoxical descriptions bordering on pantheism. Most striking is the identification with "Jesus hanging upon the tree," the image of the *Jesus patibilis* known from Augustine of Hippo's discussions of Manichaean Christology.

A Psalm of the Vagabonds

[I will] give glory to you, my God. I will give glory to you, my giver of rest to everyone, my God. I will give glory to you. [. . .] cornerstone, my God. I will give glory to you, my giver of rest to everyone, my God. I will give glory to you, cornerstone unchanging, unaltering, my God.

The foundation unshakeable, the sheep bound to the tree, the treasure hidden in the field, Jesus hanging upon the tree, the youth, son of the dew, the milk of all trees, the sweetness of the fruits, the eye of the skies, the guardian of all treasures, [. . .] that bears all things, the joy of all creatures, the rest of the worlds;

You are a marvel to tell. You are within, you are without. You are above, you are below. The one who is near, yet far, the one who is hidden, yet revealed, the one who is silent, yet speaks also: yours is all the glory, glory fitting for you.

Victory to the soul of Mary, Apa Panai, and [Theona].

Kephalaion 67: Concerning the Light-Giver
Kephalaia 165.25–166.16

This short chapter highlights Mani's role as the source of wisdom and enlightenment by playing with the parallelism between two kinds of light-giver, the sun and Mani as the spiritual illuminator. The analogy is a simple one. As the sun withdraws its shining rays from the earth when it sets, so Mani will retract his "rays," the Elect, from the earth at his departure. He will not abandon them to the darkness. The difference is that the sun's rays all depart at once, whereas Mani's Elect go one by one, "each one of them at the time of his coming forth" from the body at death. Mani stresses his ongoing connection to the Elect; they are his children and are, in effect, his continued manifestation on earth since they embody the wisdom he has bestowed upon them. The "great glorious one [that] dwells in all of them" is the Mind of Light, the personification of right attitude and understanding cultivated in the individual through exposure to Mani's teaching. Those who love Mani should demonstrate that love through support of the Elect, so that they too will not be abandoned to the darkness.

Concerning the Light-Giver

[165.27] Once again he speaks to his disciples, on the occasion when he sits in the midst of the congregation: according to the manner of the sun, the great light-giver, when it comes in its splendor, the time when it shines upon the universe, it extends its rays to the entire earth. Again, when it is about to set, its rays [disappear] and set. It does not leave [behind] a single ray [on the earth].

[165.33] This is also the way that I am like it [i.e., the sun]. In the image of flesh, in which I have been set, I have been revealed in the universe. Also, all of my children, the righteous Elect who are mine in every country, are like the rays of the sun. At the moment when I will come forth from the universe and go to the house of my people, I will gather in to that place all the Elect who have believed in me. I will draw them to me, each one of them at the time of his coming forth; I will not leave one of them in the darkness.

[166.9] Because of this I say to you: Every one who loves me, let him love all my children, the blessed Elect, since I am with them. I alone. How so? For my wisdom anoints them all; the great glorious one dwells in all of them. And every one who will love them and mix with them by his charity may live and be victorious with them, and be saved from the black universe.

Bibliography

Jackson, Abraham Valentine Williams. 1932. *Researches in Manichaeism with Special Reference to the Turfan Fragments.* New York: Columbia University Press.

Puech, Henri-Charles. 1968. "The Concept of Redemption in Manichaeism." In *The Mystic Vision,* ed. Joseph Campbell, 247–314. Princeton: Princeton University Press.

Schäder, Hans. 1924/25. "Urform und Fortbildung des Manichaischen Systems." In *Vorträge der Bibliothek Warburg,* 65–157.

— 44 —

Iamblichus, *de Mysteriis,* Book I
The *de Mysteriis*

Peter T. Struck

For many years, the *de Mysteriis* of the Late Antique Neoplatonist, Iamblichus (ca. 245–ca. 325 C.E.), languished under the stern judgments of philologists, who found his knotted prose tiresome, and historians of philosophy, who saw it as a final break with the promise of reason that had marked Greek philosophy from the classical age through the Stoics to Plotinus. While such judgments are fair enough, they are hardly the last word to be said on this pivotal tract. Running ten books, of which the first is excerpted here, the *de Mysteriis* stands as our most extensive extant tract devoted to ritual theory from the whole of the ancient period.

In this work, in which he lays out the case for a practice of ritual acts as part of a philosophical program that aims for spiritual enlightenment, Iamblichus does indeed abandon reason—but, one might say, he has good reasons for doing so. All the Neoplatonists took very seriously Plato's isolated reference to an utterly transcendent Good that lies beyond even being itself (Republic 6 509b). The founder of Neoplatonism, Plotinus (205–269/70 C.E.), understood this Good as the ontological font of the cosmos. The "One," as it became known, sat beyond being and, more pertinently for Iamblichus, beyond reason. Plotinus set the One at the center of his thought and convinced all his followers that it should be the *telos* (goal) of their philosophical project. Plotinus reconfigures philosophical thinking as an emphatically soteriological pursuit whose goal is nothing less than the thinker's union with the utterly transcendent One. In their asymptotic pursuit of this goal, the Neoplatonists leave us with the ancient world's most fully articulated thinking on the problems, and limitations, of making a rational accounting of transcendence.

Different thinkers in the school follow different strategies. Plotinus and his student and editor, Porphyry, firmly believed that by following a strict *askēsis* (asceticism) of contemplation alone, one inched ever higher through the orders of being. From the dead material world, through the levels of pure Soul and pure Nous (or Mind), the devotee eventually arrived at the doorstep of the One. While Iamblichus shares in the project of ascent, he differs from the great master on precisely how one should go about it. He was skeptical of the human intellect's power to think its way beyond itself. He suggests that the true devotee of wisdom must supplement intellectual contemplation with a program of ritual praxis.

In place of thought, he advocates certain ritual acts, which he calls "theurgy" (*theion* + *ergon*—"divine work"), that lift the enlightened celebrant into an experiential moment of hyper-rational unity with the One (chapter 2). Iamblichus argues strongly that this unity is beyond the reach of human intelligence. He claims pointedly in a later section of his work that it is not "thought" (*ennoia*) that joins theurgists to the gods, but rather "the performance of rites that are inarticulable, beyond all thought, and effected divinely" (2.11).

This view is persuasive to nearly all those who follow Iamblichus. More or less endorsed by every subsequent Neoplatonist down through Marsilio Ficino in the Renaissance, it re-situates seven centuries of philosophical speculation squarely in the service of thinking about ritual, and makes Iamblichus especially relevant for all those concerned with religious practice in the ancient Mediterranean.

Background

In Neoplatonic thinking, a philosopher's movement upward toward the One retraces the path of ontological outpouring from the One that continuously manifests and sustains the cosmos as we know it. All of reality flows from the One including the highest gods, the lowest clump of dirt, and all intermediate links in the great chain of being. All of reality contains a vestigial trace of the One and yearns (whether it knows it or not) to re-enter a primal unity with it.

Because Iamblichus's theurgic rites make use of these traces and hidden properties of matter, several scholars have treated theurgy as roughly co-extensive with magic (Dodds 1968; Sheppard 1996). Both are said to operate according to a principle of "sympathy" (*sympatheia*), the traditional ancient term for the forces by which magical rites operate. Also in support of this view, some scholars cite Iamblichus's indebtedness to the "Chaldean Oracles." This tract of shadowy provenance claimed to assemble oracles from Greek gods and sayings channeled from the soul of Plato himself and was adopted as authoritative by the later Neoplatonists.

Against this view, however, must be counted Iamblichus's own concern to distinguish his rites from those of the *goētes* (magician) (*de Myst.* 3.25, 26, 28; cf. Plotinus, *Enneads* 4.4.40): he asserts repeatedly that unlike the magicians' rites, which operate by "sympathy," his rites work according to a more divine, and less mechanistic principle, the force of "philia" (chapter 12, cf. 3.26, 4.9, 4.3, and all of 5.7–9). For Iamblichus, this term especially marks the higher orders' divine plenitude and generosity toward what they have created. We are not too far afield to find an analogous notion in Augustinian grace. Though the distinction between magic and ritual remains unstable for contemporary scholars, Iamblichus himself was concerned about it and tried to convince his detractors that his rites were not of the magical sort. If we allow Iamblichus to define his own terms, the category of ritual is a more useful description of what Iamblichus means by the term "theurgy."

Dramatic Setting

The *de Mysteriis* takes the form of a point-by-point answer to a polemical letter written by Porphyry, Iamblichus's elder Neoplatonic colleague. In the letter, Porphyry levels a very broad attack against the practice of just about any sort of ritual at all as a means of reaching the divine. For reasons that remain opaque, Porphyry addressed the letter to a putative Egyptian priest named Anebo. Iamblichus goes along with the fiction, and answers back in the persona of Abammon, Anebo's master. This critical debate over the future of Neoplatonism, then, is ventriloquized through Egyptian surrogates, an astonishing fact that still has no satisfactory explanation.

Notes on the Translation

Iamblichus's prose is turgid by any measure. Scholars only decades after his death held that opinion. Eunapius revives Plato's judgment against Xenocrates, saying that Iamblichus "has not sacrificed to the Hermetic Graces" (the governors of eloquence) (*Vit. Soph.* 5.1.4). His prose also presents special problems for the translator. Sentences break much less frequently than English will bear, antecedents are sometimes not clearly articulated, and his vocabulary forces English into gangly contortions. Especially problematic is the cluster of terms around the common Greek adjective *pathētos,* which recurs frequently in chapters ten through twelve and eighteen. In most cases, I have opted for the bulky formulation "subject to passions," though it is worthwhile to remind ourselves that by this adjective Iamblichus also means a thing's capacity to receive any kind of change or influence at all from an external source, not just a capacity to feel emotion.

I have followed des Places's text, except in one reading: *kathairēsthai* for *kathairesthai* in chapter two (des Places 1.2 [6.9]). Although not fully satisfactory, the change does help make some sense of this difficult section of text.

Finally, I thank John Dillon, who generously provided me an advance copy of his forthcoming translation, which will surely become the standard. I am indebted to his insights.

The original of this translation is found in *Jamblique: Les Mystères d'Egypte,* ed. Edouard des Places, S.J.

Iamblichus, *de Mysteriis*, Book I

The god who governs language, Hermes, has been held rightly by all priests since ancient times to be universal. The chief of true knowledge concerning the gods is one and the same everywhere, to whom even our own forefathers used to dedicate their discoveries of wisdom, handing down all their own writings under his name. Assuming that we also participate in a share of this god, which is proper and fitting for ourselves, you act properly, posing to the priests, as pleases them, questions that relate to wisdom concerning theology, and I fittingly, believing the letter sent to my student Anebo to have been written for myself, will answer your inquiries with the truth itself. For it would not be fitting that Pythagoras and Plato and Democritus and Eudoxus and many other ancient Greeks should have hit upon the proper doctrine drawing from the priestly writings current in their own time, but that you living in our time and having the same wisdom as they did should entirely miss the guidance of those now alive who are universally called teachers. I then approach the present discussion in this way, but you, if you wish, consider that the same man answers you back to whom you sent a letter, but if, on the other hand, it should appear necessary to you, consider your correspondent to be me or any other Egyptian prophet, for this makes no difference. Or still better, I suppose, set aside the one speaking, should he be worse or better, and examine whether what is said is spoken truly or falsely, having eagerly awakened your mind. First, then, let us determine how many and of what sort are the problems now at hand. Let us go through the questions and propose both from what sorts of divine theologies and according to what branches of knowledge they are being examined. Some, then, call for a sort of separation of things improperly mixed together; others concern the cause according to which each thing exists and, thus, is apprehended in thought; others draw the mind to both things, since they are proposed according to a certain opposition; and some demand the whole of our mystagogy. Since the inquiries are of this sort, they have been taken up from many points of view and from different sciences.

For some pertain to the branches of knowledge drawn out of things which the Chaldean wise men have handed down, others generate their solutions out of things which the Egyptian prophets teach, and some also pertain to the contemplations of the philosophers and pose questions fitting for them. But now there are certain others also, who draw from other opinions not worthy of discussion, and drag after them a sort of inappropriate dispute, and others are set in motion from the common conceptions of human beings. Each of these, then, in itself is complex and assembled in many forms in relation to one another. So for all these reasons, they are in need of a particular kind of discourse to guide them appropriately.

[2] We will therefore hand down to you in truth our opinion with respect to the traditional Assyrian doctrines, and our own doctrines we will wisely

reveal to you, reckoning some, with wisdom, from the ancient boundless writings, and others from those things that later the ancients assembled into a completed book, the whole of their wisdom concerning divine things.

But if you propose some philosophical question, we will decide this too for you in accordance with the ancient inscribed stones of Hermes—already in full knowledge of which Plato and Pythagoras formerly put together their philosophy—explaining away mildly and harmoniously inquiries that are foreign or illogical ones that manifest a certain quarrelsomeness, or we will make clear their absurdity. And as many things as proceed according to common conceptions we will try to discuss very intelligently and wisely. In addition, some things are accessible here only through discussion, although they require an experience of ritual actions for an accurate understanding, but others are full of intellectual contemplation and are able to be taken down completely. But it is possible to reveal signs of the ritual experience, which are fit for discussion, on the basis of which you and those like you can guide your mind concerning the essence of things as they are. As many things as are knowable through discussion none of these will we leave behind in the interest of a complete demonstration. In all cases we will render to you the proper thing in a fitting manner, we will answer theological matters theologically, theurgic matters theurgically, philosophical matters we will examine along with you philosophically. And among these as many as pertain to first causes we will follow along according to first principles and bring them to light, but as many as were spoken concerning human customs or purposes we will judge, as is necessary, according to the paradigm of human custom, and the rest in the same way according to the proper mode we will treat in order. Now let us turn to your questions.

[3] You say first, then, that you "grant that the gods exist." But the matter is not correctly stated in this way. For an innate wisdom concerning the gods coexists with us in our very essence, and it is stronger than every judgment and inclination, it pre-exists both reason and logical proof. It is both united from the beginning to the proper cause, and it coexists with the real desire of the soul for the good.

Truth be told, the link to the divine is not even wisdom. For this is separated by, I suppose, a certain alterity. The uniform continuity stretching out from the gods is self-generated and spontaneous and prior to wisdom, considering wisdom as one thing knowing some other thing. It is not fitting, then, that we assent to this, as if we were able either to grant it or not grant it, nor to consider it in both ways (for it always stands uniformly according to its own actuality), nor thus to approve it as worthy of accusing or defending as we do to run-of-the-mill things. For we are rather embraced in it and filled by it, and the very thing that we are, we hold in knowing the gods.

I have the same argument for you also concerning the superior beings that follow the gods; I am speaking of daemons and heroes and pure souls.

But you seem to believe that knowledge of the gods is the same as of any other sort of thing, and that one thing be "granted" from opposing sides, just as it is customary also in the case of propositions in dialectical arguments. But it is not in any way comparable. For knowledge of them is utterly different, and is separate from every opposition, and it does not consist in agreement for now to or in becoming, but from eternity it has coexisted uniformly in the soul.

[5] Let us go next to the solution of the problems that you posed. There is, of course, the good which is beyond being and also the good which pertains to being. I mean that "being" that is most important and honorable and exists incorporeally in itself. It is the singular quality of the gods and is present in all the classes of beings around them. On the one hand it preserves their proper distribution and order and is not detached from this, on the other hand, it nevertheless manifests itself the same, in the same way, within them all.

The essence of the good is no longer present to souls that govern bodies and are in charge of their care and, before their descent into being, are situated eternally in themselves. Nor is the cause of the good present, which is prior even to being, but a sort of hold and possession arises from it. This kind of participation of the beautiful and of virtue which we observe is very different from the sort we consider to be present in humans. For the latter has a certain ambiguity and arises like an addition among composite natures, but the other dwells within souls unchanging and unfailing, neither does it ever separate itself from itself, nor is it displaced by any other things.

[7] [The Good] is supreme, transcendent, and perfect, while [the rank of souls] is last, deficient, and rather imperfect. The one is able to do all things at once in the now uniformly; the other is not able to do everything, nor do them all at once nor instantaneously nor uniformly. The one produces and manages all things without inclining toward them; the other, by nature, inclines and turns attention to the things it generates and governs. The one initiates as the ruler and cause of everything; the other is suspended from the cause, the will of the gods, and from eternity exists as its companion. Also, the one, in a single brilliant flower, gathers the ends of all energies and essences; the other passes from one thing to another, and advances from the incomplete to the complete. Moreover, the highest and uncircumscribed one manifests itself to the former, better than every part and formless so that by no form is it circumscribed, while the latter is mastered by downward momentum, temporary condition, and decline, held in the grip of the appetite for the worse and an affinity with what is secondary, it is left behind among multiform things and is given form by parts from them. Accordingly, Nous is leader and king of existing things and is the demiurgic art of the whole, and on the one hand is always consistently present to the gods completely, and self-sufficiently and faultlessly, and by a single energy it stands inside itself purely. But soul participates in a nous that is divisible and in a multi-form state turns its attention to the managing of the whole, and it takes care of soulless things sometimes manifesting itself in some forms, other times in others.

[9] I assume, then, that you are not *really* asking the question, "Why, if the gods dwell only in the heavens, the theurgists use invocations of chthonic and subterranean beings?" for the premise is not true, that the gods range around only in the heavens—surely, everything is full of gods—but rather that you are asking, "how certain gods are said to belong to water and certain ones to the air, and some have some places while others have others, and how they are allotted portions of bodily substance, each in its own delimitation, and yet they hold power that is boundless and partless and uncircumscribed, and how they will have union with each other, if their parts are divided into distinct delimitations and considering the difference of their locations and of the underlying bodies they each take?"

Of all these and countless other similar questions, then, there is a single best solution, to survey the manner of the divine allotment. Accordingly, this allotment, whether it is assigned certain parts of the whole, for example sky or earth, or sacred cities and lands, or even certain temples or sacred statues, it illuminates everything from without, just like the sun shines from the outside upon everything with its rays. Just as light surrounds the things it illuminates, in the same way also the power of the gods has enveloped the things that partake of it from outside. Also, just as light is present in the air without being mixed with it (as is clear since nothing is left behind in it once the light source withdraws, and yet heat is present in it, when the heat source withdraws), in this way also the light of the gods illuminates while remaining separate and advances throughout the whole of things although it sits steadily within itself. Even the light, which is visible, after all is one and everywhere the same continuous whole, so that it is impossible to cut off some part of it, or to ring it off, or to set the light apart in any way from its source.

According to the very same principles, then, the whole cosmos together also is divisible and distributes itself about the single and indivisible light of the gods. But the light is one and entirely the same everywhere, and it is indivisibly present to all things able to participate in it. By a perfecting power it has filled up everything, and by some kind of boundless excess with respect to cause it finishes out all things in itself. It is both united everywhere to itself and joins together end points with first principles. Also the whole heavens imitate this very process and the cosmos goes around its cyclical revolution. It is both united to itself and it leads the elements wheeling around in a circle. It binds all existing things in each other and brings them to each other. It distinguishes by equal measures even things dispersed farthest away, and it causes end points to join to first principles; for example, earth to sky. It works out a single continuity and agreement of everything to everything.

By observing that this visible statue, so to speak, of the gods is so unified, wouldn't a person be ashamed to hold a different opinion concerning the gods, who are the causes of it, and attribute to them both divisions and distributions and circumscribe them within bodily forms? I suppose that *everyone* is disposed to consider the matter this way. For if there is neither rhyme nor reason, nor state of harmony, nor any commonality of essence, nor interweaving, potentially or actually, of what is set in order to that which sets it in order, it would be as if nothing, so to speak, has a settled place, with no extension by regular intervals, nor discrete spatial units, nor discernible distribution, and no other sort of balancing rooted in the presence of the gods. For considering things of a similar nature, in essence or potentially, or even entities that are in any way of a similar form, or even things of a similar genus, it is possible to conceive of some kind of comprehension or control, but as regards whatever is entirely transcendent over all things, can one justly conceive of any kind of reciprocal interchange in their case, or of a permeability of them as wholes, or of a distinct circumscription or extent in space, or anything at all of such things?

Rather, I believe that those things which participate in the higher principles are each of them such that some participate in them aetherially, some with respect to the air, some, the water. Observing these things, then, the art of rituals also uses the correspondences and invocations appropriate to each division and environment.

[10] Very well, let this much be said concerning the distribution into the cosmos of the higher beings. But next after this you submit another division, and you separate "the essences of the greater beings by a distinction between the passive and the impassive." But neither do I accept this division. For absolutely none of the greater types of being is subject to passions, nor is any one of them impassive in such a way that it is separated from that which is capable of receiving passions, nor in such a way that it is naturally capable of receiving passions on the one hand, but is released from them because of virtue or some other excellent condition. But since they transcend completely the opposition of being subject to passion and not being subject to passion, and since they do not possess a nature at all subject to passion, and since in essence they hold a firmness that is incapable of change, because of this, I consider impassability and unchangingness to exist in them all.

Consider if you will the lowest of the divine things, the soul unmixed with body. What need does this soul have of the creative force in pleasure, or of the return in it toward nature, when it is above nature and lives the ungenerated life? What share does it have of the pain that leads to corruption, or of the pain that dissolves the harmony of the body, seeing that it exists separately from every body and from the divided nature that surrounds bodies, and seeing that it is in every way separate from that nature that descends from the harmony in the soul into the body? But neither does it have need of the passions that govern perception, for it is not at all restrained in a body, nor, since it is not enclosed, does it in any way need to perceive through corporeal organs any other bodies that exist outside it. But since it is wholly partless and remains in one and the same form, and since it both exists in itself incorporeally and has nothing in common with the corporeal, which is subject to generation and passions, it would be affected by nothing either on account of difference or on account of alterity; nor would it at all admit of anything whatsoever that admits of change or passion.

But neither, once it has come into the body, is it subject to passions nor are the principles, which it gives to the body. For these also are forms and are simple and uniform, and admit no single disturbance nor displacement from themselves. In a thing with a composite nature, then, it is what remains that is the cause of being subject to passion, and the cause is not, of course, the same thing as the effect. Just as, therefore, the soul itself, in itself, is not susceptible to generation and corruption—even though it is the primary origin of animals with a composite nature, which come to be and pass away—so also the soul in itself is unchangeable—even though the things that participate in it are susceptible to passions and do not entirely possess life and being, but mix with the indefiniteness and the otherness of matter. The soul is unchangeable and not susceptible to generation and corruption on the grounds that it is greater, in its essence, than being subject to passions, and not on the grounds that it is something subject to passions involved in a sort of choice inclining toward both things, nor as something that, in participating with unity or of power, borrows its unchangingness as a newly acquired property.

Since, then, we demonstrated that participation with being subject to passions is impossible in case of the lowest type of the better kinds of beings, why should one apply it to the daemons and the heroes, who are both eternal and companions of the gods everywhere, and an icon of the gods' orderly arrangement of the universe, and who themselves keep a close watch on the same things, and are eternal and bring to completion the divine arrangement and never abandon it? For we know, of course, that this is in no way of itself, since passion is disorderly and out of tune and uncertain, but that it belongs to that by which it is held and to which it is a slave to the generative power. So then this belongs to some other sort of thing, more than to the thing eternally linked to the gods, which travels around both the same arrangement and the same circuit with them. Therefore the daemons also are not subject to passions and all the things of the greater types of being that accompany them.

[11] How is it, then, you ask, that many things are performed in the sacred rites toward the gods as if they were subject to passions? But I assert that this also is said by one ignorant of the sacred mystagogy. For of the things which are celebrated regularly in the rites, some have a cause which is beyond speech, in a way, and greater than reason, others have been sanctified as symbols to the higher beings from eternity, others preserve and sustain a different sort of image, in just the same way that the nature that concerns itself with generation stamped out certain visible shapes from invisible principles, others are introduced for the sake of honor, or aim at a likeness of any sort at all or even just an affinity. Some provide something useful to us or purify us, in a certain way, and remove our passions from us, or turn us away from some other of the fearful characteristics that are our companions. Still, surely no one would agree that any part of the rite is referred to the gods or daemons being worshipped as if they were subject to passions. For neither does that essence, which is in itself eternal and incorporeal, naturally admit of any change from corporeal things.

Nor, if it has in as great a degree as possible such a lack of passions, would it have ever needed humans for such a service, because it is fulfilled from itself and from the nature of the cosmos and from the entire perfection that exists in the world subject to generation. It is even, if it is possible to say this, *prior to* needing, being something self-sufficient, on account of the flawless wholeness of the cosmos and its own particular fullness, and because the stronger forms of being manifest themselves entirely full of the good things proper to them.

Let these then be our general explanations concerning the flawless divine service, since it assimilates everything else to beings higher than us, and since a pure rite is introduced to pure beings and impassive to impassive beings. But to follow up on the issues individually, we claim that the erection of phalli is a sort of symbol of generative power, and we believe that this power is invoked into the generating of the world, which is why many things are dedicated in the spring, just when the entire cosmos also receives from the gods the rejuvenation of creation as a whole. And in my view the vulgar expressions signify a token of the depravity of the beautiful surrounding the material world, and of the prior shapelessness and deformity of things that are going to be arrayed into the cosmos, things that long for order, since they are lacking it (in as great a degree as they despise the ugliness surrounding themselves). One pursues, in turn, the causes of the forms and the beautiful, when one observes the shameful from the expressing of shameful things. The act both dissuades from the shameful, while through the expressions it brings knowledge of it into the open, and it transfers one's desire to the opposite.

But another similar sort of reasoning also pertains to these things. The powers of the human affections inside us, if they are entirely blocked up, are rendered more violent, but if they are let out into activity for a short time and up to a due proportion, they are gratified and sated in a measured way, and hence they are cleansed by catharsis and are stopped by persuasion and not through force. Through this very same process, in both comedy and tragedy, when we watch the passions of others we check our own passions and work them off moderately and purge them away. Also in the divine rites, by particular sights and sounds of shameful things, we are set free from the harm that befalls shameful actions.

Such rites are introduced, then, for the care of the soul in us, and for moderation of the evils that naturally attach to it through the process of generation, and for the sake of freedom and release from its bonds. For this same reason Heraclitus fittingly called them "cures," since they heal awful things and render our souls free from the ills of the process of generation.

[12] "But invocations," you say, "are referred to the gods as if they were subject to passions, so that not only are daemons subject to passions but also the gods." But the matter is not exactly as you have assumed. For the illumination that arises through prayers is a something self-revealing and voluntary, and it stands aloof, far from being coerced, it emanates into the visible world

through its perfection and divine activity, and it surpasses voluntary movement by as much as the divine will of the good transcends the life of inclination. Through such a will then the gods radiate their light upon the theurgists without begrudging it, since they are benevolent and gracious, and they call up the theurgists' souls to themselves and orchestrate their union with them, and accustom them to stand aloof from their bodies, even while they are still in bodies, and to turn to their timeless and intelligible source.

The thing which we are just now claiming, is clear also from the acts themselves, that they are a savoir of the soul. For in seeing "the blessed sights," the soul takes another life and enacts another activity and then is not even considered to be a human, when it is considered correctly. But often, when it has abandoned its own life, it takes in exchange the most blessed activity of the gods. If, then, the ascent through invocations provides for the priests a purging of passions and a release from the process of becoming and a unity toward the divine source, why in the world does anyone attribute passions to it? For this sort of ascent does not draw down those not subject to passions and pure, toward what is subject to passion and impure, but the opposite is the case, it renders us who have become subject to passions, on account of the process of becoming, pure and permanent.

But neither do the invocations join the priests to the gods through passions, but through the divine *philia* that embraces everything they provide a communion of the indissoluble engagement of things. It is not the case, as the name on its own appears to suggest, that "in-vocations" "call down" the mind of the gods to humans, rather, according to the truth itself as it means to teach us, they render the mind of humans suitable for participating in the gods, and lead it up to the gods and adapt it through suitable persuasions. For which very reason also the names of gods that are befitting the sacred and the rest of the divine symbols that are anagogic are capable of joining them to the gods.

[13] And in addition, our "appeasements of wrath" will be clear if we consider the wrath of the gods. This is not, then, as it seems to some, a sort of ancient and enduring anger, rather it is a turning away from the beneficial care that comes from the gods, which we abandon, turning *ourselves* away, just as if we veiled ourselves from the light in the noonday sun, and set the darkness on ourselves and hardened ourselves from the gods' excellent giving. Propitiation, then, has the power to turn us toward the participation in the higher world, and to bring us forward into communion with the divine care that has been pushed back from us, and to bind to each other in due proportion what is participated and what participates. Therefore the act of appeasement is so far removed from accomplishing its work through passion that it even removes us from our troubled rejection of the gods, which is an act of the passions.

The "sacrifices that expiate" heal whatever evil is present in the places of the earth and prepare us so that not a single inclination nor any affection exists around us. Therefore, whether such an expiation should arise through the gods or through daemons, it summons these as helpers and warders-off of evil and saviors, and through them it leads away every approaching harm arising out of the passions. It is not in any way at all possible, then, that they who divert the blows of becoming and of nature, bar them through passions. And if anyone should believe that the cutting off of their care introduces any harm automatically, persuasion of the stronger orders through expiation, since it calls back again their goodwill toward caring and turns away privation, would be entirely pure and permanent.

[14] In addition, the so-called "necessary compulsions of gods" are just this, necessary compulsions that come *from* the gods, and arise in their presence. In just the same way as the Good is necessarily beneficent, thus are they disposed entirely in this particular way and in no other, and not as something from outside nor as by force. Such a necessity as this, then, is blended with an intention that has the form of the Good, and is a friend of love. By its particular station it has the sameness and permanence of the gods—since it is, in relation to the same things and in the same manner, embraced by a single boundary— and because of this steadfastness it also is never displaced. Certainly then, on account of all these things, the matter is the opposite from what you inferred: the divine turns out to be unconjurable and not susceptible to passions and not liable to compulsion, if, that is, such powers actually are truly in theurgy, as we proved.

[15] Continuing on, after this division you proceed to another, between gods and daemons: You say: "Gods are pure intellects," advancing the opinion as your hypothesis, or relating it as one acceptable to certain people, but you explain daemons as being "psychical entities that partake of mind." That these things seem to be the case to many of the philosophers has not escaped my notice either, but in speaking to you I don't suppose I need to hide the clear truth. For all such opinions have been a little confused. On the one hand, attributes of daemons are transferred to souls (for *souls* are participants of mind); on the other hand, those of gods have fallen away to the mind, which is immaterial in its activity, but which the gods, of course, utterly surpass. Why then must one assign these characteristics, which are not wholly fitting to them? With respect to the fact of differentiation let this much discussion be thought fitting (for what remains is beside the point), but the things about which you are in doubt in addition to this, since they are linked to the sacred service, let them meet up with a fitting argument.

Still more, having said that pure intellects are "unbending and unmixed with sensible things," you doubt whether it is necessary to pray to them. But I assume one ought not pray to anyone else. For the divine in us, which is both One and intell*ectual,* or if you wish "intell*igible,*" is awakened into activity during prayers, and when it is awakened it strives after what is similar to it in an exceptional manner and links itself to perfection-in-itself. But if it is plainly unbelievable to you, how something without a body hears a voice, and in what way one that also lacks perception, and even ears, hears what is spoken by us in prayers, you willfully forget the presence of the first causes both in the act of knowing and in the participation in the first causes of all things under them, for they have gathered together into a unity in themselves the whole of things altogether. Neither, then, through activities, nor through organs, do the gods receive prayers into themselves, but they comprehend within themselves the energies of the words of good men, and especially of whichever words, through the sacred rites, have been established by the gods and hit upon a unity to them. For the divine itself, at that time, is literally unified to itself and communicates with the thoughts inside the prayers (and not as one person to another).

But "the prayers of petition," as you claim, "are improperly directed to the purity of the intellect." Not at all. On account of this sort of reason: since in activity and purity and in all things we are inferior to the gods, it is the most appropriate thing of all to supplicate them in an extreme degree. For humans' awareness of their own nothingness, if anyone should judge by comparing them to the gods, makes them turn themselves spontaneously to prayers of petition, and from supplication we are led up, little by little, toward that which we supplicate, and we acquire a sameness to it, from conversing continuously with it, and from our imperfection we slowly acquire divine perfection in addition.

If one should also consider the supplications in the sacred rites, how they were sent down to humans from the gods themselves, and that they are symbols of the gods themselves and are familiar only to the gods, and that these somehow hold a power that is the same as that which belongs to the gods, how could one still justly assume that such a supplication is perceptible and not divine and intellectual? Or what affection could reasonably intrude into the supplicatory rite, in which not even an earnest human character is able to be easily cleansed.

"But the offerings," you claim, "are offered as though they were directed to beings with sensory perception and souls." Yes, if they are filled up only with bodily powers and composite ones or are ear-marked as though for the bare service of the sense organs. But since the offerings participate in incorporeal forms and in certain principles and in the simpler measures, by this fact alone is seen the proper sense of the offerings. And if some near or distant relationship or likeness exists, even this is sufficient for the connection that we are just now discussing. For not even among the things incrementally close to the gods is there anything to which the gods are not immediately present and linked. The union arising from the offerings to the gods themselves, as far as is possible, arises not as it turns out as if to beings with sense perception or souls, but in accordance with the divine forms themselves. Thus, we replied sufficiently also concerning this distinction.

[17] Let us, then, in place of this, substitute the doubts you raised against current opinion. "How," you ask, "according to your reasoning, will the sun and the moon, and the visible beings in the heavens, how will they be gods, if the gods are only bodiless?" Well, we claim that they are not circumscribed by

bodies, but that *they* circumscribe their bodies with divine lives and activities; and that they are not turned toward the body, but they hold the body, which is turned toward its divine cause; and that the body does not hinder their intellectual and bodiless perfection, nor does it produce problems for the perfection by interrupting it. On account of this, then, the body does not need extra attention, but it follows along spontaneously and in a certain way automatically, and without needing to work on its own, but by the anagogy of the gods toward the one, it also is uniformly lifted up by itself.

But if it is necessary to say this, the heavenly body is the body most closely related to the bodiless essence of the gods. For, since that essence is single, partless, and immovable, the heavenly body is simple, indivisible, and in the very same way unchangeable. And even if some one of the divine essences uniformly appends its activities under itself, even this maintains a single circuit. The heavenly body imitates also their sameness, by an everlasting motion distributed across the same things and in the same way and in the same direction, and by a single principle and in a single order of being, it also imitates the divine life by the innate life that belongs to aetherial bodies. For which very reason their body is not mixed together as if from opposing and differing things, just as indeed our body is composed, nor was soul put together with body into a single living thing from two parts. But the creatures in the heavens, among the gods, are entirely alike and united, and are wholes throughout wholes and are uniform and not composite. For the greater levels of being always and consistently dominate inside them, and the lesser levels are suspended from the head of the prior ones and never drag it down to themselves, and the wholes of things are gathered together into a single order and a single consummation; also, in a certain way, all bodiless beings, even gods, throughout the whole are gathered together, since the divine form rules in them, throughout everything, and inserts the same whole single substance everywhere.

[18] In this way, on the one hand, then, the beings visible in the heavens are all gods and in a certain way incorporeal. But your next question raises a difficulty, "How is it that some of them are beneficent and some maleficent? In fact, this opinion has surely been taken from the horoscope-takers, and totally misses reality. For all of them are good and the causes of good things alike, and they cast their attention toward a single good and uniformly conduct themselves solely according to the beautiful and the good. Nevertheless the material bodies that lie under them also themselves hold an extraordinary number of powers, some remaining only in the divine bodies themselves, others proceeding out from them into nature and its material manifestation in the cosmos, descending in order throughout all of creation, and stretching unhindered down to particulars.

And as concerns the powers that remain in the celestial divine bodies, no one would dispute that they are all similar. Let us then go through the remaining issue, which concerns those that are sent down here and mingle with the generated world. Now then, these come through for the salvation of the universe and they likewise hold together creation as a whole according to the same mode. They are both impassive and immovable, and yet they descend into what receives change and is susceptible to passions. Since creation is surely multifarious and assembled from diverse things, it receives their unity and undifferentiation with struggle and in a partial way because of its own contrariness and division. It receives what is not subject to passions, in a manner subject to passions, and entirely in accord with its own nature, not in accordance to their power, it naturally participates in them. Just as, then, what comes to be partakes of being by means of generation and the corporeal partakes corporeally of the incorporeal, so also the natural and material world within creation sometimes partakes of immaterial things and celestial bodies beyond nature and beyond the created world in a disorderly and inharmonious fashion. Then those who apply color and shape and texture to intelligible forms are absurd, since it is the things that partake in them that have such qualities; also absurd are those who attribute evil to the heavenly bodies, since it is the things that participate in them that at times have an evil nature. For there would not have been such a thing as participation in the first place, if the participant didn't have also some kind of difference from it. But if the participant receives the thing participated in as into something other and different, then doubtless this thing, as something other and among earthly things, is the evil and disordered thing.

Participation, then, becomes the cause of the great otherness in secondary things, and the commingling of material things with the immaterial emanations, and furthermore the fact that the thing which is given in one way is received by the things of this world in another way. For example, the emanation of Kronos is unifying, whereas that of Ares causes motion; however, among material things, the receptacle, which is subject to passions and generation, receives the one as rigidity and coldness, and the other as heat beyond measure. Isn't it true that the thing that corrupts and makes disproportionate comes to be on account of the differentiating, material, and passive deviation of the recipients? Furthermore, since the weakness of the material and terrestrial realms does not make room for the unmixed power and purest life of aetherial beings, it transfers its own passivity to the first causes. It is as if someone who is sick in their body and is unable to bear the life-giving heat of the sun, were to dare falsely to accuse it, because of his own problems, as if not it were not advantageous for health or life.

There might be something of this sort also in the harmony and blending of the whole, since the same things are salvation, on the one hand, to the whole and the universe, on account of the completeness both of things present in it and the things in which it is present, but for its parts; on the other hand, these same things are harmful on account of the parts' divisible asymmetry. Also in the movement of the whole, then, all the revolutions preserve the whole cosmos in the same way, but a particular one of them, in one part, is often oppressed by another part, which very thing we also see arising clearly in a dance.

So then, once again, the passivity of being corrupted and changed is innate to those things made of parts, and one ought not attribute this to the complete and primary causes, either as being in them or as having descended from them to things here. Through these things, then, it has been shown that neither the gods themselves in the heavens, nor their gifts, are malevolent.

[21] The division, which you take up, of what is subject to passions from what is not someone might equally reject as suitable to neither of the stronger forms of being, for reasons we have mentioned before. And also for this reason it is right to overturn it, that it establishes its claim from rites performed upon beings, *assuming* that they are subject to passions. For what sort of sacred rite and service, if it is performed according to sacred customs, is generated through the passions, or produces any fulfillment of passions? Was this sacred rite not legislated intellectually according to the laws of the gods and according to first principles? It imitates the order of the gods, both the intelligible order and the encosmic one. It maintains the eternal measures and wondrous tokens of the things that exist, which are sent down from the demiurge and the second father of wholes, and by which also things beyond language are brought to light through inarticulable symbols; formless things are held within forms, things greater than every image have images impressed on them, and everything is fulfilled through a single divine cause, which particular cause has been separated so far from the passions, that it is not even possible to reach a logical account of it.

This is nearly also the cause of the error of our thoughts concerning the passions. For although humans are unable to grasp wisdom by logical reckoning, they consider it to be possible and are carried along wholly toward things that are characteristic of themselves: human passions, and from them, which belong to themselves, they infer divine passions. They entirely mistake them doubly, then, both since they fall away from divine things and, when having missed the mark on these, they drag the divine down to human passions. But it is necessary with things being done in the same way toward gods and humans; for example, making prostrations and obeisances and gifts and first-fruits, not to understand them in the same way in both cases, and to set each of them apart, according to the difference in the case of the more worthy entities, and to glorify some as holy, but to consider the others as human and easy to be despised. It also must be granted that the efficacy of the human actions arises by passion both within those performing them and those to whom they are directed (for they are human and corporeal), but since the divine actions are efficacious through an unchangeable wonder and a holy condition, both of intellectual joy and steadfast wisdom, it is necessary to value differently their actual power, since they are dedicated to the gods.

Bibliography

Dillon, John. 1987. "Iamblichus of Chalcis." *Aufstieg und Niedergang der römischen Welt* 2.36.2.

Dodds, E. R. 1968. "Theurgy," appendix 2 in Dodds, *The Greeks and the Irrational*. Berkeley and Los Angeles: University of California Press.

Finamore, John. 1985. *Iamblichus and the Theory of the Vehicle of the Soul*. Chico, Calif.: Scholars Press.

Lewy, Hans. 1978. *The Chaldean Oracles and Theurgy: Mysticism, Magic and Platonism in the Later Roman Empire*. 2d ed. edited by Michel Tardieu. Paris: Etudes Augustiniennes.

O'Meara, Dominic J. 1989. *Pythagoras Revived: Mathematics and Philosophy in Late Antiquity*. New York: Oxford University Press.

des Places, Edouard, S. J., ed. 1966. *Jamblique: Les mystères d'Egypte*. Paris: Belles Lettres.

Shaw, Gregory. 1995. *Theurgy and the Soul: The Neoplatonism of Iamblichus*. University Park: Pennsylvania State University Press.

Sheppard, Anne D. R. 1996. "Theurgy." *Oxford Classical Dictionary,* 3d ed. New York: Oxford University Press.

Struck, Peter. "Pagan and Christian Theurgies." *Ancient World*. Forthcoming.

INDEX